Official PowerBuilder 6: Advanced Tools for the Enterprise

Official PowerBuilder 6: Advanced Tools for the Enterprise

Derek C.R. Ball

INTERNATIONAL THOMSON PUBLISHING COMPANY

I⟨T⟩P® An International Thomson Publishing Company

London • Bonn • Johannesburg • Madrid • Melbourne • Mexico City • New York • Paris
Singapore • Tokyo • Toronto • Albany, NY • Belmont, CA • Cincinnati, OH • Detroit, MI

Copyright ©1997 International Thomson Publishing Company

I(T)P™ A division of International Thomson Publishing Inc.
The ITP Logo is a trademark under license.

Printed in the United States of America.

For more information, contact:

International Thomson Publishing GmbH
Königswinterer Strasse 418
53227 Bonn
Germany

International Thomson Publishing Europe
Berkshire House 168-173
High Holborn
London WCIV 7AA
England

Thomas Nelson Australia
102 Dodds Street
South Melbourne, 3205
Victoria, Australia

Nelson Canada
1120 Birchmount Road
Scarborough, Ontario
Canada M1K 5G4

International Thomson Publishing Southern Africa
Bldg. 19, Constantia Park
239 Old Pretoria Road, P.O. Box 2459
Halfway House, 1685 South Africa

International Thomson Publishing Asia
221 Henderson Road #05-10
Henderson Building
Singapore 0315

International Thomson Publishing Japan
Hirakawacho Kyowa Building, 3F
2-2-1 Hirakawacho
Chiyoda-ku, 102 Tokyo
Japan

International Thomson Editores
Campos Eliseos 385, Piso 7
Col. Polanco
11560 Mexico D.F. Mexico

International Thomson Publishing France
1, rue st. Georges
75 009 Paris France

2 3 4 5 6 7 8 9 10 01 00 99 98
Library of Congress Cataloging-in-Publication Data

ISBN: 1-85032-918-4

Production: Jo-Ann Campbell • mle design • 213 Cider Mill Road, Glastonbury, CT 06033

Dedication

For Brad. Thanks for the friendship and philosophy lessons…

TABLE OF CONTENTS

Preface

This book is intended to present a concise reference for PowerBuilder™ developers who have either taken the Introduction or FastTrack to PowerBuilder course, worked with PowerBuilder on at least one project, and are ready to try and advance their skills to the next level. You may have achieved this level of experience through self education from other books or computer based training modules. Either way, you have the basics down pat and need to progress to the next stage.

This book is not intended to be the definitive bible for the PowerBuilder master. Many of the topics discussed here, the PowerBuilder master should already be familiar with. Instead, we focus on taking the intermediate level PowerBuilder developer into the realm of the advanced developer.

All of the new features in PowerBuilder 6.0 are covered in this book and are useful for developers of all levels.

The walk throughs of specific techniques are intended to allow you to either follow along with the process mentally, if you are that familiar with PowerBuilder, or actually follow along and build the walk through as you proceed through it.

Acknowledgements

The fact that you are holding this book in your hands right now is the result of an intense team effort to get it there. There are many people who I need to thank for making this book a reality. Thanks to Dave Cinderella of Sybase for keeping me in line technically providing all that information that wasn't included with the software!

Thanks to Jose Cartagena of Sybase Press for helping to iron out any wrinkles and for his support. From International Thomson, thanks to Roberta De Avila, Theron Shreve and Jim Dewolf for making the publication process seem easy (because I know its not!). And to Carol Mclendan, Cathy Elliot, and the folks at Waterside Productions for getting me hooked up with the right people.

Finally, I need to extend the biggest thanks of all to my wife Lesley, who has put up with my late nights and the huge mess I made while I pursued my writing for Powersoft Press and my other ventures. Your unending support and understanding made this all possible.

To everyone else that I haven't mentioned, thank you all. I have appreciated all the help and advice, without which I could never have completed this work. In the event you find any technical inaccuracies in this book, the responsibility for those errors are mine and mine alone.

About the Author

Derek Ball is the President of Phoenix Enterprises, an advanced technology consulting firm in Calgary, Canada. Derek is a much sought after speaker, mentor, and instructor in the arena of client/server technology and application development. His favorite tool in this field is PowerBuilder from Powersoft. Derek has been working with PowerBuilder for many years and has spent the last four years as an advanced Certified PowerBuilder Instructor teaching hundreds of people how to use PowerBuilder in all the corners of the globe from Istanbul to San Francisco.

Derek has worked with many Fortune 500 firms, helping to mentor and train their personnel in the correct techniques to be successful with client/server technology and PowerBuilder. Derek believes that learning to use PowerBuilder correctly goes beyond just how to program and write code. A successful development team has to understand the correct development methodology and architecture that will suit their environment and system requirements.

You may be familiar with some of Derek's earlier works. He has co-authored two best selling books on PowerBuilder 3.0 and 4.0 and is a member of the editorial board of the *PowerBuilder Developers Journal*. He is a frequent contributor to the PBDJ and also has a regular column entitled "Into the Looking Glass" in the *PowerBuilder Advisor*. He also writes for a number of other publications including *Computing Canada*, *Visionary Times*,

Technology in Government and *Powerline*. Derek's recent work has included a number of books from Sybase/Powersoft Press including *Advanced PowerBuilder 5.0, SQLAnywhere Developers Guide, The Official Getting Started With Power++*.

When not traveling the globe mentoring and training, Derek lives in Calgary, Canada with his wife Lesley and daughter Jamie.. If you have any comment regarding this book, please write to Derek care of the publisher, or send e-mail to dball@cadvision.com.

CHAPTER 1

Introduction

*I*nformation technology is an exciting place to work these days. Many organizations are realizing that technology holds the key to their long term success and ultimately their viability as an organization. This drive to utilize technology as a tool to achieve competitive and strategic advantage has fueled a massive industry revolving around information technology solutions. The mainstream of business activity is centered around client/server architectures and graphical user interfaces with a strong movement towards integrating Intranets and Internets into enterprise systems.

Over the past ten years, client/server architectures have made the transition from "rare" and "unusual" to "fundamental" and "mainstream." The bulk of new systems being developed in business today are rolled out in a client/server environment, although they have a definite eye towards Intranet application.

PowerBuilder in the Enterprise

Over the last six years, PowerBuilder has swept the industry, becoming the most widely used application development tool for enterprise client/server applications. Windows developers quickly adopted PowerBuilder and praised it for the improved productivity and its ease of development.

Many non-windows programmers discovered that PowerBuilder demystified the graphical user interface (GUI) and PC based Windows development. A new generation of client/server GUI application developers was rising like a phoenix from the ashes of our character based legacy systems.

How this Book is Organized

The sections of this book are laid out to help you become a better and more skilled PowerBuilder developer. It assumes that you know the basics of developing with PowerBuilder, at least to the level of having completed and understood all the materials from the Getting Started tutorial and hopefully having attended an Introduction to PowerBuilder course.

We begin by discussing some of the critical and much neglected areas of enterprise PowerBuilder projects: methodologies and architectures. People tend to jump into enterprise PowerBuilder projects like they were building a system to keep track of their stamp collection at home. Much more care and deliberation needs to be applied when the system is a mission critical system upon which your organization is betting its future!

Next we examine other predevelopment considerations that need to be worked through in the enterprise environment: how to design your application, take advantage of object orientation, and what kind of a class library should you use? These are critical components that need to be addressed before you begin the build cycle of your enterprise application.

Then in Chapter 8, we examine all the great new features PowerBuilder 6.0 brings us, and we apply them to practical situations. If you are an experienced PowerBuilder 5.0 developer and want to jump right into 6.0, this is a good place to start. You can see all the new objects and techniques put to use in the sample application that comes on the companion CD. Some of the more complex new features are covered in dedicated chapters like Internet application development in Chapter 10, Distributed PowerBuilder concepts in Chapter 9 and Compiling components in Chapter 11.

Chapters 12 through 18 address advanced development concepts. These are concepts go beyond the basic tutorials and Introduction to PowerBuilder courses (now called FastTrack to PowerBuilder). We teach you the techniques of the pros and show you how to use them in the enterprise environment.

In Chapters 19 through 22 we go into a high level of detail on DataWindows. One of the comments I had from a number of reviewers was to provide more fundamental DataWindow information, as many of the readers of this book were experienced programmers with tools like Visual Basic™ or Delphi™ and were jumping into PowerBuilder at an advanced level. Thus, they needed specific information on the role that DataWindows plays in PowerBuilder applications. Each subsequent chapter will get into more advanced topics as you move through the DataWindow area.

Finally, in Chapter 23 we round out your knowledge by examining the different types of user objects and how they should be integrated into your application. A number of examples of non-visual objects will be explained.

In the appendices you will find information about SQLAnywhere and SQLCentral. SQLAnywhere is the workplace database product that comes packaged with PowerBuilder 6.0, and SQLCentral is a handy tool for managing the database.

If you are relatively new to enterprise projects with PowerBuilder, you will probably get the most benefit from this book by reading the chapters in order. If you are already a fairly experienced enterprise developer, you can easily jump from section to section and reference the information that you currently require! Make use of the index, because I have tried to avoid any duplication of information.

This book is focused on specific techniques instead of examining a single application that you build on as you go through the book. Each of the chapters are discrete and stand alone. Often you will learn about more than one technique—allowing you to select the one that is appropriate for your situation.

Who Should Read this Book

This book is intended to provide a valuable resource to PowerBuilder developers who have a need to develop applications in the enterprise environment. It is not a beginners book and will not teach you how to paint the different controls into the window painter. We focus instead on the techniques necessary to proceed from being an intermediate developer to an advanced one. This includes advanced techniques and knowledge which is incremental to the knowledge we expect you already have. I expect intermediate and experienced PowerBuilder developers will benefit most from this book.

This book helps to round out your PowerBuilder knowledge by providing you with methodologies and architectures that work for enterprise development projects. We look at design issues for enterprise applications and discuss the concepts that help you make your applications more object oriented.

We also go into substantial depth on the new PowerBuilder 6.0 features and how to use them. This chapter alone should make this book worthwhile for all existing PowerBuilder 5.0 developers.

The advanced techniques that follow include details on how to develop the best DataWindows around, taking advantage of nested reports, drop down DataWindows, child DataWindows, sliding columns, and many other advanced features.

You learn how to construct and use non-visual business and service objects, integrate OLE 2.0 .OCX Active X controls, and much more.

What Is on the Companion CD?

The companion CD contains sample files that are referenced throughout the book. There are examples of all the new PowerBuilder 6.0 features, such as Internet hypertext linking, distributed objects, native compiled code, single level function overloading, direct DataWindow manipulation, and more! A compiled version of the sample application is included, as well as all the source code. The sample application uses the PowerBuilder sample database in SQLAnywhere, so you must have SQLAnywhere installed on your system (the database file is included on the CD in case you didn't install the sample database when you installed PowerBuilder).

The examples on the companion CD, like the chapters themselves, are discrete examples of specific techniques. To keep the examples straightforward and easy to understand, the code used does not follow pure object oriented coding techniques.

How to Install the Sample Files

To install the sample files, run the SETUP.EXE program from the CD drive. This creates a directory called ADVPB6 in your root directory. Within TFTE it creates three subdirectories:

- C:\TFTE\SAMPLES—contains all the source and compiled sample application objects. The database, if selected, is also installed here.

- C:\TFTE\DISTRIB—contains all the source and compiled files for the distributed PowerBuilder examples.

- C:\TFTE\OLEAUTO—contains all the source and compiled files for the OLE Automation example.

Setting Up the Sample Files

To set up the sample files, simply open PowerBuilder 6.0 and the application object in the TOOLS.PBL library. Make sure your current database connection is to the

PowerBuilder Demo Database. You can install this database from the CD, if you don't have it installed.

From here you can run or compile the application as you choose.

Setting Up the Distributed PowerBuilder Example

Step 1 Open and compile the PBServer and PBConsol applications. This can be done in machine code or in standard p-code without altering the effect of the example.

Step 2 Open the TCP/IP services file. This file is a text file thatis most likely in your Windows directory and should be named "Services." You can open this file with notepad. Instructions for how to format your entries are contained in comments at the top of the file.

We are going to add a new service to this file that allows PowerBuilder to communicate with the distributed object. This service has the following characteristics:

Service Name: DEMOSERVER
Port ID: 11001
Protocol: tcp
Comment: PB Book Demo
Your entry in the services file should look like:

```
DEMOSERVER        11001/tcp      #PB Book Demo
```

Step 3 Open the client application. This application object is in the PBClient.PBL library. You can either compile this application, or you can run it in the development environment directly.

Step 4 Start the PowerBuilder Demo DB V6 (THIS IS CRITICAL TO DO BEFORE STARTING THE DISTRIBUTED APPLICATION).

Step 5 Start the PB Server and PBConsol applications. Use the Run option or double click on the .EXE from explorer.

Step 6 Run the PB Client application.

Step 7 Connect to the distributed PowerBuilder application using the **PB Server Connect** command button.

Step 8   Connect to the SQLAnywhere database using the **DB Server Connect** commandbutton.

Step 9   Test the connectivity with the **Test DB Server** command button.

If you want to actually place the distributed applications on your server, follow the same steps but place the PBConsole and PBServer compiled applications on the server with the appropriate PB deployment kit libraries. Then, you must set up the appropriate port on the server and define that port in your services file for the DEMOSERVER service.

Setting Up the OLE Automation Example

Step 1   Register the OLE object. You can register the OLE object by double clicking on ole_obj.reg which will cause the object to be set up in the registry.

What's Next?

Due to various factors beyond my control, I am certain that we will not be able to get everything into this book. If I was, this book would probably be over 1,500 pages, and you wouldn't see it for another six months. With each release, I will keep adding more until the publisher tells me to stop!

In the interim, I want to leave you with some information about other places to get information on PowerBuilder and how to network with other PowerBuilder users.

The PowerBuilder documentation includes an excellent series of reference manuals including a *Programmers Reference Guide* and other valuable reference books. The online help is also very extensive and useful.

Powersoft/Sybase Press will have an excellent line of books covering the entire line of Powersoft/Sybase products that you will want to take advantage of including *Sybase SQLAnywhere Developer's Guide* and books on distributed PowerBuilder, the PFC, PowerJ, or Power++ (Powersoft's new GUI based C++ development environment).

You can go online and find Powersoft and PowerBuilder users on CompuServe (GO PBFORUM) and the Internet (http://www.powersoft.com).

You can also join up with local users groups in your area. If you can't find one, contact Powersoft to find out more details. Once a year Powersoft hosts their International Users Conference in the late summer which is an excellent opportunity to network with thousands of other PowerBuilder users and learn the latest in advanced techniques.

Last, but not least, there are a number of PowerBuilder books and publications that will help to keep you in the loop about Powersoft and PowerBuilder including the "PowerBuilder Developer's Journal" (PBDJ), the "PowerBuilder Advisor" (check out my column "Into the Looking Glass"), "Powersoft PAD," and others.

PowerBuilder Developer's Journal
Subscription Hotline
(800)513-7111
(201)332-1515
Internet: 73611.756@compuserve.com

PowerBuilder Advisor
Customer Service
(800)336-6060
(619)483-6400
Internet: 70007.1614@compuserve.com

CHAPTER 2

The Development Methodology for Enterprise PowerBuilder

"It is common sense to take a method and try it. If it fails, admit it frankly and try another. But above all, try something."

Franklin Delano Roosevelt, Address at Oglethorpe University, Atlanta, Georgia, May 22, 1932

O*ne of the most inconsistent aspects of developing PowerBuilder applications is the use of a proper development methodology. This is a component of application development which many projects overlook or ignore, often with some particularly undesirable results. For small, ad hoc development, many single developers skip any formal development process, but doing so in the enterprise development environment will quickly lead to missed deadlines and cost overruns.*

2.1 *The Evolution of Client/Server Development Methodologies*

Until recently, there have been two dominant methodologies utilized in client/server development. The first of these is the "Waterfall" methodology which although still used, is outdated and inappropriate for client/server projects. The second of these, I call the "Seat of the Pants" methodology, or in other words, no methodology at all.

It was quickly apparent to everyone using PowerBuilder to build multi-developer enterprise applications, that a new methodology needdrd to be devised. Over many different projects, we have evolved a methodology which has proven to be very successful in allowing us to deliver our projects on time and usually under budget.

A complete methodology goes beyond the scope of this book, so we focus on the highlights of the development segment of the Accelerated Client/Server Enterprise methodology (ACE). (See Figure 2-1.)

To best understand ACE, you need to understand the evolution that preceded the current model. The road to developing a development methodology suitable for PowerBuilder applications requires a lot of different approaches to be tested. The best components of each are retained and used in the ACE methodology.

ACE Methodology

Figure 2-1. The ACE Methodology has been used to deliver many enterprise PowerBuilder applications on time and on or under budget.

2.2 The Waterfall Runs Dry

In the days when we were developing custom enterprise applications in COBOL or FORTRAN we utilized a rigid methodology for structured application development. Many of you are already familiar with a methodology based on the waterfall concept.

The waterfall breaks the development cycle down into discrete steps each with a rigid, sequential beginning and end date. Each step is fully completed before the following step is started. Once a step is finished, you never go back to change it.

In Figure 2-2, we can see that the first stage in the waterfall is to plan. This encompasses the overall objectives of the system, project timelines, delivery dates, and more.

Once the planning stage is finished, the outputs from the planning process flow into the analysis process. In this stage, the users are interviewed, their requirements are analyzed, and a document is produced detailing users' requirements. Any reengineering or process redesign is incorporated into this step. Functional decomposition diagrams are created to allow the system to be broken down into manageable components.

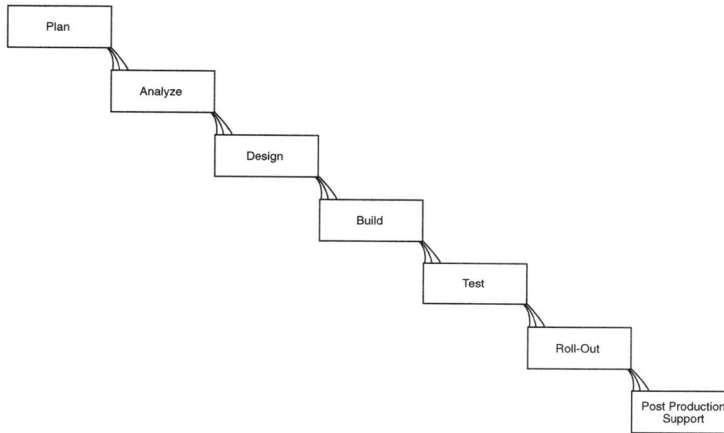

Figure 2-2. *The Waterfall methodology has been used for many years to develop systems based upon structured analysis and design and developed with procedural languages. This methodology proved to be inappropriate for use in client/server development.*

The outputs from analysis are used to develop a design of the system. Various structured design techniques are used to produce a design specification that passes on to the build phase.

In the build phase, the programmers develop the system according to the design. Once completed, the system enters the testing phase where it is unit tested, string tested, system testeds and finally user tested.

Now the system is delivered to the users in the implementation phase. Once implemented the final phase begins, this is known as post-production support.

The waterfall methodology was used by most client/server developers who entered this industry through structured development projects. This is how I first learned the waterfall. In attempting to use the waterfall, we found a number of shortcomings:

- The end users of the system were only involved in the very beginning and the very end of the process. As a result, the system that they were given at the end of the development cycle was often not what they originally visualized or thought that they asked for.

- The long development cycle and the shortening of business cycles led to a gap between what was being delivered and what was really needed. You have probably heard the famous end user quote "It's exactly what I asked for, but it's not what I need!" The lack of user involvement between the analysis and the implementation phase resulted in development time and dollars being expended to deploy systems which were no longer appropriate for the current business model.

- We expect our end users to describe in detail what they want for a system, before we begin to build. This may seem logical to developers, but to end users who haven't used a computer system before and aren't really certain what can be built, this can be ludicrous. Users usually do not know what they want until they see it and like to be presented with samples to choose from, like buying carpet for your living room!

- When we reached the "end" of a phase, we found that we really weren't done, but the methodology required that we press on anyway. If fact, you cannot really every fully complete a phase, there is always more work that can be done. When you think about it, is any system that we deliver ever "completely" finished? Probably not. The methodology we use should take this into consideration and allow us to see the progression between phases and recognize that the preceding phases are not 100% complete.

We quickly learned that the waterfall methodology was going to be woefully inadequate for our client/server development projects. Soon, after experts began to publish methodologies based upon other models, many of which were based upon a *cyclical* approach to systems development.

2.3 The Spiral Methodology

I will generalize here and lump all the first generation cyclical methodologies under the label of "Spiral" methodologies (this includes "fountain"-based methodologies). These methodologies suggest a process of working from a base and building a system incrementally. (See Figure 2-3.) Upon reaching the end of each phase, developers would always reexamine the entire structure and revisit each major stage before proceeding to the next phase.

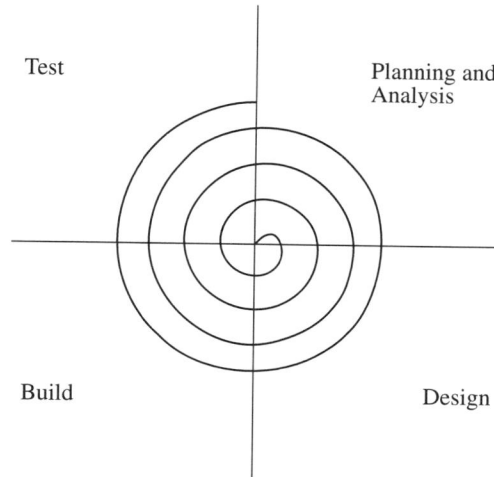

Test

Planning and Analysis

Build

Design

Figure 2-3. *The Spiral methodology allows a system to be built incrementally, revisiting each of the four major phases for each spiral through the development process.*

The spiral methodology is represented by drawing the four major phases of systems development, Planning/Analysis, Design, Build, and Test into quadrants. The process begins by performing preliminary planning and requirements analysis. Then a design is made for the base components of the system and for the functionality determined in the first step. Next this functionality is constructed and tested. This represents one complete iteration of the spiral.

Having completed this first loop, the users are given the opportunity to examine the system and enhance its functionality. This begins the second iteration of the spiral. The process continues, looping around and around the spiral until the users and developers agree that the system is complete, and developer's can proceed to implementation.

This methodology is good for ensuring that users' requirements were being adequately addressed and that the users are closely involved with the project. It also allows for the system to adapt to any changes in business requirements that occurr after the system development has begun. There is one central fatal flaw that makes this methodology fail, there is never any firm commitment to implement a working system! You can go round and round the quadrants, never actually bringing a system into production. This brings to mind the image of a crocodile killing its prey; it grabs it and spirals it down and down into the water until it is dead. Thus I affectionately call this problem "The Death Spiral." (See Figure 2-4.)

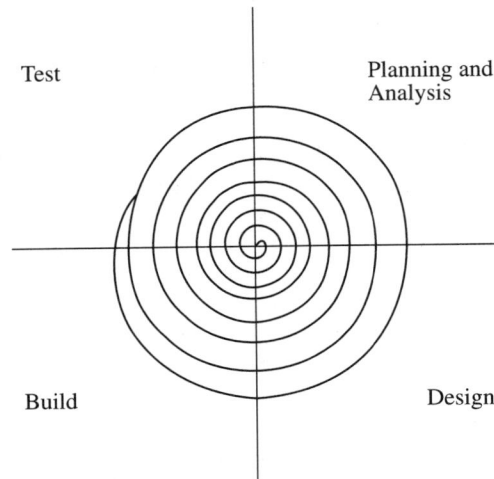

Figure 2-4. The major shortcoming of the Spiral methodology is that you can continue to add functionality over and over and never actually implement the system. This is a condition that I call "The Death Spiral" as it will surely kill your project.

While the Waterfall had proven itself to be too inflexible, the Spiral has demonstrated the exact opposite problem. If we could learn to harness and control the spiral, it would become an effective methodology for PowerBuilder development.

2.4   *The Iterative Methodology*

The Iterative methodology is an enhancement on the spiral. (See Figure 2-5.) It is intended to force the development team into actually reaching a point where the system ia implemented. The Iterative methodology recognizes that a system is never truly complete, but is evolutionary. However, it also realizes that there is a point where the system is close enough to complete to be of value to the end user.

The point of implementation is decided upon prior to the start of the system. A certain number of iterations are specified with goals identified for each iteration. Upon completion of the final iteration, the system is implemented in whatever state it is in.

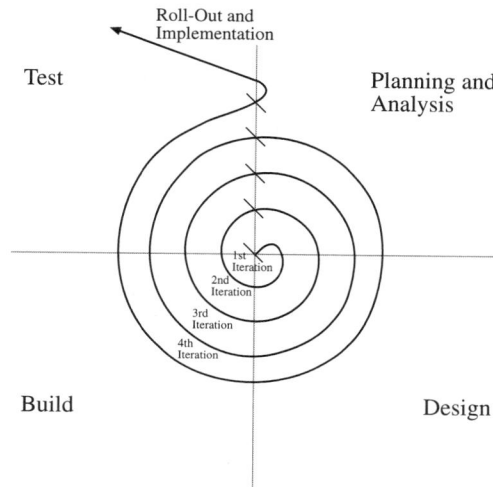

Figure 2-5. *The Iterative methodology is designed to forced the project to reach a completion point where a real, live system is implemented.*

To demonstrate this methodology, let's examine the possible iterations involved in developing a system to handle time sheet entry and tracking. The first iteration could be devoted strictly to time entry. First the time entry process is planned, the requirements are determined, and processes are modeled. The data elements are mapped to the data model or if this is a new system, the data elements are created in the appropriate data model entities. Next, the windows and objects necessary for the entry process are designed in detail. In the build phase, all the objects are constructed with PowerBuilder and if necessary, the data model entities and elements are created or revised. Then the data entry components are unit tested and, where applicable, string tested. This would end the first iteration of our cycle.

The second iteration could focus on maintenance and modification of our time details. The third could implement reporting and the fourth could develop system maintenance functions. A final fifth iteration would deal with any final changes and add a security layer to the application.

All in all we went through five complete iterations of the system. In the final stage, complete string testing and user testing would need to occur as part of the implementation process.

This methodology worked reasonably well and is still used in a number of PowerBuilder development shops today. Where we found limitations in this methodology is that it is not a strong mechanism for addressing changing business needs during the development cycle as completed iterations are not usually revisited in future iterations. The other significant drawback to this methodology is that the system's delivery time is usually much longer than one would expect, even though we are using a tool set that supports rapid application development and delivery.

This led to our development of the flattened spiral approach, which is the methodology we utilize today.

2.5 *The Flattened Spiral Methodology*

The flattened spiral approach is the current evolutionary stage of the ACE methodology. (See Figure 2-6.) I would fully expect that as we learn more, this model will continue to be refined, but for now, it has proven to perform very well in a variety of circumstances.

This approach allows you to break down the system into modules and components, like in the waterfall. It incorporates the ability to cycle through the elements of the system and revisit and improve them, like in the spiral. It has the control and built in limits of the iterative methodology. It also has more.

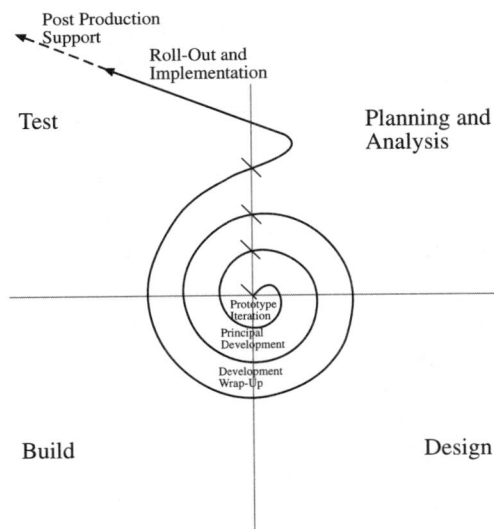

Figure 2-6. The Flattened Spiral Methodology takes some of the best features of its predecessors and combines them into a functional and effective development methodology.

The flattened spiral incorporates prototyping as a key element of its early stages in order to provide better feedback to the user and allow the organization to make a go/no-go decision early in the system process prior to investing large amounts of time and resources into a system.

When diagrammed, the flattened spiral has a look very much like the spiral and iterative methodologies. You still use the four major quadrants and work your way through each of them for each iteration of development. However, each iteration is very clearly defined and there are exactly three iterations to be performed, no more, no less.

In the remainder of this chapter, we focus on the development of a system using this methodology. The data model, if it does not already exist, should be developed in it's own spiral, which is separate from the development spiral but is tied to it in a parallel fashion. Most systems developed today in the enterprise client/server arena utilize a data warehouse concept. This means that the data model should have a life which extends well beyond the current system being developed. In the interests of remaining focused on PowerBuilder enterprise development, we do deal with data modeling in this book.

2.5.1 The First Iteration

The first iteration of development should occur within a very quick time frame. For most systems, the complete iteration should be wrapped up in four weeks. If you are taking longer than this, you are moving beyond what should be done in iteration one and are trying to perform segments of the second iteration.

2.5.1.1 Planning and Analysis

In the first phase, the objective is to deliver a preliminary functional decomposition diagram and functional specifications. (See Figure 2-7.) This can be done using a variety of techniques, but one of the most effective is to hold a Joint Application Design (JAD) session. Six or eight of the key users of the system are included in the session. An experienced JAD facilitator and scribe are also key to success. A representative from the development team is also important to ensure that the planning and analysis has a firm grounding in what can be practically accomplished. The JAD facilitator may double up and carry out this role if they have the background to do so. These sessions are very effective for driving out the details of the processes and functions involved in the system and obtaining consensus from the users on what the system must accomplish.

Planning and
Analysis

Iteration 1
Phase 1

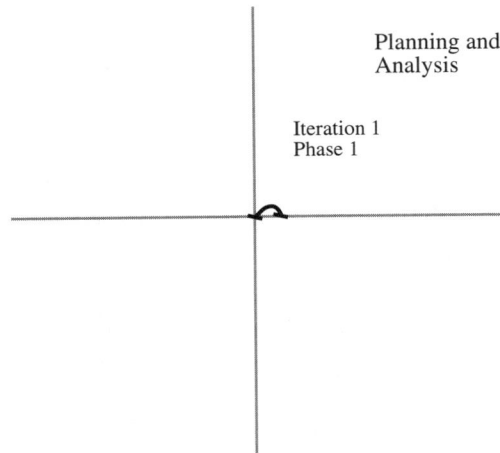

*Figure 2-7. The first phase of the first iteration is focused on
determining functionality.*

Inputs:	System objectives (from your strategic plan), user input
Deliverables:	Functional decomposition diagram, Functional Specifications
Tools Used:	Variable, tools for drawing functional decomposition (many case tools provide this functionality, or Visio™ is one that I like)
Time to Complete:	1 week

2.5.1.2 Design

In the second phase, the objective is to design some screen mock ups that can be presented to the user group to demonstrate a possible user interface for the system. (See Figure 2-8.) These mock ups must be based on the business processes that the system is intended to deliver. Business processes that are involved can often be identified here but may not be fully developed until the second iteration. These screen designs must incorporate the design and user interface standards for the organization (which implies that they have already been developed).

This phase is not usually as formally documented as other phases. If your developers are also your business systems analysts (BSA) then you may choose to have the developers mock up the screens directly in PowerBuilder. If your BSAs are somewhat PowerBuilder literate, then the same thing can be done. If your BSAs and your development team are two separate groups, the analysis can simply sketch the user interfaces on paper and pass these to the development team. There are tools on the market specifically designed for analysts in this phase, however I feel that they are a waste of money, as you can either use the manual process discussed, or use PowerBuilder as your screen building tool.

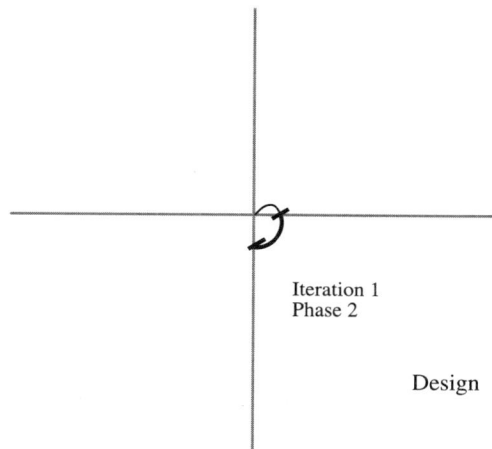

Figure 2-8. The second phase of the first iteration is focused on designing front end mock ups which support the business processes.

You don't need to spend too much time and effort here, remember that one of the goals of the first iteration is to complete it quickly and produce an online prototype at the end.

Inputs:	Functional Decomposition (from Phase 1, Step 1), Functional Specifications (from Phase 1, Step 1), development and user interface standards (from organizational standards—if they don't exist, they must be created). Logical data model (from organizational data model or as a result of a database design subproject).
Deliverables:	Quick and dirty screen designs for the user interface
Tools used:	Optional: PowerBuilder or case tool for screen mockups (not essential)
Time to Complete:	1 week

2.5.1.3 Build

In the build phase the screen designs from the previous step are turned into real windows and objects in PowerBuilder. If the data model exists then DataWindow objects can also be created where applicable. (See Figure 2-9.) This is preferable because you are maximizing the reusability of the prototype for the second phase of the system. If the data model is not yet created, then the DataWindows will have to be created in an external format for the prototype and recreated in iteration two when the data model does exist.

None of the business functionality is built into the prototype, just the look and feel of the user interface is created.

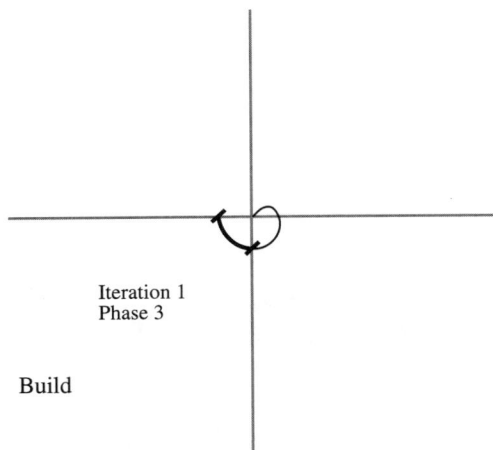

Iteration 1
Phase 3

Build

Figure 2-9. Now we can create the windows and objects for the prototype.

Inputs:	Screen designs for the user interface (from Phase 1, Step 2)
Deliverables:	Completed user interface online mock up
Tools used:	PowerBuilder, optional: class library and framework
Time to Complete:	1 week

2.5.1.4 Test

The phase in PowerBuilder application development most often skipped or ignored by development teams is the testing phase. Most of the applications being rolled out today have not been adequately tested resulting in a high level of bugs and user dissatisfaction.

The implementation of software quality assurance techniques is critical and testing needs to be taken seriously. At this stage, the quality assurance process involves checking that design prototypes adhere to the design standards implemented in the organization. It also involves ensuring that all the functions indicated in the decomposition and specifications are addressed in the prototype. Any links to navigate through the prototype which have been installed must also be tested. (See Figure 2-10.)

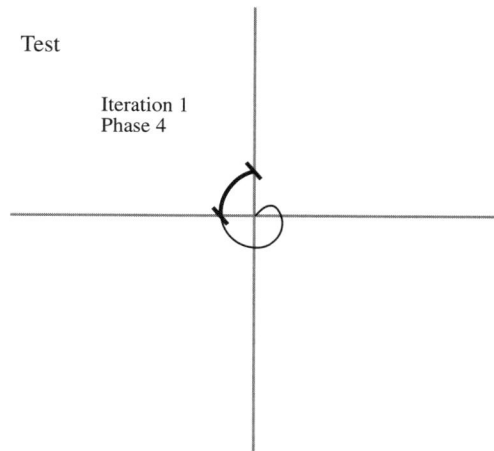

Test

Iteration 1
Phase 4

Figure 2-10. The interface should be tested before being presented to the user.

There are a number of automated testing tools that can help you improve the quality of the software you deliver to your end users. I highly recommend checking them out and taking advantage of the improvements they can make to your quality processes. Or course, testing can all be done manually but this can become a slow and tedious phase if everything is done manually.

The testing becomes more and more exhaustive with each iteration. The first iteration testing is fairly simple and straightforward but be prepared for it to get far more intensive in iterations two and three.

Inputs:	Online system mock up (from Phase 1, Step 3)
Deliverables:	Test Results Document (expected results versus actual), bug list
Tools:	PowerBuilder, optional: automated testing tool
Time to Complete:	1 week

2.5.2 The Second Iteration

The second iteration of the methodology is where the bulk of development of the business processes and functionality should occur. The time frame for this iteration is more variable and depends upon the scope of the system being developed. As a rough guideline, it will probably range from 8 weeks to 10 months. If you expect that your second iteration will take longer than this, you may want to reexamine the scope of your system and see if it can be better modularized and approached one module at a time.

2.5.2.1 Planning and Analysis

The objective of the first phase of the second iteration is to obtain user consensus on the design and final functionality of the system.(See Figure 2-11.) At the end of this stage, 90% of the functionality of the system should be fully analyzed.

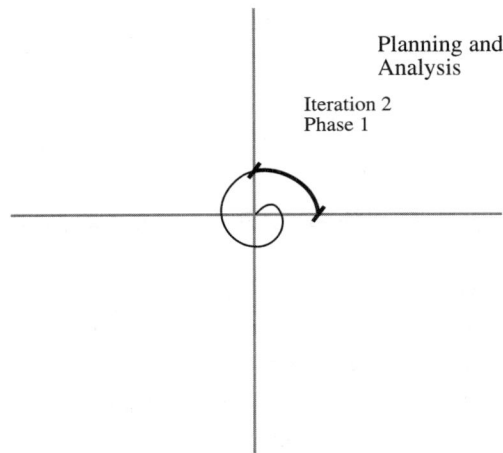

Planning and
Analysis

Iteration 2
Phase 1

Figure 2-11. The first phase of the second iteration allows the users to determine a design that will meet all the functional requirements of the system.

Again we utilize the JAD session but modified to perform a review of the prototype and solicit feedback from the users. Having a prototype to review is of tremendous value. Often end users have difficulty in determining what kind of interface would be best for their application until they are presented with some examples on which to base their feedback.

Inputs:	Tested prototype (from Phase 1, Step 4), user input
Deliverables:	Revised Functional Decomposition and Specifications, interface enhancement requests.
Tools Used:	Variable, tools for drawing functional decomposition (many case tools provide this functionality, or Visio is one that I like).
Time to Complete:	Variable: 2 days to 12 days depending on scope

2.5.2.2 Design

In the second phase, the objective is to develop detailed design specifications for each object to be built by the design team, both visual and non-visual. These designs are very detailed and include: a description of the object (covering the purpose of the object), a screen shot of the object (if applicable), how the user navigates to the object (where it is used in the system), a detailed description of all objects and controls used on the object, and any business rules or security issues associated with the object. (See Figure 2-12.)

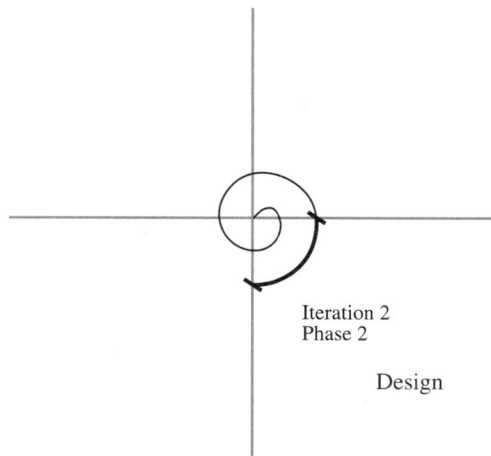

Iteration 2
Phase 2

Design

Figure 2-12. The second phase of the first iteration will develop detailed design specifications.

For each object and control placed on the first level (primary) object, a detailed description is also required. This description includes the relevant attributes and their values and any interactions with other objects or the data model. If the object is a DataWindow or data interaction object, the design should detail each data element that is involved and discuss any client based validation rules, edit masks, acceptable values and other specific information relating to the field.

The amount of detail required here depends on the business experience of the development team and if your BSAs are also your developers. User appropval of the design should be obtained at the end of this phase.

Inputs:	Revised Functional Decomposition and Specifications (from Phase 2, Step 1), development and user interface standards (from organizational standards). Physical data model (from organizational data model or from data base subproject).
Deliverables:	Detailed Design Specifications
Tools used:	Word processor of choice
Time to Complete:	Variable: 2 to 10 weeks

2.5.2.3 Build

In the build phase, the detailed designs are transformed into real objects in PowerBuilder (or in a multi-tiered architecture into service objects, RPCs, or stored procedures. See Chapter 3 for more details). The business logic is all put into place. All the necessary data fields are mapped to their physical data model data elements. Each object should be unit tested by the developer before being deemed to be completed. (See Figure 2-13.)

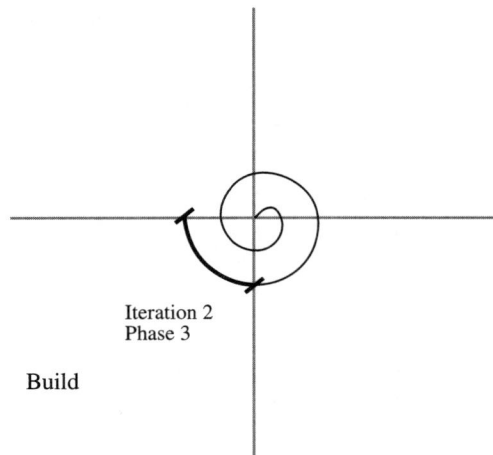

Iteration 2
Phase 3

Build

Figure 2-13. Now the real development begins as we create all the objects for the system.

This is the longest phase of the whole development life cycle, as each object must be carefully constructed and unit tested.

Inputs: Detailed Design Specifications, physical data model

Deliverables: Completed functional system

Tools used: PowerBuilder, optional: class library and framework, version control software, other third party add ins.

Time to Complete: Variable: 6 weeks to 8 months based upon scope of application

2.5.2.4 Test

The test phase will focus on performing complete unit and string testing of the application. Regression tests should be developed to allow future revisions and changes to the system to be fully tested. A documented test plan should be developed and carried out. (See Figure 2-14.)

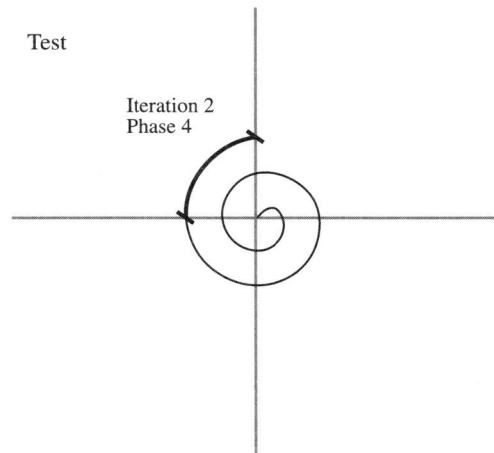

Test

Iteration 2
Phase 4

Figure 2-14. Full unit and string tests are executed to ensure the robustness of the application.

Inputs: Functional system

Deliverables: Test Results Document (expected results versus actual), bug list

Tools: PowerBuilder, optional: automated testing tool

Time to Complete: Variable: 1 week to 1 month

2.5.3 The Third (and Final) Iteration

The third iteration is the final iteration of the methodology. Here, any business changes that occurred during system development can be determined and the system adapted. This eliminates the "It's exactly what I asked for, but not what I want!" reaction from the users. The system is reviewed and any change requests, either functional or cosmetic, are documented.

Any final functionality is incorporated here. This is defined as functionality, which is important to the functioning of the system but is not necessarily an integral part of the business processes. The most common element to include is security. The time frame for this iteration is variable but is generally brief. As a rough guideline, it probably ranges from 4 weeks to 10 weeks.

2.5.3.1 Planning and Analysis

The objective of the first phase of the third iteration is to discover if any of the functionality in the system has changed or is incorrect. We also want to determine how to incorporate any layered functionality, such as security. This is the final opportunity for user input prior to implementation. (See Figure 2-15.)

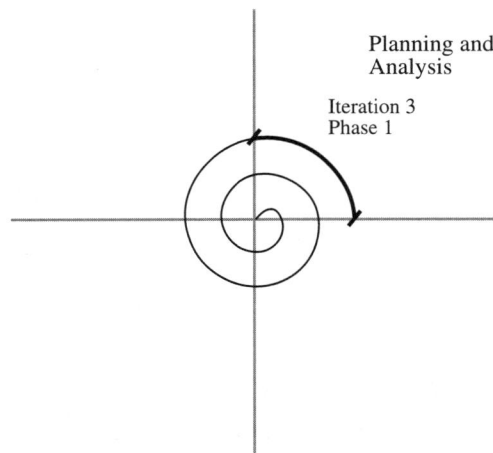

Figure 2-15. The first phase of the final iteration allows us to determine any business requirements that may have changed during development and to incorporate any layered functionality such as security.

Like before, we utilize the JAD session modified to perform a review of the functional system and solicit feedback from the users. Users are asked to specifically watch for places where the business functionality may have changed since the last user review. Users also ask them to confirm the security requirements of the system that have been previously worked out by the BSAs.

Inputs:	Tested functional system, user input, Security Requirements Document
Deliverables:	System enhancement/change requests, final Security Requirements Document
Tools Used:	Variable, word processor
Time to Complete:	Variable: 2 days to 12 days depending on scope

Design

In the second phase, the objective is to develop or revise the existing detailed design specifications for all approved enhancements, changes, and any layered functionality not yet incorporated. (See Figure 2-16.)

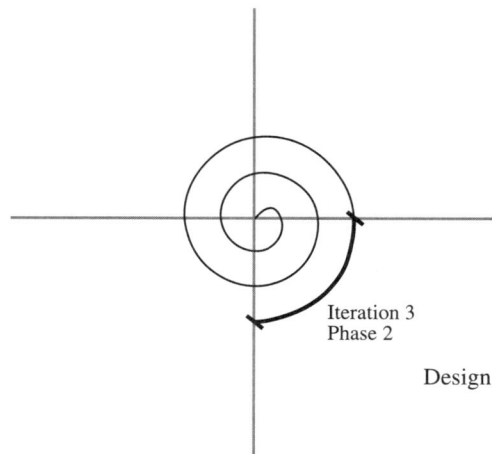

Iteration 3
Phase 2

Design

Figure 2-16. *The second phase of the final iteration will develop detailed design specifications for any approved enhancements, changes and layered functionality.*

Inputs:	System enhancement/change requests, Security Requirements Document

Deliverables:	Revised Detailed Design Specifications
Tools used:	Word processor of choice
Time to Complete:	Variable: 2 to 6 weeks

2.5.3.3 Build

In the build phase, any changes to the objects specified in the detailed design specifications are incorporated. All layered functionality is implemented. Layered functionality can often be incorporated through the use of third party tools. There are a number of good third party security tools on the market for PowerBuilder applications. If your class library does not already have a security mechanism in it, I recommend you investigate theses. (See Figure 2-17.)

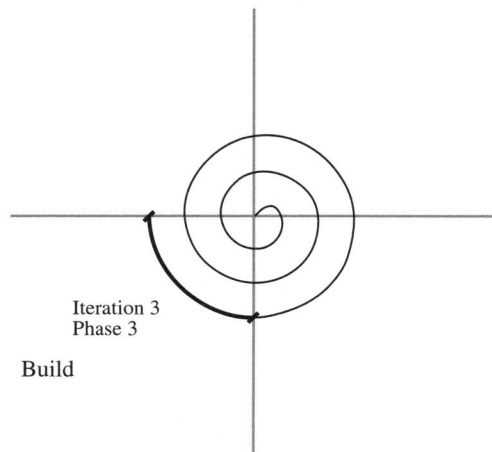

Iteration 3
Phase 3

Build

Figure 2-17. *Final polishing and development of layered functionality occurs in the third phase of the final iteration.*

Inputs:	Revised Detailed Design Specifications
Deliverables:	Final functional system
Tools used:	PowerBuilder, optional: class library and framework, version control software, other third party add ins.
Time to Complete:	Variable: 2 to 8 weeks based upon scope of application and volume of changes

2.5.3.4 Test

The final test phase, is the most extensive testing effort yet. All previous tests are reexecuted and full regression testing performed. A documented test plan are developed and carried out. (See Figure 12-18.)

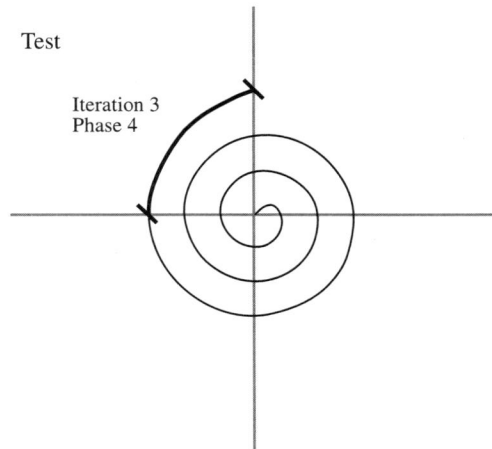

Test

Iteration 3
Phase 4

Figure 2-18. *Final complete testing of the application is conducted, including full user testing.*

Upon completion of these tests, user testing begins. Results of user testing are incorporated into the Test Results Document

Inputs:	Final system
Deliverables:	Test Results Document (expected results versus actual), bug list
Tools:	PowerBuilder, optional: automated testing tool
Time to Complete:	Variable: 2 weeks to 6 weeks

2.5.4 Implementation

The iterations are over, the system is built and tested, now it is time to deliver it to the end users. This section of the methodology is not radically different from others you may be familiar with. All the basic requirements are the same. Now you must prepare the documentation, train the users, and roll out the system to their workspaces.

2.5.4.1 Documentation

Documentation consists of two components, user and system.

2.5.4.1.1 User Documentation

The user documentation phase can actually begin earlier than this stage. The assigned technical writer can begin developing the user manuals and the online help in the build phase of the second iteration, as the system begins to take shape. The documentation can not be truly completed until the final testing of the third iteration is complete, and the system is done.

Manuals can be developed using your favorite word processing tool. To generate the online help, I strongly recommend using a help authoring tool. Anyone who has tried to develop online help only using the Windows SDK, can testify that it is not a pleasant experience. Currently, there are many available commercial help authoring tools which are excellent. Many shops no longer produce paper manuals but build only online help. This is for a variety of reasons including cost, ease of updating, and environmental friendliness.

I would strongly recommend producing quick reference cards for your end users where possible. Print these on thick card stock paper and fold it in such a way that they can stand it up like a café menu beside their monitors (this way it doesn't get lost in the stacks of paper that we all collect on our desks!)

Inputs:	Final system
Deliverables:	User Manuals, Online help, optional: Quick Reference Cards
Tools:	PowerBuilder, optional: automated testing tool
Time to Complete:	Variable: 2 weeks to 6 weeks

2.5.4.1.2 System Documentation

The purpose of system documentation is to provide the information necessary to allow the system to be maintained and repaired in the future. It also provides a paper trail that details how and why the system was designed the way it was.

All documentation produced during the system development life cycle should be gathered into one place. This includes all functional specifications, decomposition diagrams, process models, detailed design specifications, physical and logical data models, and technical print outs of all objects incorporated into the system.

Inputs: All system documentation
Deliverables: Unified System Documentation binder(s)
Time to Complete: Variable: 1 to 2 weeks

2.5.4.2 Training

The training phase of implementation involves developing a training plan and carrying it out. Depending on the number of users, the magnitude of this task varies. Users can be trained directly by one of the BSAs, in groups, or user trainer representatives can be trained in a "Train the Trainer" session. These representatives would perform all the training for their users.

Inputs: Final system and User Documentation
Deliverables: Training Plan, end user training, optional: training
                          manuals
Time to Complete: Variable: 1 to 8 weeks

2.5.4.3 Roll-out

The process of rolling out an application has a lot of the same procedures as before but there are a few new twists. A staging plan needs to be prepared for all hardware that needs to be installed. The physical networks must be established and tested. Servers need to be installed and tested. All relevant support software must be installed and tested. And so on...

Depending on how you have decided to roll out your client application, either to each individual workstation, networked on the server, or using a multi-tiered architecture, this will affect your planned roll out.

Inputs: Final system, Enterprise Architecture Plan (if available),
                          organizational hardware and network standards
Deliverables: Enterprise Architecture Plan, System Roll Out Plan
Time to Complete: Variable

2.5.4.4 Post Production Support (Help Desk)

Once the system is out and in the hands of the users, the post production support phase begins. You need to detail how user issues and system issues will be handled. Will a help desk or support line be established? Is there one already? How can a user request a change to the system? Who approves changes? And so on...

Just because a system is installed, doesn't mean the process is finished. To be complete and ensure the long term viability of the system, the above questions and more must be answered. A Post Production Support Plan should be developed to document and establish the mechanisms to manage the system now and in the future.

Inputs: Live production system
Deliverables: Post Production Support Plan
Time to Complete: Variable: 1 to 3 weeks

2.6 *Where to Go from Here*

"Our ideas are only intellectual instruments which we use to break into phenomena; we must change them when they have served their purpose, as we must change a blunt lancet that we have used long enough."

Claude Bernard

The world that we exist in changes faster than we can believe. The ACE methodology outlined above must be considered a work in progress. Take this work and use it as best you can. Change it when part of it does not apply to your situation or your world. I would be very pleased to hear any changes that you have been successful in implementing that have improved the above model.

CHAPTER 3

Architectures for Development

"The physician can bury his mistakes, but the architect can only advise his client to plant vines."

Frank Lloyd Wright, October 4, 1953, *New York Times Magazine*

*A*rchitecture plays a very important role in the success of client/server applications. When we discuss the architecture of an application we are referring to the manner in which components of the applications and functions of all the systems are stored, where they are stored, and how and where they are executed.

When developing applications using PowerBuilder, you have the flexibility to implement a variety of different types of architectures depending on your specific application or enterprise requirements. Selecting the appropriate architecture can reap substantial rewards for both the developers of the system and the users. These rewards can include a reduced development time and effort, increased application consistency, improved scalability, faster application performance, and easier maintenance.

A variety of different types of architectures can be considered, and architects are coming up with more every day. The most commonly utilized architectures today are the two-tiered architecture, the three- and N-tiered architectures, and the service based architecture.

In this chapter ,we review these architectures at a high level and tie them into different techniques in later chapters. To see how to build a basic distributed object or for more information regarding the PFC, please refer to the later chapters in this book.

3.1 Two-Tiered Architectures

Most PowerBuilder applications developed to date have been implemented using a two-tiered architecture. This architecture divides the application into two components, the *client* and the *data server*. Multiple client applications can access a single data repository on a shared database server.

The client is the component where the user interface resides. It manages the interface with the end user of the system. You may have heard this component referred to as the presentation layer. In PowerBuilder, this includes of all the visual objects such as windows, window controls, and DataWindows.

The data server is where all the data that the application accesses and manipulate is stored. This is usually contained within some kind of a relational database (RDBMS). Obviously there are other kinds of servers such as print servers, file servers, image servers, and so on, but for the purposes of this example, the only server that matters is the database server. (See Figure 3-1.)

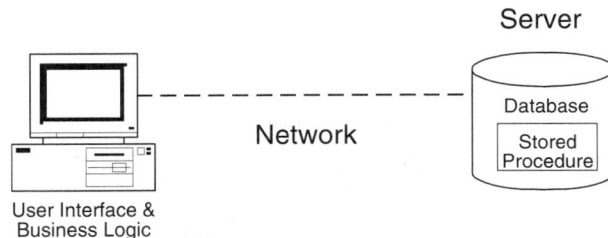

Figure 3-1. The two-tiered architecture places the user interface on the client, the data on a data server and the business rules can be programmed into either the client front end, or in stored procedures on the data server.

The business logic is programmed into the client front end, as part of the PowerBuilder code, or as stored procedures on the server database. Most existing PowerBuilder enterprise applications are a combination of both, but usually much more heavily weighted towards having the business rules coded into the PowerBuilder application. It is very rare to see a PowerBuilder application where all the business rules reside on the server, although this would help to eliminate most of the drawbacks of a two-tiered architecture discussed below.

Two-tiered architectures are particularly good for developing what we call "One Of" or "One Off" applications. These are applications where the objects involved are not likely to be reused and the business logic is not transportable across many different applications. These types of applications typically do not take advantage of any pre-built or existing business objects.

A two-tiered application can often be put together very quickly as less preparation is required to separate out the potential business logic and service objects. These objects are built right into the user interface or the relational database.

We have come to realize, after the industry has built thousands of two-tiered client/server applications, that although quick to design and build, there are some distinct limitations to this architecture. One drawback is that the business rules are all coded into either the client or the server. This means that if you select a new best of breed technology to replace one of these tiers (for example, you decide to replace your Visual Basic application with a PowerBuilder application) you will very likely have to rebuild the entire application, including your business logic.

Of even greater impact is the potential maintenance problem. If a basic business rule changes, you have to find every spot in the PowerBuilder application where that rule applies, change it, recompile the application and redistribute it to the users.

There is one other primary disadvantage to the two-tiered architecture: scalability. If you are rolling out your application to a lower number of concurrent users (the number is relative and we cannot be specific, but a rule of thumb I have heard is under 200 concurrent users), the two-tiered architecture functions adequately, however, once crossing over this dynamic threshold (the 200 user "line in the sand") application performance begins to suffer. With all the business logic on the client, these applications tend to make many small calls to the server to help them process the user input. The server gets overloaded trying to respond to all the user requests. The network tends to also slow down as the amount of data being shuffled from the server to the clients increases. This has been discussed as the "fat-client" syndrome and has plagued client centered development environments like PowerBuilder for some time.

You may encounter the term "partitioning" in your client/server documentation and training. Partitioning refers to the separation of the presentation, process/business rules and the data into three distinct and isolated units. Partitioning can be rolled out in a two-tier or multi-tier environment by selecting the location of the business logic. In PowerBuilder you can separate these components by building non-visual user objects that contain these rules. This can be a very valuable preliminary step to migrating your application from a two-tier to a multi-tier model.

3.2   *Three-Tiered Architectures*

To help overcome some of the inherent limitations of the two-tiered architecture, the concept of the three-tiered architecture was devised. In this architecture, the business logic is removed from both the client and the server and located on some other third layer. (See figure 3-3.) This third layer acts as a middleman, providing services to the user interface on the client and consolidating and managing transactions for the data server (or servers). (Note: I should point out that only in the theoretical world is all the logic removed from the client and server. Usually some of the logic still resides in these objects.)

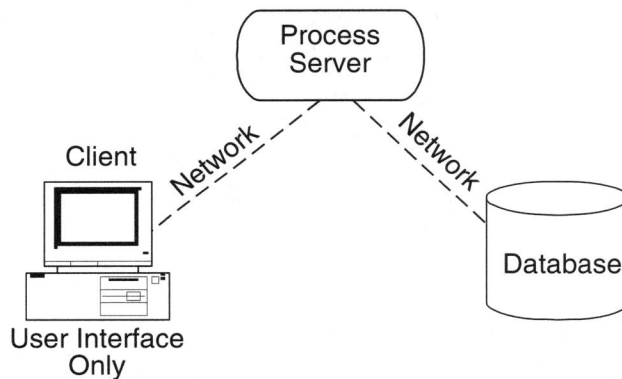

Figure 3-2. *The three-tiered architecture removes the business logic from both the client and the server and places it in some other third layer which could reside and execute on a physically separate machine from the client and the server.*

With this model, if you decide to change the front end tool for your application, you should be able to do so (if your third tier was developed in a non-proprietary format). In theory, any application development tool and any relational database can be used with the business rule objects stored on remote servers. This theory holds true if your objects are built to be DCE (Distributed Computing Environment), CORBA (Common Object Request Broker Architecture), or OLE (Object Linking and Embedding) compliant. As these standards are still evolving, most of the three-tiered applications in production today are still proprietary in nature.

With a three-tiered architecture, maintaining your business rules becomes easier, as they are all maintained in one place (in theory, although in practice, many three-tiered applications still place some business rules on the server and/or client). Many different applications can access the same business rule objects. Through centralization of objects focused on specific purposes, the burdens on the network and the database server may be able to be better managed.

Although a three-tiered architecture was conceived of to overcome some of the limitations of a two-tiered architecture, it also comes with its own disadvantages. There is a lot more up front work to be done. The investment in time and hardware for the third tier is no pittance. While you could still utilize many of the traditional structured development techniques to build applications with PowerBuilder, to build true three-tiered architectures requires that you perform proper object oriented analysis and design. These techniques have their own substantial learning curve.

A second issue with three-tiered architectures is that they become quite complex to manage and maintain. Although it becomes easy to alter an application if something like a business rule changes (all you have to do is change the appropriate business rule object on the third tier), you now find that your objects and your business logic is scattered throughout your architecture. Objects can become lost and controlling them becomes difficult. The theory of moving parts also begins to come into play: The more moving parts, the more likely a machine is to break down.

As I mentioned earlier, many of the three-tiered PowerBuilder solutions in production today rely upon sophisticated (some would say "complicated") third party products such as Novell's Tuxedo, Open Environment's Entera, IBM CICS, or Transarc Corporation's Encina. These tools, although providing some of the benefits of the three tier architecture, quickly fall victim to inflexibility and complexity.

3.3 *N-Tiered Architectures*

The n-tiered architecture is the next level beyond the three-tier architecture. In the n-tier environment, your objects can reside almost anywhere in your overall architecture. You don't have one specific piece of hardware dedicated as the "process object server." Instead, your objects are placed onto the servers where their functions are most appropriate. Through careful planning and design you can reduce load on the network. Data stores inside these distributed objects can help to reduce load on the servers. This is the type of architecture which truly allows you to scale your applications.

Like the three-tiered architecture, to be effective, an n-tiered architecture requires extensive up front planning and design effort, but they also have similar drawbacks, including the complexity factor.

3.4 Service-Based Architectures

In traditional discussions of multi-tiered architectures, the distributed objects that are usually discussed are based upon logical business entities or processes. For example, an HMO (Health Management Organization) may develop two distributed objects, one called a doctor and the other a patient. Each contains the methods and properties of their relevant business entities and can be stored and executed on a remote server.

In contrast, a service based architecture is based on taking common services that many applications require and separating them out as distributed objects. Many of these services are common amongst multiple systems and include such items as e-mail, faxing, printing, error handling, security management, and EDI (Electronic Data Interchange) to use a few of the more common examples. Services can also be driven down to a lower level and may include items like DataWindow row selection (single, multi, or other), messaging, and error handling/logging in your PowerBuilder applications.

You can begin to imagine some of the possibilities this architecture could provide. Think of an e-mail service. You could build an e-mail object that resides and executes on a remote server. When any of your internal applications need to send or work with your e-mail system, they connect through the standard interface you have constructed into the distributed object. The CPU cycles that the mail server requires are taken on the server and not on your client machine.

Developer's Tip: In PowerBuilder we usually offer services at one of three levels:

- Instance Service—when only one instance of an object in the client can use the service at a time. A separate instance of the service object would be created for each instance of a client object that requires the service.
- Class Service—when a single instance of the service object can be used to provide services to multiple instances of a given class of client object. A separate instance of the service object would be created for other classes requiring this service.
- Application Service—when a single instance of the service object can be used to provide services to all instances of all classes of client objects in the application.

There is another added benefit to this architecture. If you have five applications that all utilize e-mail, and then your organization switches from MS-Mail you could be faced with a challenge that may have an adverse impact upon your systems. If you use a standard MAPI (Messaging Application Program Interface—from Microsoft) compatible mail system you can take advantage of the built in MAPI functions that PowerBuilder supports. Then, if you decide to switch to cc:Mail which is based upon VIM (Vendor Independent Messaging—from Lotus) you will face some potentially difficult integration challenges as PowerBuilder does not have built in support for VIM. If you had used anything other than a service based architecture, you would need to modify every object that has a method that uses e-mail one at a time. Through the service based architecture, you only need to make the changes in the one object and have it take effect for all your current and future applications. The improved maintenance and the productivity gains realized across multiple applications is tremendous.

One potential disadvantage to a pure services based architecture is that the business logic can end up spread amongst a number of unrelated objects and this can become a maintenance problem.

3.5 Selecting the Right Architecture

When you were about halfway through the last subsection, you were probably thinking to yourself "But if I combine the n-tiered architecture with the services architecture, couldn't I get the best of both worlds?" and you would be absolutely correct. However, I would caution you that you are again increasing the complexity of the environment you work in and creating more "moving parts."

You cannot point at one architecture or another and say "This is the best architecture to use all the time." You must examine your corporate requirements and determine the appropriate architecture for your needs. You may be able to combine a number of the above architectures into one that works for your particular enterprise.

If you have a small company with only a dozen users and just two or three systems it might make sense to combine a two-tiered and a services based architecture. There is not a lot of opportunity to implement large scale reuse and scalability is not really an issue. The speed of development and cost effectiveness is likely to appeal to you, yet you can benefit from services which all the applications need, like providing fax services.

On the other hand, if you are a large scale corporation with dozens of custom applications of all shapes and sizes you would likely benefit from an n-tier architecture integrated with a solid foundation of distributed services.

If this is your first application with this environment and tool set, I would discourage you from trying to build a fully integrated n-tier and service based architecture. You have to learn to walk before you can run. The more complex you make the first application you approach, the greater the risk of failure. Corporate n-tier architectures should be approached by experienced personnel and professional consultant mentors if those skills are not available in house.

As a closing note, when dealing with distributed PowerBuilder applications, remember that you have to expand your thinking to imagine your local and distributed objects as one big application with some of the parts scattered around your architecture and placed where they can be more effective and useful to you!

CHAPTER 4

Designing a PowerBuilder Application

*D*esigning your PowerBuilder application correctly is a critical stage in the success of enterprise PowerBuilder systems. In this chapter, I hope to give you an overview of the considerations involved in creating a good application design. The principals are substantial enough that they could be the subject for their own book, so we will address some of the most important areas here.

There are three central components involved in building PowerBuilder applications; the data model (data server), the user interface (client), and the business processes (process server/object request broker).

4.1 The Data Model

If you are one of the fortunate, your organization may already have a corporate data model. If not, you may be saddled with small islands of data stored in a multitude of different formats throughout your organization. Or, perhaps this is the first system in your organization, and if so, what a terrific opportunity for you to build the foundation for an open corporate data model and data warehouse!

Having a well constructed data model provides you with the key to building a robust and effective PowerBuilder application. Creation of a conceptual data model is essential for starting the design of a system on the right foot. Having the physical data model in the design process is not an absolute requirement, but I would strongly recommend it before proceeding with the low level detailed design.

We will not discuss how to build a data model here, as this is one of those topics well covered by many other books. The point I wish to emphasize is that in a non-enterprise application, you may be able to get away with building the data model at the same time as you build the application. For developing larger scale or enterprise systems this is not acceptable and will result in a lot of unnecessary redevelopment. For any enterprise project the data model MUST be constructed before you design the application. I'm not implying that it has to be 100% rock solid (although it would be nice!), but it should be at least 80% stable or better.

4.2   The User Interface

Many elements combine together to make up the design of the user interface. This is an area where getting the users involved is critical. I would also recommend that you read a book by Don Norman entitled *The Design of Everyday Things*. It is a book you will find in the "architecture" section of your local book store and does not relate specifically to GUI or application design, but many of the issues that are raised in the book should be forefront in your mind when you are designing applications for your users.

4.2.1 User Centric Design

In traditional systems development, we tended to focus development of the system around the business process we were working on. We assumed that the users would have to adapt to whatever system we gave them, instead of adapting the system to the users. In traditional development, the real critical factor was that the system was able to fulfill the requirements of the process.

This is obviously no longer the case. We have come around 180 degrees in our thinking in this area. We are now developing our applications centered around the needs of the users. There are many reasons for this, including a paradigm shift that has occurred in information systems development. In the past, many of the systems we developed were tactical in nature. They addressed a specific business process, such as billing. Now the systems we develop tend to be more strategic in nature, and they address the management of entities and data rather than being designed around a single primary process.

It is critical in all PowerBuilder development projects to center your application design around the users. You need to get them involved in the initial analysis and design, and then keep them involved throughout the entire process until they actually take delivery of the completed system. This requires a great deal of bi-directional communication, but this is one of those factors that will increase the likelihood of project success by several orders of magnitude. Users must be continually updated on system development progress and be provided regular opportunities to provide feedback on the system.

PowerBuilder is an event driven tool and follows the user centric model very well. The environment allows you to provide unambiguous feedback to the user during execution, and when necessary, to hold their hand through various processes through the creation of what have become known as "wizards." The flexibility and strength of PowerBuilder allow you to build a system that fits the user instead of trying to make the user fit the system.

4.2.2 The Overall Design

The overall design of your application is a task of equal, if not greater, importance on an enterprise project than the actual application coding. If you have a bad design (or no design), then it doesn't matter how good your skills are with your chosen tool set, you will have a bad application.

You must make decisions about the overall look and feel of your application. This includes using your corporate GUI design guidelines, or if you don't have any, developing some (refer to Appendix A for more details on Design Guidelines and Standards) that will apply to this project and across the enterprise in the future. Many published standards in this arena are incomplete and inconsistent. You may be able to use them as a foundation, but you must be sure to adapt them to your requirements and evolve them as your environment changes.

The design of your application must also take into account your conceptual and physical architecture. Your design will vary if you are using a two tier versus a three tier architecture (refer to Chapter 3—Architectures for Development for more details). On the physical side, you must take into consideration the kinds of hardware involved. If your clients are running Intel based 386 PCs with 8 Mb of memory, you will design a much lighter and less processing intensive interface than if they will have Pentium 166 workstations with 32 Mb of memory. Similar considerations will have to come into play based upon the network and the server that are being used.

4.2.3 User Analysis Matrix

Part of building an application that is truly user centric is the process of analyzing the users themselves. You must evaluate their skills and abilities in order to be able to design an application that will provide the best interface for them.

I will use an example based upon an actual enterprise PowerBuilder application that I was involved with to demonstrate the use of a user analysis matrix. My role on this project was to help mentor the team in the use of client/server development concepts on PowerBuilder applications. The system was intended to help store and process student insurance policies (policies for accident, sickness, and death). The primary users of the system were defined as being the people in the claims department who would take and process insurance claims from their customers. Had they been the only user group, the system would have been quite straightforward, however, they were not. We realized there was a secondary user group who represented the executive in the company. They wanted to be able to use the system to obtain high level reports and statistics. Then we realized there was a third group, for three months of the year, they hired a number of temporary personnel who would come in and enter the new insurance policies into the system. So, we had three user groups who all required access to the same system. We had to decide what kind of an interface to build.

We assembled the three groups of users into a user requirements matrix such as the one in Figure 4-1.

	CATEGORIES	Business Knowledge	Computer Expertise	Frequency of Use
USER GROUPS				
Claims Personnel				
Executive				
Data Entry Temps				

Figure 4-1. A User Requirements Matrix contains the major user groups on the left side and has the categories of analysis across the top.

The user groups are listed down the left column, while we have the three analysis categories across the top; business knowledge, computer expertise and frequency of use.

We look at each group individually and rank them in each category as High (3), Medium (2) and Low (1). The claims people have a high business knowledge, medium computer expertise, and a low frequency of use (the number of claims processed per day is quite low). The executive also have a high business knowledge, very low computer expertise, and a low frequency of use. The data entry temps have a very low business knowledge, high computer expertise, and high frequency of use. This results in values in our matrix as we see in Figure 4.2.

CATEGORIES	Business Knowledge	Computer Expertise	Frequency of Use
USER GROUPS			
Claims Personnel	3	2	1
Executive	3	1	1
Data Entry Temps	1	3	3

Figure 4-2. The results of our user requirements matrix for the insurance example.

When we look at the numbers in the matrix, we can see that there are really two different groups of users with two very different types of interface needs. The claims personnel and the executive both have high business knowledge, low frequency of use and relatively low computer expertise. This is sharply contrasted by the temporary data entry personnel who have very little business knowledge, but high computer expertise and frequency of use. If we build an interface that is very GUI oriented, with a lot of mouse controls and push buttons, this would benefit the claims personnel and the executive who don't use the system all day long, who understand the business, and are after an intuitive interface. This style of interface would reduce the amount of time that they would need to spend in training and the amount of system detail they would need to memorize. It would also help to reduce the quantity of errors they would incur when using the system. This kind of interface would be the kiss of death to the temporary data entry people, as it forces them to remove their hands from the keyboard to use the mouse, thus slowing their productivity dramatically. This group requires an interface that allows them to enter as much data as possible as quickly as possible without having to take their fingers off the keyboard. Heavily GUI oriented interfaces which require a lot of mousing around would severely impact the productivity of this group. They require a heads down data entry display designed to move smoothly from one data entry task to the next. In fact, this was the solution that was built. The same application was constructed with two different user interfaces, one for the users with extensive business knowledge and low frequency of use, and one for the data entry personnel who had little business knowledge, but used the system all day long.

Developer's Note: If you are thinking, "This would be an ideal situation to take advantage of application partitioning!," you are absolutely correct! The business processes could be built into a set of non-visual business objects allowing us to build two completely different user interfaces with the exact same business logic and rules.

Performing this kind of an analysis on your project will help you to determine the appropriate kind of interface for your user group and see if any conflicting requirements exist among the different users. It may also force you to think outside the bounds of normal system design. It is unusual for most designers to contemplate rolling out more than one user interface for the same system.

A word of warning: Developing the correct user interface is a thankless task. If you do your job correctly, the interface will be almost transparent to the users and they will likely not give it a second thought. However, if you do it wrong, every user will be letting you know!

4.2.4 MDI or SDI?

When developing an application in PowerBuilder, you will have to decide if the application would be best developed as a Multiple Document Interface (MDI) application or as a Single Document Interface (SDI) application. Most business oriented software available, in the traditional windows platform, is MDI in design. This means that you have one primary window, the MDI Frame, and virtually all the other windows in the application are opened inside the MDI Frame. The MDI Frame acts as the desktop or workspace for the application.

Most commercial windows applications are MDI based. Some examples include Microsoft Word and Excel and even PowerBuilder itself! The advantage of choosing to build your application as an MDI application is that you can contain very diverse functionality all within the context of the same application. For example, one major university that I worked with has constructed their entire admissions system in PowerBuilder. One problem that was identified with the old system was that if someone in the Registrar's office was working on one student admission and they receive a call from a second student asking about their status, they would have to back all the way out of the student they were working on to look up the new student. With the PowerBuilder system that was developed, they used an MDI approach and now the people working on the system can have multiple students open as the same time.

MDI based applications can be further subdivided into single function MDI and multiple function MDI. A single function MDI usually performs only one relatively focused primary task. Microsoft Word is an example of a single function MDI, although you can have multiple documents open, all it really does is create and modify documents (a relatively narrow primary task). PowerBuilder, on the other hand, is an example of a multiple function MDI. Each painter develops a completely different type of object and other painters perform completely different functions such as source code management or table creation.

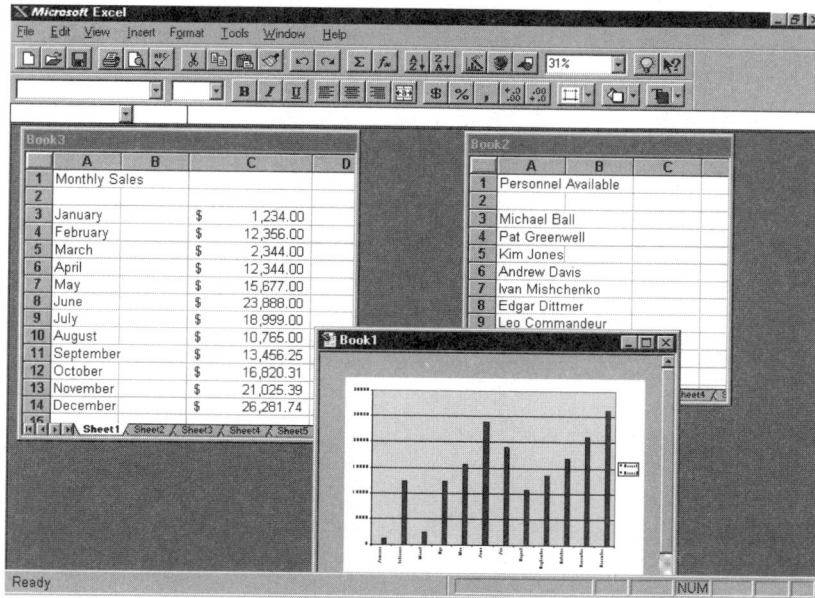

Figure 4-3. *An MDI application like Excel allows you to have multiple tasks going at the same time. In this example we have two spreadsheets and a graph all open at the same time.*

Within an SDI application, the functionality of the application is usually much more limited. Many windows can be opened simultaneously, but not having a container like the MDI Frame to help manage them makes keeping them all under control substantially more difficult. I think it is important to point out however, that the new 32 bit operating systems like Windows 95 and Windows NT seem to be slowly trending away from MDI and developing applications as complex SDI systems.

At present, most enterprise applications being developed in the windows environment are still being developed using MDI standards. From a user perspective, I feel that the MDI interface is beneficial in unifying the interface and keeping confusion to a minimum.

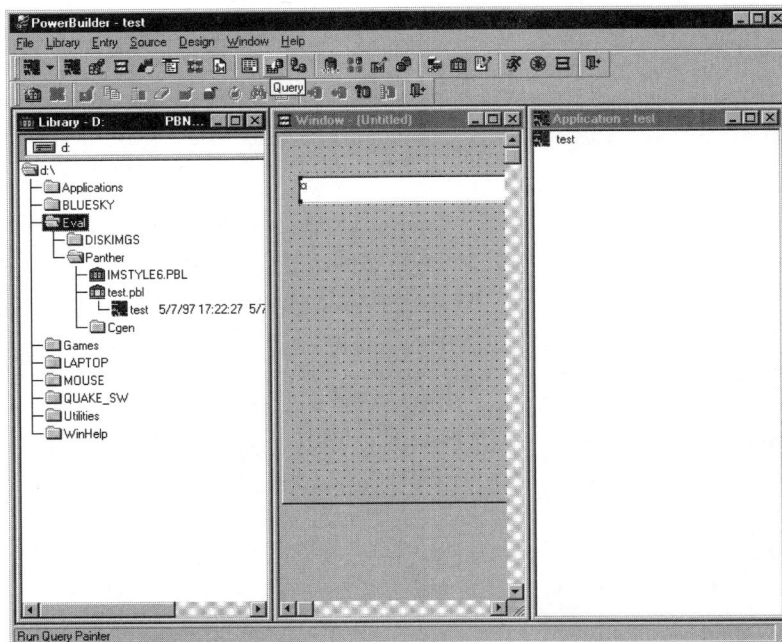

Figure 4-4. PowerBuilder is an example of a multiple function MDI application.

Developer Tip: In many business applications today there is a distinct trend towards the use of tab folder based interfaces. These are interfaces that use the real world metaphor of file folders to allow the user to access different subsets of information within a given window. This type of interface can be observed in many common commercial applications like the Microsoft Word Options dialog window shown in Figure 4-4b.

In versions of PowerBuilder prior to 5.0, we had to use third party user objects, or write our own, in order to implement tab folders. This functionality is now supported natively in PowerBuilder 5.0 and 6.0.

Tab folder implementations in applications can occur in either MDI or SDI formats.

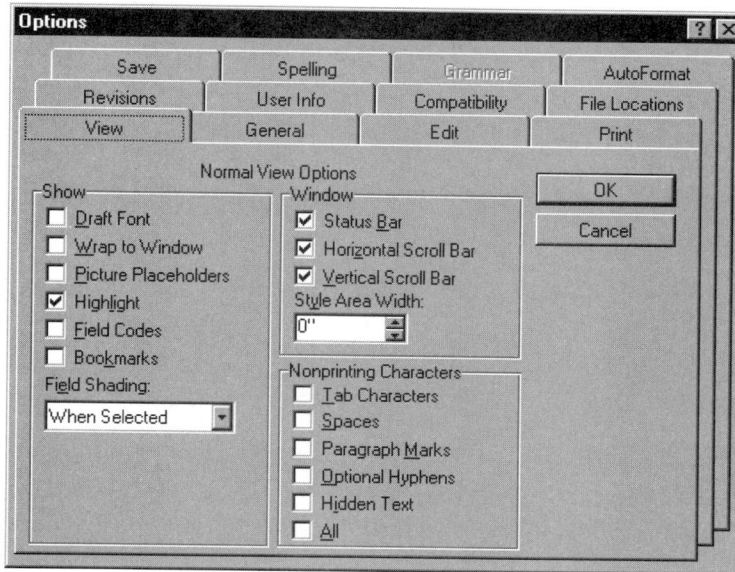

Figure 4-4b. The tabbed interface is becoming increasingly common in today's applications. This is fully supported in PowerBuilder 6.0 and can be used in both MDI and SDI type applications.

4.2.5 Choosing the Correct Window Type

Using the correct types of windows in your applications is very important. It is important to remember that the window is your primary means of interfacing with your user. The way that your chosen window will appear and behave is critical to your overall system success.

4.2.5.1 The Foundation Window

Every application has a *foundation window* or primary window. This is the main window of your application and reflects where the user will be spending most of their time. For most enterprise applications this will be the MDI frame. The MDI frame is very strong as a foundation window because it already come pre-equipped with a mechanism for managing sheets (main windows opened within the frame), displaying a toolbar with the menu, and providing feedback to the user through the MicroHelp or Status Bar.

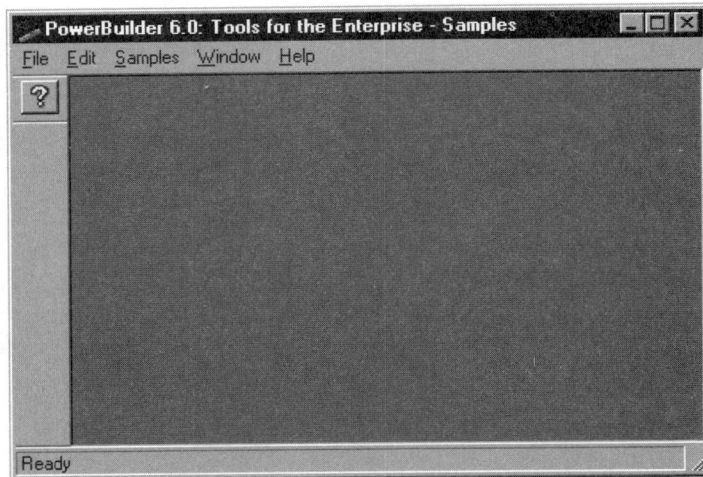

Figure 4-5. *The MDI Frame with MicroHelp is the most commonly used foundation window in enterprise applications.*

If your requirements fit appropriately, you may decide to build a SDI application. This would mean that you are creating your foundation window from a Main window. These are particularly useful for systems with a single function which are relatively simple and straightforward. For example, an amortization calculator for mortgages which you want to roll out to all the employees in a bank as a simple pop-up application would be a good use for SDI.

4.2.5.2 The Main Window

The main window type in PowerBuilder is most often used in enterprise level applications as sheets within the MDI frame. Sheets are intended to be extremely flexible. This means, among other things, that they are *modeless* and allow the user to move from sheet to sheet within the application at will. We are not forcing them down a specific route when we use main windows.

> **Developer's Note:** In versions of PowerBuilder prior to 5.0, sheets on an MDI frame were always resizeable, regardless of whether the Resizeable property was set to true or not. In PowerBuilder 6.0, if the Resizeable property is set to False, then the window cannot be resized by the user.

The main window is relatively independent. If attached to an MDI frame, it will close with the MDI frame, and if minimized, its icon will appear inside the MDI client area. If the main window is not part of an MDI application, it will only be closed when the user directly closes it, and if minimized, it will appear as its own icon in the program manager. If you are building an SDI application, your foundation window will most likely be a main window.

4.2.5.3 The Child Window

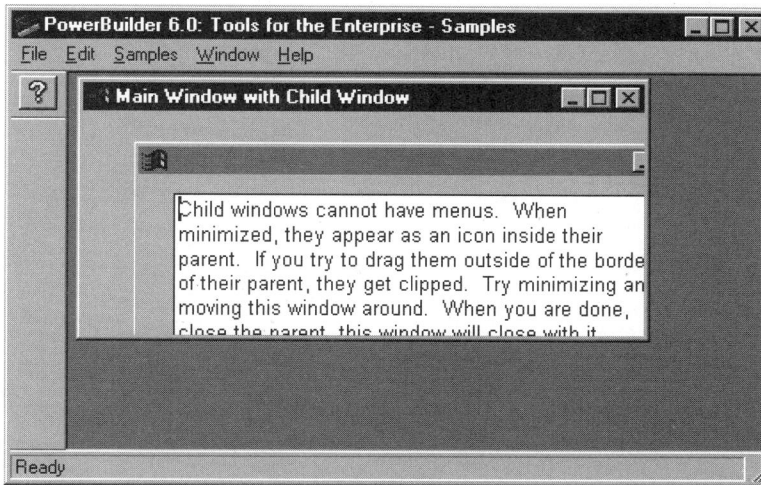

Figure 4-6. *A child window is completely dependent upon its parent. If moved beyond the borders of its parent, its edges get clipped off. This window type also never receives the activate event.*

The child window is a very interesting object. You will not use them very often due to some of their particular characteristics. The child window is completely dependent upon its parent. If you move a child window beyond the borders of its parent, the edges of the window get clipped off. If you minimize a child window, its icon appears within its parent. If you close the parent, the child closes also. The child never receives the activate event. If you click on the child window when the parent is deactivated, the parent receives the Activate event.

Development Tip: You can capture the activation of a child window through declaring an undefined system event for the window and capturing the "pbm_childactivate" event id. Refer to Chapter 18—Advanced Development Concepts for more information on setting up undefined system events.

This last characteristic is the one which makes it difficult to pass information to and from a child window. These windows do not find their way into enterprise applications often, but I have seen them used in some very creative situations. One example where I have seen it used was where we had a main window, and we wanted to place a number of small DataWindows on the main window. The DataWindow controls provided side by side drill down capability. The left most DataWindow control showed a list of countries, when a country was selected, the DataWindow next to it would show a list of states/provinces within that country. Upon selecting a state, the DataWindow to its right would show a list of counties and so on until you had drilled down to the lowest reasonable level. This could potentially involve up to eight side by side master detail DataWindows. As the window was only wide enough to display four of these at a time, the user wanted to see a scroll bar beneath the DataWindows and have the ability to scroll back and forth. There were also other controls on the window that we didn't want to scroll. In order to resolve this conflict, we placed a child window upon the main window and all the DataWindows were placed upon the child. The child was set to display no border or title bar, but would display a horizontal scroll bar. This gave us a fairly straightforward solution to what would have otherwise been a technically challenging problem.

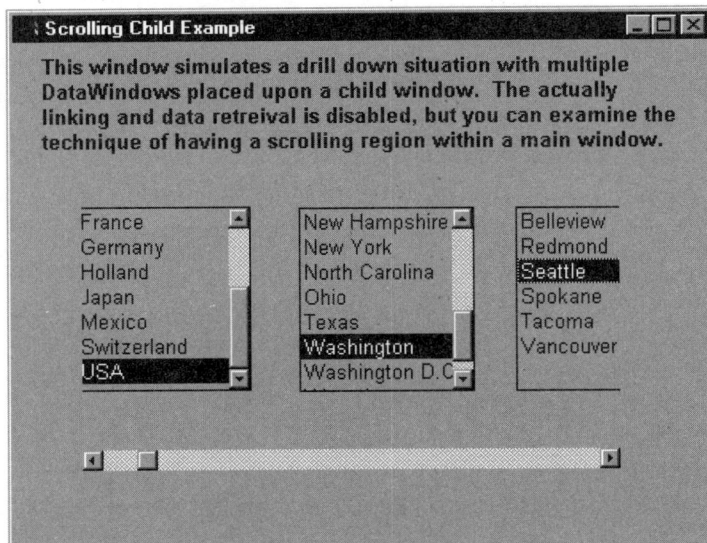

Figure 4-7. A child window was used in a production application to allow the scrolling of multiple DataWindows from side to side within a main window. This is a screen shot from the application on the companion CD.

A simulation of this solution can be found on the companion CD. The data selection logic is not there, but you can examine how the scrolling child was used.

4.2.5.4 The Popup Window

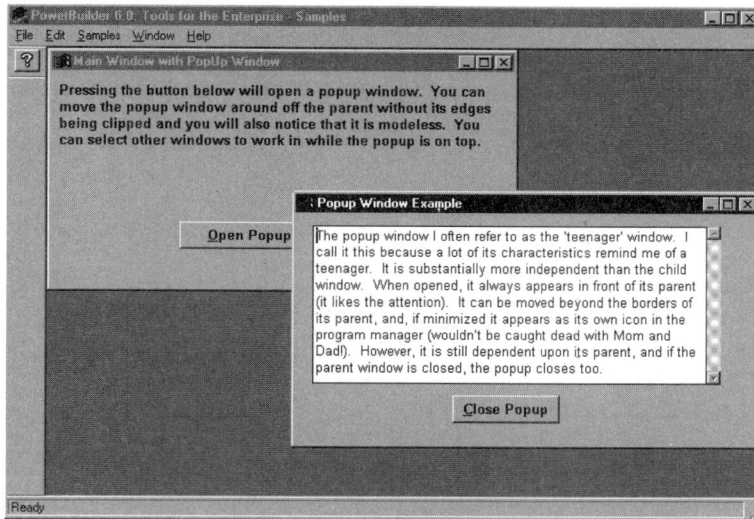

Figure 4-8. *The popup window is more independent than the child and can be moved outside its parent and minimized in the program manager.*

The popup window I often refer to as the "teenager" window. I call it this because a lot of its characteristics remind me of a teenager. It is substantially more independent than the child window. When opened, it always appears in front of its parent (it likes the attention). It can be moved beyond the borders of its parent, and, if minimized it appears as its own icon in the program manager (wouldn't be caught dead with Mom and Dad!). However, it is still dependent upon its parent, and if the parent window is closed, the popup closes too.

The popup is modeless, so you still have the ability to move from the popup to the parent and to other windows in the application, but every time you look, active or not, that popup is on top of the heap trying to get your attention!

Popup windows are used frequently in enterprise applications. You might find them used to present detail information about something in a main window. For example, a main window may contain a list of orders and double-clicking on a row would cause a popup window to be opened with the details of that specific order. You could double-click on multiple rows and see many detail windows on your screen. You should note that when a popup window is opened in an SDI application, its parent is the currently active window unless otherwise specified. This means that the script

```
Open(w_p_one)
Open(w_p_two)
```

would result in the main window being the parent of w_p_one, but w_p_one would become the parent of w_p_two. This could be resolved by specifying the parent window as the second argument in the Open function:

```
Open(w_p_one,  w_parent_name)
Open(w_p_two,  w_parent_name)
// If applicable, the reserved word PARENT or THIS can be
// substituted for w_parent_name.
// This would result in a more generic use of the function.
```

The example pictured in Figure 4-8 is a shot from the sample application that comes on the companion CD.

4.2.5.5 The Response Window

All of the windows that we have discussed so far are modeless windows. The user can move back and forth from window to window within the application whenever they choose. For the most part, this is an admirable accomplishment, however, sometimes we need to restrict the user from moving throughout the application and give us the answer we require now so we can continue. To do this, we use a window called a response window. These windows are application modal and when opened, the user can only work within that window. Attempting to move to any other window within the same application results in a chastising beep from windows. You can jump to a different application, but the application you were working in will not proceed until the response window is dealt with.

You normally want to be careful to minimize the use of this type of window because of their modal nature and the restrictions this places on the user. In many enterprise applications being built today, there is a user requirement for "wizard" like technology. Wizards are a series of response windows which lead the user by the hand (or by the nose) through the creation of some entity or process. Response windows are ideal for this type of application as opening one response window from another causes a chain to be formed and requires that to close the wizard, all the response windows must be closed in order.

You will find a sample of opening a response window in the demonstration application on the companion CD.

4.2.6 Providing Feedback to the User

Many users feel uncomfortable when the system "goes away" and does processing while the user waits for the task to finish. Often they are not even aware of what task it is that the system is trying to accomplish. It is imperative that during execution of the application you keep your user informed of what the system is doing, and what their options are. This can be accomplished through any combination of visual and auditory cues.

4.2.6.1 Visual Cues

Visual cues are mechanisms for providing information to the user through the GUI interface. This can be done through a combination of visual objects, colors, fonts and so on. For example, when the mouse passes over a column where the user is not allowed to enter data, the pointer can be made to turn into a "no-entry" symbol. You should be certain to ensure that all possible visual cues are designed into your application.

PowerBuilder has a number of features built into the standard objects for enterprise development that can assist you with the visual cues. One of these is *MicroHelp*. MicroHelp is the text that appears in the status bar at the bottom of an MDI frame. PowerBuilder will automatically use it to display information about the various options in the current menu. You can also make use of it to display information to the user about what your application is doing, such as "Connecting to the database...One moment please...."

A second mechanism for providing visual feedback is through PowerTips, PowerBuilder's version of Microsoft's balloon help. Microsoft first introduced the concept of balloon help around two and half years ago. Balloon help is a popup message that appears when your mouse stops moving over a toolbar button. You can provide this same functionality in your PowerBuilder application. This text is set in the menu painter on the toolbar tab of the properties sheet. You can enter a short text and a long text. The short text appears before the comma, and is the text that appears under the button when the ShowText for the toolbar is set to true. The long text appears after the comma. If you don't enter any long text, then the short text will be used for the balloon help, but since you can provide a better cue, you should.

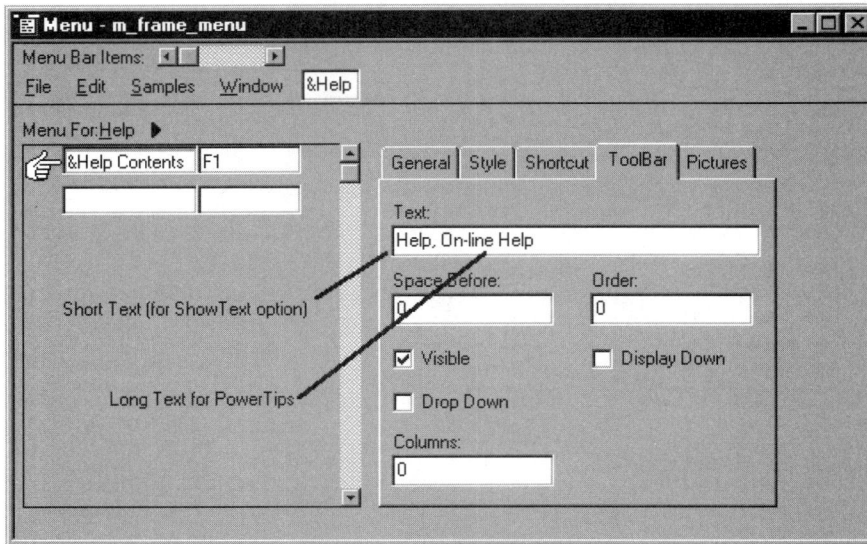

Figure 4-9. *In PowerBuilder you can have PowerTips (a.k.a. balloon help) show up for each toolbar item by entering it after the short text in the toolbar page of the menu properties page.*

Developer's Tip: The Tab Folder object that was introduced in PowerBuilder version 5.0 allows you to define PowerTips for each tab. When the user rests the mouse over the tab text, the balloon help box will pop up.

Color is the third mechanism you can use to provide feedback to your users. It is important to keep in mind however that a substantial proportion of the general population has difficulty discerning color differences and this should never be the primary mechanism for communicating information. You can use color to send a message to the user, just be certain that there is also another way that the user can receive the same information that is not dependent upon color. Many successful enterprise systems do use color to enhance the communication of data such as status of a record. For example, you can flag rows in a DataWindow by changing the background color for rows with a status of active to green and inactive to red. By also displaying a field saying "Active" or "Inactive" we are eliminating the dependence upon color as the primary communications mechanism.

4.2.6.2 Audible Cues

You can also provide audible feedback to your users in the form of beeps or .WAV files. This also is not recommended as a primary means of communication as it would preclude deaf or hard of hearing people from using your system. Sound can still be used as a user interface enhancement.

4.2.6.3 System Delays

I would strongly recommend that you be sure to provide feedback to the users whenever the system is occupied with a task. The users will appreciate being informed of progress and will be more tolerant when your system is busy. For any processes that cause a short delay (such as the opening of a window, or a short retrieval) change the pointer from the arrow to the hourglass using the SetPointer(Hourglass!) function. As the delay gets longer, the users will begin to wonder if the system has locked up. You can place a message in the MicroHelp area to inform them of what task the system is doing, and change the message as the task progresses, if applicable. For substantial delays (to be arbitrary, let's say 15 seconds) you should display some sort of a progress meter so that the user is able to see that the system is really still running and is doing something productive.

4.3 Process Objects

Whether you are building a two tier or an n-tier application, you must remember that your design needs to include not only the user interface, but also the business processes that are involved in developing the system. This may involve designing non-visual objects and service based objects, or building the business logic into the appropriate visual objects if you are using a two tier architecture.

4.3.1 Application Security

Security is one of those issues which has been severely neglected in PowerBuilder applications, and in fact, I would say in client/server applications in general. There has been a tendency in the past to rely on the database to provide security for an application. For more complex enterprise applications this is simply not sufficient.

When designing your application, you need to establish categories of users and what permissions the different categories of users can have. Permissions are simply a matter of who can do what. From a design perspective, you must be able to identify which functions and options will be visible and available to different security levels and include this in your detailed design.

There are two traditional approaches most enterprise projects take to application security. The first is to build your own non-visual security management object which would ride herd over each of your applications. The second option available to you is to purchase one of the third party security management libraries for PowerBuilder. They are gaining a lot of ground in the PowerBuilder arena and by most reports are convenient and effective.

With the PowerBuilder Foundation Class(PFC) library that is shipped with PowerBuilder 6.0 you will find a complete set of security processes and objects.

The important thing to remember when deciding on which approach to security you will implement is that it must be easy to administer and maintain, or it will slowly degrade until it is not effective. Users are notorious for developing their own workarounds when they find a system is awkward to use or doesn't meet their real requirements.

4.3.2 Other Process Objects

The possibilities for types of process objects that you might create are endless. For your specific industry alone there are probably dozens of potential process objects. For example, if you were developing systems for a hotel reservation system, you may have a process object for a guest. This object would have methods such as CheckIn, CheckOut, RoomService, GenerateBill, and so on. You could also have process objects for a room with methods for Clean, Classify, and Reserve. You could extend this model to all the entities that are involved in the reservation system, or the hotel industry (if you wanted to grow the system).

You may decide to build service based objects for managing system services such as faxing, printing or e-Mail. If you isolate these services into their own objects it will make your maintenance much easier in the future. It will also provide you with the flexibility of possibly distributing these objects onto a process server (3 and "n" tier architectures) so that multiple applications can use them (refer to Chapter 9 for more information on using distributed objects).

4.4 On-Line Help

I have seen many enterprise development projects that move forward, always telling themselves that they will write the on-line help at the end of the development cycle when they have time. Guess what? It never gets written.

On-line help needs to be taken more seriously and properly integrated into the project plan. Windows should be designed to be able to provide context sensitive help to users. One of the goals of the GUI interface is to reduce the cost of end user training. If users can look in the help file when they need more information, it will go a long way towards achieving this goal. Every major function in your functional decomposition should have a segment in the on-line help.

Writing windows help is now easier than ever before. You no longer have to get down in the mud with the Windows SDK™ to produce a help file, now we can use one of the many excellent third party tools like RoboHelp™ or Doc-2-Help™ to use our standard word processor to create fully functional help files including hot-links, screen captures and some even support video clip playback.

The help files should be written by an experienced technical writer. Any enterprise project should be able to incorporate a person with this skill set into your project. A technical writer has the skill and background to help communicate on-line help information in a format that the end user will be able to understand.

4.5 Summary

Designing a solid PowerBuilder application is still part science and part art. You must be sure when you design your application that you center the design around the users and keep them involved throughout the system development process.

Be thorough in your design, including plans for non-visual, process and service objects where appropriate. Be sure to include your plans for security implementation, on-line help and all processes which you otherwise might be tempted to leave to the end. The most successful enterprise PowerBuilder applications were built upon the foundation of a solid and thorough initial design.

CHAPTER 5

Object Oriented PowerBuilder

*P*owerBuilder is considered a flexible object oriented development tool because it allows *you to be as object oriented or non-object oriented as you choose. It was intended to allow developers who were unfamiliar with object orientation to adjust to the new concepts slowly, without having their arm twisted behind their backs. This may have been a good concept, however one serious implication is that now thousands of PowerBuilder enterprise level production applications exist with code that is half OO (pronounced "oh-oh") and half not. This means that the applications become a nightmare to maintain and are not as efficient with the system resources as they should be. They are probably also somewhat unstable and GPF (Global Protection Fault—but I am sure you are probably very familiar with that!) more regularly than a proper object-oriented application.*

If you are already familiar with object orientation, you can skip this chapter and move on to the next, however if you are new to OO or only have a fundamental grasp, I recommend spending some time with this chapter. We address some of the foundation concepts of OO including objects, classes, inheritance, encapsulation, and polymorphism. We relate these concepts to the PowerBuilder enterprise development environment and look at some sample objects to see how these concepts are used.

5.1 What Does Using OO Mean?

There are many potential benefits to using object oriented design and development techniques, however in order to realize them, the techniques must be understood and applied correctly. These techniques are particularly useful to an enterprise application developer.

It would be nice if I could tell you that OO makes it easier to develop applications; unfortunately, this is not necessarily true. It can help make a developer more productive and produce better quality applications that are easier to maintain, but it requires just as much, in fact probably more skill and effort than traditional environments.

The developer who will be successful with object oriented technology is the one who can make the paradigm shift to the object oriented concepts and grasp which components provide a practical benefit versus those that are more theoretical in nature. The successful OO developer cannot just focus on the details of the application section they are currently assigned, they must see and comprehend how the area they are currently working on fits into the big picture. This requires keeping your finger on the pulse of all the development going on throughout the project (no small task on an enterprise project!).

Although PowerBuilder gives the impression that you can tear the shrink wrap off and begin building slick applications immediately, if you do this in the enterprise environment, you will fail. To build a successful OO PowerBuilder application requires a very substantial investment in up front planning and design and no small amount of self-discipline from the development team. The quality of your up front planning will make or break your project.

There are a wealth of Object Oriented Analysis (OOA) and Object Oriented Design (OOD) tools and concepts on the market, which all advocate different methods and procedures. Peter Coad and Ed Yourdon are often spoken of as significant contributors to the world of object oriented analysis and design. Their books *Object Oriented Analysis* and *Object Oriented Design* (often referred to in OO circles as "the yellow book" and "the blue book" respectively because of the colors of their covers) are a must read for any object oriented analyst and programmer. However, in the modern arena, it is difficult to point to one OO methodology and say "This is the one you should use!" If I was to make a recommendation, I would check out the results of the joined forces of three OO powerhouses, Grady Booch, James Rumbaugh, and Ivor Jacobsen. Their new object modeling methodology called "Unified Method" seems to be getting a warm reception from the OO community.

The tools, though important, are not nearly as important as the skill and mindset of the project team. The team must be able to identify and build a system around the fundamental entities of that system, instead of trying to build it around the processes or data. This means being able to identify properties and methods of entities and model them into the structure of the object that represents that entity.

To begin to apply the concepts of OO, it is important to understand the terminology and how it relates to PowerBuilder. Some of the concepts we discuss here are not 100% in line with purist object oriented philosophy. This is because PowerBuilder bends some of the purist views a little. For the purist approach, check out the books in the bibliography relating to OO.

5.2 Why Use OO with PowerBuilder?

As we stated earlier, PowerBuilder does not require you to use OO to develop software and depending on what you are trying to develop, it may not even be worthwhile. However, for most enterprise project there are considerable advantages.

Don't be confused between object orientation and client/server. When client/server first became the rage, all the advocates said that it would reduce development time and costs. We all know that that simply isn't true. Client/server is another architecture different from mainframe computing architectures, but that doesn't make it faster or necessarily cheaper. Now OO is promising the same things and the skeptics are saying, "We heard the same story about client/server." Client/server and OO are not the same animal, although they are often found together. One does not necessarily imply the other and OO does live up to many of its promises (when implemented correctly!)

Your organization may be able to realize significant productivity gains through the adoption of object oriented project techniques for their PowerBuilder systems development. The first project you build with OO technology will be a genuine struggle and you will not deliver the system any faster than with traditional methods, in fact, it will probably take you longer. You will be trying to define and create objects that are generic enough that they can be used in other applications in the future. The real improvements in productivity will come with your second, third and fourth applications when you can begin to reuse all the functionality that you developed for your first application, and these gains can be substantial. On one client site, it took four months of intensive effort to deliver their first, medium scope application. After that, we were able to deliver the next 6 applications in less than half the time normally allotted for systems of their scope.

These productivity gains, when realized, translate directly into dollars and reduced cost, although you should be prepared to invest substantially in your first project to ensure that the results will provide the benefits that you expect. Failing to provide the proper training, tools, and mentoring for an inexperienced team will be the downfall of an enterprise project.

Maintenance of OO applications is substantially easier than with traditional systems. If implemented correctly, maintenance will cost less and be easier to perform. In traditional systems, changing one part of an application often results in unexpected failures throughout other parts of the application. This chain reaction is often called the "snowball effect." Anyone with any history in this industry has experienced this phenomenon. OO helps to eliminate this by reducing the coupling between the elements of the system and keeps a change in one area from rippling out and affecting any others.

Application execution speed and effective use of system resources can be enhanced through OO. But be warned that improper use of OO or OO implemented without proper planning can reduce execution speed and pirate system resources and not return them unless you reboot your hardware!

Given the benefits, I would strongly advocate utilizing OO for any enterprise development where the architecture is stable and the commitment exists from the organization to ensure it is performed properly. What follows is a discussion of some of these essential concepts and how they relate to PowerBuilder.

5.3 Objects

It was once explained to me some time ago that an object is merely a "thing." Since then I have used the term "thing" to describe objects to hundreds of my students. By this, I mean that an object is any thing that can be identified and named. For example, a person is an object, a car is an object, and windows (either in an application or in your home) are also objects.

When business analysts are trying to determine what the fundamental entities are in an organization, they can often begin discovering objects by extracting nouns from comments, interviews, JAD sessions, or available documentation.

PowerBuilder stretches the definition of objects a little. Everything you create is called an object. Every window, DataWindow, structure and so on is called an object, but one fundamental concept that defines an object is that they all have methods and properties, and not all PowerBuilder objects do (i.e., function "objects" have no properties). Also, the distinction between classes and instances is not as clear in PowerBuilder. This difference is discussed in the following relevant sections.

Developer's Tip: You may have heard properties referred to as *attributes* in earlier versions of PowerBuilder, or other OO documentation. Attributes is also correct nomenclature. In PowerBuilder 6.0 we have switched to using properties to be consistent with the Windows 95 and NT terminology. You may see references to both properties and methods in this book. Both terms refer to the same concept and are used interchangeably.

I will use the example of a house as our object. This example will serve us well as we describe some of the other fundamental concepts around object orientation in PowerBuilder. (See Figure 5-1.)

House

Figure 5-1. *A house is a conceptual example of an object. It is a tangible "thing" that we can identify and name.*

5.4 Properties

All objects have properties. Properties define the appearance and behavior of an object. In PowerBuilder they are like variables that belong to the object and define it. Properties include things like the width, height and color of an object.

For our house, properties would include its color, is size, how many bedrooms it has, and so on. In PowerBuilder, the properties on an object such as a window include its title, color, and position. (See Figure 5-2.)

Developer's Note: When you define your own classes of objects in PowerBuilder using the user object painter (discussed in Chapter 23) you can add your own properties to these objects by defining instance variables within the user object painter. You can also use instance variables to add to the properties of an application, menu or window class.

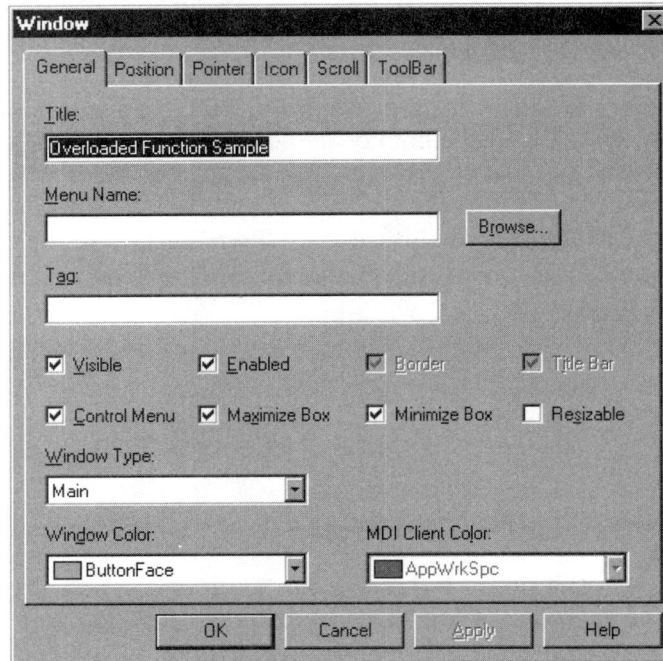

Figure 5-2. *Properties define the look and behavior of an object. Opening the properties page of any object in the PowerBuilder environment will give you access to all the properties you can modify.*

5.5 Methods

The same colleague who provided me with the definition of an object as a "thing" explained to me that a method is as simple as "things stuff do." To be a little more precise, a method is a process that is attached to an object. A PowerBuilder window, for example, has a method attached to it called Resize. When this method is called, we can alter the size of the window to a new width and height that we specify as parameters for the method. Objects usually have many methods, and they also have access to all the methods of their ancestors.

When you write a *function* or an *event script* for a PowerBuilder object, you are creating a method for that object. Global functions, which can be created in PowerBuilder, are one of those objects that are not very object oriented, for they are a method which is not attached to any object, which in a purist OO world, cannot exist.

5.6 Classes

As people begin to learn about and study OO concepts, the difference between a class and an instance is often a little confusing. You can think of a class as a more abstract definition for a group of objects, like a blueprint or template.

Let's look at our house example. I live in a house at 123 Main Street. My house is an object, but in order to have this object, someone created a blueprint that has a definition of a house. (See Figure 5-3.) This definition says that a house has four walls and a roof and one door. My house is a little different from the house next door, they are different objects, but they both fall into the class of house which is defined as having a roof, four walls and one door.

Figure 5-3. *A class is a blueprint or template for an object. This blueprint can be used to create specific objects (i.e., my house at 123 Main Street) or as a template for other classes. The general class 'house' is the abstract class for the object two story and also the abstract class for a bungalow, two different objects.*

When you create an object in a PowerBuilder painter, you are creating an object which is somewhere between the purist definition of a class and an instance, but it fits best into the definition of a class. In the purist world, a class has no values associated with its properties, for example a house has four walls and a roof, but we don't know their length, width, or height, whereas an instance has values for its properties. When we paint a window in PowerBuilder, we define a PowerBuilder class with properties (the window has a width and a height), but we also assign them values (we set a standard width and height for the object). When we actually open the window, we can override these values and set different values for its properties in the open event. You can see where the overlap in definitions is. The PowerBuilder objects are somewhere between a class and an instance.

Developer's Note: When you compile an application and distribute the
.EXE, .PBD, and .DLL files, you are providing the end user with your library
of class definitions. At runtime, these "blueprints" will be used to create
the objects that the user requires.

Classes of objects are often described in relation to other classes. For example,
we can have a class of object called "shelter." Shelter is related to the classes "house,"
"hotel," and "tent," all of which are types of shelter. (See Figure 5-4.) Shelter is a *super-class*, and house, hotel, and tent are all *subclasses* of shelter. The diagram can be continued in both directions, adding superclasses and subclasses as appropriate. We can
turn house into a superclass by adding "two story," "bungalow," and "ranch" as subclasses of house. In PowerBuilder, these relationships are formed through the use of
inheritance.

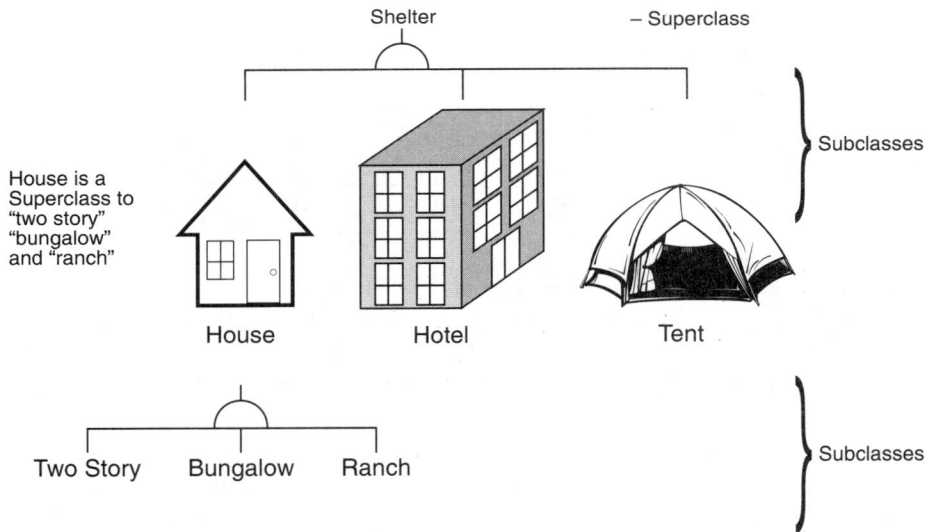

*Figure 5-4. Classes are related to each other through a superclass/subclass associa-
tion. In PowerBuilder, these associations are achieved through inheritance.*

Every descendant in PowerBuilder contains all the methods and properties of
its ancestor. The properties can be overridden in descendant classes. Methods can be
left as they are, extended or overridden. (See Figure 5-5.) These principles are discussed
further when we discuss inheritance.

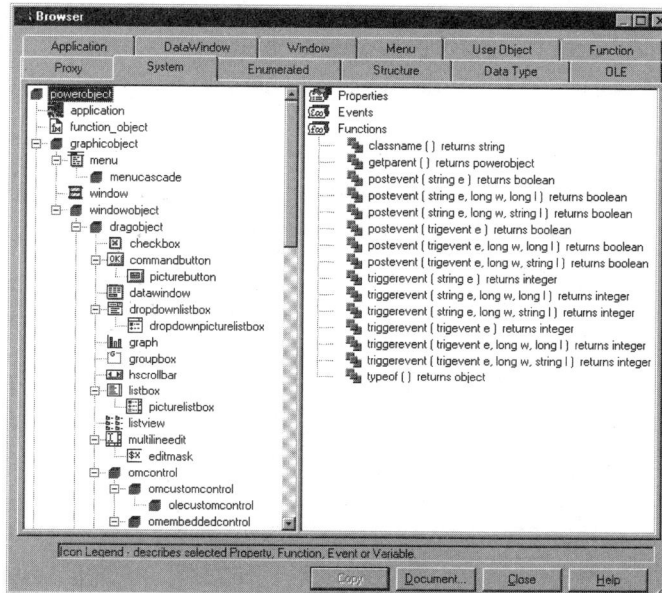

Figure 5-5. The PowerBuilder object hierarchy contains both PowerBuilder superclass objects and all the objects that you have created.

Developer's Tip: All objects in PowerBuilder exist within a hierarchy of classes/objects. You can examine this hierarchy through the Object Browser. The technique for accessing the hierarchy is not very straightforward. First you must select the System tab. Once in the system, you must click on the text of the PowerObject class in the class list on the left side. This will display a popup menu. Select the option Show Hierarchy. This will load and display the entire object hierarchy. Some of it will be hidden inside lower levels. To get the entire hierarchy visible at the same time, click again with the right mouse button on PowerObject and select Expand All (if you do it in any other order you won't see the entire hierarchy).

5.7 Instance

When you build an object in a painter in PowerBuilder, its definition is stored in your library as an object class. When you issue a command that causes that object to be created in memory (and, if visual, displayed on the screen) you have created an instance of that object. The class definition (your "blueprint") still exists in the library, and if you require, a second instance can be created from the same class definition. All object instances will have values defined for their properties. The instantiation of an object is the physical creation of the object.

With our house example, the blueprints used to create my home at 123 Main Street could be used to create an identical home next door. Now, we have two instances of the same class of home. Each house is individual and can be customized. I could paint my house green and my neighbors could paint theirs blue. (See Figure 5-6.)

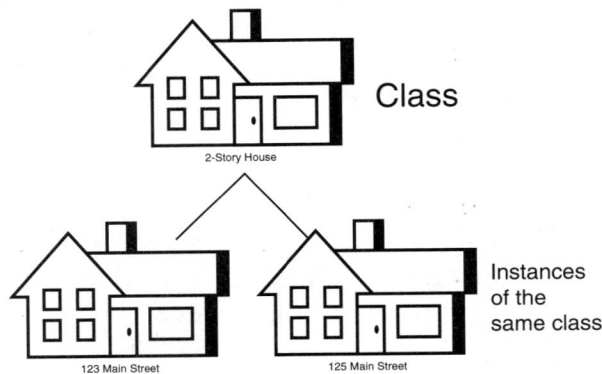

Figure 5-6. *An instance is the physical implementation of an object. A specific class of house could have multiple instances.*

This example translates to the PowerBuilder world as the creation of the same object many times. The most obvious example is the creation of multiple instances of the same window. You might have multiple sales order entry windows open at the same time in your order entry system.

5.8 Controls

In PowerBuilder, we often use objects in the construction of other objects. Some objects are intended to be building blocks for other objects, whereas others are intended to be containers. The objects that are container type objects are those that are stored independently in the library painter. We can refer to these objects as *first level objects* or *primary objects*. The Window and the User Object are examples of first level objects. When I place an object on a window, this object is referred to as a control. An example of a control would be a command button. These objects can also be referred to as *second level* or *secondary objects* as they are not stored in the library painter by themselves, but rather are only stored when they are part of a first level object.

5.9 *Inheritance*

The colloquial definition that I was provided with for inheritance is "I look just like Dad!" The allegory holds quite true. Inheritance is a process whereby a new object is created with the properties and methods from another object, just like you might inherit your fathers nose or eyes. This means that instead of building a new window from scratch you could inherit from a previously defined window, which becomes the ancestor. The new window, which is called the descendant, begins with all of the same methods and properties (including values for the properties) of the ancestor.

The concept of inheritance implies that, for the most part, descendant objects are only instantiated with the properties and methods that are different for each instance. Any commonality will remain in the ancestor class to be called when required. This prevents the duplication of a lot of superfluous code which is seldom used and allows for a more efficient use of system resources. With PowerBuilder we have the ability to either extend or override the methods in an ancestor. Methods are implemented either as scripts in events, or as object level functions.

The relationships that form between ancestor and descendant objects is referred to as a class hierarchy. An OO tool like PowerBuilder allows us to make changes to ancestor objects and those changes will automatically flow through to the descendant objects. You must be very cautious however when removing objects or making changes in an ancestor as those objects and values may be referenced in a descendant.

You gain some specific advantages through the use of inheritance. The code you place into an object can be reused by its descendants. This reduces the amount of code that a descendant class contains and the amount of time a developer has to spend creating the object.

Maintenance can be made easier by ensuring that code for a specific set of functionality is located in one place. If the need to make a change to that code arises, you need only change it in one place and any other objects that use that functionality are automatically aware of the change. No more hunting around for all the places where the functionality exists and no chance for having the alteration made differently in different locations.

Your applications will also look and behave more consistently when they draw upon a base set of objects which share a common appearance and set of functionality.

Other terms you should be familiar with when working with inheritance are abstract and concrete classes. Abstract classes are objects that are used only as ancestors. They are never physically instantiated. They are used purely as repositories to store common methods and properties for their descendant classes. This prevents the duplication of these properties and methods across multiple objects. OO designers and developers also speak of abstraction which is the technique of searching out common properties and methods among objects of similar classes and developing an abstract class to act as an ancestor to all those classes.

Concrete classes, on the other hand, are classes of objects that are physically instantiated. These classes will inherit all their common properties and methods from an ancestor class. They will layer their own additional functionality and properties on top of that which is received from their ancestor. Note that although concrete classes get instantiated, they can still serve as ancestors for other concrete classes.

One of the myths of inheritance is that using it makes an application run slower. This can be true if the inheritance is not well designed. Many experts have run empirical tests to measure this and have proven repeatedly that a solid OO application in PowerBuilder will actually improve both performance and memory efficiency.

Developer's Tip: If you are using inheritance and find that object creation is taking too long at runtime, you could instantiate the ancestor classes in memory (in a non-visual format) so that when the descendants are opened, PowerBuilder does not have to search for and instantiate all the ancestors.

This is accomplished by declaring a reference variable of the appropriate scope (perhaps an instance variable in the application service object) and calling:

```
iw_reference_window = CREATE w_ancestor_window
```

This window would not be visible to the users, but by creating it in memory will speed up instantiation of descendant classes. This technique should only be used when the client PCs have ample memory available as this object will consume resources while it is instantiated.

One other caution when it comes to using inheritance is to be careful with the complexity of your inheritance tree. Creating haphazard inheritance will make it difficult to determine where code is located and when a maintenance issue comes along you will be challenged to make the change effectively, especially if you weren't the original author of the object. Be careful to create logical and carefully layered objects and to document all objects clearly.

5.10 Encapsulation

As we continue with our plain English definitions, encapsulation would be "My insides are none of your business!" Encapsulation is the process of incorporating all the properties and methods that relate to an object inside the object itself. All the functionality and data you would care to know about the object is all contained within. These inner workings are hidden from the users, and the only way a user can interact with the properties and methods of the object is through a well defined public interface. You may hear encapsulation referred to as "information hiding" because the effect of encapsulation is to hide information from the user of the object and shield them from the object's inner complexities.

The effect of proper encapsulation is that every object can stand independently. It has no need for anything outside of itself. For example, a well encapsulated object could not depend on a value from a global variable, because if that object was used in an application where the global variable did not exist, the object would fail. These kinds of external dependencies are what create the snowball effect of changing one process or value and having that change affect many other areas.

You can begin to see how encapsulation promotes code modularity and can have a significant positive impact on the maintainability of your system. If you had a need to alter a process inside a well encapsulated object, the rest of the application would be completely unaffected assuming that the public interfaces that you built into the object remain unchanged.

A simple example of encapsulation in PowerBuilder would be the Command Button from the window painter. When you use a Command Button in your application, you automatically expect, that when it is pressed by the user it will appear to be pressed in and then released. You did not have to build this functionality into the Command Button, it was already there, encapsulated inside. You also don't have access to this process as it is hidden from you, and to use the button effectively, you have no need to access or understand the process that is involved.

Let's look at an example of encapsulation using an object that we might create for an application. We have a non-visual object called Customer. Inside this non-visual object is a process called CreateCustomer. The process is defined as a pubic object level function. When someone inside our application wants to create a new customer, they instantiate a Customer object and call the CreateCustomer function, passing the relevant details like customer name, address, and phone number. Inside the object, hidden from view of the user of the object, is a process that inserts a customer into the customer table and sets up a credit limit in the credit table of $500.00. Now, if the business rules change and it is decided that new customers will not automatically receive a $500.00 credit limit, instead, they will be given a credit status of "pending" and a flag must be placed on the record so that when the credit department logs on, they will see that they have a new credit application to approve. This process can be changed internal to the non-visual Customer object, but as long as the CreateCustomer function still accepts the same parameters and returns the same value, nothing else in the application is affected.

There is a lot more thought that must be put into designing a well encapsulated object. I would feel quite safe right now making a bet that probably 80% of the current production PowerBuilder applications in an enterprise environment are not well encapsulated. I hope this percentage will decrease substantially as more groups realize the benefits of OO.

When designing an encapsulated object, you want to be sure to insulate the methods and properties inside the object so that they cannot possibly be accessed from external objects or processes. This reduces the temptation to violate the object orientation of the system. How do we do that? We have the ability to create all our user defined properties (instance variables) and methods (object functions) as being either public, private, or protected.

Public means that these instance variables and functions can be called and referenced by objects and functions outside of this object. This is our publicly defined interface. By default, all instance variables and functions will be declared as public. For good encapsulation, instance variables should never be public, and only those functions that you want to publish as being the proper method for accessing this object should be public.

Private instance variables and functions can only be called and referenced by processes within that object. All private variables and functions are completely hidden from external processes. This includes keeping them hidden from any objects inherited from this objects. Even the descendants cannot use these variables and functions.

Protected is a little more flexible. External objects and processes cannot use protected variables and functions, but descendants of this class will have access to them and be able to call and reference them when required. (See Figure 5-7.)

You are probably familiar with how to declare an object function as public, private or protected. This is accomplished through the function definition window. The access level can only be set for object level functions, global functions are always public by definition.

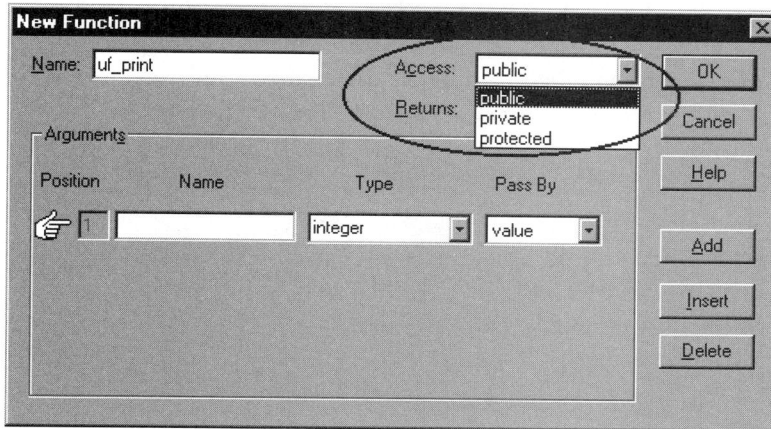

Figure 5-7. The function declaration window for an object allows you to define the function as being either Public, Private, or Protected.

What you may not be familiar with is how to change the access level of an instance variable. In this past this has been a well kept secret, but it is time that you know how it is done. In the Declare Instance Variables window you can set up three different sections simply by entering a label at the top of each section saying "PUBLIC:", "PRIVATE:" and "PROTECTED:". All variables that you declare under each of these labels will have that access level. Figure 5-8 shows an example of a public, private and protected instance variable.

Developer's Tip: In PowerBuilder 6.0, by using the keyword READONLY when declaring an instance variable we can make the variable PUBLIC for reading, but PRIVATE for writing.

```
READONLY long il_counter
```

As a general rule of thumb, your instance variables should never be public. The way you allow the outside world to modify the properties of your object is through the declaration of a public function that will change the property. You are probably thinking, "That's a lot of work when they could just access the property directly and change it when required." It is a lot more work to build a function for any property that you want to provide access to change, but when the time comes to perform maintenance and you make a change to the internal structure of the object, if that property changes in any way, you have now created the snowball effect and will have to hunt through the other objects in the application to find where the variable was referenced. With the public function as the interface, everything is internalized and encapsulated inside the object and you can make modifications without fear of being hit by a big snowball!

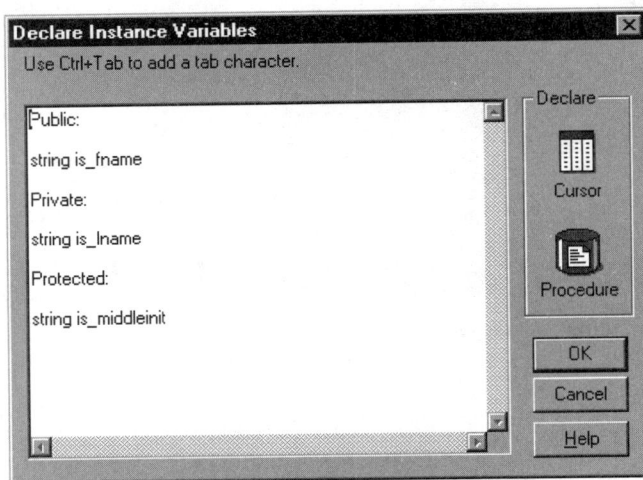

Figure 5-8. Instance variables can also be declared as either Public, Private or Protected by declaring them within subsection of the Declare Instance Variables window.

You will likely use the protected access level more than the private as you will want to ensure that the descendants of your object class will have access to the data and processes that they need to operate effectively.

Although we suggest that you make all your user defined instance variables either private or protected, remember that PowerBuilder's system attributes and events are all public.

Strong encapsulation is a critical element to the success of PowerBuilder and OO projects in general. Be sure that your objects are well thought out and planned in advance. This is not something which can be accomplished effectively by the seat of your pants method!

5.11 Polymorphism

When I think of polymorphism, the title of Frank Sinatra's famous song "[I Did It] My Way" comes to mind. Polymorphism is really the ability to call the same function on different objects, and have each object respond to the function call in a way that is specific to their requirements.

Let's look at the example of our house one more time. My house has a method called WaterLawn. If we call the method of watering the lawn on my home, it involves bring the hoses out of the shed, attaching them to the faucet, turning on the faucet, monitoring the process and shutting off the faucet at a specific time. However, watering the lawn on the bungalow across the street involves setting the timer on the underground sprinkler system which will automatically control the deployment of the sprinklers and the duration of the watering cycle. We are both watering our lawn, but our processes are different.

A good example of this in the PowerBuilder world would be the declaration of a function uf_Print() on all objects. The objective of having a general print method is straightforward: we want to be able to print the contents of the object as appropriate. Each object however is going to have different information inside of it and a different way that it might want to print it. Each object can have their own uf_Print() function declared with the specific method of executing that print method encapsulated inside the object. All we need to know is that if the user indicates they wish to print, we call the uf_Print() function on the current object.

Polymorphism can be implemented not only across multiple objects, but also within an object. This is accomplished through function overloading. Function overloading means establishing two or more functions with the same name, but different sets of parameters within the same object. At execution time, when the function is called, PowerBuilder will match the argument list for the function against the appropriate function definition and select which process that it will execute.

Developer's Tip: You can overload a function by specifying different argument sets, but you cannot overload a function by specifying a different return data type.

Let's use our example of uf_Print. Let's say that we want to have two variations of uf_Print. One takes no parameters and does a screen dump of the window. The second takes one parameter, asking if you want to show a print dialog box, and will print the contents of the window. The function list for this example is shown in Figure 5-9.

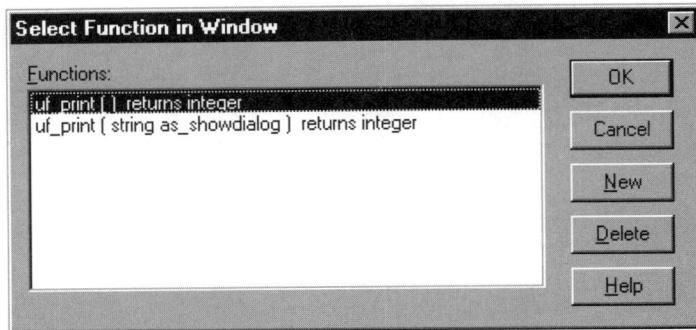

Figure 5-9. *PowerBuilder supports function overloading. This is the definition of multiple functions on the same object with the same name, but with different parameter sets or return codes.*

The companion disk contains an example of a window with two overloaded functions, both named uf_Print. One has no parameters, one has a single string parameter. You can execute the sample and then examine the code behind the window to see how it was constructed.

This powerful feature of OO languages is not always obvious to the new OO developer, however, as you begin to design and build your application you will begin to see the value this adds. In previous versions of PowerBuilder, the only way to overload a function was to use a different level of inheritance for each function variation because you weren't allowed to declare two functions with the same name at the same level. I am very pleased to announce that this is no longer the case in PowerBuilder 5.0. You can now declare all your overloaded functions at the same level simply by assigning them different argument sets or return values.

5.12 Summary

The concepts of OO, when implemented properly, lead to a system that is very easy to maintain. Across all your projects, you may be able to realize substantial productivity improvements and cost savings. The systems you build will be more flexible and *may* even run faster and consume fewer system resources than the same system in a non-OO environment. Notice that I said "may" run faster. This is a very important point which is debated amongst PowerBuilder experts and OO experts in general. You will find arguments to support the argument that proper OO can improve the speed of an application and others that say it can't. The most important factors to remember is the increase in developer productivity and ease of maintenance.

OO is apparent throughout the PowerBuilder environment. You can take advantage of it when you build any object in PowerBuilder. A critical element to integrating your OO and architecture strategies will be the use of non-visual user objects. These are discussed in Chapter 22—User Objects.

CHAPTER 6

Class Libraries and Frameworks

"Libraries are not made; they grow."

Augustine Birrell, 1850–1933, *Obiter Dicta. Book Buying*

*N*ow there is a fundamental truth if I ever heard one! (Okay, he was referring to books, but I think it is equally applicable to PowerBuilder libraries.) The one basic concept that is imperative for me to impart to you in this chapter is that a library of PowerBuilder objects and classes should always be considered a work in progress. You must be prepared to continually evolve and improve the contents, adding new objects and improving processes wherever possible. Any library which never changes, quickly grows stagnant and becomes obsolete.

So what are libraries and frameworks and why would I want them? Good question! A framework provides a library of objects that allow you to develop your applications much more quickly, with a higher degree of robustness and improved application consistency. They accomplish this through the power of inheritance, encapsulation, and polymorphism as we discussed in the last chapter. A solid framework will provide a standard set of base objects which contain many of your commonly used processes and application logic. This can then be reused without having to recode the functionality. With this chore out of the way, you can focus on the business solution without having to worry about many of the low level programming details such as setting up every single DataWindow control in your application to either single select or multi select the rows it contains.

Objects in a framework tend to all be necessary parts of a whole. They represent all the required elements and foundation upon which you can build your application. You can take advantage of all the existing functionality and support that the framework provides.

Often, however, when it comes to a framework, you must take all of it, or nothing. This can sometimes result in you having to bring a lot of excess baggage into your application that you weren't planning on including.

Object libraries are a little different from frameworks (although many third-party vendors use the two terms interchangeably). Object libraries, like frameworks, also have a great deal of logic and functionality built into their components that you can reuse or inherit. The fundamental difference is that each object in an object library stands on its own. It does not require the framework or any other objects to be in existence in order for it to function correctly. You don't have the excess baggage problem because you only use what you need. Object libraries are good for specific techniques or problems, but remember that the object library does not provide the general foundation that every good enterprise application requires. That is where the framework comes in.

So which one should I have? A framework or an object library? You should probably have both. The framework is going to provide you with the solid foundation that will help to make your project a success, and the object library will enhance the tools that you have available to accomplish your business objectives.

6.1 A Single Library Should Support All Your Enterprise Applications

When you create or purchase a library of objects and a framework for your organization, be sure to think beyond the current project. The library should be general enough to support all the applications that the organization uses. Each application can have its own library which contains any objects which are particular to just this application, or are customized versions of objects from the corporate library.

Your object library's configuration will depend upon what architecture your organization uses. Most corporate environments should be working on attempting to isolate their business processes into business objects, and standard services into non-visual service objects. This would result in a corporate class library which contains three primary libraries, one for each class of object, like in Figure 6.1. More details on these libraries is available in the section entitled, "What Kinds of Objects Should a Library Have?"

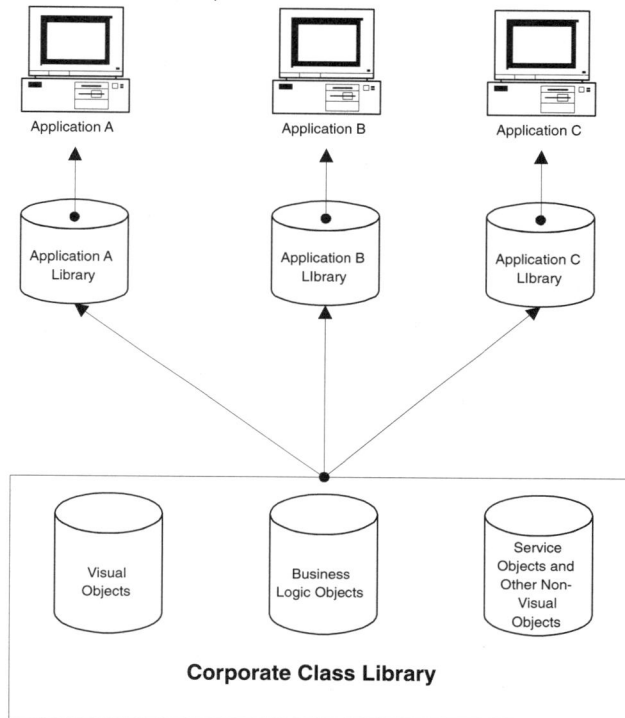

Figure 6-1. *A single corporate class library should service all of the PowerBuilder applications in your organization.*

6.2 The Build Versus Buy Dilemma

When an organization first acquires PowerBuilder, or launches their first significant project, they are faced with the dilemma "Should I buy a class library or build my own?" There is no right or wrong answer here. Which way is correct for you depends on a variety of factors.

How tight are the project timelines? Short timelines might suggest that buying an existing library may help accelerate your development cycle. You have to remember to factor in sufficient time to come up the learning curve on the new library. If you are under no time pressure to deliver (not likely, but it happens once in a while…a long while…) then you may have a significant window to develop a strong class library, or if you have the ability to factor the time into the project schedule.

How much skill and experience does your team have? If your team is really green when it comes to PowerBuilder, buying an object library might be an inexpensive way to put some expertise on your side. On the other hand, if your team has strong PowerBuilder skills, building a robust object library would probably be a very useful and productive exercise.

What is the cost? You must weigh the cost of third-party libraries against the cost of developing it internally (usually measured in time). Many third-party libraries have hundreds of person hours of development time behind them.

There are many other factors to consider such as the complexity of your applications, the environment they are operating within and so on. You have to consider all the factors and then make the decision that is right for your organization.

6.3 Building Your Own

The primary goal when designing the class library is to maximize reusability and reduce the amount of coding required to deliver an application to your users. This requires a great deal of planning and forethought.

Be aware that simply building your own class library is not quite as simple as it sounds. Most of the class libraries in use in the corporate environment are the result of a tremendous investment of development time and a great deal of work and rework by some very dedicated personnel.

Probably the biggest single advantage to building your own class library is that you understand every object that is inside. You know how it all works because you built it. Many of the commercial class libraries which you can purchase have become so complicated that learning to use them is like learning a whole new language and programming tool (not to mention, marrying yourself to that firm for upgrades as new release of PowerBuilder become available).

When you build it yourself you can also be reasonably certain that you are not bringing along any functionality that you don't need ("excess baggage"). A lot of the libraries that you can purchase try to solve 80% of your problems before you incur them. As a result, 50% of the code that is in the object, is almost never used, but eats up system resources anyway!

The other final significant factor to building your own custom class library is that you have the opportunity to make it truly custom for your organization's business requirements, instead of implementing a relatively generic third-party product.

With PowerBuilder 5.0, Powersoft has given you a tremendous leg up when it comes to developing your own class library. The PowerBuilder Foundation Class (PFC) contains a set of base objects that form the basis of a very solid class library. The PFC is quite comprehensive in its scope and is build using up to date development techniques. I would highly recommend using it as your starting point if you are going to develop your own class library. See Chapter 7, Using the PFC for more details on the foundation class library.

There are a number of potential gains to building your own class library and with the new PFC on your side, doing so is now easier than ever before. You should still keep in mind that many of the third-party libraries have been built by experts with a great deal of experience and talent.

6.4 *Purchasing Third-Party*

So you have decided to purchase a class library. Now you have to wade out into the jungle and fend for yourself among the wild animals all trying to sell you their "state of the art" class library. I don't mean to scare you off, but the maxim for consumers in the PowerBuilder library market is "caveat emptor"—let the buyer beware.

There are hundreds of class libraries available for sale, they range in price from $99.00 to $40,000.00 (no kidding!). The average price for a class library is somewhere between $800.00 to $3,000.00 per developer (run time licenses are usually free). The ratio of good libraries to poor libraries is quite extreme. Be very careful when investing in one of these. Be sure to get an evaluation copy and to take it apart and examine it closely. If you are new to PowerBuilder, hire a seasoned expert to help you evaluate them.

When you look at the manuals for the library, it should read like PowerScript. Don't buy it if the manual looks like you are getting into a whole new language. You didn't decide to use PowerBuilder because you wanted to layer another language on top of it!

Don't buy libraries which have every conceivable option either. Look for ones that have functionality you will use 80% of the time. If the bulk of the functionality you think you would never use, then that library is probably not appropriate for you. You would just end up wasting your available system resources.

Look for consistent and correct use of GUI and development standards. The library should also have a published set of standards that you can follow for your application development. Along with the standards should be complete documentation of the objects and samples of how they are used.

Never buy an object library unless you get the source code with it! Although it is not advisable to go modifying a commercial class library (instead you should have an inherited layer that you can modify) you will still want full access to the code so you can break an object down and understand how it functions. Having the source code also eliminates your dependence on the vendor if you require something to be changed or if the vendor goes out of business!

You should try to find a class library that contains a solid security methodology and a good set of independent object classes. This is critical in enterprise application development. Many of the major vendors now have security libraries that they sell separate from their class libraries. If you decide to build your own class library, you may still want to consider one of these third-party security libraries to help safeguard your applications (check out the security functionality of the new PFC also!).

Developer's Tip: Many of the third-party class libraries on the market are based upon concepts from PowerBuilder 3.0 (or even 2.0) and have much of the functionality attached to the window objects, or other places where it doesn't really belong. Be aware of this if you are evaluating libraries to purchase. You should really focus on a library that was architected to take advantage of the strengths of PowerBuilder 6.0.

Since the PFC was first introduced in PowerBuilder 5.0 there have been a number of third-party class libraries that have come to market. One of the ones that I have used and found to be excellent was CornerStone™ by Financial Dynamics.

6.5   What Kinds of Objects Should a Library Have?

Whether you buy or build your object library, there are some standard objects that should be part of it. These fall into one of three general classes: visual objects, business objects, and service/non-visual objects.

6.5.1 Visual Objects

The visual objects are those that make up the user interface of your application. They contain standard logic that is common throughout most applications. Examples of these objects include various types of windows such as sheets, response windows, MDI

Frames, query windows, pick lists, login windows, single-row updates, multi-row updates, and so on. Other visual objects include menus, OLE objects and user objects. (See Figure 6-2.)

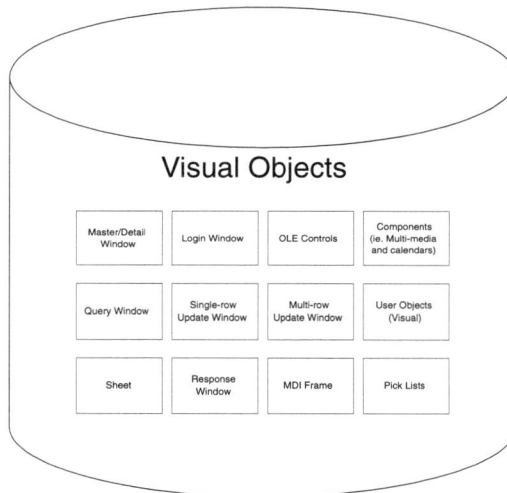

Figure 6-2. Visual objects are used to develop the user interface of your application.

There is an increasing supply of third-party objects that fill specific niches. You can now obtain multi-media objects, calendars, spreadsheets, word processors, and internet access objects.

6.5.2 Business Objects

Your library should contain objects that contain the business logic that is applicable to your organization. These may be difficult to purchase from third-party vendors unless your industry is one of those which has been well serviced by the third-party software development houses, like the oil and gas industry (which seems to be well serviced by everyone!).

If you are using a two tiered architecture, you will likely not be developing business logic, but instead rolling your business logic into your visual objects. If you are developing under a three or n-tiered architecture then this area will develop over time and become more complete as you roll out more applications.

The kinds of objects you find here will relate to the primary entities which house business logic. If you are building a system for an education center, you may have a business object for a student, one for a company and another for a course. (See Figure 6-3.)

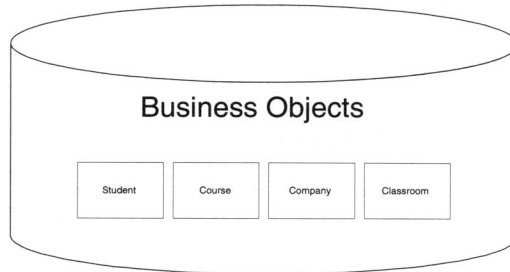

Figure 6-3. Business objects are used in three and n-tiered applications to contain methods and properties for specific business objects.

6.5.3 Service/Non-visual Objects

This library will contain any non-visual and service objects that you will use in your applications. The service objects include things like e-mail objects, fax objects, modem controllers and security objects. Non-visual objects could include things like sheet managers. (See Figure 6-4.)

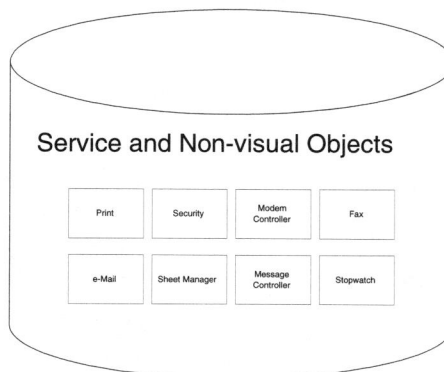

Figure 6-4. Service and non-visual objects libraries are used to contain objects that provide application services as described in Chapter 3—Architectures for Development.

6.6 *Conclusion*

Using a robust class library is a key factor in the success of any enterprise development project. Whether you decide to buy or build you should ensure that you factor in the appropriate time to integrate the class library into your project. The combined benefits of reduced development time, improved robustness and the ease of post implementation maintenance make the use of a class library a hands down winner for all projects.

Whether you choose to buy or build your libraries, be sure to check out the functionality of the new PowerBuilder Foundation Class library. It is well constructed and provides a great deal of your essential functionality.

CHAPTER 7

Using the PFC

*I*n *this chapter, we will introduce you to the PowerBuilder Foundation Class library, referred to as the PFC. Earlier in the book we introduced you to the different types of object libraries. The PFC is both a service-oriented framework and a class library. These objects are developed in native PowerBuilder format and are delivered with full source code to allow you to understand and modify the classes as desired. The library takes advantage of advanced PowerBuilder object-oriented coding techniques.*

Most of the objects that you will work with in the PFC are part of an overall framework and are designed to be used together. Other objects in the library are meant to stand on their own as independent entities that you only use to enhance the functionality of your application.

The PFC was introduced in version 5.0 of PowerBuilder. It is designed to help you to build more robust applications more quickly. It is not required that you use it when building applications with PowerBuilder, but if you are starting a new application, you will probably find it to offer numerous advantages including:

- *Faster development of your applications through the reuse of pre-built components.*

- *Easier maintenance through the use of thin, less complex objects which adhere to a consistent set of naming conventions and development standards.*

- *More optimized use of available resources as only necessary components are instantiated in memory.*

7.1   *The Service-Oriented Structure*

In a service-oriented framework, key functionality is encapsulated in reusable non-visual *service* classes. When the functionality of the service class is required in the application it is called via a *requester* class.

Requester classes are objects that contain predefined methods for instantiating and calling methods in service classes. Through these methods they are able to pass processing to the service objects as required. The requester classes also maintain the responsibility for destroying any instances of service objects that get created. The process of a requester class passing work on to service classes that it "owns" is known as *delegation*.

Service classes are designed to handle specific processes. They contain encapsulated business or functional logic to accomplish their task. The instances of service classes will always maintain a reference to the requester object that called them to allow them to communicate the results of their processes.

As an example of this requester/service relationship, think of a standard DataWindow control. Instead of writing your own code on the control for doing searches within the DataWindow, you would use a requester class of DataWindow which would instantiate a non-visual service object specifically designed for searching. When the user initiated a search (perhaps through a right mouse click option, triggering a ue_search user event on the DataWindow control) this processing would be redirected from the requester object to the service object as shown in Figure 7-1.

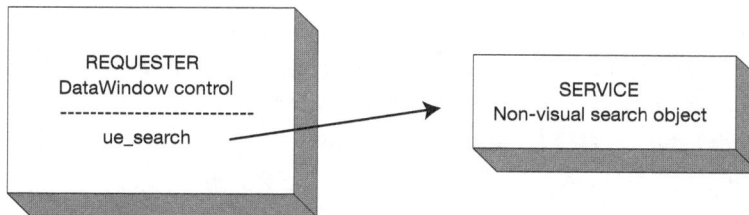

Figure 7-1. The search process request is passed from the DataWindow requester object to the non-visual search service object.

By using this requester/service structure the PFC increases the reusability of the object classes and reduces the amount of excess "baggage" that each object places in memory. With the requester/server orientation, only those services that are required are actually instantiated. No more putting everything but the kitchen sink into your object libraries! This also has the added advantage of being able to instantiate objects more quickly because the objects themselves are much thinner. As each object is less complex, you will spend less time maintaining your architecture and more time on producing your business functionality.

The following sections will focus on specific knowledge that you will require in order to begin using the PFC effectively.

7.2   *The PFC Libraries*

The PFC includes *base class* framework objects such as windows, menus, DataWindow controls, and user objects. It also provides many custom class non-visual user objects for providing services. Other libraries include *extension class* libraries which inherit from the base classes listed above. These will be used to allow you to perform your own customizations to the PFC. Also included are a set of *utility classes* which can be used both within PFC based applications and in other applications that are not based on the PFC.

The PFC consists of a set of twelve main PowerBuilder libraries (PBLs). In these libraries you will find all the base class, service class, extension class, and utility class objects. We can divide these twelve libraries into three groups of four; the ancestor libraries, the extension libraries, and the QuickStart libraries.

7.2.1 The Ancestor Libraries

The ancestor libraries contain all the original PFC objects and source code. They can be identified easily by the library names, which all start with "PFC" such as "PFC-MAIN.PB." You should NEVER modify any of the objects or source code in the PFC ancestor libraries. Doing so would make it impossible to apply bug fixes or PFC upgrades in the future without destroying your modifications and possibly rendering your applications unusable.

There are four main ancestor libraries and two auxiliary libraries. The main libraries are:

- PFCMAIN.PBL—contains standard visual objects for all window types and control types. Services are contained in the other libraries.

- PFCAPSRV.PBL—contains non-visual objects for providing application services such as the application manager and debugging.

- PFCDWSRV.PBL—contains non-visual objects for providing DataWindow services such as sorting, resizing, and row selection.

- PFCWNSRV.PBL—contains non-visual objects for providing window services such as resizing. This library also contains standard menu objects from which you can inherit to create the menus you will use in your application.

The two auxiliary PFC libraries are PFCSECAD.PBL and PFCSECSC.PBL which contain the objects that you can use to provide application security. The first library provides security administration services while the second provides security scanning services.

7.2.2 The Extension Libraries

Every PFC ancestor library has a matching extension library which will contain unmodified descendant classes inherited from the ancestor in the ancestor library. You will use these objects for customizing the PFC functionality to be more specific to you requirements.

The extension levels are critical because without them you would be unable to modify your ancestor classes without limiting your ability to upgrade the framework as PFC versions and features change. To understand this better, consider a framework without extension classes. In Figure 7-2 you can see an ancestor class w_m_main which has two descendants w_employee and w_benefits.

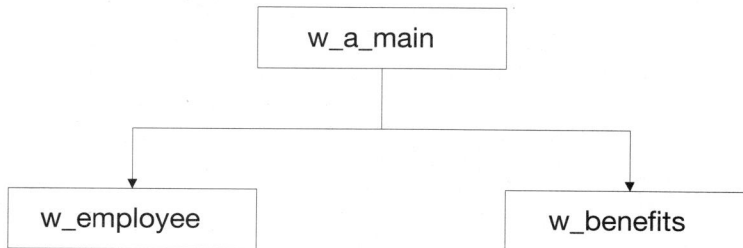

Figure 7-2. A framework without extension levels.

If you decide you want to modify the ancestor to add a new of_Save() method which can then be called on both descendant classes for the purpose of initiating DataWindow updates you can do so. (See Figure 7-3.)

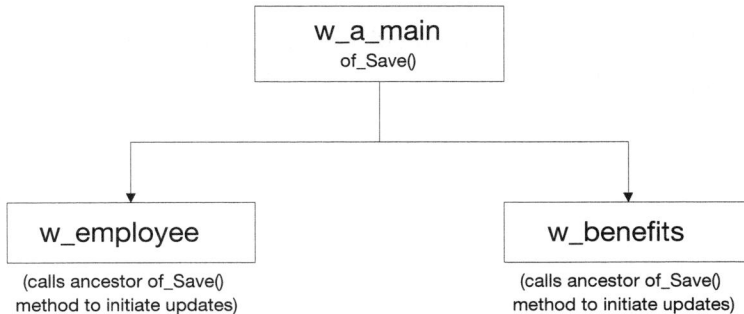

Figure 7-3. Adding of_Save() to the ancestor class.

This will work fine, until a new version of the ancestor library is released, and you decide that you want to integrate it into your application. When it is installed, it will replace the w_m_main ancestor that you modified with a new ancestor that doesn't have your modifications. (See Figure 7-4.)

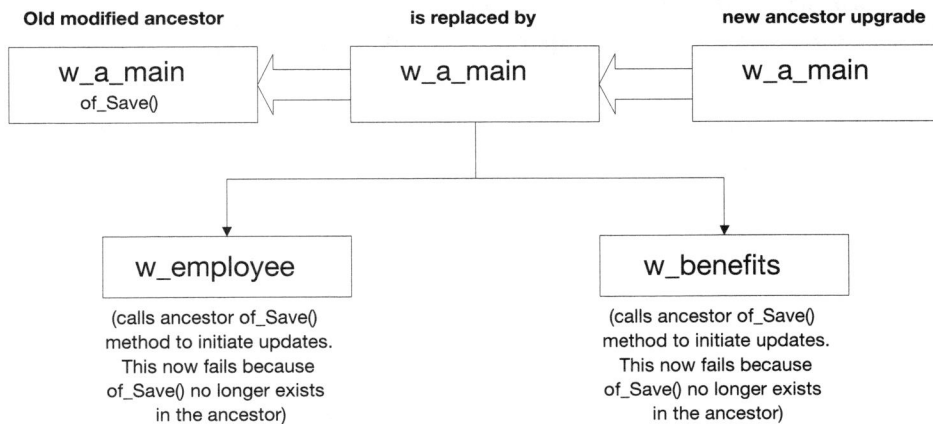

*Figure 7-4. Upgrading the ancestor object to the latest release
has some negative side effects.*

Now the descendant object scripts, which call of_Save() will fail because the of_Save() method no longer exists in the ancestor. You could manually attempt to replace all the code that you modified in the ancestor, but then you are being unproductive and repetitive. Not to mention, there could be conflicts with code in the new ancestor which may prevent you from adding the functionality you desire.

If we insert an extension level between the ancestor and the descendant classes, then we have the ability to add and modify ancestor functionality without negatively impacting the future upgradability of the framework. (See Figure 7-5.)

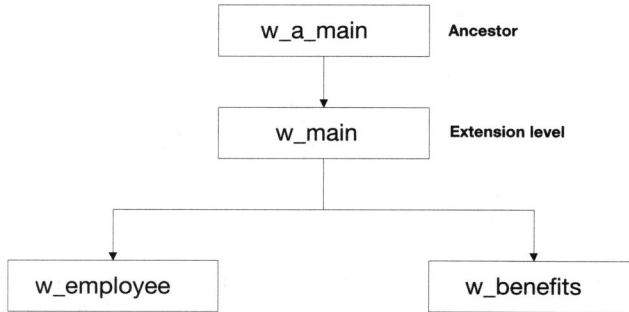

```
           ┌──────────────┐
           │   w_a_main   │        Ancestor
           └──────────────┘
                  │
           ┌──────────────┐
           │    w_main    │        Extension level
           └──────────────┘
                  │
        ┌─────────┴─────────┐
 ┌──────────────┐    ┌──────────────┐
 │  w_employee  │    │  w_benefits  │
 └──────────────┘    └──────────────┘
```

***Figure 7-5.** We can add an extension level to allow us to upgrade the framework without affecting our modifications.*

Now if we want to add an of_Save() method, we do this in the extension level, so that when the time comes to upgrade our main object w_a_main, none of our changes are wiped out. (See Figure 7-6.)

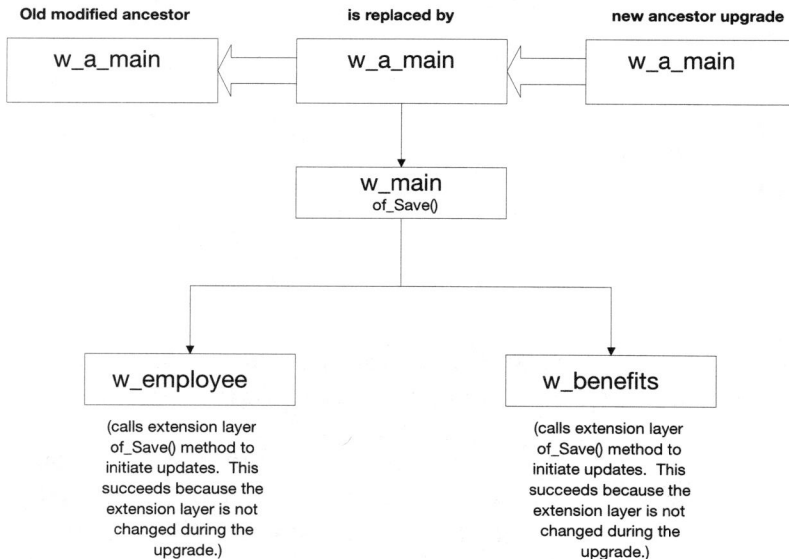

```
   Old modified ancestor        is replaced by              new ancestor upgrade

  ┌──────────────┐        ┌──────────────┐          ┌──────────────┐
  │   w_a_main   │◁═══════│   w_a_main   │◁═════════│   w_a_main   │
  └──────────────┘        └──────────────┘          └──────────────┘
                                 │
                          ┌──────────────┐
                          │    w_main    │
                          │   of_Save()  │
                          └──────────────┘
                                 │
                      ┌──────────┴──────────┐
              ┌──────────────┐      ┌──────────────┐
              │  w_employee  │      │  w_benefits  │
              └──────────────┘      └──────────────┘
```

(calls extension layer of_Save() method to initiate updates. This succeeds because the extension layer is not changed during the upgrade.)   (calls extension layer of_Save() method to initiate updates. This succeeds because the extension layer is not changed during the upgrade.)

***Figure 7-6.** Now when we upgrade our ancestor object in the framework, all of our customizations are preserved.*

The extension level libraries can be identified by their names. They all start with the characters "PFE" such as "PFEMAIN.PBL."

7.2.3 The QuickStart Libraries

The QuickStart libraries are available for you to use to set up a new application quickly. They contain extension level classes and descendant classes that contain precoded events and methods. These are very much like the PowerBuilder template in that they will set up a standard application object, a standard MDI frame, standard sheet, and standard menu for you. This way you can begin concentrating on the business purpose for building your application instead of trying to construct the underlying architecture.

The QuickStart libraries can be identified by the first three characters of their name. They all start with the letters "PFQ" such as "PFQMAIN.PBL."

7.3 The PFC Objects

The PFC contains many different objects. Each of these objects relates to and relies upon other objects within the framework. We will look at each of the different types of objects and show you where they fit into the framework.

7.3.1 Naming Conventions

All the objects in the PFC follow this basic set of naming conventions:

Table 7-1. *Naming conventions for PFC objects.*

Prefix	Object Type	Example
m_	Menu	m_frame
n_	Standard class user object	n_tr (transaction object)
n_cst_	Custom class user object	n_cst_appmanager
s_	Structure	s_paper_attrib
w_	Window	w_main

All objects in the ancestor libraries will use the same naming conventions, but they will have an additional prefix of "pfc_" such as "pfc_n_tr" to tell you that they are ancestor objects and should not be modified.

7.3.2 Windows

In the PFC you will find classes for all the standard window types. These types are all inherited from a single PFC window class called *pfc_w_master*. Any windows which you create should be inherited from the extension level descendant of this class called *w_master*.

Now things will get a little more complex. The diagram in Figure 7-7 shows how objects in the ancestor libraries can actually be inherited from objects in the extension class libraries.

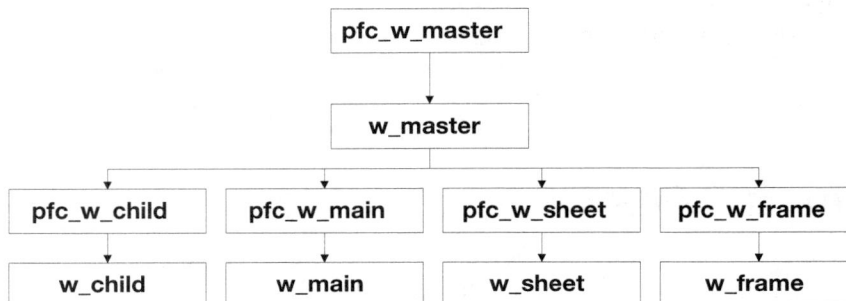

Figure 7-7. Objects in the ancestor libraries are sometimes inherited from objects in the extension class libraries.

You can see that w_master is inherited from pfc_master. However, the various PFC level window classes are inherited from w_master in the extension level. This allows you to make modifications to the hierarchy at any level. Just be sure you don't try to change the names of the objects in the extension classes (you can modify them, just don't rename them).

Developer's Note: Remember to ALWAYS inherit any new windows you create from an extension level class starting with a "w_" prefix.

7.3.3 Menus

Menus for your application should be created by inheriting from either m_master or m_frame in the extension class libraries. The m_master class contains most of the standard menu functionality and also conforms to Microsoft menu layout standards.

The menu m_frame is a descendant class of m_master which is in turn descended from pfc_m_master as shown in Figure 7-8.

```
┌─────────────────┐
│  pfc_m_master   │
└─────────────────┘
         │
         ▼
┌─────────────────┐
│    m_master     │
└─────────────────┘
         │
         ▼
┌─────────────────┐
│    m_frame      │
└─────────────────┘
```

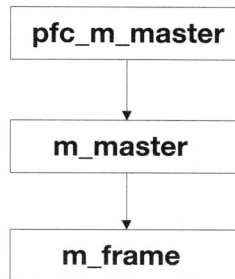

***Figure 7-8.** The menu hierarchy in the PFC.*

In addition to the m_master and m_frame menus, there are four other menu objects in the PFC. These are used to provide right mouse button functionality on other PFC visual objects, such as DataWindows. These objects are:

- **m_dw**—provides right mouse button popup support on DataWindow controls descended from u_dw.

- **m_edit**—provides right mouse button popup support on editable PFC visual controls like the multi line edit.

- **m_oc**—provides right mouse button popup support for OLE controls inherited from u_oc.

- **m_view**—provides right mouse button popup support for listview controls inherited from u_lv.

7.3.4 Standard Visual Objects

The PFC contains a standard visual user object for each of the standard PowerBuilder window controls. All the predefined methods and attributes of these controls have been integrated with the PFC services such as:

- All editable controls now have Cut, Copy, Paste, and other editing functions which can be accessed by the user using the right mouse button on the control. This affects the dropdown listbox, dropdown picture listbox, DataWindow, edit mask, multiline edit, OLE custom control, rich text edit, and single line edit controls.

- The DataWindow control contains extensive service functionality which will be addressed alter in this chapter.

- Most controls contains precoded functionality in the GetFocus event to provide for functionality such as showing the tag attribute in the Microhelp bar.

7.3.5 Non-Visual User Object (Class Objects)

The PFC contains many other user object classes covering both standard and custom classes.

7.3.5.1 Standard Classes

The standard class objects cover most of the system objects that you will already be familiar with such as the transaction and error objects. The hierarchy for these objects appears as shown for the transaction object in Figure 7-9

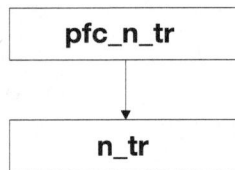

```
┌─────────────────┐
│    pfc_n_tr     │
└─────────────────┘
          │
          ▼
┌─────────────────┐
│      n_tr       │
└─────────────────┘
```

Figure 7-9. The hierarchy for the standard system class transaction object.

In Table 7-2 you can see a list of all the standard system objects which have PFC classes created for them.

Table 7-2. PFC equivalents of standard system objects.

System Object	PFC Ancestor	Extension Level Object
Connection	pfc_n_cn	n_cn
DataStore	pfc_n_ds	n_ds
Error	pfc_n_err	n_err
Mail Session	pfc_n_ms	n_ms
Message	pfc_n_msg	n_msg
Pipeline	pfc_n_pl	n_pl
Transaction	pfc_n_tr	n_tr
Transport	pfc_n_trp	n_trp

7.3.5.2 Custom Classes

Custom class user objects are often referred to in PowerBuilder circles as "non-visual objects" or NVOs. These objects contain discrete components of business and/or functional logic. You can call methods on these objects and set attributes, but you will never see these objects. These hidden powerhouses are how most of the PFC services are implemented.

The rest of this chapter focuses heavily on how these services are implemented. They can be classified into five primary categories:

- **Application services**—includes objects to provide services to the application as a whole (as opposed to a specific window or DataWindow) such as debugging, error handling, security, and more.

- **Window services**—includes objects designed to provide services specific to window processing such as resizing.

- **Menu services**—includes objects designed to provide services to menus and functions implemented through menus like the message manager.

- **DataWindow services**—includes objects for sorting, querying, row selection, and much more. By using these object this functionality can be added to your DataWindows with virtually no coding.

- **Utility services**—includes objects designed to provide general services such as file handling.

7.4 A Closer Look At The Architecture

The PFC architecture makes extensive use of requester/service object relationships as well as leveraging events and functions.

7.4.1 Requesters

As we mentioned earlier in the chapter when we first introduced requesters, we know that they contain predefined methods and instance variables that allow them to call and work with service objects.

The instance variables are often variables passed by reference. Using these allow the requester and service objects to maintain pointers to each other and thus be able to communicate effectively. For example, on the u_dw requester object, there are many instance variables that point to the different custom class service objects. The instance variable inv_sort is used to store a pointer to the instantiation of the n_cst_dwsrv_sort custom class object that provides sorting functionality to the DataWindow.

These variables are set up as pointers and then the requester object can instantiate only those services that it required. Predefined methods exist in the PFC requester classes to automatically handle the creating, destroying, and linking of any service objects that are required. All that you will do as a developer is to call the SetService(TRUE) function for the particular service that you want to turn on. For example, to enable row sorting in the DataWindow you would call the SetSort(TRUE) function to instantiate the n_cst_dwsrv_sort object. The following code in the constructor event of a DataWindow control would turn on sorting and row selection for the DataWindow.

```
dw_customer.SetSort(TRUE)
dw_customer.SetRowSelect(TRUE)
```

Once you have enabled a service, predefined events in the requester object will automatically kick in to redirect service requests to the appropriate objects. As a developer, there is nothing more you have to do. In fact, the requester object will even clean up after itself by turning off the service and destroying the object in the Destructor event for the requester object.

7.4.2 Services

The service objects are the other side of the requester/service relationship. All service objects will contain a reference variable that points to the requester object that instantiated it. That allows it to perform functionality on the requester object.

The code within a service object is fully encapsulated and you will not be able to access instance variables or call methods on a service object with the exception of the Get and Set functions that are made public to allow requesters to call the appropriate methods.

You don't really need to know what goes on inside a service object in order to use it effectively. However, if you are curious about what goes on within the object, take a look at the source code of an object in the PFC libraries.

7.4.3 Events

PFC objects have all the events of standard PowerBuilder objects as well as many other events that have been defined for use specifically with the PFC. These PFC defined events come in two categories; those that are used internally by the PFC objects and have predefined code that will perform functions based upon user actions (like selecting a menu item), and those that are empty events that will be triggered by the PFC where you will add business logic code specific to your application.

> **Developer's Note:** If you ever decide that you want to redirect an event that is part of the PFC defined events, you must be sure to pass all the arguments with the event, otherwise predefined PFC functionality may not work correctly.

7.4.4 Functions

You will notice that the PFC makes extensive use of user-object functions. These functions are all preceded with the prefix "of_" for Object Function.

There are two types of predefined functions that you will see in PFC objects:

- Public functions that are used to allow communication between objects such as the of_SetRequestor() function that is used to allow a DataWindow service to work with a specific DataWindow control.

- Public functions that are used for general application processing like of_CreateDirectory(). These functions can be called by your PowerScript business logic code as they are required.

There are also private functions within the objects, which you will see if you spend any time investigating the objects at the PFC level. But thanks to encapsulation, you don't need to be aware of these as a developer unless you are curious!

7.5 Using Specific Services

In the following sections we will focus on explaining the purpose of and how to use the different services that are part of the PFC. These services are divided into their major groups.

7.5.1 Application Services

Application services are all managed through the custom class object `n_cst_appmanager`. This object is referred to as the *application manger*. With this object you will enable and disable the various application services as appropriate.

7.5.1.1 Application Manager

The application manager is a non-visual custom class object that allows to you enable and disable the various application services. It will also contain all the code that would normally be contained in the application object. Since the application manager is an object that can be inherited, this give the added advantage of allowing you to use object orientation to reuse application object code that normally would have to be copied into every application because the application object itself cannot have descendants.

All PFC based applications must have an application manager defined. To do this you will need to create a global variable called gnv_app which will be used to reference the application manager. It is imperative that you name this global reference variable correctly because this is the name that all other objects in the framework will use to reference the application manager.

Your global variable declarations must contain a line like this:

```
n_cst_appmanager    gnv_app
```

The n_cst_appmanager may be a different class, as long as the class is inherited from n_cst_appmanager.

Since we will put all the code for application object events in the application manager, we will need to redirect all the application object event calls to the application manager. The event scripts in your application object should look like those in Table 7-3.

Table 7-3. Code redirection for all application object events.

Application Object Event	PowerScript Code
Open	`gnv_app = CREATE n_cst_appmanager` `gnv_app.EVENT pfc_Open(commandline)`
Close	`gnv_app.EVENT pfc_Close()` `DESTROY gnv_app`
ConnectionBegin	`RETURN gnv_app.EVENT pfc_ConnectionBegin(&` `        user_id, password, connectstring)`

(continued)

Table 7-3. *(continued)*

Application Object Event	PowerScript Code
ConnectionEnd	`gnv_app.EVENT pfc_ConnectionEnd()`
Idle	`gnv_app.EVENT pfc_Idle()`
SystemError	`gnv_app.EVENT pfc_SystemError()`

Developer's Note: The QuickStart libraries contain an application object that already has all the redirection scripts in place. You can copy this application object into your application library and have all the setup in place, ready for use.

The application manager contains a number of predefined events that you will use to write scripts to respond to various actions in the application. These events are listed in Table 7-4.

Table 7-4. *Application manager events.*

Application Manager Event	Description
Constructor	Fired when the application manager is instantiated. Can be used to set up any global parameters.
Destructor	Fired when the application manager is destroyed. Can be used to clean up any outstanding garbage, processes and connections.
pfc_Close	Fired when the application close event is called. Also can be used for clean up.
pfc_ConnectionEnd	Fired when the application ConnectionEnd event is called. Used for distributed computing. Refer to Chapter 9 for more details on this event.
pfc_ConnectionBegin	Fired when the application ConnectionBegin event is called. Used for distributed computing. Refer to Chapter 9 for more details on this event.
pfc_Exit	Used to close the frame window, shutting down the application.
pfc_Idle	Fired when the application Idle event is called. Whatever logic you choose to execute when the application becomes idle would be entered here (such as logging the user off or locking the workstation).

(continued)

Table 7-4. *(continued)*

Application Manager Event	Description
pfc_Logon	Fired when the user clicks on the OK button in the logon window (w_logon). It receives the user id and password as parameters. This is where your script should be for connecting to the database.
pfc_Open	Fired when the application Open event is fired. Here is where you should write the script to open the frame or the first window in the application. Any other script which you might normally locate in the open event should also be located here.
pfc_PreAbout	This event controls the display of the application's About dialog box. It is fired when the user selects the Help>About menu item from a PFC menu. It will set up the n_cst_aboutattrib custom class object with the application name, logo, version, and copyright information which will then be used in the About dialog window.
pfc_PreLogonDlg	This event controls the display of the Logon (w_logon) dialog window. Like pfc_PreAbout this event will set up the n_cst_logonattrib structure the user_id, application name, and logo information.
pfc_PreSplash	This event is fired by the of_Splash() function. It will set up the anv_splashattrib argument with the application name, logo, version and copyright to be displayed in the splash window.
pfc_SystemError	This event is fired by the application SystemError event. You should place any of your standard system error handling code here.

You will enable any application services that you wish to use, and set any application level attributes in the constructor event of the application manager. The following example tells the application which file to use for the application INI file:

```
THIS.of_SetAppINIFile("c:\myapp\myapp.ini")
```

Table 7-5 shows you the functions that you can use in the application manager to set and get information about your application.

Table 7-5. *Some of the key functions in the application manager.*

Application Manager Function	Description
of_SetAppINIFile(filepath)	Allows you to specify the INI file used for the application. It accepts a string argument containing the file and path name.
of_GetAppINIFile()	Returns a string containing the name and path of the application INI file.
of_SetCopyRight(copyright_string)	Sets the copyright statement that you want to appear in the Logon and About dialog windows. Accepts a string argument containing the statement.
of_GetCopyRight()	Returns a string containing the copyright string that you set for this application.
of_SetHelpFile(filepath)	Allows you to specify the help file used for the application. It accepts a string argument containing the file and path name.
of_GetHelpFile()	Returns a string containing the name and path of the application help file.
of_SetUserINIFile(filepath)	Allows you to specify the user specific INI file used for the application. It accepts a string argument containing the file and path name.
of_GetUserINIFile()	Returns a string containing the name and path of the user specific INI file.
of_SetVersion(version_string)	Sets the version that you want to appear in the Logon and About dialog windows. Accepts a string argument containing the version.
of_GetVersion()	Returns a string containing the version that you set for this application.
of_SetAppKey(key_string)	Specify the registry key under which application information can be found. Accepts a string argument with the key information.
of_SetFrame(frame)	Assigns the active frame window to the iw_frame instance variable. This function is called by the Activate event for the w_frame object.
of_GetFrame()	Returns a reference to the current active frame stored in the iw_frame instance variable.

(continued)

***Table 7-5.** (continued)*

Application Manager Function	Description
of_SetLogo(filepath)	Allows you to specify the logo file used for the application. It accepts a string argument containing the file and path name.
of_GetLogo()	Returns a string containing the name and path of the logo file.
of_SetMicroHelp(TRUE/FALSE)	Allows you to enable or disable automatic MicroHelp display.
of_SetUserID(userid_string)	Allows you to specify the user id used for the application. It accepts a string argument containing the user id.
of_GetUserID()	Returns a string containing the current user id.
of_SetUserKey(key_string)	Allows you to specify the registry key where user information will be stored. It accepts a string argument containing the key value.
of_Splash(seconds)	Displays the w_splash window for the number of seconds specified in the numeric argument.
Of_LogonDlg()	Displays the w_logon dialog window and then calls the pfc_Logon event where you can log the user on to the database.

There are more functions than these for the application manager, but this will be all you need to begin building PFC applications. Refer to the PFC online help for details on other application manager functions.

When you choose to utilize any of the other application services, you will enable those by using other application manager functions. Table 7.6 shows the set of functions that will be used to call each of the other services listed in this section.

***Table 7-6.** Application manager functions for enabling and disabling other application services.*

ApplicationObject Function	Description
of_SetDWCache(boolean)	Enables (TRUE) or disables (FALSE) the DataWindow caching service.
of_SetDebug(boolean)	Enables (TRUE) or disables (FALSE) the debugging service.
of_SetError(boolean)	Enables (TRUE) or disables (FALSE) the error handling service.

(continued)

***Table 7-6.** (continued)*

Application Object Function	Description
of_SetTrRegistration(boolean)	Enables (TRUE) or disables (FALSE) the transaction registration service.
of_SetSecurity(boolean)	Enables (TRUE) or disables (FALSE) the PFC security services.

7.5.1.2 Error Handling

PFC Error Handling services are handled by the extension library object n_cst_error which is inherited from pfc_n_cst_error. This object is designed to be able to handle all your standard error handling needs. It contains the necessary logic to display error messages for application, SQL, DataWindow, and system level errors. It also has functionality for logging error messages to a system file, sending error message notifications via e-mail, and logging error messages in the database.

To enable the error handling service you must call the of_SetError() function in the application manager constructor event like:

```
THIS.of_SetError(TRUE)
```

The PFC logic will take care of all the rest.

In Table 7-7 you will find a listing of the PFC error handling functions that you should be familiar with.

***Table 7-7.** Error handler functions.*

Error Handling Function	Description
of_CreateLogText(string)	This function will add the specified text string to the log file.
of_CreateNotifyText(subject, string)	This function will create the text and subject for an e-mail error notification message.
of_GetBeep()	Returns a boolean variable indicating if the PFC will sound a beep before displaying the w_message window.
of_GetLogFile()	Returns a string containing the name of the log file uses for logging error messages.
of_GetLogSeverity()	Returns an integer specifying the log severity level.

(continued)

***Table 7-7.** (continued)*

Error Handling Function	Description
of_GetNoifyConnection(mailsession)	Returns a reference (passed into the reference argument) to the mail session that is currently being used for error message notification.
of_GetNotifySeverity()	Like of_GetLogSeverity(), this function will return the severity level for the current e-mail notification.
of_GetNotifyWho(users)	Returns a string array (passed into the users argument) containing a list of users who are to be notified when an error occurs. The function also returns an integer specifying how many users are in the users array.
of_GetPredefinedSource(source)	This function will return to you the file name or transaction object that is being used to link to the database of predefined messages. If these messages are stored in a text file, then a file name is returned. If they are stored in a database, then the transaction object reference is returned.
of_GetPredefinedSourceType(string)	Returns a string containing either "File" or "Database" to indicate if the error handler is getting its predefined messages from a DOS file or a database table.
of_GetTimeOut()	Returns an integer specifying the number of seconds that the w_message dialog window will stay open until it closes automatically.
of_GetUser()	Returns a string containing the name of the current user.
of_LoadPredefinedMsg()	This function will load (or reload) the message cache from the current predefined message source.
of_Message(message)	Opens the w_message dialog window displaying the message text, or if the message argument points to a predefined message, it is loaded from the ids_messages DataStore.
of_ProcessLog()	Writes a message to the log file.

(continued)

***Table 7-7.** (continued)*

Error Handling Function	Description
of_ProcessMessage()	Will process a message, logging it in the log file and notifying administrators if required.
of_ProcessNotify()	Will send an e-mail message to the list of users specified with the of_SetNotifyWho() function.
of_SetBeep(boolean)	Specifies if the PFC will trigger a beep before opening the w_message dialog window.
of_SetLogFile(filepath)	Specifies what log file to use for logging error messages. If no log file exists at this path/file then one will be created.
of_SetLogSeverity(level)	Specifies what the log severity level should be. When errors occur, their severity level must be greater than this value in order to be logged.
of_SetNotifyConnection(mailsession)	Sets the mail session object to be used for automatic e-mail error notification.
of_SetNotifySeverity(level)	Specifies what the notify severity level should be. When errors occur, their severity level must be greater than this value in order to trigger the sending of an e-mail.
of_SetNotifyWho(users)	Sets the list of users (passed in the string array "users") to whom an e-mail should be sent when an error occurs. **Note:** This functionality works with MAPI compatible e-mail systems only.
of_SetPredefinedSource(file/tran_object)	Specifies where the system will look for predefined messages. This can be either a file/path name or a transaction object (for loading from the database).

To use the error handler, after instantiating it you would set up any parameters that it requires in order to function. The following code could exist in the application manager constructor event:

```
THIS.of_SetError(TRUE)
// Point to the predefined error message file
THIS.inv_error.of_SetPredefinedSource("g:\myapp\errmsgs.txt")
// OR we could use a database message file
// THIS.inv_error.of_SetPredefinedSource(itr_error)
// Specify name of a log file (if used)
THIS.inv_error.of_SetLogFile("g:\myapp\errlog.txt")
```

7.5.1.3 Transaction Object

The PFC includes a customized transaction object which has a great deal of built in functionality that you can take advantage of including processing for performing commits, rollbacks, connects, and disconnects. The object that you will use is n_tr which is inherited from pfc_n_tr. This object should be substituted for SQLCA in your global variable preferences. This is done by accessing the application painter and displaying the properties sheet. On this sheet you will see the variable types tab. Replace the object "transaction" in the SQLCA box with the object "n_tr." Then click OK and save your changes. (See Figure 7-10.)

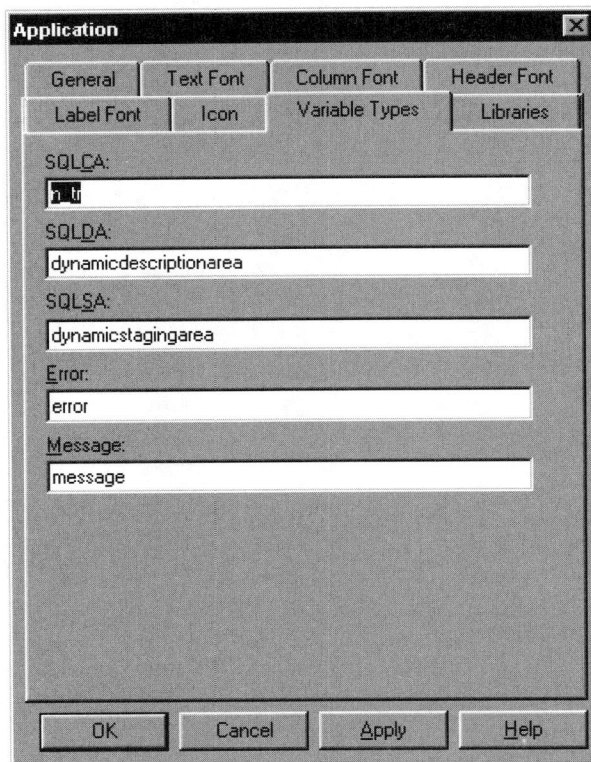

Figure 7-10. Setting SQLCA to use n_tr.

If you are using multiple transaction objects in your application, you can take advantage of the PFC transaction registration service.

In Table 7-8 you will find a listing of the PFC transaction object functions that you should be familiar with.

Table 7-8. Transaction object functions.

Transaction Object Function	Description
of_Begin()	This function is a placeholder that doesn't currently contain any functionality. It is intended to be a spot where you can add the logic specific to your database on how to begin a transaction.
of_Commit()	Issues a COMMIT statement. This should be used in place of the standard in-line COMMIT using SQLCA; code.
of_Connect()	Connects to the database.
of_CopyTo()	Copies the contents of one transaction object to another.
of_Disconnect()	Disconnects from the database.
of_DistinctValues()	Returns a list of distinct values from the specified database column.
of_End()	Like of_Begin, this is an empty placeholder where you can add the code specific to your database for ending a transaction.
of_Execute()	Executes the specified SQL statement immediately.
of_GetAutoRollback()	Returns a value indicating if you have enabled the PFC AutoRollback feature.
of_GetName()	Returns the transaction name that you specified using the of_SetName() function.
of_GetSQLState()	Returns the SQL state being returned by the database.
of_GetTrace()	Will indicate if tracing is enabled or not.
of_Init()	Initializes the transaction object with the values passed as arguments.
of_IsConnected()	Returns a boolean indicating if the current transaction object is connected to the database.
of_Rollback()	Issues a ROLLBACK statement. This should be used in place of the standard in-line ROLLBACK using SQLCA; code.

(continued)

Table 7-8. *(continued)*

Transaction Object Function	Description
of_SetAutoRollback()	Enables or disables the AutoRollback feature of the PFC, which initiates a rollback when a database error occurs.
of_SetName()	Specifies the transaction object name to be used by the transaction registration service.
of_SetTrace()	Used to enable or disable the PowerBuilder database trace option.
of_SetUser()	Used to specify the database user id and password.

7.5.1.4 Transaction Registration

The PFC transaction registration service is used to track all the transaction objects being used by your application. All the transaction objects being tracked MUST be of the class n_tr or descended from that class.

This service will automatically destroy all open transactions when the application is closed. If the AutoRollback feature (mentioned in the previous section) is set to TRUE, closing transactions will cause a COMMIT. If it is FALSE, this will cause a ROLLBACK.

You turn on transaction registration with the following line of code:

```
gnv_app.of_SetTrRegistration(TRUE)
```

Then to register a particular transaction object you use:

```
gnv_app.inv_TrRegistration.of_Register(SQLCA)
```

7.5.1.5 Debugging

The PFC has built in debugging features which will display messages when the PFC encounters conditions that indicate an error. This functionality is intended for the development environment only, and for obvious reasons should not be enabled in a production application.

This service is activated by calling:

```
gnv_app.of_SetDebug(TRUE)
```

There are no other functions or tuning that you need to worry about, its all automatic!

7.5.1.6 Security

With the built in PFC security features you can secure Menu items, Window controls and columns in a DataWindow. There may be more sophisticated security products available from third parties if you need more functionality than this, but for 90% of the applications in production, this is more than sufficient.

The security service object is n_cst_security which is inherited from pfc_n_cst_security.

In order to use the security service, you must have developed a security plan. This plan will define all the users of the system and will set them into specific groups. From there you must determine which users and/or groups will have access to which windows, controls, and DataWindow columns.

Then you must set up the appropriate security tables in the database. The PFC ships with security administration objects in the PFC security related PBLs. These will populate the database tables that are required (refer to your PFC documentation for the specifics of setting up these tables).

Once you have done this you are ready to begin implementing the security for the application. You can instantiate the security service by calling the of_SetSecurity() function in the application manager pfc_Open event as follows:

```
THIS.of_SetSecurity(TRUE)
```

Next you must establish a transaction object that the security service can use to determine access levels as defined in the database. In this example, we will use an instance level transaction object:

```
itr_sec = CREATE n_tr
```

If your security tables are in the same database as your SQLCA tables, you can use the same transaction object, or if you want to keep the objects separate, use the PFC of_CopyTo() function to move the details from SQLCA to your new transaction object.

```
SQLCA.CopyTo(itr_sec)
```

Then you should connect to the database.

```
itr_sec.of_Connect()
```

Initialize the security object by calling the of_InitSecurity() function.

```
THIS.inv_security.of_InitSecurity(itr_sec, "MYAPP", &
    gnv_app.of_GetUserID(), "Default")
```

Then in any windows where you want to apply security, you would call the of_SetSecurity() function in the pfc_PreOpen event as follows:

```
IF NOT gnv_app.inv_security.of_SetSecurity(THIS) THEN
    MessageBox("Security Failed","Unable to set security for this" &
        +"window. Please see your System Administrator.",StopSign!)
    Close(THIS)
END IF
```

Finally, remember to disconnect and destroy your transaction object in your application manager close event (or alternatively, register it with the transaction registration service).

7.5.1.7 DataWindow Caching

DataWindow caching is something that many advanced developers have been doing for many years. It is discussed in the advanced DataWindows chapters of this book. The PFC has automated this process for us by providing us with a DataWindow caching service. This provides a single source of data sets, eliminating redundant database retrievals. This data is stored in DataStores on the client.

A typical use for this type of service would be to cache a list of states, genders, or other relatively static lookup codes. Once this data is cached, then it can be used in multiple places improving the performance and efficiency of your application.

The PFC DataWindow cache object is n_cst_dwcache which is inherited from the PFC object pfc_n_cst_dwcache.

In Table 7-9 you will find a listing of the PFC DataWindow caching functions that you should be familiar with.

Table 7-9. *DataWindow caching functions.*

DataWindow Cache Function	Description
of_GetCount()	Returns the number of objects currently registered with the DataWindow cache.
of_GetRegistered()	This function will access the cached data and return either: • reference to the data store matching the passed object id. This would be used for accessing a specific set of data, like a list of states. • a string array of Ids for all the objects cached in the DataWindow cache. This would allow you to search for a specific ID. • an array of DataStores (passed by reference) that you can sort through and select information from.
of_IsRegistered()	Returns a 1 if the passed ID is registered with the service, a 0 if it is not and a -1 if an error occurs.
of_Refresh()	Refreshes one, or all the DataStores cached with the caching service. If no argument is passed, all DataStores are refreshed. If a specific ID is passed, only that DataStore is refreshed.
of_Register()	Caches data for a specified DataWindow object. There are several possible syntaxes depending on the source of the data. In general, data can come from a DataWindow object, a DataStore, a file or from a SQL statement.
of_RegisterArgs()	If one of the registered caches requires retrieval arguments, this function is used to set the arguments based upon the object id.
of_UnRegister()	Removes one, or all the DataStores cached with the caching service. If no argument is passed, all DataStores are removed. If a specific ID is passed, only that DataStore is removed.

7.5.2 PFC Windows

As demonstrated in Figure 7-7 earlier in the chapter, all PFC windows are inherited from w_master. There is a descendant class of w_master for each of the different window types (w_child, w_frame, w_main, w_popup, w_response, w_sheet). Each of these windows is built to be a requester object that can implement services through functions, events and instance variables.

In the w_master class functionality exists to enable and disable all the other window services. Instance variables are used to allow you to reference each custom class service object that is to be used. You will also find many predefined custom events used by the PFC for the performance of specific window services, when enabled. There are also many empty predefined custom events where you will place specific business logic as it applies to your application.

Table 7-10 lists the window services that are available to you.

Table 7-10. Window services.

Window Service	Description
Basic window services	*n_cst_winsrv:* Standard window processing like automatic close query, message router, and toolbar functionality.
Preference Service	*n_cst_winsrv_preference:* Provides functionality for saving and restoring user window preferences.
Sheet Management Services	*n_cst_winsrv_sheetmanager*: For managing multiple sheets in an MDI application.
Status Bar Service	*n_cst_winsrv_statusbar*: Provides custom details such as date/time and more in the window status bar.
Resize Service	*n_cst_resize*: Provides functionality for automatic resizing of window controls when the window is resized.

7.5.2.1 Basic Window Services

All PFC windows come equipped with the functionality for basic window services. This functionality includes automatic implementation of CloseQuery processing, message routing, toolbar management, saving, and window centering.

CloseQuery process is automatically utilized to check for unsaved changes in any DataWindows when the window is closed. If unsaved changes are found, the user is given the opportunity to save, not save, or cancel the closing of the window. If you don't want this functionality in a given window, override the CloseQuery event with your own processing (or no processing if applicable). If you want to override this functionality in all windows in the application you can override this functionality at the w_master level.

Also included is the standard message router functionality which allows a window to receive and respond to messages send from a menu or another object. The message router is discussed in more detail in the PFC Menus section below.

Toolbar control is provided through the pfc_Toolbars user event in the frame window If you want to trigger the dialog box for configuring the toolbars you can use the following line of script:

```
gnv_app.of_GetFrame().EVENT pfc_Toolbars()
```

Updating and saving to the database is also an automated process with the PFC basic window services. It is called automatically in response to the user selecting the File→Save menu item, or during the CloseQuery process if required. If you want to initiate a save yourself in your processing you can do so by triggering the pfc_Save() event.

Window centering is the last of the window services. In order to use this service you must first call the of_SetBase() window to establish the basic services such as:

```
THIS.of_SetBase(TRUE)
```

and then call the of_Center() function:

```
THIS.inv_base.of_Center()
```

7.5.2.2 Preference Service

This service can be used to save and restore a users preferred window settings such as window size, toolbar settings, and window position.

To activate the service you will call the of_SetPreference() function in the Open event such as:

```
THIS.of_SetPreference(TRUE)
```

Table 7-11 contains a listing of all the functions for the n_cst_winsrv_preference user object.

Table 7-11. *Preference service functions.*

Preference Function	Description
of_SetMenuItems ()	If set to TRUE, the service will save menu item properties.
of_GetMenuItems()	Returns the TRUE or FALSE condition of this property.
of_SetWindow()	If set to TRUE, the service will save window properties.

(continued)

Table 7-11. *(continued)*

Preference Function	Description
of_GetWindow()	Returns the TRUE or FALSE condition of this property.
of_SetToolbars()	If set to TRUE, the service will save toolbar properties.
of_GetToolbars()	Returns the TRUE or FALSE condition of this property.
of_SetToolbarTitles()	If set to TRUE, the service will save toolbar titles.
of_GetToolbarTitles()	Returns the TRUE or FALSE condition of this property.
of_SetToolbarItemOrder()	If set to TRUE, the service will save the order of toolbar buttons.
of_GetToolbarItemOrder()	Returns the TRUE or FALSE condition of this property.
of_SetToolbarItemSpace()	If set to TRUE, the service will save the spacing of toolbar buttons.
of_GetToolbarItemSpace()	Returns the TRUE or FALSE condition of this property.
of_SetToolbarItemVisible()	If set to TRUE, the service will save the visible property of toolbar buttons.
of_GetToolbarItemVisible()	Returns the TRUE or FALSE condition of this property.
of_Restore()	Restores all the window, toolbar, and menu settings from a registry area or an INI file.
of_RestoreMenu()	Restores only menu items from a registry area or an INI file.
of_RestorePositiveNumber()	Checks a registry or INI file to make sure that the window save information value exists.
of_Save()	Saves all the window, toolbar, and menu settings to a registry area or an INI file.
of_SaveMenu()	Saves only menu items to a registry area or an INI file.

The two functions that you will need to really be aware of if you are planning on using the preference service are of_Save() and of_Restore().

You can save the window settings on exiting the window by placing the following script in the CloseQuery event:

```
INTEGER li_rcode
li_rcode = THIS.inv_preference.of_Save(gnv_app.of_GetUserINIFile(),&
    THIS.Name + "Settings")

IF li_rcode = -1 THEN
    // Unable to save window settings.  Display a message (if desired)
    MessageBox("Window Preferences",&
    "Unable to store window preferences.")
End IF
```

To restore a saved set of window settings you would code the following into your Open event of your window:

```
THIS.inv_preference.of_Restore(gnv_app.of_GetUserINIFile(),&
THIS.Name+"Settings")
```

You could also check the return code, but chances are that if it isn't restoring the preferences, then there may not be any preferences to restore, so I don't think we need to show an error message here!

To control which items are saved and restored when you use those functions you can call the individual functions listed in the above table such as of_SetWindow-(TRUE) to ensure that window properties are saved or of_SetToolBarTitles(FALSE) to stop the preferences from saving the toolbar titles.

7.5.2.3 Sheet Management Service

This service can be used to manage multiple sheet windows in an MDI frame. The functions available from this service include the ability to count the number of sheets, order the sheets by type or title and to undo a sheet rearrangement.

To activate the service you will call the of_SetSheetManager() function in the Open event such as:

```
THIS.of_SetSheetManager(TRUE)
```

Table 7-12 contains a listing of all the functions for the n_cst_winsrv_sheet-manager user object.

***Table 7-12.** Sheet manager service functions.*

Sheet Manager Function	Description
of_GetSheetCount()	Returns the number of sheets open for the current frame.
of_GetSheets()	Returns an array of windows with references to all the frame's open sheets.
of_GetSheetsByClass()	Returns an array of windows with references to all the frame's open sheets sorted by class.
of_GetSheetsByTitle()	Returns an array of windows with references to all the frame's open sheets sorted by title.

(continued)

Table 7-12. *(continued)*

Sheet Manager Function	Description
of_GetCurrentState()	Returns the current sheet arrangement style for the purpose of undoing the arrangement.
of_SetCurrentState()	Sets the current sheet arrangement style for the purpose of undoing a sheet arrangement.
of_SetRequestor()	Associates a window with this object.

7.5.2.4 Status Bar Service

This service will allow you to display significantly more information in the application status bar such as the date, time, available memory and some user defined text. This functionality is the result of interaction between the n_cst_winsrv_statusbar custom class object which handles all the processing, and the w_statusbar popup window which actually displays the custom status bar information.

To activate the service you will call the of_SetStatusBar() function in the Open event of your frame window (w_frame) such as:

```
THIS.of_SetStatusBar(TRUE)
```

All cleanup, closing, and destroying of status bar related objects will be performed automatically by the PFC when the application terminates.

Table 7-13 contains a listing of all the functions for the n_cst_winsrv_statusbar user object.

Table 7-13. *Status bar service functions.*

Status Bar Function	Description
of_SetGDI()	Available in 16 bit environments only, this will enable or disable the displaying of GDI memory resources in the status bar.
of_SetMem()	This will enable or disable the displaying of free memory in the status bar.
of_SetTimer()	This will enable or disable the displaying of date and time in the status bar.
of_SetUser()	Available in 16 bit environments only, this will enable or disable the displaying of user defined text in the status bar.

7.5.2.5 Resize Service

This service will allow you have windows automatically move and resize the controls within them whenever the user resizes a window or a tab. You can specify how controls resize, or if they should resize at all.

To activate the service you will call the of_SetResize() function (on either a descendant of the w_master or u_tab classes) in the Open event of your window or constructor event of your tab object such as:

```
THIS.of_SetResize(TRUE)
```

After initiating the resize service, you will need to specify which controls will participate in the resizing and how they will participate by using the of_Register() function to register each control and how it should respond to a resize. This function is called using the following syntax:

```
THIS.inv_resize.of_Register(control_name, behavior)
```

where control_name is the name of the window control that you are registering and behavior is how that control should respond to the resize. The options for behavior are:

- FixedToRight.
- FixedToBottom.
- FixedToRight&Bottom.
- Scale.
- ScaleToRight.
- ScaleToBottom.
- ScaleToRight&Bottom.
- FixedToRight&Bottom.
- FixedToRight&ScaleToBottom.
- FixedToBottom&ScaleToRight.

The behavior argument as passed as a string like this:

```
THIS.inv_resize.of_Register(dw_customer, "ScaleToRight")
```

You can also specify a minimum size for the window. Below that size the resize service will not resize any of the controls. This is done by using the of_SetMinSize() function as follows:

```
THIS.inv_resize.of_SetMinSize(300,400).
```

To set the window so that it cannot be resized any smaller than its original size you would place the following line in your open event:

```
THIS.inv_resize.of_SetMinSize(THIS.Width,THIS.Height).
```

Table 7-14 contains a listing of all the functions for the n_cst_resize user object.

Table 7-14. *Resize service functions.*

Resize Function	Description
of_GetMinMaxPoints()	Determines the four extreme points of all controls within a window.
of_Register()	Registers a control with the resize service so that it will be automatically resized if the user resizes the window.
of_Resize()	Forces the movement of the controls as specified in the of_Register() function.
of_SetMinSize()	Sets a minimum size for the window below which the resizing service will not modify any of the controls.
of_SetOrigSize()	Sets the current window size.
of_TypeOf()	Determines the object type of a window control.
of_UnRegister()	Removes a window control from the list of registered controls that participate in resizing.

7.5.3 PFC Menus

The PFC conforms to the object oriented model of not putting any business logic into a menu object. The menu object merely sends messages to other objects when the user selects a menu option.

All menu functionality is derived from the m_master class. This class contains the necessary processes to implement the message router logic and the individual menu item events that will use the message router to perform the user selected functionality.

When you create your own menus for your application you should use m_master as the ancestor for your sheet menus. Alternatively, you could create your own menus from scratch, but you will need to manually add the code to utilize the of_SendMessage() function.

7.5.3.1 Inheriting From PFC Menus

When you inherit your new menus from the m_master class, you will find that the Shift Over/Down property of the m_master menu items will cause the items that you add to appear in the middle of the menu. This is good because that is generally the behavior that we desire.

In the main menu bar, any items that you add will be inserted between the Tools menu item and the Window menu item. This conforms to Microsoft menu building standards which have the Window and Help menu items always at the far right.

Under the File menu bar item, any items that you add will be added above Delete. In the Edit menu, they will be added above Update Links; the View menu above Ruler; the Tools menu above Customize Toolbars; the Window menu below Undo Arrange; and the Help menu above About.

When using inheritance, in the descendant menu, if a specific menu item is not applicable, make it invisible. If the menu item does apply to the window the menu is attached to, you will need to check the PowerScript code for the user event on the window that is triggered by the menu item.

7.5.3.2 The Message Router

The PFC message router is used handle communication between menus and windows in your application. It can also be used for general message passing between objects within the PFC framework. The functionality for this is built into all PFC menus and windows, so you do not have to do anything special to make it work.

When the message router works, it uses a search algorithm to determine which object is supposed to receive the message. In the case of a menu communicating with a window, the message is only told what event is to be called by the of_SendMessage() function. They will determine the current window on their own and if necessary, the control on the window that needs the message. This means that you don't have to code events on the window solely for the purpose of triggering events on window controls such as a DataWindow. This will mean that you won't have to remember to maintain as many user events in a PFC application.

The of_SendMessage() function always takes a string argument containing the name of the user event that you wish to trigger. When this function is called in the Clicked event script for a menu item, the pfc_MessageRouter event on the active window is called. This event, in turn calls the appropriate user event on the appropriate control.

The message router event looks for the user event first in the active sheet. If the event exists in the active sheet, then the event is triggered and the message router is finished its job. If the event does not exist in the active sheet then the message router checks the current control. If it doesn't find the event there, then it will check the last active DataWindow control. If the event isn't found there, then the message router will call the event in the frame window.

7.5.4 PFC DataWindows

The PFC contains many services to provide more functionality to the DataWindows in our applications. In this section we will examine drop down, multitable update, print preview, query mode, reporting, row management, row selection, and sorting services.

7.5.4.1 Basic DataWindow Services

Like the window class, the PFC adds a number of basic services to the DataWindow class including the functions necessary to enable and disable other DataWindow services.

To enable basic DataWindow services we must first call the of_SetBase() function in the contructor even like this:

```
THIS.of_SetBase(TRUE)
```

With this service active, there are many new functions that you will be able to use on the DataWindow, some of which are listed in Table 7-15.

Table 7-15. *Some of the DataWindow service functions.*

DataWindow Function	Description
of_Describe()	Used like the Describe() DataWindow method to extract information on DataWindow properties and objects.
of_Modify()	Used like the Modify() DataWindow method to set DataWindow properties and object properties.

(continued)

Table 7-15. *(continued)*

DataWindow Function	Description
of_GetItem()	Will retrieve the formatted text of any column regardless of data type. The return value will include any display formats, edit styles, and so on.
of_SetItem()	Works like the SetItem() function except that it is not datatype dependent. The value that you pass will be converted into the correct data type by the of_SetItem() function.
of_GetHeaderName()	Will determine the header name for a specific DataWindow column.
of_GetHeight()	Will return the total height of the DataWindow object.
of_GetObjects()	Will return a list of the names of the objects within a DataWindow.
of_GetWidth()	Will return the total width of the DataWindow object.

7.5.4.2 Dropdown Search Services

The dropdown search service will automatically scroll dropdown DataWindows to items that begin with the letter entered by the user. If the user enters a D in the dropdown DataWindow entry field, the service automatically scrolls the list to the first time that begins with D.

This service is activated by calling the of_SetDropDownSearch() function on the DataWindow control on which we are enabling dropdown search services such as:

```
THIS.of_SetDropDownSearch(TRUE)
```

if the script is placed in the constructor event for the DataWindow control.

There are two other steps involved still. You must also place a call to the service in the EditChanged and ItemFocusChanged events like this:

```
EditChanged
inv_dropdownsearch.EVENT pfc_EditChanged (row, dwo, data)

ItemFocusChanged
inv_dropdownsearch.EVENT pfc_ItemFocusChanged (row, dwo)
```

These will redirect these events so that when they are triggered they will fire off the appropriate functionality in the n_cst_dwsrv_dropdownsearch object.

7.5.4.3 Multitable Update Service

If you need to update multiple tables from a single DataWindow, you can use the PFC multitable update service object n_cst_dwsrv_multitable.

This service, once enabled, will be automatically invoked when the pfc_Save event is called on any class or subclass of w_master. To enable this service you must call the of_SetMultiTable() function in the constructor event of the DataWindow which will be performing multitable updates such as this:

```
THIS.of_SetMultiTable(TRUE)
```

After doing this, you must call the of_AddToUpdate() function for each additional table that you want to send updates to. This function requires that you pass not only the table names, but the column names that will participate in the update. If we want to update not only the employee table, but also the department table, we would call the of_AddToUpdate() function as follows:

```
STRING ls_deptcols[ ] = {"dept_id","dept_name"}
THIS.of_AddToUpdate("department",ls_deptcols)
```

7.5.4.4 Print Preview Service

The PFC print preview service allows you to easily provide DataWindow print preview capability in your application. This function will be automatically available in menus that are descended from the m_master PFC menu.

To enable this service all you need to do is to turn the service on in the constructor event of the DataWindow like this:

```
THIS.of_SetPrintPreview(TRUE)
```

7.5.4.5 QueryMode Service

The PFC query mode service allow you to use the DataWindow built in query mode functionality to provide dynamic search capabilities to the user in your DataWindow. You can use this service to turn query mode on and off, indicate columns that can be used in the query, and save and load queries from a file.

To active the query mode service, in the constructor event of the DataWindow you would add:

```
THIS.of_SetQueryMode(TRUE)
```

This enables the service, but does not turn query mode on. When you want to turn query mode on you code:

```
dw_control.inv_querymode.of_SetEnabled(TRUE)
```

To turn query mode off you will call the same function passing FALSE as the argument.

You can call the of_SetQueryCols() function on the service object to set which columns should be included in the query. They are passed as a string array parameter like this:

```
STRING ls_cols[ ]
ls_cols[1] = "dept_name"
ls_cols[2] = "city"
dw_control.inv_querymode.of_SetQueryCols(ls_cols)
```

To allow the user to save and load queries from a file, you will call the of_Save() and of_Load() functions on the querymode service object. Both functions will open up dialog windows to get the user to specify the filename and path to save to or load from.

7.5.4.6 Reporting Service

The PFC reporting services is intended to allow you to modify and view a DataWindow. This includes adding items to the DataWindow, combining multiple DataWindows into a composite DataWindow for printing, formatting and print a DataWindow, setting background, color and border for DataWindows, and also zooming a DataWindow.

This service is enabled by calling the of_SetReport() function in the DataWindow constructor event like:

```
THIS.of_SetReport(TRUE)
```

Once activated, there are many functions on the service that you can call. For adding items to the DataWindow you could use one of the functions in Table 7.16.

Table 7-16. *Report service functions for adding to a DataWindow.*

Report Function	Description
of_AddCompute()	Used to add a computed field to the DataWindow.
of_AddLine()	Used to add a line drawing object to the DataWindow.
of_AddPicture()	Used to add a bitmap image to the DataWindow.
of_AddText()	Used to add a static text field to the DataWindow.

To combine multiple DataWindows into a single composite DataWindow so they can be printed as one report you use the of_CreateComposite() method as follows:

In this example we will combine the d_customer and the d_order DataWindows into one composite DataWindow stored in dw_result which we assume has already had the report services enabled.

```
STRING   ls_datawindows[ ], ls_trailfooter [ ], ls_slidedw[ ]
STRING   ls_rcode
INTEGER li_rcode
BOOLEAN lbl_vertical = TRUE
BORDER   lbo_border [ ]

//Set first DW
ls_datawindows[1] = "d_customer"
ls_trailfooter[1] = "No"
ls_slidedw[1]     = "AllAbove"
lbo_border[1]     = Lowered!

//Set second DW
ls_datawindows[2] = "d_order"
ls_trailfooter[2] = "No"
ls_slidedw[2]     = "AllAbove"
lbo_border[2]     = Lowered!

//Create composite DW
li_rcode = dw_result.inv_report.of_CreateComposite(&
    ls_datawindows, lb_vertical, ls_trailfooter, &
    ls_slidedw, lbo_border)

IF li_rcode = 1 THEN
    dw_result.SetTransObject(SQLCA)
    dw_result.EVENT pfc_Retrieve()

    //Now print it.
    dw_result.inv_report.of_PrintReport(TRUE,FALSE)
END IF
```

As demonstrated in the above example, you can call the of_PrintReport() function to print a DataWindow.

To set defaults, colors and borders for DataWindows you can call one of the functions in Table 7-17.

***Table 7-17.** Modification functions for the report service.*

Report Function	Description
of_SetDefaultBackColor() of_SetDefaultBorder() of_SetDefaultCharset() of_SetDefaultColor() of_SetDefaultFontFace() of_SetDefaultFontSize()	Any of these functions will modify the default attribute that they specify.
of_SetBoder	Allows you to change the border for one or more objects in the Datawindow.
of_SetColor	Modifies the color or background color of one or more objects in the DataWindow.

To set up zooming for a DataWindow you can use the of_SetRelativeZoom() function which will alter the zoom percentage relative to the current zoom percentage. If your DataWindow is currently displaying at a zoom factor of 200%, calling of_SetRelativeZoom(50) would change the zoom percentage to 100%. This function is called like this:

```
dw_control.inv_report.of_SetRelativeZoom(50)
```

7.5.4.7 Row Management Service

You can use the PFC row management service to provide basic add, insert, delete and undelete functionality to your DataWindows.

To active this service you will add the following line in the constructor event of your DataWindow:

```
THIS.of_SetRowManager(TRUE)
```

Once this is active you can perform the actions in the table by issuing the related script in your code. (See Table 7-18.)

***Table 7-18.** Code examples for DataWindow actions.*

DataWindow Action	PowerScript Code
Add a row	This script will add a row at the end of the current result set: `dw_control.inv_rowmanager.EVENT pfc_AddRow()`

(continued)

Table 7-18. *(continued)*

DataWindow Action	PowerScript Code
Insert a row	This script will insert a new row before the current row: `dw_control.inv_rowmanager.EVENT pfc_InsertRow()`
Delete a row	This script will delete the current row, or if multple rows are selected, all selected rows: `dw_control.inv_rowmanager.EVENT pfc_DeleteRow()`
Open undelete dialog window	This script will open a dialog window allowing the user to undelete rows: `dw_control.inv_rowmanager.EVENT pfc_RestoreRow()`

7.5.4.8 Row Selection Service

The PFC row selection service allows you to provide single row selection, multiple row selection or "extended" row selection functionality in your DataWindow.

To enable this service you will call the following in the constructor event for the DataWindow:

```
THIS.of_SetRowSelect(TRUE)
```

Then you must specify which style row selection you want using the of_SetStyle() function such as:

```
THIS.inv_rowselect.of_SetStyle(2)
```

The possible values for row selection style are listed in Table 7-19.

Table 7–19. *Row selection style values.*

Row Selection Style	Description
0	**Single row selection** only one row can be selected at a time.
1	**Multi row selection** user can select multiple rows with single mouse clicks. A row is toggled on or off by clicking on it with the mouse.
2	**Extended selection** user can select multiple rows by holding down the CTRL keys to toggle rows on and off, or the SHIFT key to select a range or rows. This is similar to most Windows row selection functionality.

7.5.4.9 Sort Service

The PFC sort service makes it very easy for you to provide flexible sorting functionality to your DataWindows. All you have to do is to activate the service and set the style that you want to use.

To enable the service, in the DataWindow constructor event add:

```
THIS.of_SetSort(TRUE)
```

and then follow this with the style of sorting that you want:

```
THIS.inv_sort.of_SetStyle(1)
```

The possible styles for sorting are listed in Table 7-20.

Table 7-20. *Row sorting style values.*

Sorting Style	Description
0	**PowerBuilder Sort Dialog** the sort service will open the standard PowerBuilder sort dialog.
1	**Drag and Drop** he sort service will use drag and drop to let the user select sort order at runtime.
2	**Single column sorting** allow the user to sort at runtime by clicking on the column headers.
3	**Multicolumn sorting** allow the user to sort at runtime by clicking on multiple column headers to specify sorting priority.

Another useful function of the sorting service is the ability to sort based upon either data values or display values. To use display values you call the of_SetUseDisplay() function like this:

```
dw_control.inv_sort.of_SetUseDisplay(TRUE)
```

7.5.4.10 Filter Service

The PFC filter service makes it easy for you to provide your users with filter functionality within the DataWindow. Once this service is enabled you can call a filter dialog box to allow the user to enter filter criteria. There are three different filter dialog boxes that you can choose from.

First you must enable the service by adding this code to the constructor event of the DataWindow:

```
THIS.of_SetFilter(TRUE)
```

and then follow this with the style of filter dialog box that you want:

```
THIS.inv_filter.of_SetStyle(1)
```

The possible styles for filter dialog boxes are listed in Table 7-21.

Table 7-21. Filter dialog box style values.

Sorting Style	Description
0	**PowerBuilder Filter Dialog** the filter service will open the standard PowerBuilder filter dialog window.
1	**Dropdown Listbox** the filter service will a simplified dropdown listbox style interface to allow for filtering. This is much better for less technical users.
2	**Extended Filter Dialog** the filter service will open a dialog window that is designd to be more user friendly, but still quite powerful. This window utilizes a tab format to allow the more sophisticated user to access more flexible filters.

Another useful function of the filtering service is the ability to show the column header names instead of the column names which may be easier for the users to understand. To do this you must call the of_SetColumnNameSource() function with a value of 2 like this:

```
dw_control.inv_filter.of_SetColumnNameSource(2)
```

Refer to the PFC documentation for details on other filtering functions if you wish to go beyond the filtering functionality described in this section.

7.5.4.11 Find and Replace Service

With the find and replace service, you can add this standard text manipulation tool to your DataWindow. When triggered the user will be presented with either a Find dialog window (w_find) or a Replace dialog window (w_replace). If you enable the service

these boxes will be displayed automatically when the user selects Edit→Find or
Edit→Replace from the menu.

To enable this service you will enter the following code in the DataWindow
constructor event:

```
THIS.of_SetFind(TRUE)
```

Everything else is automatic. If you want to manually trigger a find process or a
replace process you can call the pfc_FindDlg() and pfc_ReplaceDlg() events in your code.

7.5.4.12 Linkage Service

The linkage service is used to bind two DataWindows together in either a master/detail
relationship, or for coordinated processing.

To enable this service, it must be enabled for all DataWindows involved in the
linkage. In each DataWindow constructor events you would add:

```
THIS.of_SetLinkage(TRUE)
```

Alternatively, you might choose to set up the relationship in the open event for
the window. Then you would need to specify the names of the DataWindows involved
such as:

```
dw_master.of_SetLinkage(TRUE)
dw_detail.of_SetLinkage(TRUE)
```

Obviously this isn't enough to complete the linkage. The next step is to make
sure that the transaction object for all DataWindows in the linkage is set up correctly.
You can do this in one step by calling the function:

```
dw_master.inv_linkage.of_SetTransObject(SQLCA)
```

which will set all the DataWindows in the linkage with the SQLCA transaction object.
Now we must specify which DataWindow is the master and which is the detail by calling the of_LinkTo() function:

```
dw_detail.inv_linkage.of_LinkTo(dw_master)
```

With the two DataWindows now aware of their relationship, we need to inform them about which columns are related between the two DataWindows. In the master DataWindow the key column is the "dept_id" column. This same column exists in the detail window which shows a list of all employees in the department. To set this up in the linkage service we call the of_SetArguments() function:

```
dw_detail.inv_linkage.of_SetArguments("dept_id","dept_id")
```

Next we will specify what action we want to occur in the detail DataWindow when the row changes in the master. We have three options; we can [1] use the column(s) from the master to filter the data in the detail, [2] use the columns from the master as retrieval arguments in the detail, [3] use the columns from the master to scroll to the matching data in the detail. To set this we use the number of the option as a parameter for the of_SetUseColLinks() function:

```
// Retrieve new detail data if the row in master changes
dw_detail.inv_linkage.of_SetUseColLinks(2)
```

To retrieve the result sets for all the linked DataWindows we call the of_Retrieve() function on the linkage service object. It will then in turn retrieve all the data sets needed through the chain:

```
dw_master.inv_linkage.of_Retrieve()
```

The master DataWindow should also have the following code added to the pfc_Retrieve event to ensure that the user can reinitialize the retrieval of data:

```
RETURN THIS.Retrieve()
```

If you are allowing the user to update data in the linkage chain, and the data must be updated in a reverse order up the linkage chain, you should also call the of_SetUpdateBottomUp() function:

```
dw_detail.inv_linkage.of_SetUpdateBottomUp(TRUE)
```

otherwise updates will occur from the top down by default.

7.5.4.13 Required Column Service

In order to make it easier to handle interdependent columns within DataWindows, the PFC provides us with a required column service for DataWindows which enables and disables default DataWindow processing for required fields as needed. This has the effect of deferring required field processing until the user has completed entering their data.

When the service is enabled, required field checking occurs when the pfc_Save event is triggered. To activate the service call this line of code in the DataWindow constructor event:

```
THIS.of_SetReqColumn(TRUE)
```

If there are any columns that you don't want to defer the required field checking on, you can specify them using the of_RegisterSkipColumn() function on the required column service object as follows:

```
dw_control.inv_reqcolumn.of_RegisterSkipColumn("last_name")
```

7.5.5 Utility Services

The utility services provided in the PFC are class library services that you can use in any application even if that application is not based upon the PFC framework. Because they are not part of the framework, that means that you will be responsible for setting up any variables that the service requires and destroying it (cleaning up) after you have finished using it.

The utility services include file services, INI file handling, platform information services, date/time services, string services, data selection services, conversion, parsing, and numerical services.

7.5.5.1 File Service

The file services make it easy for you to access and manipulate files from your PowerBuilder application. This object is platform specific so it will instatiate the appropriate platform specific class when you set it up.

There are many different functions in this object. For the complete list, refer to your online help or Table 7-22. The kinds of functions you can perform include file sorting, copying, renaming, deleting, moving, directory creation, directory changing, directory listing, file writing, access file date and time information ,and much more.

To enable the service you will need to declare a variable to contain the reference to the file service object. If you are only using the file service locally, you can create a local variable. If you are using it within a specific object, you might create an instance variable. If it will be used throughout your application then you can create a global variable. After setting the variable you will call the f_SetFilesrv() global function passing the reference placeholder variable. You can then call the methods on the variable. When you are finished you must then destroy the object.

A complete local transaction might look like:

```
n_cst_filesrv  lnv_FileSrv

f_SetFileSrv(lnv_FileSrv, TRUE)

lnv_FileSrv.of_FileCopy("c:\oldfile.txt","c:\newfile.txt")

DESTROY lnv_FileSrv
```

The following table contains the list of functions for n_cst_filesrv. This list is subject to change, so refer to your online documentation for the latest updates.

Table 7-22. *File services utility functions.*

File Service Function	Description
of_AssemblePath	This function will compile a fully qualified directory path from the component parts passed as arguments (drive, path, filename, and extension).
of_CalculateFileAttributes	This function will calculate a file's attribute information to determine if it is a readonly, hidden, system, or archive file.
of_ChangeDirectory	Changes the current directory to the new directory specified.
of_CreateDirectory	Creates a new directory with the specified directory name.
of_DelTree	Recursively deletes a directory along with all of the files and subdirectories it contains.
of_DirAttribToDS	Copies the directory attribute structure to a DataStore
of_DirectoryExists	Verifies the existence of the specified directory.
of_DirList	Returns a directory list into a n_cst_dirlistattrib variable. This can then be copied to a DataStore using the of_DirAttribToDS() function.
of_DSToDirAttrib	Copies a specific row from a DataStore to the n_cst_dirlistattrib variable.
of_FileCopy	Copies one file to another with the option of appending to the destination file.
of_FileRead	Reads a file into a BLOB or a string array.

(continued)

Table 7-22. *(continued)*

File Service Function	Description
of_FileRename	Renames a file to the new name specified.
of_FileWrite	Writes a file from a BLOB or a string.
of_GetCreationDate	Returns the date that the specified file was created.
of_GetCreationDateTime	Returns the date and the time that the specified file was created.
of_GetCreationTime	Returns the time that the specified file was created.
of_GetCurrentDirectory	Returns the current fully qualified directory path.
of_GetDiskSpace	Returns the available free space on the specified disk.
of_GetDriveType	Returns information about the drive type of the specified drive.
of_GetFileAttributes	Allows you access to see if a file is a read only, archive, hidden, or system file.
of_GetFileSize	Returns the size of a file in bytes.
of_GetLastAccessDate	Returns the date that the specified file was last accessed.
of_GetLastWriteDate	Returns the date that the specified file was last written to.
of_GetLastWriteDateTime	Returns the date and time that the specified file was last written to.
of_GetLastWriteTime	Returns the time that the specified file was last written to.
of_GetSeparator	Returns the directory separator character.
of_ParsePath	Separates a fully qualified path and filename into its component parts (drive, path , directory path, file name, and extension).
of_RemoveDirectory	Deletes a specified directory.
of_SetCreationDateTime	Set the creation date and time for a file.
of_SetFileArchive	Set a file's archive property to on (TRUE) or off (FALSE)
of_SetFileAttributes	Set all of a files properties (read only, hidden, system, archive) in one function using boolean values to turn each option on or off.
of_SetFileHidden	Set a file's hidden property to on (TRUE) or off (FALSE).

(continued)

Table 7-22. (continued)

File Service Function	Description
of_SetFileReadOnly	Set a file's read only property to on (TRUE) or off (FALSE).
of_SetFileSystem	Set a file's system property to on (TRUE) or off (FALSE).
of_SetLastAccessDate	Set the file last accessed date.
of_SetLastWriteDateTime	Set the last written date and time for a file.
of_SortDirList	Sorts the directory list by either file name, extension, last write date/time, or size. Sorting can be either ascending or descending.

7.5.5.2 INI File Service

With the PFC INI file service we now have much more control over the use and management of INI files that was previously available with just the PowerBuilder Profile() functions. You will still use the ProfileInt(), ProfileString(), and SetProfileString() PowerScript functions to read and write a single INI file line at a time. What the INI file service adds is the ability to retrieve all the keys for an INI file section, retrieve all the sections from an INI file, delete lines from an INI file, and delete whole sections from an INI file.

This service is provided by the custom class object n_cst_inifile. Unlike the file services utility service, this class is set to AutoInstantiate, so you will need to declare it, but you are not required to issue CREATE or DESTROY statements.

There are many different functions in this object. For the complete list, refer to your online help (the full list was not available at the time of this writing).

7.5.5.3 Platform Service

With the PFC platform service you can issue standard calls to determine the amount of free memory, free system resources and the height and width (in PBUs) of a given text string. The method for determining this is different on every platform, but the platform service insulates you from this allowing you to issue a general function call which it will then translate to the appropriate function call for the platform it is currently executing on.

This flexible functionality requires the PFC to create a platform specific descendant class of n_cst_platform. As a result, you must manually take care of destroying the object when you are finished with it.

To enable this service you must first declare a variable of the appropriate class, call the global f_SetPlatform() function. Then you can call any of the standard calls for this object which are listed in Table 7-23

Table 7-23. *Platform service utility functions.*

Platform Function	Description
of_GetComputerName	Returns the currently defined system name (not available in 16 bit windows).
of_GetFreeMemory	Returns the amount of free memory.
of_GetFreeResources	Returns the amount of free resources (supported on 16 bit windows only).
of_GetPhysicalMemory	Returns the total amount of physical memory (not supported on 16 bit windows).
of_GetSystemDirectory	Returns location of the system directory.
of_GetTextSize	Returns all the details about text that is used within an object (not supported on Macintosh).
of_GetUserID	Returns the current user ID (based upon the of_SetUserID() function).
of_IsAppRunning	Returns a boolean to indicate if an application is currently running (supported on 16 bit windows only).
of_PageSetupDlg	Displays the w_PageSetup dialog window allowing you to control print settings.
of_PlaySound	Will play the soundfile specified using the appropriate routines for the current platform.
of_PrintDlg	Displays the w_PringDlg dialog window to allow you to set options for and initiate printing.

7.5.5.4 Date/Time Service

The PFC date/time service provides you with many functions that can be used when doing calculations involving dates and times. These services include:

- Conversion functions to convert; Julian dates to Gregorian dates, Gregorian dates to Julian dates, seconds to hours, seconds to days.

- Determine intervals between two date/time values in seconds, milliseconds, years, months, or weeks.

- Determine if a date is a weekday or weekend.

- Halt processing until a specific date/time.

This object does use the AutoInstantiate feature, so you will need to declare the appropriate level of variable, but you will not need to CREATE or DESTROY the object.

7.5.5.5 String Handling Service

The string handling service is used to provide a large set of functions for string manipulation including loading a delimited string into an array (and back), determining the case of a string, doing global replaces, occurrence counting, removal of spaces, and nonprinting characters and more.

To enable this service you must first declare a variable of the appropriate class. The variable uses the AutoInstantiate feature, so you do not need to perform a CREATE or DESTROY. Once declared, you can call any of the standard calls for this object which are listed in Table 7-24

Table 7-24. String service utility functions.

String Handling Function	Description
of_ArrayToString	Converts an array into a delimited string.
of_CountOccurrences	Returns a count of the number of times that particular string occurs within a second text string.
of_GetKeyValus	Returns the right side of a *keyword = value* string (returns the *value*).
of_GetToken	Removes tokens from a string. A token can be any set of characters separated by a delimiter.
of_GlobalReplace	Replaces all occurrences of string1 with string 2 within string 3.
of_IsAlpha	Returns true if the specified string contains only Alphabetic characters.
of_IsAlphaNum	Returns true if the specified string contains only Alphanumeric characters.
of_IsArithmeticOperator	Returns true if the specified string contains only arithmetic operators like (.),+,-,/,* and ^.
of_IsComparisonOperator	Returns true if the specified string contains only comparison operators like <, >, and =.

(continued)

Table 7-24. *(continued)*

String Handling Function	Description
of_IsEmpty	Returns true if a string is empty or NULL.
of_IsFormat	Returns true is the specified string contains only format characters which are all nonAlphanumeric printable characters.
of_IsLower	Returns true is the specified string contains only lower case characters.
of_IsPrintable	Returns true is the specified string contains only printable characters (ASCII values 32 through 126)
of_IsSpace	Returns true is the specified string contains only spaces.
of_IsUpper	Returns true is the specified string contains only upper case characters.
of_IsWhitespace	Returns true is the specified string contains only white-space characters which are newline, tab, vertical tab, carriage return, form feed, backspace, and space.
of_LastPos	Searches backwards through a string to find the last occurrence of another string.
of_LeftTrim	Returns a string with any spaces and non-printable characters removed from the left side.
of_PadLeft	Returns a string padded with spaces on the left until it is a specified length.
of_PadRight	Returns a string padded with spaces on the right until it is a specified length.
of_ParseToArray	Parses a delimited string into array elements.
of_Quote	Encloses a string in double quotes.
of_RemoveNonPrint	Removes all non-printable characters from a string.
of_RemoveWhiteSpace	Removes all whitespace characters from a string.
of_RightTrim	Removes all spaces and non-printable characters from the right of a string.
of_SetKeyValue	Sets the *value* portion of a string containing a *keyword = value* expression.
of_Trim	Removes all spaces and non-printable characters from both the right and the left of a string.
of_WordCap	Sets the first letter of each work in a string to upper case and all other letters to lower case.

7.5.5.6 Selection Service

The PFC selection service allows you to pop open a selection window with a set of data from the database. The user can then select a specific row in the selection window and it will be passed back to the application. This is often referred to as "lookup" functionality. For example, you need to enter a customer for an order form DataWindow. The user could double click on the field to be presented with the selection list of all the customers. They could then choose one and pass it back into the order form.

This service is provided by the n_cst_selection class. To use it, you declare a variable of the appropriate scope. You don't need to worry about CREATE or DESTROY statements because this object uses the AutoInstantiate option.

Once declared you can open w_selection using the of_Open() function. There are three variations on this function:

- **Display rows retrieved from the database**. With this option w_selection will use a DataWindow object that you specify to retrieve the selection list from the database. You will also specify what data is to be returned, any retrieval arguments that will be used and a title for the selection window.

- **Display rows passed as a function argument**. This option is the same as the first option, except that instead of data being retrieved from the database, it is passed in as an argument to the of_Open function.

- **Display rows already in the DataWindow**. This option will use a specified DataWindow, but will display the data current in the buffers instead of loading a new result set from either the database or a function argument.

7.5.5.7 Conversion Service

The PFC conversion service allows you to convert values from one datatype to another. These functions are in addition to the conversion functions that already exist in PowerScript. With the conversion service you can convert:

- Integers and String to Boolean.

- Boolean, ToolbarAlignment, or SQLPreviewType to String.

- Boolean to Integer.

- String to ToolbarAlignment.

- Button to String.

- Icon to String.

- String to SQLPreviewType.

Refer to your online documentation for syntax details on these functions (this information was not available at the time of writing).

7.5.5.8 SQL Parsing Service

The PFC SQL parsing service is designed to allow you to assemble and parse SQL statements. You can use the n_cst_sql service object and the n_cst_sqlattrib to either construct a SQL statement from its components or to break an existing SQL statement down into components.

Once you have declared a variable of the n_cst_sql object at the appropriate scope, you can begin to call the functions to either assemble the values you have inserted into your local n_cst_sqlattrib class into a SQL statement or have the service accept a SQL statement and place its values into the n_cst_sqlattib class variable that you specify. You do not need to call the CREATE or DESTROY statements for this object.

Refer to your online documentation for syntax details on this service (this information was not available at the time of writing).

7.5.5.9 Numerical Service

The PFC numerical service allows you to perform bit level processing and convert binary to base 10 and back.

You enable this service by declaring a variable at the appropriate scope of the class n_cst_numerical. You do not need to call the CREATE or DESTROY statements as this class uses the AutoInstantiate option.

Once declared you can call the functions in Table 7-25.

Table 7-25.

Numeric Functions	Description
of_Binary	Determines the binary equivalent of a positive base 10 number. The result is stored in a string variable.
of_BitwiseAnd	Performs a bitwise AND operation on each bit of two passed values. (1 and 0 evaluates to 0, 0 and 0 evaluates to 0, 1 and 1 evaluates to 1)

(continued)

Table 7-25. *(continued)*

Numeric Functions	Description
of_BitwiseNot	Performs a bitwise NOT operation on each bit of a passed values. (1 evaluates to 0, 0 evaluates to 1)
of_BitwiseOr	Performs a bitwise OR operation on each bit of two passed values. (1 and 0 evaluates to 1, 0 and 0 evaluates to 0, 1 and 1 evaluates to 1)
of_BitwiseXor	Performs a bitwise exclusive or (XOR) operation on each bit of two passed values. (1 and 0 evaluates to 1, 0 and 0 evaluates to 0, 1 and 1 evaluates to 0)
of_Decimal	Determines the base 10 equivalent of a binary number (passed in as a string variable).
of_GetBit	Determines if the specified binary bit of a passed base 10 argument is on (1) or off (0).

7.6 Customizing the PFC For Your Own Use

The extension libraries are where you will inherit all the objects that you are going to use in your application. You will also perform any modifications and additions that you wish to make to the PFC at this level. This will ensure that you will be able to upgrade the PFC as newer versions become available.

As you work with the PFC you will think of changes, improvements and additions that you will want to integrate. You will need to keep in mind as you make modifications to the PFC that you need to be sure to insulate the modifications so that they remain intact and stable when you apply future upgrades to the PFC base class libraries. Remember to never make any changes in the PFC base class libraries (those that start with the letters PFC) or in any objects that start with "pfc_".

Depending on the complexity and functionality required at your site, you may choose to implement one of the following three strategies when making changes to the PFC:

- Use the built-in PFC extension level.

- Add extension levels and insert them into the hierarchy (for departmental or corporate levels).

- Add custom services.

The PFC extension layers contain unmodified descendants of the ancestor classes in the PFC base class libraries. Through inheritance, you have access to all the instance variables, events and functions of the ancestor classes when you make modifications to the extension layer classes.

When implementing changes to the PFC extension layers, you should consider if you want the change to apply to all applications or only a certain group of applications. If you are applying the change to all applications, then modification of the extension level is appropriate. If you only want to change the functionality for a subset of the applications in your organization, you may want to consider adding another extension layer or creating a new service object to provide the functionality.

7.7 Upgrading the PFC With Maintenance Releases

As long as you have not modified anything in the PFC base class layer, upgrading to newer versions of the PFC should be relatively pain free. To install an upgrade, follow the steps below.

1. Make a full backup of all your PFC and extension layer PBLs (just to be safe).

2. Move all of your extension level libraries to a temporary holding area. This will ensure that they are not overwritten when the new version of the PFC is installed.

3. Run the PowerBuilder installation utility, selecting to install the PFC. This option can be found under the Advanced Developer Toolkit heading.

4. Check for any new objects in the installed extension PBLs. If any exist, copy those objects to your extension PBLs.

5. Copy your extension PBLs back over the installed extension PBLs.

6. Open your application object and ensure that the library search path is correct.

7. Open the project painter and do a full rebuild of your application to ensure that all the ancestor/descendant relationships are synchronized correctly.

CHAPTER 8

What's New In PowerBuilder 6.0

*P*owerBuilder 6.0 is full of new and exciting features to help you develop better applications with greater efficiency. If you are already familiar with PowerBuilder 5.0, this
is a good place to start in order to discover the new and improved version 6.0 features
*and how to use them. Some of the new features are explained in detail in this chapter, where-
as others are described here, but discussed in detail in the chapters where they are relevant
(such as with the new Internet functionality and the distributed computing enhancements).
In the latter case, this chapter will point you in the right direction to get all the details.*

8.1 PowerBuilder on the Internet

PowerBuilder has always been a best of breed client/server application development
tool. I never used to think of it as an Internet development tool, but with some of the
recent changes and additions, it is certainly worth trying.

With PowerBuilder 5.0, Powersoft introduced an add on tool called the Internet
Developer Toolkit which included Web.PB and the PowerBuilder Window and
DataWindow plug-ins, allowing you to leverage your existing PowerBuilder knowledge
to deploy database applications on the Internet.

With Internet development becoming mainstream and applications looking to
deploy Intranet and Extranet applications based on Internet standards, this growth area
of PowerBuilder is one of the most critical. Powersoft's commitment to this new technology arena is readily apparent in PowerBuilder 6.0 which now includes the Internet
Developer Toolkit as part of its standard set of features. With this you can begin creat-

ing full, web based applications, or web-enable your existing application. How to do this is the subject of a full chapter in this book, Chapter 10—PowerBuilder and the Internet.

If you are already familiar with this area, here is a summary of the changes for version 6.0 (how to use each is discussed in Chapter 10).

8.1.1 Window Plug-In/Active X Enhancements

The Window plug-in has had a three key enhancements:

- It now supports secure encrypted communications to ensure that your application data is not being observed by a third party.

- PowerBuilder global variables can now be used in your window.

- There are new MIME types for the two plug ins; the standard widow plug in is "application/vnd.powerbuilder6" and the new secure window plug in is "application/vnd.powerbuilder6-s."

Also, now the Window plug-in is available as an ActiveX control. As an ActiveX control you have all the functionality of the plug-in, plus the ability to access the child window's events and functions via JavaScript or VBScript. More detail is provided on this control in Chapter 10.

8.1.2 Web.PB Enhancements

Web.PB has been enhanced in version 6.0 to take advantage of the new PowerBuilder distributed computing features such as shared objects, asynchronous function calls and server push. These are discussed further in the section on "Enhanced Distributed Computing" and in Chapter 9—Building Distributed PowerBuilder Applications.

8.1.3 Cookie Support

The Internet Developer Toolkit comes with a class library for developing windows intended for Internet deployment. A major new feature of this class library is the support for cookies. Now you can embed information in a cookie to be read by a different window. This allows you to now deploy Internet applications that span more than one window.

8.1.4 DataWindow HTML Generation

In version 5.0, Powersoft first introduced us to the ability of a DataWindow to generate HTML code. This allowed us to dynamically generate a DataWindow using Web.PB and save the output on our webserver and then point the client to the result set file. Suddenly, we had dynamic content on our web pages.

In version 6.0, this functionality has been significantly expanded in the following ways:

- New DataWindow properties that allow us to control cell formatting and borders when the HTML code is generated.

- PowerBuilder 6.0 now converts certain DataWindow presentation information into an HTML cascading style sheet. This style sheet is then saved the StyleSheet and HTMLTable properties of the DataWindow. Then if you call the SaveAs() function with the HTMLTable option the style sheet is embedded in the generated HTML syntax.

- Now you can not only create HTML pages with data output from a DataWindow, but you can also now create HTML forms using DataWindows with the freeform or tabular presentation style. The generated form will also retain any special formatting such as radio buttons or check boxes. With the new command button control for DataWindows (see new DataWindow enhancements below), you can also include buttons on your forms with predefined actions such as scrolling or submitting the form.

8.1.5 Toolbar Web Links

This new feature doesn't have anything to do with deploying PowerBuilder applications on the Internet, but this seemed like the best place to put it. In PowerBuilder 6.0, you can add buttons to your toolbar which will launch your Internet browser and link to a web site that you use often. Up to four web links can be specified. To define these links you enter weblink definitions in your PB.INI file under the [pb] section. The definition contains a weblink number, a name for the link and the URL address. This will be something like the following:

```
[pb]
WebLink1=&Powersoft,http://www.powersoft.com
```

```
WebLink2=&Sybase,http://www.sybase.com
WebLink3=&ITCP,http://www.itcpmedia.com
WebLink4=&AceNet,http://www.aceonline.com
```

The first parameter after the WebLink# is the name of the link which will appear under the Help menu in your PowerBuilder development environment. The ampersand (&) character defines the accelerator key for the menu item. Then a comma separates the link name from the URL address.

8.2 *Enhanced Distributed Computing*

In version 5.0, Powersoft introduced distributed computing that allowed us to deploy and execute our non-visual components on a third tier. This was the first step towards PB distributed computing, but it was a very tentative step. Key components were missing, such as the ability to request a service from the distributed computer and have it execute while we performed other tasks, and then signal us when it was done. The ability to have the distributed server share information between different client connections was also missing.

All of this is available in version 6.0 with the addition of asynchronous processing, server push and shared objects. Refer to Chapter 9 for more details on distributed computing.

8.2.1 Asynchronous Processing

In PowerBuilder 5.0, distributed computing implementations, all calls to distributed objects were *synchronous*. This meant that if you made a function call to the server, the client application stopped executing until it received a response back from the server.

The new *asynchronous* calls in version 6.0 mean that when the client calls a process on a distributed server, the client is free to continue executing without having to wait for a response from the server. This is very useful for doing enterprise applications such as:

- Having a distributed server that performs all batch processing.

- Building a report server to do all report generation off-line.

- Perform large data mining queries off line and then call the client (using server push) when the result set is available.

- Any other process where the client does not require an immediate response from the process before proceeding.

When an asynchronous call is made to the server, the call is placed in a queue and executed when the server has the free time to do so. This also ensures that asynchronous calls are executed in the order they are received.

To make an asynchronous call instead of a synchronous call, the syntax is exactly the same except you add the POST keyword in the function call like this:

```
// Global connection object variable defined as:
// connection gc_Remote
// Instance variable for remote NVO defined as:
// nvo_SetBatch invo_SetBatchInstance

gc_remote.CreateInstance(invo_SetBatchInstance)
invo_SetBatchInstance.POST CallBatch("update_summary")
```

> **Migration Note:** The CreateInstance() function replaces the SetConnect() function from PowerBuilder 5.0. SetConnect() will still work to allow for reverse compatibility, but you should use the CreateInstance() function for all new development.

There are some restrictions to using asynchronous calls with remote objects:

- If the function being called uses a return value, the return value will be ignored.

- All arguments passed to a remote object function must be passed by value. Attempting to pass by reference will pass the compiler, but will cause execution errors.

- Clients that have made asynchronous calls cannot poll or inquire to find out the status of the call. The only direct way to communicate the status of a call is if the server uses server-push to send the information to the client.

- Asynchronous calls will be executed by the server in the order in which they are received, but timing may very extensively due to many factors such as load, number of calls in queue and so forth.

- In the event of a server crash, any queued requests will be lost. If the client that made the call crashes, the results may be unpredictable. Therefore, you should institute a way to track and verify that calls have executed successfully. This could be accomplished by using your relational database as a logging device for asynchronous call status.

- Synchronous calls to the server always take priority over asynchronous calls.

8.2.2 Server Push

Server push is a technique that allows messages to be sent from the distributed server to the client. There are many possible uses for this type of process including:

- Informing the client when an asynchronous call that they had requested is completed.

- Informing system administrators when certain users have logged on to the system.

- Broadcasting messages to connected users (i.e., "The server will be going down for maintenance in 10 minutes, please save your work and exit."),

- And, many other ideas only limited by your creativity!

The mechanics of how server-push works are very similar to the way that clients make requests of distributed server objects. The server connects to the client application and then makes a request of an object in that application. Like calls to the server, these calls can be either synchronous (where the server waits for a response from the client) or asynchronous (where the server doesn't wait for a response from the client).

In order for the server-push technique to work, the client must have passed a valid object reference to the server. This object will be the object that the server will connect to in order to communicate with the client. I predict that most class libraries will soon have a non-visual object for distributed communications to manage the messages between the client and the server.

8.2.3 Shared Objects

In PowerBuilder 6.0, we now have the ability to have a single object on the server which is shared by multiple client connections. In version 5.0, this wasn't possible. Each connection to the server would cause the server to create a new instance of the object being connected to. This meant that information couldn't be shared between client connections.

Now we can have persistent, shared data on a server side object. For example, a list of employees could be buffered in a shared object on the server instead of each connection hitting the database and building its own list of clients (very inefficient!).

This technique can also be used in conjunction with Web.PB to provide the same functionality to your Internet applications.

> **Platform Limitation:** Shared objects cannot be used where the client is running Windows 3.x or Macintosh 68K because these platforms are not capable of the necessary server based support.

There are many different uses for shared object such as managing state in an Internet application, serving out data that doesn't change frequently to clients to help reduce the load on the database, managing workflow processes between multiple clients, providing real time transaction resolution (such as in a stock trading environment) and more.

8.2.4 DataWindow Synchronization

In a distributed application you might have a DataWindow on a client and a DataStore on the server application which are using the same or similar information. This becomes a real hassle to keep the data in these two distinct locations correctly synchronized. PowerBuilder 6.0 now has created five new functions specifically designed to help keep your data in sync:

- **GetFullState()**—This function can be called on a DataWindow or DataStore to capture the current state of the data. This can be used to set the identical state on another DataWindow or DataStore using the **SetFullState()** function. This will ensure that all the update flags on both data sources are the same.

- **GetChanges()**—This function can be called on a DataWindow or DataStore to capture all the changes on that object. Then you can use the **SetChanges()** method to apply all those changes to another DataWindow or DataStore.

- **GetStateStatus()**—This funtion can be called on a DataWindow to learn all the details about its state and evaluate if you should call the GetFullState() and GetChanges() functions to synchronize the DataWindow with another.

All of these functions return their data into a blob variable called a "cookie."

8.3 New Debugger

The PowerBuilder 6.0 debugger is a completely rewritten tool. It is much more user friendly and provides more debugging options than ever before. You now have the ability to set conditional breakpoints, break on variable changes, observe the call stack and more. The new pane and window interface also makes it easier to watch and observe the execution of your application.

PowerBuilder 6.0 also introduces "just-in-time" debugging, allowing you to break into the debugger in the event of an application error, even if you started your application using the "running person" icon.

A full description of and instructions on using the new debugger are available in Chapter 16—Debugging and Optimizing your Application.

8.4 Profiling and Tracing

Completely new in version 6.0 is the ability to collect and analyze information about the execution of your application. Trace data is collected by using the Profiling tab on the System Options dialog box, inserting Trace() functions into application scripts, or adding tracing windows to your application to turn tracing on and off dynamically (a window for this is available and can be added to your class library from the Profile.pbl library).

Using the tracing data you can evaluate where bottlenecks are in your application's execution. This is half the battle when it comes to improving the execution speed of your application. Then you can rewrite or change the process to remove the bottleneck.

There are several new system objects and many functions that are available to provide profiling and tracing information. You can get full details on how to use these in Chapter 16—Debugging and Optimizing your Application.

8.5 PFC Enhancements

The PowerBuilder Foundation Classes (PFC) has had several enhancements added to give this service architecture class library even more functionality. The following chart outlines the new objects and services that are available or proposed. (Check your final release documentation to ensure that all of these services, which are in the beta release are also in the final release that ships. See Table 8-1.)

***Table 8-1** New objects and Services.*

Service	Related Object	Description
DataWindow Resize Service	n_cst_dwsrv_resize	Provides automatic resize functionality for objects within a DataWindow object.
Calendar Services	u_calendar	Displays a calendar for selecting dates. Also appears inside drop downs for date fields within DataWindow objects.
Calculator Services	u_calculator	Displays a calculator for calculating numeric values. Also appears inside drop downs for numeric fields within DataWindow objects.
Progress Bar	u_progressbar	Used to display a standard progress bar for long running processes.
Application Preference Service	u_apppreference	Used to allow the setting of preferences for the application.
Splitbar Service	u_st_splitbar	
Most Recently Used Service	n_cst_mru	Displays a list of most recently used windows or other sheet-specific items.
Linked List Service	n_cst_link	
Message Manager Service	n_cst_broadcaster	
Timer Service	n_cst_timer	
MetaClass Service	n_cst_metaclass	
Toolbar Customization Service		
Balanced Binary Tree service		

In addition to the above new services and classes you will find changes to the PFC in the following areas:

- Constants are now used by many objects for return codes. This helps to make the code more readable, similar to enumerated data types.

- The windows sheet manager service has been enhanced.

- u_dw and u_em have been set to use the new Calculator and Calendar services.

- The pfc_Save process has been enhanced.

- The Window Status Bar service has been enhanced.

- Enhancements to the Error Message service.

- DataWindow caching has been improved.

- Row Selection service has been enhanced.

- Security services have been improved.

- The supplied code examples have been expanded significantly.

For more information on using the PFC, refer to Chapter 7—Using the PFC.

8.6 *Changes to the Application Object*

Application objects can now be registered, checked out and checked in properly. PowerBuilder will now undertake a number of tasks in the background when you check out an application object including:

- The current application will be changed to the current application.

- The library path of the checked out application object will be modified to include the check out library.

- The configuration for the checked out application object will be set to the same configuration file for the main application object.

When you check the application object back in, PowerBuilder will undo the above actions, setting the main application object back to the current application.

8.7 *Internationalization*

Powersoft has always striven to make PowerBuilder a true development tool for the world. PowerBuilder is available in many different native languages, supports double byte characters, right to left cursor movement and more. In PowerBuilder 6.0, the international features of PowerBuilder have been further enhanced including Unicode support, Japanese Double Byte Character Support (DBCS), Arabic and Hebrew right to left cursor movement, a translation toolkit and international versions of the PFC.

8.7.1 Unicode Support

Unicode is a standard for character encoding that has the capacity (by using double byte character storage) to encode all characters for all common written languages around the world. A special version of PowerBuilder 6.0 for NT is available with full support for Unicode. You would use this if you want to produce an application that uses any of the character sets supported within the Unicode standard.

Unicode PowerBuilder Libraries are different from the ANSI PowerBuilder libraries. If you have an ANSI PowerBuilder application and want to migrate it to Unicode, there are special migration features in the Unicode PowerBuilder Library painter. A reverse migration is also possible, but any custom characters that are not supported in ANSI may cause unpredictable results.

Note that although Unicode PowerBuilder supports these alternate character sets, text in built in GUI objects like dialog boxes will display in English, but everything typed by the user will display in the appropriate Unicode characters. Also, when deploying PowerBuilder Unicode applications, you will require special deployment .DLLs that are different from the standard ANSI PowerBuilder deployment .DLLs.

There are two new functions that you will see in PowerScript to deal with conversions to and from Unicode. These functions are **ToANSI()** and **ToUnicode()**.

8.7.2 Japanese DBCS

If you need to build an application in Japanese, the Japanese version of PowerBuilder for Windows (3.x, 95 and NT) platforms now supports integrated double byte character sets. Like the Unicode version of PowerBuilder, this version of PowerBuilder requires special deployment .DLLs and also supports conversion to and from this format.

8.7.3 Arabic and Hebrew Support

There are also special versions of PowerBuilder 6.0 with enhanced Arabic and Hebrew support. They support special character sets as well as displaying and entering text in a right to left order. Special deployment .DLLs are required for these versions of PowerBuilder also.

There are eight new functions to support the Arabic and Hebrew versions of PowerBuilder:

IsArabic() will check a string to see if it contains Arabic characters. Neutral characters are ignored.

IsAllArabic() will check to see if a string contains ONLY Arabic characters.

IsArabicAndNumbers() will check to see if a string contains Arabic characters and numbers.

AnyArabic() will check to see if a string contains any Arabic characters.

There are the four equivalent functions for Hebrew: **IsHebrew()**, **IsAllHebrew()**, **IsHebrewAndNumbers()**, and **AnyHebrew()**.

Another feature to support Arabic and Hebrew is the addition of an EditMask masking character to allow you to require the user to enter either an Arabic or Hebrew character.

Like the Japanese and Unicode versions of PowerBuilder, you can migrate ANSI PowerBuilder applications to the Hebrew and Arabic versions, and also migrate them back, if desired.

8.7.4 Translation Toolkit

Although it is not available at the time of writing of this book, Powersoft is planning to release, as an enhancement to PowerBuilder 6.0 Enterprise, a Translation Toolkit which contains a number of tools which are intended to help you translate your application into another language. I can tell you what the tools are, but I must caveat this by saying that I haven't been able to try them myself due to their lack of availability. The first tool is the **Phrase Extractor** which is used to create an object called a "translation project" which will search for and extract phrases from PowerBuilder libraries. These phrases are then passed to the **Translator Tool** which translates the extracted phrases. Then you use a third tool, the **Project Translator Tool** to replace the phrases in your PowerBuilder libraries with the translated phrases.

There are three other support tools that round out the Translation Toolkit: The **Database Administration Tool** is used to manage the translation database by importing glossaries, defining new languages and deleting unused phrases and images. The **Text Analyzer Tool** examines the text that is being replaced and lets you know where command buttons and other controls need to be resized due to a translated phrase that is larger than the original. And finally the **Microsoft International Glossaries™** are included to help you translate common phrases in the same what that Microsoft does.

8.7.5 Localized Versions of PowerBuilder Foundation Class Libraries

Powersoft has also promised to release with PowerBuilder 6.0, versions of the PFC that are customized for regional issues. However, these are not yet available for testing, and no further information is available at the time of writing of this book.

8.8 Deployment and Cross Platform Changes

PowerBuilder 6.0 contains a number of improvements in the area of application deployment. There are also three significant cross platform changes in PowerBuilder 6.0. New UNIX support, font mapping, and a new definition for PowerBuilder Units.

8.8.1 Development/Deployment in 16 bit Windows and 68K Macintosh

One important change that will impact any organizations who are still using Windows 3.1 as a development platform is that PowerBuilder 6.0 will not be available for

Windows 3.1 or the Macintosh 68K. You can continue to deploy to these platforms, but not develop on them. For the first time you will be able to build 16 bit P-code executables from your 32 bit development environment (in version 5.0 we could only create 16 bit machine code executables from our 32 bit development platforms) see Table 8-2.

Table 8-2 *PowerBuilder 6.0 Development and Deployment Platforms.*

Platform	Development	Deployment
Windows 3.1 (Intel 16 bit)	No	Yes
Windows 95/NT (Intel 32 bit)	Yes	Yes
Sun Solaris UNIX	Yes	Yes
HP/UX UNIX	Yes	Yes
IBM AIX UNIX	Yes	Yes
Macintosh 68K	No	Yes
PowerMac	Yes	Yes

8.8.2 Other Deployment Changes

Deployment and deployment environment management have always been one of the hassles of developing your applications in PowerBuilder. Powersoft has helped to make this easier by reducing the number of .DLLs, giving us more information about them, and also providing a tool for verifying deployment environment .DLLs are current.

8.8.2.1 Fewer DLLs

The majority of the .DLLs in the deployment kit have been combined into one .DLL called PBVM060.DLL. The "VM" stands for *virtual machine* (a term borrowed from the Java environment). This has reduced the number of .DLLs and the overall size of the deployment kit. There is another separate .DLL for the DataWindow functionality (PBDWE060.DLL), one for Rich Text functionality, one for Distributed PowerBuilder, and then the same .DLLs that we have always had for native database drivers. You only need to deploy those .DLLs that are required for your applications (instead of all of them, like in version 5.0). For example, if you aren't using distributed computing, you don't have to deploy that .DLL.

8.8.2.2 DLL Name Changes

Another problem with deployed PowerBuilder applications was determining if the .DLLs that were in the deployment environment were up to date or not. In version 6.0, the .DLLs will contain the build number in the name, along with the version number (which has always been there).

The names will also be slightly different for each different international deployment platform (refer to the section on "Internationalization" for changes in Internationalization features). The following chart shows a list of the naming variations.

Platform	Naming Convention
English 32 bit	PBxxx060
English 16 bit	PBxxx060w
Hebrew 32 bit	PBxxx060h
Hebrew 16 bit	PBxxx060i
Arabic 32 bit	PBxxx060a
Arabic 16 bit	PBxxx060b

8.8.2.3 Synchronization Tool (PBSync)

In addition to .DLL name changes, Powersoft is also packaging a new "utility" with PowerBuilder called PBSync. PBSync is actually a complete set of runtime functionality for synchronizing any two sets of files that you may care to compare. This can be in a standard file structure, or if you are building web-based applications, from a client machine to a server machine (like updating the ActiveX or Netscape Plug-In™ files that are running on a client browser).

One example of using this tool would be to verify, when the user starts running an application built in PowerBuilder, that the version of the deployment .DLLs they are using is really the current version. Another good example, is that sometimes to reduce network traffic or improve object loading speed, a PowerBuilder application that may have been placed on the server is instead placed on the client system hard drive. This becomes a maintenance nightmare because every time that you want to deploy a new executable you must then run around and copy it to each individual hard drive. Using the PBSync functionality, when the application starts, it could automatically check for updated files from a central location and copy them down to the hard drive if a new version of the executable has been released.

As this is a significant change, I felt that it warranted its own section in this chapter. Please refer to the section on "PowerScript Changes" for full details on using the PB Sync tool.

8.8.3 New UNIX Platforms

With the release of PowerBuilder 6.0, you can now build and deploy PowerBuilder applications on two new flavors of UNIX: HP-UX version 10.20 and IBM AIX version 4.14.

8.8.4 Font Mapping

You can also take advantage of user defined font mapping by mapping your cross platform fonts into an .INI file. The font files to use are defined in the following table.

Platform	File
Windows	c:\windows\pbfont60.ini
UNIX	~user/.pbfont60.ini
Macintosh	disk:System:Preferences:Powersoft Font Preferences

In this file you will need to create a section called [FontSubstitution] where you will map font1 to font2 like this:

```
[FontSubstitution]
Times = Times New Roman
Arial Narrow = Arial
```

8.8.5 PowerBuilder Units (PBUs) Redefined

PowerBuilder Units used to be defined in earlier versions of PowerBuilder as 1/32 the size of the system font. The intent behind the PBU was to make sure that your applications looked the same regardless of the properties of the monitor it was being displayed on. This didn't always translate well across platforms, so for PowerBuilder 6.0 the PBU has been redefined in terms of the *logical inch*. A logical inch is defined in the operating system of your platform as being a fixed constant number of pixels.

Migration Note: The change in how PBUs are defined could cause an existing application to display differently if you migrate it to 6.0. Be sure to back up your .PBLs before you migrate them in case you have a conversion issue. This issue may be able to be fixed by altering your logical inch definition in your system parameters or resizing the objects in your application.

8.9 *PowerScript Changes*

As with each new release of PowerBuilder, there are some new PowerScript features that you should be aware of.

8.9.1 Intellimouse Support

You have probably seen the new mouse that Microsoft has produced called the *Intellimouse™*. It works the same as a standard two or three button mouse, except that there is a small wheel between the two buttons. When this wheel is turned, it will cause a scrolling action in your application. Clicking on the wheel produces the same result as clicking on the middle button of a three button mouse.

In previous versions of PowerBuilder, all actions on the "wheel" had no results. Now in PB 6.0, a user can scroll a DataWindow object by rotating the wheel. The user can also zoom a DataWindow larger or smaller by holding down the CTRL key while rotating the wheel.

List Views and Tree Views can also be scrolled by rotating the wheel.

8.9.2 New Timer Object

If you have ever wanted to create a timer that was independent of a window, now you can. The new PB 6.0 Timer Object is a non-visual object that provides timer functionality without the need to attach it to a window.

These timer objects can be used as global application timers or on distributed PB applications where each client connection does not have its own window.

The timing object has two methods: Start() and Stop(). The Start() method takes a numeric argument to specify the interval in seconds between timer events (yes, you can use fractions of seconds). When the specified interval has passed, the Timer event on the Timer object is triggered. Calling the Stop method stops the timer from running.

8.9.3 Control Arrays of Windows and Tab Objects

Often in the past we couldn't count on Window or Tab object control arrays to be accurate because any controls or user objects that we added dynamically at runtime wouldn't be included in the array. This has been changed in PB 6.0. If you previously used your own array you should be careful when migrating these applications to PB 6.0 to avoid any conflicts that may arise.

8.9.4 AncestorReturnValue

Now if you extend a script in a descendant class you find out the value of what the return value of the ancestor script was by accessing the *AncestorReturnValue* argument which is now part of all descendant class events.

If you have any local variables with the name "ancestorreturnvalue" this will cause an error during migration. But if we were all following good coding practices and naming conventions this won't be an issue, will it?

8.9.5 Populating the Error Object

There are two new ways in PowerBuilder 6.0 to populate the global Error object: with the new SignalError() function and the PopulateError() function.

The SignalError() function allows you to populate the Error object with an error number and message of your choosing *before* the function triggers a SystemError event. This makes it much easier for you to initiate your own system errors in your applications.

The PopulateError() function allows you to populate the Error object without triggering a SystemError event.

8.9.6 Garbage Collection

In previous versions of PowerBuilder, the process of "garbage collection" was something that was completely beyond our control, and therefore we didn't worry about it (although we did find it convenient to blame any mysterious errors we were having on "garbage collection problems"). PowerBuilder would automatically check a class of objects when an object was destroyed to see if there were no current users of that class. If not, the class was removed from memory. Periodically PowerBuilder would also check all the classes to look for "orphans" (classes that have an instance in the class pool, but aren't being referenced by anything in the PowerBuilder application) and remove them.

Now in PowerBuilder 6.0, we have the ability to take control of the garbage collection process through three new functions; GarbageCollect(), GarbageCollect-GetTimeLimit(), and GarbageCollectSetTimeLimit(). We want to use these functions to ensure that unused objects are cleared from memory as efficiently as possible, thus freeing up the memory for other more important tasks.

8.9.6.1 GarbageCollectGetTimeLimit()

This function can be called at any time to determine the current system minimum garbage collection interval. This is the minimum amount of time that PowerBuilder will wait before initiating garbage collection procedures. The syntax for this function is simply:

```
long ll_time
ll_time = GarbageCollectGetTimeLimit()
```

Which returns a long containing the current time limit during which garbage collection is guaranteed not to occur.

8.9.6.2 GarbageCollectSetTimeLimit()

This function can be used to change the current system minimum garbage collection interval. It takes one argument, a long, with the time in milliseconds that you want to set as the minimum garbage collection interval. The syntax for this is as follows:

```
long ll_NewMinTime = 2000   /*2 second minimum interval*/
GarbageCollectSetTimeLimit(ll_NewMinTime)
```

This function will return a long containing the time interval that existed before the change. You can effectively stop garbage collection from occurring by setting this value to a very large number, but remember, this means that unused classes will not be cleared from memory.

8.9.6.3 GarbageCollect()

This function can be used to initiate an immediate garbage collection cycle. There is no return value for this function. The syntax for calling it is:

```
GarbageCollect()
```

with no arguments and no return value.

8.10 DataWindow Changes

There are many new features for DataWindows in PowerBuilder 6.0 which will help to make your DataWindows more powerful and more user friendly.

8.10.1 DataWindow Command Button Controls

Almost every PowerBuilder developer, at one time or another, has wanted to put a command button on a DataWindow. Now with PowerBuilder 6.0, you can! The button object is now a standard DataWindow Object (DWO) just like a column or a text field. When the user clicks on the button at execution time it can be programmed to either cause a predetermined action (like filtering or sorting) or it can trigger a **ButtonClicked** event allowing you to write custom code for the button.

To place a button on your DataWindow, you select the command button object from the toolbar and place it onto your DataWindow just like you would with any other DWO. Then you can set its properties by selecting it with the right mouse button and choosing **Properties...** from the pop up menu. This will open the Properties Page as shown in Figure 8-1.

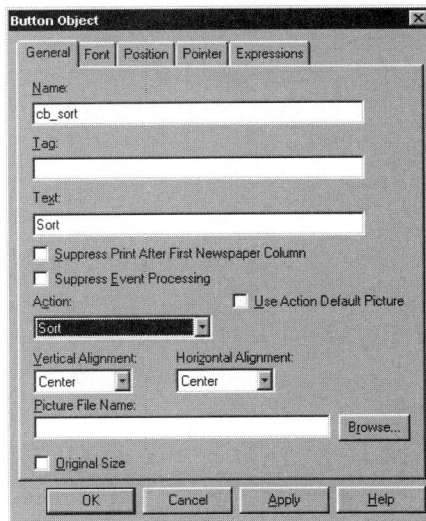

Figure 8-1. The Properties Page for a DataWindow Command Button.

On this page you should assign the appropriate properties to the button. The various properties include:

- **name**. This is a unique name for the button. This will allow you to define custom actions for it in the ButtonClicked event.

- **tag**. Like other tag properties, this can be any string. It doesn't impact the functioning of the button.

- **text**. This is the text that will appear on the button. The font and style of the text can be changed on the Font tab of the properties page.

- **suppress print after first newspaper column**. This checkbox allows you to set the button to only print once if you are using the newspaper column formatting in a tabular DataWindow.

- **suppress event processing**. A button can trigger either a predefined action, specified in the "action" property, or it can trigger a custom user defined action through the ButtonClicked or ButtonClicking events. If you are using a predefined action then you should disable event processing by selecting this checkbox. This will stop the DataWindow from triggering the ButtonClicked and ButtonClicking events.

- **action**. This drop down list box allows you to select from a set of predefined actions that the button can trigger, or a user defined action. If you choose a predefined action, then the ActionReturnCode argument in the button clicked event will contain a different value depending on the action you choose. The set of predefined actions includes: (See Table 8-3.)

Table 8-3

Action	Description	ActionReturnCode
User Defined (default)	Will trigger the Button Clicked and ButtonClicking events allowing you to program any custom script that you choose.	N/A
Retrieve(Yield)	Retrieves data from the database with the "yield" option turned on. The yield option allows the user to cancel the retrieval prior to its completion.	Contains the number of rows retrieved or -1 if retrieve fails.

(continued)

Table 8-3 *(continued)*

Action	Description	ActionReturnCode
Retrieve	Retrieves data from the database with no option to yield.	Contains the number of rows retrieved or -1 if retrieve fails.
Cancel	Cancels a retrieval that has been started with the yield option.	0
Page Next	Scrolls to the next page of data.	Contains the row number of the row displayed at the top of the DataWindow control when the scroll to next page is complete. Contains -1 if an error occurs.
Page Prior	Scrolls to the previous page of data.	Contains the row number of the row displayed at the top of the DataWindow control when the scroll to prior page is complete. Contains -1 if an error occurs.
Page First	Scrolls to the first page of data.	Contains 1 if successful or -1 if an error occurs.
Page Last	Scrolls to the last page of data.	Contains the row number of the row displayed at the top of the DataWindow control when the scroll to last page is complete. Contains -1 if an error occurs.
Sort	Displays the standard sort dialog window allowing the user to change the sort order.	Contains 1 if successful or -1 if an error occurs.
Filter	Displays the standard filter dialog window allowing the user to change the filter criteria on the DataWindow.	Contains the number of rows filtered or a negative value if an error occurs.
DeleteRow	The functioning of this button is dependent on where it is placed. If it is in the detail band of the DataWindow it deletes the row that it is associated with, otherwise it deletes the current row.	Contains a 1 if successful and -1 if an error occurs.

(continued)

Table 8-3 *(continued)*

Action	Description	ActionReturnCode
AppendRow	Inserts a row at the end of the DataWindow.	Contains the row number of the newly inserted row.
InsertRow	The functioning of this button is dependent on where it is placed. If it is in the detail band of the DataWindow it inserts a new row using the row number that it is currently on (meaning prior to the row the button was on), otherwise it inserts a row before the current row.	Contains the row number of the newly inserted row.
Update	Saves changes to the database. If successful, a commit will be automatically issued, and if it fails, a rollback will be issued.	Contains 1 if the update succeeded and -1 if it failed.
Save Rows As	Displays the Save Rows As dialog window allowing the user to save the data in any of the standard formats.	Contains 1 if successful, and -1 if it fails.
Print	Prints a single copy of the DataWindow.	0
Preview	Toggles between regular view and print preview.	0
Preview With Rulers	Turns the rulers on and off (toggle).	0
Query Mode	Turns query mode on and off (toggle).	0
Query Sort	Allows the user to use Query Mode to specify sorting. This option forces Query Mode on.	0
Query Clear	Clears the Where clause from a Query Mode query (if one existed).	0

- **use action default picture**. Pictures can be defined to appear on the button, and if you are using one of the predefined actions, you can check this checkbox to have the default picture for the action you selected loaded.

- **vertical alignment.** Specifies how the text in the button should be vertically aligned. The options are top, center, bottom or multiline.

- **horizontal alignment.** Specifies how the text in the button should be horizontally aligned. The options are left, center, or right.

- **picture file name.** Allows you to specify a filename for a picture that you want to appear on the button. If you do not specify a name, only the text will appear on the button.

- **original size.** If you are showing a picture, click here to display the picture in its original size. If not selected, the picture will be resized to fit the button.

In addition to these properties, you can set two new properties on the DataWindow itself to control if the buttons show up when the DataWindow is printed, or in Print Preview.

To write scripts for these buttons for user defined actions, or for additional processing related to a predefined action you would write code in the ButtonClicked or ButtonClicking event. The ButtonClicking event is triggered when the user clicks on a DataWindow button, but before the action is executed. The ButtonClicked event is triggered after the action is executed. Here is some sample code from a ButtonClicked event:

```
LONG ll_next_key

CHOOSE CASE dwo.name
    CASE "cb_get_next_key"
            SELECT Max(customer_id) INTO :ll_next_key
            FROM customer;

            ll_next_key++

            THIS.SetItem(row,"customer_id",ll_next_key)
    CASE "cb_retrieve"
            IF ActionReturnCode < 0 THEN
                    //Error occurred
                    MessageBox("Error","Retrieve Failed")
            ELSE
                    //Success
                    MessageBox("Success",String(ActionReturnCode)+&
                    " rows returned.")
            END IF
END CHOOSE
```

8.10.2 DataWindow Group Box Controls

Another thing that I am sure every PowerBuilder programmer has done is to simulate group boxes in their DataWindows using rectangle objects and text objects. That, thankfully, is a thing of the past now that PowerBuilder 6.0 has Group Box controls built right in to the DataWindow.

The Group Box control is a purely visual enhancement and doesn't add any functionality to the DataWindow but it is very useful for group logical sets of fields together.

8.10.3 Centered Checkboxes

If you use checkboxes and want to center justify them within a field, now you can. In order for centering to work, the field must not have any associated text and the Left Text property must be set to true.

8.10.4 RowFocusChanging Event

The new RowFocusChanging event on a PowerBuilder 6.0 DataWindow is triggered when the user or the system has requested to change the row focus but before the RowFocusChanged event is triggered.

This event has two arguments: CurrentRo, and NewRow. CurrentRow contains the row number of the current row before the row focus changes. NewRow contains the row number of the row that the focus will be changing to.

At this point you can choose to either allow the row focus to change by using a return code of 0 (the default) or stop the row focus from changing by returning a value of 1.

There are many reasons why you might want to stop the row focus from changing such as the user has unsaved data on the current row and you want them to save it before proceeding.

8.10.5 Print Preview Scrollbar Support

Prior to version 6.0, the scroll bar only showed the current page when the DataWindow was in Print Preview mode. Now the scroll bar will let you scroll through all the pages in the result set.

8.10.6 SaveAs Excel 5

The SaveAs() function can now save the data in a DataWindow as an Excel spreadsheet using the Excel 5.0 format.

8.10.7 SaveAsASCII Function

A new function has been added to allow you to save the contents of a DataWindow or DataStore as an ASCII text file. You will specify a file name and if desired what character you want to use to delimit values, the character to use to wrap values, and the character, you want for a new line. The last three parameters will default to a tab, no character and a carriage return respectively.

8.10.8 Border Painting

Borders used to be a little flaky in earlier versions of PowerBuilder. Particularly when dealing with zooming in Print Preview mode, border repainting, and cell borders within grid DataWindows. These issues have all been corrected in PowerBuilder 6.0.

8.10.9 Display Formats

Until now, edit styles always took precedence over display formats. Now in version 6.0, if you have a Drop Down DataWindow edit style and a display format defined, when the column has focus the edit style is used, but when the cell doesn't have focus, the display format is used.

You may find some migration issues with this change. If you accidentally left an old display format in place and then applied a Drop Down DataWindow edit style later, everything worked fine. But after migrating to version 6.0, now the old display format will come back to haunt you. Keep this in mind if you notice some strange DataWindow display behavior after converting.

8.10.10 N-Up Row Selection

N-Up DataWindows have not been used extensively in production applications due to a number of problems that they experience. One of those issues is that all the cells on a row get selected no matter which column you were trying to select. That has now been fixed in version 6.0.

8.10.11 Longer DWSyntax Strings

There used to be a limit on the maximum size of DataWindow Syntax strings that you could work with. This limit was 32K and this forced you to not work with complex DataWindows in this fashion. This limit has been removed in PB 6.0

8.11 OLE Changes

There are two key areas of enhancement of OLE functionality in PowerBuilder 6.0; server features and error handling.

For server features, PB 6.0 now provides the following:

- Support for Microsoft's DCOM standard with two new functions **ConnectToRemoteObject()** and **ConnectToNewRemoteObject()**. With these two functions, when you connect to an OLE object (using the PB OleObject data type to hold it) you can pass the name of a remote host where a COM server resides.

- You can also assign user events to an OLEObject variable by making a user object descendant class of OLEObject.

- Using the **SetAutomationPointer()** function you can assign the OLE automation pointer used by OLE into a descendant class of OLEObject.

- Using the **SetAutomationTimeout()** function you can control the timeout period for OLE procedure calls from a PowerBuilder client to a server. Otherwise the default is 5 minutes.

- Overall performance of OLE automation has been improved.

- The PowerBuilder object browser will now display the enumerated data types for all OLE automation servers.

For error handling, PB 6.0 now provides the following:

- An OLE control can now provide its own "stock Error event" that is called when the control calls the MFC FireError method. This enables you to write separate error handling events for FireError triggered error messages and standard PB error messages.

8.12 Object Generator

The underlying architecture of how executables are created has been altered in PowerBuilder 6.0 to allow you the flexibility of generating many different kinds of objects from your source code. In the project painter you will now be presented with a dialog window asking which type of object you want to generate. Initially, this list will be limited, but will expand as more generators become available for PB 6.0.

Currently you have the choice of building Applications (either as machine code,or native format), Proxies, or C++ files. Planned generators, which will be released as soon as they are available, include CORBA and DCOM object types along with Jaguar Component Transaction Server components (as OLE automation servers), Microsoft Transaction Server components and Java Bean proxies.

More details on this are available in Chapter 11.

8.13 New Component Gallery Changes

PowerBuilder 6.0 now includes in the Component Gallery a number of ActiveX components for trial use. This means that you can't put them into production applications, but you can test drive them in your development environment.

Included in the component set are objects for database and network access, message handling, telecommunications, multi-media,and more.

These components are not included in the current beta release, so check your PowerBuilder documentation for more details.

CHAPTER 9

Building Distributed PowerBuilder Applications

Unless you have been hiding in a dark room without any outside communication you will have seen (and maybe read) dozens of articles on three-tiered, n-tiered and distributed computing with PowerBuilder. These articles have all focused on the pros and cons of distributed computing and discussed the theory of how it would be applied. In this chapter we will focus specifically on how the mechanics of building a distributed PowerBuilder application work. We will look at the distributed computing objects introduced in PowerBuilder 5.0 and extended in PowerBuilder 6.0 that are involved in making distributed computing work and we will build a simple application which we will partition and then distribute.

This chapter has a descriptive section and a detailed sample exercise. If you are one of those people who learn by doing you might want to start with the sample exercise and then return to the detail to get the in-depth information.

9.1 Distributed PowerBuilder

Distributed computing has had its share of the spotlight recently in the information technology (IT) industry. With many companies having completed their "experiments" with client/server and many moving on to enterprise development, a distributed architecture has become a significant part of their IT strategy. Powersoft, realizing the benefit of this architecture, has implemented distributed computing capabilities in PowerBuilder 6.0.

9.1.1 Distributed PowerBuilder Concept

To this point, the PowerBuilder model for application development has been designed with two components: a client application and the database server. The client application contains the user interface, application navigation controls, data validation and editing, as well as business logic. The database server may contain some part of the business logic but is primarily used as a data source for PowerBuilder clients. (See Figure 9-1.)

Figure 9-1. The 2-tier architecture model with client and server.

The new model using PowerBuilder 6.0 allows for distributed application development. Non-visual business or service objects can be installed and executed on a physically separate third server. Using a three-tier model as an example, the components of distributed PowerBuilder applications are the PowerBuilder client application, an application server (or object server), and the database server. In this model, the user interface is separated from the business logic. The PowerBuilder client will control the application navigation, GUI standards, and simple application validation. PowerBuilder objects and functionality that perform critical business processes can be physically moved to the application server. The application server can execute these PowerBuilder objects in a distributed environment through the *transport* and *connection* objects in PowerBuilder 6.0. The Transport object is used by the server application to process the requests from a PowerBuilder client application. The Connection object specifies the parameters that PowerBuilder uses to connect to a server application.

By locating these business objects on a single distributed server, maintenance for all applications using that object can be centralized. The database server will still act as the data repository. (See Figure 9-2.)

The advantages of this new distributed PowerBuilder model include:

• Ability to "thin out" the client application ("thin" clients will require fewer resources to run effectively).

- Take advantage of server processing and resources.

- Allows the design to be scalable over time.

- Business functionality centralized in one location.

- Centralizes support, maintenance, distribution.

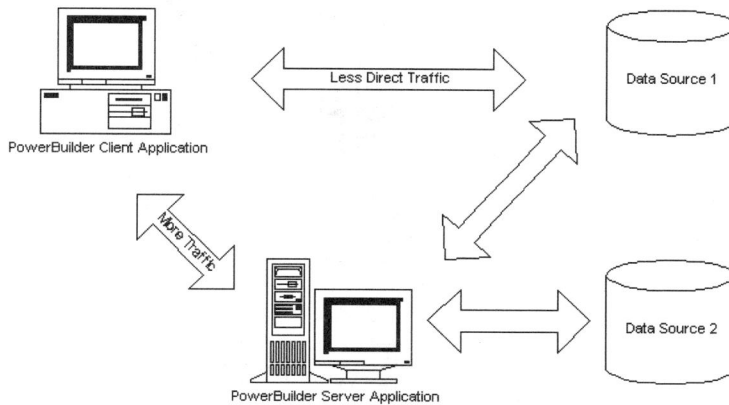

Figure 9-2. The three-tier model with client, application server, and database server.

The distributed model can be further extended into an "n-tier" model by distributing the business functionality to multiple remote servers. The functionality of each server may be different in terms of either implementation or business logic. The multiple application server model may also be used to replicate functionality in the event of a failure on one or more servers. The objects distributed on these application servers can take advantage of the processing power and resources of each individual server platform.

In order to take advantage of a multi-tiered model, you must first clearly identify the business specific elements of the application. These business entities will be deployed as non-visual PowerBuilder custom class user objects on one or more application servers. The properties and methods of the user objects will map to the business elements and their associated functionality. The client application can instantiate a copy of the business object (on the application server) and set properties or execute functionality as necessary. The actual execution of the functionality occurs on the server and is communicated back to the client. (See Figure 9-3.)

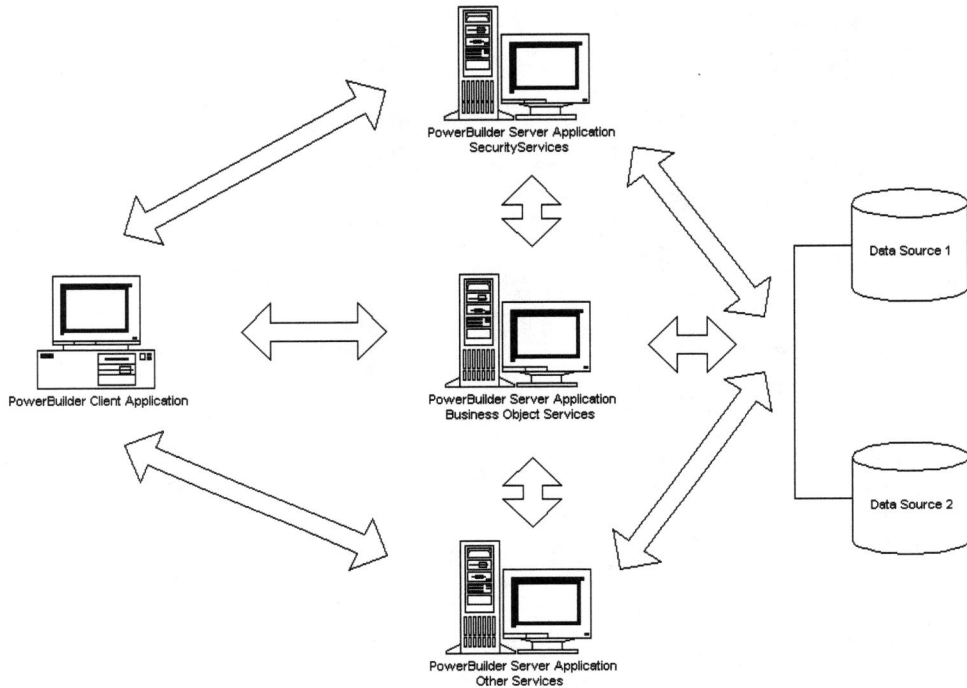

Figure 9-3. *The n-tier model can have multiple application servers that interact with each other and also with multiple databases.*

These business objects are implemented using familiar PowerBuilder objects and PowerScript code. If you are in the build phase of your application, you can initially design and implement the objects locally on your client. The application can be scaled up to multiple distributed servers as you are ready to roll out or as you discover an increased need for more throughput or processing power.

Key areas of the design include:

- Separation of business and/or service logic from user interface.

- Partitioning the application.

- PowerBuilder client to application server communication.

- Data flow.

- Error processing.

9.1.2 Objects Involved in Distributed Computing

Several PowerBuilder 6.0 classes exist to provide the distributed capabilities in PowerBuilder. These classes are inherited from either the non-visual object or the structure object.

9.1.2.1 Inherited from the NonVisualObject

9.1.2.1.1 ConnectObject

The ConnectObject is the ancestor object class for both the Connection and Transport objects.

Connection

The Connection object is used to connect a PowerBuilder client to a PowerBuilder server application. Once the connection is established, the client application can call object methods for those remote objects located on the server in the same manner as is it were a local object method. The connection object works in conjunction with the Transport object.

Several properties exist for this object:

ApplicationName(string)—name of the PowerBuilder server application.

For the *WinSock* driver, this specifies the port on the server machine that contains the application. This can be done either directly, by specifying the port number (i.e., "11000") or indirectly by specifying the service name which is specified in the TCP/IP services file on the client machine. Every server application must have a unique port on the server machine that it "listens" to.

For the *NamedPipes* driver, this specifies the application portion of the pipe name.

For the *OpenClientServer* driver, this specifies the query service (SQL.INI).

For the Local driver, this is ignored.

ConnectString(string)—application specific text sent to the ConnectionBegin event of the server application object. You can use this to pass parameters to the server application which you can then evaluate in your scripts in the ConnectionBegin event. For example, you could pass the user id and password for a database connection.

Driver(string)—communications driver used between client and server. The valid values for this driver are:

WinSock—use the Windows Sockets driver which provides the interface between Windows and TCP/IP

NamePipes—interprogram communications method using Application Program Interfaces (API).

OpenClientServer—Sybase middleware which provides interprogram connectivity.

Local—a special driver built into PowerBuilder which allows you to test a distributed application locally without having to get caught up in all the communication protocol issues. PowerBuilder will simulate the remote server for you (thus eliminating, at this level, the need for a transport object –discussed below).

ErrCode(long)—code indicating success or failure of most recent operation. A value of 0 indicates success. Anything greater than 0 indicates failure. Refer to the chart that follows the methods section or your PowerBuilder documentation for a full list of failure codes.

ErrText(string)—text string describing the success or failure of most recent operation. The ErrCode and ErrText attributes function very much like the SQLDBCode and SQLErrText of the database Transaction object.

Location(string)—specifies location of the server application.

For the WinSock driver, specifies the specific server host. This can be done by naming the host (as specified in the TCP/IP hosts file), giving the specific IP address (such as 225.15.15.15), or by using the literal "LocalHost" which indicates to PowerBuilder that the server application actually resides on the client machine.

For the NamedPipes driver, specifies the location portion of the pipe name if not specified then a local pipe is constructed using dot (.) as machine name.

For the OpenClientServer driver, this is ignored.

For the Local driver, this is ignored.

Options(string)—allows you to specify communication options such as:

BufSize—sets the size of the Windows Sockets buffer (for WinSock only).

MaxRetry—sets the maximum number of times that the client application will try to connect to the server if the server's listening port is busy.

NoDelay—allows you to override the default packet sending delay to send with no delay. This is very specific to your network and should not be used without consulting your network administrator as it could cause significant performance degradation. Use "NoDelay = 1" to activate this option (for WinSock only).

PacketSize—specifies CTLIB packet size (OpenClientServer only).

RawData—allows you to override the default data passing method of the network (which obscures the data) and pass the data in its raw format. The benefit to this setting is a potential improvement in performance of distributed objects. In order for this to work, the server application must be expecting data in raw format or it will not be able to understand it. Use "RawData = 1" to activate this option (for WinSock only).

This argument is ignored for NamedPipes and Local drivers. If you want to specify multiple options for this argument, separate them with a comma. For example:

```
my_connection.Options = 'MaxRetry=4,NoDelay=1'
```

Password(string)—Server password. This application specific text is not used by PowerBuilder.

Trace(string)—specifies the tracing options for debugging purposes such as

Level—setting "Level = 1" will turn on the Console, ObjectCalls, and ObjectLife trace options.

ObjectLife—allows you to trace each attempt to create/destroy a remote object and its success or failure. This option is set by specifying "ObjectLife=1."

ObjectCalls—allows you to trace which methods have been invoke and with what parameter types. It will also specify if the method was called successfully. This option is set by specifying "ObjectCalls=1."

ThreadLife—trace thread life creation/destruction

Log—will specify the file name that will contain the log information. All new information will be appended to this file (not overwritten). Each connection object must have its own specific log file.

Console—enables console logging (Windows 95 and NT only). This is extremely useful for letting you see in a console window all the communication and between the client and server. Activate this option by specifying "Console=1."

Userid(string)—User ID of the user who is connecting to the server. This application specific text, like Password, is not used by PowerBuilder

Several methods exist for the Connection object:

ConnectToServer()—connects a client to the application server specified in its arguments above. Returns a 0 if the connection was successful, or one of the distributed error codes (greater than zero) if an error occurred. Refer to the chart below for the full set of error codes.

DisconnectServer()—disconnects a client from the application server it was connected to.

GetServerInfo()—allows a client (with administrative privileges) to retrieve server information. This is done by passing an array of datatype *connectinfo* (described in detail in a subsequent section). This is a structure specifically created for this purpose. With this the administrative level client can perform such actions as finding out which other clients are connected and could disconnect them with a RemoteStopConnection() function. This method returns a long containing the number of elements in the connectinfo array.

RemoteStopConnection()—allows an administrative level client to disconnect another client by specifying that client's remote id as an argument. The remote id is obtained from the GetServerInfo() method.

RemoteStopListening()—allows an administrative level client to instruct the server to stop listening for client requests.

All methods, except GetServerInfo(), return long data type with a value of 0 for success and a value greater than zero for an error. The possible errors are:

Code	Description
50	Distributed service error
52	Distributed communications error
53	Requested server is not active
54	Server is not accepting requests
55	Request was terminated abnormally
56	Response to request was incomplete
57	Not connected
62	Server is busy

Transport

The Transport object is a PowerBuilder server side object that enables the server application to listen for clients requests. A method called Listen() enables this process and can be initialized in the same way transaction object is initialized.

Several properties exist for this object many of which are similar to those defined for the connection object:

ApplicationName, Driver, ErrCode, ErrText, Location, and **Trace** all have the same definition and possible values as specified for the connection object.

Options(string)—specifies communication options but has a different set of options than the connection object:

BufSize, MaxRetry, NoDelay, RawData, and PacketSize are the same as for the connection object.

MaxServerConnections—specifies the maximum number of open connections that are allowed on an OpenServer client (for OpenClientServer only).

MaxServerThreads—specifies the maximum number of threads that the Open Server application can use (also for OpenClientServer only).

NetBufSize—sets the maximum I/O buffer size of the network for client connections (OpenClientServer only).

TimeOut—sets the maximum length of time that client applications can be inactive before the server will automatically disconnect that client. If you leave this option unspecified there will be no automatic disconnection of clients.

The methods for the Transport object include:

Listen()—instructs the server to listen for client requests. Returns a 0 if successful or a greater than zero error code as specified in this table:

Code	Description
50	Distributed service error
52	Distributed communications error
55	Request was terminated abnormally
56	Response to request was incomplete

StopListening()—instructs the server to stop listening for client requests. Returns a long of 0 if successful or an error code from the table above if unsuccessful.

RemoteObject

PowerBuilder remote objects are nonvisual objects that exist on the server and can issue any nonvisual PowerBuilder function and/or issue database commands. They may also use the new nonvisual DataStore object which has all the data intelligence functionality of a DataWindow, but without the visual user interface. The remote objects is functionally equivalent to a procedure call in the sense that it supports parameter passing and return values for all nonclass or simple PowerBuilder data types.

> **Development Tip:** Be sure to use only simple data types in your remote object functions. If you use complex or class types these methods will not be allowed in the remote form of your object and the PowerBuilder compiler will flag and remove them.

9.1.2.2 Inherited from the Structure

9.1.2.2.1 ConnectionInfo

The structure connectioninfo holds information that describes the connections in place on the server. The members of the structure are:

Busy (boolean)—is the connection busy processing.

CallCount (long)—total number of calls made by the client.

ClientId (string)—the Id of the client that has established a connection.

ConnectTime (DateTime)—date and time of client connection.

LastCallTime (DateTime)—date and time of the last client request.

Location (string)—machine where client resides.

UserID (string)—the user id of the client.

9.1.2.2.2 ProxyObject

The proxy object is an optional part of the nonvisual user object (NVO). If a proxy name is defined for an NVO, then every time the NVO is saved the proxy is also saved. The proxy is the signature for the NVO. The signature defines the methods and interface for the remote NVO. When we distribute an application by moving the business NVOs to the server, the corresponding proxy objects for those NVOs are left on the client. The calls to the NVOs are replaced with calls to the proxy. The method call is routed through the connection object to the server where it executes. The proxy is similar to the Interface Definition Language (IDL) used by the Distributed Computing Environment (DCE) and Microsoft.

To create a proxy object you would open the remote user object in the user object painter, click on it with the right mouse button and select the Create Proxy **Object...** option from the pop up menu. This object will be placed in the same .PBL as the distributed object. You will need to move it to the appropriate library.

9.1.3 Other Issues

Data sharing issues exist with a distributed application. The server creates separate client context areas for each client connection so data may not be shared across client connections. Within each client context, variable and object scope rules are similar to a standard PowerBuilder application (i.e., global variables are initialized at application startup).

Also keep in mind that the distributed functionality can only be called synchronously. The client will wait for the server to finish a process prior to any other events executing. The application object now has events for ConnectionBegin and ConnectionEnd to signal connection to and disconnection from a PowerBuilder server.

Another area that will take some planning is error processing. The error processing for a distributed PowerBuilder application is that if an error occurs on the server, the error information is populated for the current client thread and sent to the current client. On the client side, an application error will fire and the appropriate logic must be coded. The error can be processed in the Error event of the connection object using one of the four new enumerated error types ExceptionFail!, ExceptionRetry!, Exceptionignore!, or ExceptionSubstituteReturnValue!.

Finally, the server component of PowerBuilder 5.0 has been architected so that a single misbehaved client will not terminate the server. An exception handler within the server will attempt to locate the misbehaved client and terminate the thread gracefully, freeing resources if possible.

9.2 *Distributed Application Example*

In this section, we are going to walk through the construction of a distributed PowerBuilder application. This example will go through a number of steps and is a great exercise to get the basic concepts under your belt.

9.2.1 Step 1: Build A Partitioned Application

The first step that we are going to take is to construct a simple application that is partitioned. This application is going to connect to the PowerBuilder demo database that ships with PowerBuilder enterprise and count the number of employees in the employee table. We will encapsulate the methods for connecting to the database, counting the number of employees and disconnecting from the database all within a non-visual user object.

Begin by creating a new application object and storing it in a new library. Next create a window with two command buttons, a checkbox and a single line edit as shown in Figure 9-4. Name each object appropriately and disable the Count Employees command button (we will enable it once we have successfully connected to the database). Save the window as "w_emp_count."

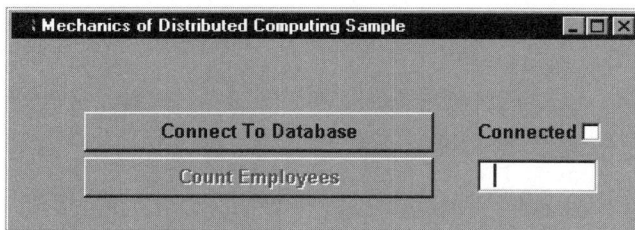

Figure 9-4. Create the window for the client application as it appears here.

Next, we want to build the non-visual user object which contains the processes to connect, count employees and disconnect. Open the user object painter and select a new custom class object. (See Figure 9-5.)

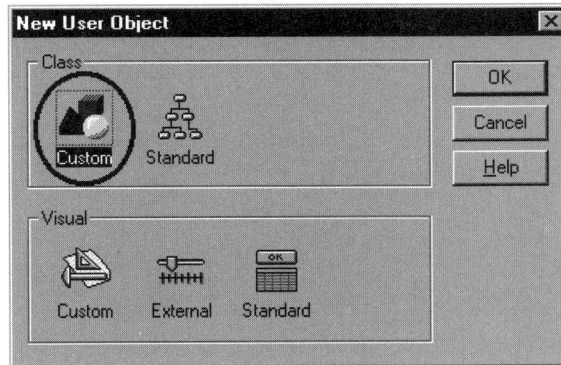

Figure 9-5. *Our non-visual object is created by opening the user object painter and selecting a new Custom Class user object.*

The user object painter will open with what appears to be a window workspace. Remember that the custom class object is non-visual, so you cannot place controls on the workspace. What we want to do in this painter is create user object functions (methods) that we will call from our application.

The first method we will create is for connecting to the database. From the **Declare** menu bar item, select the User Object Functions... menu item. When the selection list appears, choose **New**. We could declare the function with no arguments, assuming that the object was going to pick up its database connection information from somewhere else (perhaps the system registry or an .INI file). Alternatively, we could have the function accept arguments for the key database parameters and then pass these at runtime. For our application, we will hard code in the database parameters and declare the function with no arguments. Define a return code of long with public access and call the function "of_dbconnect." In the script painter, write the following method to connect to your database.

```
SQLCA.DBMS = "ODBC"
SQLCA.DBParm = "ConnectString='DSN=Powersoft Demo DB V6;UID=dba;PWD=sql'"

CONNECT USING SQLCA;

RETURN SQLCA.SQLCode
```

Exit the function painter to save the application.

The second method that we will write is the disconnect. Follow the same steps but declare the new function as "of_dbdisconnect" and use the following script.

```
DISCONNECT USING SQLCA;

RETURN SQLCA.SQLCode
```

The final method that we will add to the non-visual object is the one that actually counts the number of employees in the employee table and returns that value. Declare the new function as "of_count_emp" and use this script:

```
long ll_count

SELECT      count(*)
INTO        :ll_count
FROM        employee;

IF SQLCA.SQLCode = 0 THEN
    //Successful query
    RETURN ll_count
ELSE
    //Query failed
    RETURN -1
END IF
```

Save the non-visual user object as "n_emp_count."

Now we need to integrate our encapsulated business process into our application. Go back to the window painter and open the window "w_emp_count." Declare a protected instance variable of the class "n_emp_count" called "inv_emp_count." We will use this reference variable to instantiate and call the business processes in the non-visual object. (See Figure 9-6.)

Simply declaring the reference variable does not provide us with a tangible instance of this class. The next thing that we have to do is to instantiate this class in the open event of the window. Use the CREATE reserved word as in the following script:

```
inv_emp_count = CREATE n_emp_count
```

Now we can call the processes in the non-visual as required in our application. In the clicked event for the Connect To Database command button we add the script:

```
IF inv_emp_count.of_dbconnect() = 0 THEN
    //Successful connect
    cbx_dbconnect.Checked = TRUE
    cb_count.Enabled = TRUE
ELSE
    //Unsuccessful connect
    cbx_dbconnect.Checked = FALSE
    cb_count.Enabled = FALSE
    MessageBox("Database Connection Failure",&
        "Error Code: "+String(SQLCA.SQLCode) +&
        "~n~r~n~rError Message: "+SQLCA.SQLErrText)
END IF
```

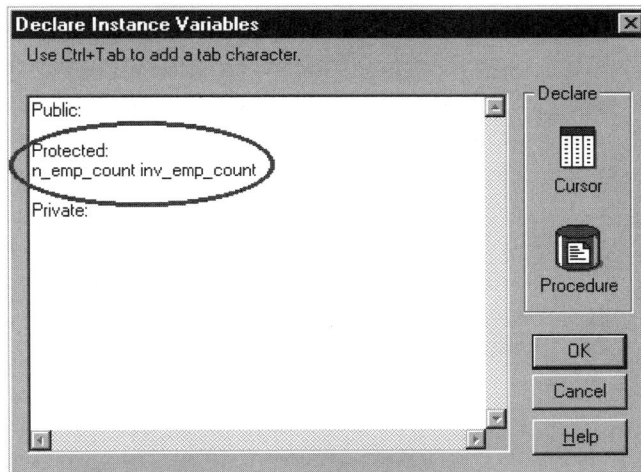

Figure 9–6. *Declare a protected instance variable of the class "n_emp_count" called inv_emp_count.*

In the clicked event for the Count Employees command button we add:

```
sle_empcount.Text = String(inv_emp_count.of_count_emp())
```

to display the total number of employees, or a -1 if an error occurred.

The last thing we should do is to make sure that we clean up after ourselves. In the close event for the window we need to disconnect from the database and destroy our instance of our non-visual object. The script to do this is as follows:

```
inv_emp_count.of_dbdisconnect()
DESTROY inv_emp_count
```

If you don't destroy your non-visual instances, when the window closes, the reference variable will pass out of scope, but the object will still occupy system resources in your instance memory pool. You have just "orphaned" this object and created a memory leak in your application.

Your application is ready to run. Save the changes to your window, add a script in the application object open event to open w_emp_count and run the sample. You have just created a simple partitioned application. Now let's distribute it!

9.2.2 Step 2: Distributing a Partitioned Application

To turn our partitioned application into a distributed one, we need to build a second application which will run on our server. The server application is not all that different from the client application. It will still use an application object and have some visual component. The major difference is that a server application listens for and responds to requests from other client applications instead of listening for and responding to requests from a user.

In order to enable our application to listen for requests from other we will use some of the new objects discussed earlier in the chapter. Two of these objects are the Connection and Transport objects. These objects serve very similar purposes. Both are necessary to allow one application to communicate with another. (See Figure 9-7.)

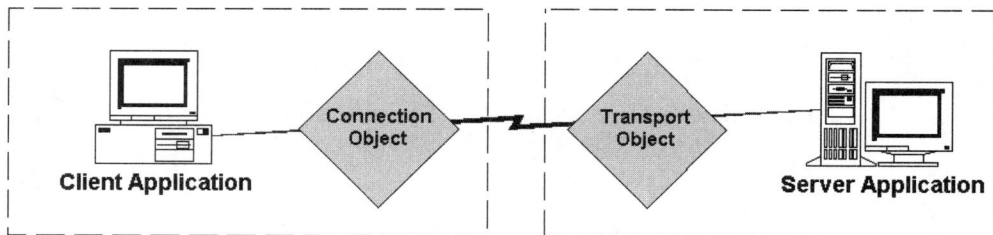

Figure 9-7. The Connection and Transport objects in PowerBuilder allow two PowerBuilder applications to communicate together in a distributed environment.

The Connection object resides on the client application (the one making the request). It functions in a very similar way to the Transaction object that you use to connect to the database. The difference of course is that you are connecting to another application. There is no global reference variable predeclared for you like the SQLCA

Transaction object. You must declare and instantiate your own connection object at the appropriate scope. Once you have done this you must set up the properties of the object. Like the Transaction object you won't require all of them, for full details, see the appropriate section earlier in this chapter.).

Driver—this is a string containing the name of the communications driver that you are using to connect to your server application. The possible values here are:

Winsock if you use the Windows Sockets driver to provide the interface from Windows to TCP/IP.

NamedPipes for interprogram communications using Application Program Interfaces (API).

OpenClientServer if you use the Sybase Open Client Server middleware.

Local for a special driver built into PowerBuilder which allows you to test a distributed application locally without having to worry about the communications driver.

Our sample assumes that you are using a Winsock driver. If you aren't you can modify the sample as appropriate.

Application—this is also a string which contains the identifier for the PowerBuilder server application. The values here will differ depending on what value you have in the driver attribute:

For the *WinSock* driver, this specifies the port on the server that contains the application. This can be done directly by specifying the port number (i.e., "11000") or indirectly by specifying the service name as specified in the TCP/IP services file on the client machine. Every server application must have a unique port on the server machine that it "listens" to.

For the *NamedPipes,* driver this specifies the application portion of the pipe name.

For the *OpenClientServer,* driver this specifies the query service (SQL.INI).

For the *Local* driver, this is ignored.

Location—this string attribute specifies location of the server application. Like ApplicationName the appropriate value for this attribute is dependent upon which driver you are using:

For the *WinSock* driver, this string will specify the specific server that the PowerBuilder server application resides on. This can be specified by naming the host (as specified in the TCP/IP hosts file), giving the specific IP address (such as 225.15.15.15), or by specifying "LocalHost" which indicates to PowerBuilder that the server application actually resides on the client machine.

For the *NamedPipes* driver ,this string will specify the location portion of the pipe name. If you don't specify a location then a local pipe is constructed using dot (.) as machine name.

For the *OpenClientServer,* driver this is ignored.

For the *Local* driver, this is ignored.

These are the three attributes that need to be set at a minimum for our client to communicate with the server application. Other attributes for the connection object include ConnectString, ErrCode, ErrText, Options, Password, UserID, and Trace.

The connection object will manage the client side of the distributed conversation. In order for it to connect to and disconnect from the server application we use functions **ConnectToServer()** and **DisconnectServer()**. These methods do not require any arguments. The first method will establish the server conversation, automatically passing the values stored in the ConnectString, UserID, and Password attributes of the connection object to the server application. The DisconnectServer() method will terminate the conversation with the server application.

On the server side of the conversation, we have the Transport object which provides very much the same function as Connection object, but on the receiving end of the conversation. It shares many of the same attributes of the Connection object. We will use the same settings for the Application, Driver, and Location attributes. We will add a fourth attribute that we will set on our server to allow us to monitor and observe the conversations that occur over our communications protocol. This attribute is the **Trace** attribute and is used as follows:

Trace—is a string attribute which contains instructions on what level of tracing you want to use. You can set multiple tracing options by separating them with a comma within the string. For example, in our sample application, our transport object will have a value of "Console=1,All=1." The first part of this will turn on the Console window (on Windows 95 and NT only) allowing you to view all the communication occurring between the server application and the clients it services. The second part (All = 1) tells the system that you want to see all the messages. You can choose to see only a limited set of messages depending on what specific functionality you are trying to trace.

The Transport object only has two methods that we use, **Listen()** to tell the server application to begin listening for client requests, and **StopListening()** to tell it to stop.

9.2.3 Step 3: Build the Server Application

Let's build the server application for our distributed example. You will need to create a new application object and store it in a new library.

As I mentioned earlier, even though your server application is not designed to interact with an end user, you must build a visual component for the application. Remember that a PowerBuilder application without a visual component triggers the close event of the application object and shuts down. We will build a window for our server application that has three command buttons and a picture control as shown in Figure 9-8.

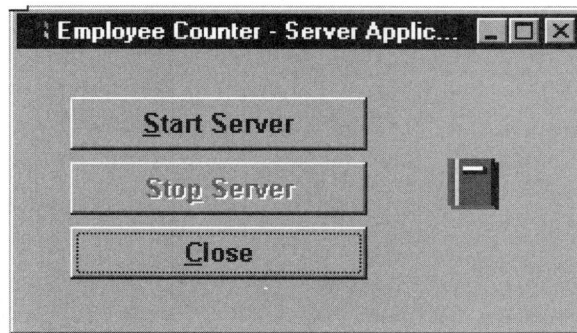

*Figure 9-8. Every server application must have a visual component.
Our sample will have a window that appears like this.*

The next step is to move our non-visual object from our client application to our server application. Do this in the Library painter.

Now define and instantiate your transport object. Define the transport object as a protected instance variable in the server application window. Do the same thing for your non-visual employee count class. Instantiate these objects in the clicked event for the command button Start Server. (See Figure 9-9.)

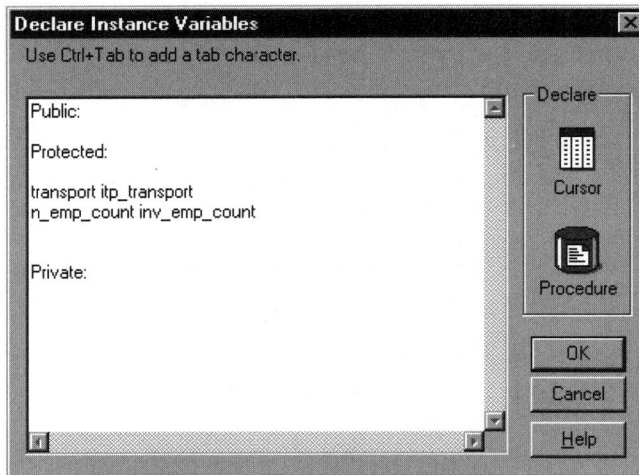

Figure 9-9. Define instance variables for the Transport and non-visual objects. Instantiate these objects in the clicked event for the command button Start Server.

Also in the clicked event we will initialize the Transport object setting the driver to "Winsock," the application to "EMPCOUNT," the location to "Localhost" and the trace to "Console=1,All=1." See the complete code listing for this event for details.

Next in this event, we will ask the application to start listening for client requests. We do this with the Listen() function as shown in the code listing. If the listen is successful, then we set the timer event (to begin animating our bitmap) and enable the Stop Server command button. We also disable the Close command button so that a user on the server won't press it and shut down the server while it is listening.

Code listing for the clicked event of the command button cb_start:

```
// Instantiate Transport and non-visual objects

itp_transport = CREATE Transport
inv_emp_count = CREATE n_emp_count

// Initialize the Transport Object

itp_transport.Driver = "Winsock"
itp_transport.Application = "EMPCOUNT"
itp_transport.Location = "Localhost"
itp_transport.Trace = "Console=1,All=1"
```

```
// Begin Listening for client requests

IF itp_transport.Listen() = 0 THEN

        //Successful

        // Set up the timer event and enable/disable the
        // appropriate objects

        Timer(.15)
        THIS.Enabled = FALSE
        cb_stop.Enabled = TRUE
        cb_close.Enabled = FALSE
ELSE
        // Listen Failed
        RETURN
END IF
```

For the Stop Server command button (cb_stop) we want to stop the server from listening and destroy the transport and non-visual objects.

Code listing for the clicked event of cb_stop:

```
// Stop the server from listening

itp_transport.StopListening()

// Destroy the transport and non-visual objects

DESTROY itp_transport
DESTROY inv_emp_count

// Stop the timer event

Timer(0)

// Enable/disable the command buttons

THIS.Enabled = FALSE
cb_start.Enabled = TRUE
cb_close.Enabled = TRUE
```

For the command button cb_close, code a script to close the parent window.

For the CloseQuery event of the parent, stop the window from closing if the transport object is still listening:

```
IF NOT cb_close.Enabled THEN
        // Still listening
```

```
        MessageBox("Cannot Shutdown","Please stop the server from"+&
" listening before closing this window.")
        RETURN 1
END IF
```

In the timer event for the window, we want to write a script which will rotate the picture to provide some animation. The example on the companion CD ROM uses a book with turning pages. You could borrow the animated globe or ABNC trash can or use the CT_CLIP control that comes in the component gallery if you haven't loaded the samples from the CD. Our script looks like:

```
Choose Case Lower(p_book.picturename)
case "book1.bmp"
            p_book.picturename = "book2.bmp"
    case "book2.bmp"
            p_book.picturename = "book3.bmp"
    case "book3.bmp"
            p_book.picturename = "book4.bmp"
    case "book4.bmp"
            p_book.picturename = "book5.bmp"
    case "book5.bmp"
            p_book.picturename = "book6.bmp"
    case else
            p_book.picturename = "book1.bmp"
End Choose
```

Save the window and close the window painter.

In the application painter, write a script for the open event that opens your server window. We have to write a script for one other event in the application object, the Connection Begin event. This event fires whenever a client application tries to connect with the server. It is in this event that we can perform security checks, user validation and other functionality to decide if we want to let this user connect or not.

The ConnectString, UserID,and Password attributes of the client Connection object are passed to this event as paramenters. We can evaluate those parameters and return one of three possible return codes (which as you will notice are enumerated data types):

- *ConnectPrivilege!*—allows the user to connect with standard user privileges.

- *NoConnectPrivilege!*—declines the client application access to the server application.

- *ConnectAdminPrivilege!*—gives the user full administrative access to the server application including the ability to view and disconnect other clients and to tell the server to stop listening.

For our ConnectionBegin event we will take a very simple approach and give everyone access by coding:

```
RETURN ConnectPrivilege!
```

The server application is complete except for two things, we need to create a proxy object and we need to compile the application.

A proxy object is created from the non-visual process object that you have in your server application. To create it you must open the non-visual object in the user object painter. Click on the object with the right mouse button. From the popup menu select the option to **Set Proxy Name...**. A dialog window will open asking you to specify a name for the proxy object that will be automatically generated when you save the user object. Enter "ro_emp_count" ("ro" for remote object).

The proxy serves as a stub or placeholder for all the function calls that the client application with make to the server application. The proxy knows the names of all the public methods of the non-visual object, but acts as a pointer to these objects on the server rather than actually containing the code in itself. (See Figure 9-10.)

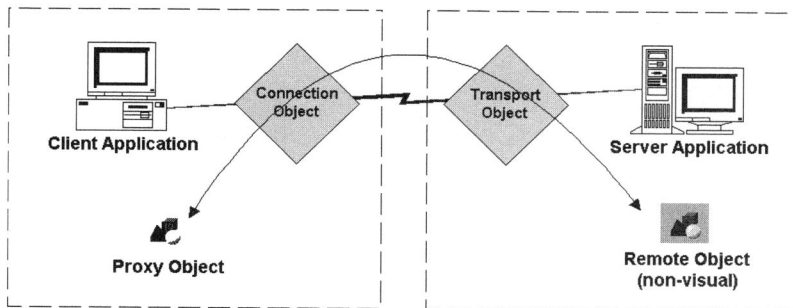

Figure 9-10. *The proxy object acts as a placeholder or stub allowing our client application to call methods stored on a distributed non-visual object.*

Saving the user object now will cause the object "ro_emp_count" to be created in your server library. Move this object to your client library in the library painter. It will take the place of the non-visual object that used to be there.

Compile your server application (either as machine code or p-code, it doesn't matter which). Now we are done with the server application. It is time to alter our client.

9.2.4 Step 4: Altering the Client Application

Our client application is the same application that we build for our partitioned sample. We just need to redirect its calls to the non-visual object to the remote object. In order to do this we must also instantiate and initialize a connection object.

Define a connection object as a protected instance variable. Change the definition of the non-visual object to use the proxy object. (See Figure 9-11.)

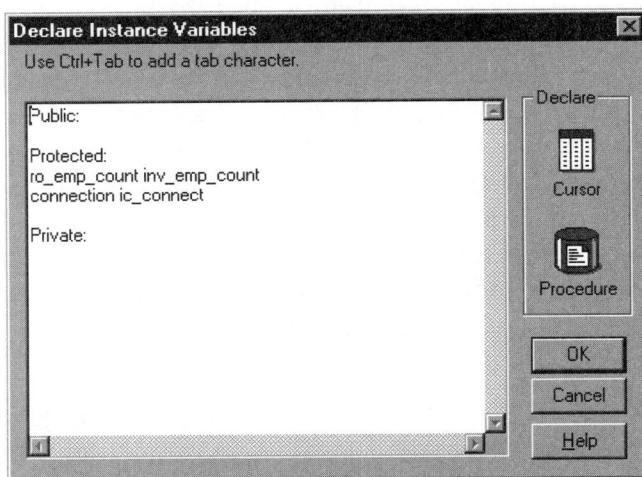

Figure 9-11. *Define an instance of the connection object and change the non-visual to declaration to use the proxy object.*

In the open event for the window we need to instantiate the remote object ro_emp_count and the connection object as shown in the code listing. Next we need to initialize the connection object setting the attributes that we discussed earlier.

Code listing for the open event of w_emp_count

```
// Instantiate remote object and connection object
inv_emp_count = CREATE ro_emp_count
ic_connect = CREATE connection
```

```
// Initialize the connection object
ic_connect.Driver = "winsock"
ic_connect.Application = "EMPCOUNT"
ic_connect.Location = "localhost"

// Connect to the Server application
IF ic_connect.ConnectToServer() = 0 THEN
        // Set the remote object to use the ic_connect connection object
        inv_emp_count.SetConnect(ic_connect)
ELSE
        // Inform user that the connection was unsuccessful
        MessageBox("Unable to Connect",ic_connect.ErrText)
        Close(THIS)
END IF
```

You don't need to modify any of the process scripts. They will be blissfully unaware that anything has changed. You do need to change the close event for the window. Currently we have script to disconnect from the database and destroy the non-visual object. We are no longer responsible for the destruction of the non-visual object, but we do need to destroy our connection object. Change the close event of w_emp_count to look like:

```
inv_emp_count.of_dbdisconnect()
DESTROY ic_connect
```

Save your window.

We now have completed our client and server application. We need to instruct our middleware on the location of our server. This example uses TCP/IP, so we will change our "Services" file (which you will find in your client Windows directory) and add our EMPCOUNT service.

Open this file with notepad and add:

```
EMPCOUNT    11000/tcp       #distributed PowerBuilder example
```

to the end of the file. This defines an application named "EMPCOUNT" listening to port 11000 on a tcp/ip connection. Save this file. You many need to restart your computer depending on your TCP/IP configuration.

If you desire, you can install the server application on a physically separate server and define the port and location properties as appropriate. We will assume that you are running both client and server on one PC for now.

9.2.5 Step 5: Run the Example

Now we are ready to make it run! Start up your server application. You should see your window appear on your screen. Press the Start Server command button. The tracing console should appear and show a successful start of the server. The pages of the book should begin to turn.

Make sure you start up the database manually. The server application will assume that the database is running. If you don't do this the results could be unpredictable.

Now return to PowerBuilder and run your client application. Upon starting up, the application will connect to the server application. You can watch the communication that occurs in the trace window. Press the Connect To Database command button. You will see the of_dbconnect() function execute on the server application and return it's status to the client application. Now press the Count Employees button. This will execute the appropriate method on the server and return the number of employees to the client application.

Congratulations! You have build a distributed PowerBuilder application!

9.3 *Improvements in PowerBuilder 6.0*

PowerBuilder 6.0 represents the second release of the PowerBuilder product to contain distributed computing. Many of the functions in the 5.0 versions of distributed PowerBuilder were very limiting. Powersoft has tried to improve that with three key improvements in version 6.0: Shared Objects, Server Push, and Asynchronous Processing.

9.3.1 Shared Objects

In version 5.0, objects on the server application could not be shared. That made it necessary for every client to have their own copy of the data being worked with on the server. This was both operationally and memory intensive and impractical. In version 6.0 we can create persistent, shared data in a distributed application through the use of server side *shared objects* which can be shared between multiple client connections. By using these objects you no longer have to retrieve the same data for each client connection which reduces the number of database accesses lightening the load on the server.

Developer's Note: Shared objects cannot be deployed on Windows 3.x or Macintosh because these platforms do not support server side processing.

Shared objects require client objects to register themselves by using the SharedObjectRegister method. Each client connected then can call the SharedObjectGet function to obtain an object instance that references the shared object. Now the server is free to perform the requested operations in its main thread instead of having to spin off separate client sessions.

9.3.2 Server Push

In version 6.0, we now have the ability to do something totally new. We can now have our server application send messages to our client applications using *server push*. This is particularly useful for batch asynchronous processing where we want our clients to make a request to the server to do something (like run a batch report) and then allow us to continue running as normal, but to be informed when the server has finished its task.

The ability to make both synchronous and asynchronous calls goes both ways in this relationship. The client can make both types of calls against the server and the server can do the same with the client. In order to allow the server to send a message back to the client, the server must know which client side object to send the message to. This is accomplished by having the client pass an object reference to the server when it makes the request. The server will then create a remote object reference which it can then call functions on at some future point. These function calls are passed back over the network to the appropriate client side object.

The client application calls the function on the server object using the POST keyword such as:

```
remote_object.POST functionname(response_object_reference)
```

The response_object_reference would be the object that the server can call functions on to pass messages back to the client.

That means that on the server, the function "functionname" must receive this argument and then call a function on this object reference in order to pass the message back such as:

```
uo_object_type    luo_passed_object
long                     ll_somevalue=1
// do some processing
// now tell the client we are done and pass back the value
luo_passed_object.POST ReturnValue(ll_somevalue)
```

The response_object on the client would have a function called "ReturnValue" which might have script like:

```
MessageBox("Server Processing Complete","Process Complete.   "+&
Final value is " + String(arg_value) +".")
```

9.3.3 Asynchronous Processing

The server push example above also takes advantage of *asynchronous processing* where the client can call a function on the server without having to suspend all processing waiting for a result. This is done simply by using the POST keyword.

There are some restrictions that apply if you are planning to do asynchronous processing however:

- If the server function has a return value, that value will be ignored.

- Parameters cannot be passed by the client to the server by reference.

- The client cannot use polling to try to determine if a process has completed. The only way to indicate this is to use the server push technique described above.

- Asynchronous calls are all executed in the order that they are received.

- If either the server or the client should crash before the processing is completed, any queued processing requests will be lost.

- Synchronous requests always take priority over asynchronous requests.

9.4 Where To Go From Here

Although distributed PowerBuilder is still fairly new, and does not yet have all the bells and whistles distributed theories promise, enterprise developers now have the opportunity to begin to push the envelope and extend the functionality of their applications beyond the "fat" two-tiered clients we have always worked with to date. The largest benefits will accrue to two types of organizations; those that are deploying many

PowerBuilder applications and can benefit from removing some of the common functionality (such as security) and centralizing it, and to organizations trying to push forward with client server but have limited hardware resources. This latter group could distribute intensive processing on a few more powerful machines and leave the resource strapped clients running lower powered "thin" applications. Another large benefit is the ability to queue batch processes to execute on a different machine.

CHAPTER 10

PowerBuilder 6.0 Internet Features

by Nicholas D. Evans

10.1 Introduction

In this chapter we'll be taking a close look at the Internet features in PowerBuilder 6.0. This Chapter will start by introducing you to the basic concepts and the tools that PowerBuilder 6.0 makes available to you for constructing web-enabled applications. Later in the chapter we'll go into more detail and will present several code examples that you can try out for yourself.

PowerBuilder was first given its Internet capabilities with the release PowerBuilder 5.0 and the Internet Developer Toolkit (IDT) in 1996. The IDT included all the so-called "enabling technologies" for web-enabling PowerBuilder applications: the DataWindow Plug-In, Window Plug-In and Web.PB. These technologies are the core web-enabling technologies that are still used in PowerBuilder 6.0 today. The PowerBuilder 6.0 release takes these features and builds upon them with enhancements and several new features such as the Window ActiveX control. If you have read my recent book from Powersoft Press, *PowerBuilder 5.0 Application Development for the Internet and Intranet*, your investment in learning can easily be leveraged into the world of PowerBuilder 6.0. If you haven't read the book and are interested in PowerBuilder development for the web, then I encourage you to purchase it since the entire book is devoted to what we only have a chapter to cover here.

In addition to the Internet features in PowerBuilder 6.0, I encourage you to take a look at some of the other tools in the PowerStudio product suite including PowerSite and Jaguar CTS. These tools complement Powerbuilder 6.0 and extend its reach into the Internet arena.

10.2 Internet Tools

PowerBuilder 6.0 now combines the Internet Developer Toolkit into the core product and names it the Internet Tools. The IDT was previously an additional package that could be purchased for $99. In this section we'll see how to install the software, look at each of the Internet Tools with some high-level details, and see which types of applications can be constructed with each tool. You'll find that some of the Internet Tools are more suited to Internet applications while others are more appropriate for intranets, where you can make more assumptions about the client desktop.

10.2.1 Installation

When you install PowerBuilder 6.0 you'll be given the option of installing the Internet Tools as shown in Figure 10-1.

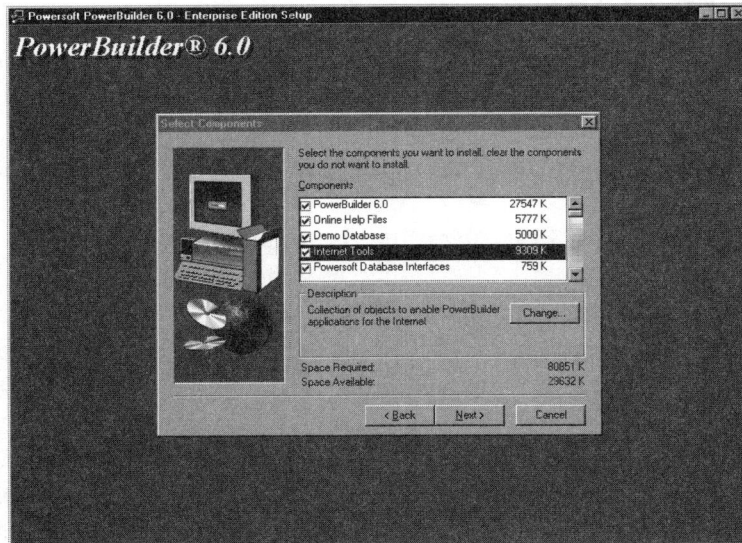

Figure 10-1. PowerBuilder 6.0 Enterprise Edition Setup showing the Internet Tools component.

The total disk space required for installation of the Internet Tools is small. As you can see in Figure 10-1, the total requirement is 9,309K—that's under 10MB. When you install the Internet Tools, you get the following choices:

- Window Plug-in (Standard)   36K
- Window Plug-in (Secure)   35K
- Web.PB   2,725K
- Internet Class Libraries   2,700K
- DataWindow Plug-in   1,674K
- Window ActiveX (Standard)   40K
- Window ActiveX (Secure)   40K
- Tutorial   120K
- Examples   1,764K
- Internet Tools Help Files   172K

After installation, you'll find the software under the c:\program files\power-soft\pb6\it folder. The Internet Tools also come with O'Reilly's WebSite 1.1 web server. You can use WebSite to test the web applications that you develop using PowerBuilder 6.0. WebSite is an easy-to-use web server that can run on either Windows 95 or Windows NT. It is the same web server that was provided in the Internet Developer Toolkit with PowerBuilder 5.0.

10.2.2 DataWindow HTML Generation

PowerBuilder 6.0 has enhanced functionality for creating HTML Forms and Tables from the data in a DataWindow or DataStore. (A DataStore is a non-visual form of a DataWindow typically found in the middle-tier of Web.PB and Distributed Power-Builder applications. It provides a way to use the power of the DataWindow technology for data access in a non-visual manner.) You may remember from PowerBuilder 5.0 that you could create an HTML Table from a DataWindow or DataStore by using the HTMLTable attribute or by using the SaveAs function with the HTMLTable! enumerated datatype.

With 6.0, Powersoft has added more features including more HTMLTable properties which allow you to customize table display by using StyleSheets, CellPadding, CellSpacing and so on. Listing 10-1 shows some sample PowerScript code to do just this.

```
String ls_html

ds_1.Modify("datawindow.HTMLTable.GenerateCSS='yes'")
ds_1.Modify("datawindow.HTMLTable.NoWrap='yes'")
ds_1.Modify("datawindow.HTMLTable.width=5")
ds_1.Modify("datawindow.HTMLTable.border=5")
ds_1.Modify("datawindow.HTMLTable.CellSpacing=2")
ds_1.Modify("datawindow.HTMLTable.CellPadding=2")

ls_html = "<HTML>"
ls_html += ds_1.object.datawindow.HTMLTable.StyleSheet
ls_html += "<BODY>"
ls_html += "<H1>DataWindow with StyleSheet</H1>"
ls_html += ds_1.object.DataWindow.data.HTMLTable

ls_html += "</BODY>"
ls_html += "</HTML>"

return ls_html
```

Listing 10-1. *PowerScript code for creating an HTML Table from a DataStore.*

Another feature is the new GenerateHTMLForm PowerScript function which can convert the contents of a DataWindow or DataStore into an HTML Form for capturing user input from the browser. Listing 10-2 shows some sample code. This function is used on FreeForm and Tabular DataWindows or DataStores.

```
String ls_syntax, ls_style, ls_action
String ls_html
Integer li_return

ls_action = &
  "/cgi-bin/pbcgi060.exe/myapp/uo_webtest/f_emplist"
li_return = ds_1.GenerateHTMLForm &
(ls_syntax, ls_style, ls_action)
IF li_return = -1 THEN
    ls_html = "Unable to create HTML form."
ELSE
    ls_html = "<HTML>"
    ls_html += ls_style
    ls_html += "<BODY>"
    ls_html += "<H1>Employee Information</H1>"
    ls_html += ls_syntax
    ls_html += "</BODY></HTML>"
END IF
Return ls_html
```

Listing 10-2. *Using the GenerateHTMLForm function to create an HTML form from a DataStore.*

10.2.3 DataWindow Plug-In

The PowerBuilder DataWindow Plug-In provides an easy way to interact with Powersoft Report files (PSR) in a browser environment. A Plug-In is an extension to the browser environment and appears as a window within the Web page. A PSR file is a report that contains both a presentation style and data. Any DataWindow presentation style can be used for a PSR except for the rich text edit (RTE) style.

PowerBuilder DataWindow Plug-Ins are supported by Microsoft's Internet Explorer 3.0 and above and Netscape's Navigator 3.0 and above (including Netscape Communicator).

Using DataWindow Plug-Ins, you can take advantage of existing PSR files and deploy them on the Internet. By using Web.PB as well, you can create PSR files on the fly and include a reference to them within the HTML string that is returned to the browser from a DPB server application's non-visual user object method.

Figure 10-2 shows an HTML page containing a PowerBuilder DataWindow Plug-In. When a user accesses an HTML page containing a PowerBuilder DataWindow Plug-In, the PSR is automatically downloaded to the client machine by the browser. The user can right-click within the PSR in order to display a popup menu, page through a report, print it, or save it to disk.

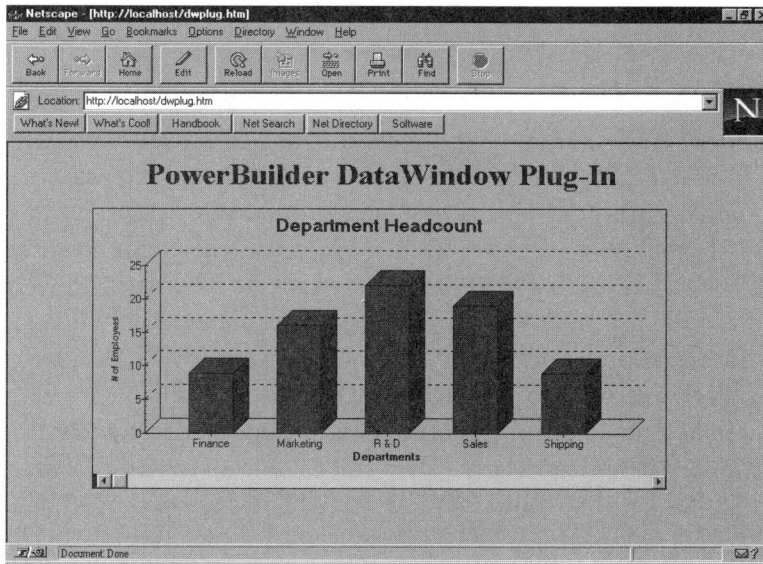

Figure 10-2. PowerBuilder DataWindow Plug-In.

10.2.3.1 Types of Applications

A DataWindow Plug-In is well-suited to intranet applications where the necessary client software can be pre-installed. The DataWindow Plug-In is a lot lighter, in terms of client-side software requirements, than the Window Plug-In and only requires the DataWindow Plug-In DLL to be installed.

Table 10-1 shows the client and server-side software requirements for the DataWindow Plug-In. It can also be used for Internet applications in conjunction with Web.PB, providing the Web.PB application with a mechanism for rich graphical content, created on the fly. The DataWindow SaveAs function, which returns a DataWindow as an HTML table, does not support the graphic presentation style so the DataWindow Plug-In fills this gap quite nicely.

Table 10-1. Client and Server-side requirements for PowerBuilder DataWindow Plug-Ins.

CLIENT-SIDE REQUIREMENTS	SERVER-SIDE REQUIREMENTS
HTML Browser	WEB Server
PowerBuilder DataWindow Plug-In (DLL)	Powersoft Report File (PSR) HTML pages which reference the DataWindow Plug-In (HTM)

10.2.4 Window Plug-In

The PowerBuilder Window Plug-In is a powerful way to host a PowerBuilder application within a Web page. As mentioned earlier, a plug-in is an extension to the browser environment and appears as a window within the Web page. When you run a PowerBuilder Window Plug-In, the code is executed on the client machine.

Using Window Plug-Ins, you can take advantage of existing PowerBuilder code for deployment to the Internet. You may have to make some minor code changes, however, since the application must be based on a Child window. A Child window is a specific PowerBuilder window type assigned in the Window Painter.

You can place any controls onto the Child window. The Tab control, which was new in PowerBuilder 5.0, is especially useful since it allows the user to navigate through several tabbed pages within a child window allowing more content to be placed in the window.

Figure 10-3 shows an HTML page containing a PowerBuilder Window Plug-In. When a user accesses an HTML page that contains a PowerBuilder Window Plug-In, the PowerBuilder dynamic library (PBD) for the Child window is automatically downloaded to the client machine by the browser.

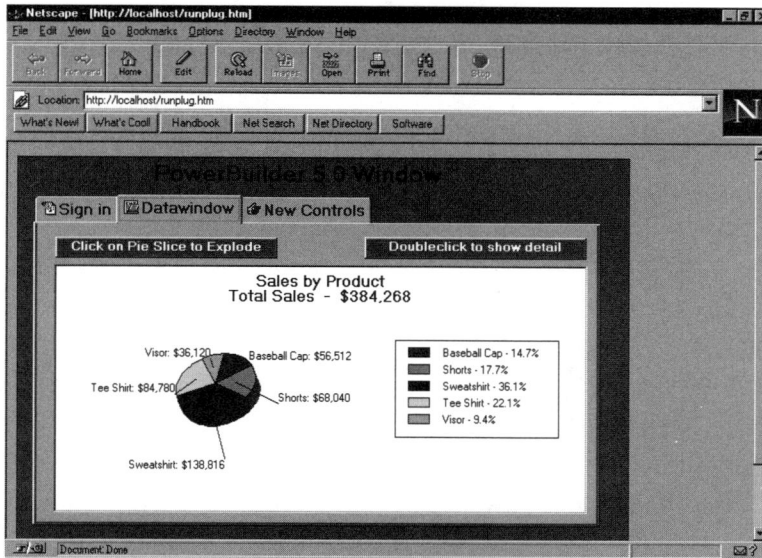

Figure 10-3. PowerBuilder Window Plug-In.

10.2.4.1 Types of Applications

With the PowerBuilder Window Plug-In, you can build various kinds of Internet and intranet applications. The Window Plug-In is especially suited to intranet development since it requires the PowerBuilder runtime libraries and the Window Plug-In DLL on the client side. Table 10.2 lists the client and server-side software requirements. In an intranet environment, it's a lot easier to ensure that the client PCs all contain the software necessary to run the plug-ins. If you're developing an Internet application, however, you could simplify things by providing a way for a user to download the necessary software. If you do this, be sure to provide users with information on how to install the software.

Another reason that the Window Plug-In is suited to intranets rather than Internet applications is that it uses plug-in architecture that is proprietary to Netscape. HTML browsers other than Netscape will not be able to see the Window Plug-In within the HTML page. An exception to this is Microsoft's Internet Explorer 3.0 and above which now supports the EMBED tag. The Explorer browser can display both Window and DataWindow Plug-Ins.

Table 10-2. Client and Server-side requirements for PowerBuilder Window Plug-Ins.

CLIENT-SIDE REQUIREMENTS	SERVER-SIDE REQUIREMENTS
HTML Browser	WEB Server
PowerBuilder Window Plug-In (DLL)	PowerBuilder application with Child window (PBD)
PowerBuilder RunTime Libraries (DLL)	HTML pages which reference the Window Plug-In (HTM)
Client-side Database Connectivity Software	RDBMS and Server-side Database Connectivity Software

In addition to using tabs on child windows, you can also increase the scale and flexibility of applications by adding links to other Web pages which contain Plug-Ins. This way, HTML pages become the framework for PowerBuilder applications. An advantage of dividing an application into multiple child windows on a Web site is that the users will only have to download the function they need. This way, you can reduce the wait time for end users as they download the required PBD. For example, a user could download an order entry child window without having to access the order status page.

10.2.5 Window ActiveX

Support for the Window ActiveX control is a welcome addition to PowerBuilder 6.0. In 5.0, Powersoft only supported the Window Plug-In—this gave developers a way to run PowerBuilder Child Windows within a browser but there was no way to write client-side script against the Window. With the Window ActiveX Control, you can now actually write JavaScript or VBScript client-side script that can invoke methods and events within the window thus providing a higher level of user-interaction with the window.

To create a PowerBuilder Window ActiveX control you create a Child window within PowerBuilder that contains all of your required controls such as DataWindows, TreeViews and so on. You then compile this window within a PowerBuilder Dynamic Library (PBD) file. It's important to note that you are not actually creating an OCX file—you're creating a PBD file which can be controlled and displayed by the PowerBuilder Window ActiveX control, named PBRX60.OCX, which is supplied with PowerBuilder. The PowerBuilder Window ActiveX requires that the client workstation contain the PowerBuilder deployment DLLs as well as a registered version of the PowerBuilder Window ActiveX.

After creating the PBD file, all you need to do is create an HTML page to host the control. Listing 10-3 shows a sample page that contains a window named w_activex:

```
<HTML>
<BODY>

<H2>PowerBuilder 6.0 Window ActiveX Control</H2>

<OBJECT ID="PBRX1" WIDTH=400 HEIGHT=300
 CLASSID="CLSID:CEC58653-C842-11CF-A6FB-00805FA8669E">
    <PARAM NAME="_Version" VALUE="65536">
    <PARAM NAME="_ExtentX" VALUE="2646">
    <PARAM NAME="_ExtentY" VALUE="1323">
    <PARAM NAME="_StockProps" VALUE="0">
    <PARAM NAME="PBWindow" VALUE="w_activex">
    <PARAM NAME="LibList" VALUE="activex.pbd;">
    <PARAM NAME="PBApplication" VALUE="activex">
</OBJECT>

</BODY>
</HTML>
```

Listing 10-3. HTML code for the PowerBuilder Window ActiveX Control.

10.2.6 Secure Mode for Window Plug-ins and ActiveX

Both the existing Window Plug-In and the new Window ActiveX control now include an option for secure mode. This secure mode is similar to the Java security model in that it limits the access that the plug-in or control has on the client machine. This restricted functionality also goes a long way toward preventing a rogue Window Plug-In or ActiveX control from damaging a client machine. Table 10-3 lists the types of activity that are restricted by secure mode.

Table 10-3. Types of activity restricted by secure mode for the Window Plug-In and ActiveX Control.

ACTIVITY	EFFECT
External functions	Calling an external function causes a runtime error.
Certain PowerScript functions	Calling a restricted PowerScript function causes a runtime error.

(continued)

Table 10-3. (continued)

ACTIVITY	EFFECT
Database connection	Calling PowerScript functions that result in database access causes a runtime error.
Internet access	Applications running in secure mode can only establish an internet connections to the current Web server.
E-mail	Calling PowerScript Mail functions causes a run time error.
OLE (restricted in Netscape plug-in only)	Calling PowerScript OLE functions causes a run time error.
Distributed PowerBuilder	You cannot connect to PowerBuilder application servers.
Dynamic Data Exchange (DDE)	Calling PowerScript DDE functions causes a runtime error.

There are actually 52 PowerScript functions which are restricted by secure mode. These include all the functions for working with files (such as FileExists(), FileRead(), ImportFile(), ProfileInt(), SetProfileString() and so on) and all the functions for working with the registry (such as RegistryDelete(), RegistryGet(), and so on).

You can implement secure mode by deploying special versions of the Window Plug-In or the Window ActiveX control on the client machine. These files are listed below:

PRODUCT	DEFAULT VERSION	SECURE VERSION
PowerBuilder Window Plug-In	NPPBA60.DLL	NPPBS60.DLL
PowerBuilder Runtime ActiveX	PBRX.OCX	PBRX_S.OCX

10.2.7 Web.PB

Web.PB is a key technology for bringing PowerBuilder applications to the Internet, allowing HTML browsers to act as clients for Distributed PowerBuilder (DPB) applications. A DPB server can therefore communicate with both Windows-based and browser-based (or universal) clients. Non-visual user objects within a DPB server application can be called with or without parameters and the results can be returned as dynamic content to the browser. The return type of this content can be either "String" or "Blob."

These two datatypes cover virtually any type of data for a browser. HTML content can be returned using either String or Blob datatypes and richer content such as images and sounds can be returned using the Blob datatype.

Web.PB supports CGI forms and URL-based invocation. This means that a user can enter data into a form on a Web page and have that data sent to the DPB server application for processing. The data is sent via the Web server which recognizes the request and forwards it to the application via the Common Gateway Interface (CGI). The non-visual user object function within the DPB server application accepts the data from the form as arguments. It returns it to the browser in HTML format. Figure 10-4 shows the path taken during a typical dialog between an HTML browser and a DPB server application using Web.PB.

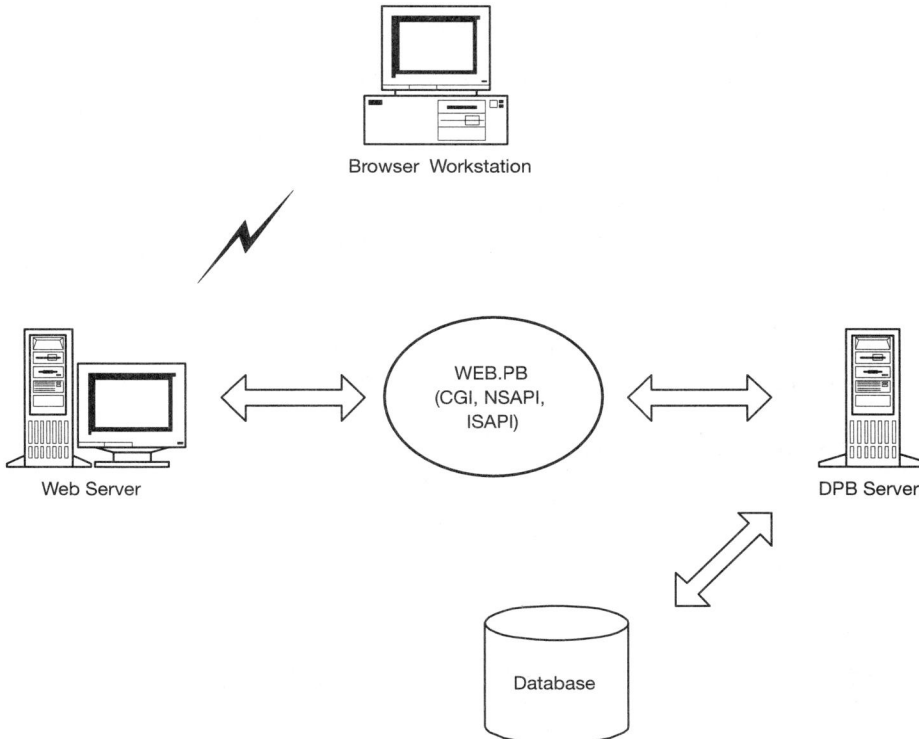

Figure 10-4. Web.PB Architecture.

Web.PB supports Web servers that in turn support CGI standard programming. It also provides in-process DLL support for ISAPI and NSAPI. ISAPI is Microsoft's Internet Server Application Programming Interface, developed jointly by Microsoft and Process Software. This interface allows third parties to extend the functionality of Microsoft's Internet Information Server (IIS) just as CGI extends other Web servers. NSAPI, the Netscape Server Application Programming Interface, is used by Netscape Web servers such as Netscape Enterprise Server.

The ISAPI and NSAPI interfaces run much faster than standard CGI because:

- They share the same address space as the Web server and therefore can be called more quickly than CGI scripts.

- They do not spawn a new process for each request as CGI scripts do.

- They do not need to be interpreted as CGI scripts do.

ISAPI or NSAPI is recommended when you have a high-volume Web site and need the fastest response possible.

Web.PB can also access CGI environment variables which contain useful information about the current browser and Web server communication. If the Web server has assigned values to these variables, you can access them within the DPB server's user objects by including the relevant variable names as arguments to the user object's functions. An example might use the REMOTE_USER CGI environment variable to get the name of a server-authenticated user.

10.2.7.1 Types of Applications

With Web.PB you can build many types of Internet and intranet applications. It is especially suited to Internet development since all that is required on the client side is the HTML browser. Table 10-4 describes the client and server-side software requirements.

Table 10-4. Client and Server-side requirements for Web.PB.

CLIENT-SIDE REQUIREMENTS	SERVER-SIDE REQUIREMENTS
HTML Browser	WEB Server
	DPB Server Application
	Web.PB Software
	HTML pages which reference the DPB functions

10.2.8 Other Internet Features

Besides the major Internet Tools such as the DataWindow Plug-in, Window Plug-in, Window ActiveX, and Web.PB, there's a couple of other items worth looking at: customizable web jumps from within PowerBuilder, the Web.PB wizard on the toolbar, and context information.

10.2.8.1 Customizable Web jumps from within PowerBuilder

This feature provides up to four links to the World-Wide Web from within the PowerBuilder development environment. You can customize these links by editing the PB.INI file (usually under the C:\Program Files\Pwrs\Pb6 folder) and changing the WebLink keys within the [PB] section. Here are some example settings which go out to the Powersoft, Netscape, Microsoft, and Sybase web sites. The default settings included with the product provide links several areas within the Powersoft and Sybase web sites including the Developer Resource Web Site at http://www.powersoft.com/products/panther/protected/pb6devsrc.html.

```
[PB]
WebLink1=&Powersoft Web Site, http://www.powersoft.com
WebLink2=&Netscape Web Site, http://www.netscape.com
Weblink3=&Microsoft Web Site, http://www.microsoft.com
WebLink4=&Sybase Web Site, http://www.sybase.com
```

The menu items appear under the Help menu, above the About menu item as shown in Figure 10-5.

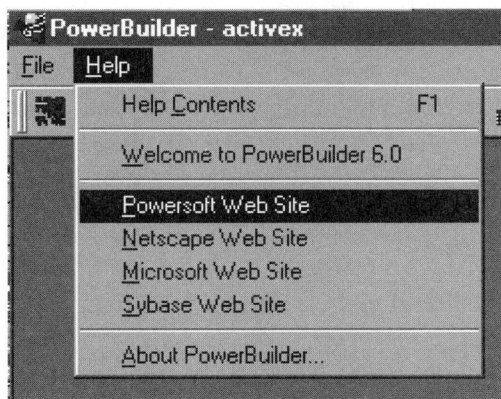

Figure 10-5. *The customizable web jumps in the PowerBuilder 6.0 development environment.*

10.2.8.2 Web.PB Wizard on the Toolbar

There is now a toolbar icon that allows you to launch the Web.PB wizard directly from the PowerBuilder development environment. The wizard guides you through a series of screens which prompt you for information in order to create an HTML page that accesses DPB user object functions. The wizard assists you in the creation of the client component for Web.PB applications. For more information about the Web.PB wizard, see section 10.7.1 later in this chapter.

10.2.8.3 Context Information

A new set of objects in PowerBuilder 6.0 are the Context Objects. Here are the four new PowerBuilder objects which relate to Context:

- ContextInformation.
- ContextKeyword.
- Inet.
- InternetResult.

These objects allow the developer to find out information about the context in which a PowerBuilder application is running. These services provide environment-specific functionality for the following environments (also called contexts): PowerBuilder execution time (default context), Window plug-in, and Window ActiveX.

The context objects provide functionality similar to the COM QueryInterface. Typical uses for the context objects include opening the default browser and displaying a URL from within a PowerBuilder application, accessing application arguments and environment variables, and determining the execution context, modifying the application's look, feel, and processing depending on the environment.

An example might make working with contexts a little more clear. Here's an example which will start the default browser with a specified URL. This can be achieved by calling the Internet service's HyperLinkToURL function.

To hyperlink to a URL:

1.   Declare an instance or global variable of type Inet:

```
Inet  iinet_base
```

2.   Create the Internet service by calling the GetContextService function:

```
GetContextService("Internet", iinet_base)
```

3.   Call the HyperLinkToURL function, passing the URL of the page to display when the browser starts:

```
iinet_base.HyperlinkToURL("http://www.microsoft.com")
```

Contexts can help to integrate client/server and Internet applications. If you try the above example you'll start to see what's possible with just a few lines of code.

10.2.9 Supported Platforms

Table 10-4 summarizes the current platform support for each of the PowerBuilder Internet Tools. The SaveAs HTML feature is also listed since it is an easy way to produce HTML syntax directly from DataWindows or DataStores.

Table 10-4. *Platforms supported for each of the PowerBuilder Internet Tools.*

FEATURE	WINDOWS 3.1	WINDOWS 95, NT (INTEL)	SOLARIS	MACINTOSH
Web PB		Yes	Yes	
Window Plug-In	Yes	Yes		Yes
DataWindow Plug-In	Yes	Yes		
SaveAs HTML	Yes	Yes	Yes	Yes

10.2.10 Summary

The Internet Tools of Web.PB, the PowerBuilder Window Plug-In and the DataWindow Plug-In provide tools to tie PowerBuilder applications to the Internet. Web.PB links HTML browsers to Distributed PowerBuilder application servers in order to create dynamic Web-based applications. The PowerBuilder Window Plug-In leverages existing PowerBuilder applications, re-hosting them on the Web with little HTML coding. The PowerBuilder DataWindow Plug-In lets users of InfoMaker and PowerBuilder make their Powersoft Report files available to browser-based clients. DataWindow Plug-Ins can also be used in Web.PB applications in order to provide a rich graphical presentation of reports.

10.3 Hardware and Software Requirements

10.3.1 Introduction

Building an Internet or intranet application using PowerBuilder 6.0 involves quite a few software options. Not only do you have to select a suitable database management system, but you also need a Web server, Web browsers, and operating systems for these components to be developed and deployed on.

Software selection should be performed on a case by case basis. If you are building an application for your corporate intranet and your company has already standardized on a particular browser then you'll want to test your Web pages on that browser. Your company may have also standardized on Web server, network environment and operating systems.

If you're developing from scratch, you obviously have more choices. If deploying an application for the Internet, you should plan to test it on most, if not all of the popular browsers including Internet Explorer and Netscape Navigator (and Communicator).

Some other factors to consider are security and performance. How sensitive is the data that will be accessed on your site? Will you need to use encryption techniques? What response times are acceptable? Does your server have enough horsepower to service hundreds of simultaneous connections?

In the next couple of sections we'll explore answers to these questions by looking at the required hardware and software for typical Web site implementations. We'll examine the requirements for a large-scale Internet site servicing thousands of users per day and we'll also look at a smaller-scale intranet site with tens or hundreds of users.

10.3.2 Required Hardware

The caliber of the hardware must also match the requirements of the application. If you're developing a large Web site, expecting thousands of hits per day, you'll obviously need a more robust and high-performing server than if you're targeting a fifty-person intranet. Production Web servers for the Internet typically contain vast amounts of memory, often up to 1.0 Gb or more.

You should also consider how your application will be physically distributed. Will there be separate Web servers, database servers and Distributed PowerBuilder application servers? Will it be handled by a single machine?

Table 10-5 contains requirements for a small-scale intranet servicing around fifty users.

Table 10-5. *Typical hardware requirements for a small-scale intranet.*

	WEB SERVER	**CLIENT PC'S**
CPU	Pentium or higher	486 or higher
RAM	32 Mb or more	8-16 Mb
Hard Drive	1 Gb or more	120 Mb or higher

For a small-scale intranet, the hardware requirements on the Web server are quite small. You can probably get by with a Pentium/100 and 32 Mb or so of memory. The minimum requirements for the server depend on the type of application you are running and the amount of Web site content that you are providing on the server. O'Reilly's WebSite recommends a 486 or higher CPU, with 16 Mb of memory for NT or 12 Mb of memory for Windows 95. WebSite itself requires only 10 Mb of free disk space. Microsoft's Internet Information Server can run with just 13 Mb or memory (16 Mb is recommended) and 5 Mb of available hard disk space. Of course, these are just minimum recommendations—any web site that's doing anything useful will require at least a Pentium chip and 32 Mb of memory. If you're publishing a few static HTML documents, you can get by with a small hard disk. If you're delivering a lot of rich content such as multimedia, and you're providing a library of files which can be downloaded, you'll need a much larger hard disk. The amount of memory should be based on the number of simultaneous connections you expect.

Table 10-6 gives requirements for a large-scale internet servicing thousands of accesses per day.

Table 10-6. *Typical hardware requirements for a large scale Internet-based client and server.*

	WEB SERVER	**CLIENT PC'S**
CPU	Dual-Pentium	486 or higher
RAM	256 Mb or more	8–16 Mb
Hard Drive	4 Gb or more	120 Mb or higher

A large-scale Internet setup will typically have one or more servers with dual-Pentium processors and 256 Mb or more of memory. The computers are usually power-protected by an uninterruptable power supply (UPS) system and are connected to the

Internet using ISDN, T1 or T3 connections (see the section on Connectivity below for a definition of those standards). The Internet connection goes to a local Internet Service Provider (ISP) who in turn connects to the Internet backbone.

10.3.3 Required Software

Software selection includes the following choices:

- Network Operating System.
- Client and Web Server Operating systems.
- HTML Browsers.
- Web Server.
- RDBMS.

10.3.3.1 Network Operating System

Windows 95 and Windows NT make great choices for creating a network. Another advantage is that these operating systems support many browsers and servers and are the standard for developing and running PowerBuilder applications.

The main requirement of the network operating system is that it can support TCP/IP. Neither intranets or Internets can run without TCP/IP communications. Windows 95 and Windows NT have networking functionality built in.

If you have Windows NT running, you can set up an NT domain where all administration and security can be handled from a central location. If you run a network of Windows 95 machines, without NT, you can set up peer-to-peer networking where users control access to their machines.

10.3.3.2 Client and Web Server Operating Systems

A typical client for intranet use might be Windows 95. This includes Microsoft TCP/IP which is required to make the connection to the Web server. You can also use Windows 3.1 provided you have the necessary TCP/IP protocol loaded.

On the Internet side, the client operating system could be any version of Windows, Macintosh or any of the many varieties of UNIX. Part of the appeal of the Internet is that it supports a universal client.

The choice of server operating system should be made based on the type of security you need for your Web site. Some servers take advantage of the security mechanisms provided by the underlying operating system. For example, Internet Information Server uses the security provided by NT. You can set up the Web server so that it requires a valid NT login and password before allowing access to its Web pages.

10.3.3.3 HTML Browsers

The choice of browser depends on a number of factors. If you intend to develop state-of-the-art Web pages using the latest HTML specifications you'll probably need Internet Explorer or Netscape Communicator. Version 4.0 of both browsers are available, supporting many new HTML features too numerous to mention.

If you're more conservative and you don't want to keep downloading the latest browsers, (which seem to appear every couple of months), then you can use virtually any browser you like.

Web.PB is really not concerned with the type of browser used since no software, other than the browser itself, is required on the client PC. If you're returning DataWindows in HTML table format you'll want to use the Netscape and Microsoft 3.x browsers or above since they can display tables well thanks to their enhanced support of the HTML <TABLE> tag.

If you're extending Web.PB by using DataWindow or Window Plug-Ins then you'll need a Plug-In capable browser. Explorer 3.0 includes support for Netscape Plug-Ins so either Navigator or Explorer should be fine.

10.3.3.4 Web Server

The three main choices for Web server operating systems are UNIX, Windows 95 and Windows NT. There are also servers for Macintosh and OS/2. Web server software initially ran mostly on UNIX platforms, but is now increasingly appearing with support for the Windows family of operating systems. Since we're going to be developing Web.PB and Plug-In applications we'll need to choose a server that is supported by this software.

To run Web.PB you can choose from the following Web Servers:

- Microsoft Internet Information Server 1.0 and higher.

- Netscape Commerce and Communications Servers.

- Netscape FastTrack and Enterprise Servers.

- O'Reilly & Associates—WebSite 1.1 and higher.

- Any Web Server that supports CGI Standard programming.

The great thing about developing Web applications is that the HTML standard means that you can develop on a small scale using a single machine and later deploy the application on machines running different Web servers and operating systems.

10.3.3.5 RDBMS

If you're developing Web.PB applications, you can use any database supported by PowerBuilder. This includes major databases such as Oracle, SQL Server and Sybase. The database you choose depends upon your specific requirements and whether your organization has standardized upon a particular vendor's database. You may choose a database that provides additional functionality for a PowerBuilder Web site. For example, SQL Server 6.5 has an option to create HTML pages from its data based on a user-defined schedule. The HTML page can be built periodically or you can have it built when the data reaches a certain size.

10.3.4 Connectivity Requirements

10.3.4.1 Connecting your Web Server and Browsers to an Intranet

The major connectivity requirement for building intranets (or using the Internet) is TCP/IP. This is the "language of the Internet" and stands for Transmission Control Protocol/Internet Protocol. If you've used UNIX, you may be familiar with it, since it's been used for UNIX networking for years. TCP/IP has become very popular because it provides communications in a heterogenous network and is routable. Almost all major network operating systems support TCP/IP, including, Microsoft Windows operating systems. Windows-based machines can easily be set up as clients in a network environment. Figure 10-6 shows the TCP/IP configuration option in the Network dialog box under Windows 95. This dialog box is accessed from the Settings | Control Panel folder from the Start icon on the taskbar. If you see a TCP/IP entry in this box then you know that your PC is running the protocol.

TCP/IP protocol defines how data is moved from one machine to another. It's part of a larger networking model called the OSI Reference Model which is shown in Figure 10.7. The OSI model breaks network communications into seven layers. Each layer communicates with the layer immediately above and below it. TCP defines the Transport layer and IP defines the Network layer.

If your Web server is running on a local network along with your client machines, and TCP/IP is running, you can get directly to your Web server quite easily. All you need to do is enter the URL for the server into your browser. For example, the

Web.PB application that we discuss in the next chapter was installed on an Windows NT 4.0 server named `ntserver.nick.com`. With DNS running, the server can be accessed by typing the domain name in the URL as follows: `http://ntserver.nick.com/`

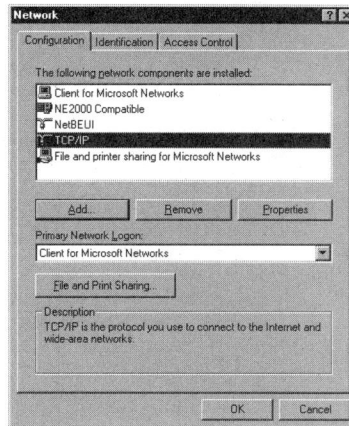

Figure 10-6. TCP/IP Configuration Option in the Network dialog box.

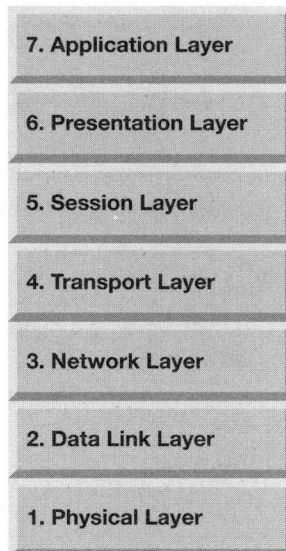

Figure 10-7. The OSI Reference Model.

DNS stands for Domain Name Service, it maps domain names to IP addresses. In this example it provides the following mapping:

```
ntserver.nick.com    167.14.85.137
```

If you don't have DNS running, or you haven't added your Web server to the DNS name registry, then the client machine will not know how to access the Web server by its domain name. In this case, you can enter the IP address as follows:

```
http://167.14.85.137/
```

Of course, you'll need to know the IP address of your Web server. You can determine this by any of the following techniques:

If your Web Server is running on Windows 95:

1.   Choose Start | Programs | MS-DOS Prompt.

2.   Enter WINIPCFG at the DOS Prompt.

3.   Read the IP address in the IP Configuration dialog box (Figure 10-8).

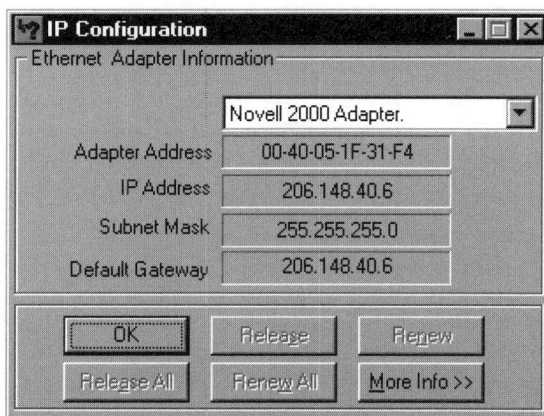

Figure 10-8. IP Configuration dialog box under Windows 95.

If your Web Server is running under Windows NT 4.0:

1.   Choose Start | Programs | Command Prompt.

2.   Enter IPCONFIG /ALL at the DOS Prompt.

3.   Read the IP address from the resulting IP configuration information.

The following lines show typical output from the IPCONFIG /ALL command on Windows NT 4.0:

```
Windows NT IP Configuration
  Host Name . . . . . . . . . . . . . . . . .: ntserver.nick.com
  DNS Servers . . . . . . . . . . . . . . . :
  Node Type . . . . . . . . . . . . . . . . .:          Hybrid
  NetBIOS Scope ID . . . . . . . . . .:
  IP Routing Enabled . . . . . . . . . :          No
  WINS Proxy Enabled . . . . . . . . :     No
  NetBIOS Resolution Uses DNS :    No
Ethernet adapter NE20001:
  Description  . . . . . . . . .  . . . . . . :     Novell 2000 Adapter.
  Physical Address . . . . . . . . . . . :     00-40-05-1F-31-F4
  DHCP Enabled . . . . . . . . . . . . . :     No
  IP Address . . . . . . . . . . . . . . . . :     206.148.40.6
  Subnet Mask . . . . . . . . . . . . . .. : 255.255.255.0
  Default Gateway  . . . . . . . . . . . :
  Primary WINS Server . . . . . . . . :   206.148.40.6
```

If you have an IP address which has been specified (hard-coded) locally rather than assigned automatically, you can view it by opening the Networking application in the Control Panel as follows:

Windows 95:

1.   Choose Start | Settings | Control Panel.

2.   Choose the Network icon.

3.   Click on the TCP/IP network component and choose Properties.

4.   The TCP/IP Properties dialog box will display showing the IP address tab.

5.   The IP address will be listed here, if it has been specified (Figure 10-9).

Note: If your Web server is available on the Internet, your IP address will be assigned to you by InterNIC. This is because once you make your server available to the outside world it needs a unique IP address in order to uniquely define your machine. Within a corporate intranet this is not a problem since outside users cannot access those machines. You can use any IP addresses that you like provided they are unique within your intranet network.

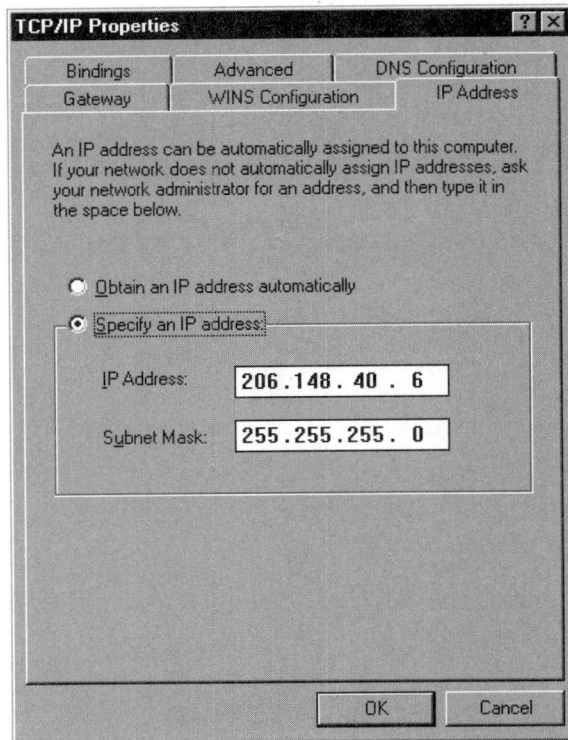

Figure 10-9. IP Address tab in the TCP/IP Properties dialog box.

The techniques above can be used to find the IP address of any machine that is running TCP/IP under Windows 95 or NT. Be sure not to change any TCP/IP configuration settings unless you have the permission of the network administrator.

10.3.4.2 Connecting your Web Server to the Internet

If you're developing an Internet Web page you'll also need to have your server connected to the Internet via an Internet Service Provider or ISP. ISPs provide Internet access for customers and organizations throughout the world. America Online and CompuServe provide Internet access to millions of customers via a dial-up connection using a PC's modem. Most customers use a 28.8 Kb modem to gain access to the Web. This is actually quite a bottleneck since it provides a very narrow bandwidth for large binary files such as graphics and multimedia to pass through. You've probably experienced this when you visit many Web sites and have to wait for all the graphics to be downloaded. Even 33 or 56 Kb modems can be slow to download and display graphics and multimedia. For this reason, you need to review the content of your site to make sure that its contents are as compact as possible. If you're using Plug-Ins, you should review the size of any PowerBuilder objects, such as PBD and PSR files, as well as graphics and multimedia content.

Your Web server's connection to the Internet will probably use an ISDN, T1 or T3 line. We'll take a quick look at each of these connectivity options.

10.3.4.2.1 ISDN

ISDN, Integrated Services Digital Network, is an inter-LAN digital connectivity specification. It is a service provided by telephone carriers with a monthly charge for usage. ISDN provides a faster connection than the standard telephone line since it operates at 64 Kbps per channel and can use multiple channels simultaneously for a much higher throughput. Basic rate ISDN has three channels. Two of these operate at 64 Kbps and can be used for data. The third channel operates at 16 Kbps and is used for signaling and link management. Combining the two data channels give a throughput of 128 Kbps which is almost ten times faster than a 14.4 Kbps modem.

ISDN is designed to be used primarily as a dial-up service. It does not require the use of a modem since the data is sent digitally. (A modem converts the computer's digital signal to an analog equivalent which is then sent across the telephone line. A modem on the other side of the connection, then converts the analog signal to a digital format and passes it on to the receiving computer).

10.3.4.2.2 T1 and T3

For a permanent, high-speed connection between your Web server and your Internet Service Provider, you can use a T1 or T3 line. These are digital lines that use two-wire pairs to transmit data at the rate of 1.544 Mbps. One wire sends data while the other receives data. T1 and T3 lines can be used to transmit data, voice and video signals. There are 24 pairs of wires in a T1 line, to make things more cost-effective you can subscribe to one or more of these pairs in order to have a Fractional T-1 line which operates at 64 Kbps per pair. T3 is one of the highest capacity leased line services available today, with a throughput of 6 to 45 Mbps.

10.3.5 Summary

The choice of hardware and software for creating and using a Web site is a big decision. This part of the process should be planned carefully to ensure that the site has the capacity to handle the necessary volume of client requests and provides the required security for data and applications.

Internet sites require some additional planning since domain names must be registered with InterNIC and high-speed connections need to be established with Internet Service Providers. Be sure to start these processes early in your project.

The amount of work required to set up an intranet will depend on the types of operating systems you have within your organization and whether you are running the TCP/IP protocol. If you have TCP/IP and your client PCs are all equipped with browsers, an intranet can be set up very quickly. The implementation of the intranet should be planned to ensure that the right people and departments have access to the Web site and that the outside world is restricted.

To make the best decisions about hardware and software selection, you should already have a plan for your Web site project which includes the type of security required, the necessary performance, an approximate idea of the number of users that will be accessing the site per day, and the number of simultaneous connections. It's better to over-estimate the number of users, especially for an Internet site, so that your hardware and network connections can service requests from client browsers as quickly as possible. An Internet Web site shows the public what your company or organization can do and they'll undoubtedly be expecting a quick response and easy access to the information they need. As with any other software development project, a carefully-planned hardware and software architecture is vital to the success of your project.

10.4 Advanced Internet Tools

In addition to the Internet Tools that we describe in section 10.2 above, Powersoft also makes available several other Internet tools and technologies both within PowerBuilder 6.0 and in other products within the PowerStudio Enterprise product suite. Some of these tools and technologies include the component generator (which will be appearing in a point release of PowerBuilder 6.0), PowerSite and Jaguar CTS. In this section we'll review these products and see how they can be used to enhance Internet applications built using PowerBuilder 6.0.

10.4.1 Component Generator

Perhaps the most eagerly anticipated feature of PowerBuilder 6.0 is the project generator infrastructure. This generator will allow you to write PowerScript code and then deploy industry standard components anywhere. Generating multiple component types from PowerBuilder objects will enable an easy transition from one component model to another. Powersoft is planning support for CORBA, COM/DCOM, DPB and JavaBeans Proxy as shown in Figure 10-10. The component generator will allow thousands of PowerBuilder developers to create distributed objects using a language that they are familiar with.

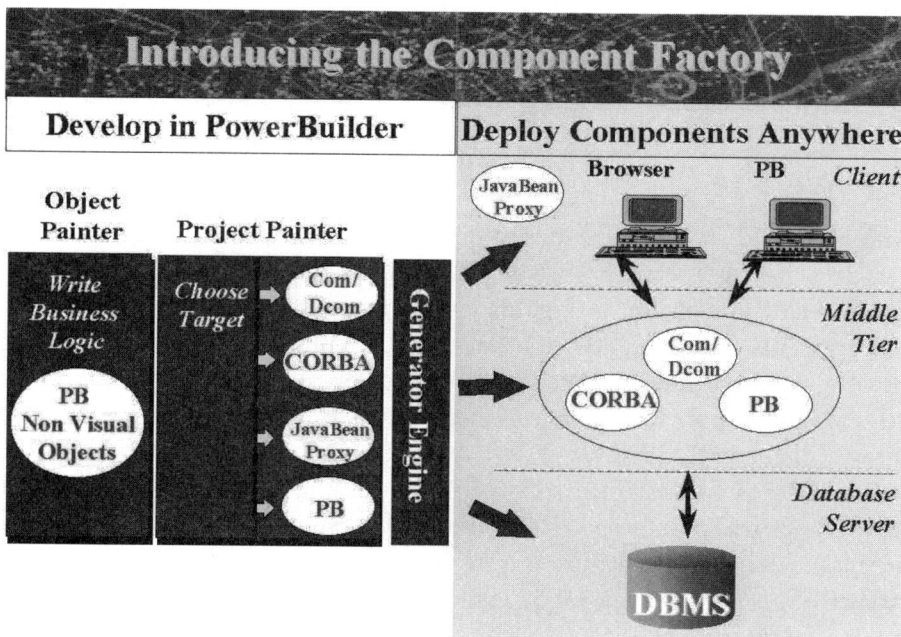

Figure 10-10. The Component Generator will be able to create a variety of middle-tier components from a PowerBuilder non-visual user object.

According to Powersoft, here's how the generator will function. When you create a new project in the Project painter, the New Project dialog box shows the types of project you can build. Among the choices is Application, which lets you build a standard executable and dynamic libraries for either Pcode or machine code executables. The other choices available depend on which generators are installed. Each generator will produce a different set of output file types. When you deploy generated components, you may need to deploy the PowerBuilder virtual machine (PBVM60.DLL) on the same machine.

In addition to the Application generator, the dialog box also displays the Proxy library generator, which builds a proxy object that you can deploy with the client in a distributed PowerBuilder application. When you install other generators, they will appear in this dialog box.

When you select a generator, the Select Objects dialog box opens so that you can choose the objects you want to use to generate a component. Depending on the generator, you may also need to set some properties of the component.

As this book goes to press we do not yet have access to the generator functionality. It will be interesting to see how this exciting technology is turned into a reality for PowerBuilder developers.

10.4.2 PowerSite

PowerSite is an end-to-end RAD environment for building, managing, and deploying dynamic, data-driven enterprise Web applications. If you were to categorize Powersite, it is a component integration tool similar to Microsoft's Visual InterDev.™ It is a tool where components are assembled in order to create fully functioning web applications that include database access. According to Powersoft, it is intended for project-oriented team development and management efforts critical for building large, scalable applications for the enterprise.

PowerSite is a total, open solution; it streamlines the development of complex site content by providing all aspects of building, managing, and deploying applications. Perhaps the most appealing feature of PowerSite is that it is not tied into a single proprietary Web application server but instead has a common object model that can deploy to a number of supported Web application servers. These servers include Microsoft Active Server Pages, Netscape LiveWire and Sybase PowerDynamo. PowerSite applications can also be deployed to a range of web servers including Microsoft Internet Information Server and Netscape Enterprise Server. PowerSite supports third-party HTML editors, multiple component types (scripts, JavaBeans, ActiveX, PB), clients (Microsoft Internet Explorer, Netscape Navigator), and languages (JavaScript, VBScript, DynaScript, Java).

For those of you who are looking to create truly open web applications this may be just the tool. In addition to creating open applications on both the browser-end and the database-end, PowerSite has the potential to allow you to create fully open applications where even the choice of web server and application server is open. The next product that we'll discuss, Jaguar CTS, has a similar philosophy.

10.4.3 Jaguar CTS

The Jaguar CTS product is designed for delivering scalable transactional applications in a multi-tier distributed computing environment. It offers connection management, session management, multi-database connectivity, and point-and-click administration.

Sybase is particularly pushing the use of Jaguar in developing scalable applications for the Internet, intranets or extranets. In fact, they have even coined a new phase for this type of environment which they call Net Online Transaction Processing (NetOLTP). Jaguar was specifically designed for NetOLTP and it's features include a platform-independent execution engine, component-based development with support for all leading component models including: ActiveX, JavaBeans, C++ and CORBA objects, full internet security support including SSL encryption and authorization and application-level access control lists, flexible transaction management with support for both synchronous and asynchronous transaction processing.

The Jaguar SDK includes support for components built using C/C++ or ActiveX. Sybase has partnered with VisiGenic Software in order to license their VisiBroker for C++ and VisiBroker for Java object request brokers (ORBs) and include them as an integrated product in Jaguar. By so doing, Sybase will be able to offer support for the CORBA and IIOP standards developed by the Object Management Group (OMG).

Jaguar CTS is part of a new breed of tools which combine the features of an Object Request Broker (ORB) and a TP Monitor. Microsoft's Transaction Server is another example. Figure 10-11 shows the architecture for the Jaguar CTS with its kernel and session management, transaction management and connection pooling functionality. The Jaguar kernel is multi-threaded, has multi-processor scalability, and has extensive tuning parameters for optimal performance. The session manager and connection manager work together in order to funnel a large number of browser sessions into a smaller number of database connections. This improves scalability and gives more uniform response times with varying workloads.

As you can see from the figure, a Jaguar application consists of a client application such as Java applet or application and Jaguar server components. The client application executes the methods in the server components via the Jaguar server. The components can then execute business logic and access databases as necessary.

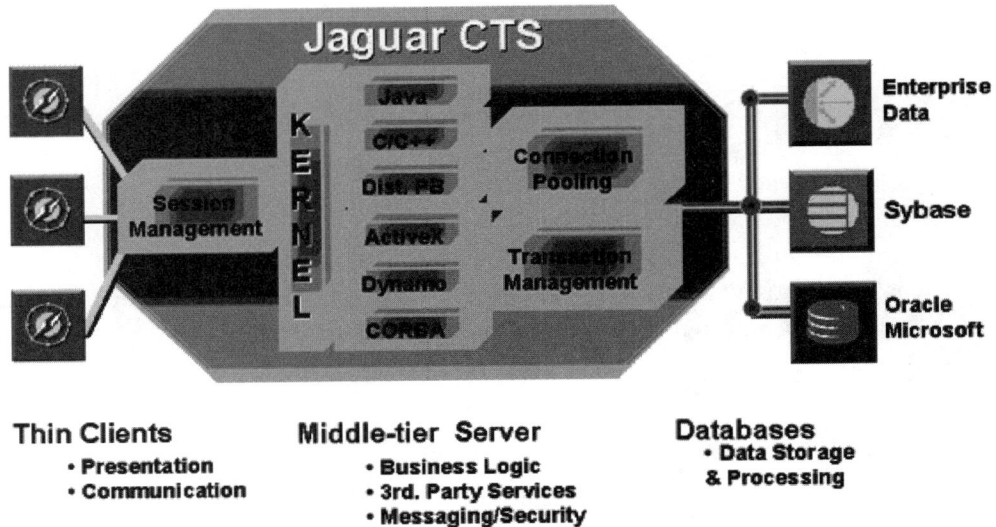

Figure 10-11. The Jaguar Architecture (courtesy of Powersoft).

Jaguar provides high-speed connectivity with a data streaming protocol called TDS (Tabular Data Stream). Database connectivity can be achieved using ODBC, JDBC or the Sybase EnterpriseConnect data access products. Sybase also offers jConnect for JDBC which is a JDBC driver written purely in Java. This supports both applet to servlet and servlet to database communications.

The nice feature with Jaguar's Transaction Manager is that it supports both synchronous and asynchronous processing. Asynchronous processing is achieved using a new dbQ service which employs database queuing technology in order to provide transactional integrity.

10.4.4 Summary

Powersoft is definitely moving in the right direction in terms of their PowerBuilder 6.0 product and their supporting tools and technologies. The market is getting increasingly competitive as vendors such as Microsoft bring out suites of application development tools with amazing levels of integration between the operating system, web servers and their client/server and Internet development tools. The best way for Powersoft to remain competitive is exactly what they are doing—bringing client/server to the Internet world and the distributed component-based development world with support for all the major distributed models such as CORBA, COM/DCOM and JavaBeans. The component generator will have a major role to play and a role that will be watched closely by developers and analysts alike.

Powersoft's Jaguar Component Transaction Server (Jaguar CTS) is another tool that complements PowerBuilder 6.0 with its management of server-side components for creating OLTP applications for the web ("NetOLTP"). This product promises to help deliver the enterprise scalability that was somewhat lacking in the original DPB server applications of PowerBuilder 5.0.

PowerBuilder 6.0 brings the next round of Internet tools to the client/server developer. After the first generation of Internet tools in PowerBuilder 5.0, this second generation product builds upon the first and adds some valuable enhancements.

10.5 Developing DataWindow and Window Plug-In Applications

10.5.1 Introduction

In this section, we'll go through the steps required to build an application that uses both the PowerBuilder Window Plug-In and the PowerBuilder DataWindow Plug-In. These application types are particularly suited for use on an intranet due to their dependence on client software.

An advantage of Window and DataWindow Plug-Ins is that you can leverage existing PowerBuilder application code and DataWindows. The Window Plug-In provides the ability to use the rich graphical user interface components of PowerBuilder such as tabs, tree-view and list-view controls. When running a PowerBuilder Window Plug-In you can break away from the HTML page metaphor and host an entire PowerBuilder application within a single HTML page.

To run Plug-Ins within a browser, software needs to be loaded on the client machine. In the case of the DataWindow Plug-In, all you need is the Plug-In DLL supplied by Powersoft. To run an application which uses the Window Plug-In, you'll need the Plug-In DLL plus the PowerBuilder runtime libraries and client-side database connectivity software. The requirements for client-side software make a Plug-In application better suited to intranet usage where the installation of the software can be more easily administered.

The fact that Plug-Ins are suited for intranets does not preclude using their technologies in an Internet scenario as well. In this case, you could provide the user with a way to download the required software from a Web page and include instructions on how to install it. You might even want to do this for your intranet users as well in order to simplify administration. In the case of a DataWindow Plug-In, this installation is very simple since it involves just one file.

10.5.2 Creating the Plug-In Application

10.5.2.1 Working with Child Windows

When building an application using the PowerBuilder Window Plug-In there are a couple of restrictions. First, the PowerBuilder runtme dynamic libraries and the Window Plug-In DLL must be installed on the client machine. Second, the application must be created with a child window.

Using a Child window is not as limiting as it might seem. One great way to provide navigation control and access to multiple "pages" is to use tab controls. This way, you can place a full-featured application on a single Web page. Users interact with the controls within the plug-in in the same way as with a regular PowerBuilder application. The script for the events and functions within the code executes on a client machine. Of course, database access is also possible.

You can also extend an application by having multiple Web pages, each with their own associated Window Plug-In. For example, one page could be used, for customer maintenance and another (with its own plug-in) for producing reports.

In these scenarios the browser is acting like an operating system by providing a way to host an application—just as an operating system hosts traditional applications.

10.5.2.2 Working with Other Window Types

One way to extend Window Plug-In applications is to open other windows and menus from within the child window embedded on the Web page. Here are some window and menus that can be used:

- MessageBox.
- Popup Window.
- Response Window.
- Popup Menu.

A MessageBox can easily be displayed from within a child window by using the MessageBox PowerScript function. In addition, you can use the Open statement to open other window types such as popup and response windows. Finally, you can take advantage of the PopMenu PowerScript function to display a popup menu from within a child window. The code necessary to do this is shown below:

```
m_sample_menu NewMenu
NewMenu = CREATE m_sample_menu
NewMenu.m_sample.PopMenu(PointerX(), PointerY())
```

In this sample code, `m_sample_menu` is a pre-defined menu which is instantiated prior to display with the CREATE statement. The menu is then displayed using the PopMenu function. The PointerX() and PointerY() functions return the current location of the cursor on the screen and are used to define the position of the popup menu. This code can be placed in the clicked event of a command button, in the rbuttondown event of the child window, or anywhere else within the child window that is appropriate.

10.5.2.3 Registering the MIME Type

Since PowerBuilder Window Plug-Ins and DataWindow Plug-Ins are extensions of the browser environment, we need to give the browser a way to handle them. The Web server must also inform the browser of the type of content it is sending so the browser can act accordingly.

The Web server informs the browser by including a description of the content type in its HTTP header response. The content type is usually plain HTML:

```
content-type: text/HTML
```

In the case of the Plug-Ins, we need to define the content type to the Web server:

application/datawindow	PSR files	Powersoft Report Files
application/vnd.powerbuilder6	PBD files	PowerBuilder Dynamic Libraries
application/vnd.powerbuilder6-s	PBD files	PowerBuilder Dynamic Libraries (Secure Mode)

We define the content by registering the MIME type with the Web server. MIME stands for Multiple Internet Mail Extensions. A Web server will usually have many MIME mappings defined, such as Microsoft Internet Information Server 3.0, which includes over 100 default mappings.

Once we have defined the MIME type with the server, it can send the appropriate content-type description to the browser.

10.5.2.4 The EMBED Tag

The EMBED tag is a special HTML tag that first appeared in Netscape browsers as an extension to HTML. The EMBED tag is used to reference both PowerBuilder Window Plug-Ins and DataWindow Plug-Ins.

The syntax for the EMBED tag, when applied to Window Plug-Ins, is as follows:

```
<EMBED SRC=URL WIDTH=120 HEIGHT=250 WINDOW=w_child_win >
```

where URL is the Uniform Resource Locator for the PBD to be downloaded.

Relative or complete URL references are used as shown here:

```
app.pbd                                     (relative URL)
/pbds/app.pbd                               (relative URL)
http://ntserver.nick.com/pb/pbds/app.pbd   (complete URL)
```

w_child_win is the name of the child window that is found within the PowerBuilder Library file referenced above.

WIDTH and HEIGHT are the dimensions of the window that appears in the HTML browser. The dimensions are in pixels.

Here's a sample HTML file containing the EMBED tag for a Window Plug-In:

```
<HTML>
<HEAD>
<CENTER><TITLE>Employee Information</TITLE></CENTER>
</HEAD>
<BODY>
<CENTER>
<H1>Employee Information</H1>
<I>Powered by </I><ALIGN=center><IMG SRC="PB5.jpg" ALIGN=top
     WIDTH=200 HEIGHT=25>

        <P>

<EMBED SRC="emp_dir.pbd" WIDTH=640 HEIGHT=350 WINDOW=w_emp_plugin>
</CENTER>
<HR>
Back to the <A HREF="/hr/index.htm">Home Page</A>
</BODY>
</HTML>
```

In this example, the child window named `w_emp_plugin` is displayed in the browser with a width of 640 pixels and a height of 350 pixels. It is contained in the `emp_dir.pbd` PowerBuilder library, which is found in the same directory as the HTML page being displayed. This example is taken from an application which uses a Window Plug-In for viewing employee phone numbers, birthdays and addresses (Figure 10-12).

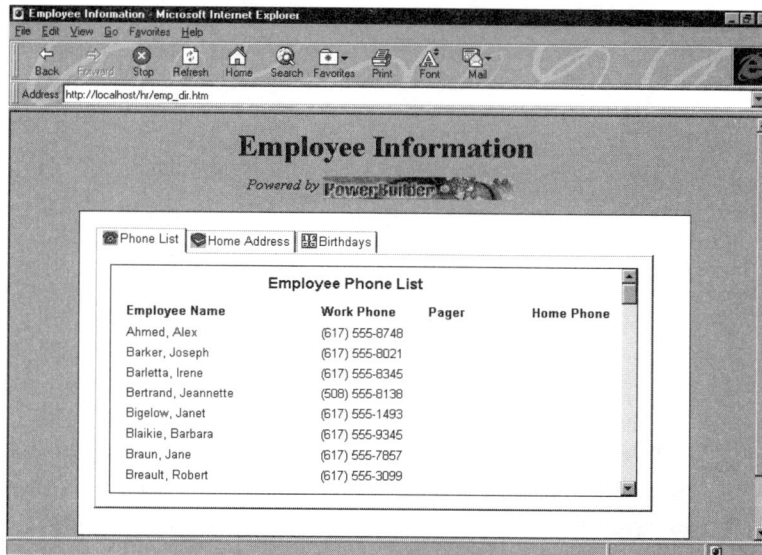

***Figure 10-12.** An example of a PowerBuilder Window Plug-In.*

The syntax for the EMBED tag, when applied to DataWindow Plug-Ins, is as follows:

```
<EMBED SRC=URL WIDTH=120 HEIGHT=250>
```

where URL is the Uniform Resource Locator for the PSR file to be downloaded.

Once again, relative or complete URL references are allowed as follows:

```
report.psr                               (relative URL)
/psrs/report.psr                         (relative URL)
http://ntserver.nick.com/pb/psrs/report.psr  (complete URL)
```

WIDTH and HEIGHT are the dimensions of the PSR report that appears in the HTML browser. The dimensions are in pixels.

Here's a sample HTML file containing the EMBED tag for a DataWindow Plug-In:

```
<HTML>
<HEAD>
<CENTER>
<TITLE>Investment Plan - Description of Funds</TITLE>
</CENTER>
</HEAD>
<BODY>
<CENTER>
<H1>Investment Plan - Description of Funds</H1>
<I>Powered by </I><ALIGN=center><IMG SRC="PB5.jpg"ALIGN=top
  WIDTH=200 HEIGHT=25>
<P>
<EMBED SRC="funds.psr" WIDTH=740 HEIGHT=350>
</CENTER>
<HR>
Back to the <A HREF="/hr/index.htm">Home Page</A>
</BODY>
</HTML>
```

In this example, the Powersoft Report, funds.psr, is displayed in the browser with a width of 740 pixels and a height of 350 pixels. The PSR file is in the same directory as the HTML page. This example is taken from the HR Info application and shows the General Fund Information page with the DataWindow Plug-In for viewing the various fund descriptions and risk levels (Figure 10-13).

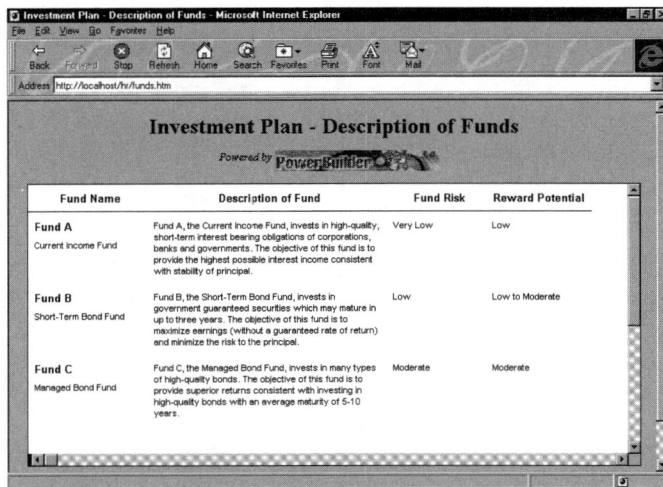

Figure 10-13. *An example of a PowerBuilder DataWindow Plug-In.*

10.5.2.5 PSR Files

Since DataWindow Plug-Ins display PSR files, it's worth examining them to see how they're created and used. A PSR file is a PowerSoft Report which can be created either in PowerBuilder or InfoMaker. It's important to note that a PSR file contains both the presentation style for the data and the actual data values themselves. It's a static file containing a hard-copy report that has been generated from the database earlier.

PSR files are used by InfoMaker users who can click on the file within File Manager, Explorer or a Mail message, and then view the report in the Report Painter. When InfoMaker is installed, the file extension .PSR is associated with the InfoMaker program, which enables this process.

Within PowerBuilder you can create a PSR file by choosing File | Save Rows As from the menu bar and selecting Powersoft Report from the Save As dialog box as shown in Figure 10-14.

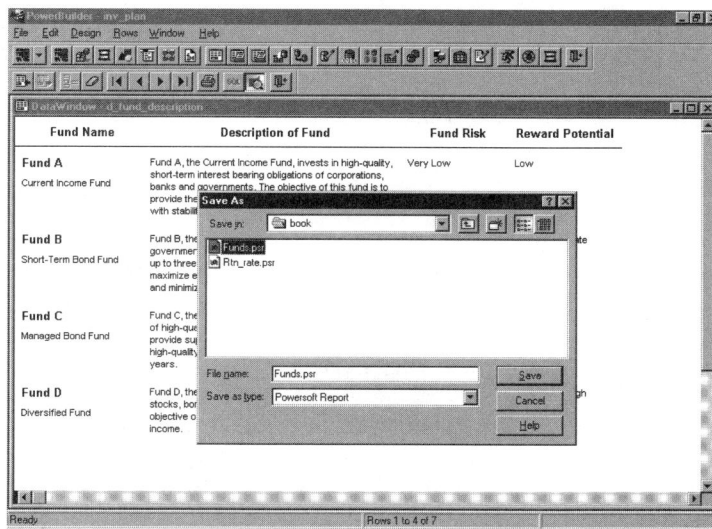

Figure 10-14. *The Save As dialog box for saving DataWindow reports as PSR files.*

To open a PSR file from within PowerBuilder:

1.   Go into the Report Painter.

2.   Select File | Open File... from the menu.

3.   In the Select a File Name dialog box, enter the file name of the PSR file you want to view.

4.   Select the Open button to open the file.

5.   Choose Design | Preview... to preview the report.

PSR files can have the presentation styles of any DataWindow except the Rich Text presentation style. Here's a list of available styles:

- Tabular.

- Group.

- Freeform.

- Crosstab.

- Grid.

- Composite.

- Graph.

- N-Up.

- Label.

Notice that one of the presentation styles is a graph. PSRs are a great way to present database reports graphically within an Internet or intranet application.

10.5.2.6 Viewing DataWindow Plug-Ins in the HTML Browser

When you've accessed an HTML page with a DataWindow Plug-In, the PSR file is copied from the Web server to the client machine and displayed in the browser. The Plug-In has vertical and horizontal scroll bars for viewing the report and contains a popup menu which is accessible by right-clicking from anywhere within the Plug-In.

The popup menu offers the following options:

- Save Rows As....

- Print....

- First Page.

- Prior Page.

- Next Page.

- Last Page.

Figure 10-15 shows the popup menu as it appears in the browser. The four page navigation options appear only if the DataWindow needs to scroll in order to display its entire report. Smaller reports will only show two options: Save Rows As.. and Print....

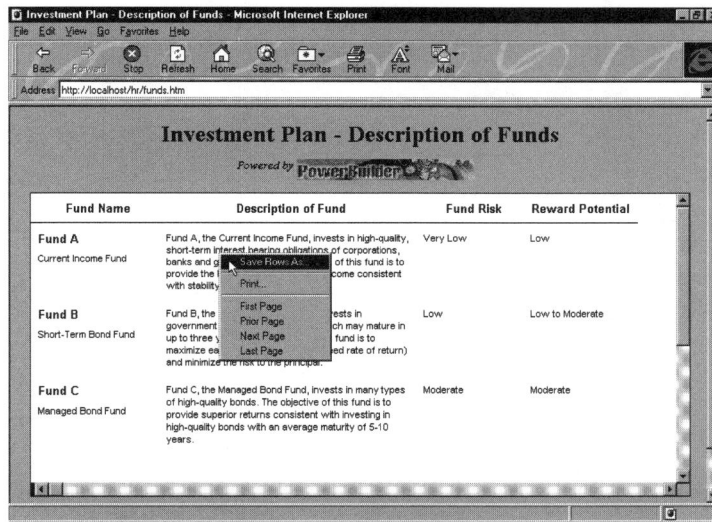

Figure 10-15. DataWindow Plug-In showing the popup menu.

If you choose the Print... menu item, the DataWindow report is immediately sent to the default printer. The entire report is printed even if it is not completely displayed within the Plug-In window. This is in contrast to the print function of the browser which prints the HTML page `without` the Plug-In.

If you choose the Save Rows As... menu item, you are presented with the Save As dialog box as shown in Figure 10-16. It lets you save the data to disk in a selected file format.

These file formats are supported:

- CSV.

- CSV with headers.

- dBASE 2.

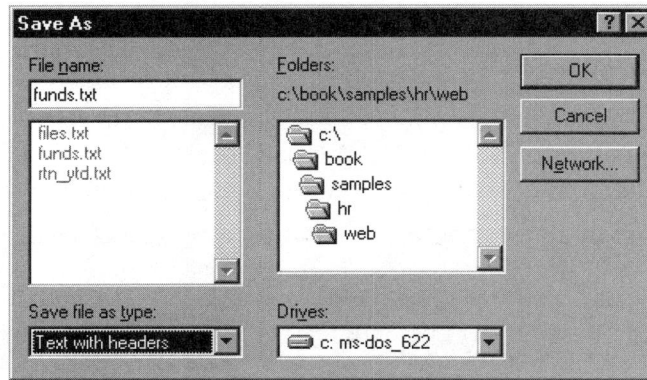

Figure 10-16. *The Save As dialog box for the DataWindow Plug-In.*

- dBASE 3.
- DIF.
- Excel.
- Excel with headers.
- HTML Table.
- Powersoft Report.
- SQL.
- SYLK.
- SYLK with headers.
- Text.
- Text with headers.
- WKS.
- WKS with headers.
- WK1.
- WK1 with headers.
- Windows Metafile.

If you save the file as "Text with headers" (or any other file format with headers) be sure to code the SQL statement that generates the PSR file so that it has user-friendly column names. This way, the column descriptions in the text file will be more meaningful to the user. Here's a sample SQL statement that shows how to create user-friendly column names:

```
SELECT "fund_401k"."fund_name" "Fund Name",
          "fund_401k"."fund_desc" "Fund Title",
          "fund_401k"."fund_long_desc" "Fund Description",
          "fund_401k"."fund_risk" "Risk",
          "fund_401k"."fund_reward_potential" "Reward Potential"
    FROM"fund_401k"
ORDER BY "fund_401k"."fund_name" ASC
```

The first few lines of the sample output file might look like this:

```
Fund Name    Fund Title          Fund Description
Fund A       Current Income Fund  Fund A, the Current Income Fund...
Fund B       Short-Term Bond Fund Fund B, the Short-Term Bond Fund...
```

10.5.2.7 Viewing PowerBuilder Window Plug-Ins in the HTML Browser

When you've accessed an HTML page that has a PowerBuilder Window Plug-In, the PBD file is copied from the Web server to the client machine and displayed in the browser. The Plug-In has vertical and horizontal scroll bars for viewing the child window.

If the application references any files external to the PBD, they must be stored on the client machine along with the PowerBuilder runtime libraries. Examples include INI files which contain database connection information and OCX controls which extend the functionality of the application.

Once the PBD file has been coped to the client machine, the application can run from within the browser just as with any regular PowerBuilder application. The PowerScript code executes on the client machine.

It's important to note that when running a PowerBuilder Window Plug-In application, the HTTP transaction has completed and you're no longer using the Web. All database access occurs via the regular network connections to a database using the client side database connectivity software. The advantage of the Window Plug-In is that you can centrally administer application code to ensure that users always have the latest version. You just need to have one copy of the application loaded on the Web server.

If the PowerBuilder runtime libraries and the database connectivity software are stored on the server, users can download all components of an application from a central location.

10.5.2.8 Compiling the PBD Files

When building PBD files, be sure to remove any objects that are not needed. This reduces the size of the resulting PBD file to an absolute minimum.

To test the child window:

1. Create another PowerBuilder Library which contains a window of type Main which can open the child window.

2. Create an application object inside this new library which can be used for testing.

3. Place code to open the main window from the application object's open event.

4. Place code to open the child window from the main window's open event.

5. Run the application and test the child window.

By using another library for your test application object and main window, the size of the actual PBD file can be kept to a minimum. Alternatively, you can create these objects within the same library as the child window and then move them out to another library prior to building the PBD.

To build a PBD, go to the Project Painter and choose the PBD checkbox for your library. Figure 10-17 shows the Project Painter ready to build a PBD for the Employee Information application.

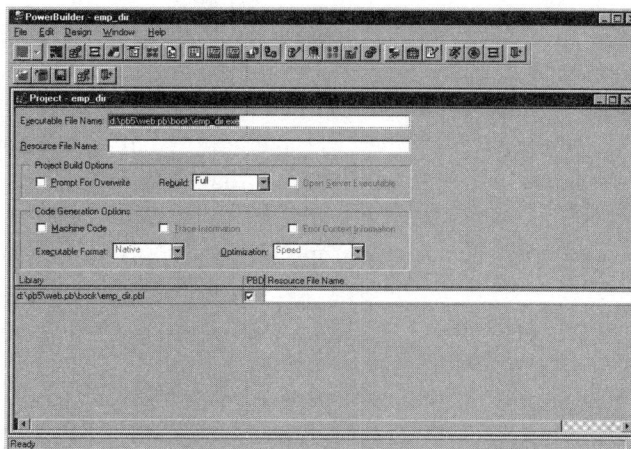

Figure 10-17. *Project Painter where you can create the PBD files for the Window Plug-In.*

Be sure that the "Machine Code" code generation option is left unchecked. If it is checked, the Project Painter creates a DLL file instead of a PBD. The Window Plug-In functionality only works for PBD files.

When you've successfully compiled your application and created a PBD file, you can move it to the server. Its location should match the location referenced in the EMBED tags in the HTML pages. The location can either be the same directory as the HTML page or a different directory or machine.

10.5.3 Summary

In this section we've covered Window and DataWindow Plug-Ins and have seen how they can be placed in an HTML page by using the EMBED tag. Each type of Plug-In has its merits for certain circumstances; a combination of HTML pages and Plug-In components can produce an effective and flexible Web-based application. A Plug-In enabled application combines the ease of use of the Web with database access, sophisticated GUI controls, and the report presentation styles of regular PowerBuilder applications.

10.6 Developing Web.PB Applications

10.6.1 Introduction

In this section, we'll cover the essential techniques for developing Web.PB applications. As when building a Distributed PowerBuilder (DPB) Application, a Web.PB application has three main areas to be considered: the client, the middle layer and the server. While these three components are usually deployed on two or three different machines in a production environment, we can carry out our development on a single machine, without being concerned about the physical implementation details. After the code has been written and tested locally, we can make a few minor changes to test the application in its real life production implementation.

For tools, we need an HTML editor for developing the client content, PowerBuilder 6.0 for the middle layer, and a relational database for the server. We might also want to take advantage of an image map editor such as MapThis! and a graphics editor such as PaintShop Pro in order to enhance our Web application with image maps and custom graphics.

Before we start, let's see how the components of a Web.PB application fit together. The client code consists of standard HTML pages displayed by a browser. These pages contain the code necessary to invoke user object functions, with or without parameters, within a middle-layer Distributed PowerBuilder Application. The database server delivers information to the DPB server which then goes to the browser. This is converted to HTML format by the DPB server application and appears on the browser as a new Web page.

10.6.2 Creating HTML Pages to Access DPB Functions

10.6.2.1 Accessing DPB Functions via HTML Forms

The key to understanding how to access DPB functions from Web pages lies in the HTML form tag and the anchor tag.

10.6.2.1.1 Using the <FORM> tag

To call a DPB function using Web.PB you use the following HTML syntax:

```
<FORM METHOD="GET/POST"
      ACTION="/URLPath/Web.PB/ServerAlias/Object/Method">
input_text<INPUT NAME="ParameterName">
..
<INPUT TYPE="SUBMIT" VALUE="submit_text">
<INPUT TYPE="RESET" VALUE="reset_text">
</FORM>
```

The values shown above in italics should be replaced with specific application names as follows:

URLPath	URL path to the Web.PB software.
Web.PB	Name of the Web.PB software.
ServerAlias	Name of the DPB server alias.
Object	Name of the DPB user object.
Method	Name of DPB method.
ParameterName	DPB variable name for DPB Method.
Input Text	Text beside the entry field.
Submit Text	Text for the Submit button.
Reset Text	Text for the reset button (Optional).

Here's an example of a DPB function call using the <FORM> tag:

```
<FORM METHOD="POST" ACTION=
  "/scripts/pbcgi060.exe/bankweb/uo_general/f_feedback">
Enter Name:<INPUT NAME="as_name">
Comments:<TEXTAREA NAME="as_comments" ROWS="6", COLS="50">
  </TEXTAREA>
<INPUT TYPE="SUBMIT" VALUE="Submit">
<INPUT TYPE="RESET" VALUE="Reset">
</FORM>
```

You can pass as many parameters to the DPB object method as you want. The above example just shows two parameters collected via the HTML form interface and passed to the DPB method. You can use either the GET or POST method to submit the data to Web.PB. The POST method is generally recommended.

The data goes to the Web server and then Web.PB when a user clicks on the Submit button. The submit button can have any name but its type must always be `submit`. Some examples:

```
<INPUT type="submit" value="Submit">
<INPUT type="submit" value="OK">
<INPUT type="submit"value="Send">
```

The reset button clears the form by erasing any values in the text fields (or other styles of field) on the form.

There's a wide range of interface components that can be placed in HTML forms: edit fields, checkboxes, radiobuttons, list boxes, drop-down listboxes, hidden fields, multi-line edit fields and so on. Remember, these interface components can either belong to a static Web page on disk or can be dynamically created from PowerBuilder using the appropriate HTML syntax. You can even populate components such as list boxes from data in the database before returning the Web page to the browser!

10.6.2.1.2 Using the Anchor tag

The second way to access DPB functions from within HTML is by using the anchor tag reference as follows:

```
<A HREF="/URLPath/Web.PB/ServerAlias/Object/Method
  ?parm1value+parm2value">text</A>
```

The names in italics should be substituted with values appropriate to the application. Notice that the parameters to the DPB object's method are passed on the same line and separated from the method name by a question mark. Parameters are delimited from each other by a plus sign.

Here's an example of a DPB function call using the anchor tag:

```
Click on the hypertext link below to see the values of the CGI
  environment variables:
<P>
<A HREF="/scripts/pbcgi060.exe/bankweb/uo_general/f_cgivars?p1">
  CGI Variables</A>
```

The two methods for accessing DPB functions described here are not specific to PowerBuilder. Use of the form tag and the anchor tag are general techniques for calling CGI scripts from within HTML. In this case, the CGI script happens to be Web.PB which passes the information to the DPB server application.

10.6.2.1.3 Reading the PBWEB.INI file

When the Web server receives a request from a browser which refers to Web.PB, it passes the rest of the URL string to Web.PB for processing. In the above example, Web.PB would receive the following string:

```
/bankweb/uo_general/f_cgivars?p1
```

Web.PB interprets the string by breaking it down into its component parts. In this example, the server alias is named bankweb, the remote object is named uo_general and the method is named f_cgivars. Web.PB must now determine how to access the bankweb server. It does this by reading the pbweb.ini file which should be located in the Windows root directory. If you look at the pbweb.ini file included with PowerBuilder 6.0, you see that there's an entry as follows:

```
[idkdemo]
application=pb_net_examples
location=localhost
driver=winsock
```

This tells Web.PB that the DPB server resides locally and is running the winsock communications driver. You may have noticed that the pbweb.ini file contains a [DEFAULT] section. You can use this section to reduce the amount of information that you need to specify in the URL. If you don't specify the server alias or the user object name in the URL, Web.PB will use the values specified in the [DEFAULT] section. The following lines set the default server alias to `bankweb` and the default user object to `uo_finance`.

```
[Default]
serveralias=bankweb
serverobject=uo_finance
```

By using the [DEFAULT] section of the `pbweb.ini` file, the following URL's can produce the same result:

```
/URLPath/Web.PB/ServerAlias/Object/Method
/URLPath/Web.PB/Object/Method
/URLPath/Web.PB/ServerAlias/Method
/URLPath/Web.PB/Method
```

10.6.3 Creating the Distributed PowerBuilder Application

We'll now develop the main component of our application, the Distributed PowerBuilder (DPB) server application. In this section, we'll concentrate on the Web.PB specifics and assume knowledge of DPB terminology such as Connection and Transport objects.

10.6.3.1 Requirements

The Distributed PowerBuilder Server Application is the main mechanism for communication between the HTML Web pages and the database. It can accept queries from a form on an HTML page, query the database, and return dynamic content to the browser. A Distributed PowerBuilder Server Application written for Web.PB is the same as a normal DPB application except that it wraps HTML tags around the content returned to the client. These HTML tags perform the browser formatting.

A DPB Server application written for Web.PB usually contains an application object, one or more windows, and several user objects containing many methods. Although DPB servers are essentially non-visual applications which run unattended, it's a good idea to develop a window for an administrator to start and stop the listener. This window can even contain a bitmap, in the form of a traffic light, to provide a strong visual clue as to the status of the DPB server. The bitmap could be switched between a red and a green light depending on whether the server is listening or not.

Another useful component for a DPB server application is a console window for monitoring client connections. It can also be used to terminate client connections if required.

In order to communicate with external applications, you'll need to create a transport object and start the Listener to monitor client requests.

The main part of the DPB Server application is the application-specific logic that is placed in non-visual user objects. You can use the DataStore, a non-visual form of the DataWindow, to perform database queries and return data back to the browser.

In summary, your DPB server application will most likely include the following:

- A window for starting and stopping the Listener.

- A console window to monitor all client connections to the server.

- Non-visual user object methods for processing the business logic of the application and returning the results to the browser in HTML format.

10.6.3.2 Remote Objects

Remote objects comprise the core of Web.PB applications. It's here that you place the application logic to access the database (if necessary) and return dynamic content to the browser. Let's take a look at the arguments and return values that are allowed for Web.PB server applications.

10.6.3.2.1 Return Values

You can return one of two datatypes to the browser from your non-visual user object methods: `Strings` and `Blobs`. Here are the typical uses for these datatypes:

String	For returning HTML Web pages.
Blob	For returning HTML Web pages.
	For returning binary files such as graphics or multimedia.
	For returning URL redirections to other web pages.

Strings and blobs are processed differently by Web.PB. Web.PB calls a method that returns a `blob` datatype repeatedly until the method returns a `null blob` value. In contrast, Web.PB calls a method that returns a `string` datatype one time only.

The easiest type of data to return to Web.PB is `string` data. This is because Web.PB will automatically add the content-type identifier, `text/html` to the string that it returns to the browser so you don't need to code it yourself.

If you're returning a `blob` datatype to Web.PB you'll need to do a little more coding to make it work. You need to end each portion of the data with a carriage-return and line-feed combination and you also need to specify the content-type that you're returning. See the section entitled "Returning Blob Datatypes to the Browser" for more detail and some examples.

10.6.3.2.2 Arguments

A method in a Web.PB server application can accept any standard datatype as an argument with the exception of arrays and structures. If a user does not enter a value on an HTML form submitted to Web.PB, a NULL value will be sent to the method. (This is assuming that no default value was coded in the field in the HTML form itself.) The method is responsible for handling any NULL values it receives in the appropriate manner. For example, you might want to supply a default value within the method or return an HTML page that asks the user to fill out the form completely.

10.6.3.2.3 Returning String Datatypes to the Browser

To return a `string` datatype to the browser, build the HTML syntax in the user object method and use the `Return` statement. Be sure to include the <HTML> and </HTML> tags at the start and end of the string in order to properly identify the HTML text to the browser.

Here's an example of a simple page that is returned from the method to the browser:

```
String ls_header, ls_footer, ls_detail

ls_header = "<HTML><HEAD><TITLE>Basic Web Page</TITLE></HEAD>"
ls_detail = "<BODY>This is a basic web page</BODY>"
ls_footer = "</HTML>"
ls_rtn = ls_header + ls_detail + ls_footer

Return ls_rtn
```

As you build your HTML syntax you can often reuse components of the syntax for other pages. For example, when returning Web pages via Web.PB you can often include standard header and footer syntax. Reusing this syntax will not only speed your development efforts but it will lead to a more consistent interface for the browser's user.

The standard header usually contains some of the following elements:

- <HTML> tag.

- Title for the Web page created using the <TITLE> tag.

- Logo or graphic for the site or company displayed using the <A> tag.

- Heading for the page using the <H1> tag or similar.

- Horizontal rule using the <HR> tag.

The standard footer may contain some of the following elements:

- Horizontal rule created using the <HR> tag.

- Logo or graphic for the home page, using the <A> tag.

- URL to take the user back to the home page, using the <A> tag.

- E-mail address of the Webmaster, using the <A> tag.

- </HTML> tag.

In order to encapsulate some of this reusable code, you may want to create special non-visual user object with methods that return the appropriate HTML syntax. One example might be an `f_page_footer` method that returns an entire footer for a Web page as follows:

```
Return '<HR>Back to the ' + &
  '<A HREF="/bank-web/index.htm">Home Page</A></HTML>'
```

The Internet Tools features an extensive class library of user objects and methods similar to the example above. See section 10.7.2 for a complete discussion of the Web.PB Class Library.

If you build methods such as these, be sure to check your HTML tag so that you always have the starting and ending tags where required. For example, every <HTML> tag must have a corresponding </HTML> tag. One way to make it easy to remember which methods belong in pairs is to use a similar naming convention. Here are some examples from the Web.PB Class Library:

f_BeginForm	Creates HTML syntax to begin a FORM by supplying the <FORM> tag along with it's ACTION and METHOD attributes
f_EndForm	Creates HTML syntax to end a FORM by supplying the </FORM> tag
f_BeginTable	Creates HTML syntax to begin a TABLE by supplying the <TABLE> tag along with it's many attributes
f_EndTable	Creates HTML syntax to end a TABLE by supplying the </TABLE> tag

10.6.3.2.4 Returning Blob Datatypes to the Browser

Web.PB handles `blob` datatypes returned from a method differently than it handles `string` datatypes. For each program request, Web.PB calls a method that returns a string just once. In contrast, Web.PB calls methods that return `blob` datatypes repeatedly until a `null` `blob` value is returned. The method that returns a `blob` datatype must also include a description of the content type as in the following examples:

```
content-type: image/gif    For returning gif files
content-type: image/jpeg   For returning jpeg files
```

You can return any type of content in a `blob` return type, even plain HTML! For example, you can build an HTML Web page as a `string` and then convert it to a `blob` datatype prior to returning the data to Web.PB. Each portion of data returned by the method should be delimited with carriage-return and line-feed characters. To define these characters within PowerScript code, you can use the following string: "~r~n."

It's important to separate the content-type definition (which constitutes the HTTP header response) from the actual data by using a double carriage-return and line-feed as shown here:

```
graphic = Blob("content-type: text/plain~r~n~r~n")
graphic += Blob(<text for display within the browser goes here>)
```

10.6.3.2.5 Returning Graphics to the Browser

The following example shows how to return a graphic file to the browser. This example is based on the examples in the Web.PB documentation from the Internet Developer Toolkit, because the technique is well-established.

```
// Define variables
Blob graphic
Boolean lb_file_exists
Long ll_flen, ll_bytes_read
String ls_image_type

// Return a null blob value in order to terminate the processing
IF TerminateProcessing = TRUE THEN
  SetNull(graphic)
  Return graphic
END IF

// Execute this code the first time the method is invoked
IF fnum = 0 THEN
```

```
TerminateProcessing = FALSE
lb_file_exists = FileExists(picture_name)
IF NOT lb_file_exists THEN
   graphic = Blob("content-type: text/plain~r~n~r~n Picture '" + &
   picture_name +"' does not exist~r~n")
   TerminateProcessing = TRUE
   Return graphic
END IF

// Get the file length, and open the file
ll_flen = FileLength(picture_name)
fnum = FileOpen(picture_name, StreamMode!, Read!)

IF fnum = -1 THEN
   graphic = Blob("content-type: text/plain~r~n~r~n picture '" + &
   picture_name + "' could not be opened for read~r~n")
   TerminateProcessing = TRUE
   fnum = 0
   Return graphic
END IF

// Build the HTTP header response
ls_image_type = Right(picture_name,3)
graphic = Blob("content-type: image/" + ls_image_type + "~r~n")
graphic += Blob("content-length: " + string(ll_flen) + "~r~n~r~n")
Return graphic
END IF

// Read the file
ll_bytes_read = FileRead(fnum, graphic)

// Check for the end of the file
IF ll_bytes_read <= 0 THEN
   FileClose(fnum)
   SetNull(graphic)
   fnum = 0
END IF

Return graphic
```

You can see from the source code that the graphic file is accessed using the standard `FileOpen` and `FileRead` functions within PowerScript. The name of the file, `picture_name`, is passed into the method as an argument. The variables, `fnum` and `TerminateProcessing`, are defined as instance variables. This allows them to retain their values from one invocation of the method to the next. Note how the HTTP header response is constructed using the "content-type" syntax and a double carriage-return/line-feed is used to separate the HTTP header from the data that's being returned.

When returning a graphic to the browser, it's also necessary to define the length of the file that's being returned by using the "content-length" definition. It's only necessary to have a single carriage-return/line-feed between the "content-type" and "content-length" definitions.

10.6.3.2.6 Returning DataWindow content to the Browser

There are two ways to create HTML syntax from a DataWindow: the `SaveAs` function and the `HTMLTable` property. The `SaveAs` function writes the HTML syntax for the DataWindow to a file on disk. The `HTMLTable` property can be used to save the HTML syntax into a string variable.

SaveAs Function

The first method is the `SaveAs` function which includes a format called `HTMLTable`. You can use the `SaveAs` function either from within the PowerBuilder development environment or from a PowerBuilder application.

The `HTMLTable` Property

The contents of DataWindows can be returned to the browser by using the `HTMLTable` property. You can assign this property to a string variable using the following syntax:

```
ls_html = ds_datastore.Object.DataWindow.Data.HTMLTable
```

The variable, `ds_datastore`, refers to a datastore object defined in the code. Before assigning the HTML syntax to the string variable, make sure that the datastore object has connected to the database and performed a `Retrieve`.

You can use the `HTMLTable` property to create HTML syntax for most DataWindow presentation styles. A rich text edit presentation style is not supported, however, since it is not supported in distributed PowerBuilder applications. Some presentation styles produce better results than others when they are viewed in a browser. This is a list of the styles that produce the best results:

- Crosstab.
- Freeform.
- Grid.

- Group.

- Tabular.

The HTML syntax for other presentation styles such as Composite, Graph and OLE 2.0, is based on the data only and not the actual presentation style.

10.6.3.2.7 Performing a URL Redirection

A URL redirection directs the browser to another Web page which is often external to the current server. This is commonly performed when you want to return a page from the World Wide Web, such as the Powersoft home page, instead of returning your own dynamically-created pages.

To perform a URL redirection from a PowerBuilder method, construct the syntax for the new Web location and return it to the Web server for processing. Return the data as a `blob` datatype with an HTTP header that includes the location URL syntax as shown in the example below.

```
location: http://www.powersoft.com
```

The full code for the method that performs URL redirection would look something like this:

```
String ls_rtn
Blob lb_blob

IF il_callcount = 0 THEN
  ls_rtn = "location: http://www.powersoft.com/" + "~r~n~r~n"
  lb_blob = Blob(ls_rtn)
  il_callcount = il_callcount + 1
ELSE
  SetNull(lb_blob)
END IF

Return lb_blob
```

10.6.3.2.8 Accessing CGI Environment Variables

`CGI` environment variables contain useful information that can often be used in applications. These variables can contain information about the Web server, the browser and the CGI transaction that is currently taking place. The listing below shows the typical CGI variables and gives a description of each one.

SERVER_SOFTWARE	Name and version of the web server software.
SERVER_NAME	Hostname of the web server.
GATEWAY_INTERFACE	Type of web server interface. e.g., CGI.
SERVER_PROTOCOL	Web server protocol. e.g., HTTP.
SERVER_PORT	Port number associated with the request. e.g., 80.
REQUEST_METHOD	Request method. e.g., GET or POST.
HTTP_ACCEPT	File name for the MIME types and content types.
PATH_INFO	Extra path information (logical path).
PATH_TRANSLATED	Path information (physical path).
SCRIPT_NAME	Path information for the script (executable path).
QUERY_STRING	Data associated with the GET request method.
REMOTE_HOST	Hostname of the browser making the request.
REMOTE_ADDR	IP address of the browser making the request.
REMOTE_USER	Remote user name.
CONTENT_TYPE	The content type of POST data.
CONTENT_LENGTH	The size of the content file.

The `pbweb.ini` file contains an entry in its [Web.PB] section for storing the CGI keywords. There are three variables that store these keywords: `ISAPIKeywords` `CGIKeywords`, and `NSAPIKeywords`.

If you want to access any of the CGI variables within the PowerScript code, you need to declare the relevant CGI variable as an argument to your user object's method. For example, if you want to access the `REMOTE_ADDR` CGI environment variable within a method named, `f_login`, you would declare an argument named `REMOTE_ADDR` of type string for the `f_login` method. You do not need to do anything in order to ensure that the CGI variable is passed from browser to server since this is handled automatically by the HTTP protocol. For example, when you're calling the `f_login` method, you don't need to pass `REMOTE_ADDR` as a parameter in the form or anchor tag within the HTML source code.

10.6.3.3 Compiling the Web.PB Application

To compile a Web.PB application, use the Project Painter as you would with regular PowerBuilder Applications. For the best performance, build the executable as a 32-bit machine code file. Figure 10-18 shows the Project Painter as it appears for a sample application. This application has a single PBL and uses a resource file, `dpb_srv.pbr`, for the bitmaps used to display the traffic light signals for starting and stopping the listener.

If you are using DataStores in an application to return database content to the browser using the `HTMLTable` syntax, be sure to check the PBD checkbox in the Project Painter next to any PBLs that reference DataWindows to be associated with the DataStores. Since these DataWindow names are being associated with the DataStore at runtime rather than being set initially, a PBD file is required.

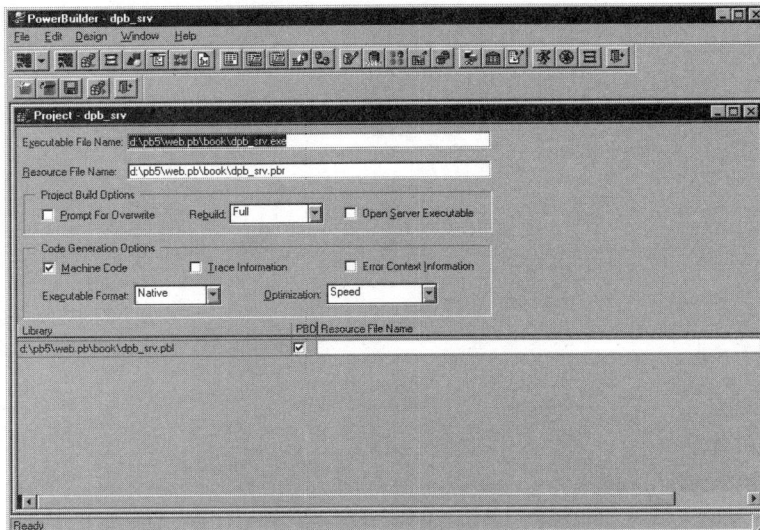

Figure 10-18. Project Painter showing the code generation options and the PBD checkbox.

10.6.4 Summary

In this section we've explored some of the techniques for building Internet applications using PowerBuilder 6.0 and Web.PB. We've covered both the creation of HTML pages to access Distributed PowerBuilder methods and the creation of the actual user objects and methods themselves.

PowerBuilder 6.0 and Web.PB provide powerful tools for Internet development. The Internet Tools within PowerBuilder 6.0 can also help speed you on your way by providing extra tools to get the job done. In the remaining section we'll look at some of these supporting tools.

10.7 Web.PB HTML Wizard and Class Library

In this section we'll took at two tools that are designed to assist you in creating Web.PB applications: the Web.PB HTML Wizard and the Web.PB Class Library.

10.7.1 Using the Web.PB HTML Wizard

The Web.PB HTML Wizard is a standalone executable program named pbwizard.exe, that you can use to rapidly build HTML source code that accesses custom class user objects using the HTML form or anchor tags. The wizard is almost identical to the wizard that was included in the Internet Developer Toolkit with PowerBuilder 5.0. As we discovered earlier in this chapter, you can also access the wizard via the Toolbar from within the PowerBuilder 6.0 development environment.

The wizard is useful for novice and experienced HTML developers alike. For developers relatively new to HTML coding, it provides a level of abstraction and makes it easy to create HTML forms that access DPB user object methods. For experienced developers, it provides a quick way to generate HTML code which can be further customized via an HTML editor later on.

Here are the steps involved in created an HTML form using the HTML Wizard:

1. Start the Web.PB HTML Wizard program, `pbwizard.exe`, from either the icon on the PowerBuilder toolbar or from Windows 95 explorer.

2. Enter the full path and filename for the PBL containing the user object function you want to access from your HTML form.

3. Select the custom class user object containing the function you want to access from your HTML form.

4. Select the user object function you want to access from your HTML form.

5. Select the arguments to create an input field for, or pass directly to, the function from your HTML form.

6. Select your Internet server type, the URL which locates Web.PB, and the type of HTML tag (anchor or form) by which to invoke the method.

7. Select the `pbweb.ini` file that you want to use and the Server Alias from the file.

8.   Enter initial values and field labels for each of the arguments that you selected above, the form method (Get or Post), the label for the Submit button, the HTML header text, and the full path and filename of the HTML file you wish to create.

9.   Choose Preview to preview the HTML that will be created.

Now that we've reviewed the required steps, let's walk through the creation of an HTML form using the Wizard. We'll use a method named f_payment_htm in a user object named uo_finance. This method is from an example in *PowerBuilder 5.0 Application Development for the Internet & Intranet* and calculates the monthly loan payment in a sample banking application called BankWeb.

First of all, start the Web.PB HTML Wizard by choosing the wizard icon from the toolbar. You should now see the first page of the wizard as shown in Figure 10-19.

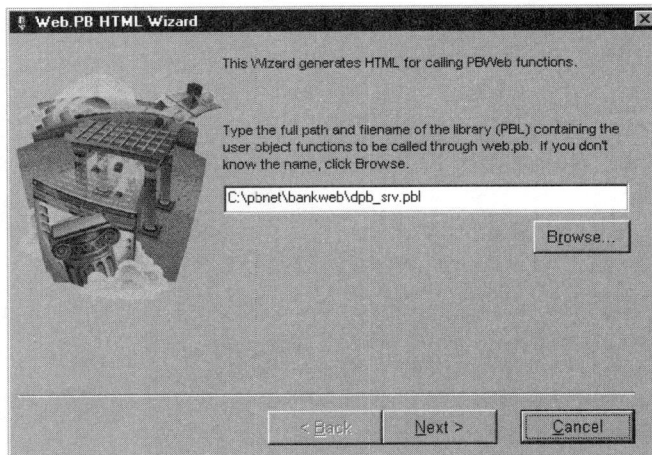

Figure 10-19. The opening page of the Web.PB HTML Wizard.

In this first page you'll choose the PowerBuilder Library (PBL) file that contains the user object you want to work with. Click on the Next button when you've finished selecting the file.

The next page to appear is shown in Figure 10-20. Here you choose the custom class user object containing the method you want to invoke from the HTML form. In this example we've chosen the uo_finance user object.

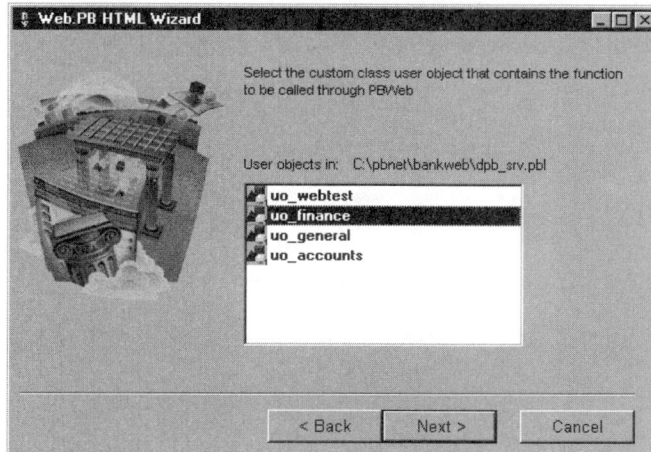

Figure 10-20. *Choosing the custom user object from the Wizard.*

Next, you'll see the page shown in Figure 10-21. Now that we've selected the user object, we need a method. In this example we've chosen the `f_payment_htm` method.

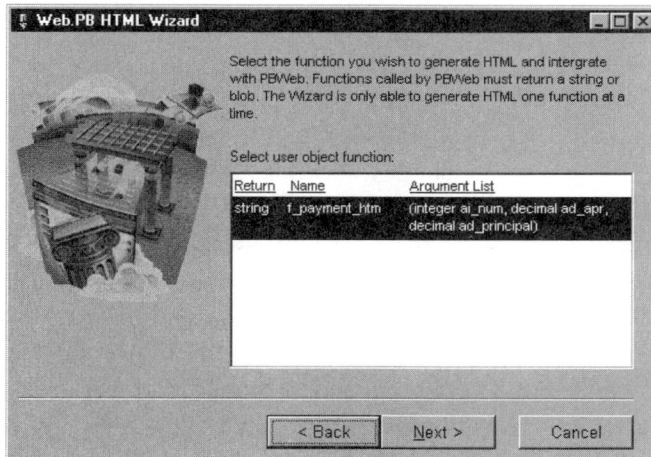

Figure 10-21. *Choosing the method from the Wizard.*

You'll now see a select list allowing you to choose which arguments you want to either provide input fields for on the form or pass directly to the PowerBuilder method (Figure 10-22). By default, all arguments are selected. Since we want all three arguments on our loan calculation form, you can leave the arguments selected and simply click on the Next button to proceed.

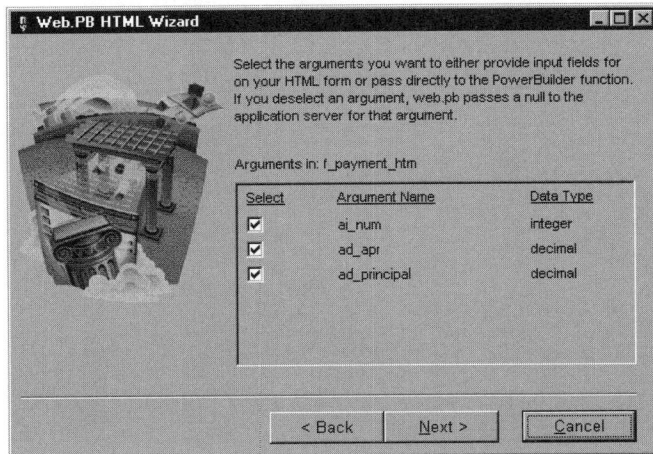

Figure 10-22. Choosing the arguments for the HTML form or anchor element.

On the fifth screen, you have a few more choices to make (Figure 10-23). Choose your Web server from among the choices in the "Select your Internet Server" group box, so the wizard knows which Web.PB file to use. Since you're probably using WebSite, (it comes with the Internet Tools), select that option. You should also enter the CGI location. This will probably have been set to /scripts, a standard mapping for the CGI directory. Finally, select the HTML style that you'd like to use to invoke the method, the anchor tag or the form tag. If you choose form, you generate an HTML form which will prompt the user for input. If you choose anchor, you generate a hypertext link that invokes the user object method without requiring the user to fill out any fields on a form. Select the form option here and then click on the Next button to proceed.

The next page lets you to select the pbweb.ini file (Figure 10-24). This tells the wizard how to complete the server alias section of the URL syntax for accessing the PowerBuilder method. Remember that Web.PB uses the server alias to read the pbweb.ini file, determine the port number for the DPB server application, and the communications driver it uses. Click on the Next button to proceed.

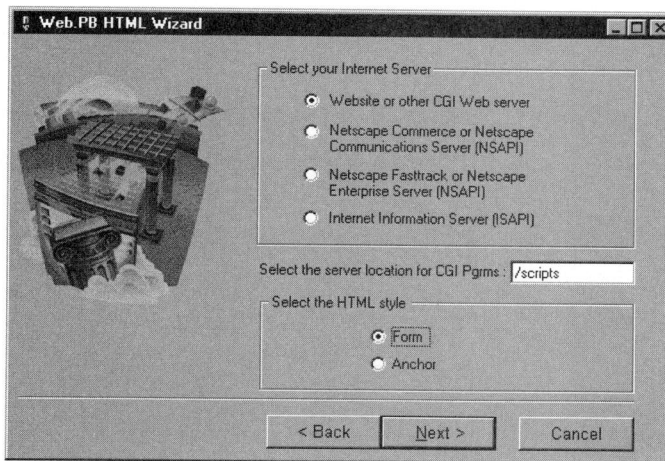

Figure 10-23. *Choosing the Internet server and HTML method of invocation.*

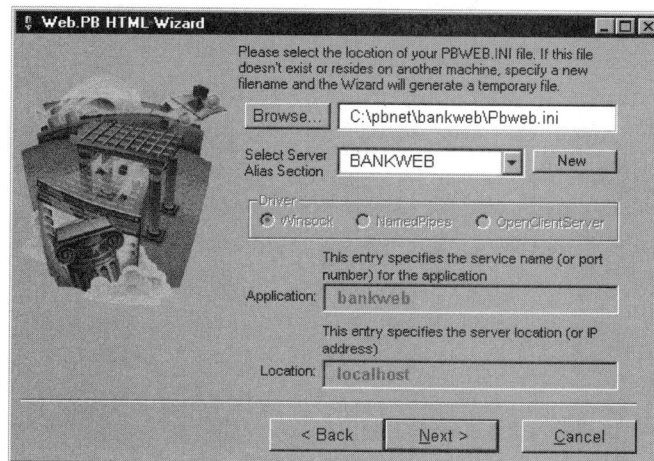

Figure 10-24. *Choosing the pbweb.ini file.*

The final page that you need to complete depends on the style of invocation that you chose for the PowerBuilder method. Since we chose the form tag, the page contains the entries for the HTML forms field labels and initial values (Figure 10-25). You can choose whether to use the GET or POST method for the CGI transaction. Enter the following values into the "Input Field Label" entry fields:

```
Enter Number of Months:
Enter APR:
Enter Principal:
```

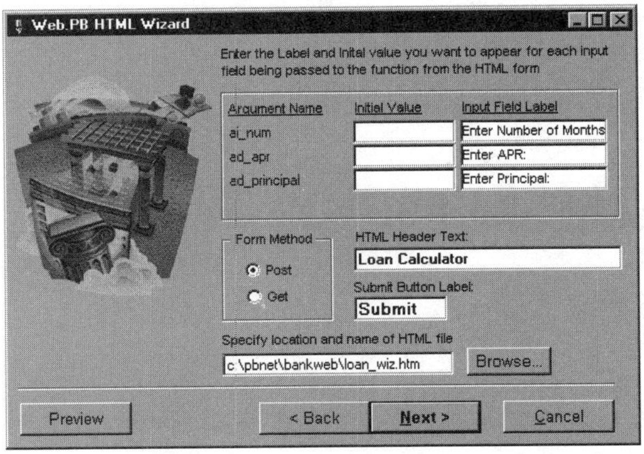

Figure 10-25. *Choosing the field labels and creating the HTML file.*

We'll leave the "Initial Value" entry fields blank since we don't want to make any assumptions about the loan calculation parameters. Now enter "Loan Calculator" in the "HTML Header Text" field and allow the Submit button label to default to "Submit."

If you choose the anchor tag instead of the form tag, the final page asks for values for each of the arguments selected earlier. Figure 10-26 shows the Wizard page for the anchor tag.

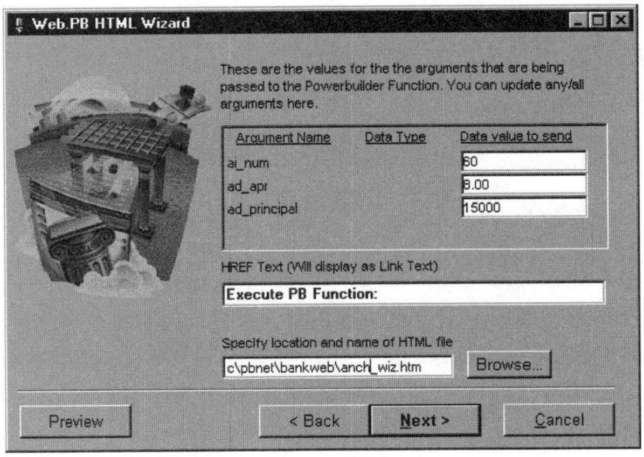

Figure 10-26. *Setting parameter values for the anchor tag.*

Continuing with the creation of an HTML page using the form tag, a full path and filename for the HTML file is needed. In this example, the path is set to `c:\pb_web\samples\bankweb\loan_wiz.htm`.

Congratulations, you're finished! You can click on the preview button to preview the HTML syntax that will be generated (Figure 10-27). One of the nice things about the wizard is that you can use the Previous button to backtrack and make changes to any of the earlier screens. When you're ready to create the HTML file, just click on the Next button.

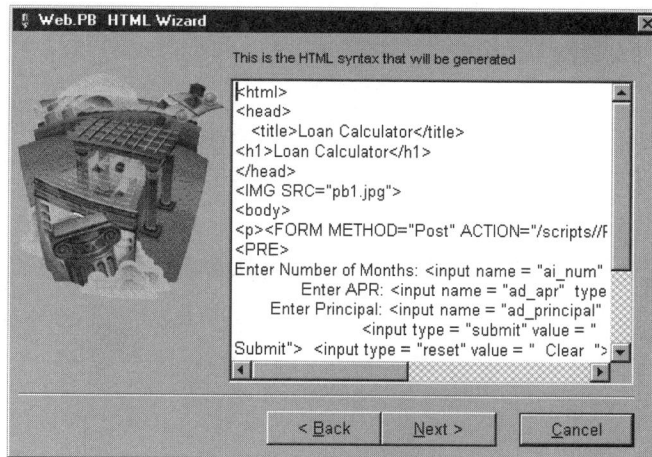

Figure 10-27. Previewing the HTML.

The final checkered flag page is shown in Figure 10-28. You've crossed the finish line! This page gives instructions on how to test the page. After using the Wizard just a couple of times, you'll be able to complete the process in a fraction of the time it's taken to read this section.

Figure 10-29 shows the unaltered HTML page generated by the Wizard.

You can test this page (or other pages generated by the wizard) by starting the DPB server application, completing the form, and clicking on the Submit button.

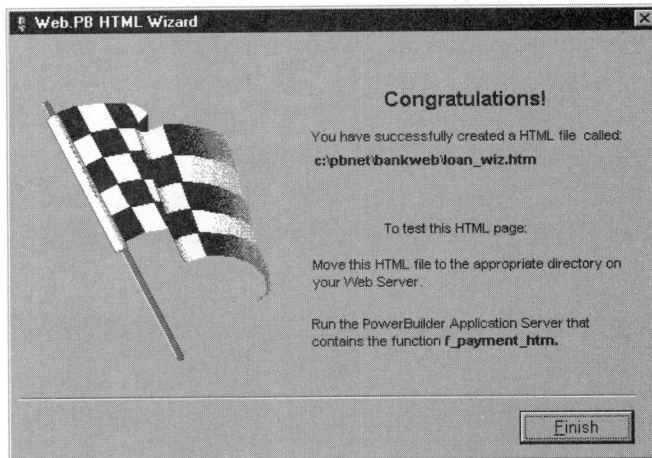

Figure 10-28. Congratulations! You've created an HTML form that accesses a PowerBuilder method.

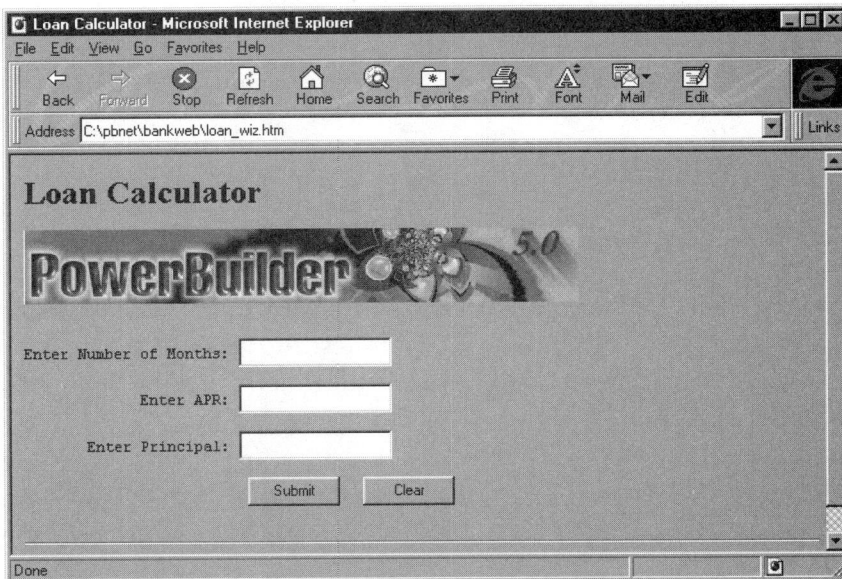

Figure 10-29. A wizard-created Web page.

10.7.2 Using the Web.PB Class Library

Included in the Internet Tools is a class library consisting of five custom class user objects, stored in a PowerBuilder library file named `webpb.pbl`.

Here's a listing of the five user objects and their purpose:

u_html_form	Methods for creating HTML syntax for form elements such as buttons, edit fields, listboxes, dropdown listboxes, checkboxes and radiobuttons.
u_html_format	Methods for creating HTML syntax for general page elements such as page headers, tables, lists, applets, images and links.
u_html_template	Methods to read an HTML template file and make replacements to predefined substitution text. The substitution parameters can be prefixed with two ampersands (&&) or other characters as required.
u_session	Methods for Session Management. This object contains methods for establishing a session and maintaining user, state and transaction information about the session. This method uses the www_session and ww_session_argument tables in the webpb database included with the Internet Tools.
u_transaction	Methods for Transaction Management. This object contains methods for maintaining transaction information. A transaction is an application-specific unit of work. There can be zero or more transactions within a session. This method uses the www_transaction, www_transaction_argument, and www_transaction_page tables in the webpb database included with the Internet Tools.

The class library is designed to ease the development of Web.PB applications. Instead of having to remember all the HTML syntax for dynamically created Web pages, you simply call the required user object methods in order to build page. The user object methods create the HTML syntax.

The user objects also contain more advanced functions for session and transaction management. These functions are contained in the `u_session` and `u_transaction` objects. They basically help solve the "persistence of state" problems which most Web developers encounter eventually. By using the methods within these user objects, you can keep track of the users on your Web site as they move from one page to the next.

This can be useful for sites where you need to keep track of items the user has selected as part of a "shopping basket," so you can display a grand total when finished.

Here are the five user objects in more detail.

10.7.2.1 Form Processing Service—u_html_form

The user object named `u_html_form` is the Form Processing Service. This object creates HTML syntax for a variety of form elements. Methods such as this are extremely useful since you can create dynamic Web pages with listboxes and other form elements that contain up-to-date selection criteria from the database.

For example, the `f_MakeDDLB` method within the `u_html_form` user object creates HTML syntax for a dropdown listbox. It uses a column name from a DataStore object passed to the method. Here's some sample code that illustrates the use of the `f_MakeDDLB` method:

```
DataStore lds_product
...
lds_product = CREATE DataStore
lds_product.dataobject = "d_product"
lds_product.SetTransObject(SQLCA)
IF lds_product.Retrieve() < 1 THEN
 Return("Retrieval Error")
END IF
...
ls_product = inv_html_form.f_MakeDDLB("as_product", lds_product, &
 "product_id", "product_name")
...
```

This example shows how a DataStore containing product information is first created and retrieved. After data has been retrieved into the DataStore, the `f_MakeDDLB` method creates HTML syntax for a dropdown listbox using the DataStore values. This method could be used order to build a dynamic HTML form. The first argument, `as_product`, is the name of the dropdown listbox used in the HTML form. Remember, if this form invokes another user object method, the name of the listbox must match the name of one of the arguments within the method. The `f_MakeDDLB` method also has optional arguments for specifying the beginning and ending rows in the DataStore which are to be included in the dropdown listbox.

To use the Forms Processing Service within your Web.PB applications, declare an instance variable within your user objects of type u_html_form as follows:

```
u_html_form inv_html_form
```

You can now invoke any of the methods contained in `u_html_form` by simply prefixing the methods with the name of the instance variable. You should also be sure to include the `webpb.pbl` file in your library search path. `Webpb.pbl` is found in the `c:\program files\powersoft\pb6\it` directory by default.

10.7.2.2 HTML Generation Service—u_html_format

This user object is the HTML Generation Service. It's more generic than the form processing service since it can create most of the standard HTML syntax required for Web page development. Some of the methods return very simple strings, `f_BeginPageHeading` returns <HEAD> to denote an HTML page heading. Other methods contain more advanced functions such as `f_BeginTable` which creates a tag to begin a new table. With this method, you can specify additional attributes for the table such as the alignment on the page, the cell padding and spacing, and the border width. `f_BeginTable` also uses function overloading so it can be called using four sets of arguments. These arguments define whether the function will create syntax for generic browsers, Netscape extensions, Explorer extensions, or both Netscape and Explorer extensions to the HTML table syntax.

The `u_html_format` user object contains several instance variables which can be referenced. Two common variables are `ii_errorcode` and `is_errormsg`. These instance variables can also be used in the other four user objects as well. The instance variable `ii_errorcode` contains an error code for the last `u_html_format` method to be invoked. Likewise, the `is_errormsg` variable contains an error description for the same method. These variables should be read when the `u_html_format` method returns an empty string.

Here's a list of the other instance variables and structures accessible to the `u_html_format` user object:

```
is_column, ist_columns[]    DataWindow column information
is_font, ist_fonts[]        Font formatting information
is_table, ist_tables[]      Table formatting information
```

10.7.2.3 HTML Template Service—u_html_template

The `u_html_template` user object is the Template Service. Its methods can be used to read an HTML template file and make replacements to predefined substitution text. This can be useful if you have Web pages which have a standard header or footer, or which need elements replaced such as page counts. To read the template file into a string variable you can use the `f_OpenTemplate` method. To perform the text substitutions you can use either the `f_Replace` or the `f_ReplaceAll` method.

To use the Template Service to make replacements to some of the text in a template file:

1. Create an HTML template file that contains substitution parameters prefixed with suitable characters such as two ampersands, e.g., `&&Start`.

2. Declare an instance variable in your user object of type `u_html_template`. This lets you reference `u_html_template` methods within your user object.

3. Call the `f_OpenTemplate` method to read the template file into a string variable.

4. Call the `f_Replace` or `f_ReplaceAll` method to make the substitutions.

5. Return the HTML template string to the browser.

The Template Service uses two instance variables to maintain information about the template files:

```
is_templatedir    Template Directory
is_documentdir    Document Directory
```

The `f_SetEnvironment` method is used to set these instance variables. The template directory instance variable, `is_templatedir`, is provided in case you store your template files in a directory below the main document directory, `is_documentdir`. By using `f_SetEnvironment` to set these directory paths, there is no need to specify a full pathname in the `f_OpenTemplate` method when you open the template file.

10.7.2.4 Session Management Service—u_html_session

The session management service keeps track of users as they move from page to page within a Web.PB application. This service and the transaction management service make use of the tables in the `webpb` database. See the section "Class Library Database Tables" for more information on these tables.

The methods available in the session management service allow you to save data regarding the session via the `f_SetArgumentValue` method. The data saved can be anything you want to maintain. For example, you could store information about which Web pages the user visited, for the purposes of improving your Web site in the future. Once you have saved this session data, you can retrieve it at any time using the `f_GetArgumentValue` method.

Developer Note: It's interesting to note that the session management service uses hidden fields on the Web pages it returns to the browser. The `session id` can be placed as a hidden field on an HTML page by using the following syntax:

```
ls_sessionid = inv_html_form.f_MakeHidden("as_sessionid", ll_sessionid)
```

The `session id, as_sessionid,` is then passed as an argument to the user object method that is invoked by the `ACTION` attribute.

10.8.2.5 Transaction Management Service - u_html_transaction

The transaction management service is similar to the session management service in that it keeps track of users as they move from one page to another. There can be zero or more transactions per session. A transaction, in this context, is an application-specific unit of work, not a database transaction.

You can use the `f_MakeHidden` method within the `u_html_form` object to maintain `transaction ids`. With this method, you can place hidden fields on dynamic Web pages which store the `transaction` and `session ids` of the user. An example of a transaction might be an Order Entry application where the user chooses line items for purchase. You can save data regarding the transaction using the `f_SetArgumentValue` method. This will store data in the `www_transaction_argument` table. You can access the data later using the `f_GetArgumentValue` method. If the user selects a "Cancel Order" or similar option, you can clear out the data using the `f_SetArgumentValue` method to reinitialize the order information. You can also clear out a transaction by using the `f_CleanUpTransactions` method. This method will delete all transactions which occurred before a specified date and time.

In addition to the methods described above, the transaction management service also lets you cache data from a DataStore into the `www_transaction_page` table for later use. The methods to do this are `f_SetTransactionPage` and `f_GetTransactionPage`. With `f_SetTransactionPage` you can also break up the data in a DataStore and save it in multiple rows in the `www_transaction_page` table. This lets you present the DataStore information across several Web pages.

Although the transaction management service is not related to actual database transactions, you may think of them in the same way, since they both help manage a unit of work within an application.

10.7.2.6 Class Library Database Tables

In addition to the user objects, there's also an SQL Anywhere 5.x database named `webpb`. This database contains tables used by the `u_session` and `u_transaction` user objects at runtime. Here's a listing of the tables:

`www_new_session_id`	Table used to generate session ids
`www_new_transaction_id`	Table used to generate transaction ids
`www_session`	Table used to store session details such as Session Id, IP Address, and first and last access date and time.
`www_session_argument`	Table used to store user-defined session argument names and values.
`www_transaction`	Table used to store transaction details such as Transaction Id, Session Id, and creation date and time.
`www_transaction_argument`	Table used to store user-defined transaction argument names and values.
`www_transaction_page`	Table used to cache data from DataStores. Used by the f_GetTransactionPage and f_SetTransactionPage methods within u_transaction.

The primary and foreign key relationships between the tables are shown in Figure 10-30.

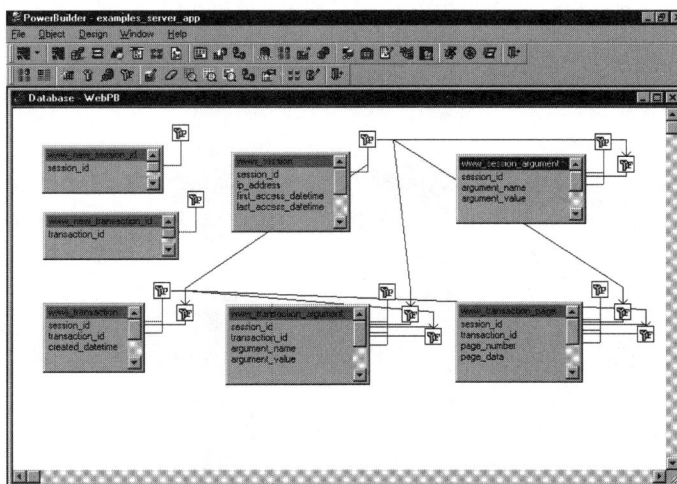

Figure 10-30. *Relationships between the tables in the Web.PB Class Library*

10.8 Running the Code Examples

The examples included in the Internet Tools are divided into three sections as shown in Figure 10-31. You can run them by opening the `sample.htm` file after installing all required components of the Internet Tools into the appropriate directories on your PC. For complete installation and configuration instructions, read the `runexamp.htm` Web page.

"Distributed PowerBuilder Web Examples" provide some useful code examples for Web.PB. In particular, the "Using the Web.PB Class Library" example provides an insight into the use of the Web.PB Class Library. It shows how to dynamically generate an HTML form which lets a user select a department to view its employee names.

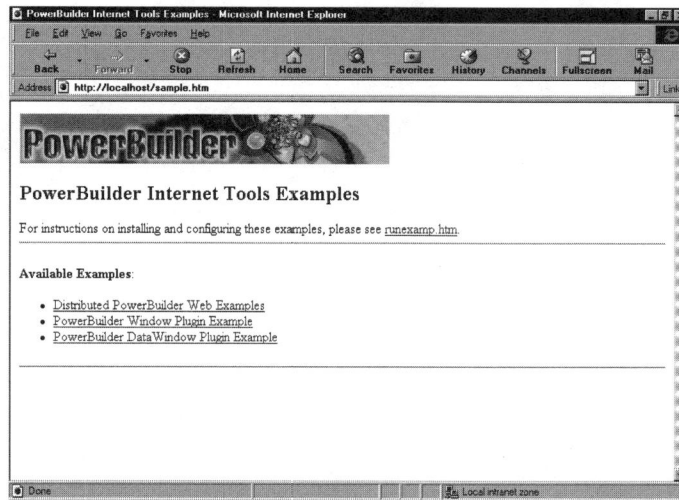

***Figure 10-31.** PowerBuilder Internet Toolkit Examples.*

Figure 10-32 shows the first page from the example. You can see the generated listbox showing department names, created using the `f_MakeLB` method within the `u_html_form` user object. The entire page was created using a combination of methods from the `u_html_form` and `u_html_format` user objects. For example, text was placed on the form using the `f_InsertParagraph` method and the horizontal lines were created using the `f_InsertHRule` method.

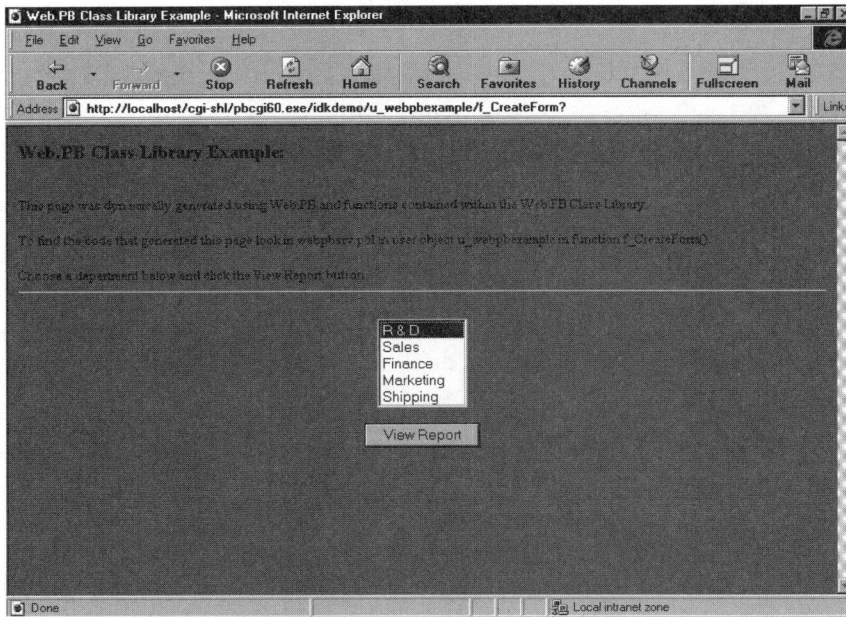

Figure 10-32. *A dynamic Web page created by the Web.PB Class Library example.*

Once a department is selected, you are presented with the employee records as shown in Figure 10-33. This page is again dynamically created by PowerBuilder; demonstrating the use of `u_session` and `u_transaction` for session and transaction management. The employee records are displayed across multiple pages which can be accessed via buttons on the form. The data for these pages, obtained via a DataStore, is stored in the `www_transaction_page` table in the `webpb` database using the `f_SetTransactionPage` method.

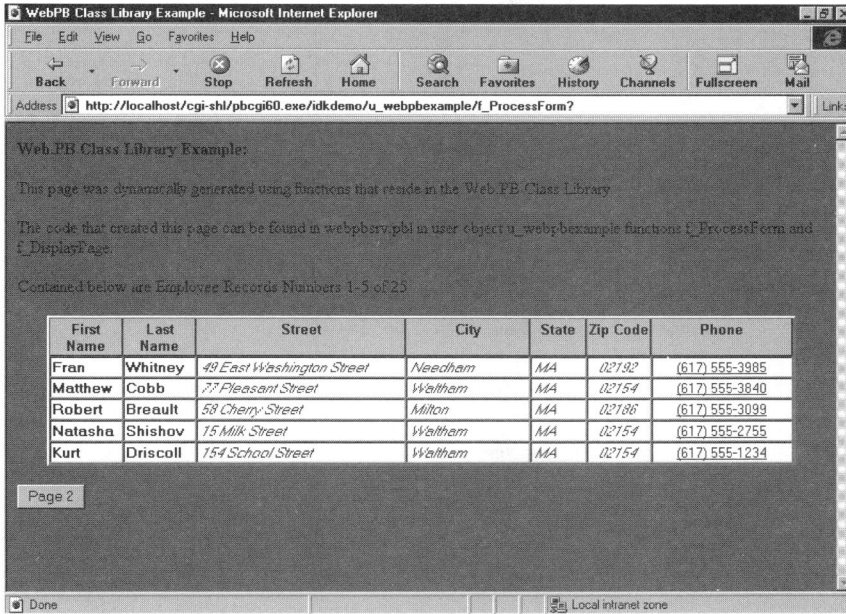

Figure 10-33. *A dynamic Web page showing Employee Information created by the Web.PB Class Library example.*

CHAPTER 11

Compiling Your Applications

*P*owerBuilder 6.0 has made a fundamental change in the way that we create our applications. The product now incorporates a project generator infrastructure that enables future support for generating many different types of targets such as CORBA, DCOM or other industry standard object types. The idea behind this is that you can build one set of source code, but then generate that source code into many different types of component and/or object models as you require. In the future, if Powersoft is able to swing it, you may see such generators as a JavaBeans generator or something similar.

The place where you will choose what your target is going to be is the Project Painter. When you select to create a new project you will be given a dialog window showing which targets are currently available to be generated as shown in Figure 11.1.

Currently you have the option to build an application, a proxy library or a C++ header file and source file.

11.1 Application

The application choice will allow you to build a standard PowerBuilder compiled application like you have always done in previous versions of PowerBuilder. Since version 5.0 we have had the option of building the executable with P-Code or in machine code.

11.1.1 P-Code

P-Code is the standard interpreted format of executable that PowerBuilder has relied upon since its first version. Most of your development and testing will be done using

P-code executables as they are much quicker to build and easier to work with. However, you may choose to generate your final production version of your application using machine or native compiled code for speed.

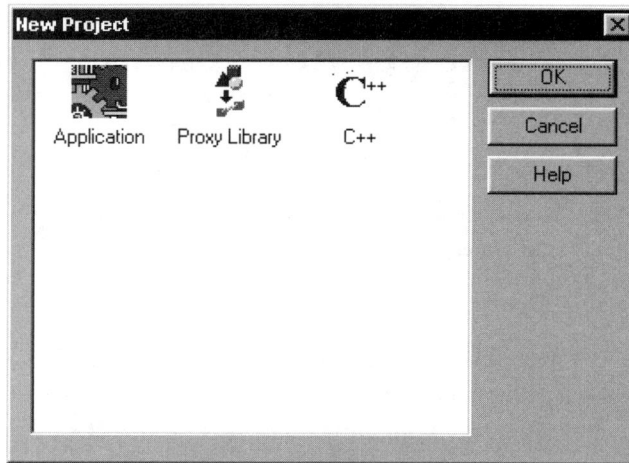

Figure 11.1. The Project Painter now utilizes a project generator infrastructure to allow us to build many different types of targets.

11.1.2 Native Compiled Code

One of the most common complaints that I have heard about PowerBuilder applications over the years has been "My applications run too slow!". Many of the trade magazines and industry experts regularly put down the 4GL tools because of their interpreted code and the resulting overhead in the execution of enterprise applications.

Since PowerBuilder 5.0, we have had the option of compiling our applications in machine code to improve the performance. We can still generate p-code executables, but when we are ready for production, we can have PowerBuilder generate C code which is passed to the embedded Watcom compiler and compiled into a machine code executable. (See Figure 11-2.)

Developer's Tip: Generating a machine code executable can take an extremely long time, even for a small application. It is not unusual for compile times to be several hours or more. Compile to p-code until you are fairly close to your final product to avoid wasting time waiting for compiles.

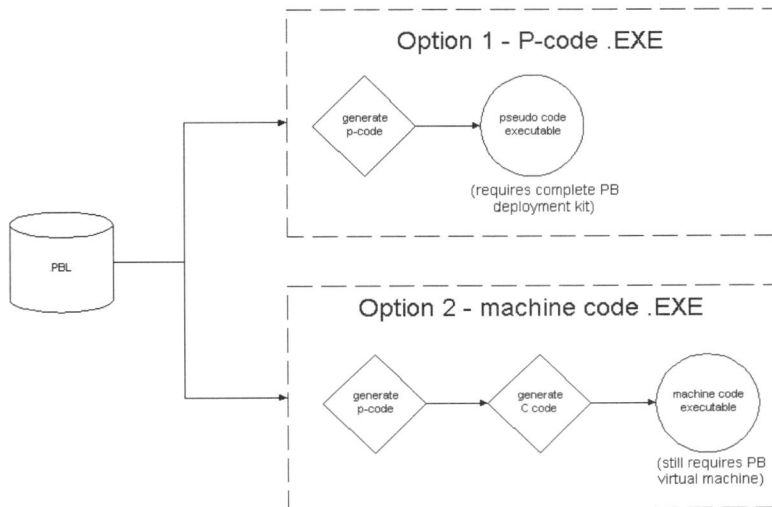

Figure 11-2. *You can generate either p-code or machine code executables with PowerBuilder 6.0. When you generate a machine code executable, PowerBuilder first generates C code which is then passed into the compiler. The C code generation is all behind the scenes and cannot be accessed by the developer.*

The magnitude of performance improvement you will see from machine code compilation will vary tremendously depending on your application. The compiling will improve the performance of your PowerScript which formerly was interpreted. It will not improve the speed with which your windows open or your data is retrieved from your data base. Specifically within your scripts you should see improved performance in the areas of:

- Access to variables.

- Execution of operations such as assignments, string concatenation and general math.

- Flow of control statements such as IF/THEN and CHOOSE CASE statements.

- Calling functions.

The ability to generate machine code is available in the Windows 95 and Windows NT versions of PowerBuilder 6.0. The objects from any version of

PowerBuilder can be recompiled in the 95 or NT versions and 16 bit machine code executables can be produced for Windows 3.11 from either of the 32 bit environments (although registry functions work differently in 16 and 32 bit environments).

When you compile your application into machine code, the .EXE file becomes a native executable. However, you must still distribute the PowerBuilder Virtual Machine (PBVM060.DLL) as it contains key components that you may have called in your application. These could have been rolled into the .EXE, but Powersoft decided that doing so would add too much unnecessary bulk to the EXE. You may notice the machine code EXE is larger than the p-code EXE but that is all right, it will still run faster!

Developer's Tip: The processing of compiling a machine code executable can take a significant amount of time. To help to improve the speed of .EXE generation, ensure that you have the maximum amount of RAM available to PowerBuilder by; physically increasing your RAM, changing a temporary swap file to a permanent swap file, and increasing the size of virtual memory when applicable.

Under machine code generation, your PowerBuilder Dynamic Libraries (.PBDs) will become Dynamic Link Libraries (.DLLs). However, these DLLs, unlike the .DLLs that we call in the External Functions (see Chapter 18) examples, cannot be called by external applications.

The process for generating a machine code executable is very straightforward. You enter the project painter where all executable files are generated. You will see the window in Figure 11-3.

You select "Machine Code" in the Code Generations Options group box. Then you press the Build button in the toolbar. PowerBuilder does the rest! You can choose to optimize your generation for speed, space or no optimization (I can't imagine too many situations where you would optimize for anything but speed).

Development Tip: Local and instance variables will execute faster than global and shared variables. Yet another reason for avoiding these variables!

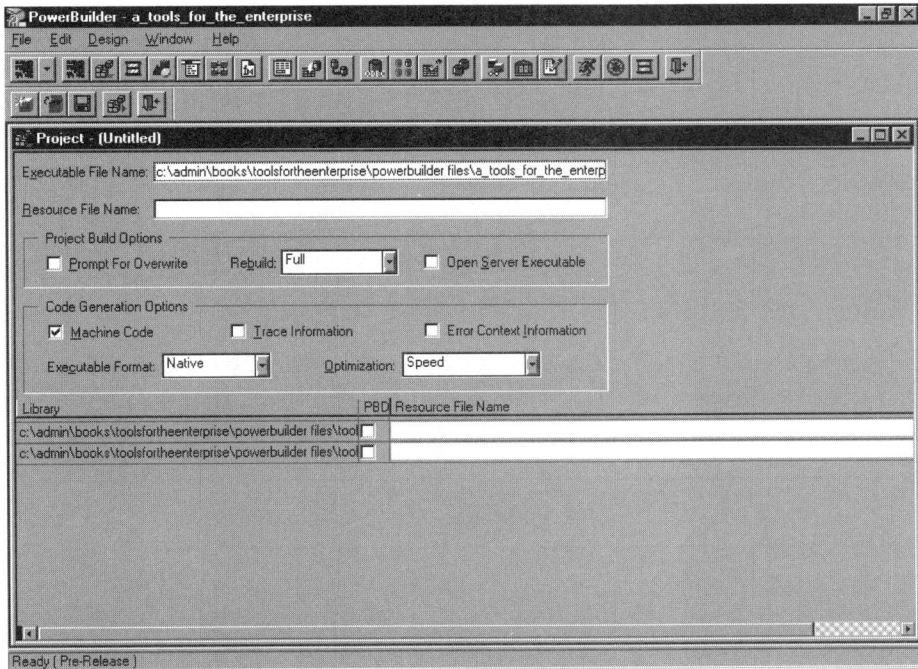

Figure 11-3. *In the project painter you can select machine code executable to allow you to build true compiled code executables.*

Development Tip: Do not compile into machine code until you have reached your final stage of testing. If you use the p-code version for testing you can still take advantage of switches like PBTRACE that allow you to shadow the execution of a p-code compiled executable and track where errors are occurring.

11.2 Proxy Library

If you select to generate a proxy library, the Project Painter will generate proxy objects for any of your applicable non-visual objects. These objects will then be deployed with your client application if you are building a distributed PB application. Refer to Chapter 9 for more information on Proxy objects.

When you select this generator, you will be presented with a list of custom class (non-visual) user objects from which you will select those that you wish to generate. You will be given a report detailing which objects were examined and which proxy objects were generated.

> **Author's Note:** This generator is not yet functional in the beta version of the software. Refer to your documentation for more details.

11.3 C++ Generator

The C++ generator will create a C++ header file and a source or binary file that is the C++ equivalent of the custom class (non-visual) user objects that you specify in the object selection dialog.

> **Author's Note:** This generator is not yet functional in the beta version of the software. Refer to your documentation for more details.

CHAPTER 12

Using Inbound OLE Automation

*I*n Chapter 9 we examined how PowerBuilder 6.0 implements distributed computing. This concept relied very heavily on the use of non-visual objects to provide the processes that the application server could execute. A close relative of distributed computing is the creation of OLE (Object Linking and Embedding) process servers (also referred to as "inbound OLE automation").

OLE process servers are objects that contain methods (processes) that have a standard interface which can be accessed through any OLE compliant tool. This means that you could develop processes in Visual Basic and access those processes like a regular NVO (nonvisual object) in PowerBuilder. Also, you could take a PowerBuilder NVO and generate it as an OLE process server and access these methods from Visual Basic, or any other OLE compliant tool.

OLE process servers are an essential part of Microsoft's distributed computing strategy. If your organization is intending to implement distributed computing following Microsoft's model you will be creating many of these objects.

OLE process servers are also particularly useful if you are a development shop that uses more than one development tool and want to be able to share processes between them.

Let's examine how we generate an OLE process server in PowerBuilder 6.0. Then we will see how we can access an OLE server from within our application, regardless of whether that process server is written in PowerBuilder, Visual Basic or any other language. Finally we will look at an example of how our PowerBuilder generated OLE process server can be accessed from Visual Basic.

12.1 The Sample Application

The sample application will require three objects, an application object, a window and a non-visual user object. If you refer back to Chapter 9, we constructed a non-visual object called n_emp_count. This non-visual object had three functions defined for it:

- Of_connect()—established a connection to our sample database.

- Of_disconnect()—terminated the connection with the sample database.

- Of_emp_count()—counts the number of employees in the database.

It had no instance variables or other characteristics that were different from the default settings. In this example we will turn this NVO into an OLE process server.

If you are following along and haven't built the objects from Chapter 9, you can create the NVO now adding the following three user functions in the source code listings. Alternatively, you can load it from the CD-ROM that came with this book. Create a new application called *ole_exercise*. Save it in a .PBL called "CLIENT.PBL." Add the non-visual object *n_emp_count* to this library. Build the three functions described in the code listings.

Script for of_connect() for non-visual object n_emp_count

```
SQLCA.DBMS = "ODBC"
SQLCA.DBParm = "ConnectString='DSN=Powersoft Demo DB V5;UID=dba;PWD=sql'"

CONNECT;

RETURN SQLCA.SQLCode
```

Script for of_disconnect() for non-visual object n_emp_count

```
DISCONNECT;

RETURN SQLCA.SQLCode
```

Script for of_test() for non-visual object n_emp_count

```
LONG ll_emp_count

SELECT count(*)
INTO :ll_emp_count
FROM employee
;

RETURN ll_emp_count
```

This non-visual object is the processing component of our simple partitioned application. Next we will need to add the window object w_ole_client. Construct the window as shown in Figure 12-1.

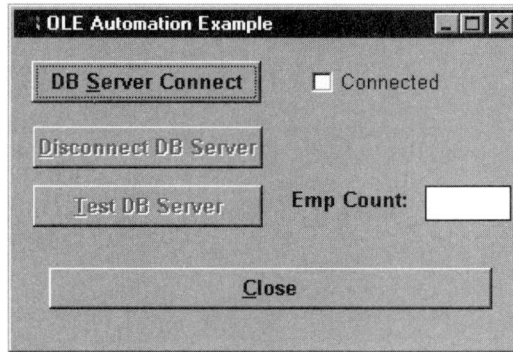

Figure 12-1. The Sample Application.

Add scripts for the objects as shown in the code listing.

Instance variables for w_ole_client

```
n_emp_count invo_emp_count
```

Script for Open event of w_ole_client

```
invo_emp_count = CREATE n_emp_count
```

Script for Clicked event of cb_connect on w_ole_client

```
IF invo_emp_count.of_connect() <> 0 THEN
    // Connect Unsuccessful
    cbx_dbserver.checked = FALSE
    cb_disconnect.enabled = FALSE
    cb_testdb.enabled = FALSE
ELSE
    // Connect Successful
    cbx_dbserver.checked = TRUE
    cb_disconnect.enabled = TRUE
    cb_testdb.enabled = TRUE
END IF
```

Script for Clicked event of cb_disconnect on w_ole_client

```
IF invo_emp_count.of_disconnect() <> 0 THEN
    // Disconnect Unsuccessful
    MessageBox("Disconnection Unsuccessful",&
            "Unable to disconnect from database")
ELSE
    // Disconnect Successful
    cbx_dbserver.checked = FALSE
    cb_disconnect.enabled = FALSE
    cb_testdb.enabled = FALSE
END IF
```

Script for Clicked event of cb_test on w_ole_client

```
LONG ll_count

ll_count = invo_emp_count.of_count_emp()

sle_count.text = String (ll_count)
```

Script for the Clicked event of cb_close on w_ole_client

```
// Close the OLE client window
Close(PARENT)
```

Script for the Close event of w_ole_client

```
DESTROY invo_emp_count
```

For the application object we only need to open the OLE client window. The script for the open event of the application object is:

Script for application object Open event

```
//  open the OLE server interface window
open(w_ole_client)
```

This is the starting point for our example. Run the sample application and you should be able to connect to the database and count the number of employees in the database. Next we will see how this is turned into an OLE process server.

12.2 Turning the NVO Into an OLE Process Server

There are four steps involved in turning our n_emp_count non-visual object into an OLE process server that can be accessed from other applications.

Step 1 *Move NVO into a new library.*

Create a new library called COUNT.PBL. Move the non-visual object into this new library.

Step 2 *Generate a runtime version of the new library.*

Create a runtime version of the library. This runtime version can be either p-code (a PBD.) or machine code (a .DLL). This is accomplished by clicking on the library containing the nvo in the library painter with the right mouse button. A popup menu will appear as shown in Figure 12-2.

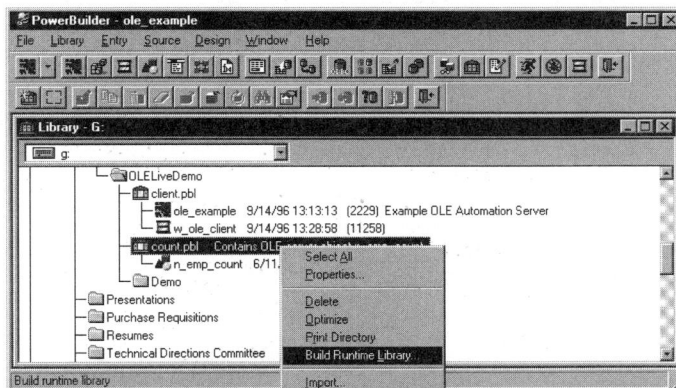

Figure 12-2. *Creating the runtime version of the library from the library painter.*

Select **Build Runtime Library...** from the menu. This will open the window in Figure 12-3.

In the Build Runtime Library dialog window you will choose your compilation options. First you will select if you want a p-code or machine code runtime library. Then you will select the appropriate compilation options. With the current builds of PowerBuilder, if you are going to generate a machine code library I strongly suggest setting the Build Type to "Full" and the Optimization to "No Optimization" to ensure your library is built correctly. When you are finished, press the **OK** command button to generate the library. A new file will be created called COUNT.PBD or COUNT.DLL depending on if you built a machine code or p-code library.

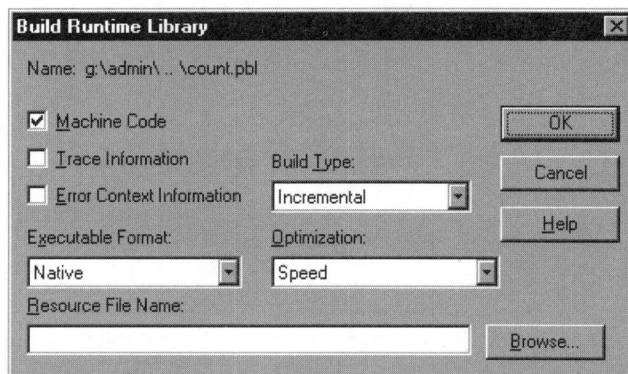

Figure 12-3. The Runtime Library Generation options.

Note: If you don't add the COUNT.PBL to the library search path of the ole_client application, this is acceptable as it is not required. However, if you don't you will see a warning message appear when you try to build the runtime library for the NVO saying that the window w_ole_client cannot find the object n_emp_count. This will not stop the generation of your runtime library.

Step 3   *Run PBGENREG application to obtain a GUID, create .REG, and .TLB files.*

There are a number of functions inside PowerBuilder that you can use to manually build your own application to generate all the files necessary to create an OLE process server. Luckily you don't have to create your own. Use the PBGENREG application that comes with PowerBuilder to do all the dirty work for you. It is a very handy utility that you will find in the PowerBuilder directory. It is a .PBL file so you will need to move out of your CLIENT.PBL application and into the PBGENREG for a few minutes.

Open the PBGENREG application object and press the Run icon to run the application. The window for this application is shown in Figure 12-4.

The first section is called "Globally Unique Identifiers" and is used to uniquely identify this object from any others that may be generated already or in the future. The only part you fill in here is the program id (Prog ID), which is the unique name that you want to recognize this object as. Call ours "count_emp.object."

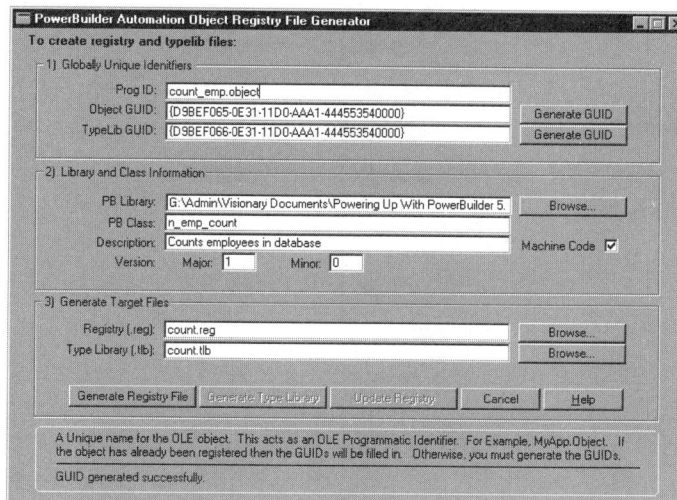

Figure 12-4. *The PBGENREG application helps us to construct the necessary files to build our OLE process server.*

The next two fields are for the Globally Unique IDentifiers (GUID) for the object itself and the type library (the type library is used to describe this object to other applications that may wish to use it). Press the **Generate GUID** buttons for both fields to have the system get a unique identifier for you.

The second section of the window is where you specify which library the nvo is in and what the name of the nvo is. You should use the full file and path name for the location of your .PBD or .DLL. If you don't know the location you can press the **Browse...** command button. Next give your object a description, a major release and minor release number (this will default to version 1.0) and indicate if it is a machine code or p-code object.

The third and final section is where you specify the file names for the OLE target. You must generate a .REG file (for the registry) and a .TLB file (for the type library). Enter the names COUNT.REG and COUNT.TLB respectively.

Now we must generate these files. Press the **Generate Registry File** command button at the bottom of the window. Very Important: Be SURE to check the message at the bottom of the window to see the status of your operation. If it was successful you will see a message saying "Registry File Generated Successfully." If it failed you will see an error code. An error code usually means that you entered something wrong in the first two sections such as forgetting to flag the Machine Code setting correctly or making a mistake in the path of the runtime library. If this failed, you must fix the problem and try again.

If you were successful, then press the command button **Generate Type Library**. This, like the previous operation, will tell you if the operation was successful, or will return an error code. If it was unsuccessful, do not try to update the registry. Fix the problem and try again.

If it was successful you will now have .REG and .TLB files. These files are the OLE version of your non-visual object.

Step 4   *Update the registry.*

Now that the OLE object has been created, we have to add it to the registry so that we can use it. You can do this from within PBGENREG by clicking on the **Update Registry** command button. Alternatively, from Explorer you could double-click on the COUNT.REG file and it would do the same thing. You will get a message indicating if your object was successfully inserted into the registry. Our object is now ready to be used by PowerBuilder, Visual Basic or any other OLE compatible tool.

12.3 Changing Our Application To Use The OLE Server

We want to alter our sample application so that instead of trying to use the NVO, that now it will access the OLE server. Close PBGENREG (if you haven't already) and reopen your CLIENT.PBL application object.

In w_ole_client we need to make some changes. Begin with the instance variables. We want to remove our variable we declared for our NVO (n_emp_count invo_emp_count) and replace it with a variable of type OLEObject.

Instance variables for w_ole_client

```
OLEObject iole_emp_count
```

Now in the open event we no longer want to create our NVO, we want to create the OLEObject container variable. We also want to try to connect to our OLE process server. If we are successful connecting we will continue with the application, if we are unsuccessful we will disconnect. The function that we use to connect to the OLE server is **ConnectToNewObject(OLEserver)** and it takes as an argument a string containing the name of the OLE object that you want to connect to (this is the unique name that you defined in the PBGENREG application).

Script for Open event of w_ole_client

```
long ll_status
iole_emp_count = CREATE OLEObject

// Connect to OLE server
ll_status = iole_emp_count.ConnectToNewObject(&
          "count_emp.object")
IF ll_status <> 0 THEN
          // Unable to connect
          MessageBox("Connection Failed",&
                 "Unable to connect to OLE server")
          Close(THIS)
ELSE
          // Successful connection
END IF
```

Upon successful connection to the OLE process server, you are ready to execute any of the methods that you called before. You only need to replace any reference to invo_emp_count with iole_emp_count.

Script for Clicked event of cb_connect on w_ole_client

```
IF iole_emp_count.of_connect() <> 0 THEN
        // Connect Unsuccessful
        cbx_dbserver.checked = FALSE
        cb_disconnect.enabled = FALSE
        cb_testdb.enabled = FALSE
ELSE
        // Connect Successful
        cbx_dbserver.checked = TRUE
        cb_disconnect.enabled = TRUE
        cb_testdb.enabled = TRUE
END IF
```

Script for Clicked event of cb_disconnect on w_ole_client

```
IF iole_emp_count.of_disconnect() <> 0 THEN
        // Disconnect Unsuccessful
        MessageBox("Disconnection Unsuccessful",&
               "Unable to disconnect from database")
ELSE
        // Disconnect Successful
        cbx_dbserver.checked = FALSE
        cb_disconnect.enabled = FALSE
        cb_testdb.enabled = FALSE
END IF
```

Script for Clicked event of cb_test on w_ole_client

```
LONG ll_count

ll_count = iole_emp_count.of_count_emp()

sle_count.text = String (ll_count)

Script for the Clicked event of cb_close on w_ole_client

// Close the OLE client window
Close(PARENT)
```

On the close of the window instead of destroying the non-visual object we will simply disconnect from our OLE process server using the **DisconnectObject()** function.

Script for the Close event of w_ole_client

```
iole_emp_count.DisconnectObject()
```

Run and test your application. Congratulations, you have just created an inbound OLE automation server from a PowerBuilder non-visual object.

12.4 Calling This Object From Visual Basic

I am not a VB expert, but I will take a stab at showing you the code of connecting to this object from Visual Basic.

To connect to the OLE server

```
Dim PBObject as object
PBObject = CreateObject("count_emp.object")
if PBObject is nothing then
        REM handle the error
else
        REM call methods as required
end if

To connect to the database.

if PBObject.of_connect() <> 0 then
        REM couldn't connect to the database
        REM handle error and disable buttons
else
```

```
        REM connection to DB successful
        REM set options and enable button
   end if
```

The methods are the same for accessing any of the other functions, so I won't be redundant and repeat them. The important thing to notice is that you can treat the methods and properties of the non-visual object just like you would in PowerBuilder.

12.5 Summary

OLE automation servers are very valuable for allowing you to generate and maintain one set of business processes that are shared between different development tools. It also provides a standardized (albeit Microsoft's standards) method for storing and referencing business objects. If Microsoft has their way and the world's distributed computing architectures all become based upon OLE Automation, then you will definitely find yourself building more and more of these types of objects.

CHAPTER 13

PowerScript Painter and PowerBuilder 6.0 PowerScript Enhancements

I make the assumption in this book that you are already familiar with writing PowerScript and the basic functionality of the PowerScript Painter. The goal of this chapter is to familiarize you with some of the more advanced customization and productivity tools available to you in this painter, beyond the basic code and compile.

We also address the new enhancements that are available in PowerBuilder 6.0, and in case you are upgrading from PowerBuilder 4.0, we also review what was new in PowerBuilder 5.0.

13.1 Leveraging the PowerScript Painter

For years PowerBuilder developers coveted the color coded Visual Basic and Delphi script editors. In the past two versions of PowerBuilder, Powersoft has cured this "editor envy" by implementing an enhanced script painter that has all the vivid colors of the rainbow. You can select custom colors to represent data types, functions, flow of control statements, comments, and literals.

Along with custom colors you also now have the ability to have the script painter auto indent, perform multiple levels of Undo, change fonts, and customize which drop down options you would like to have appear at the top of the painter. (See Figure 13-1.)

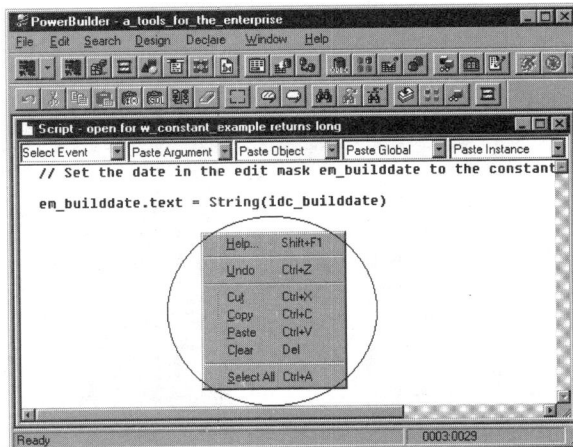

Figure 13-1. *Advanced features of the script painter include clicking with the right mouse button to access to a menu of functions for undoing, using the clipboard or accessing help. To alter the properties of the script painter you must select the* ***Options...*** *menu item from the design menu.*

To access the advanced features of the script painter, PowerBuilder uses the right mouse button access in the script painter workspace. This will pop up a menu with options including undo, clipboard function, and access to help information (Figure 13-2).

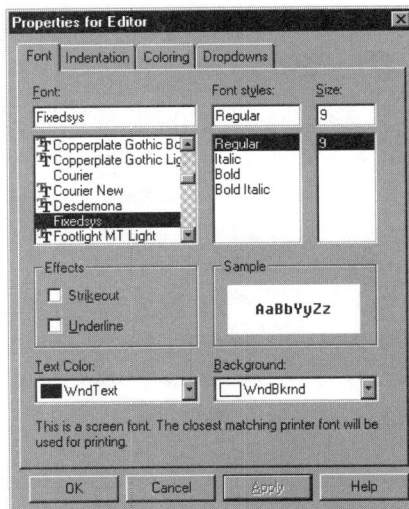

Figure 13-2. *The Properties page allows you to customize the script. The Font tab allows you to alter the font that the script is displayed in.*

The Font tab of the properties page allows you to adjust the font that the script in the editor displays in. This can be useful if you have good eyes and want to make the script smaller so you can see more, or perhaps the reverse, your eyes are poor (or your screen is small) and you want to make the font larger and easier to read.

Another advantage to changing the font is that it also affects your printer. In version 4.0, all print outs of your code came out in that daisy wheel reminiscent Fixedsys font. If you change the font or font size, you may be able to print more text on your printer (again trading off size for readability). (See Figure 13-3.)

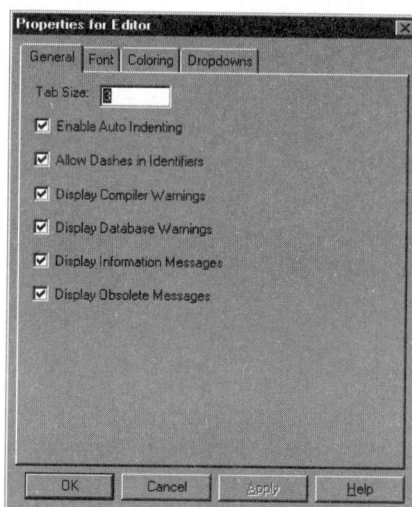

Figure 13-3. The General tab allows you to adjust the size of a tab indentation and if you want the system to automatically manage your indents for flow of control statements.

The General tab is where you will adjust the size of a tab indentation and can turn auto indenting on or off. If auto indent is set to on, when you enter a flow of control statement, PowerBuilder will automatically indent the next line one tab stop. Subsequent to that, if you enter a reserved word from the flow of control statement, for example, "ELSE," then it will automatically remove the indent for that line and keep all the statements blocked appropriately.

This seems like a nice idea, but I am not sold on it yet. Having developed PowerBuilder code for many years, it has become habitual for me to automatically insert tab stops and do indenting. The auto indenting initially slowed me down as I had to continuously remove the extra tabs that I normally inserted by habit, however, now that some time has gone by since this feature was introduced, I now have new habits and am an avid user of the AutoIndenter. If you are not a habitual indenter now, then this feature will probably be good for you, but if you are like me, it may take you a little while to adjust. (See Figure 13-4.)

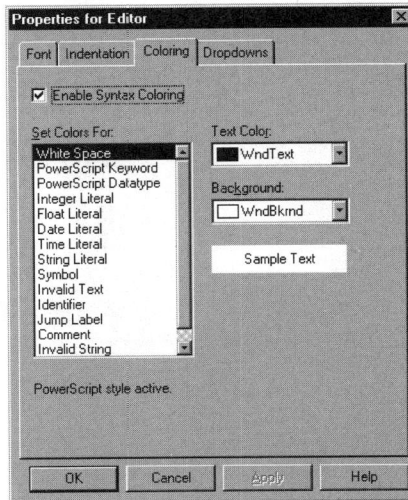

Figure 13-4. *The coloring tab is where you can customize the colors that PowerBuilder uses to represent the different types of text in the script editor.*

This tab will also allow you to control other aspects of the script painter including:

- Do you want to allow dashes in your identifier names? I strongly discourage this practice.

- Do you want to display compiler and database warnings? This is generally a good idea. It helps you to ensure that your code is correctly written.

- Do you want to display information messages? These are messages that aren't necessarily errors but the system is just letting you know something that may be useful. I would recommend leaving these on.

- Do you want to display "obsolete" messages? These messages will appear when you use a function that is considered obsolete in version 6.0. This isn't a bad idea for those of us who have been working with PowerBuilder 5.0 and earlier versions. It will help to correct our habitual usage of functions which may not be relevant now, like "SetActionCode."

One nice thing about the color coding is that it is user customizable. If you really don't like one, or any of the colors that are provided by default, you simply select the type of object that you want to change the color on and select your preferred color choice.

If you want to really make something stand out, you can change not only the color of the font, but the color of the background also. For items like Invalid Text or Invalid String, having the color invert would really make those incomplete or syntactically incorrect strings stand out. In version 6.0, invalid text show up immediately as it is being typed in (such as when you have an open quotation for a string, but haven't yet entered the close quotation). (See Figure 13-5.)

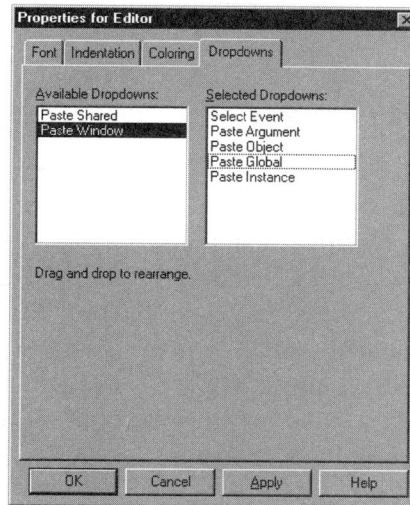

Figure 13-5. *The Dropdowns tab allows you to alter the script editor by selecting which of the available drop down lists you would like to display at the top of the editor.*

As a final method of customization, the Dropdowns tab on the properties page allows you to select which drop down lists you would like to display at the top of the editor. You are given several to choose from. The available set will change in each instance of the painter as appropriate. For example, the Window painter allows you to display any combination of Select Event, Paste Argument, Paste Instance, Paste Global, Paste Window, Paste Shared, and Paste Argument.

The version 6.0 script painter has one other advanced function worth mentioning. It supports drag and drop for cutting and pasting blocks of code. You can select a block of code, then drag it to a new location within your script using the mouse. The initially selected block will be deleted and inserted into the new cursor location.

13.2 PowerScript 6.0 Code Enhancements

There are fewer new general PowerScript enhancements in this latest release from Powersoft. General enhancements are those which cross multiple object classes as opposed to new objects which have new methods (such as in distributed PowerBuilder). These types of PowerScript enhancements are discussed in their relevant sections within this book.

13.2.1 Control Property Arrays

Windows and tab controls have an instance level array called the *control array*. These arrays contain pointers to all the controls that are on the object. In previous versions of PowerBuilder, if you added controls to your window or tab page dynamically at runtime, these new controls were not inserted into the control array. In version 6.0 the control array will be updated automatically when you call these functions: OpenTab( ), OpenUserObject( ), OpenTabWithParm(), OpenUserObjectWithParm( ), CloseTab( ), CloseUserObject( ), or MoveTab( ).

This means that you can now loop through the control array when wanting to perform a general action against a group of controls. For example, you can now use the control array if you want to loop through and find all the DataWindow controls and execute the Update() method against them.

> **Migration Note:** Many class libraries and enterprise level applications used their own custom control arrays to provide this type of functionality. This should not be a serious migration issue as the old arrays will continue to work, however, you can free up memory and resources if you can modify your routines to use the control array instead. This may improve your application performance.

13.2.2 AncestorReturnValue

A new local variable is declared in any script which is an extension of an ancestor script or which uses the CALL reserved word to execute an overriden ancestor script. This new variable is called `AncestorReturnValue` and it contains the return value from the ancestor script.

The intention behind this enhancement is to allow you to obtain the return value of the ancestor script without have to go through the onerous process of having to override the ancestor, then call it, pass in the variables, and trap the return code.

Migration Note: There are no migration concerns with this new variable UNLESS you already have a variable called `AncestorReturnCode` in which case the migration will likely produce an error as it tries to regenerate the script in PB 6.0. If you have followed standard naming conventions, then you shouldn't have any variables with this name.

13.3 PowerScript 5.0 Code Enhancements

In version 5.0 Powersoft made quite a few changes and enhancements to PowerScript. If you haven't yet converted to 5.0, or have, but are not familiar with the new functionality, I am including descriptions of that functionality here. You can skip this section of you already understand the 5.0 enhancements.

13.3.1 Keywords

There have been a number of changes to the use of keywords in PowerBuilder 5.0

13.3.1.1 CONSTANT

This keyword is used to modify a variable declaration so that it will be turned into a constant value at compile time. For variable values that do not change, this has the effect of increasing application performance. This can be used with variables of any scope.

The following is an example of how this would be used. You can enter the keyword CONSTANT before a variable declaration. The compiler will then go through the script and anywhere that it finds that variable it will replace it with a constant value.

```
CONSTANT lic_daysinweek = 7

w_demo.text = ii_totaldays/lic_daysinweek
```

The second expression would evaluate the variable total days (an instance variable) and divide it by the constant value of 7.

Figure13-6 shows an instance constant declaration for the build date of the object. As this is determined at compile time, this date will always show the date the object was last compiled or regenerated. This example is available in the demonstration application on the companion CD.

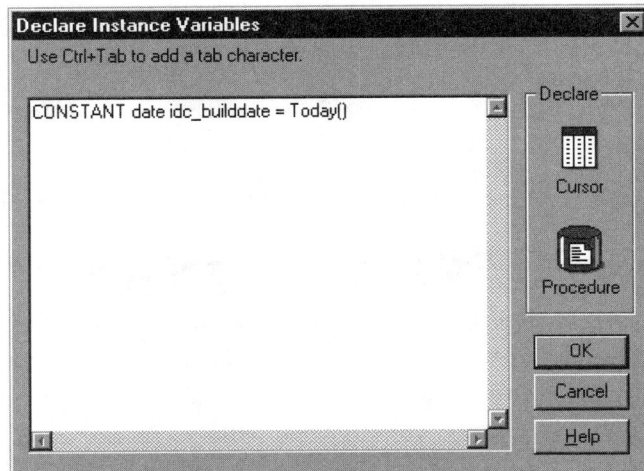

Figure 13-6. Declaring an instance level constant.

13.3.1.2 "::" For Global Variable Access

This topic relates to an issue you should hopefully never encounter except in very exceptional circumstances. In the event that you have a variable (of any scope) with the same name as a global variable, the keyword :: (double colon) when placed in front of the variable will tell the script to access the global variable instead of accessing the local, shared or instance variable. The reason I say that you should never encounter this is that if you follow proper naming conventions for your variables, you would never have two variables of different scopes with the same name!

In the event you do encounter the above problem, when you try to exit your script, the compiler will notify you that you have a conflict between the name of a global variable and your local, shared or instance variable. This is an informational message and not an error, so you can ignore it and proceed if you choose.

13.3.2 Variable Declaration

In PowerBuilder 5.0, you can use functions to determine the initial value of a variable during declaration. For example, you could declare a local variable containing the RGB value for green like this:

```
LONG ll_green = RGB(0,255,0)
```

This would have given you a syntax error in PowerBuilder 4.0.

13.3.3 Read Only Function Arguments

When you created arguments for user defined functions in PowerBuilder, you have always had the option to select if you wanted to pass the arguments by value or by reference. Now you can also choose to pass your arguments in a "read only" format. This format passes the argument by reference, but does not allow the function to modify the passed argument in any way. (See Figure 13-7.)

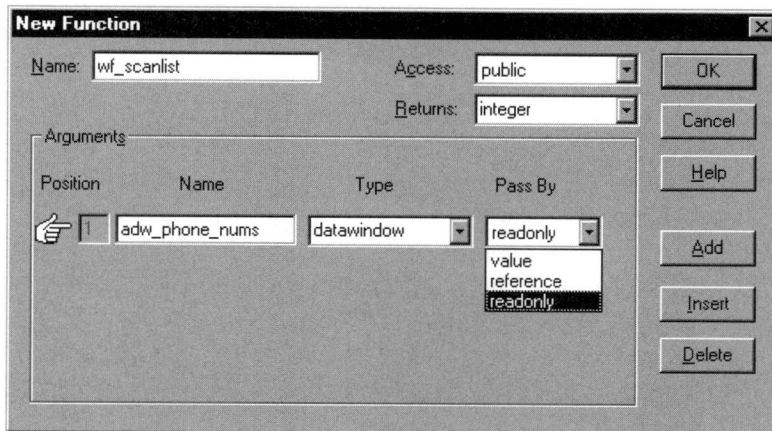

Figure 13-7. We now have the ability to pass user defined function arguments in a "read only" fashion. This means that the argument is passed by reference but the function cannot alter the argument in any way.

13.3.4 GetParent Function

To determine the parent of an object, we have traditionally used the keyword PARENT. This keyword limited us to only see one level up our hierarchy. I have been asked by students innumerable times, how can I do a PARENT.PARENT to get at the parent of the current parent. Until now, this was extremely difficult. With the GetParent() function, we now have this ability. This value in this function becomes particularly relevant with controls that will be placed upon a tab page where the tab page is the parent to the control, the tab object is the parent to the tab page, and the window is parent to them all.

The following script is on the **Show Parents Parent** command button from the sample application w_getparent_example window:

```
PowerObject lpo_parent

// Get the parent of the current object
lpo_parent = THIS.GetParent()

// Show the class name of the parent of the parent of this object
MessageBox("Parent",classname(lpo_parent.GetParent()))
```

The companion CD contains an example of using the GetParent() function in the way described above. Examine the window w_getparent_example and look at the scripts behind the command buttons to see a live example of how the GetParent() works.

13.3.5 Registry Functions

Instead of using initialization files (.INI files) to store startup and other details in a DOS file, Windows 95 and NT use something called the system registry. If you use one of these platforms, you will be familiar with this. The registry contains an entry for each piece of software registered with the operating system (usually they are registered upon installation).

This registry is arranged as a treed hierarchy of keys. A key represents a single branch in the tree. Each key can have subkeys, and each of those can have further subkeys, and so on. There are four root keys in the registry; HKEY_CLASSES_ROOT, HKEY_LOCAL_MACHINE, HKEY_USERS, and HKEY_CURRENT_USER.

Developer's Note: If you are going to use the registry functions in a Windows 3.1 environment, they will work, because there is a registry in Windows 3.1. The registry, however, only has one root key, HKEY_CLASS-ES_ROOT and each key can only have a single value name which is actually unnamed. This is not usually used in Windows 3.1 deployed PowerBuilder applications.

Keys operate very much like the old DOS directory structure. Each subdirectory or in our case, subkey, is separated from its parent by using a backslash ("\").

If you are going to roll out your application in either Windows 95 or NT, you can use this registry as a repository for information very similar to the .INI file. The functions that we use to access the registry include RegistryValues(), RegistryGet(), RegistrySet(), RegistryKeys(), and RegistryDelete().

Developer's` Tip: All the registry functions return a value of 1 if the function was successful and a -1 if the function failed.

13.3.5.1 RegistryValues()

The RegistryValues() function will allow you to query the registry and find out the names of all the value fields within a particular key. The syntax for this function is:

```
RegistryValues ( key, valuename[ ] )
```

where

key contains the name of the key for which you want to get the names of all the value fields. This is a string variable.

valuename[ ] is an array of strings that will contain an entry for each value field within the key. If this is a variable size array, then calling the UpperBound() function will tell you how many values are contained within the key. If this is a fixed array, you must ensure that it is large enough to contain all the values.

With the information from this function, you can use the other registry functions to extract the actual value for a specific registry value name. The following example allows us to extract all the registry value names for the Microsoft Schedule application:

```
string ls_valuename[]

RegistryValues(&
"HKEY_LOCAL_MACHINE\SOFTWARE\Microsoft\Schedule+\Application",&
 ls_valuename)
```

13.3.5.2 RegistryGet()

Once you have the list of value names (which you may have gotten using the RegistryValues() function) you can obtain the specific value for a value name using the RegistryGet() function. The syntax for this function is:

```
RegistryGet ( key, valuename, value )
```

where

> **key** contains the name of the key for which you want to get the value for the value name specified.

> **valuename** contains the name of the value name in the registry you want the value for. If you specify an empty string, it will return the value for the "default" or "unnamed" value. A single unnamed value exists for each key in the registry. A registry does exist for Windows 3.1, but it only supports unnamed values and is limited in its functionality.

> **value** a reference variable of type string which will contain the value for the value name specified if the function is successful.

This example will get the "MailPath" value for the Microsoft Schedule+ application and store it in a string variable:

```
string ls_mailpath

RegistryGet(  &
 "HKEY_LOCAL_MACHINE\SOFTWARE\Microsoft\Schedule+\Application",&
 "MailPath", ls_mailpath)
```

13.3.5.3   RegistrySet()

The RegistrySet() function works exactly the same as the RegistryGet() function but in reverse. It allows you to set the value for a specific value name in a specific field. The syntax is identical except for the last parameter which will contain either a literal or variable with the value that you want to set for the value name. For example, to set the mail path for Microsoft Schedule+ we would code:

```
string ls_mailpath
ls_mailpath = "C:\Notes\mailbox"

RegistrySet( &
 "HKEY_LOCAL_MACHINE\SOFTWARE\Microsoft\Schedule+\Application",&
 "MailPath", ls_mailpath)
```

13.3.5.4 RegistryKeys()

This function will obtain a list of the subkeys for a specified key. The syntax for this function is:

```
RegistryKey ( key , subkey[ ])
```

where

> **key** contains the name of the key for which you want to get the list of subkeys. This is a string variable.

> **subkey[ ]** is an array of strings that will contain an entry for each subkey within the key. If this is a variable size array, then calling the UpperBound() function will tell you how many subkeys are contained within the key. If this is a fixed array, you must ensure that it is large enough to contain all the keys.

The following example would return a list of all the subkeys in the key value Microsoft:

```
string ls_subkey[]

RegistryValues("HKEY_LOCAL_MACHINE\SOFTWARE\Microsoft", ls_subkey)
```

13.3.5.5 RegistryDelete()

The RegistryDelete() function allows you to remove a value name or an entire key from the registry. The syntax for this function is:

```
RegistryDelete( key , valuename )
```

where

> **key** contains the name of the key for which you want to delete a value name or delete the entire key. This is a string variable.

> **valuename** contains the name of the value that you want to remove from this key. If you wish to remove the entire key, specify an empty string ("") for this argument.

For example, to remove all reference to Microsoft Schedule+ from our registry we would code:

```
RegistryDelete ("HKEY_LOCAL_MACHINE\SOFTWARE\Microsoft\Schdule+", "")
```

CHAPTER 14

Advanced Menus

*T*he interface that you will work with to build your menus in PowerBuilder uses a tab folder metaphor for navigation and has since version 5.0 was released. If you are migrating from version 4.0 this will be a significant change. All the same properties that you are accustomed to in version 4.0 of PowerBuilder are still here, just moved around a little.

There are several advanced menu concepts that will be addressed in this chapter. As in other parts of this book, I assume that you already know the basic menu components and how to navigate through the menu painter.

14.1 Drop Down Toolbars

One user interface tool that is often overlooked by PowerBuilder developers (possibly because it was only released in recent versions of PowerBuilder) is the Drop Down Toolbar. You've seen them before; PowerBuilder uses these in the development environment. For example, the Drop Down Toolbar is the icon that you can see in the PowerBuilder development environment for the controls in the Window painter, or the different painters in the PowerBar. It appears as a single icon with a drop down arrow next to it. When you select it, a listbox full of icons drops down. You can then select the icon you want. The last selected icon is the one that will appear beside the drop down arrow in the toolbar.

You can use this kind of functionality in your application toolbars. The sample application contains a drop down toolbar for the Edit menu item. Let's walk through how it was constructed. (See Figure 14-1.)

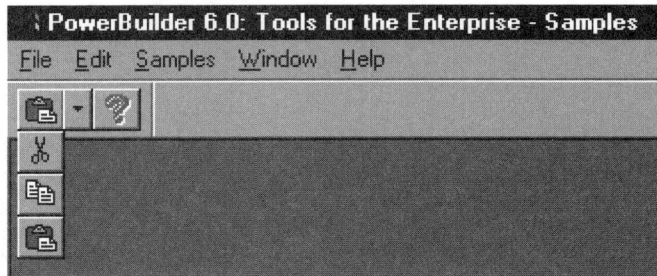

Figure 14-1. *The sample application contains a Drop Down Toolbar for the Edit menu bar option.*

Step 1 Build your menu. Build your menu as you normally would, with all menu items, cascades, and toolbar icons.

Step 2 Define the MenuCascade. Every menu item has a new property called MenuCascade. When this property is set, all menu items with toolbar icons contained within that item will appear as a drop down toolbar. This property is set on the Toolbar tab of the menu painter for the parent menu item (in this case, the Edit item). (See Figure 14-2.)

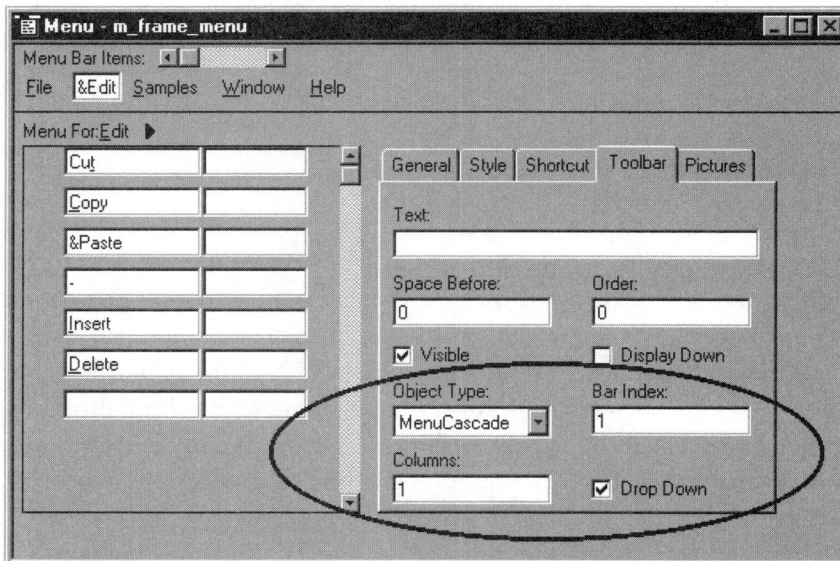

Figure 14-2. *The menu painter now has a series of properties that allow us to define drop down toolbars. These properties are found on the Toolbar tab.*

Set the Object Type drop down list box to MenuCascade. The Drop Down checkbox must also be checked (which it is by default). If you uncheck this listbox, the toolbar items will appear in their normal format.

Step 3 Define the number of columns. We can select how many columns we want our pictures to display in when the drop down area appears. This is set in the Columns field on the Toolbar tab. The default value is 1 column.

Step 4 Save and preview. You can run the window containing this menu to examine its functionality. Note that any menu items within the drop down toolbar which are defined as MenuCascade will not be contained within the drop down toolbar of the parent.

14.2 Creating Multiple Docking Toolbars

PowerBuilder also allows us to create multiple toolbars in our applications and our development environment. You do not define multiple menus for the window, but rather split the toolbar itself into multiple sections.

To define multiple toolbars for your application is very easy. On the Toolbar tab of a menu item there is a field called Bar Index. In this field you can specify a toolbar number that you wish this particular toolbar item to appear on. PowerBuilder will automatically instantiate as many toolbars as you specify. You can have up to eight toolbars on a sheet and four on an MDI frame. Using this technique effectively allows you to split a single toolbar into many toolbars. This would allow you to show and hide different toolbars as you wish to reveal different sets of functionality.

14.3 Menu Inheritance

Menus are part of the family of inheritable objects in PowerBuilder, although as an advanced developer you should be aware that menu inheritance contains significant performance and development considerations.

Although Powersoft has been working hard to reduce the impact of menu inheritance, inheritance for this object is still very inefficient and it is generally recommend to never have more than 2 levels of inheritance in a menu object inheritance tree.

Also, if you are using menu inheritance and need to change and ancestor menu, after doing so you should immediately regenerate all the descendant menus. Failing to do so can cause nasty corruption problems in your .PBLs which are unrecoverable. You will lose significant amounts of work and will probably have to restore your files from a previously backed up uncorrupted copy.

Now having scared the heck out of you, let me continue by saying that it is acceptable to use menu inheritance as long as you are careful. In my projects I generally have one ancestor frame menu which has the majority of the functionality in it. Then from it I create a descendant sheet menu. Whenever a need another menu I open the descendant sheet menu, do a Save As... to save it with a new name, and then modify it as appropriate.

With descendant menus, menu items can be appended to the end of an existing menu bar, drop down or cascading set of ancestor menu items. Descendant menu items cannot be placed in between ancestor menu items and ancestor menu items cannot be removed (they can, however, be hidden).

If you want your descendant menu items to appear in the middle of a set of ancestor menu items, this can be accomplished. For example, we might want to put the menu item **Print** in the middle of the **File** drop down menu set which currently contains **Open** and **Exit**. To do this we set the Shift Over/Down attribute for the ancestor menu items that we want to move to the right (in the case of the menu bar) or down (in the case of drop down or cascading menu items). In the descendant menu any items that you append, even though they appear at the bottom of the list of menu items in the designer, they will be inserted between any ancestor items which are set to Slide Over/Down and those that are not. You can verify that your descendant items are appearing in the correct position using the Preview option in the menu painter.

Performance Tip: Changing the visibility of menu items causes significant performance degradation in PowerBuilder applications. This is because every time a menu item is hidden (or made visible), the original menu is destroyed and then recreated and redrawn. Therefore, it is generally not recommended to be changing the visible property of a menu at runtime.

14.4 Menus and MDI Frames

Menus behave a little differently within MDI frames. These are some tips and reminders about some of the differences.

If a sheet within an MDI frame does not have a menu, then PowerBuilder will display the frame menu in your application MDI frame. This is different from earlier versions of PowerBuilder (3.0 and earlier) where the sheet would just use whatever menu was used from the sheet before it (the current method is far more logical).

A good rule of thumb is that if one of your sheets is going to have a menu, then they should all have menus. This will help to prevent user confusion and is generally considered good GUI design.

14.5 Saving User Runtime Toolbar Settings

One common feature of most GUI applications today is that they remember the configuration used by the last user and restore it the next time the same user starts a session. You can have the same functionality in your application through the use of a set of functions specifically for toolbar management.

14.5.1 GetToolbar() and SetToolbar()

The GetToolbar() function allows you to query a window and get information back about its toolbar such as its alignment, visibility and title. The syntax for the function is as follows:

```
window.GetToolbar( index, visible {,alignment {, title}})
```

where

window is the name of the window (must be an MDI Frame or sheet) which you want the toolbar information from.

index is an integer for which toolbar (there can be multiple) for which you want information.

visible is a boolean reference variable which will contain TRUE if the toolbar is visible and FALSE if it is not.

alignment is a reference variable of the enumerated datatype ToolBarAlignment which will indicate what the current alignment of the toolbar is.

title is a string reference variable which contains the title for the toolbar that is displayed if the toolbar alignment is *Floating!*

The function will return a positive 1 if the function succeeds and a -1 if it fails.

The SetToolbar() function is the reverse of GetToolbar() in that it allows you to set the visibility, alignment, and title of a toolbar. The attributes for SetToolbar() are identical to those for GetToolbar() except that the reference variables must all now contain real values.

14.5.2 GetToolbarPos() and SetToolbarPos()

The GetToolbarPos() function allows you to query a window and find out the position of a toolbar. There are two different versions of the function depending on whether the toolbar in question is docked or floating.

If the toolbar is docked, the syntax for the function is as follows:

```
window.GetToolbarPos( index, row, offset)
```

where

window is the name of the window (must be an MDI Frame or sheet) which you want the toolbar position from.

index is an integer for which toolbar (there can be multiple) for which you want the information.

row is an integer reference variable which will contain the row number that the toolbar is in. Row numbers are determined from top to bottom and from left to right (depending upon alignment).

offset is an integer reference variable which will contain the numeric offset value for the toolbar (how far from the docking edge it is).

The function will return a positive 1 if the function succeeds and a -1 if it fails.

The SetToolbarPos() function is the reverse of GetToolbarPos() in that is allows you to set the row and offset for a specific toolbar. The syntax for SetToolbarPos() is as follows:

```
window.SetToolbarPos( index, row, offset, insert)
```

where all the arguments are the same as GetToolbarPos (except that they are real values, not reference variables) with the exception of the new fourth argument which is:

insert is a boolean variable which indicates if you want any existing toolbars that overlap with the position of this toolbar to be bumped over. If FALSE, and you are inserting a toolbar with an offset of 1, but a toolbar with an offset of 1 already exists, the toolbar that you are placing will be placed at the end of the row. If TRUE and the same situation happens, the toolbar you are placing will be placed at position 1 which all other toolbars on the same row will have their offset increased by 1.

If the toolbar is floating, then there is a slightly different version of the GetToolbarPos() and SetToolbarPos() functions. The syntax for this version is:

```
window.SetToolbarPos( index, xcoor, ycoor, width, height)
```

where

window is the name of the window (must be an MDI Frame or sheet) which you want the toolbar position from.

index is an integer for which toolbar (there can be multiple) for which you want the information.

xcoor is an integer reference variable which will contain the X coordinate of the floating toolbar (if the toolbar is docked when you call this function, it will return the last known floating coordinate for this toolbar).

ycoor is an integer reference variable which will contain the Y coordinate of the floating toolbar (if the toolbar is docked when you call this function, it will return the last known floating coordinate for this toolbar).

width is an integer reference variable which will contain the current or last known width of the floating toolbar.

height is an integer reference variable which will contain the current or last known height of the floating toolbar.

Like the previous functions, this will return a positive 1 if the function call is successful and a -1 if the toolbar doesn't exist or the call fails. The SetToolbarPos() function for floating toolbars has the same argument list as the GetToolbarPos() function, but substituting real values for the reference variables.

14.5.3 A Code Example of Saving Toolbar Settings

Using the above functions it is fairly easy to write a script that will save the current toolbar settings in an INI file, into the database or maybe the system registry.

The following example uses an INI file to store the details about the location of the toolbar. There are two events that we use to do this, the window Close event and the window Open event.

The Window Close Event (saves toolbar details)

```
Integer li_Row, li_Offset, li_X, li_Y, li_Width, li_Height, li_BarNum
Boolean lbl_Visible
ToolbarAlignment ltba_Current
String ls_Title, ls_Alignment, ls_WindowName, ls_Visible

// We will need to loop through and find all the valid toolbars.
// There are nine possible toolbars so we will need to loop nine times.
FOR li_BarNum = 1 to 9

    IF THIS.GetToolbar(li_BarNum, lbl_Visible, ltba_Current,  ls_Title) = 1
THEN

        // This is a valid toolbar, save the data to the INI file.

        // First get the window name.  This will be the INI file section.
        ls_WindowName = THIS.ClassName()

        // Next, convert the boolean to a string value
        IF lbl_Visible THEN ls_Visible = "TRUE" ELSE ls_Visible = FALSE

        // Set this value to the INI file
        SetProfileString( gstr_app.s_ClientINI, ls_WindowName,&
        "Visible"+String(li_BarNum), ls_Visible)

        // Now convert the alignment enumerated data type to a string
        CHOOSE CASE ltab_Current
            CASE AlignAtLeft!
                ls_Alignment = "Left"
            CASE AlignAtRight!
                ls_Alignment = "Rignt"
            CASE AlignAtTop!
                ls_Alignment = "Top"
            CASE AlignAtBottom!
                ls_Alignment = "Bottom"
            CASE Floating!
                ls_Alignment = "Floating"
        END CHOOSE

        // Set this value to the INI file
        SetProfileString( gstr_app.s_ClientINI, ls_WindowName,&
        "Align"+String(li_BarNum), ls_Alignment)

        // Set the title value to the INI file
        SetProfileString( gstr_app.s_ClientINI, ls_WindowName,&
        "Title"+String(li_BarNum), ls_Title)

        // Get the Row and Offset details
        THIS.GetToolbarPos( li_BarNum, li_Row, li_Offset)
```

```
            // Set these values in the INI file
            SetProfileString( gstr_app.s_ClientINI, ls_WindowName,&
            "Row"+String(li_BarNum),String(li_Row))
            SetProfileString( gstr_app.s_ClientINI, ls_WindowName,&
            "Offset"+String(li_BarNum),String(li_Offset))

            // Get the coordinates and size details
            THIS.GetToolbarPos( li_BarNum, li_X, li_Y, li_Width, li_Height)

            // Set these values in the INI file
            SetProfileString( gstr_app.s_ClientINI, ls_WindowName,&
            "X"+String(li_BarNum),String(li_X))
            SetProfileString( gstr_app.s_ClientINI, ls_WindowName,&
            "Y"+String(li_BarNum),String(li_Y))
            SetProfileString( gstr_app.s_ClientINI, ls_WindowName,&
            "Width"+String(li_BarNum),String(li_Width))
            SetProfileString( gstr_app.s_ClientINI, ls_WindowName,&
            "Height"+String(li_BarNum),String(li_Height))

        ELSE
            // There is no toolbar for this bar number, so blank out the
            // section in the INI file.
            SetProfileString( gstr_app.s_ClientINI, ls_WindowName,&
            "Visible"+String(li_BarNum), "unused")
        END IF
NEXT
```

The Window Open Event (loads toolbar details)

```
Integer li_Row, li_Offset, li_X, li_Y, li_Width, li_Height, li_BarNum
Boolean lbl_Visible
ToolbarAlignment ltba_Current
String ls_Title, ls_Alignment, ls_WindowName, ls_Visible

// We will need to loop through and find all the valid toolbars.
// There are nine possible toolbars so we will need to loop nine times.
FOR li_BarNum = 1 to 9
    // First get the window name.  This will be the INI file section.
    ls_WindowName = THIS.ClassName()

    // Check the toolbar's visibility.
    ls_Visible = ProfileString(gstr_app.s_ClientINI, ls_WindowName,&
    "Visible"+String(li_BarNum),"unused")

    // If the visibility is "unused" then we skip this restore, else set the
    //boolean appropriately
    CHOOSE CASE ls_Visible
        CASE "unused"
            CONTINUE
```

```
         CASE "True"
             lbl_Visible = TRUE
         CASE "False"
             lbl_Visible = FALSE
     END CHOOSE

     // Now convert the alignment string to an enumerated data type
     ls_Alignment = ProfileString(gstr_app.s_ClientINI, ls_WindowName,
     "Align"+String(li_BarNum),"")
     CHOOSE CASE ls_Alignment
         CASE "Left"
             ltba_Current = AlignAtLeft!
         CASE "Right"
             ltba_Current = AlignAtRight!
         CASE "Top"
             ltba_Current = AlignAtTop!
          CASE "Bottom"
             ltba_Current = AlignAtBottom!
         CASE "Floating"
             ltba_Current = Floating!
     END CHOOSE

     // Now get the title
     ls_Title = ProfileString(gstr_app.s_ClientINI, ls_WindowName,
 "Title"+String(li_BarNum),"")

     // Now set the toolbar details.
     THIS.SetToolbar( li_BarNum, lbl_Visible, ltba_Current, ls_Title)

     // Get the location details
     li_Row = ProfileInt( gstr_app.s_ClientINI, ls_WindowName,
 "Row"+String(li_BarNum),0)
     li_Offset = ProfileInt( gstr_app.s_ClientINI, ls_WindowName,
 "Offset"+String(li_BarNum),0)
     li_X = ProfileInt( gstr_app.s_ClientINI, ls_WindowName,
 "X"+String(li_BarNum),0)
     li_Y = ProfileInt( gstr_app.s_ClientINI, ls_WindowName,
 "Y"+String(li_BarNum),0)
     li_Height = ProfileInt( gstr_app.s_ClientINI, ls_WindowName,
 "Height"+String(li_BarNum),0)
     li_Width = ProfileInt( gstr_app.s_ClientINI, ls_WindowName,
 "Width"+String(li_BarNum),0)

     // Set the toolbar location details
     THIS.SetToolbarPos( li_BarNum, li_Row, li_Offset, FALSE)
     THIS.SetToolbarPos( li_BarNum, li_X, li_Y, li_Width, li_Height)
 NEXT
```

14.6 Adding "Undo" Functionality To Your Menus

Most GUI applications these days provide a means to "undo" a previous action. There is a fairly straightforward way to add this functionality to your Edit menu. PowerBuilder has two functions that make this simple: **Undo()** and **CanUndo()**.

These two functions can be called against DataWindow controls, edit masks, multi line edits and single line edits. The CanUndo() function returns a boolean value which indicates if the control in question has the ability to undo its last change. If it can, the Undo() function commands it to do so. The following sample code listing shows how you might implement this in an Undo menu item.

Clicked event for m_undo

```
// Declare variables
GraphicObject lgo_InFocus
Datawindow ldw_Current
EditMask lem_Current
MultiLineEdit lmle_Current
SingleLineEdit lsle_Current

// Get the current object in focus
lgo_InFocus = GetFocus()

IF NOT IsNull( lgo_InFocus) THEN
    // Valid object in focus
    CHOOSE CASE lgo_InFocus.TypeOf()
        CASE DataWindow!
            ldw_Current = lgo_InFocus
            IF ldw_Current.CanUndo() THEN ldw_Current.Undo()
        CASE EditMask!
            lem_Current = lgo_InFocus
            IF lem_Current.CanUndo() THEN lem_Current.Undo()
        CASE SingleLineEdit!
            lsle_Current = lgo_InFocus
            IF lsle_Current.CanUndo() THEN lsle_Current.Undo()
        CASE MultiLineEdit!
            lmle_Current = lgo_InFocus
            IF lmle_Current.CanUndo() THEN lmle_Current.Undo()
    END CHOOSE
END IF
```

Developer's Note: If you are deploying your application in a Windows 95 environment, this environment already has built into it a convenient pop up edit menu, including Undo, for all editable controls.

14.7 In-Place OLE and Menus

Some advanced developers have chosen to implement in-place OLE activation in their PowerBuilder applications. In this situation, the OLE application becomes part of the deployed PowerBuilder application. For example, if you use an OLE object on a window which is a spreadsheet of data and then use MS-Excel™ to edit it in place, then Excel appears inside your PowerBuilder application, and the menu for your PowerBuilder application gets replaced with the Excel menu. This allows you to access all the Excel functionality while editing the spreadsheet OLE object.

As an advanced developer, you have the option of merging menu items from your PowerBuilder application into the OLE server menu. This is accomplished through the **MergeOption** attribute in the Menu painter. The drop down list of valid options is shown in Table 14-1 with an explanation of how that option affects the menu.

Table 14-1 Drop Down List of Valid Options.

Merge Option	Explanation
Exlcude (default)	This is the default setting for all PowerBuilder menu options. This menu item will be excluded from the OLE server's menu.
Merge	Will add this menu item and any items that cascade from it into the OLE server menu.
File	Will add this menu item will be used in place of the OLE server's File menu item. This is usually your own File menu bar item.
Edit	Will add this menu item will be used in place of the OLE server's Edit menu item. This is usually your own Edit menu bar item.
Window	Will add this menu item will be used in place of the OLE server's Window menu item. This is usually your own Window menu bar item.
Help	Will add this menu item will be used in place of the OLE server's Help menu item. This is usually your own Help menu bar item.

Remember that OLE options are only available on the Windows platforms.

14.8 Summary

In this chapter we have reviewed some advanced techniques that relate to menus including drop down toolbars, docking toolbars, menu inheritance, save toolbar configurations, and using menus with OLE.

It is important to remember that menus are one of the areas of PowerBuilder that is not 100% bullet proof and you should use care when working with advanced techniques such as menu inheritance as to avoid corrupting your source code. And as in any development environment, you should be backing up your source code on a regular basis!

CHAPTER 15

Data Pipelines

*S*ince version 4.0, PowerBuilder has provided developers with a powerful tool for moving data from one location to another. Sometimes this data needs to be moved from one
database to a different database and sometimes it is moved within the same database.
    Many developers have written routines to do this manually, but PowerBuilder devel-
opers can use the Pipeline object to automate much of this process.

15.1 What is a Data Pipeline?

The need to move data is an ever present issue in application development. Whether
you are moving data from a production to a test database or moving historical records
from an active OLTP table to a historical data warehouse the basic requirement is the
same. The PowerBuilder Data Pipeline is an object designed to perform just this task.

    The pipeline can move data between databases of different types (for example,
moving data from a Sybase™ table to an Oracle™ table) and different physical locations
or can be used to simply move data between tables within a single database. Both situations have practical real life application. The pipeline can also be used to synchronize
data between two tables to ensure that both are up to date.

    When creating a data pipeline you must specify the source database, the desti-
nation database, the table (or tables) that you want to move data from and the table to
which you want to move the data. If this destination table does not exist, you can
request that the pipeline create the table for you. In addition you must specify the operation that you want the pipeline to perform, for example, do you want it to drop the

data from the destination table and insert new records? Or perhaps append new records to the data that already exists in the destination table? You will also specify how often the pipeline will commit the new records that it is creating, how many errors you will tolerate before you want the process to abort and if you want to copy any of the table's extended attributes.

15.2 Building a Pipeline

Data Pipelines are created using the Pipeline Painter. The icon to launch the Pipeline Painter is shown in Figure 15-1.

Figure 15-1. The icon to launch the Data Pipeline Painter.

When you open the painter you will be given the standard PowerBuilder dialog window for selecting an existing object to open or if you want to create a new one. If you select the New command button you will begin the process of creating a new pipeline.

The first step in creating a new pipeline is to choose your source and destination databases and the data source (QuickSelect, SQLSelect, Query or Stored Procedure, like in the DataWindow painter) where your data will be coming from. This all comes from the New Data Pipeline dialog window that will automatically appear as shown in Figure 15-2.

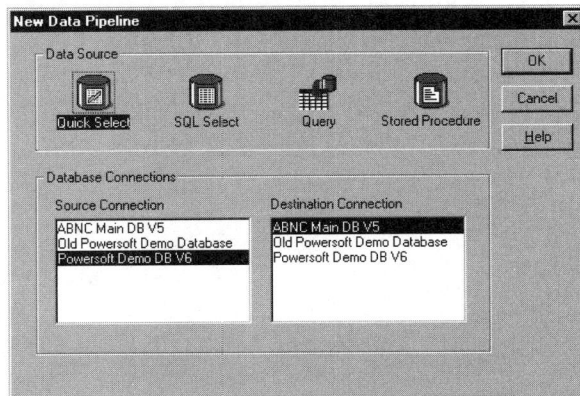

Figure 15-2. The New Data Pipeline dialog window allows you to specify the source and destination databases and the data source.

The bottom half of this window is where you will specify the source and destination databases. All the connection profiles that you have previously defined in your PowerBuilder environment will appear in the lists. Whatever database you last connected to will be used as the default source database.

The top half of the window is where you will select the type of data source that you wish to use. The options available to you are the same as the database data source options in the DataWindow painter; QuickSelect, SQLSelect, Query object, or Stored Procedure. The option you select must provide a result set appropriate for copying to the destination database.

When you press the **OK** command button you will be taken to the appropriate painter to define the SQL statement that will create the result set of data that you want to copy. These work exactly the same as they do in the DataWindow painter. If you are not familiar with any of these, refer to Chapter 19 for an overview of creating DataWindows. As with DataWindow data sources, you can define retrieval arguments for the pipeline to refine the data set that you want to pipe to the destination database.

When you have exited the appropriate designer for the data source you selected you will see the Data Pipeline painter workspace as shown in Figure 15-3.

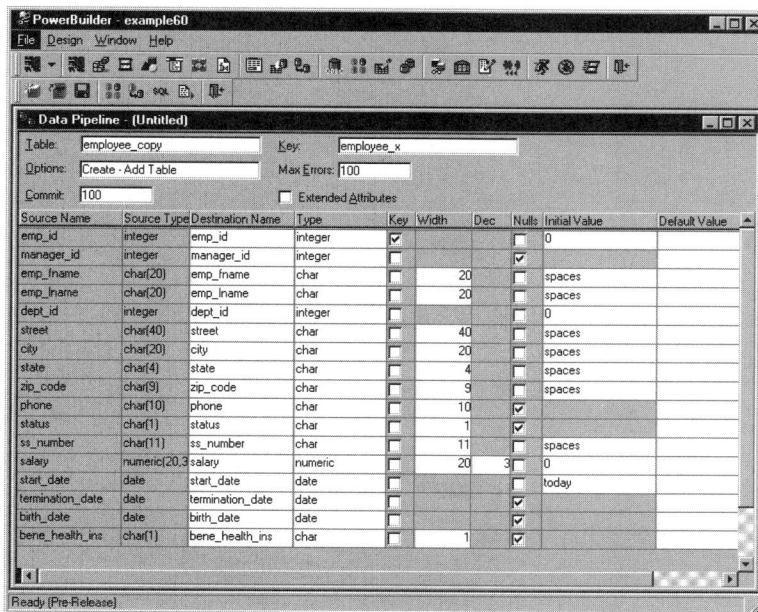

Figure 15-3. The Data Pipeline painter workspace.

This workspace can be divided into two parts. The top part contains the fields that define what the destination for the pipeline is and how the pipeline will execute. The bottom part contains a table listing all the columns in the result set that are being copied and their characteristics.

15.2.1 Source and Destination Tables

If we look at the bottom portion of the pipeline workspace and examine the table we see the name and datatype of the column in the source table. To the right of that we see the name and datatype that this field will have in the destination database. If you desire, you can change theses names and types as appropriate to your destination. The next column indicates if the column is part of the primary key. After that are two columns for specifying the width of the field and number of decimal places (if appropriate). The Nulls column allows you to specify if NULL values are allowed in this column on the destination database. The initial value column specifies what value will be inserted into the destination table if the value in the source table is NULL. The default column specifies if the destination table will have a default associated with it such as a time-stamp, current date, current time, NULL, user id or perhaps an auto-increment value.

The destination table is listed in the single line edit in the top left of the workspace. This is a value that you can edit at any time along with the name for the primary key in this table. The other four fields in the top of the pipeline workspace are all used to set pipeline options.

15.2.2 Options

In the pipeline options you will specify what kind of action you want the pipe to take. The possible options are: Create—Add Table, Replace—Drop/Add Table, Refresh—Delete/Insert Rows, Append—Insert Rows, Update—Update/Insert Rows. These options are listed in the following table along with an explanation of the action they perform. (See Table 15-1.)

Table 15-1 *Pipeline Options.*

Option	Explanation
Create—Add Table	This option will create a new table in the destination database and insert all the data from the pipeline result set into the new table. If a table with the same name already exists, the pipe will fail. This option also allows you to modify the table and key structure of the destination table.

(continued)

Table 15-1 *(continued)*

Option	Explanation
Replace—Drop/ Add Table	This option is the same as Create except that if the table already exists in the destination database it will be dropped and all data in the dropped table will be lost. This option also allows you to modify the table and key structure of the destination table.
Refresh—Delete/ Insert Rows	This option will delete all the rows from the destination table (which must already exist or the pipe will fail) and then inserts all the rows from the result set.
Append—Insert Rows	This option will insert all the rows from the source result set into the destination table (which must already exist or the pipe will fail) adding them to any rows that already exist in the destination table. Be careful about causing duplicate key errors when using this option.
Update—Update/ Insert Rows	This option will generate an update SQL statement for any rows in the source result set that have the same key as an existing row in the destination table (which must already exist or the pipe will fail), thus updating the data in the destination table. If no matching key is found in the destination table, then the source row is inserted into the destination table.

Another option in the workspace that you must set is the Commit setting. This option controls how many rows will be passed to the destination table before a COMMIT is issued. If you specify a commit value of ALL then the data will only be committed after all the rows have been piped to the destination database. You can also specify NONE as the commit option which means that no COMMIT will be issued to the database once the pipeline action is concluded.

The Max Error option is used to specify how many errors that you are willing to tolerate before you want the pipeline to abort the piping action.

The Extended Attributes checkbox is used to indicate if you want the pipeline to copy the extended attributes associated with the source columns to the destination table. If an extended attribute already exists in the destination table, then the source attribute is not piped over.

15.2.3 Handling BLOBs

The pipeline is capable of handling Binary Large OBjects (BLOBs) but they must be handled a little differently (this was introduced in version 5.0 of PowerBuilder). To include a BLOB in the result set, you select the Database BLOB… menu item from the **Design** menu in the pipeline workspace. This will open the BLOB definition dialog window shown in Figure 15-4.

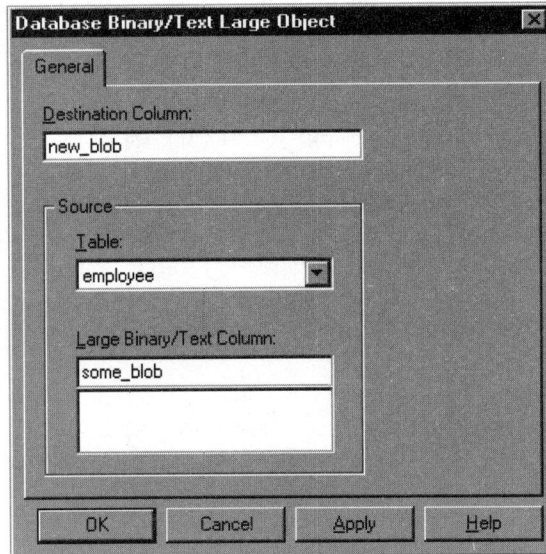

Figure 15-4. BLOBs can be copied in the pipeline but must be handled separately.

You must specify in this window the name of the BLOB column in the destination table, which source table the BLOB is coming from (if there are multiple) and what the BLOB column is. When you have finished this you can press the **OK** command button and the BLOB will now be piped with the rest of the data.

15.3 Executing a Pipeline

Once you have built your pipeline you can then choose to use it interactively, or incorporate it into an application.

To execute the pipeline interactively you simply select the Execute icon from the painterbar or choose the **Execute** menu item from the **Design** menu.

PowerBuilder will then execute the pipe according to your specifications. If you have included retrieval arguments, you will be prompted for those before the source result set is constructed. You can observe the progress of the pipeline activity by watching the MicroHelp bar at the bottom of the screen. This area will show you how many rows have been reach, how many written, how many errors have occurred and how long the process has taken.

If no errors are shown at the end of your pipeline action, then you are finished and you can save and exit the pipeline painter. If errors occurred, you will need to proceed to the error handling step.

15.4 Handling Errors

Errors can occur from any number of sources. Anything that causes an integrity error will show up as an error in the pipeline such as trying to insert a duplicate key. When errors occur the pipeline painter will open a special window for displaying and correcting errors as shown in Figure 15-5.

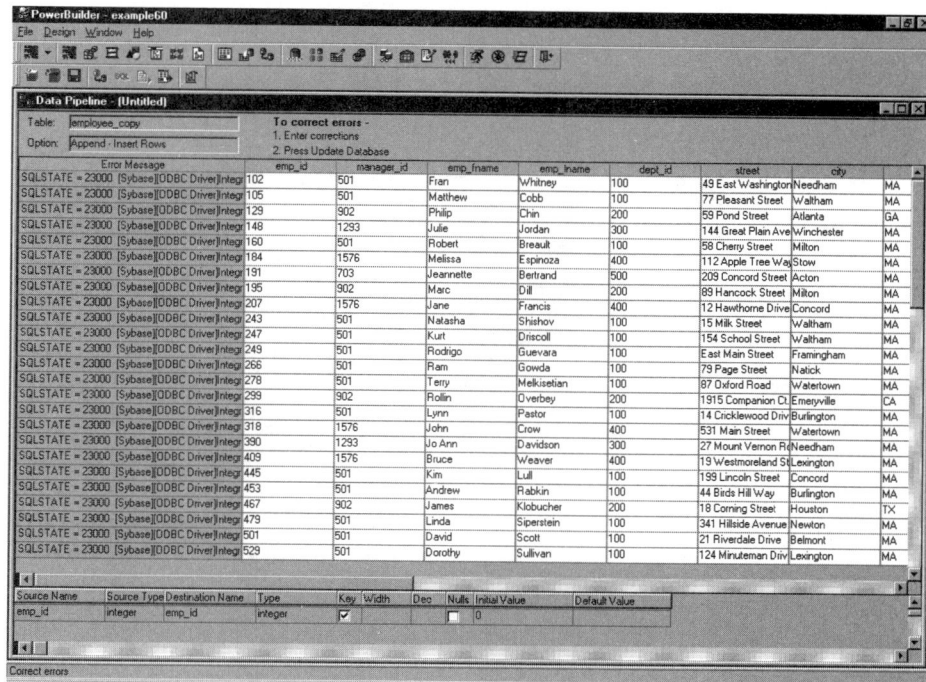

Figure 15-5. The pipeline error correction window.

All the rows that are in error are displayed. You can then manually correct the errors, if desired, and re-pipe them to the destination database by clicking on the Update icon in the painterbar.

15.5 Using Pipelines Within an Application

The second method of using a Data Pipeline is to embed the pipeline directly into a PowerBuilder application.

To best explain this, we will walk through a simple demo of using a pipeline. First, build the pipeline shown in the above figures by using the Demo Database as both your source and your target. Build a SQL data source that uses all the columns in the employee database. Use the Replace option. Save the pipeline with the name p_pipe_demo. Your pipeline workspace should look the same as Figure 15-3 except to have the option of Replace instead of Create.

Now we need to create a standard pipeline user object in order to place our pipeline on a Window. Launch the User Object Painter and select the option to create a new user object. When the New User Object dialog window opens (as shown in Figure 15-6) select a Standard Class object.

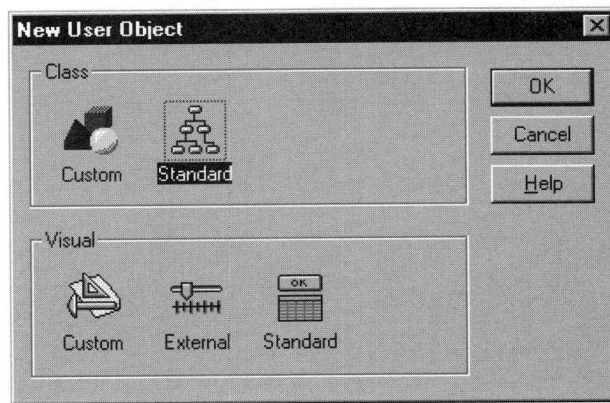

Figure 15-6. We need to create a Standard Class user object to contain our pipeline on the window.

After pressing the **OK** command button you will be shown a second dialog window (Figure 15-7) in which you will select the standard class type that you want to create, in our case a "pipeline."

One technique commonly used amongst advanced pipeline users to relay the progress of your pipeline to the user is to use three static text reference variables to contain the read, written and error information. To do this, declare three instance variables for the pipeline user object as shown in Figure 15-8.

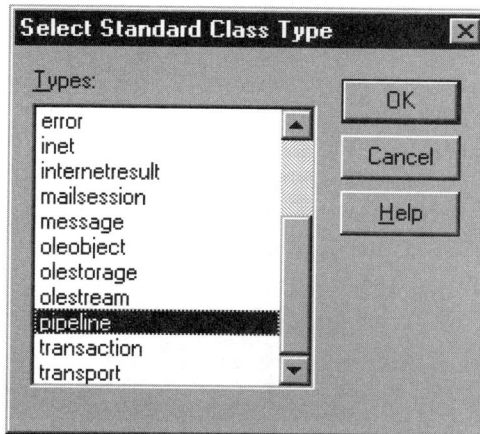

Figure 15-7. *Next we need to select our standard class type of "pipeline" to create.*

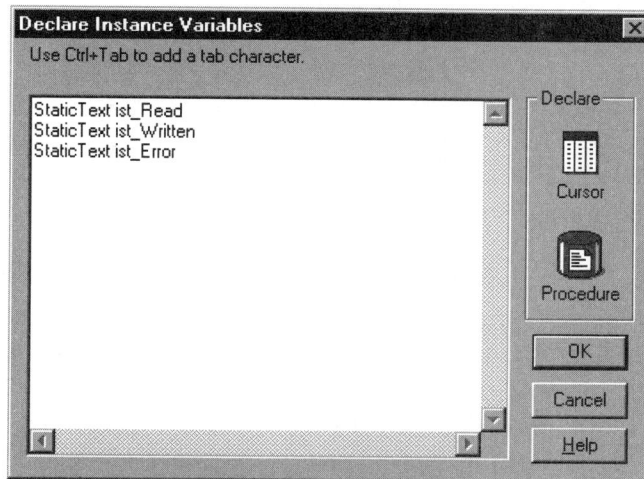

Figure 15-8. *Static Text instance variables used to track the progress of the pipeline.*

We will add code in the PIPEMETER event to update these variables. The PipeMeter event is triggered every time the statistics for the pipe change. There are three arguments which we use to update our instance variables: RowsRead, RowsWritten, and RowsInError. See the following code listing for the PipeMeter event.

PipeMeter event for u_pipe_demo

```
ist_read.text = String(RowsRead)
ist_written.text = String(RowsWritten)
ist_Error.text = String(RowsInError)
```

Now save the user object as u_pipe_demo and close the user object painter.

The next step is to create a new window that we will use as the container for our pipeline action. Create a window similar to the one shown in Figure 15-9 with six static text fields, three command buttons and one DataWindow controls.

Figure 15-9. *Build a window with the components arranged something like this.*

Three of the static text controls will be the labels for the counter boxes, which are the other three static text controls. These last three static text controls should be names *st_read, st_written,* and *st_error* respectively. The three command buttons should be named *cb_start, cb_repair,* and *cb_cancel* and should be labeled as shown in Figure 15-9. The DataWindow control will be used to display any pipeline errors. You can give it a title bar with the title Pipeline Errors and be sure to set the scroll bars to on.

Now declare two instance variables for the window as shown in Figure 15-10. The first instance variable is a transaction object that we will use to define and connect to our destination database. For our example, this will be the same as our source. The second instance variable is our pipeline user object u_pipe_test.

Next a script is needed for the window open event that will set up the source and destination transaction objects and connect them to their respective databases.

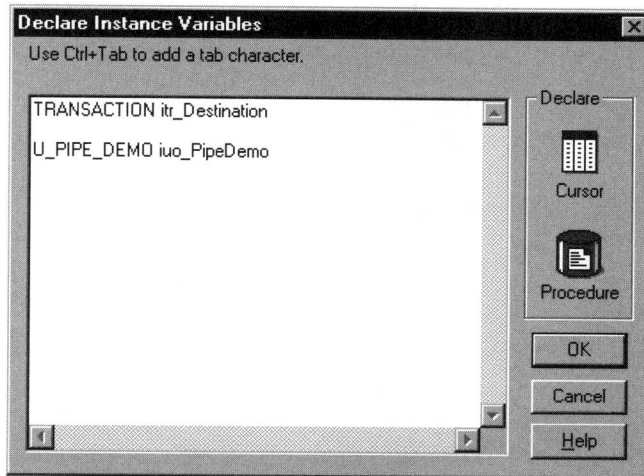

Figure 15-10. *Declare instance variables for the destination transaction object and for the pipeline user object.*

Open event for wm_pipeline_demo

```
// Set up values for source transaction object - SQLCA
SQLCA.DBMS = "ODBC"
SQLCA.DBParm = "Connectstring='DSN=Powersoft Demo DB V6'

CONNECT using SQLCA;

IF SQLCA.SQLCode < 0 THEN
        MessageBox("Connection Failed","Unable to connect to source database.~n~r"+&
                "Error: "+String(SQLCA.SQLErrText), Stopsign!)
        RETURN
END IF

// Set up values for the destination transaction object - itr_Destination
itr_Destination = CREATE transaction
itr_Destination.DBMS = "ODBC"
itr_Destination.DBParm = "Connectstring='DSN=Powersoft Demo DB V6'

CONNECT using itr_Destination;

IF itr_Destination.SQLCode < 0 THEN
        MessageBox("Connection Failed","Unable to connect to destination"+&
        database.~n~r"+&
                "Error: "+String(itr_Destination.SQLErrText), Stopsign!)
        DISCONNECT using SQLCA;
        RETURN
END IF
```

I like to make sure that all the clean up work is done first, so next we will write the script for the CloseQuery event that destroys the instance variable objects. This will free up any resources that are currently being held by these objects.

CloseQuery event for wm_pipeline_demo

```
DISCONNECT using SQLCA;
DISCONNECT using itr_Destination;

DESTROY iuo_PipeDemo
DESTROY itr_Destination
```

Now we will write the scripts that do all the real work of running the pipeline. Normally these scripts would be contained in user events on the window or on the pipeline object itself to be more object oriented. To keep this demo simple, we will write this code directly into the Clicked event of the appropriate command button.

First we will write the script for the cb_start command button. Before we can do anything we must instantiate an instance of our pipeline user object and associate the appropriate pipeline with it (like we would associate a DataWindow object with a DataWindow control. Then we will link the three static text counters to the appropriate instance variables on the static text variables on the pipeline user object. These will be updated automatically by the scripts that we wrote earlier for the pipeline user object.

Now that we are all set up, we will execute the pipeline using the Start() function. The syntax for the Start() function is as follows:

```
pipeline.Start( source_tran, dest_tran, error_dw)
```

where

pipeline is the pipeline that you are going to execute.

source_tran is the source database transaction object.

dest_tran is the destination database transaction object.

error_dw is a DataWindow control in which any pipeline errors will be diplayed.

The following is the code listing for the cb_start Clicked event:

Clicked for cb_start

```
INT li_ReturnCode
```

```
// Instantiate the pipeline
iuo_PipeDemo = CREATE u_pipe_demo
iuo_PipeDemo.DataObject =  "p_pipe_demo"

// Link the static text counters to the user object variables
iuo_PipeDemo.ist_Read =  st_Read
iuo_PipeDemo.ist_Written  =  st_Written
iuo_PipeDemo.ist_Error  =  st_Error

// Execute the pipeline
li_ReturnCode = iuo_PipeDemo.Start(SQLCA, itr_Destination, dw_1)

IF li_ReturnCode < 0 THEN
        // Error Occurred
        MessageBox("Pipeline Error","Pipeline failed.  Error code:"+&
        "+String(li_ReturnCode),StopSign!)
ELSE
        // Successful pipeline
        MessageBox("Pipeline Complete","Data Pipeline transfer is complete!")
END IF
```

If everything is working successfully, this is the only script that you will need to execute out of the three command buttons. However, if any errors occur, you will want to be able to correct the errors and "repair" the pipeline. The user will correct the errors in dw_1 where they were all listed during execution. Then the user will press the Repair command button to execute the repair process. To execute this process we will call the Repair() function which has syntax as follows:

```
pipeline.Repair(dest_tran)
```

where

pipeline is the pipeline that you are going to execute.

dest_tran is the destination database transaction object.

Clicked for cb_repair

```
// Execute the repair of the pipeline
INT li_ReturnCode

li_ReturnCode = iuo_PipeDemo.Repair(itr_Destination)

IF li_ReturnCode < 0 THEN
        // Errors occurred
        MessageBox("Repair Failed","Repair failed.  Error code:"+&
        "+String(li_ReturnCode),StopSign!)
```

```
ELSE
        // Successful repair
        MessageBox("Repair Complete","Repaired data successfully transferred!")
END IF
```

If any new errors occur, or any rows that weren't repaired properly will reappear in the DataWindow error list where the user can try again to repair them.

During execution of the pipeline, the user might decide that they want to cancel the process. That is the function of the Cancel command button. This button will call the function Cancel() to stop the pipeline from proceeding. The syntax for this function is:

```
pipeline.Cancel()
```

where

pipeline is the pipeline that you are going to execute.

Clicked for cb_cancel

```
// Stop execution of the pipeline
INT li_ReturnCode

li_ReturnCode = iuo_PipeDemo.Cancel()

IF li_ReturnCode = 1 THEN
        // Successful cancel
        MessageBox("Pipeline Canceled" , "Pipeline canceled successfully.")
ELSE
        // Cancel failed
        MessageBox("Cancel Failed" , "Unable to cancel pipeline execution.", StopSign!)
END IF
```

Now you can try executing this example to see an embedded pipeline actually running!

15.6 Quick Reference for Pipelines

The following sections provide some quick reference sheets for using Pipelines.

15.6.1 Attributes

Table 15-2 *Attributes.*

Attribute	Description
DataObject	Like the DataWindow control, DataObject is the name of the Pipeline object that you created previously in the pipeline painter.
RowsRead	The number of rows that have been read from the source database. This number is updated continuously during execution of the pipeline.
RowsWritten	The number of rows that have been written to the destination database. This number is updated continuously during execution of the pipeline.
RowsInError	The number of rows that could not be transferred to the destination database. If this number exceeds that maximum number of errors set in the pipeline painter then execution of the pipeline will be halted.
Syntax	The description of the properties of the pipeline object. Contains information such as the source, destination, commit level and error tolerance.

15.6.2 Events

Table 15-3 *Events.*

Event	Description
Constructor	Fires when the object is created using the object_instance = CREATE pipeline_object syntax.
Destructor	Fires when the object is destroyed using the DESTROY object_instance syntax.
PipeStart	Fires at the start of the pipeline execution when the pipeline_object.Start() function is called.
PipeMeter	Fires every time a complete block of reads and writes completes. The size of this block is defined by the pipeline's commit block setting.
PipeEnd	Fires at the end of the pipeline execution.

15.6.3 Functions

Table 15-4 contains only pipeline specific functions.

***Table 15-4** Pipeline Specific Functions.*

Function	Description
Cancel	Can be called during pipeline execution to halt the transfer of data. Returns a 1 for success and a -1 for failure.
Repair	Re executes the pipeline processing any error rows encountered during the last execution. These errors are found in the linked DataWindow control where the user will have modified them before trying to call the repair function. Returns a 1 for success or a negative number for an error (see error codes QuickReference).
Start	Executes the pipeline. Returns a 1 for success or a negative number for an error (see error codes QuickReference).

15.6.4 Repair and Start Return Codes

***Table 15-5** Repair and Start Return Codes.*

Return Code	Description
-1	Pipe open failed.
-2	Too many columns.
-3	Table already exists.
-4	Table does not exist.
-5	Missing connection.
-6	Wrong arguments.
-7	Column mismatch.
-8	Fatal SQL error in Source.
-9	Fatal SQL error in Destination.
-10	Max number of errors exceeded.
-11	Invalid window handle.
-12	Bad table syntax.
-13	Key required but not specified.
-15	Pipe already in progress.
-16	Error in source database.
-17	Error in destination database.
-18	Destination database is read only.

15.7 Summary

Data Pipelines are very useful tools to help enterprise developers move data from place to place and table to table. It can be used for historical archiving, data warehousing and executable roll out to name a few uses.

I have used Data Pipelines either interactively or natively on almost every enterprise project that I have worked on since they were introduced in PowerBuilder 4.0. You will be surprised at how well they work.

CHAPTER 16

Debugging and Profiling Your Application

*A*s we discussed in Chapter 2, testing is a critical stage of every application development project. Unfortunately, the testing stage is the area that that is most often cut
back or skipped altogether due to time or budget constraints. There are many books
on the market suggesting different ways of testing, so we won't discuss testing philosophies
in this chapter. What we will discuss in this chapter is specifically how to use the new
PowerBuilder 6.0 Debugger and profiling options to find and correct errors in your application and identify performance bottlenecks.

16.1 The Debugger

The Debugger is a painter that allows you to set breakpoints in your code and execute
your application scripts line by line to observe its execution. When PowerBuilder hits
a line of code with a breakpoint, execution stops and you have the option to check
and/or alter variable values, step through the code line by line, or continue executing
until the next breakpoint is hit.

The functionality of the debugger is very important in any application development situation, but traditionally PowerBuilder has been very weak in this area. In
PowerBuilder 6.0, Powersoft has completely rewritten the debugger to provide us with
conditional breakpoints, Just-In-Time debugging, multiple application views and more!

To open the Debugger, press the "no bugs" icon in the toolbar. (See Figure
16-1.)

Figure 16-1. The Debugger icon.

When the Debugger opens, you will notice that the interface is completely different from what it was in version 5.0. The new interface uses panes and views to allow you to access the different functions of the Debugger. The default setup of the Debugger is shown in Figure 16-2.

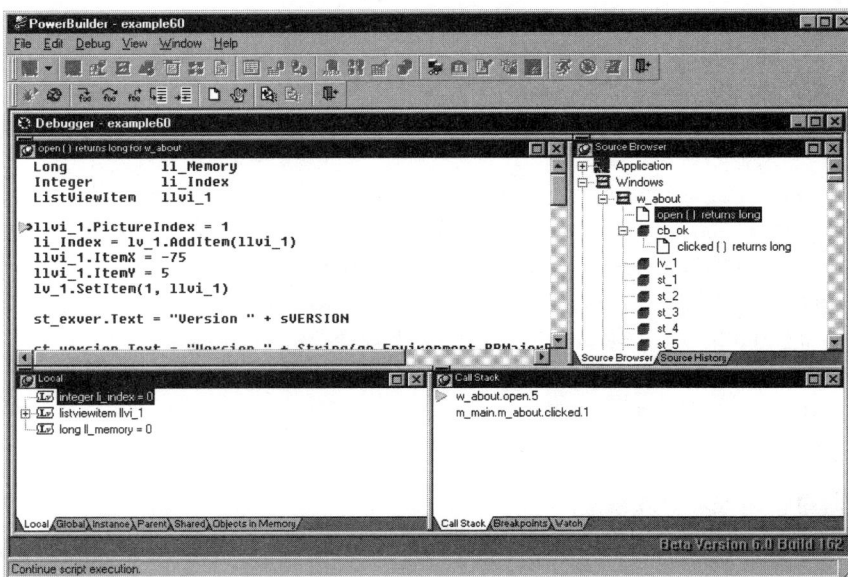

Figure 16-2. The new Debugger uses panes and views to let us access all of its functionality.

Panes are simply rectangles within the painter workspace that you can customize to show information. Views are the different types of information that you can see within the panes. You can customize this configuration to show as many panes as you like (up to one for each view). Panes that show multiple views will contain tab folders allowing you to move between views.

For example, the default Debugger configuration shown in Figure 16-2 has four panes, some of which contain only one view, some of which contain many. The upper left pane contains only one view, the script that you are looking at. This view should be familiar as this was the same as the top pane in the old Debugger interface. Immediately to the right of that is a pane containing two views, the Source Browser and the Source History. We will explain all these views below. On the bottom left is a pane which contains all the variable views. There is one view for each of Local, Global, Instance, Parent, Shared, and Objects In Memory. The pane on the bottom right contains three views: the Call Stack, Breakpoints, and Watch.

In the example in Figure 16-2, each pane has a title bar showing. By default, only the title bar for the script view shows. Each of the other panes has a hidden title bar which becomes visible when you pass the mouse over it. This is to provide you with more work space while debugging. If you are unfamiliar with the views and want the title bars to stay visible, click on the "thumbtack" icon on the top left corner of the title bar to make it permanent. Click the thumbtack again to make it go away. (See Figure 16-3.)

Each view provides a different function in the debugging process.

Figure 16-3. *Click on the thumbtack icon in the top left corner of the pane to make the title bars permanent or temporary.*

16.1.1 Source View (or Script View)

In the Source view you can see the script for a specific object/event or function. You can also set breakpoints within the script by double clicking on the script line that you want to break on (the break occurs *before* executing the line). In this view you cannot set breakpoints on comments, variable declarations or empty lines.

In Figure 16-4, you can see an example of a line with a breakpoint set. It shows as a small red stop sign beside the line. The current line (which will be executed next) is also shown using a yellow arrow icon.

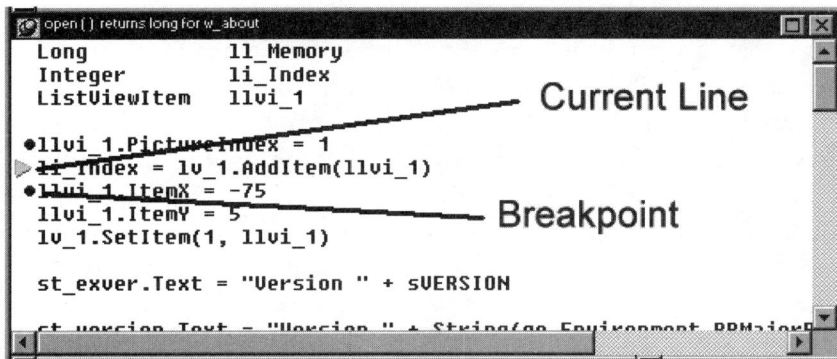

Figure 16-4. *Breakpoints and the current line are visible as icons beside the respective line.*

Clicking with the right mouse button on breakpoints in this view will allow you to manipulate breakpoints and also to move through the script if in the middle of a debug session.

16.1.2 Source Browser

This view provides you with an expandable hierarchy where you can drill down to select any script in your application to work with. Double-clicking on an event or function will open that script in the Source view area. (See Figure 16-5.)

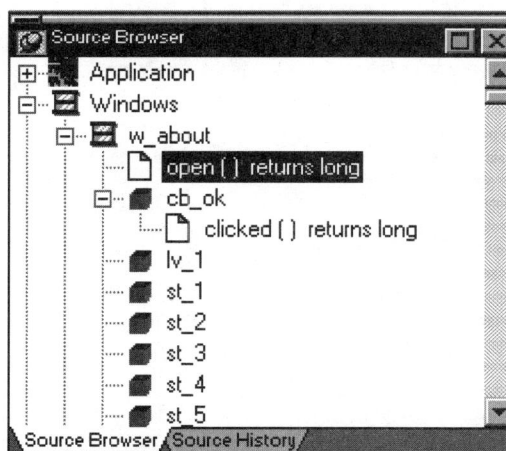

Figure 16-5. *The Source Browser allows you drill down into the hierarchy of objects in your application to find scripts.*

16.1.3 Source History

This view will display a historical list of the scripts that you have been looking at in the Source view as shown in Figure 16-6.

Figure 16-6. The Source History view displays a list of the most recently viewed scripts.

By double-clicking on a script, the Script view will change to display the specified script. This makes it easy to move between multiple scripts. Alternatively you can drag and drop from the Source History view to the Source view to display that script.

16.1.4 Variable Views

The Variable views are used for viewing the runtime variables and their values. In the default configuration of the Debugger, there are five variable views shown. One for each of Local, Global, Shared, Instance, and Parent. If you haven't started your debug session yet, these views will be blank. For complex variables such as objects and structures, you can expand the branch to see all the elements inside the variable, as shown in Figure 16-7.

Each variable view can show any combination of the five different variable views. For example, if you click on the view with the right mouse button and select Local and Global from the pop up menu, you will see both local and global variables in your view (and the title on the view will change accordingly).

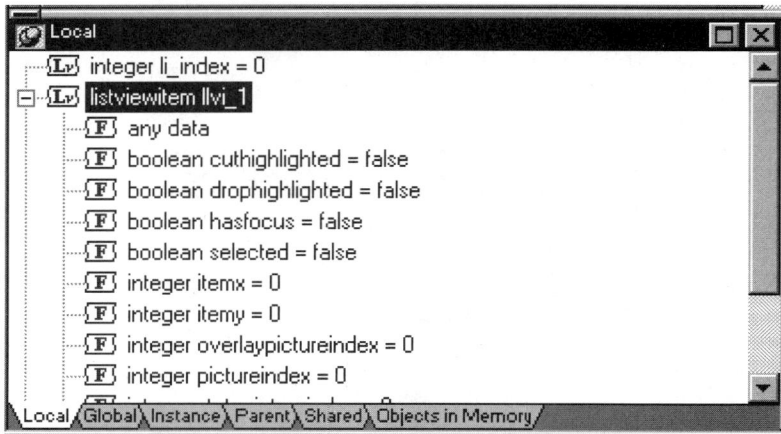

Figure 16-7. A Variable view showing a complex local variable.

On this same popup menu you will see an option to modify a variable during the debug session. This is very useful if you want to force an error to occur to test your error handling process, or if you want to correct a value which was wrong due to an earlier error to allow the script to carry on. In PowerBuilder 5 you accomplished this by double clicking on the variable. This doesn't work in PowerBuilder 6.0 any more (at least not in the Beta version, maybe they will change this by the release date).

When you select **Edit Variable...** from the popup menu, the Modify Variable dialog window will appear as shown in Figure 16-8.

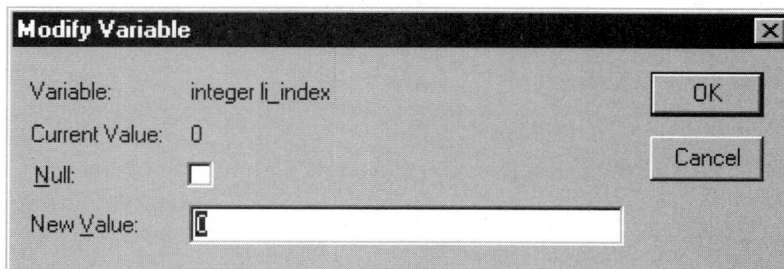

Figure 16-8. The Modify Variable dialog window allows you to change the value of a variable during execution.

This window shows you the variable name and its current value. You can enter a new value in the single line edit field or you can set it to NULL by clicking on the Null checkbox. Press **OK** to alter the value of this variable in the application.

Another option on the popup menu is to add the variable to the Watch view. This can also be accomplished using drag and drop to drag the variable to the Watch view. See below for details on the Watch view.

16.1.5 Objects In Memory View

This view will display a list of the names and memory locations of all objects that are currently instantiated in memory. You can also expand each object to view its properties as shown in Figure 16-9.

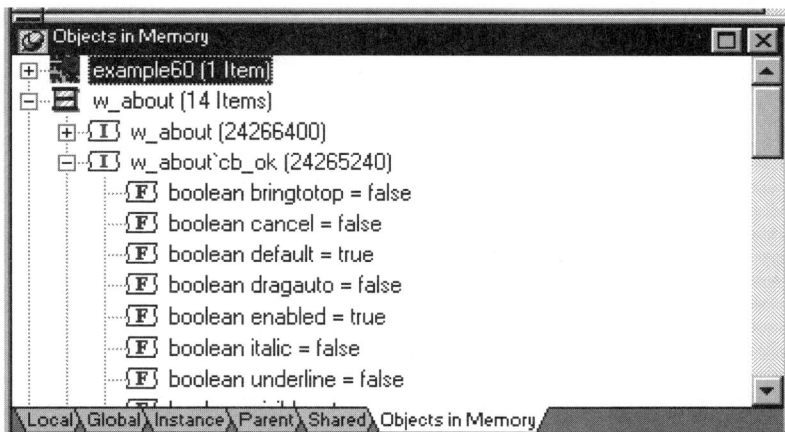

Figure 16-9. The Objects In Memory view allows you to see all the currently instantiated objects, their memory locations, and property values.

This view is refreshed when you select the Objects In Memory tab. It can take a while for this view to open, so be patient. In my tests it sometimes took as long as two minutes for the tab to open.

This view is very useful for monitoring for orphans (instantiated objects with no handle that consume resources but cannot be used by the application) and verifying that objects exist and have the correct properties before you try to access them in your scripts.

16.1.6 Call Stack View

The Call Stack view is a tremendous addition to the PowerBuilder 6.0 debugger. Finally PowerBuilder developers can see the order with which events and functions are called.

This has been a constant thorn in the side of advanced PowerBuilder developers. This view displays the sequence (from top to bottom) of all the events and functions that are scheduled to be called (or are in the middle of being called).

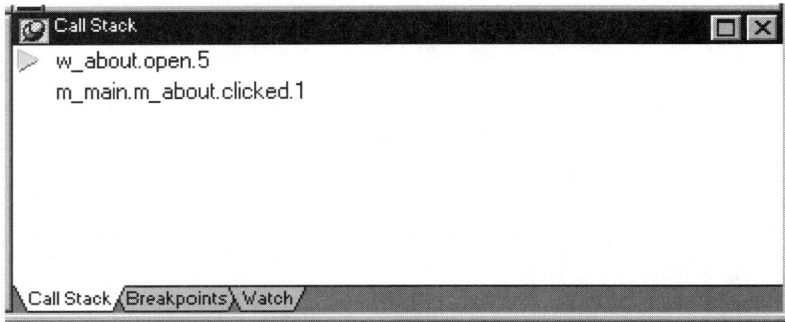

Figure 16-10. *The Call Stack view allows us to see the sequence of events and functions as they are being executed by the system.*

In our example in Figure 16-10, the view shows the event on the top of the stack as "w_about.open.5." This tells you that the w_about open event is the current event being executed by PowerBuilder, and that it is currently at line 5. The line below that shows "m_main.m_about.clicked.1." This tells you that when the open event finishes executing, then the next event that will execute will be the clicked event of m_main.m_about starting after line 1. In our situation, it was the Open(w_about) script in the m_main.m_about clicked event that caused the w_about.open event to be triggered. So when the w_about.open event is concluded, then the m_main.m_about event can conclude (remember the difference between posting and triggering).

If you want to see where the stack pointer is for another event on the Call Stack, you can double click on that event/function and see the script with a green pointer beside the current line in the Source view. Alternatively, you could click on the event/function with the right mouse button and select **Set Context** off the popup menu to do the same thing. This step can be a little slow, taking approximately five seconds to trace the stack, so be patient.

16.1.7 Breakpoints View

This view allows you to see and modify all the breakpoints that are set for this debug session. To the left of each breakpoint is an icon that will show you if the breakpoint is enabled (a small red octagon) or disabled (a clear octagon).

By clicking on a breakpoint with the right mouse button you can enable, disable, or clear a breakpoint. You can also choose to enable, disable or clear ALL the breakpoints from this menu (be careful, there isn't an undo for this action!). You can also view the script in the Source view that contains this breakpoint by choosing **Open Source** from the menu. Choosing the **Breakpoints** menu item or double clicking on a breakpoint will open the Edit Breakpoints dialog window where you can edit breakpoints, make conditional breakpoints and set breakpoints on variables. This is discussed later under Custom Breakpoints. (See Figure 16-11.)

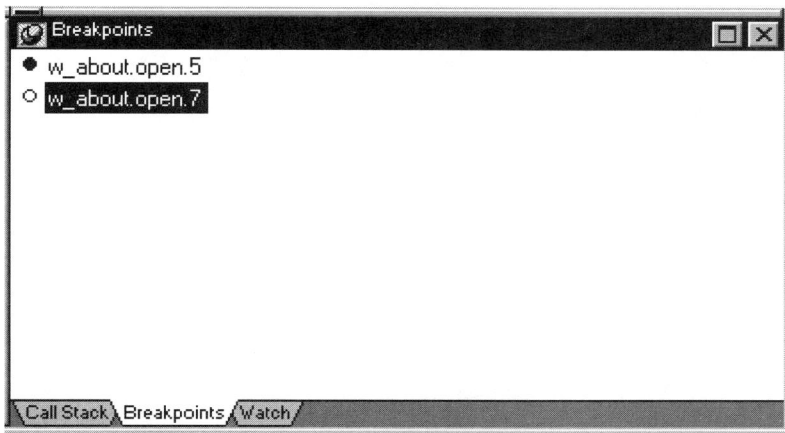

Figure 16-11. *The Breakpoints view showing an enabled and a disabled breakpoint.*

16.1.8 Watch View

The Watch view allows you to keep an eye on a specific sub set of variables that you specify. This functions the same as it did in PowerBuilder 5.0, allowing you to select variables from the Variables view and drag them to the watch area to keep them in sight at all times. This helps you to focus your attention on the variables that are of specific interest to you.

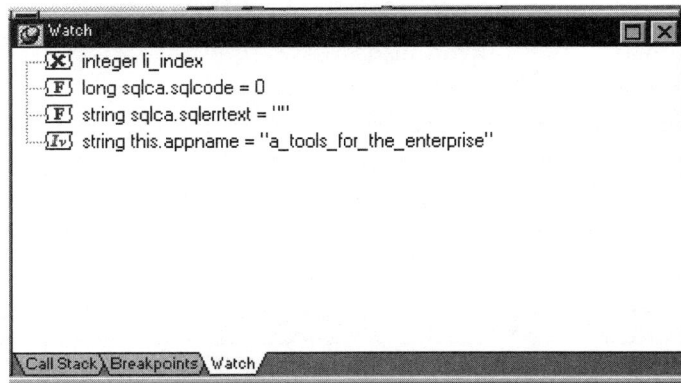

Figure 16-12. The Watch view for viewing a set of variables.

16.2 Using Breakpoints

Just in case you were unsure, a breakpoint is a specific point in your code where you want the application to temporarily stop executing so that you can examine and manipulate the context of the application execution (such as viewing and changing variable values).

When breakpoints are set on a line of your code, the execution will be stopped before the line is executed. Breakpoints are also saved to the PB.INI file when you exit the debugger. This allows you to keep the same breakpoints from one debug session to another.

Breakpoints can be static breakpoints, which will stop execution any time that they are hit, or conditional breakpoints, which evaluate an expression to determine if they should stop execution or continue. Conditional breakpoints are discussed in the next section.

16.3 Editing Breakpoints and Setting Conditional Breakpoints

As a new feature in PowerBuilder 6.0, we can now set our breakpoints to evaluate a logical expression and only halt execution if the expression is TRUE. To adjust your Breakpoint to be a conditional breakpoint, you must open the Edit Breakpoints dialog window as shown in Figure 16-13.

This window replaces the PowerBuilder 5.0 Edit Stop dialog window. On the Location tab, the box at the top will show you a list of all the breakpoints currently defined in your debug session. Each line represents one breakpoint. The text on the line will be the fully qualified object name and location of the script. This will be followed by the line number where the breakpoint is. For example, in the Figure 16-13 above you can see:

```
w_drag_drop.pb_trash.dragdrop.38
```

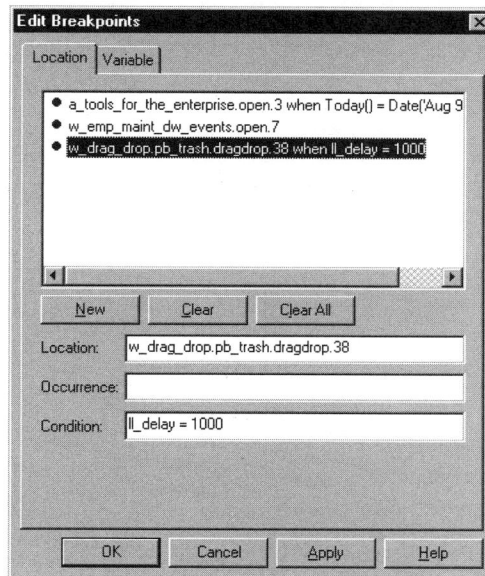

Figure 16-13. *The Edit Breakpoints dialog window is where you will set conditional breakpoints.*

This means that the breakpoint is in the window w_drag_drop on the picture button control pb_trash in the dragdrop event on line 38. You will also notice that after this statement, on the same line you will see:

```
when ll_delay = 1000
```

This means that this break point is conditional and only breaks if the variable ll_delay is equal to 1000 when the breakpoint is triggered (see Setting A Conditional Breakpoint below).

If the breakpoint has nothing after it, then it is triggered every time it is hit. If after the breakpoint you see:

```
occurrences = 4
```

This means that this breakpoint is set to trigger every fourth time that it is encountered (see Breaking On An Occurrence in the next section).

Below the location box you will see three command buttons: New, Clear, and Clear All. The New command button will allow you to define a new breakpoint using the syntax above to fully qualify the location of the breakpoint. Remember that all breakpoints must be placed on executable lines of code. It is unusual to define your breakpoints here, usually we will doubleclick on the appropriate executable line in the Source view. The Clear command button will clear the currently selected breakpoint in the location box. The Clear All command button will clear all the breakpoints in the current debug session.

At the bottom of the tab are three single line edits for entering or modifying the details of a breakpoint. You can change the location, occurrence or condition associated with the currently selected breakpoint.

16.3.1 Breaking on an Occurrence

The Occurrence entry field can be used to tell the debugger not to break every time it encounters this breakpoint, but every X times that it does. For example, setting a value of 4 in this field would only trigger a breakpoint every fourth time that the breakpoint is hit.

16.3.2 Setting A Conditional Breakpoint

The Condition entry field can be used to tell the debugger to only break at this breakpoint if the expression that you enter here evaluates to TRUE. You can use standard PowerScript functions as well as variables in this expression. In the current beta release, trying to set the condition to use an attribute of an object (i.e., SQLCA.SQLCode) triggers an error because it doesn't like the period used to separate the object from the attribute. Hopefully this will be changed by the final release.

Examples of conditions that you might set would be:

```
ll_variable = 133
```

This would only break if the local variable ll_variable was equal to 133.

```
ll_variable < ll_othervariable
```

This would only break if the local variable ll_variable was less than the local variable ll_othervariable.

```
Today() = Date('Aug 8, 1997') OR ld_InvoiceDate = Today()
```

This would only break if the system date was equal to August 8, 1997, or if the local variable ld_InvoiceDate was equal to the system date.

16.3.3 Breaking When a Variable Changes

You can also set a breakpoint to occur when a specific variable changes. To set this up you must switch to the Variable tab as shown in Figure 16-14.

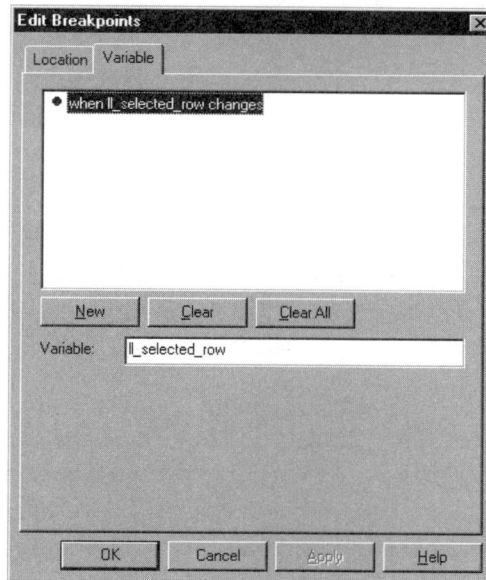

Figure 16-14. Breakpoints can be set to open the debugger whenever a specified variable changes.

If you press the **New** command button you can define a new breakpoint by entering the name of the appropriate variable in the entry field below the list box.

16.4 Stepping Through Your Code

When you reach a breakpoint in your code you have a number of choices of how to begin moving though your application. You can press the **Continue** button on the toolbar to continue the execution of the application until it reaches the next breakpoint.

Alternatively, you can step through the code. In PowerBuilder 5.0, you only had one way to do this–line by line. The new features of PowerBuilder 6.0 give us a number of alternatives as to how we can step:

- **Step In.** This is like the PB 5.0 step command. This will cause the current line of code to execute and the cursor to move to the next line. If the line being executed contains a function, you will step into that function. The current line of code that shows will now be the first executable line in the function.

- **Step Over.** The Step Over button will function the same as the Step In, except if there is a function to be executed in the current line. With Step Over, the function will be executed as if it was a single logical line of code. You will not need to step through all the code within the function.

- **Step Out.** If you Step In to a function and then decide you want to execute the rest of the function and return to the line that called the function in the first place, you can use the Step Out button. Like the name implies, you are stepping to the first executable line that is outside the function you are currently in.

- **Run To Cursor.** This allows you to select some point in your script (in the Source view) and then execute your code until it reaches the line that you have currently selected. You don't have to set a breakpoint on that line. This is very useful for situations such as a loop where you have stepped through the first loop, but don't want to have to step through them all.

- **Set Next Statement.** This allows you to change the current line of code that is to be executed to a different line. This is a very powerful, but also very dangerous feature. You must be careful not to upset the logical functioning of your application. For example, doing a Set Next Statement in the middle of a loop that hasn't been initialized yet will cause an unpredictable error that is sure to be unpleasant.

16.5 Just-In-Time Debugging

Just-In-Time debugging is another new PowerBuilder 6.0 feature that you will find very useful. If you click on the run icon, and then, while running, decide that you really want to be running through the debugger, you can now do this.

In order to accomplish this feat, you must have turned on the Just-In-Time debugging system option. By default, when you install PowerBuilder, this option is set to OFF. To enable this option, open the System Options dialog window by clicking on the System Options icon in the PowerPanel. On the General tab of this window you can turn on the Just-In-Time debugging option as shown in Figure 16-15.

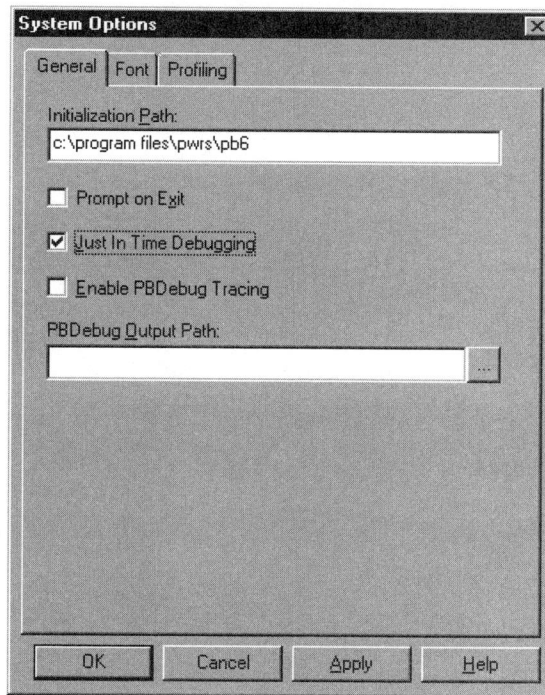

Figure 16-15. *The Just-In-Time debugging option can be enabled in the System Options window.*

Now, to activate the Just-In-Time debugging while running your application from the Run icon, you simply switch applications to PowerBuilder. This will cause the dialog window shown in Figure 16-16 to open.

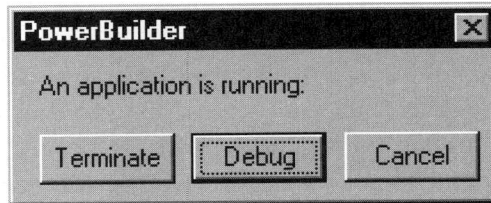

Figure 16-16. *The Just-In-Time debugging feature can be activated by switching to PowerBuilder while your executable is run from the running person icon.*

Macintosh Note: The method for switching into debug mode on a Macintosh platform is a little different. To do it you press the OPTION-ESC keys.

If you press the **Debug** command button, a debug session will be started in PowerBuilder.

You may need to open a script painter and then define breakpoints for the application if none exist from a previous session. The views that only update when in context like the Variable and Call Stack views will be blank until you hit one of the breakpoints that have been set.

This functionality can also be accessed through a new function called *DebugBreak()*. The syntax for this function is straightforward because it is a system function and has no arguments:

```
DebugBreak()
```

This could be embedded in error handling conditional statements to allow you to check the context when an error occurs such as:

```
IF SQLCA.SQLCode < 0 THEN DebugBreak()
```

If you accidentally compile your application and leave DebugBreak() calls in your code, they will be ignored. They will also be ignored if Just-In-Time debugging is not enabled (as we discussed earlier).

16.6 Using PBDEBUG

Sometimes you may find problems in an executable version of your application that doesn't seem to appear in the debugger. Or your application may hang, but you cannot identify what line of code is causing it to do this. PowerBuilder is equipped with another utility that allows us to trace the creation and destruction of objects, execution of scripts and functions, even in a compiled application.

If you are building a P-code executable, these functions are already built into your executable. If you are building a machine code executable, then you must select the Trace Information check box in the Project painter as shown in Figure 16-17.

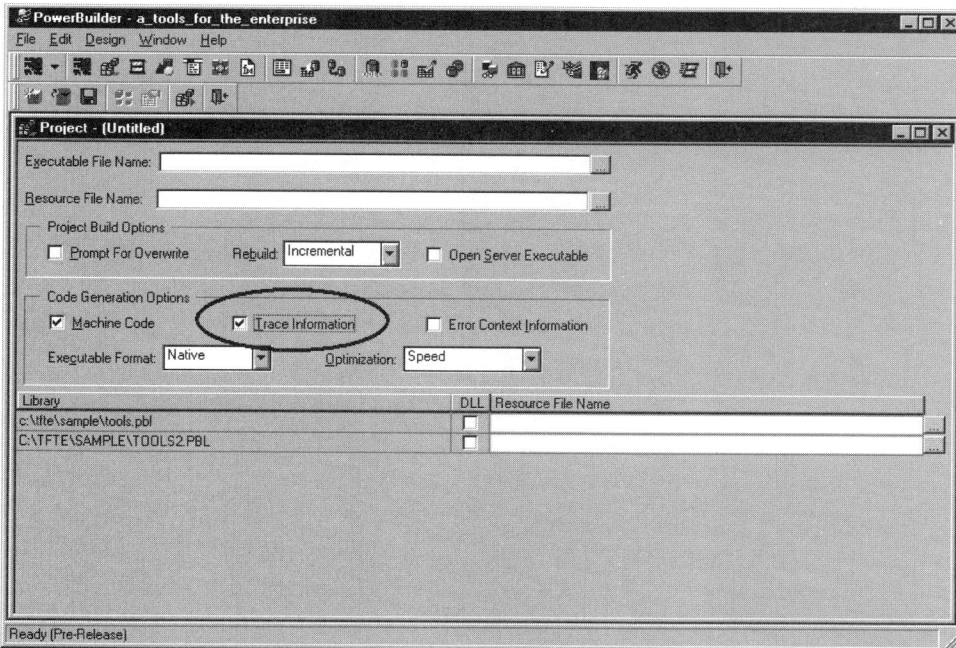

Figure 16-17. *To activate PBDEBUG features in a machine code executable, you must active the Trace Information option in the Project painter.*

To activate the tracing feature on a compiled PowerBuilder application, you must append the /PBDEBUG execution parameter to your run command. For example:

```
C:\pathname\myapp.exe /PBDEBUG
```

This will cause an output file to be created with the same name as your executable, but with a .DBG extension. This file will appear in the same library as the executable. This file can then be viewed using any text editor.

Due to bugs in the beta version (which will be eliminated in the final production version I am sure) do not allow me to compile either the sample application or the Tools For The Enterprise demo application. I have created a simple application called Demo Debug using the PowerBuilder application template. I then compiled this application and ran it using the debugger. I have extracted a section of the debug file in the following listing:

```
End event +OPEN for class A_DEBUG_DEMO, lib entry A_DEBUG_DEMO
Executing event +CLICKED for class CB_ADD, lib entry W_GENAPP_SHEET
   Executing instruction at line 1
   Executing object function ADDITEM for class LB_1, lib entry W_GENAPP_SHEET
     Executing system dll function
   End object function ADDITEM for class LB_1, lib entry W_GENAPP_SHEET
   Executing instruction at line 2
End event +CLICKED for class CB_ADD, lib entry W_GENAPP_SHEET
Executing event +CLICKED for class CB_ADD, lib entry W_GENAPP_SHEET
   Executing instruction at line 1
   Executing object function ADDITEM for class LB_1, lib entry W_GENAPP_SHEET
     Executing system dll function
   End object function ADDITEM for class LB_1, lib entry W_GENAPP_SHEET
   Executing instruction at line 2
End event +CLICKED for class CB_ADD, lib entry W_GENAPP_SHEET
Executing event +CLICKED for class M_EXIT, lib entry M_GENAPP_FRAME
```

This file will show you every step that is occurring in the execution of your application including which object is currently being created, executed, or destroyed. In the above excerpt the Open event for the application object has just ended (this is where all the objects are created and initialized. This was over 30Kb of code, so I left this out). The next line shows me clicking on the Add command button in the window w_genapp_sheet. This has a one line script which adds text from a single line edit to a list box. This is shown by the execution of the instruction at line 1 of the script, and then another line follows telling you which object functions are being executed.

This feature is particularly useful when your application crashes after it has been compiled, but runs fine in the debugger. Using this file you can jump to the end of the file and see the last line of code that executed. This is likely the step that caused the system to crash and where you should being examining your application for a problem.

> **Developer's Note:** You should be very careful about using the PBDEBUG option in a production environment, as turning this on causes your application performance to degrade considerably. Also, the debug output file can grow very large, very quickly, so be sure you have enough disk space to manage the file, or you could bring your system or even your network to a grinding stop!

16.7 Using Profiling and Tracing

PowerBuilder 6.0 has a new developer tool that I think is one of the most significant developer changes in the new release. You can now analyze your PowerBuilder executable to look for bottlenecks and profile exactly how it runs. This has been a key issue in enterprise projects and will help developers to eliminate slow running processes to improve overall application performance.

These profiling and tracing features are available only in the Enterprise version of PowerBuilder.

There are three stages involved in using profiling and tracing: data collection, analysis, and display.

16.7.1 Data Collection

In the data collection stage of profiling you will run your application with options enabled that will create a trace file. Unlike the PBDEBUG file, this file is binary and cannot be read by a text editor. Instead you will use, or write, special performance analysis tools. This will be discussed further in the next section.

In order to generate a trace file you must turn the trace option on in the system dialog or select the tracing information check box in the project painter if building a machine code executable. This trace file contains a log of timer values at certain activity points in your application. You have control over what points will cause a trace file record to be created. This can be done either by setting options in the system dialog window before running your application or by using the new PB 6.0 system functions to initiate a tracing activity.

Table 16-1 shows all the predefined logging points which can be enabled or disabled by you as you choose. The enumerated data types shown in the table are for using the tracing methods described below.

Table 16-1 Predefined logging points.

Logging Point	Enumerated Datatype
Standard (routine) entry or exit from the application.	ActRoutine!
Start and end of logging.	ActBegin! (Note: an activity of this type is automatically recorded in the trace file when you begin and end tracing.
Execution of any line in any script or function.	ActLine!
Embedded SQL call entry and exit (very useful for determining how long an embedded SQL command takes to execute).	ActESQL!
Creation of an object.	ActObjectCreate!
Destruction of an object.	ActObjectDestroy!
A specific user defined activity.	ActUser!
System error or warning.	ActError!
Standard garbage collection.	ActGarbageCollect!
Combination 1: At routine entry and exit, embedded SQL, object creation and destruction and garbage collection.	ActProfile!
Combination 2: All activities except script line execution.	ActTrace!

16.7.1.1 Using the System Options Dialog Window

The System Options dialog window has a tab for Profiling as shown in Figure 16-18.

On this tab you can turn tracing on for your entire application and select if you want the system to prompt you before it overwrites an existing trace file. You can set the path and file of your trace file. This file will, be default, have the same name and path as your .EXE file, or your .PBL locations, but it will have a .PBP extension (for PowerBuilder Profile).

The trace label option allows you to specify a string that will be inserted into the trace blocks in your trace file, but this is not required in order for tracing to run.

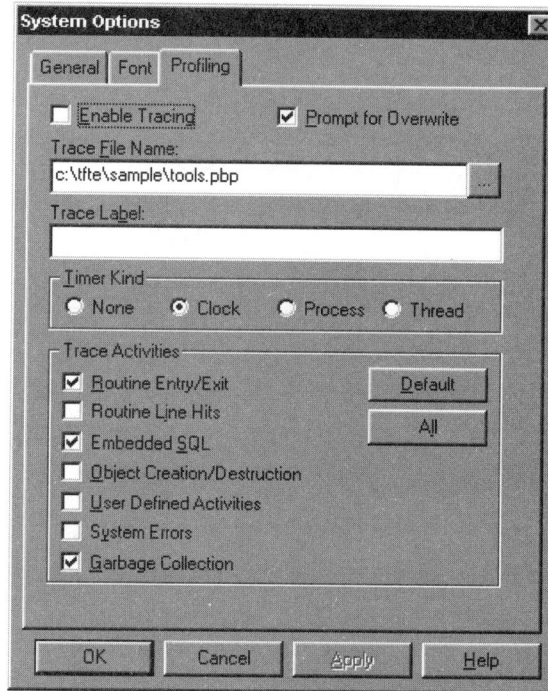

Figure 16-18. *The System Options dialog has a tab for setting all your tracing options.*

The Timer Kind radio buttons allow you to select how you want timer information to be recorded in your tracing file. The options are:

- **None** will not record any timing information.

- **Clock** will use the system clock to record times (this is the default for Windows 95 and NT). Time will be measured in microseconds, and if your system processor is fast enough, portions of a microsecond.

- **Process** will use the process timer to record times. This time is measured in microseconds (no portions of microseconds). The process timer should provide you with a more accurate time for the execution of specific processes, but has a lower resolution for the time that is recorded.

- **Thread** will use the thread time to record times. Time is measured in microseconds (no portions of microseconds). This timer should be used when you are timing distributed applications.

If you are running on a different platform other that Wintel 32 bit different timers will be used regardless of what you select in the System Options dialog:

- **Windows 3.1** the timer used will always be the Windows function GetTickCount() which measures time in milliseconds since Windows was started, but only measures in increments of 13 milliseconds.

- **UNIX** the timer used will always be the thread timer which captures time in nanoseconds.

- **Macintosh** at the time of writing of this book, timing was not available on the Macintosh platform, although this may have changed by release time. Please refer to your system documentation.

Developer's Note: The time it takes to actually write the trace data to the trace log file will be excluded from the timer values, so you don't have to worry about this.

The Trace Activities group box contains a set of check boxes while allow you to select which activities you want to generate a trace log entry. Each of these options is described in table 16.1 above. The Default command button will select the default activities (Routine Entry/Exit, Embedded SQL, and Garbage Collection). The All command button will select all the check boxes.

16.7.1.2 Using the Trace Functions

An alternative method for capturing trace information is to insert function calls in your application to turn tracing on and off, or set tracing options as you desire. This can also be done by calling the standard window class that has been provided in the PRO-FILE.PBL library to activate tracing options.

The functions for managing tracing include TraceOpen(), TraceClose(), TraceBegin(), TraceEnd(),Trace Error(), TraceEnableActivity(), TraceDisableActivity(), and TraceUser().

16.7.1.2.1 TraceOpen()

This function will open a trace file with the name and path that you specify. You will also specify the timer type that you want to use (refer to timer types in the previous section). After calling this function the system will automatically begin tracing activities as defined in the User defined activities defaults. You can use the TraceEnableActivity()

and TraceDisableActivity() functions to change which activities are logged after calling TraceOpen().

The syntax for the TraceOpen() function is:

```
TraceOpen(filename, timer_type)
```

where

filename is a string variable or literal containing the path and filename of the trace file to be created.

timer_type is a variable of the enumerated type TimerKind which has possible values of Clock!, Process!, Thread!, or TimeNone!

This function will return an enumerated data type of type ErrorReturn with the possible values:

- **Success!** Trace file was opened successfully.

- **FileAlreadyOpenError!** TraceOpen was already called previously and the file has not yet been closed with a TraceClose() function call.

- **FileOpenError!** The file could not be opened.

- **EnterpriseOnlyFeature!** You tried to call this function from PowerBuilder Desktop, but it is only supported in PowerBuilder Enterprise.

If the filename argument for the function is NULL, the return value will also be NULL.

TraceClose()

This function will close the trace file opened with the TraceOpen() function. Prior to calling this function, the TraceEnd() function should be called.

The syntax for the TraceClose() function requires no arguments:

```
TraceClose()
```

This function will return an enumerated data type of type ErrorReturn with the possible values:

- **Success!** Trace file was closed successfully.

- **FileNotOpenError!** TraceOpen function hasn't been called prior to the calling of the TraceClose().

- **FileCloseError!** This error indicates that the log file is full, or you have run out of disk space.

- **EnterpriseOnlyFeature!** You tried to call this function from PowerBuilder Desktop, but it is only supported in PowerBuilder Enterprise.

16.7.1.2.3 TraceBegin()

This function will insert a record into the trace file to indicate that tracing has started. All enabled application tracing activities will now be logged. The trace file must have been opened with the TraceOpen() function before calling TraceBegin(). Each set of TraceBegin() and TraceEnd() is called a *tracing block*. Each tracing block can be given a label to help you identify different sets of results in your analysis.

The syntax for the TraceBegin() function is:

```
TraceBegin(tracing_block)
```

where

tracing_block is a string variable or literal containing the label that you want to assign to the current tracing block. If this variable is Null, then an empty string will be used as the tracing block label in the trace file.

This function will return an enumerated data type of type ErrorReturn with the possible values:

- **Success!** Trace was begun successfully.

- **FileNotOpenError!** TraceOpen hasn't been called yet.

- **TraceStartedError!** A tracing block is already open (TraceBegin() has already been called without a matching TraceEnd()). Only one tracing block can be open at a time.

- **EnterpriseOnlyFeature!** You tried to call this function from PowerBuilder Desktop, but it is only supported in PowerBuilder Enterprise.

16.7.1.2.4 TraceEnd()

This function will end the currently open trace block and place an activity type value into the trace file to indicate that logging has stopped. If TraceClose() is called before a tracing block has been ended, the system will automatically call the TraceEnd() function.

The syntax for the TraceEnd() function requires no arguments:

```
TraceEnd()
```

This function will return an enumerated data type of type ErrorReturn with the possible values:

- **Success!** Trace was ended successfully.

- **FileNotOpenError!** TraceOpen hasn't been called yet.

- **TraceNotStartedError!** TraceBegin() hasn't been called yet, and as such, there is no current tracing block to end.

- **EnterpriseOnlyFeature!** You tried to call this function from PowerBuilder Desktop, but it is only supported in PowerBuilder Enterprise.

16.7.1.2.5 TraceEnableActivity()

This function will enable logging of a specific trace activity. Each activity must be specified separately. A list of all the possible activity enumerated data types is given in table 16.1 earlier in this section. This function can only be called outside of a tracing block (i.e. before TraceBegin() is called). Each time the TraceOpen() function is called, the enabled activities reverts to the default activities defined in ActUser! You cannot call this function with the ActError! and ActUser! enumerated data values as they both require additional data to be passed. These must be called with the TraceError() and TraceUser() functions.

The syntax for the TraceEnableActivity() function is:

```
TraceEnableActivity(activity_type)
```

where

activity_type is an enumerated data type of type TraceActivity specifying which activity to begin logging for. The list of possible TraceActivity types is provided in Table 16.1.

This function will return an enumerated data type of type ErrorReturn with the possible values:

- **Success!** This activity will now be logged.

- **FileNotOpenError!** TraceOpen hasn't been called yet.

- **TraceStartedError!** A tracing block is already open (TraceBegin() has already been called without a matching TraceEnd()). You cannot alter the logging in the middle of a tracing block.

- **EnterpriseOnlyFeature!** You tried to call this function from PowerBuilder Desktop, but it is only supported in PowerBuilder Enterprise.

16.7.1.2.6 TraceDisableActivity()

This function is the reverse of TraceEnableActivity(). It allows you to disable the tracing of a specific activity type. It also must be called outside of a tracing block.
The syntax for the TraceDisableActivity() function is:

```
TraceDisableActivity(activity_type)
```

where

activity_type is an enumerated data type of type TraceActivity specifying which activity to end logging for. The list of possible TraceActivity types is provided in Table 16-1.

This function will return an enumerated data type of type ErrorReturn with the possible values:

- **Success!** This activity will no longer be logged.

- **FileNotOpenError!** TraceOpen hasn't been called yet.

- **TraceStartedError!** A tracing block is already open (TraceBegin() has already been called without a matching TraceEnd()). You cannot alter the logging in the middle of a tracing block.

- **EnterpriseOnlyFeature!** You tried to call this function from PowerBuilder Desktop, but it is only supported in PowerBuilder Enterprise.

16.7.1.2.7 TraceError()

This function will allow you to log your own error messages into the trace file. Each message will have a severity level and a text description. The activity type for this message will be ActError!

The syntax for the TraceError() function is:

```
TraceError(severity, error_message)
```

where

severity is a long with the value that you want to use to indicate the seriousness of the error.

error_message is a string variable or literal that contains the text that you want to log in the trace file as the error message.

This function will return an enumerated data type of type ErrorReturn with the only possible value being Success! If either of the two arguments are Null, then the return code is Null and no entry will be made in the trace file.

16.7.1.2.8 TraceUser()

This function will allow you to log an activity of type ActUser! to the trace file with a numeric identifier and message of your choosing.

The syntax for the TraceUser() function is:

```
TraceUser(identifier, message)
```

where

identifier is a long with the value that you want to use to reference the logged activity.

message is a string variable or literal that contains the text that you want to log in the trace file as the user message.

This function will return an enumerated data type of type ErrorReturn with the only possible value being Success! If either of the two arguments are Null, then the return code is Null and no entry will be made in the trace file.

16.7.1.3 Using the w_starttrace Window

A window class is provided for you in the PROFILE.PBL library that is installed with your PowerBuilder Enterprise development environment. You can copy the window w_starttrace into your application library and use it to allow you at runtime to set tracing options (although you should probably remove this before deploying the application in production!). To open the window you simply use the Open() function such as:

```
Open(w_starttrace)
```

> **Author's Note:** This PBL was not available at the time of writing. Please refer to your PowerBuilder documentation for more details on this feature.

16.7.2 Analyzing the Trace File

Once the trace file has been generated, it needs to be analyzed. This can be accomplished using the supplier Application Profiler, or you can write your own analysis routines using the functions and objects provided in the PROFILE.PBL.

16.7.2.1 Using the PowerBuilder Application Profiler

The Application Profiler (a.k.a. the "Profiler") is an application written in PowerBuilder which is provided with your PowerBuilder Enterprise license. It is the compiled version of the Profiler application that you will find in the PROFILE.PBL. A compiled executable version is installed for you, ready to go, or you can look at the uncompiled version if you want to see how it works.

You can use the Profiler to view and analyze the trace file that is created in the data collection stage. Among other things, you can learn which functions and events called other specific functions and events, how long every piece of script took to execute and where bottlenecks exist in your application. Having spent a tremendous amount of time manually trying to profile and optimize PowerBuilder applications, I know that this tool will have a tremendous impact on improving my application execution speeds.

When you first start up the Profiler, you will see a standard MDI frame and a dialog box. The dialog box allows you to select the trace file that you want to analyze. Once you have opened the trace file, you can open three views: the *Class View*, the *Routine View*, and the *Trace View*.

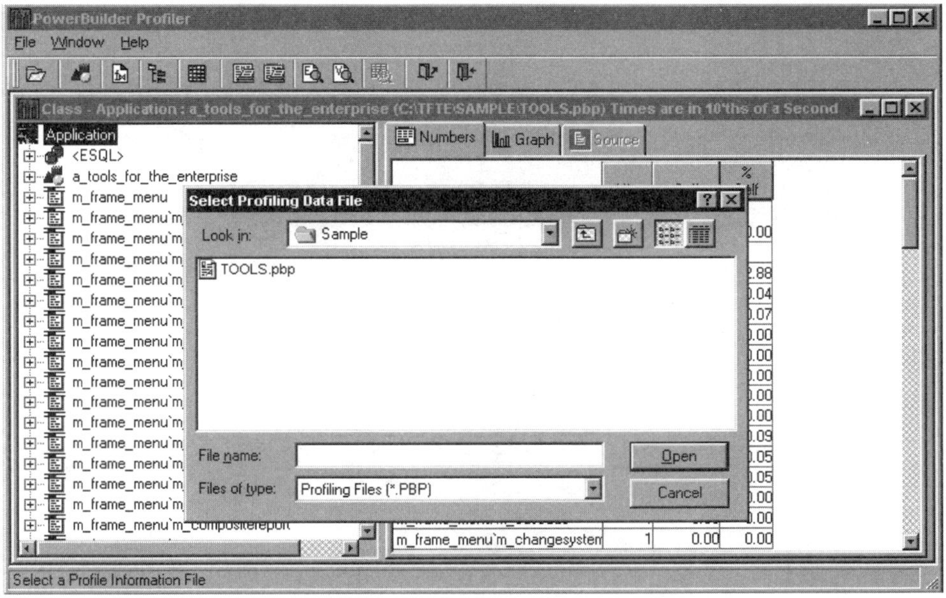

Figure 16-19. *The Application Profiler allows you to view and analyze the trace file created in the data collection stage.*

16.7.2.1.1 The Class View

In the Class View you can see statistics for any of the PowerBuilder objects, functions and events that were active while the trace file was being created.

If you examine the Class View sample in Figure 16-20 you can see a tree view control on the left side shows all the objects that have statistics in the trace file. This list will include both system level objects and user defined classes. You can expand each branch of the tree to drill down into routines that were called by the objects.

There are three possible branch types in the tree view control: the *application*, an *object*, or a *routine*.

- When the **application** is selected, in the right pane you will see the statistics for each object in the trace.

- If an individual **object** is selected in the left pane, the right pane will show the cumulative statistics for the object as well as detailed statistics for the routines that belong to the object.

- If a specific **routine** is selected in the tree view, then the right pane shows the cumulative statistics for that routine and shows the details for any routines that were in turn called by the selected routine. (Figure 16-20.)

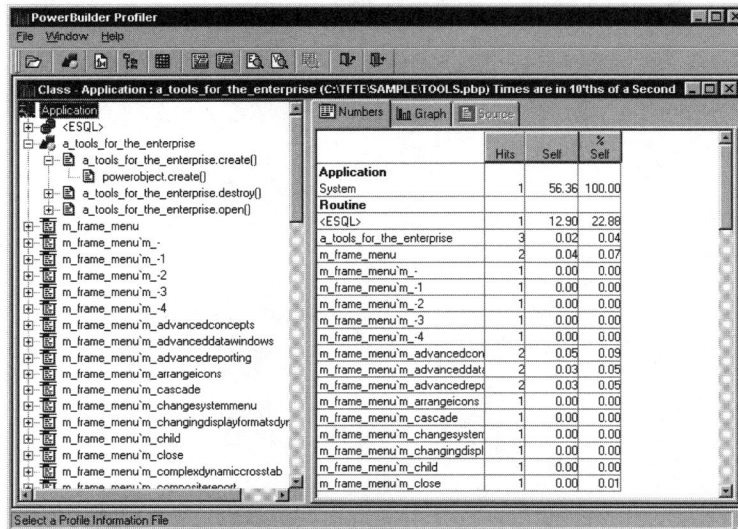

Figure 16-20. The Class View of the Application Profiler.

The right pane shows five different types of statistics:

- **Hits.** The number of times that a routine was executed (in the current instance)

- **Self.** The total time spent in this routine or line. Any time spent in routines called by this routine is not included. If the routine was executed multiple times this is the total time spent in the routine. The time is displayed in the time scale selected in Preferences (discussed later). This time scale defaults to tenths of a second.

- **%Self.** This is the percentage of time that this routine took up in the period that the calling routine was active. For example, in Figure 16-20, the %Self shown for a_debug_demo is 1.24. This indicates that a_debug_demo took up 1.24% of the execution time of the routine that called it, which happened to be the main system routine.

- **Self+Called.** The total time spent in the current routine (or line) and in any routines (or lines) called from the current routine. Like self, if the routine was called more than once, this value is the total time spent.

- **%Self+Called.** Like %Self, but shows Self+Called as a percentage of the total time that tracing was enabled.

Developer's Note: Remember that percentages captured in the trace file are based upon the total time that the trace was active. This means that any idle time in the application could throw of the performance metrics. If you are checking percentages, you will get the most accurate application profile if you control tracing using the trace functions discussed earlier as opposed to creating a trace file for an entire application.

Detailed reports can also be generated and printed by selecting the appropriate icon from the toolbar or using the **File|Print** menu option. You can print a report for the current entry only, or for the entire view.

In the right pane you will also notice a tab labeled Graph. This provides you with a graphical view of the statistical information in the tabular view. A sample of the graph is shown in Figure 16-21.

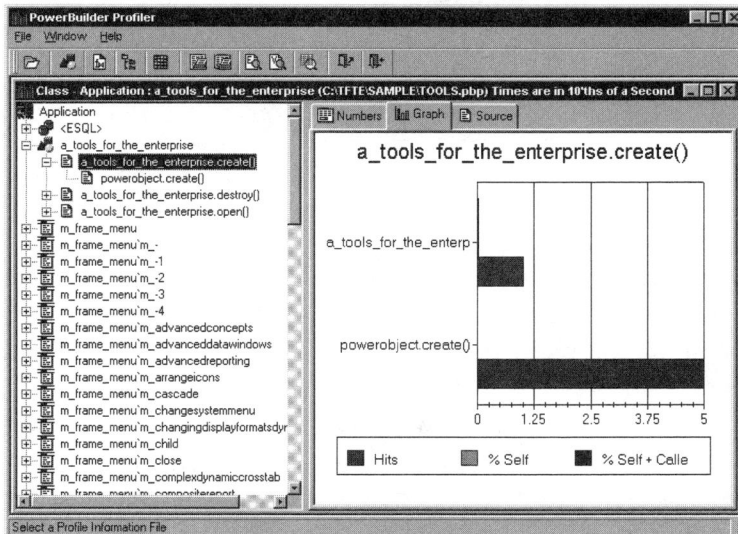

Figure 16-21. *The Graph tab gives you a graphical representation of the statistical information for the current entry.*

16.7.2.1.2 The Routine View

The Routine View uses the same data as the Class View, but extracts to show calls, hits and timing for each routine in the application. You can also examine the relationships between routines, see when one routine calls another and statistics relating to that interaction. (See Figure 16-22.)

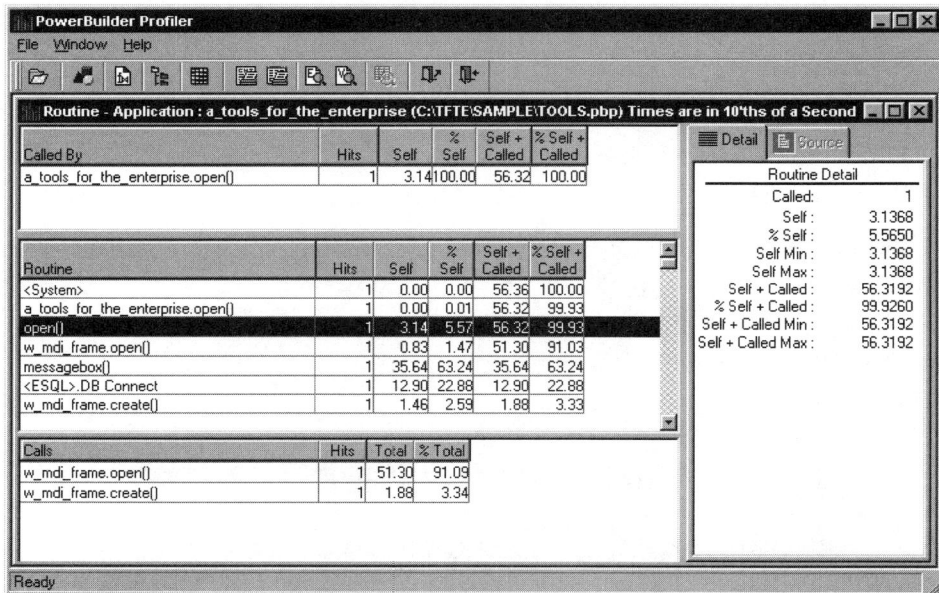

Figure 16-22. The Routine View of the Application Profiler.

There are four panes in the Routine view. The one that you will probably use most is the middle pane on the left. This pane contains the list of all routines that were run when the trace was generated. When you select a routine from this pane, the top pane will show all the routines that call the selected routine, and the bottom pane will show all the routines that are called by the selected routine.

The pane on the right will show the statistics for the selected routine (refer to the Class view for descriptions of what all these statistics terms mean). The Source tab in the right pane will allow you to see line by line all the source code for the selected routine and see specific statistics on how each line executed.

16.7.2.1.3 The Trace View

The Trace View will show you all the routines and objects that were called in sequential order. This allows you to walk through the execution of the application and look for bottlenecks. (See Fgure 16-23.)

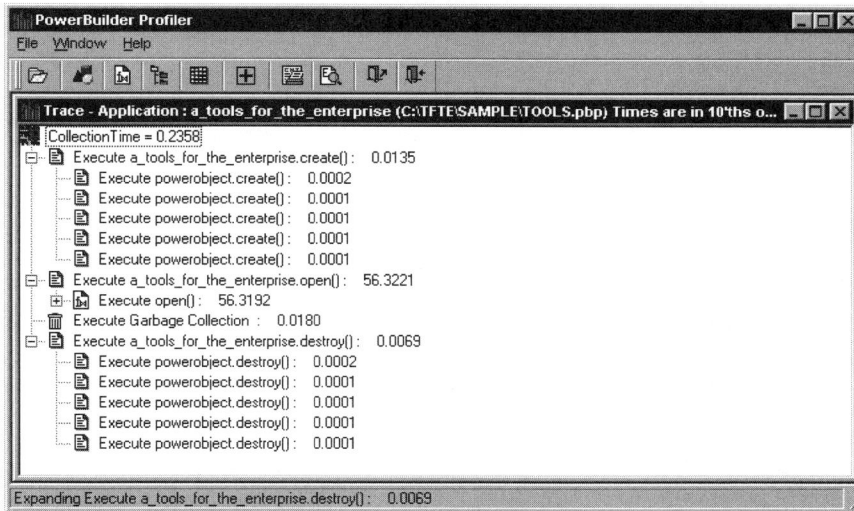

Figure 16-23. The Trace View of the Application Profiler.

Each branch of the trace can be expanded to see the specific details that make up that segment of the trace.

CHAPTER 17

Using the Object Browser

A *lthough simply using the Object Browser is not a particularly advanced topic, I am including it in this book because so few developers use this tool effectively. One of the reasons that this is so is because prior to version 5.0, the Object browser was not particularly useful, however, in the last two versions of PowerBuilder, a completely new object browser has been added, and is worth understanding how it is used.*

17.1 What is the Object Browser?

The Object Browser is a tool that helps you to become a more efficient developer by providing means to familiarize yourself with all the system and user created objects in your application. It also helps you to write better code by giving you a way to examine the attributes and properties of every object.

This second characteristic of the Object Browser can be particularly useful when you are performing actions that are working with properties of objects that are accessed using a string variable. For example, if you want to extract the value from the column in a DataWindow that contains an employee's first name, but you can't remember if the column was called "emp_name" or "emp_first_name" you can browse the DataWindow object in the object browser to get a list of all the column names (and other properties) for that object. This is important because the code you might write to perform this action would be:

```
String ls_EmpName
ls_EmpName = dw_1.GetItemString( dw_1.GetRow(), "emp_name")
```

Because the column name is passed to the function as a string, there is no way for PowerBuilder to evaluate if the column name is valid until runtime when it will try to access the column (and if you got the name incorrect, return a runtime error).

17.2 Looking At the Object Browser

The Object Browser in PowerBuilder 6.0 is fully integrated and utilizes the tab dialog format to access every object within the PowerBuilder environment. This includes all the system objects, enumerated data types, OLE objects, distributed proxy objects, data types, application, DataWindow, window, menu, structures, user objects, and functions. (See Figure 17-1.)

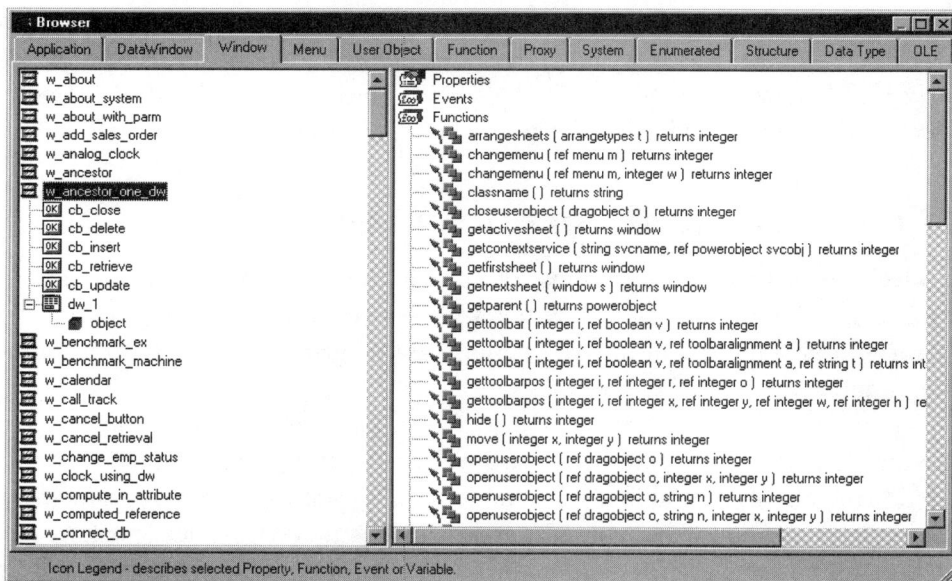

Figure 17-1. The PowerBuilder 6.0 Object Browser allows easy access to all the objects in the PowerBuilder environment. Inside an object you can see all the controls or other components that are part of that class. On the right side you can examine the selected object's properties, functions, events, variables, and structures.

You can select the type of object you wish to browse from the tabs on the top of the page. The objects will appear in the left list box. Double clicking on the object will expand the object so you can see the components that are part of it.

PowerBuilder 5.0–6.0: Note that the buttons for Copy, Document, Close, Regenerate and Help in PowerBuilder 5.0 have been replaced by pop up menu options that are accessed via a right mouse click.

The list box on the right side of the browser will allow you to browse the properties, functions, events, variables and structures (local) in the object. Some items, like functions, can be selected and pasted back into your script painter.

The browser also has a feature to help you prepare documentation for your objects (something all enterprise projects should ensure is done). If you select an object on the left list box and click the right mouse button on the object, you will see a pop up menu option for **Document...** If you select this option it will open the PowerBuilder documentation window. This window produces a rich text edit with all the details of the object inside. You can save this out as an RTF file and import it into a word processor document, or you could cut and paste it into the clipboard. (Figure 17-2.)

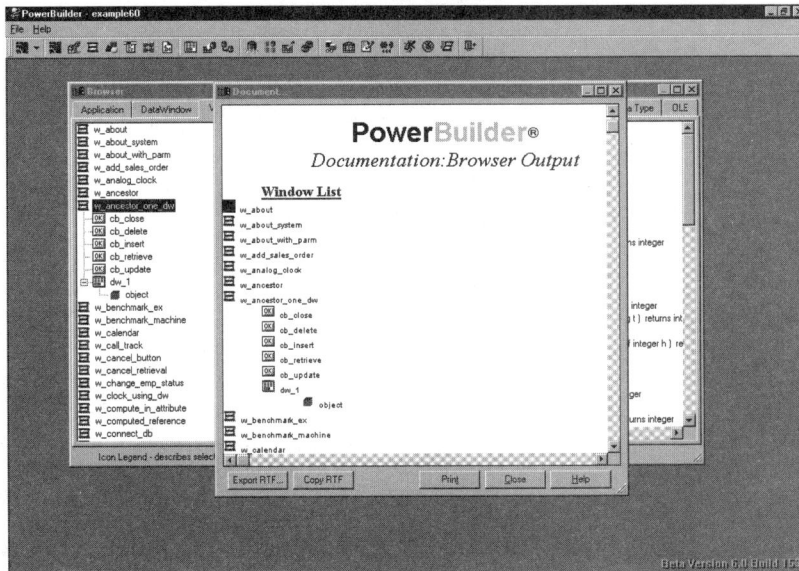

Figure 17-2. The documentation feature of the PowerBuilder 6.0 object browser will make it easier to document your objects for enterprise applications.

PowerBuilder 6.0 Enhancement: The Browser window in PowerBuilder 6.0 has been made non-modal which makes it much easier for you to move between the script painter and the browser for cutting and pasting functions and properties.

17.3 Showing the Inheritance Hierarchy

Another very useful feature of the Object Browser is the ability to view the entire object hierarchy of a system object, or the inheritance tree of any object that you created. By default the browser does not show this. To enable this feature, you click with the right mouse button on an object in the left pane of the browser. A pop up menu will appear with options that you can select. One of the options is Show Hierarchy which will display the left pane hierarchically sorted. You will probably also want to select the right mouse button option Expand All so that all of the objects are visible.

When I perform these two actions on the application object when the System tab is selected, I see results as shown in Figure 17-3.

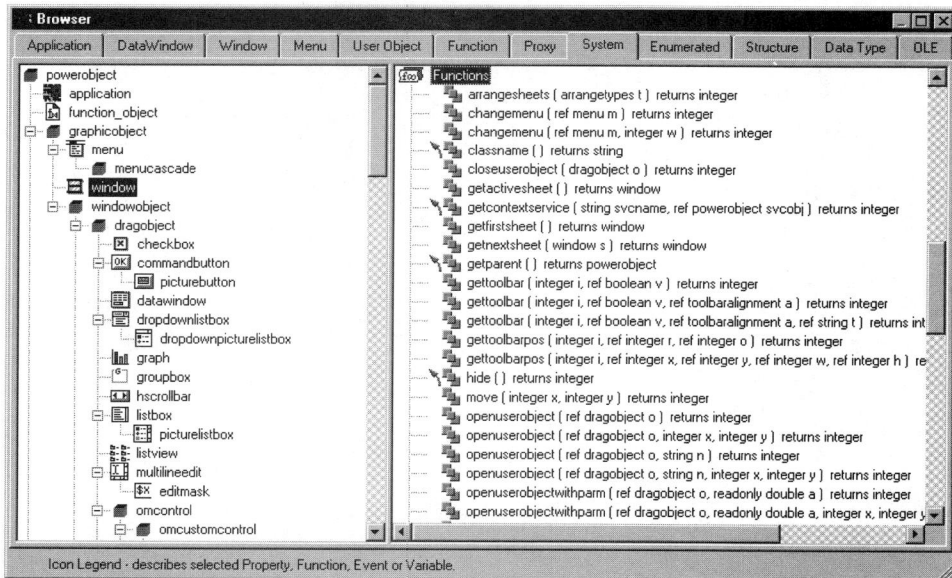

Figure 17-3. The entire system object inheritance tree shown hierarchically sorted.

The browser also helps you to see which properties and functions of an object are native to the current level of the object, or were inherited from an earlier version. Note the functions listed in the right pane of Figure 17-3. Some of these functions have an icon before the function name which shown and arrow pointing to the left. This indicates that this function was inherited from an earlier level in the inheritance tree.

17.4 Regenerating an Object Tree

Sometimes when you make a change in an ancestor object, and then recompile your application, you don't always see the changes in the descendant objects. This happens because the descendant objects need to be regenerated to be brought into sync with the ancestor objects. This can be a real chore if you have changes a base ancestor class which has many descendants.

To make this take easier, you can use the Object Browser! If you browse the ancestor class that you modified, then click on it with the right mouse button, you will see an option on the pop up menu for Regenerate. If you select this option, the entire inheritance tree will be regenerated starting from the ancestor and working its way down. This save you having to hunt through all your libraries to find all the descendant classes (and being sure to regenerate them all in order if you have multiple levels of descendant classes).

17.5 Using the Context Sensitive Help

Another new feature in PowerBuilder 6.0 is the context sensitive help that is available from the popup menu in both panes of the browser. Depending on what you have selected, the Object Browser will open up a help window that relates to the selected item. For example, if you have a function name selected, the help engine will open up the help topic relating to the specific function. Or if you have a specific object selected, the help engine will show you the topic that relates to that specific object class.

17.6 Popup Menu Quick Reference Chart

Table 17-1 is intended to provide an easy reference to the functions that are available on the popup menu.

Table 17-1 *Functions on the Popup Menu.*

Popup Menu Item	Browser Pane	Action
Edit	Left	Opens the select object in the appropriate painter. If a control on an object is selected, then the parent object is opened (i.e. if you select Edit on a command button on a window, the window is opened in the window painter).
Copy	Left/Right	Copies the name of the selected object into the clipboard so that it can be used in scripts.
Paste	Left/Right	If the script painter is open when you open the Object Browser, selecting Paste will paste the name of the selected object into the script.
Expand All	Left/Right	Expands all the objects or controls within the selected object (often used in conjunction with Show Hierarchy).
Regenerate	Right	Regenerates the selected object and all of its descendant objects.
Show Inherited	Left	Allows you to display or not display any properties, functions, events and variables which are inherited from ancestor objects.
Show Legend	Left	Allows you to display or not display the text that describes the currently selected property, function, event or variable.
Show Hierarchy	Left	Allows you to display or not display the inheritance hierarchy for the objects in the display. If this is set to not display, then objects are shown in alphabetical order.
Document	Left/Right	Opens a rich text preview window with a description of all the properties, events, functions and variables for the selected objects (along with a list of all the objects of the same class, which isn't necessary and you may want to edit out). This information can then be printed, saved as an RTF file or copied to the clipboard (an pasted into another document such as MS-Word™).
Help	Left/Right	This will display context sensitive help information related to the selected object, function or property. For example, selecting help while the Retrieve function is selected will open the Retrieve function help topic from the on-line help.

17.7 Summary

The Object Browser is a particularly useful tool for helping a developer to view all the objects in their application and the relationships between them. It also provides a set of tools to help with the documentation and regeneration (synchronization) of the objects.

CHAPTER 18

Advanced Development Concepts

*D*espite some of the claims of Powersoft, there is a considerable leap to be made to move from being a PowerBuilder beginner to being an intermediate or expert developer. Experience and networking have been two of the ways that we have been required to learn in order to become better developers. These are still excellent learning tools and will never be replaced, but we hope to provide you with many of these advanced skills in this chapter and the ones that follow.

These skills relate to almost all areas of PowerBuilder. In this chapter we will address concepts that relate to objects in general. In the following chapters we will address specific subjects including the DataWindow object, reporting, and more.

18.1 Setting Up Object Events

PowerBuilder works within an event driven model. The objects that we create respond to messages sent by the operating system and we build our code into the events to allow our program to carry out its purpose. Every PowerBuilder OO object comes with a set of predefined events. Beyond those we have the ability to define other system events, define custom events or our own user defined events.

Predefined System Events
Activate, Clicked, Close,
CloseQuery, Open, etc.

Custom Events
Events with event ids
from pbm.custom 01
to pbm.custom 75

Undefined System Events
pbm_dwn processenter, pbm_hscroll,
pbm_move, pbm_vscroll, etc.

User Defined Events
Events defined for an object,
but not assigned an event id.

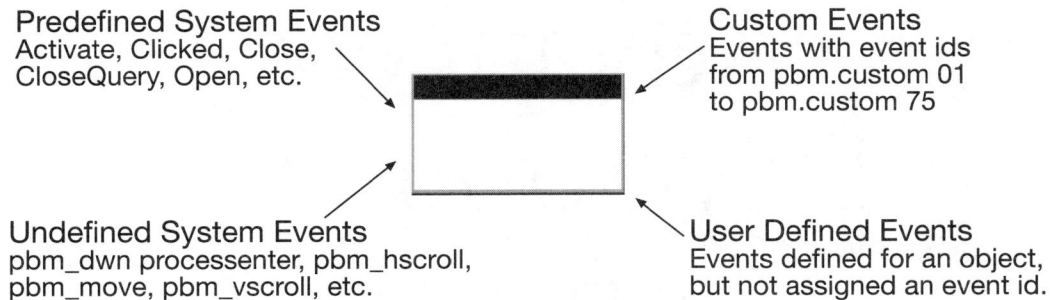

Figure 18-1. PowerBuilder operates within an event driven model. Predefined system events are built into all OO objects. We also have the ability to define other system events, define custom events or our own user defined events.

18.1.1 Predefined System Events

In the Windows environment, there are literally hundreds of messages that an object could listen and respond to. To provide access to all those objects would make the PowerBuilder programming environment far more difficult to use, and having all those stubs could affect the performance of our objects. To avoid these problems, Powersoft has selected the system events that you are most likely to need for each object and built stubs into those objects to allow you easy access to events for inserting your application code.

The predefined system events are the ones that you have used a lot in the past. What is different from pre release 5.0 PowerBuilder versions is the ability to pass arguments into an event. In the system defined events, these arguments replace many of the functions which you are accustomed to. For example, in the ItemChanged event for a DataWindow control, you no longer call GetText() to find out what data the user has entered, it is now obtained through an event argument called *data*.

Arguments can be used in your scripts for a great deal of the system specific information you need to know during execution such as what row was clicked on and the X and Y coordinates of the pointer in the Clicked event of a DataWindow control. This replaces the ClickedRow(), PointerX() and PointerY() functions used in previous versions of PowerBuilder. (See Figure 18-4.)

Predefined System Events

Clicked	LoseFocus
Constructor	Other
DBError	PrintEnd
Destructor	PrintPage
DoubleClicked	PrintStart
DragDrop	RButtonDown
DragEnter	Resize
DragLeave	RetrieveEnd
DragWithin	RetrieveRow
EditChanged	RetrieveStart
Error	RowFocusChanged
GetFocus	ScrollHorizontal
ItemChanged	ScrollVertical
ItemError	SQLPreview
ItemFocusChanged	UpdateEnd
	UpdateStart

DataWindow Control

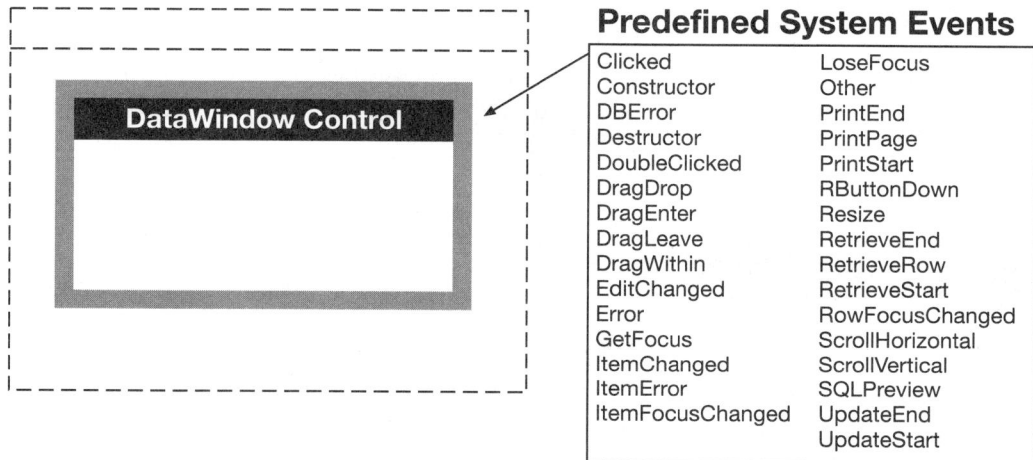

Figure 18-2. Every PowerBuilder OO Object has its own set of predefined system events. These are the events that Powersoft has determined that developers will require most often.

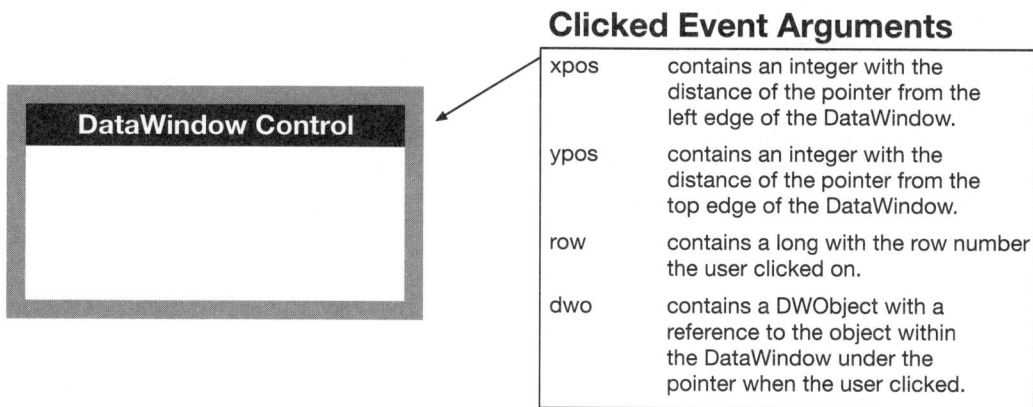

Clicked Event Arguments

xpos	contains an integer with the distance of the pointer from the left edge of the DataWindow.
ypos	contains an integer with the distance of the pointer from the top edge of the DataWindow.
row	contains a long with the row number the user clicked on.
dwo	contains a DWObject with a reference to the object within the DataWindow under the pointer when the user clicked.

DataWindow Control

Figure 18-3. Arguments within a predefined system event can be used to provide system specific information. They are static and cannot be changed.

Developer's Tip: If you use a TriggerEvent() or PostEvent() function to trigger any system event (predefined or one you define yourself) the arguments that are provided will be empty. Be aware of this when you write scripts for these events and be careful when forcing a system event to fire.

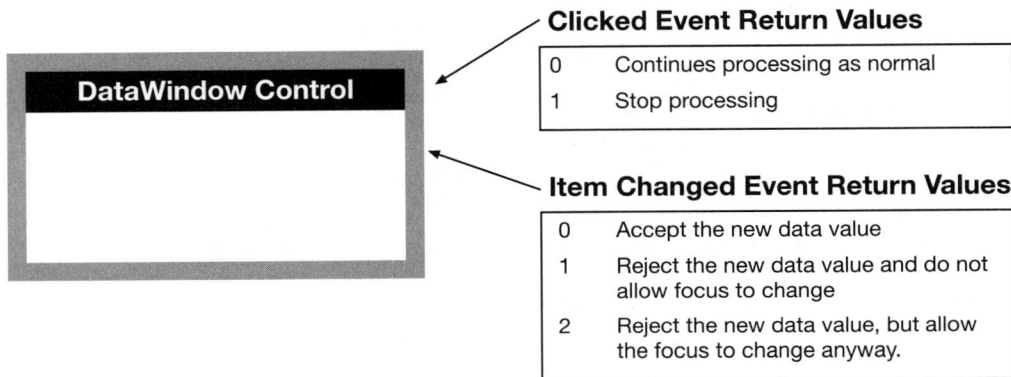

Clicked Event Return Values

DataWindow Control

0	Continues processing as normal
1	Stop processing

Item Changed Event Return Values

0	Accept the new data value
1	Reject the new data value and do not allow focus to change
2	Reject the new data value, but allow the focus to change anyway.

Figure 18-4. Return values for system defined events allow you to alter the default system processing that would occur when an event ends. These are static and cannot be changed.

The return value allows you to change the default system processing that would occur when an event ends. In earlier versions of PowerBuilder this was accomplished through either a function, as in the case of SetActionCode() in the DataWindow control, or through setting the ReturnValue in the Message object (i.e., Message.ReturnValue = 1 in the CloseQuery event of a window would stop the window from closing).

Here is an example of a script in the ItemChanged event of a DataWindow control. You can see the use of the argument *data* for this event to allow us to validate the value, and the use of the return code to tell the system whether we wish to accept the data or not. This script is from the demonstration application on the companion CD and can be found in the DataWindow control dw_employee_list on the window w_emp_maint_dw_events.

Sample Note: In the sample application on the companion CD (and in the script example below) only one column is updateable by the end user, the Salary column. This means that we don't need to check in the script which column is being validated. In a situation with a DataWindow where there are multiple updateable columns, you will need to do a CHOOSE CASE statement to determine which column was clicked on and execute the appropriate valiation rule.

As a second note, many experts recommend that the error message be displayed in the ItemError event and I agree. This is because it is possible for the DataWindow to have encountered an error and triggered the ItemError event before reaching the ItemChanged event. The inclusion of all messaging in the ItemError event helps to properly encapsulate your object. The error is included in this event for the purpose of clarity.

```
// Validates entry to ensure that employee salary has not been increased
// above limit in em_max_salary

DECIMAL ldec_max_salary

IF em_max_salary.GetData(ldec_max_salary) < 1 THEN
        // Invalid value in edit mask
        MessageBox("Invalid Maximum Salary","Maximum Salary does not"+&
            "contain a valid value, please correct before changing"+&
            " salaries")

        // Reject value, but allow the focus to change
        RETURN 2
ELSE
        // Validate new data
        IF IsNumber(data) THEN
            // Valid number entered
            IF Dec(data) > ldec_max_salary THEN
                // Salary exceeds maximum limit
                MessageBox("Salary Too High","The salary entered is"+&
                    " above the allowable maximum")
                // Reject value, but do not allow the focus to change
                RETURN 1
            ELSE
                // Accept the new value
                RETURN 0
            END IF
        ELSE
            // Invalid number entered
            MessageBox("Invalid Salary","The salary you entered "+&
            "is not valid.")
            RETURN 1
        END IF
END IF
```

18.1.2 Undefined System Events

The predefined system events will probably meet 90% of your system event requirements. To allow you to fulfill the other 10%, we have the ability to define our own events that can be linked to any of the currently undefined system events.

Developer's Note: In some of the PowerBuilder documentation and educational materials predefined and undefined system events are referred to as "mapped events."

These undefined system events all have a unique event id. PowerBuilder filters these event ids so they do not appear precisely as they will in your Microsoft Windows SDK or other windows programming manual. Instead you will see them prefixed with a "pbm" identifier (for **P**ower**B**uilder **M**essage) and there will be some events that you won't find listed in your windows guide because they are unique to PowerBuilder (specifically, those that relate to DataWindows). This also allows PowerBuilder applications to use the same objects across multiple platforms as the message from the relevant operating system will be translated to a PowerBuilder Message. (See Figure 18-5.)

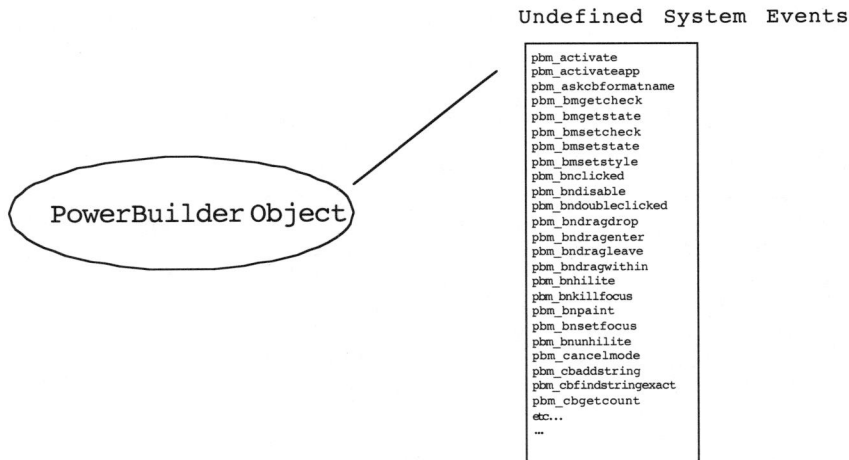

Undefined System Events

```
pbm_activate
pbm_activateapp
pbm_askcbformatname
pbm_bmgetcheck
pbm_bmgetstate
pbm_bmsetcheck
pbm_bmsetstate
pbm_bmsetstyle
pbm_bnclicked
pbm_bndisable
pbm_bndoubleclicked
pbm_bndragdrop
pbm_bndragenter
pbm_bndragleave
pbm_bndragwithin
pbm_bnhilite
pbm_bnkillfocus
pbm_bnpaint
pbm_bnsetfocus
pbm_bnunhilite
pbm_cancelmode
pbm_cbaddstring
pbm_cbfindstringexact
pbm_cbgetcount
etc...
...
```

PowerBuilder Object

Figure 18-5. Undefined system events are those events that respond to system messages, but do not have stubs predefined in the object. All undefined system events have unique event ids, all prefixed with "pbm."

If you are going to be working in the windows environment, most messages still retain the same name and can be looked up in your windows guide to determine their function. If you don't have a windows programming guide, or the Microsoft SDK, and you hope to utilize undefined system events, or other underlying windows functionality, I strongly recommend you acquire one.

To incorporate the undefined system events into your application, you must first open or select the object for which you want to define a new system event. Once opened/selected you will select the **User Events...** menu item from the **Define** option on the menu bar. This will cause the window in Figure 18-6 to open.

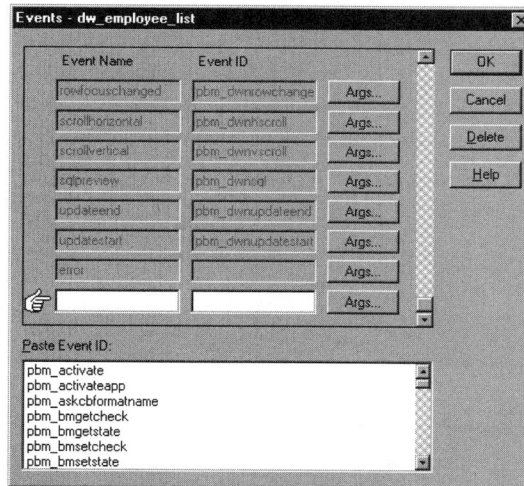

Figure 18-6. *The events window lists all the events currently defined for an object and their respective event ids. You can enter new events here, but you cannot alter events that have been defined at a higher level within the object hierarchy.*

From this window, you can see all the existing predefined system events. They are the ones that are grayed out and you do not have access to them (any undefined system events, custom events, or user events that you have incorporated into ancestor objects will also be grayed out).

To add an undefined system event to the event list, you must move to the bottom of the existing list and enter a name for the new event. The name for the event should have a prefix that allows you to identify it as an event that you have defined. In previous versions of PowerBuilder, many people named these events with a "ue_" prefix for "user event." With the significant difference between the different types of user events, I would recommend different naming standards for each type. For user defined system events, I would stick with the standard naming that Powersoft has used for the predefined system events. For example, if defining an event for pbm_mousemove, call the event MouseMove. I don't feel there is a need to add a prefix to this event type as they are essentially predefined events that simply weren't predefined. If you are more comfortable adding a prefix to the name of the event then use "se_" for "system event." For the other user defined events, I would recommend using "ce_" for the custom events, "ee_" for the external events (pbm_uonexternal01 to 25), for the visual basic events (pbm_vbxevent01 to 50) "vbx_" and for other user events "ue_."

This is an increase in complexity in the naming of user events, but it will allow the developer to discern at a glance what kind of stimulus would trigger a particular event.

Next, to create a previously undefined system event you must select the appropriate event id from the event list. In Figure 18-7 we have created an undefined system event pbm_rbuttondblclk and given it the name "RButtonDblClick." This event will now appear in the event list for this object and all objects inherited from this object. It will be triggered when the user double clicks the right mouse button on this window.

Like the predefined system events, these events have arguments predefined for them. You can view these arguments by pressing the **Args...** button, but you cannot alter them. Each system event will have a different set of arguments.

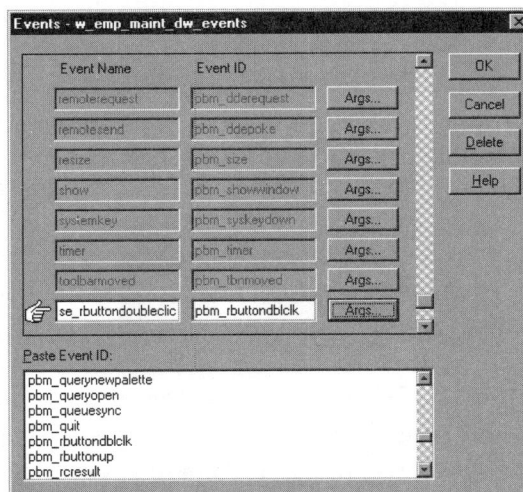

Figure 18-7. *An example of creating a previously undefined system event pbm_rbuttondblclk and assigning it the name "RButtonDblClick." This event will be triggered when the user double clicks the right mouse button on this window.*

18.1.3 Custom Events

The next type of event you might decide to create in an object would be a custom event. In previous versions of PowerBuilder these were referred to as user events. They were given event ids ranging from pbm_custom01 to pbm_custom75. The intention of these events was that the user could call them when they were required using the TriggerEvent() and PostEvent() functions. (Figure 18-8.)

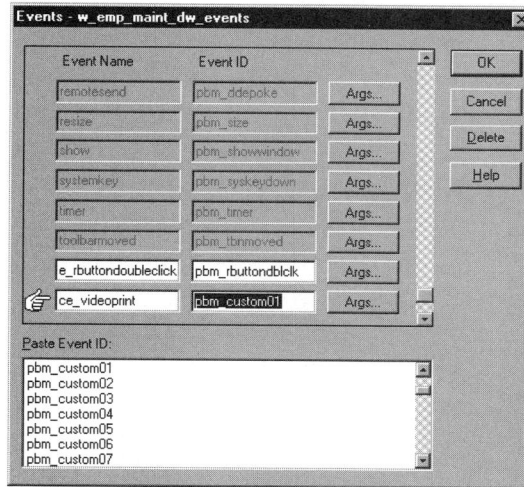

Figure 18-8. *The custom event is an event that you create and is given an event id between pbm_custom01 to pbm_custom75.*

There were two problems with these events. First, there were only 75 stubs (placeholders for custom events). For most PowerBuilder developers this was plenty, but for some of the really involved applications, or the really hefty class libraries, this was not quite enough room. The second problem was that although these were supposed to be user events, they could actually be triggered by certain system messages. Some third party object developers would use these events (quite correctly) to pass messages into the PowerBuilder application from their object. This became a problem if the third party developer passed a message pbm_custom32 and you had defined a different event to occur on that message than the third-party software developer had intended. Suddenly your user defined events became system events.

For this reason, the class of event called a user event was created. See the following section for details on how to use these events.

You may still want to use custom events. If you are migrating an application up from a third-party class library developed under version 4.0, you will definitely still be using them. If, on the other hand, you are developing a completely new application in PowerBuilder 5.0, you will probably want to not use the custom event unless you do desire the event to be triggered by some external party. For purely internal events, use the user event.

All the custom events have two arguments predefined for them, *wparam* which is an unsigned long and *lparam* which is a normal long. You may recognize these from the Message.WordParm and Message.LongParm attributes that we used to use in PowerBuilder 4.0 to pass parameters to events. You cannot change or alter these arguments. This ensures reverse compatibility with previous versions of PowerBuilder.

18.1.4 User Defined Events

The name user defined event has been around for a long time, but as we discussed above, in PowerBuilder 5.0 it means something new. This name now refers to a very special class of event that has a name, but is not linked to a specific system event id. These events are specifically intended to allow you to attach your own methods to an object and then have them triggered only when you call a TriggerEvent() or PostEvent() function. (Figure 18-9.)

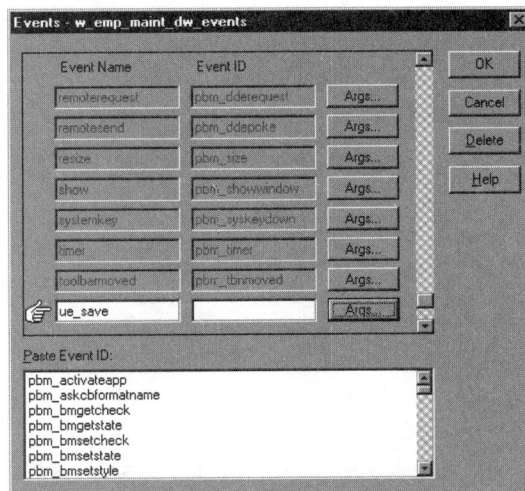

Figure 18-9. To create a user event you simply give the event a name and leave the event id blank.

To create one of these events is very straightforward. You simply give the event a name and leave the event id blank. If you choose you can define arguments and a return value for the event by pressing the **Args...** button. (Figure 18-10.)

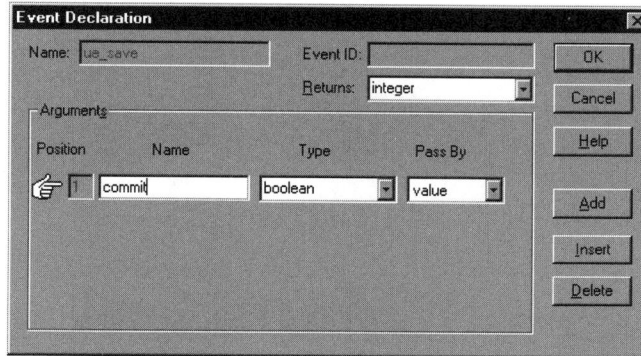

Figure 18-10. *You can define arguments for the events in the Event Declaration window, as you would in the Function Declaration window.*

18.2 *Functioning with Functions*

Functions are an essential part of any development tool. PowerBuilder comes equipped with a very substantial set of built in PowerBuilder functions (at last count I think it was somewhere between 500 to 700) and also supports functions that are defined by the user and functions defined external to the PowerBuilder environment and saved as .DLLs.

Each of the classes of functions are important for providing the functionality and flexibility of PowerBuilder.

18.2.1 PowerScript Functions

PowerBuilder's built in PowerScript functions will fulfill the bulk of your requirements for your processing related development efforts. There are functions for manipulating variables and arrays, functions for opening and closing objects, functions for communicating with the user and more. (Figure 18-11.)

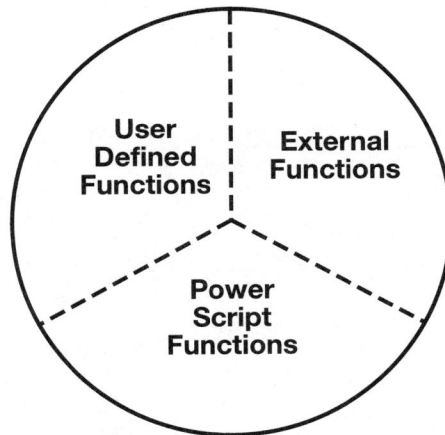

Figure 18-11. There are three primary classes of functions in PowerBuilder, PowerScript functions, user defined functions, and external functions.

Two types of PowerScript functions exist; global and object level. Global PowerScript functions are not attached to any specific objects. They can be used anywhere in your application. They include functions such as Open(), Close(), Today(), Now() and so on. Object level functions are functions which are encapsulated within a specific object class. These functions are only applicable to that class to which they belong. For example, the DataWindow control has functions for Retrieve() and SetRow() that are only of use on the DataWindow control. These functions would serve no purpose on an object such as a command button.

Like all other functions, PowerScript functions accept arguments and return values to the script that called them. Precise explanations of all the PowerScript functions can be found in your PowerBuilder Function Reference Manual or your on-line help.

18.2.2 User Defined Functions

There is always some business process, system process or other functionality that won't exist in the tool and language you decide to work in. PowerBuilder allows you to develop your own user defined functions as required. These functions can accepts arguments, perform processing and return a value just like any PowerScript function.

User Defined Functions

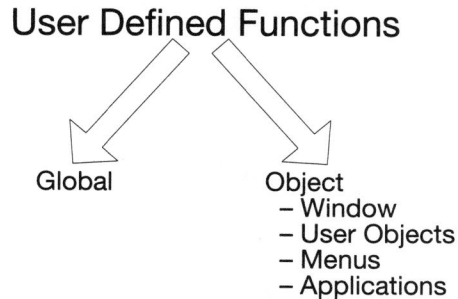

Global

Object
   – Window
   – User Objects
   – Menus
   – Applications

Figure 18-12. User defined functions can exist at two possible levels, global or object (in the form of functions attached to windows, user objects, and menus).

Functions in PowerBuilder can exist at two possible levels, global or object. Object functions can only be declared for windows, user objects, application objects and menus. (Figure 18-12.)

18.2.2.1 Global

The global function has been created to allow you to develop methods that you want to have accessible anywhere in your application. These objects are not really considered OO for two reasons; the exist at a global level which is contradictory to the rules of encapsulation, and they are processes with no substance. A function has a method, but has no properties.

Global functions are declared from the main PowerBar. This icon looks like the script painter icon, a piece of paper with the corner folded over, except that the function painter icon has an "F(x)" symbol on it. This painter exists solely for the purpose of creating global functions, object level functions are created in the painter of the object for which they are created.

In the function declaration window for a global function, you must provide the function with a unique name. This name serves a dual purpose, it is the name that the function object will be saved under in the library, and it is the name that you will use to call the function in your scripts. The name can be up to forty characters in length and is not case sensitive. You can use alphanumerics, underscores, dashes, pound characters (#) and percent characters (%) in the function name although these last three are not recommended (see the Development Tip on the next page).(Figure 18-13.)

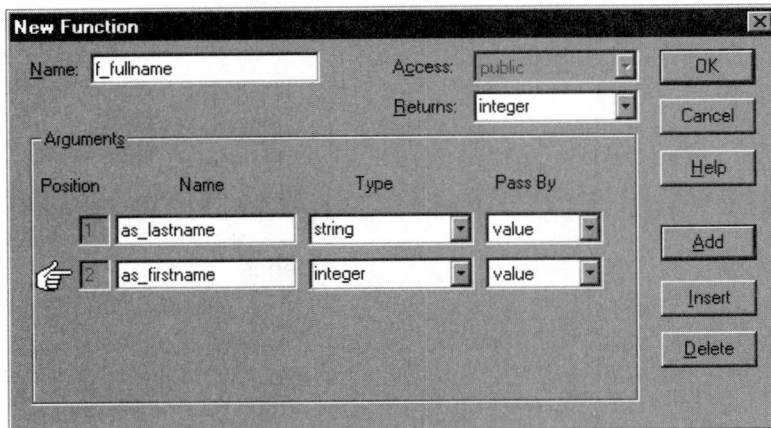

Figure 18-13. The function declaration window for a global function allows you to define the name, arguments, and return values of the function.

Development Tip: Although the name of a function can include dashes, pound, and percent characters, you should not use them in the naming of your functions. These characters can have special meanings and this can be confusing for developers. Consider this example: If you have a variable named A and a variable named B. If you have another variable named A-B it is hard to differentiate from A minus B (A - B).

The access level of a global function is always public. This is necessary as the purpose of this kind of a function is to allow the process to be called from anywhere in the application.

The return type of a global function can be anything in your class hierarchy. The default return value is integer, but you could return a string, a DataWindow, a structure, a window, or any other object anywhere in your class hierarchy (including classes that you have defined with the PowerBuilder painters).

Optionally, you could choose a return type of "(None)." This means that the function will not return a value to the script that called it. This type of function is commonly referred to as a *subroutine*.

You can declare as many arguments for a function as you like (or you could declare none at all). To declare an argument you must decide upon a name for the argument (I recommend prefixing all arguments with a{datatype}, such as as_lastname). The name conforms to standard PowerScript identifier rules. You must also assign the argument a data type. Any data type from within the class hierarchy is acceptable, including any classes that you have defined.

The final element that must be defined is how the argument is to be passed. You have a choice of passing the argument by value, reference, or read only. Passing an argument by *value* means that when the argument is used in the function, you are using a copy of the original value. If you make any changes to the argument the original value from the calling script is not affected.

Passing an argument by *reference* is the exact opposite. What is passed when an argument is sent by reference is not a value, but rather a pointer to where the value can be found. This means that when you use the argument in the function, if you make any changes to the argument these changes will affect the variable which contained the argument in the calling script.

Anything other that a simple datatype (i.e., string, integer, long, etc) is always passed by reference (even if you specify value). This includes objects like DataWindows, windows, menus and so on. If you want to ensure that any object passed by reference cannot be changed in the function you are declaring, you can declare the arguments as *read only*. Any attempt to change the argument or pass it to another function or event will cause a compile time error.(Figure 18-14.)

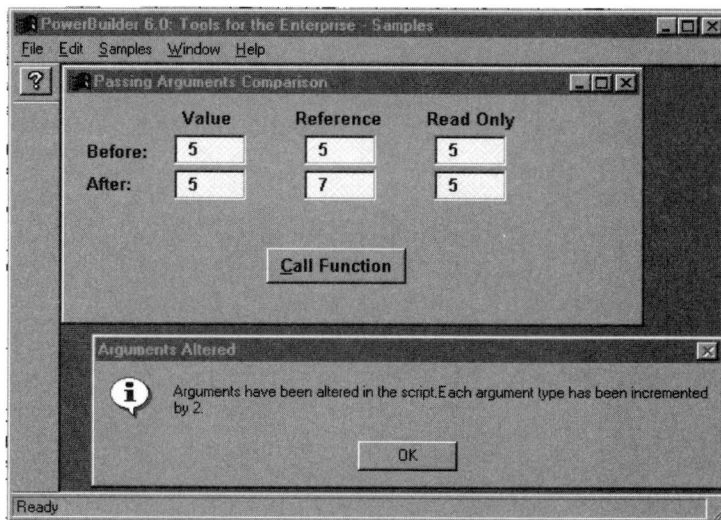

Figure 18-14. The companion CD contains a window with scripts that demonstrate the passing of arguments of all three types.

On the companion CD we have an example which demonstrates the passing of arguments of all three types. You can open the window `w_passing_arguments` to observe the above scenarios. In the Clicked event for the command button Call Function we have three local variables declared: `ll_value`, `ll_reference` and `ll_readonly`.

Each of these local variables is set to a value of 5. The values of each are displayed in a set of single line edit controls, one for each category. Then the function is called and each of the variables is passed in their respective positions. When the function is over the values of the variables are displayed in a separate set of single line edits so that you can compare the differences.

Script for Clicked Event of cb_callfunction on w_passing_arguments:

```
long ll_value, ll_reference, ll_readonly

// Set Before Values

ll_value = 5
ll_reference = 5
ll_readonly = 5

sle_value_before.text = String(ll_value)
sle_reference_before.text = String(ll_reference)
sle_readonly_before.text = String(ll_readonly)

// Call function
wf_arguments(ll_value,ll_reference,ll_readonly)

// Set After Values
sle_value_after.text = String(ll_value)
sle_reference_after.text = String(ll_reference)
sle_readonly_after.text = String(ll_readonly)
```

Within the function wf_arguments the script tries to increment each argument by two. The script compiles for the value and reference types, but does not compile for the read only type. If you wish to see the error message, remove the comments from the line that tries to modify the read only argument. The function concludes by sending a message to the user indicating that the arguments have all been incremented.

Function wf_arguments for w_passing_arguments:

```
// All three arguments will be received.  They will all be altered by adding
2 to each.

al_value=al_value + 2
al_reference = al_reference + 2
```

```
//al_readonly = al_readonly + 2   This statement is not valid.
//                                Trying to execute it would result
//                                in an error at compile time

RETURN MessageBox("Arguments Altered",&
"Arguments have been altered in the script."+&
    "Each argument type has been incremented by 2.")
```

Your application should not require many global functions. Most functions that we would have written as global functions in earlier versions of PowerBuilder should now be included as methods attached to objects (often non-visual).

An example of where global functions have been often used in enterprise systems is in the area of error handling. Figure 18-15 shows a diagram detailing how database errors have often been funneled through our system. A database error can occur in one of two places, after embedded SQL or in a DataWindow. The embedded SQL has often been trapped by a global function like f_check_sql_error(transaction). This function determines the error code (i.e., SQLCA.SQLDBCode) and error message (i.e., SQLCA.SQLErrText) and passes them to f_handle_error(error code, error message) to handle. The DataWindow error causes a DBErrorEvent to be fired. In this event the error code and message are determined by using the DataWindow functions DBErrorCode() and DBErrorMessage(). These are also passed to f_handle_error(error code, error message). The function f_handle_error would then be responsible for tasks such as managing the error, communicating with the user and informing systems support. (See Figure 18-16.)

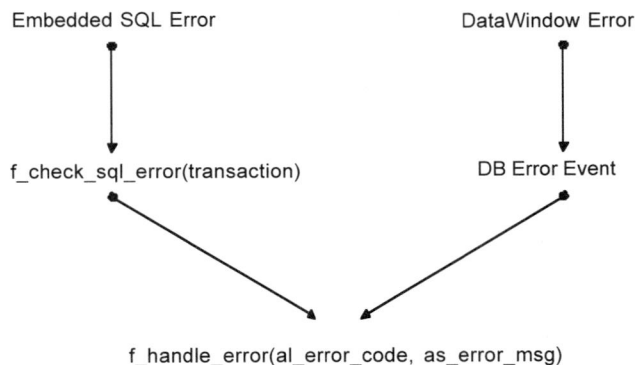

Figure 18-15. *Global functions have often been used in enterprise systems in areas that cross over many boundaries such as error handling.*

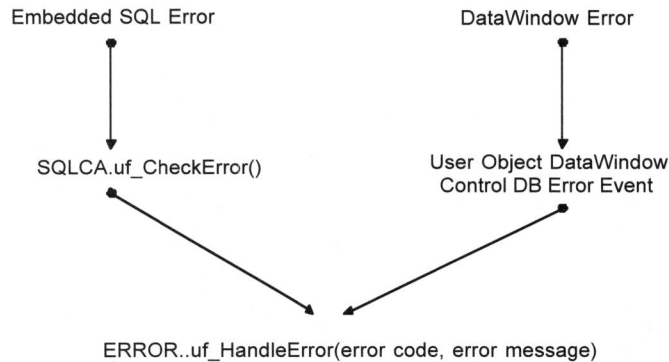

Figure 18-16. In the PowerBuilder applications we build today, methods that may have otherwise become global functions are now being located inside non-visual objects.

All these functions would now be located in different places in today's enterprise development environment. The global function for error checking would be built into the transaction object. This is more in line with the rules of encapsulation. All the methods that belong to the transaction object should be contained within the object. The DBErrorEvent script is contained inside of a user object DataWindow control that serves as the ancestor for all required DataWindow controls. These two methods still call a common error handling routine, but this routine instead of being global is now a part of the non-visual standard Error class that you have modified (refer to Chapter 12 for specific details on how to modify and use the standard class objects.).

18.2.2.2 Object Level

Object level functions are used a great deal in any OO PowerBuilder application. These functions are the mechanism that we use to attach methods to specific objects. We also use this level of function extensively in user object method definition and to build the public interface for any user objects (further discussion on this can be found in Chapter 12—User Objects).

Defining an object level function is very similar to defining a global function. Where it is defined is quite different. You do not use the function painter to create an object level function, instead you use the painter for the object for which you wish to create the function. Under the **Declare** option on the menu for the Window, Menu,

Application, and User Object painters you will see an option that says **Window Functions...**, **User Object Functions...**, **Application Functions...** or **Menu Functions...** as appropriate. Selecting this option will open a similar window to the global function selection window. The one that opens will display all the existing user defined functions for this object. You can open one of the listed functions or create a new one by pressing the **New...** command button. (Figure 18-17.)

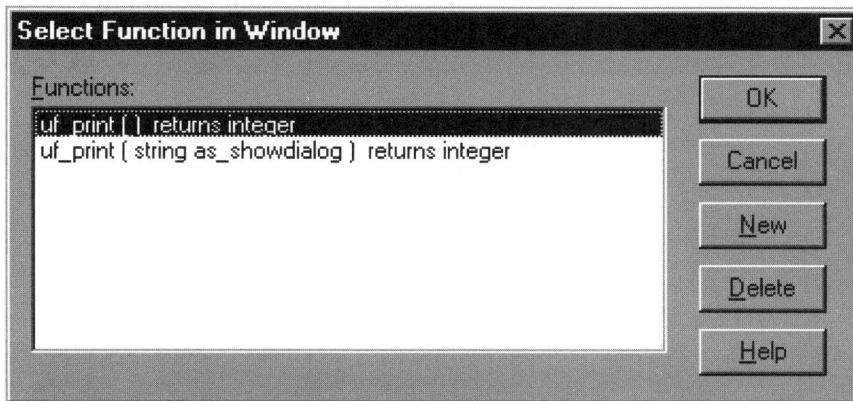

Figure 18-17. The user function selection window for an object level function displays all the functions for the current object.

> **Developer's Tip:** Although it has never been well documented, you can create object level functions in the Application painter for the application object. These are almost global in scope because the application object exists as long as the application is running, but this is a better solution as the rules are at least encapsulated within the application object.

If you select new, you will be taken to the user function declaration window. This window is identical to the one for global user function declarations except that you can now change the access level of your function. You can select from Public, Private or Protected. A *public* access level means that this function is visible and can be called by other objects outside of the current object. For example, from a script on the window for the event ue_retrieve, we can call:

```
dw_employee.Retrieve()
```

This is because Retrieve() is a public function of a DataWindow control. If the function was private or protected, the above script would cause a compile error in the script painter.

Being able to declare a function as private or protected is essential to the concept of encapsulation. It is this process of hiding the functionality within an object that has led to the colloquial definition of encapsulation as 'information hiding'.

Declaring a function as *private* will limit its access to only those scripts actually contained within that object, or on controls on that object. Even descendants of this object will not be given access to the function. An example of this would be a window with a 'flashwindow' function that causes the background color of the window to change at regular intervals. This function could be declared private, and as such could only be called from other scripts and functions on the window or from events on controls on that window. Scripts on controls on a descendant of the window (i.e., a command button clicked script for a command button placed on a window inherited from this window) could not access this function.

To allow descendant classes to access the functions in an object, you would declare your function as *protected*. All the same rules apply as the private access level, but now we are going to be generous and share the functionality with our descendant classes.

In a strong OO application, you should have a substantial quantity of private and protected functions.

The other difference that you will find in an object level function is that you have access to all the same variables, properties and objects that the window event scripts do. You can directly access the window's instance variables, the attributes of a control on the window and so on. Calling functions on controls or on the object directly is not considered negative with regards to OO because the control and the function exist on the same class of object. That means these references are not coupling two classes independent classes together which violates the rules of OO.

18.2.3 External Functions

External functions allow you to integrate functions written in other languages like C, C++, MicroFocus COBOL and Object Pascal into your PowerBuilder applications. In fact, PowerBuilder external functions can access standard windows compliant .DLLs (Dynamic Link Libraries) written by any other language (as long as they have been declared with the standard pascal calling sequence).

There are three primary reasons why you might choose to incorporate external functions into your application:

- The functionality does not exist in native PowerScript (i.e., playing a .WAV file or connecting to an external device).

- The performance of a native language .DLL will exceed the performance that we can obtain out of PowerBuilder. For example, while working on a project with a large telecommunications firm, we needed to calculate the resistance of a standard copper telephone cable. The calculations were quite complex, and although they could be performed in PowerScript, writing them into a C .DLL would result in much faster execution. This was the solution we implemented.

- There are .DLL's already written which will provide the functionality that you require without you having to reinvent the wheel.

Like user defined functions, external functions can be either local or global in scope. Global external functions can be declared in any painter, but are stored in the application object. These functions can be called from anywhere in your application. Local external functions are declared in the painter for the object that you wish to define them for and can only be called by referencing that object first using the traditional "dot" notation. Like user defined functions, local external functions can be given access levels of public, private or protected.(Figure 18-18.)

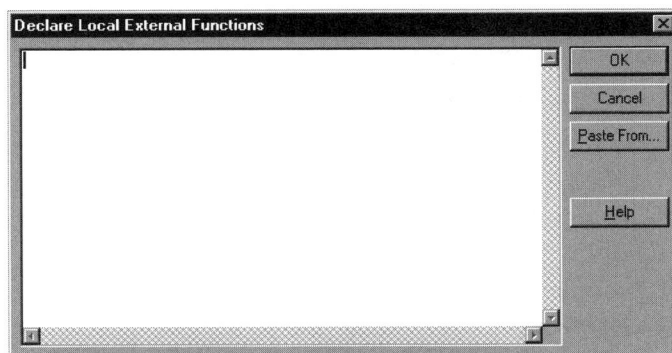

Figure 18-18. The Declare Local External Functions allows you to declare local functions for the current object that are written outside of PowerBuilder. These functions are stored in a .DLL and could be written in C, C++, Object Pascal or another language.

To declare an external function, you will select either **Global External Function...** or **Local External Function...** from the **Declare** menu item. That will open the window shown in Figure 18-18. The window appears the same for both global and external declarations with the exception of the title. The locally declared function will be stored as part of the definition of the object you are currently in whereas the global external will be stored as part of the application object for the current application.

In this window, you must declare all the different components of the external function. The syntax is as follows:

{*access* - PUBLIC, PRIVATE or PROTECTED - only applicable for Local declarations} FUNCTION *return_type function_name* ({{*passed_by* - REF or empty} *argument1_datatype argument1_name,* {*passed by*} *argument2_datatype argument2_name,* ...} LIBRARY *library_name* {ALIAS FOR *extension_name*}

This may look a little complicated, but it really isn't once you get a handle on the different variables:

access. This is the access level for the function. If you don't declare this, it will assume it is public. Global external functions can only be public. Local external functions can be declared as public, private or protected. This argument is optional.

return_type. This is the data type of the value that the function will return to you.

function_name. This is the name of the function within the .DLL that you are accessing. If the function name in the .DLL is not a valid PowerBuilder name, you can use an alias for the function name. This requires appending the ALIAS FOR keywords at the end of the function (see below).

passed_by. This argument is used to define each of the function arguments as being passed either by reference or by value. Many windows API calls utilize variables passed by reference. To indicate a variable passed by reference, enter REF, for all others leave this argument out.

argument_datatype. This is the data type of the argument that you are passing into the function. There will be one of these for every argument that is being passed in.

argument_name. This is the name of the argument that you are passing into the function. You will also need one of these for each argument that the function requires.

LIBRARY library_name. This is the name of the .DLL that contains the function (enclosed in quotations as the data type is string). This .DLL must also be available in your executable environment. LIBRARY is a keyword and must be included before the library name.

ALIAS FOR extension_name. This variable contains the name of the function within the .DLL. This is an optional argument and is only used if you want to use a different name as the function name to call this function, or if the name of the function is not a valid PowerBuilder name. The extension name must be passed within quotation marks (i.e., "sndPlaySndA"). ALIAS FOR are keywords that must precede the extension name variable. You can see the ALIAS for in use in the sample application contained on the companion CD.

An example of declaring a local external function might look like this:

```
PUBLIC FUNCTION uint GetModuleHandle(string ModuleName) LIBRARY "kernel.exe"
```

You call this function with the syntax

```
integer li_handle

// Determine if MS-Word is running

li_handle = THIS.GetModuleHandle("word.exe")

IF li_handle <> 0 THEN
    MessageBox("Found It!","Word is currently running.")
ELSE
    Run("word.exe")
END IF
```

This script uses the external function to determine if Microsoft Word is running already, and if not, it starts it. Two examples of using external functions follow this section, one can be used for playing wave (.WAV) files and the other can be used for altering the system menu on a window.

Developer's Tip: Much of the documentation for third party .DLLs that you may want to integrate will describe the arguments in terms of C data types. Here is a conversion chart for these data types to standard PowerBuilder data types:

C Data Type	PB Data Type	Description
UNSIGNED	UINT	16 bit unsigned integer
LONG	LONG	32 bit unsigned integer
BYTE,CHAR	CHAR	8 bit unsigned character
BOOL	BOOLEAN	16 bit signed integer
WORD	UINT	16 bit unsigned integer
DWORD	ULONG	32 bit unsigned integer
LPSTR	STRING	32 bit far pointer to a char string
LPBYTE	STRING	32 bit far pointer to a char string
LPINT	STRING	32 bit far pointer to a character
LPWORD	STRING	32 bit far pointer to an unsigned integer
LPLONG	STRING	32 bit far pointer to a long
LPDWORD	STRING	32 bit far pointer to a double word
LPVOID	STRING	32 bit far pointer to any data type
HANDLE	UINT	16 bit handle to a window object
PSTR_NPSTR	not supported	

Along with external functions, we also have external subroutines. External subroutines use very similar syntax, but do not return a value. The syntax for an external subroutine is:

{*access* - PUBLIC, PRIVATE or PROTECTED - only applicable for Local declarations} SUBROUTINE *function_name* ({{*passed_by* - REF or empty} *argument1_datatype argument1_name*, {*passed by*} *argument2_datatype argument2_name*, ...} LIBRARY *library_name* {ALIAS FOR *extension_name*}

As you can see, the only difference is the keyword SUBROUTINE instead of FUNCTION and the elimination of the return_datatype parameter.

18.2.3.1 Example—Playing a Wave File

You might decide that you want to provide the ability to play sound bites to your user from time to time. We can use an external function to provide this functionality. I can recall one PowerBuilder application where the ancestor window played the sound effect of opening doors on Star Trek (that distinctive "shoop" sound) when the window opened and then played the sound of the same doors closing when you exited from the window. (Figure 18-19.)

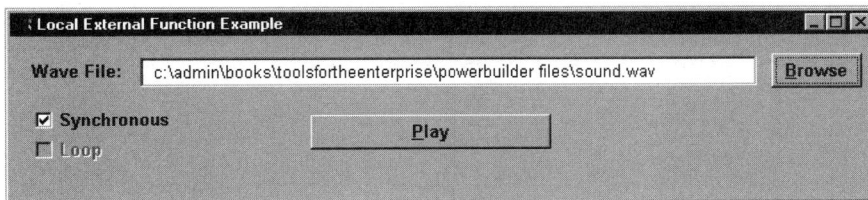

Figure 18-19. *The Companion CD example application contains a window which will call a local external function to play a wave (.WAV) file.*

To make this work, we need to declare two local external functions. You can follow this example along by examining the object w_local_external_function in the sample application that comes on the companion CD.

The declaration for these local external functions is as follows (the declaration shows both the 32 bit and 16 bit variations):

```
// This set of functions is declared for 32 bit operating environments.
// If you have a 16 bit environment, please comment out the lines below
// and uncomment the section labeled "16 bit local external functions"

FUNCTION boolean sndPlaySoundA(string SoundName, uint Flags)&
        LIBRARY "WINMM.DLL"
FUNCTION uint waveOutGetNumDevs () LIBRARY "WINMM.DLL"

//16 bit local external functions

//FUNCTION boolean sndPlaySound (string SoundName, uint Flags)&
//        LIBRARY "mmsystem.dll"
//FUNCTION uint waveOutGetNumDevs () LIBRARY "mmsystem.dll"
```

The WaveOutGetNumDevs() function is used to determine if we have a valid device for playing .WAV files. If we have a valid device, it will return a number greater than zero. If no device exists, then it will return a zero.

The sndPlaySoundA() function actually passes the name of a wave file to an external API which takes care of the process of playing it. By setting the flags parameter, you can alter if it plays synchronously, asynchronously, loop the sound until you tell it to stop, and other options. (Figure 18-20.)

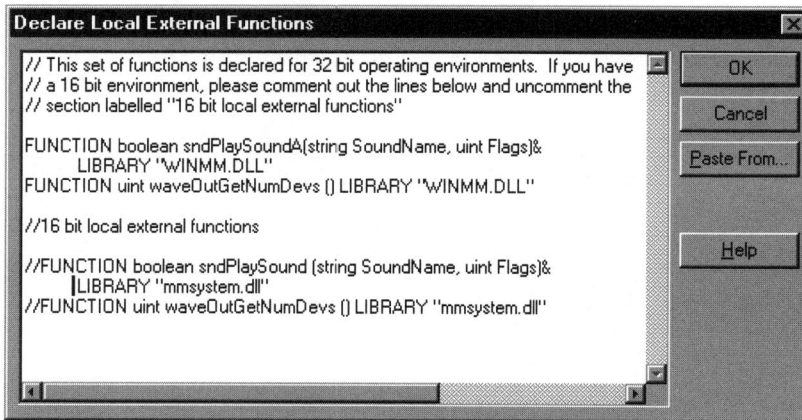

Figure 18-20. *By declaring two local external functions as they appear here, we are sound enabling our object.*

The names of these functions can be a little cryptic, so we can take advantage of the ALIAS FOR keyword to simplify our interface with the external functions. The new declaration looks like this:

```
FUNCTION boolean PlayWave(string SoundName, uint Flags) &
        LIBRARY "WINMM.DLL" ALIAS FOR "sndPlaySoundA"
FUNCTION uint  GetWaveDevice() &
        LIBRARY "WINMM.DLL"  ALIAS FOR "waveOutGetNumDevs"

//16 bit local external functions
//FUNCTION boolean  PlayWave(string SoundName, uint Flags) &
//          LIBRARY "mmsystem.dll" ALIAS FOR "sndPlaySound"
//FUNCTION uint GetWaveDevice()
//          LIBRARY "mmsystem.dll" ALIAS FOR "waveOutGetNumDevs"
```

The script we call in the Clicked event of our Play command button looks like this:

```
// Options for playing sound with the windows API.
// These values can be added together to achieve the desired
// combination.
// (i.e. asynchronous sound with looping would be 1+8 = 9)
```

```
//SND_SYNC       Value: 0  // play sound synchronously (default)
//SND_ASYNC      Value: 1  // play sound asynchronously
//SND_NODEFAULT  Value: 2  // don't use default sound
//SND_MEMORY     Value: 4  // lpszSoundName (the first argument) points //
                    to a memory file
//SND_LOOP       Value: 8  // loop the sound until next sndPlaySoundA
//                                function call
//SND_NOSTOP     Value:10  // don't stop any currently playing sound

uint lui_numdevs
integer li_options=0

// Set synchronous option
IF NOT cbx_sync.checked THEN li_options = li_options + 1
// Set Loop option
IF cbx_loop.checked THEN li_options = li_options + 8

SetPointer(Hourglass!)
lui_numdevs = GetWaveDevice()
IF lui_numdevs > 0 THEN
    PlayWave(sle_filename.text,li_options)

ELSE
    MessageBox("Wave Failure","Cannot play requested .WAV file."&
          +"No device available.")
END IF
```

Now you can have fun adding sound to your PowerBuilder applications! (remember not to use sound as a primary means of communicating with the user as this would not be a good interface for people who are hearing impaired. Use sound purely as a secondary means of communications).

18.2.3.2 Things to Remember

If you are planning on rolling your application out across both 16 and 32 bit platforms, you will need to be careful. Most .DLLs that you might want to access are different in the 16 and 32 bit environments. You will need to keep separate versions of any objects that use external functions like that.

Remember that when rolling your application out to your end user, any .DLLs being accessed must be available in the Windows directory, the current directory or somewhere in the library search path. They will not be rolled into the .EXE that you are creating.

18.3   Calling Events and Functions from Scripts

You have a choice in how you would like to call your functions and events within your scripts. In previous versions of PowerBuilder, we would call global functions simply by naming them:

```
f_check_sql_error(SQLCA)
```

and we could either Post or Trigger an event using the PostEvent() and TriggerEvent() functions such as:

```
w_employees.TriggerEvent(Clicked!)
```

or

```
dw_employees.PostEvent("ue_save")
```

Triggering an event caused it to be executed immediately, whereas posting an event meant that it was placed in the queue to be processed after the current script was complete. You can still call your function and trigger or post your events with this syntax, however, for PowerBuilder we have expanded functionality available to us, and in order to take advantage of it, we need to use the updated syntax.

We now have the capability of not only choosing between post and trigger for events, but now also for functions. The syntax has been standardized so that we can use the same format for both.

{*objectname.*}{*type* - FUNCTION or EVENT}{*call_type* - STATIC or DYNAMIC}{*when* - TRIGGER or POST} *method_name* ({*argument1, argument2, …*})

The components that make up this syntax are:

objectname. This is the name for the object which the method (function or event) exists on. If this is a global function, then objectname would be excluded from the above syntax. If used, objectname must be followed by a period ("."). This is the dot notation separator.

type. Contains a keyword which indicates if you are calling a FUNCTION or an EVENT. If you leave out this optional parameter, it will assume that you are calling a FUNCTION.

call_type. By default, PowerBuilder will confirm the existence of the function or event you are calling and its correct syntax. In certain situations, such as using abstract classes of objects, you may want to access a function that does not exist in this object, but may exist in a descendant (this object is never instantiated, but its descendants are). To accomplish this, we must tell PowerBuilder not to check the syntax now, but to check it at runtime. We specify this by using the DYNAMIC key word here. After using this in your script, you will not get a compile error on the method, but you could trigger a runtime error. If you do not specify DYNAMIC, the alternative is STATIC, which is also the default if you do not specify a call type.

when. Here is where you decide if you are going to TRIGGER or POST your method. Triggering the method will cause it to execute immediately, whereas posting it will cause it to execute when the current script ends. The default if you do not specify a when keyword is to trigger the method.

method_name. The name of the function or event that you will to call. You can use either predefined PowerScript functions and events, or you can use user defined functions and events. The syntax is the same in all cases.

argumentn. (**Note:** arguments will match the declaration for the object method.) The arguments that you are passing to the method. Both functions and events can receive arguments. Refer to the function reference guide or objects and controls manual for details on which arguments are required for the method you are using.

The functions and events within PowerBuilder are becoming more alike with each new release of the product. The *type*, *call_type* and *when* keywords above can be placed in any order and PowerBuilder will be able to understand, just be sure to place them between the dot and the method name.

Here are some examples of the method calling syntax in use.

18.3.1 Triggering an Event

Triggering an event will cause it to be executed immediately. This will cause the user defined event ue_print on the object w_employees to execute:

```
w_employees.EVENT STATIC TRIGGER ue_print("landscape",2)
```

Note that the keywords STATIC and TRIGGER did not need to be included as they would have defaulted if we had entered:

```
w_employees.EVENT ue_print("landscape",2)
```

The event ue_print is set up to accept two arguments. Due to this, we could not use the traditional syntax, TriggerEvent() to call this method as it does not support this type of argument passing.

18.3.2 Posting an Event

Posting an event will cause it to be placed in the queue of methods waiting to be executed for the current object. This method will run when its turn comes up. We will add a twist to this example, we are declaring this script on the ancestor object w_a_base which never gets instantiated. All the descendants that can print are descendants of w_a_print_base, a direct descendant of w_a_base. We decide to put the call to the print method in the ancestor w_a_base event though it only exists on the descendant.

```
THIS.EVENT DYNAMIC POST ue_print("landscape",2)
```

Remember that the keywords can be in any order. We could just as easily have entered:

```
THIS.DYNAMIC EVENT POST ue_print("landscape",2)
```

Traditional PostEvent() function syntax does not check for the existence of dynamic user defined events until runtime, but it will check for system defined events if you use enumerated data types to call them. For example:

```
THIS.PostEvent("ue_print")
```

would not check for the existence of ue_print until runtime, but,

```
THIS.PostEvent(Clicked!)
```

will check for a clicked event immediately. Either way, the traditional syntax still could not be used due to the custom arguments being passed.

18.3.3 Posting Functions

For the first time, now you have the ability to make a function execute after the current script has finished running. You can also now define a function to be called dynamically, this means that the function does not need to exist on your current object. Prior to this, functions were always declared statically and if you only wanted to place a function in a descendant, you had to declare the function in the ancestor in order to provide a stub that would allow the function to compile.

You must use the new syntax to post a function. For example:

```
dw_dept.FUNCTION STATIC POST Retrieve()
```

or

```
dw_dept.FUNCTION DYNAMIC POST wf_update("COMMIT")
```

where wf_update() may not exist on this object, but will definitely exist on the descendant(s) which will use this method.

18.3.4 Triggering Functions

Triggering functions is the easiest of all four of these methods. You can use the traditional syntax such as

```
dw_dept.Retrieve()
```

which will cause the function to execute immediately and the function must exist at compile time in order for the above to be syntactically correct.

The same thing could be accomplished with the 5.0 syntax as follows:

```
dw_dept.FUNCTION Retrieve()
```

although using the FUNCTION keyword is redundant as this is the default. You can use the keywords in any order you choose. If I wanted to use a function called ChangeData that does not exist now, but would at runtime (through inheritance) I would call it from my script like:

```
dw_dept.DYNAMIC ChangeData()
```

18.4 Implementing Drag and Drop

The Graphical User Interface (GUI) has revolutionized the way that people interact with computers in their day to day lives. It has enabled many non-technical people to have regular interactions with information systems. When the GUI revolution arose a number of years back, one of its primary differences was the ability to use the mouse to "pick up" something and "drop" it somewhere else. The term that came to describe this is known as *drag and drop*.

18.4.1 What Is Drag and Drop?

The concept behind drag and drop is to allow the user to interact with the computer the way they would interact in the real world. When designing applications we call this a *real world metaphor*. An example of a real world metaphor that you are likely already familiar with would be to pick up something (perhaps a file from file manager, or an icon in your Windows 95 desktop) and drag it to a trash can icon (or "Recycling Bin"in the environmentally conscious Windows 95). When you drop the object/file on the trash can, it deletes it. Just like throwing something into your trash bin in real life.

Another example of drag and drop in an application you are probably familiar with is the Windows 3.11 File Manager, or the Windows 95 Explorer. In these applications, you can copy and move files simply by dragging them and dropping them in their new locations.

18.4.2 How Should Drag and Drop Be Used?

The end user of your system will initiate a drag and drop by selecting the object they wish to "pick up" by pressing the left mouse button while the pointer is over the object and holding it down through the drag process. The mouse pointer should now change to an icon that indicates to the user that they have picked up the object. Now the user will move the mouse (still holding down the left mouse button) to the object where they wish to drop what they picked up. Releasing the left mouse button above the object the user wishes to "drop" on triggers the appropriate action.

When you perform the final act of drag and drop, the "drop," a variety of actions can occur. There are certain types of business processes to which this techniques lends itself well. (Figure 18-21.)

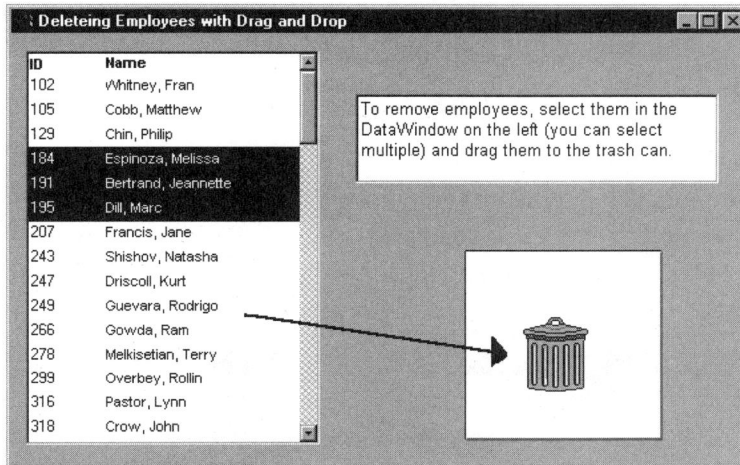

Figure 18-21. Drag and Drop allows the user to interact with the system in a way that models the way they interact with the real world.

18.4.2.1 Copy and Move Objects or Data

Drag and drop is often used to copy or move selected items from one object into another. This is the type of process being modeled in the Windows Explorer. In a PowerBuilder application, we may have a window with two or more DataWindow objects and we might want to drag and drop rows between them. On the companion CD is a sample window with three DataWindow controls as shown in Figure 18-22.

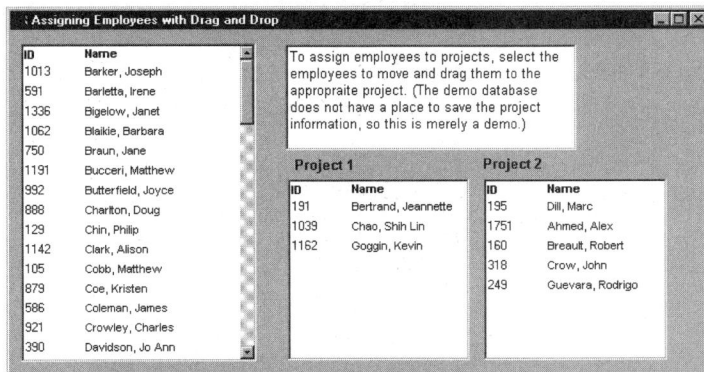

Figure 18-22. Copying and moving objects and data is a common use for drag and drop.

You can select personnel from any of the DataWindow controls and drag it to another. You can also select multiple people to move at one time. We will examine the details of these two samples later in this section.

18.4.2.2 Change Properties

Drag and drop is often implemented in situations that allow us to change the properties of the source object or data. On the companion CD there is a window that allows us to see the changing of data for an employee via drag and drop. This is the window pictured in Figure 18-23.

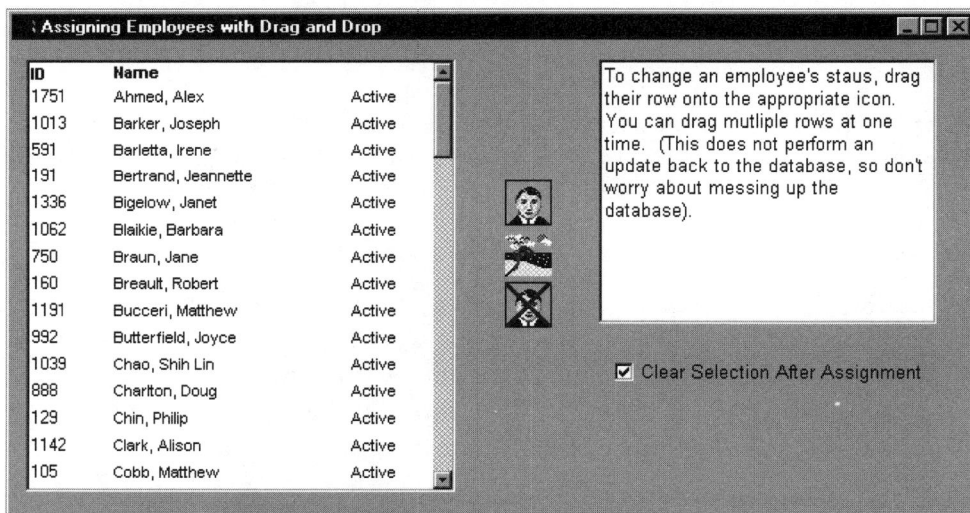

Figure 18-23. *Drag and drop can also be used to change the properties of an object or data.*

In this window we can select an employee, or multiple employees, and drag them onto the picture that represents their current status. This will allow us to perform a mass change of status for any grouping of employees.

18.4.2.3 Process Data

The drag and drop interface can be used to initiate processing on an object or a set of data. In the example in Figure 18-21, we use drag and drop to initiate the DeleteRow() process against any set of employees that we selected.

Another example of this would be taking a document in the Windows 95 desktop and dropping it onto the printer icon or the fax icon. The former would send the document to the printer, the latter to the fax machine. I have worked on an application where a completed where a completed order was scheduled for delivery by dragging the order onto a picture of a delivery truck.

18.4.3 How Does Drag and Drop Work?

In order to use drag and drop within your application, you must first identify a *source object* (the object that will be dragged) and a destination or *target object* (where the source object can be dropped). You may have many source and many target objects, but both must exist in order for drag and drop to work. (Figure 18-24.)

Figure 18-24. *To use drag and drop you must have at least one source object (to be dragged) and one target object (to be dropped upon).*

All PowerBuilder controls can be dragged with the exception of drawing objects which have no events (lines, ovals, rectangles, round rectangles). The reverse is also true, anything that can be dragged is also a valid target object. Objects can be dragged to any window or object within a PowerBuilder application, but you cannot drag an object to a non-PowerBuilder application.

Developer's Tip: To obtain a list of objects that can be dragged, go to the Object Browser and select the System tab. Click on DragObject with the right mouse button and select **Show Hierarchy** from the popup menu. Then click again and select **Expand All**. All the objects that appear under DragObject are valid source and target objects. This includes any objects that you create as user objects or descendants of standard windows objects and controls.

18.4.4 The Drag and Drop Events

When an object is being dragged, it will cause certain events to fire in any valid target objects that it comes into contact with. (Figure 18-25.)

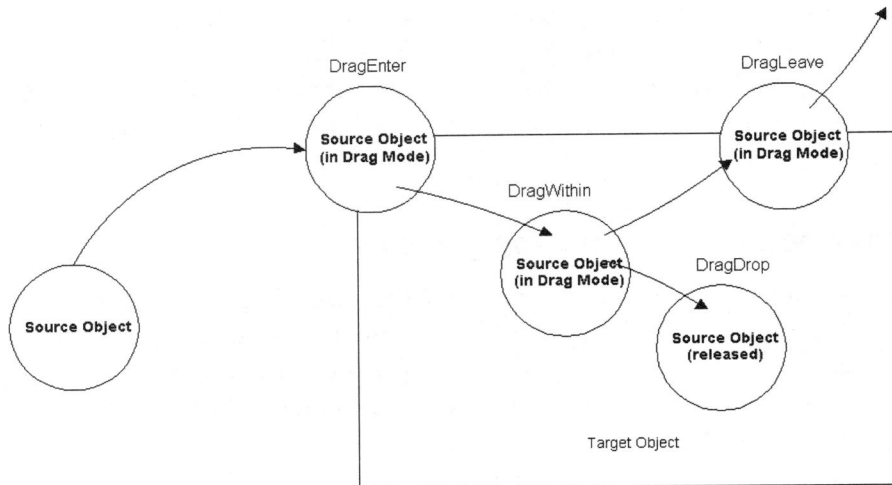

Events

DragDrop	The source object is dropped on a target object. The left mouse button is released.
DragEnter	The center of the source object crosses over the border into the target object.
DragWithin	The source object is dragged within the border of the target object.
DragLeave	The center of the source object crosses over the border passing outside the target object.

Figure 18-25. When an object is being dragged, it may initiate DragDrop, DragEnter, DragWithin, and DragLeave events on valid target objects it comes into contact with.

In Figure 18-25 you can see the different events that fire as we drag our source object. When the center of the source object passes over the border of a valid target object, a DragEnter event is triggered on the target object. If you continue dragging the source object inside the target object, a DragWithin event is triggered. If you drag the object all the way through the target object and out again, a DragLeave event is triggered as the center of the source object passes over the border of the target. The most important event that you will want to catch will be the DragDrop event which occurs when the source object is dropped on the target by releasing the left mouse button.

It is up to you to write the scripts for these events that will determine what action will occur when the object is dropped.

18.4.5 Drag Properties

All objects that can be dragged have two properties that relate to the way they appear and behave when they are being dragged:

- **DragAuto.** This is a Boolean value that determines whether you will be setting drag mode on in your script, of if you want PowerBuilder to do it for you.

- **DragIcon.** The icon that will display at the pointer for the source object currently being dragged.

18.4.6 Drag Mode

When an object is being dragged, we say that the object is in *drag mode*. On any given source object we can set the DragAuto attribute to determine if PowerBuilder will automatically place a control into drag mode when a user clickes on it (DragAuto = TRUE), or if you must code a script that will start drag mode (DragAuto = FALSE). A DragAuto value of FALSE (which is the default) means that the drag mode must be initiated using the Drag() function in your script.(Figure 18-26.)

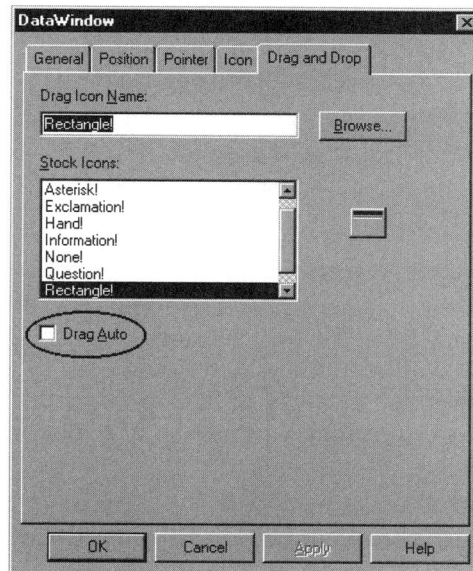

Figure 18-26. The DragAuto property can be set on the Drag and Drop tab page of the Properties window for any valid source object.

You may decide that you like DragAuto for some of your controls to be set to TRUE. As a warning, you need to remember that if DragAuto is TRUE, the clicked event on that object never gets triggered by the system. Instead the object is placed into drag mode. This means that for objects where we do want to deal with the clicked event, such as a DataWindow or a list box, we must use DragAuto = FALSE and manually initiate the drag mode.

The DragAuto property can be set on the Drag and Drop tab page of the properties window for any valid source object. This is also where you will set the DragIcon property.

Developer's Tip: Always make sure that you do not interfere with the normal behavior of an object or control when you implement drag and drop. For example, setting DragAuto to TRUE in a listbox would result in the user never being able to select an item from the listbox.

18.4.6.1 Using the Drag() Function

To initiate drag mode manually we will use a function called *Drag()*. This function can be used to both begin and end drag mode, although it is primarily used to begin drag mode and drag mode automatically ends when you drop the source object.

The syntax for the Drag() function is:

```
objectname.Drag(dragstatus - Begin!, End! or Cancel!)
```

The parameters that compose the syntax are:

objectname. This is the name of the object for which you want to change the drag mode.

Dragstatus. Specifies whether you want to begin, end or cancel drag mode. The values in this parameter are enumerated datatypes: Begin!, End! or Cancel!. Drag mode automatically ends when the user releases the left mouse button. For all but exceptional circumstances, the only drag status you will use is Begin!.

So where do I code this function? It should be coded in some event that relates to the mouse, such as Clicked, DoubleClicked, MouseMove, LeftButtonUp and so on. If you code the function in an event which is not related to the mouse, for example, the open event of a window, then the user will be dragging the object without needing to hold down the left mouse button. In order to restore normal functioning of the mouse, the user will need to click on something to cancel the drag mode. This is not standard windows behavior.

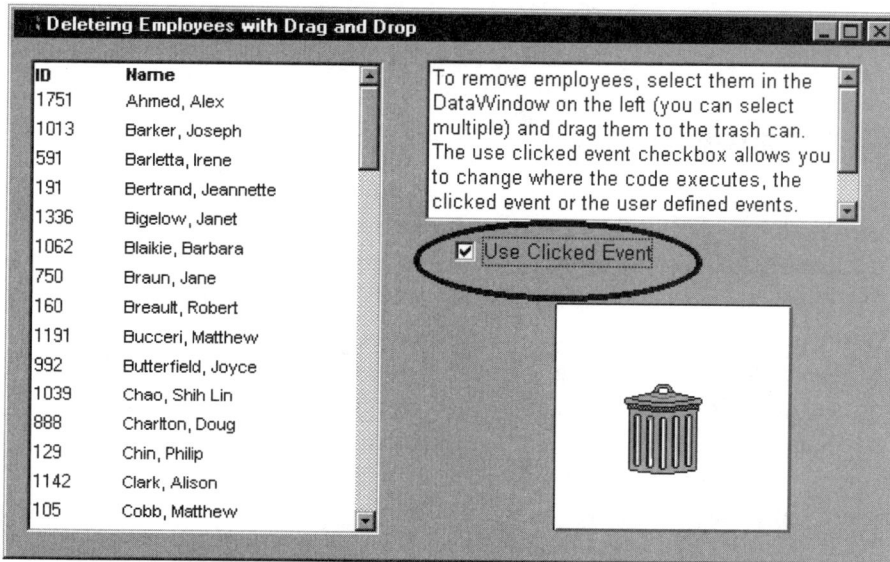

Figure 18-27. *In the sample application, you can choose whether you want to initiate drag mode in the clicked event, or in the user defined events, MouseMove and LeftButtonUp.*

Which event you will code the function in is dependent upon the precise functionality you require. The sample application on the companion CD demonstrates the difference between coding the Clicked event and coding the MouseMove or LeftButtonUp events. You can select the option to use one or the other, as indicated in Figure 18-27.

If you use the LeftButtonUp and MouseMove events, the individual rows are not selected or deselected in the process of trying to begin drag mode. If you use the clicked event, they will be. The clicked event script requires less code, but I feel that using the combination of LeftButtonUp and MouseMove provides a better user interface. See the section "Looking At The Code" to see how the object from the companion CD functions.

The return value of the Drag() function will tell you if the control was successfully placed into drag mode (a return value of 1) or if it failed (a return value of -1). The two reasons that this function might fail are:

- You tried to put a control into drag mode when another control was already in drag mode. Only one control can be in drag mode at a time.

- You tried to cancel drag mode for a control that wasn't currently in drag mode.

18.4.7 Setting the Drag Icon

When you drag an object in a PowerBuilder application, PowerBuilder will show an outline in the shape of the object as the dragged object. This is not always the most visually appealing way of indicating to the user that they are dragging an object. To use a more compact icon you can set the DragIcon property of a control to a custom icon that will appear in place of the standard mouse pointer.

An example of using a drag icon can be seen in the Windows 3.1 File Manager. When you select a file from the listbox, instead of seeing an outline of the entire listbox, you see an icon which shows and arrow and a sheet of paper (representing a file).

You can use the DragIcon attribute to provide a visual cue to the user as to when they can perform certain actions. For example, you can place the object into drag mode and set the drag icon to be a picture of the object (i.e., a file folder if you are moving a file). Then, when the user drags the file over a valid target object, you could use the DragEnter event to change the DragIcon attribute to a different icon (i.e., a round target). It is also useful for indicating areas where the user cannot drop this object by changing the icon to a "no.cur" indicating that dropping on that target is not valid.

Developer's Tip: You can create your own icons and cursors using any drawing application that can create .ICO and .CUR files. The Watcom Image Editor which comes with PowerBuilder enterprise can create both of these types of files.

Developer's Tip: PowerBuilder will automatically turn the drag icon into a no-drop icon whenever the user moves the pointer to any spot that is an invalid drop zone (such as outside the window or onto the control menu).

18.4.8 Looking at the Code—w_drag_drop

In the sample application on the companion CD there are three different drag and drop examples; w_drag_drop, w_drag_drop_2 and w_drag_drop_3. These windows all show the different variations of drag and drop discussed in the sections above.

The key events in w_drag_drop include events on the DataWindow control (se_mousemove and se_lbuttonup) and events on the picture button (dragdrop).

On the DataWindow control dw_emp_list we have a user defined event "se_mousemove" which is linked to the windows message pbm_mousemove. This event contains:

```
IF flags = 1 THEN
        THIS.Drag(Begin!)
        ib_drag = TRUE
END IF
```

Note: "flags" is an argument defined for the system event pbm_dwnlbuttonup. At the time of the development of the sample application, this functionality was not working. It is working in the final release. In the actual scripts for mouse move in the sample application you will see `Message.WordParm` for each instance of "flags" above.

This event checks the argument that is passed to the event (flags) to see if the left mouse button is being held down (flags = 1). If it is, it initiates drag mode on this control and sets the Boolean variable ib_drag to TRUE.

Also on the DataWindow control dw_emp_list we have a user defined event "se_lbuttonup" which is linked to the windows message pbm_dwnlbuttonup. This event contains:

```
IF NOT ib_drag THEN
        THIS.SelectRow(row,NOT THIS.IsSelected(row))
ELSE
        //Set IB_DRAG to FALSE
        ib_drag = FALSE
END IF
```

Note: "row" is an argument defined for the system event pbm_dwnlbuttonup. At the time of the development of the sample application, this functionality was not working. It is working in the final release. In the actual scripts for mouse move in the sample application you will see THIS.GetRow() for each instance of "row" above.

This event checks to see if the instance variable ib_drag is set to true, indicating that the control is currently in drag mode. If it is, then set the variable back to FALSE, resetting it for the next use. If the control is not in drag mode, then the script will select or deselect the current row as appropriate.

On the picture button "pb_trash" we use the predefined system event "drag-drop" to handle the process we initiate when the user drops the DataWindow control. This event contains:

```
// Declare local variables
long ll_delay, ll_time=12000, ll_selected_row=0
datawindow ldw_source

// Let's check to be sure that the source is really a datawindow
IF source.TypeOf() = DataWindow! THEN

        // Cast the variable into a DataWindow variable
        ldw_source = source

        ll_selected_row = ldw_source.GetSelectedRow(0)

        IF ll_selected_row = 0 THEN
                MessageBox("Nothing Selected",&
                        "No rows were selected to delete.")
                RETURN
        END IF


        DO UNTIL ll_selected_row = 0

                ll_selected_row = ldw_source.GetSelectedRow(0)
                IF ll_selected_row > 0 THEN
                        // We don't want to really discard any
                        // employees, so we'll just remove the rows from
                        // the primary buffer

                ldw_source.RowsDiscard(ll_selected_row,&
                        ll_selected_row,Primary!)
                        // IF we really wanted to delete the rows, we
                        // would have coded:
                        // ldw_source.DeleteRow(ll_selected_row)
                END IF
        LOOP

        // Animate the Icon, just for fun!
        THIS.picturename = "Trash4.bmp"
        FOR ll_delay = 1 to ll_time
        NEXT

        THIS.picturename = "Trash3.bmp"
        FOR ll_delay = 1 to ll_time
        NEXT

        THIS.picturename = "Trash2.bmp"
        FOR ll_delay = 1 to ll_time
        NEXT

        THIS.picturename = "Trash1.bmp"
    END IF
```

We use the event argument "source" to determine what object was dropped on us.

We execute the TypeOf() function on the source argument to determine what class of object the dropped object is. We should be sure that it is a DataWindow before we try to call any DataWindow functions against it.

Once we have confirmed that it is indeed a DataWindow, we cast the generic object "source" into a specific variable we declared of the class DataWindow (ldw_source).

Now we can begin executing DataWindow control functions against the dropped object. We use the GetSelectedRow() function to determine the first selected row in the source object. If there are no selected rows, we inform the user that they must select rows in order for us to initiate processing. If there are rows selected, we loop through all the selected rows discarding them one by one. If this was a production application, we would be using the DeleteRow() function to initiate the deletion of the rows from the primary buffer and eventually from the database. Instead, we use the RowsDiscard() function to remove them from the buffer without affecting the underlying database.

After completing this, we add in a little icon animation for fun. We show a happy face being placed into the trash can!

Developer's Tip: For a more sophisticated DragDrop event where you want to perform different functionality depending on which type of control was dropped on the target you can use the TypeOf() or ClassName() functions embedded inside a CHOOSE CASE flow of control statement as in the following example:

```
// Declare local variables for each class of object involved
SingleLineEdit lsle_dragged
DataWindow ldw_dragged

CHOOSE CASE source.TypeOf()
    CASE SingleLineEdit!
            // Cast the generic object 'source' into
            // its appropriate class variable
            lsle_dragged = source

            // Clear the text out of the SLE
            lsle_dragged.text = ""

    CASE DataWindow!
            // Cast the generic object 'source into a
            // DataWindow class variable
            ldw_dragged = source
```

```
                    // Delete the current row from the DataWindow
                    ldw_dragged.DeleteRow(0)
      END CHOOSE
```

18.5 *Summary*

Using these advanced techniques you can go beyond the skills of the beginner and take advantage of the flexibility and versatility of the PowerBuilder environment. Don't be afraid to experiment and push the limits of what you think is possible. That is how you will move from being an intermediate programmer to becoming an expert.

CHAPTER 19

Using DataWindows

*T*his chapter has been added to the second edition as a direct request from readers who were experienced programmers, but didn't have in depth knowledge of the DataWindow. The intention in this chapter is to provide you with some of the fundamental knowledge of DataWindows and how they work. If you are already familiar with DataWindows, you may want to skip to the next chapter.

Once of the reasons for the tremendous success of PowerBuilder is the DataWindow object. The DataWindow object is a custom control that Powersoft has developed and patented. It is not a native Windows control, such as a list view. The DataWindow is an incredibly powerful and flexible object for allowing the end user to work with data from the database in a method that is easy for the developer to implement and maintain.

19.1 What Is a DataWindow Object?

DataWindow objects represent the real strength behind client/server PowerBuilder applications. The primary role of a DataWindow object is to manipulate, update and present data. It is an intelligent database control that handles all the interaction with a relational database or other data source (such as a dBase .DBF file), as well as controlling what data is displayed to the user and how it is viewed.

When you utilize the intelligence built into a DataWindow object, the data can be used in a way that is most meaningful to the user. The foundation for the DataWindow's intelligence is made up of two primary components: the source of the data and the presentation style.

The data source for a DataWindow can be any one of a number of items. Data can come from relational databases, text and dBase files (.TXT and .DBF), Dynamic Data Exchange (DDE) with other windows applications, Object Linking and Embedding (OLE), or it can be input by the user directly. The DataWindow performs data validation based upon what it knows about the data (the data type—string, numeric, and so on) and any rules that have been defined (for example, the age of an employee must be greater that 18, but less that 65).

The DataWindow displays the data to the user based upon the format specified. DataWindows have a wide variety of presentation styles, including Freeform, Tabular, Graphs, and Crosstabs. These presentation styles provide a default format for displaying the data. However, there is still a wide latitude for enhancing the default format to meet your specific needs.

When paired with a DataWindow control (the object that you place on a window in the Window painter to accommodate DataWindow objects), this object provides an interface in two directions—an interface to the user and an interface to the database.

This chapter will cover a great deal of information including, how to launch the DataWindow Painter and construct a DataWindow object, the different data sources and presentation styles that you can use, how to integrate the DataWindow object into your application, and more. (Figure 19-1.)

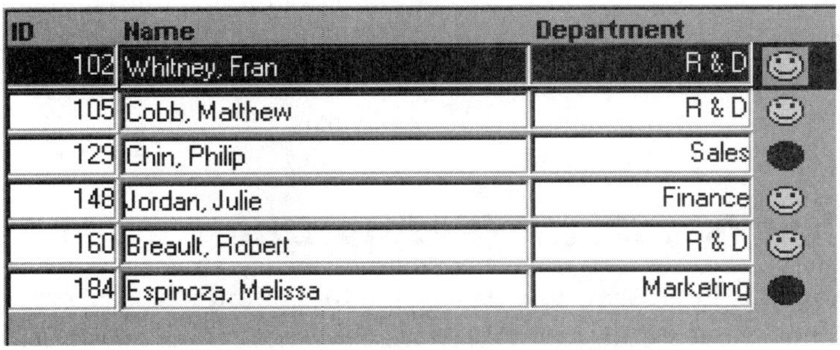

ID	Name	Department	
102	Whitney, Fran	R & D	☺
105	Cobb, Matthew	R & D	☺
129	Chin, Philip	Sales	●
148	Jordan, Julie	Finance	☺
160	Breault, Robert	R & D	☺
184	Espinoza, Melissa	Marketing	●

Figure 19-1. A typical DataWindow.

19.2 Launching the DataWindow Painter

The DataWindow Painter is launched from the main PowerBuilder toolbar. The icon is shown in Figure 19-2. Note that this is the same icon that is used to place a DataWindow control on a Window.

Figure 19-2. The icon to launch the DataWindow Painter.

The DataWindow will automatically utilize the current database connection that you are using in PowerBuilder.

19.3 Selecting a DataWindow

When you open the DataWindow Painter it will open the Select DataWindow dialog window. In this window, you can select the DataWindow that you want to work with, or choose **New** to create a new DataWindow object. All the DataWindows in the current library will be shown in the list along with any comments that were entered when they were saved. (Figure 19-3.)

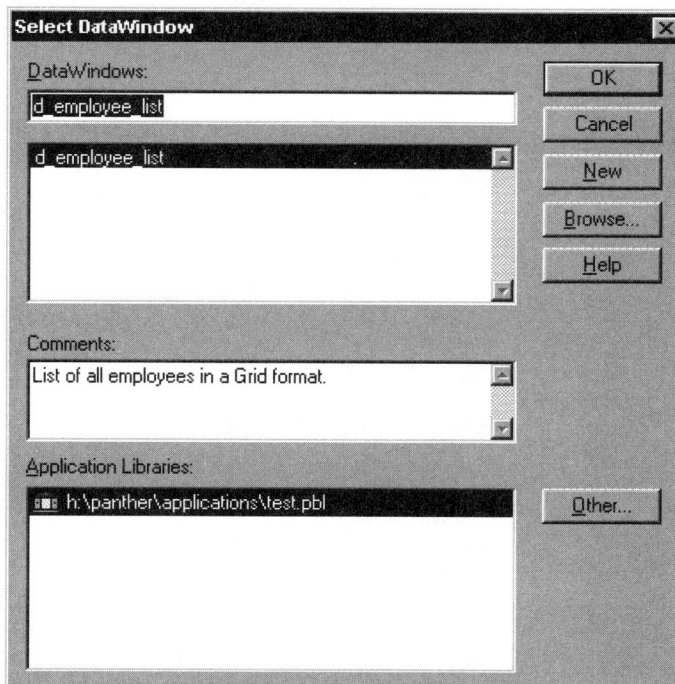

Figure 19-3.The Select DataWindow dialog window is used to choose the DataWindow that you want to work with, or to begin creation of a new one.

The **OK** button will allow you to open a DataWindow object that you have selected in the list box on the top left. Once open, you can modify the SQL statement and the layout of the DataWindow object.

Pressing the **New** button will allow you to begin building a new DataWindow object starting by specifying the *data source* and the *presentation style* that you want to use.

19.4   Sources of Data

Before the DataWindow can be created, the DataWindowPainter needs to know exactly where the data it will be using is coming from. You have five options to select from: QuickSelect, SQLSelect, Query, External, or Stored Procedure. All data sources except External retrieve data from a database. The data source, Stored Procedure, only appears if the database you are connecting to supports stored procedures that are capable of returning a result set. When you specify **New** in the Select DataWindow dialog, the first thing you will see is the dialog window in Figure 19-4 where you will select your data source and presentation style. (Figure 19-4.)

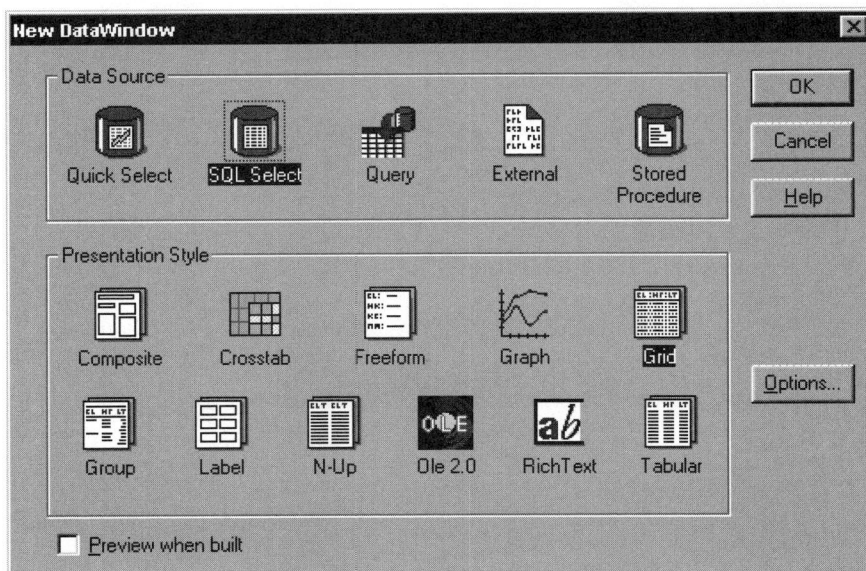

Figure 19-4. The New DataWindow dialog window allows you to specify the data source and presentation style for your new DataWindow.

19.4.1 QuickSelect

QuickSelect is one of the quickest ways to define a data source, although its capabilities are limited. It is designed for simple database queries. A QuickSelect data source will create a DataWindow populated with data retrieved usually from only a single table in a relational database. Multiple tables can be included as long as the relationship between the tables is defined with a primary/foreign key relationship. After specifying the tables that you will include in the SQL select statement, you will specify the columns that will be included, a simple WHERE clause and simply sorting. With QuickSelect you cannot perform grouping, computed columns, provide retrieval criteria or more complex SQL operations.

19.4.1.1 Steps in Building A QuickSelect

When you decide to use QuickSelect as your data source, the DataWindowPainter opens the QuickSelect window as shown in Figure 19-5. To simplify the use of this window, all items that can be set to define the result set are entered in this location. At the top of the window are instructions to guide you through the QuickSelect definition. There are two list boxes in the window: the first lists all the tables and views in the current database, and the second lists all the columns in any table or view selected from the first list box.

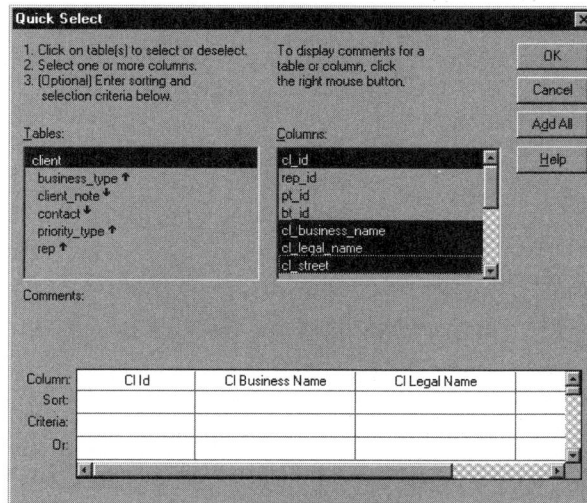

Figure 19-5. The QuickSelect window for building simple SQL queries.

19.4.1.2 Selecting a Table and Columns

To begin the process, select the table you want to retrieve data from. If you want to retrieve data from multiple tables, the first table you select should be the main table that all the other tables are related to, although, if you are planning to join more than two tables, it is generally recommended to use the SQLSelect data source. Once you have selected your first table, other tables that are related to the selected table will be listed and indented, below the selected table. If you want to include one of the related tables, you can select it also. You will notice an arrow beside each of the secondary tables. The arrow represents the "many" condition. For example, in Figure 19-5, the client table is the primary table and the contact table is the secondary table. The arrow pointing down indicates that the contact table is the many table. This would read "The contact table may have many records for each record in the client table." This process will repeat until you have selected all the tables that you wish to include.

All the columns that exist in the selected table or tables will appear in the columns list box. If you have selected multiple tables, then the columns will be prefixed with the table name. From the columns list, select the columns that you want to include in the result set. You can view the comments about a column (as declare in the extended column attributes, if you are using a case tool to define them) by pressing and holding the right mouse button over the column for which you want to see the comment .

You can select all the columns at once by pressing the **Add All** command button on the right side of the window. If you change your mind about including a column in the result set, click the column name in the list with the left mouse button to deselect it. The selected columns appear in the grid at the bottom of the window.

19.4.1.3 Ordering, Sorting and Setting Criteria

To rearrange the order of the columns, select the column that you want to move (pressing and holding the left mouse button over the column name), drag it to the desired position.

The DataWindowPainter works through the columns from left to right to establish sorting criteria. Set the DataWindow to sort by a certain column name, select the sort box below the column name and choose Ascending or Descending from the drop down list box as appropriate (see Figure 19-8). The example in Figure 19-6 would sort first by business name (CL_BUSINESS_NAME) in an ascending manner and then it would sort by contact last name (CT_LAST_NAME) in a descending manner. The client ID (CL_ID) column is not sorted even though it appears before the business name and last name columns because it has been flagged as "(not sorted)."

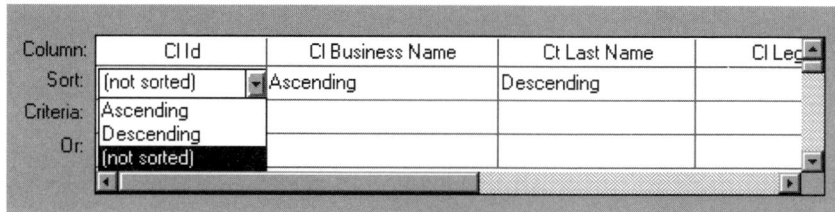

Figure 19-6. Entering sorting details in a QuickSelect DataWindow.

If you want to sort in a different order, rearrange the columns by dragging and dropping them in the new sort order.

Selection criteria, contact criteria that are not altered at runtime, can be specified in this grid. However, retrieval criteria, dynamic selection criteria that are defined only at runtime, cannot. The criteria should be entered in the grid space below the appropriate column heading. The edge of the grid may restrict the entry of criteria. If you run out of space, you can enlarge the grid by dragging the grid line in the column header like you might in a spreadsheet program like Excel™.

Any standard SQL relational operator can be used within the criteria. These include equal (=), greater than (>), less than (<), not equal to (<>), greater than or equal to (>=), less than or equal to (<=), LIKE, NOT LIKE, IN and NOT IN. If you enter only a value in the criteria area, the operator is assumed to be "=." Logical operators OR and AND can also be used to connect expressions. If multiple expressions are entered and no logical operator is used, the operator is assumed to be OR.

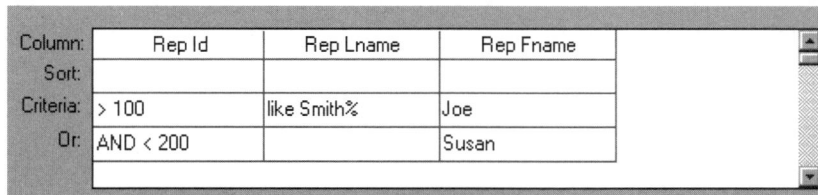

Figure 19-7. An example of entering selection criteria in a QuickSelect window.

The QuickSelect example in Figure 19-7 would result in a DataWindow being built with the following SQL select statement:

```
SELECT  rep.rep_id,
        rep.rep_lname,
        rep.rep_fname
FROM    rep
WHERE   (((rep.rep_id > 100)
```

```
AND      (rep.rep_id < 200)
 AND      (rep.rep_lname LIKE 'Smith%')
 AND     ((rep.rep_fname = 'Joe')
  OR      (rep.rep_fname = 'Susan'))
```

When you are finished defining the QuickSelect, click the OK command button to close the dialog window and open the DataWindow Painter design workspace.

> **Developer's Note:** After a QuickSelect statement has been created, you can add items to it, such as retrieval arguments, that couldn't be included in the initial definition. You can do this by moving from the DataWindow Painter design workspace back to the SQL painter. Any DataWindow created using QuickSelect will have its SQL maintained using the standard SQLSelect painter discussed in the next section.

19.4.2 SQLSelect

SQLSelect is arguably the most commonly used DataWindow data source. Like QuickSelect, a SQLSelect data source will result in a DataWindow that is populated by a SQL select statement. With SQLSelect you have more control over the formation of the select statement than QuickSelect. The data can come from one or more tables in your relational database. All possible select statement clauses can be included in the SQLSelect statement. This is the type of data source to use if you need to specify retrieval arguments that are only available at runtime. An example of this would be to show all the employees who work in a department, but to allow the user to specify the department at run time. The department id would be passed in to the SQL statement as a retrieval argument.

19.4.2.1 Steps in Building A SQLSelect

Choose SQLSelect as the data source for a DataWindow to open the DataWindow Painter SQL "painter" (no, that's not a type, it is the "SQL painter" inside the DataWindow "painter"). This tool allows us to develop a SQL select statement in a graphical point and click environment.

19.4.2.2 Selecting Tables

The Select Tables window, as shown in Figure 19-8, will appear immediately after you choose SQLSelect as your data source and close the New DataWindow dialog window.

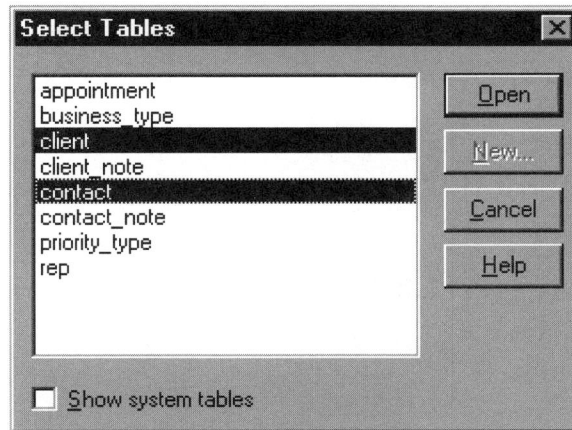

***Figure 19-8.** The Select Tables dialog window allows you to choose the tables that will be included in your SQL select statement.*

This window enables you to choose the tables that you want to include in the select statement. All the tables and views defined in the current database are available in the list. To select an individual table, click it with the left mouse button. You can select tables one at a time, or a click on multiple tables to choose more than one.

When all the desired tables are selected, you can open them by clicking the Open command button or double-clicking on the last selected table. If you want to open the tables one by one, you can double click on them and see them open in the workspace behind the Select Tables window.

19.4.2.3 Joining Tables

Any tables that you have selected that have a primary/foreign key relationship will be joined automatically. If the tables in your result set are not associated through primary/foreign key relationships then the DataWindowPainter will attempt to automatically join them based on any columns with identical names that it finds. You should always manually verify any automatic joins that the DataWindowPainter made on your behalf to ensure that you don't end up with a join on some generic column like "description."

To set up a manual join, select the join icon from the toolbar and then select the columns in the respective tables that you want to join. For example, if there was no automatic join between the tables in Figure 19.9, I would select the join icon, click on the CL_ID column from the client table, and then click on the CL_ID column for the contacts table.

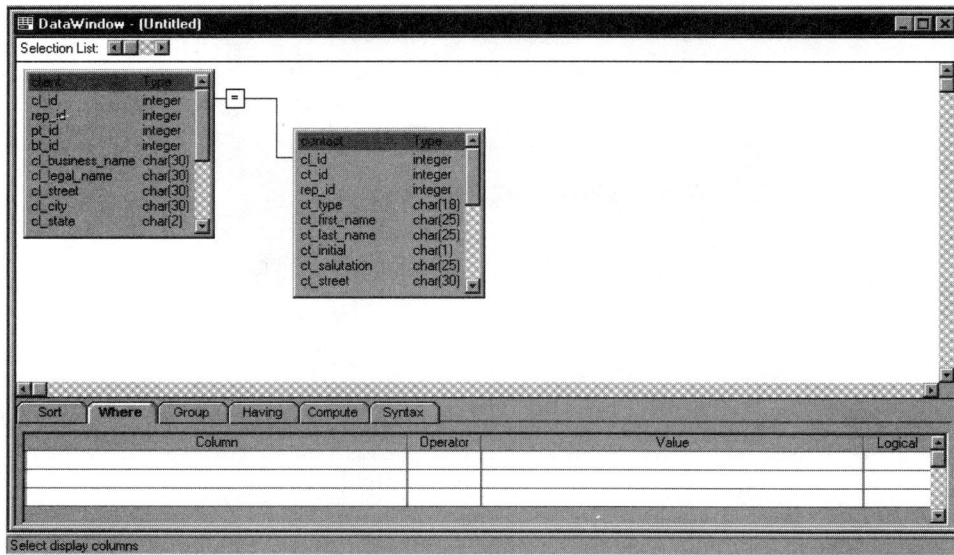

Figure 19-9. *The SQL painter workspace with two tables that have an automatic join indicated by the line connecting the joined columns.*

By default, all joins are created with an "equal" condition (meaning that the value in one table must match the value in the other field exactly). If you are doing some advanced SQL and you wish to build a join condition with a different operator, or if you want to create an outer join condition, click the join operator box (the box containing the operator symbol on the red join line) with the left mouse button. This opens the Join window shown in Figure 19-10. In this window you can select an expression for a different join operator (such as greater than or less than) or an outer join condition (such as all the rows from client, even if no matching contact row exists).

In this window you can also delete a join you no longer want by pressing the **Delete** command button.

19.4.2.4 Selecting Columns

To build the columns that will compose the result set for your select statement you, choose them with the mouse. They become highlighted in the column lists, and appear in the selection list at the top of the workspace, as shown in Figure 19-11, in the order in which they will be retrieved from the database.

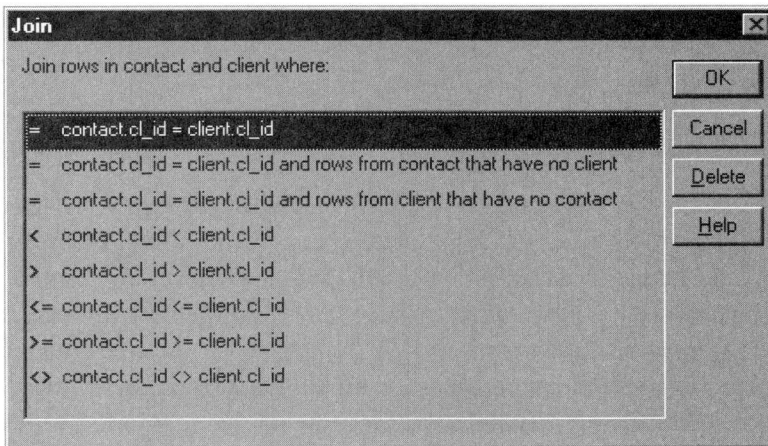

Figure 19-10. The Join dialog window allows you to set different operators for your join condition, define an outer join or delete a join.

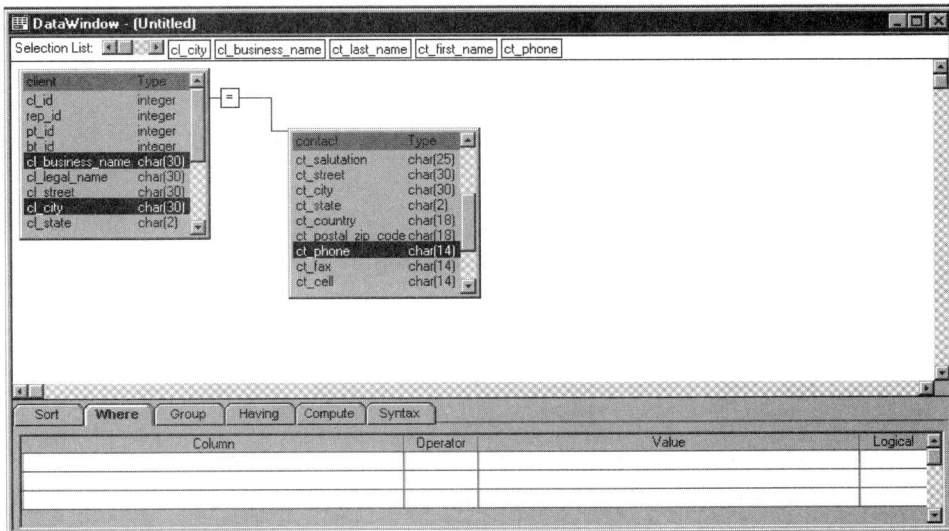

Figure 19-11. Selected columns in the SQL painter appear highlighted and are listed at the top in the Selection List area of the workspace.

To reorder the sequence of the columns in the select list, move the mouse pointer over the list of columns in the Selection List. The pointer will switch from an arrow to a hand to indicate that you are in "move" mode. Click and hold the left mouse button on the column you want to move, and then drag it to the appropriate position.

You can select or deselect all the columns in a table at once by choosing the appropriate option from the popup menu that will appear if you right mouse click on the title bar of the table in the workspace.

19.4.2.5 Retrieval Arguments

As we mentioned earlier, sometimes you want to pass values into your select statement at runtime. In order to do this, you must define these values as a type of variable. In the DataWindow Painter these variables are referred to as *retrieval arguments*. These arguments are usually used in the WHERE clause (discussed below) to limit the result set of the query to a more specific set of rows.

To specify retrieval arguments, select **Retrieval Arguments...** from the **Design** menu. This will open the Specify Retrieval Arguments dialog window shown in Figure 19-12. Each argument you want to use must be given a unique name and an appropriate data type. The Position edit box identifies the position in the Retrieve function that this argument will occupy at run time. For example, to retrieve the data for the DataWindow using retrieval arguments as defined in Figure 19-12, we would use the retrieve function:

```
dw_control.Retrieve( 100, "Houston")
```

to retrieve the employees in department 100 in Houston.

Press the **Add** command button to add new retrieval arguments, **Delete** to remove an existing argument or **Insert** to add an argument into the middle of your list. Once you have specified all your retrieval arguments press the **OK** command button to close the window.

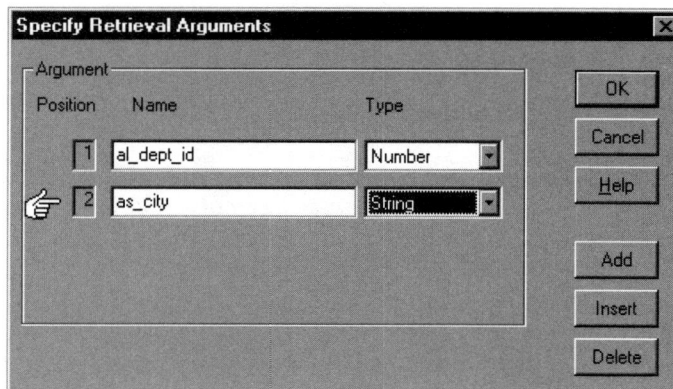

Figure 19-12.DataWindow retrieval arguments are defined in this dialog window.

19.4.2.6 The SQL Toolbox

At the bottom of the workspace in the SQL painter you will see a series of tab folders. This area is referred to as the *SQL Toolbox*. In this part of the window you will define Where clauses, sorting, grouping, and computed columns for your select statement.

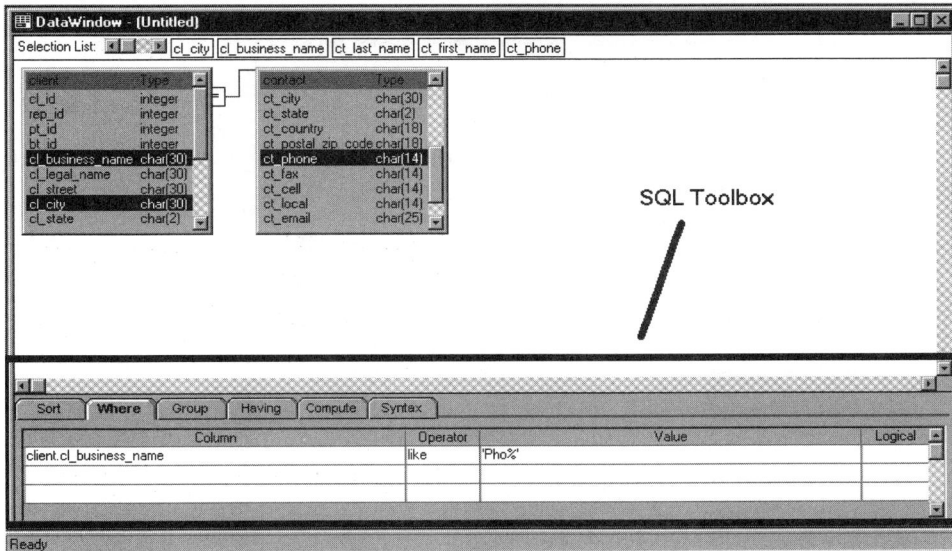

Figure 19-13. *The SQLToolbox allows you to define where clauses, sorting, grouping, and computed columns.*

19.2.4.7 Using WHERE Clauses

You may want to set limits on your SQL query to refine the result set that you will retrieve, as we did in the QuickSelect example. You may want your DataWindow to only show employees from a particular department or city. These types of limiting criteria can be included in a WHERE clause in the SQL select statement.

Where clause statements can be either static, or make use of retrieval arguments to dynamically retrieve data. Expressions to be used in the WHERE clause can be entered on the Where tab in the SQLToolbox. (See Figure 19-14.)

Expressions consist of combinations of database columns, literal values, operators, database functions, and retrieval arguments. Examples of each of these include:

- **Database Columns** client.cl_business_name , contact.ct_first_name.

- **Literal Values** 1, 33, "Phoenix", "3/15/97."

- **Operators** =, >, < , >=, LIKE, IN, IS.

- **Retrieval Arguments** :al_rep_id, :as_last_name.

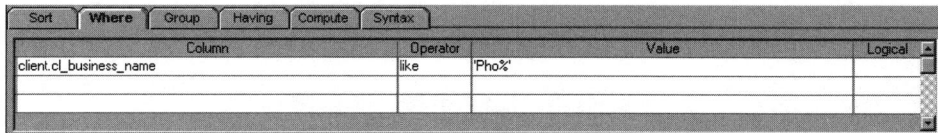

Figure 19-14. The Where tab of the SQLToolbox.

Expressions usually have at least one database column and one literal value or retrieval argument joined by an operator. For example:

```
contact.ct_last_name = 'Smith'
```

or if we use a retrieval argument for the name of the contact we are searching for:

```
contact.ct_last_name = :as_last_name
```

You can type column names, retrieval arguments, literals, and operators directly into the cells in the where clause entry fields as shown in Figure 19-14. Often you may find it easier to use some of the ease of use functions that are built in to the where tab to help you select. In the Columns field, you can click on the drop down arrow to get a list of all the column in the tables that make up the select statement. You can also click with the right mouse button to open a pop up list box of all the columns or a list box showing all the database functions (These are database functions, not PowerScript functions, as they are executed on your database server. The specific set of functions that are available to you will vary from database to database. Refer to your database manuals for details on the different functions).

The operator can also be selected from the drop down list in the Operator column. Then, in the Value column you can enter a literal value, a retrieval argument, or another column (forming a manual join between tables). You can also use database function in the Value field.

Another option is to write a *nested subselect* statement in the value field which you are joining a column in your query to a completely separate query. A simple example of doing this would be a query where you want to select all the employees in Houston who earn more than the average corporate salary. If we have an employee table that includes their name, city, and salary, we can write the following SQL select statement:

```
SELECT last_name, first_name

FROM    employee
WHERE   salary >= (SELECT Avg(salary)
                   FROM       employee)
AND     city = 'Houston'
```

To build the nested subselect, you can type the subselect statement into the field directly (SELECT Avg(salary) FROM employee), or you can click on the field with the right mouse button and choose the **Select...** option from the pop up menu to launch a nested version of the SQLSelect painter where you can graphically build your subselect.

You will also notice on this pop up menu the ability to select a column from a list of columns from the tables in the query, a retrieval argument from a list of predefined retrieval arguments, a function from the available database functions or a "value." When you select the **Value...** option a pop up selection list will open. It will display all the distinct values from the database that are contained in the column specified in the Columns field. In our example in Figure 19-15, selecting the Values pop up menu option gives us the ability to select the business name for one of our contacts. (Figure 19-15.)

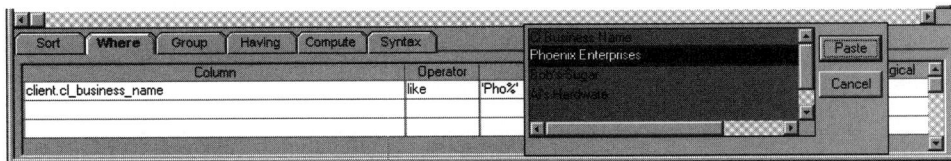

Figure 19-15. *The Values... menu item allows you to select from all the current possible values for the specified column.*

To include multiple expressions in your where clause, a logical operator (either AND or OR) must be defined in the field labeled "Logical." If you go to the second line of the Where clause tab, the DataWindowPainter will automatically insert a logical AND between the two expressions that you define.

Some example where clauses:

employee.emp_id = :emp_id. "Include in the result set only those rows of data where the employee ID in the employee table is equal to the employee ID that I'm passing in the retrieval argument."

employee.emp_age >= policy.early_retire_age. "Include in the result set only the employees who are eligible for early retirement based solely on their age."

19.4.2.8 Sorting the Result Set

A sort clause can also be included in the SQL select statement allowing you to order the result set based upon any column or columns in the query. You can choose to sort in an ascending or descending manner. The sort order is specified on the Sort tab in the SQLToolbox which is shown in Figure 19-16.

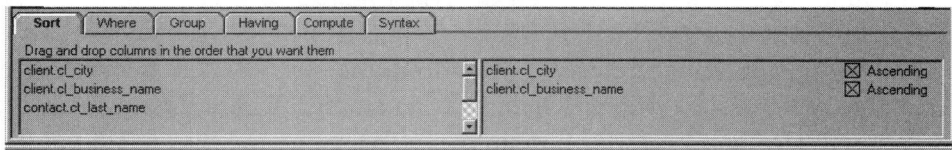

Figure 19-16. The Sort tab allows you to order your result set.

All the columns in the query will be listed in the box on the left size of the tab. Using your mouse you can drag and drop the columns from the left side of the tab to the right side. The columns on the right represent the sort order and if the sort will be ascending or descending. You can change the order by rearranging the columns on the right using the mouse and selecting or deselecting the ascending checkbox.

The example in Figure 19-16 would sort by the city column in ascending manner, and then for any two records that are in the same city. It would sort by the business name in an ascending manner.

> **Developer's Note:** Setting the sort criteria in the Sort tab tells the database which order to return the result set to the client. It has nothing to do with the Sort() PowerScript function or sorting in the DataWindow designer, which we will discuss later, as these are all client functions that manipulate the data that is buffered on the client and does not involve the server.

19.4.2.9 Grouping the Result Set

You can use the Group tab in the SQLToolbox to have the server return the result set ordered into groups. We won't spend a lot of time here as this is not a common function that is used when building DataWindows. Usually grouping on the server is done to return summary information from the database, but when data is summarized like this, it becomes impossible for the DataWindow to perform any updates to the data.

An example of where we might use the Grouping tab would be if we wanted to define a query where we would list all the clients and the total number of contacts in each. To do this, we would use the grouping tab to indicate that we wanted to group by client ID. Then we would define a computed field to count the number of contacts in each client. This might create a SQL statement and result set such as:

```
SELECT CL_ID, CL_BUSINESS_NAME, COUNT(CT_ID)
FROM        client, contact
GROUP BY CL_ID
```

result set:

```
CL_ID           CL_BUSINESS_NAME        COUNT of contacts
1               Phoenix Enterprises     3
2               Bob's Sugar             2
3               Al's Hardware           0
4               Valley Wines            4
```

Because each line is a summary record, the DataWindow cannot use its data updating strengths to allow any database update.

19.4.2.10 The Having Tab

On the Having tab you can define what is essentially a Where clause for the group by statement. It appears and functions the same way as the Where tab discussed above, but its expressions are applied to the GROUP BY clause only.

For example, if we wanted to modify the query in the previous section to only include companies with 2 or more contacts, we could define a having clause like this:

```
SELECT CL_ID, CL_BUSINESS_NAME, COUNT(CT_ID)
FROM        client, contact
GROUP BY CL_ID
HAVING COUNT(CT_ID) >= 2
```

If you don't have a grouping expression, then you won't have a having clause. Thus, like the GROUP BY, having clauses are seldom used in DataWindows.

19.4.2.11 Computed Server Fields

Like many of the options in DataWindows, you can often perform the functionality on the client or on the server. The same is true with computed fields. If you want the server to perform computations for you and return them in your result set, you define them on the Compute tab in the SQLToolbox.

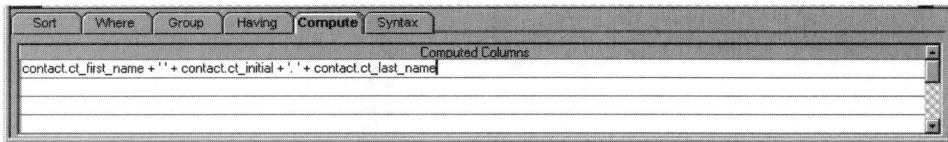

Figure 19-17. The Compute tab allows you to define server side computed fields.

The example in Figure 19-17 would produce a computed field that produces the full name of a contact by combining the first name, middle initial, and last name of the client with the following expression:

```
contact.ct_first_name + ' ' + contact.ct_initial + '. ' + contact.ct_last_name
```

You enter your expression directly into the box and you can use the right mouse button to paste in column names and functions.

Remember that since the fields are computed in the server, the client application has no idea that they are computed fields. To the DataWindow, this is just another standard field that is represented in the result set. The implications of this will be discussed later in the chapter when we discuss client side computed fields.

19.4.2.12 Graphic Mode vs. Syntax Mode

On the Syntax tab of the SQLToolbox, you can see the SQL select statement that the DataWindowPainter is creating as you paint your SQL statement. This can be a good tool for experienced SQL developers to verify that the SQL that is being generated is what they expect, or for SQL neophytes who can see how the results of their painting activities affect the SQL statement. (Figure 19-18.)

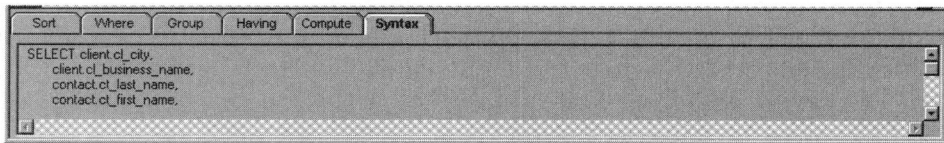

Figure 19-18. The Syntax tab allows you to view the SQL statement that is generated by the DataWindowPainter.

This tab is not editable, but if you are a SQL wizard and want to enter your SQL manually, you can convert the SQL painter from *graphic mode to syntax mode*. In the Design menu you will find a Convert To Syntax option which opens the SQL painter as a standard text editor window as shown in Figure 19-19. Here you can manually create your SQL statement or tweak one that you created graphically.

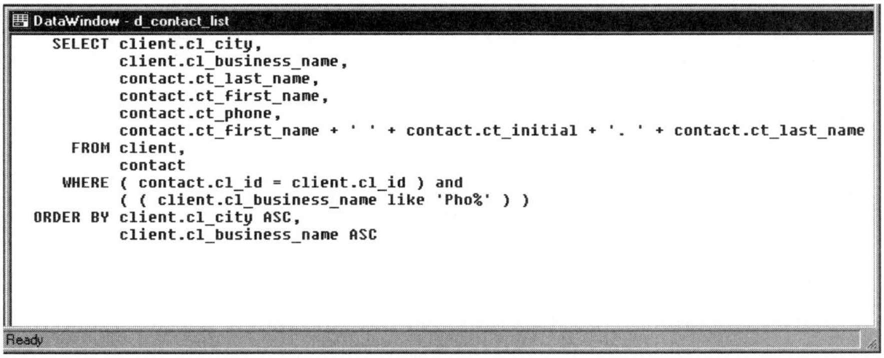

```
DataWindow - d_contact_list
    SELECT client.cl_city,
           client.cl_business_name,
           contact.ct_last_name,
           contact.ct_first_name,
           contact.ct_phone,
           contact.ct_first_name + ' ' + contact.ct_initial + '. ' + contact.ct_last_name
      FROM client,
           contact
     WHERE ( contact.cl_id = client.cl_id ) and
           ( ( client.cl_business_name like 'Pho%' ) )
  ORDER BY client.cl_city ASC,
           client.cl_business_name ASC



Ready
```

Figure 19-19. You can flip between graphical and syntax views of your SQL select.

You can also do the reverse. You can convert from syntax mode to graphic mode by select Convert To Graphics from the Design menu. There is a caveat attached to this action: you can only convert back to graphics if the syntax can be graphically represented. It is very rare to not be able to convert back to graphics, but if you get a message indicating that the SQL statement cannot be converted to graphic mode, then you have implemented something in your SQL which the painter cannot represent and you will need to either remove it, or stay in syntax mode.

19.4.2.13 Other SQL Functions

The DataWindowPainter also allows you to include other SQL functionality into your DataWindow such as DISTINCT and UNION clauses. Distinct can be turned on and off by choosing the Distinct option from the Design menu. To create a Union, you will select the Union option from the Design menu and will then define the select statement that will be unioned with your first select statement (very much like the nested subselect in the Where clause).

The SQL select statement that you build in the DataWindow SQL painter can be saved and reused. The saved select statement is called a *query object* and is discussed in the next section. To save your SQL select statement as a query object select **Save Query As...** from the File menu. Alternatively, you can load a query into the SQL painter by choosing **Open Query...** from the File menu.

19.4.3 Query

A query data source performs the same functions as a SQL select data source. However, the Query data source utilized a predefined SQL select statement. The statement must have been previously defined and saved in the SQL painter as detailed in the section entitled, "Other SQL Functions" or using the Query painter.

19.4.3.1 Steps in Building a Query Object

To define a Query object to be used as a data source for a DataWindow, open the Query painter by clicking the Query painter icon in the tool bar.

The Query object painter launches directly into the SQL painter, where you define the SQL select statement exactly as you did previously in the SQL select option. The statement is then saved as a Query object in your library.

To associate the Query object with the DataWindow, select the appropriate Query object from the selection list that opens when you tell the DataWindow painter to create a Query object source DataWindow.

19.4.4 External

External data source DataWindows are the only ones that don't link to a relational database directly. The data to be used in these DataWindow objects is provided either by scripts coded into your application or from direct user input. Each column and data type must be individually defined in the DataWindow. External data sources can be used when the data is to be accessed from a text file (.TXT), a dBase file (.DBF), a Dynamic Data Exchange (DDE) session, or some other non-DBMS source.

> **Developer's Note:** The External data source serves many other uses as well. There are times when you want to take advantage of a DataWindow's intelligence in your user interface, even if the data isn't coming from or going to a database. If user entries need to be validated, a DataWindow with a validation rule can be used rather than having the user code it manually. The ability to use DataWindows to represent other Windows objects (such as radio buttons or check boxes) can also be very useful to a developer.

19.4.4.1 Steps in Building an External DataWindow

When you choose External as the data source for your new DataWindow, the Result Set Description dialog window opens as shown in Figure 19-20.

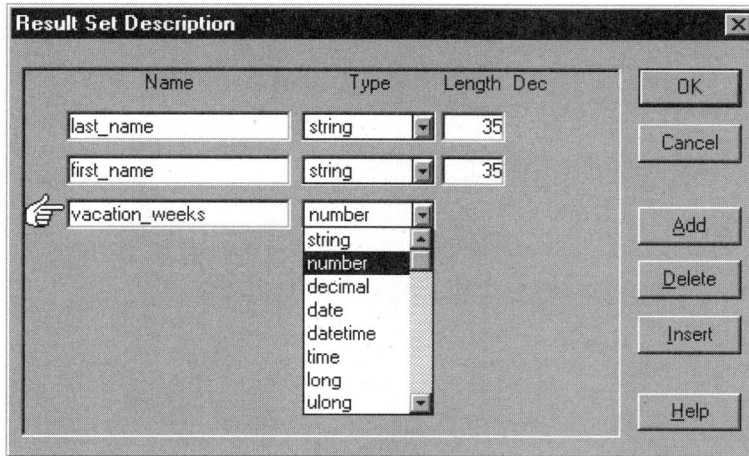

Figure 19-20. *You define the data fields in an External DataWindow in the Result Set Description dialog.*

Here you must specify all the columns and their descriptions (type and length) that you want to comprise the result set. You can add more columns by selecting the **Add** or **Insert** command buttons and may remove columns by selecting the **Delete** command button.

Select the **OK** command button when you have finished defining the data result set for the External DataWindow. You will now be placed directly into the DataWindow designer workspace.

19.4.5 Stored Procedure

With a Stored Procedure data source, the DataWindow will execute a database stored procedure and utilized the data returned in the result set (if the procedure returns multiple result sets, you can select which one you want the DataWindow to use, but only one can be used). This option is only available (and visible) if the database you are connecting to supports stored procedures that return result sets.

> **Developer's Note:** Stored Procedures can be used to improve the performance of your SQL queries by reducing the number of steps involved for a DataWindow to receive a result set from the server and by reducing network traffic (stored procedures are pre-compiled and pre-optimized and are stored on the server, not the client).

19.4.5.1 Steps in Building a Stored Procedure DataWindow

When you choose Stored Procedure as the data source for your new DataWindow, the Select Stored Procedure dialog window opens as shown in Figure 19-21.

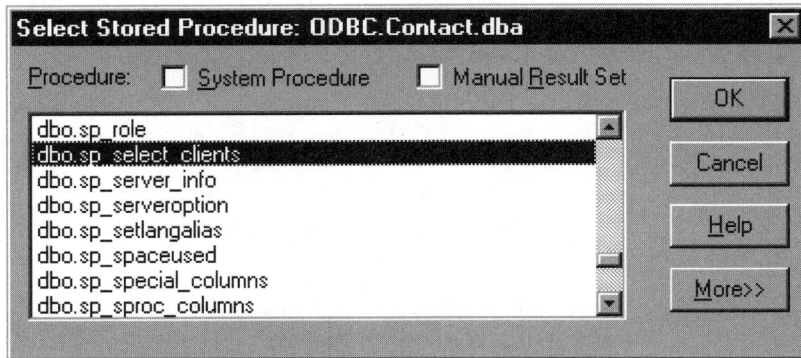

Figure 19-21. *The Select Stored Procedure dialog window is used to choose which stored procedure you will be using for your data source.*

This window contains a list box with all the stored procedures currently stored in your DBMS (not including system procedures you can include these in the list by selecting the Show system procedures check box). After selecting the stored procedure that you desire you can press the **More...** button to see the stored procedure source code, if your database supports this. If it doesn't you will see a message in the box saying that PowerBuilder was unable to read the source code. This is not an error, it only means that you can't preview the stored procedure, and it will still run fine.

The other checkbox on the window is used if you want to manually define a result set. By default, the DataWindowPainter will execute the procedure and build a result set to match what is returned. If for some reason the result set at runtime is different that it will be at design time, then you can select this checkbox to define what the result set will be like. If you have selected this box, when you press the **OK** button the Result Set Description window described in the External data source section will open. You must define the result set that will be returned by the stored procedure the same way you did for an External DataWindow. This is necessary so that the DataWindow knows what kind of data it will be receiving from the DBMS.

If you have an automatic result set, or when you have finished defining the manual result set, you will be placed in the DataWindow designer.

> **Developer's Tip:** If you don't have access to a tool for developing stored procedures, you can use the DB Administration tool from the Database Painter toolbar to create them.

19.5   *Presentation Style*

The presentation style is the second decision you must make when creating a new DataWindow. This will define how the DataWindowPainter will format the data in the DataWindow and display it to the end user. Each style is a different predefined default format. Each of these formats is only a default, and you can modify them to meet your specific needs.

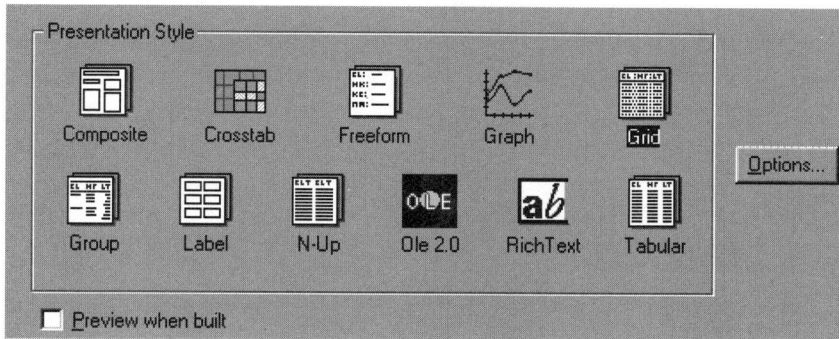

Figure 19-22. Selecting a DataWindow presentation style.

19.5.1 Options Button and Preview

Before we discuss all the different DataWindow presentation styles, there are two other controls on the New DataWindow dialog window that you should understand, the **Options...** button and the Preview checkbox.

The **Options...** command button in the New DataWindow dialog enables you to specify the default colors and borders for the new DataWindow. Click this button to open the DataWindow Options window as shown in Figure 19-23.

There are three tabs on the Generation Options window. The first tab, shown in Figure 19-23, allows us to set which presentation style for which we are setting the options. From the other drop down list boxes on the tab you can select the default colors to be use for the text, columns, and background. All of the system colors are available. You can also choose the Windows system colors and have your DataWindow dynamically pick up the colors that the end user has defined for their Windows environment.

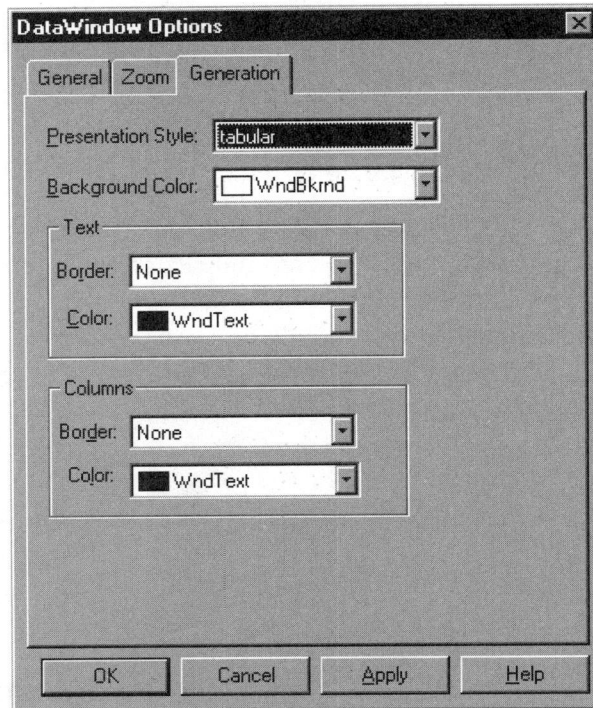

Figure 19-23. *The Data Window Options dialog window allows us to set defaults for a particular presentation style and for the designer.*

You can also select the border that you want text fields and columns to have when the DataWindow is first created. You can choose from 3D lowered, 3D raised, box, shadow box, underline, or no border at all. Remember that the borders and colors are just defaults, and you can change them later in the DataWindow designer.

The Zoom tab allows you to define the default zoom ratio that you want the DataWindow to have when it is opened in the designer. As anything but a 100% zoom factor will make the DataWindow read only in the designer, this is generally an impractical tab and you shouldn't change the value from the default 100%.

The General tab allows you to set options for how the DataWindow painter will behave. You can set the size of a snap to grid, choose to display it and choose if you want the objects on the DataWindow to align themselves to the grid. You can also choose to display a ruler. This is particularly helpful if you are laying out a report that is to be printed on an unusually sized piece of paper. The show edges checkbox specifies if you want to be able to visually discern where the edges of the objects in the DataWindow are. Retain data to design means that when you preview your DataWindow, it will only actually retrieve a result set from the database the first time you preview, after that it will display the same result set which it has buffered in memory. Retrieve on preview will cause the DataWindow to automatically retrieve a result set when you enter preview mode (instead of waiting for you to trigger a retrieve manually). And Preview On New is the same as the Preview When Built checkbox on the New DataWindow dialog. When checked, this means that the first time you move from the SQL painter to the DataWindow designer (when the DataWindow is newly built) it will automatically drop into preview mode before moving to the DataWindow designer.

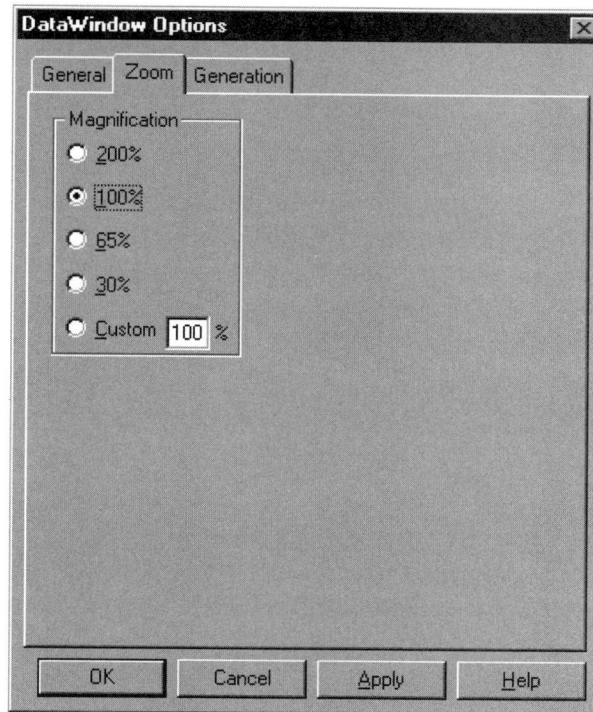

Figure 19-24. The Zoom tab should be left at 100%.

Once you set the options for a particular presentation style, the DataWindow-Painter will retain those default options indefinitely, until you decide to change them. This is true even if you shut down and restart the DataWindowPainter.

19.5.2 Tabular Style

In a Tabular presentation style, as shown in Figure 19-25, data is presented in columns placed horizontally across the DataWindow with appropriate headers above each column. The number of rows of data that are displayed at one time is dependent upon the size of the DataWindow control that the object is placed in (we will discuss Data-Window controls in more depth later in this chapter). The tabular layout is very flexible and can be easily reorganized to move columns into a different order, set up groups of data, add custom headers, and so on. The tabular style is one of the most commonly used presentation styles. You can implement split scrolling with the tabular presentation style.

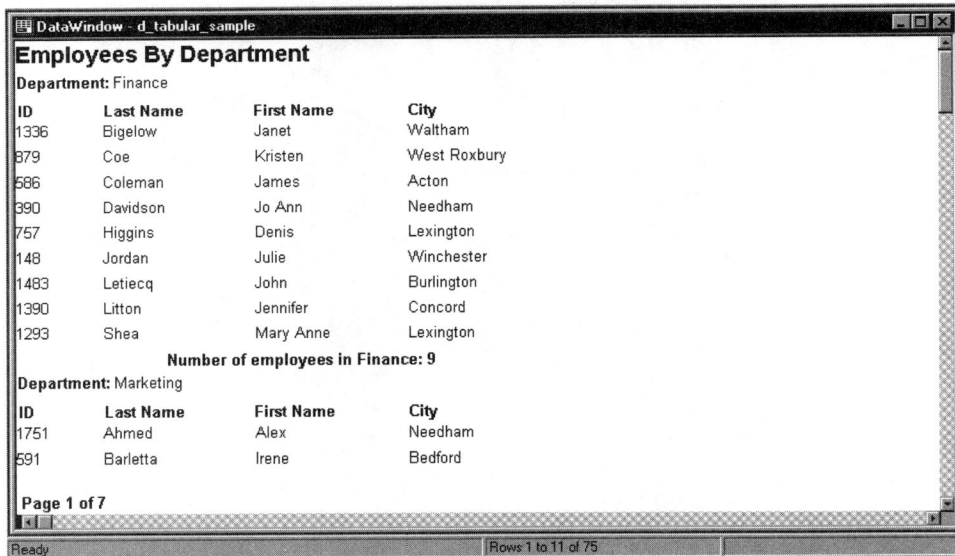

Figure 19-25. An example of the Tabular presentation style.

19.5.3 Grid Style

The grid presentation style, as shown in Figure 19-26, is very similar to the Tabular style. Data is also displayed in a row and column format, but in this style there are grid lines diving the rows and columns. The vertical grid lines can be selected and dragged to allow the user to resize the columns dynamically at runtime. The left to right ordering of the columns can also be reorganized by the end user using drag and drop techniques. As a designer, you are more restricted as to how you can lay out where columns appear as all the columns must be placed into the grid. Special titles and header information cannot be added because it doesn't fit into the grid. This type of display is often good if you want to use split scrolling.

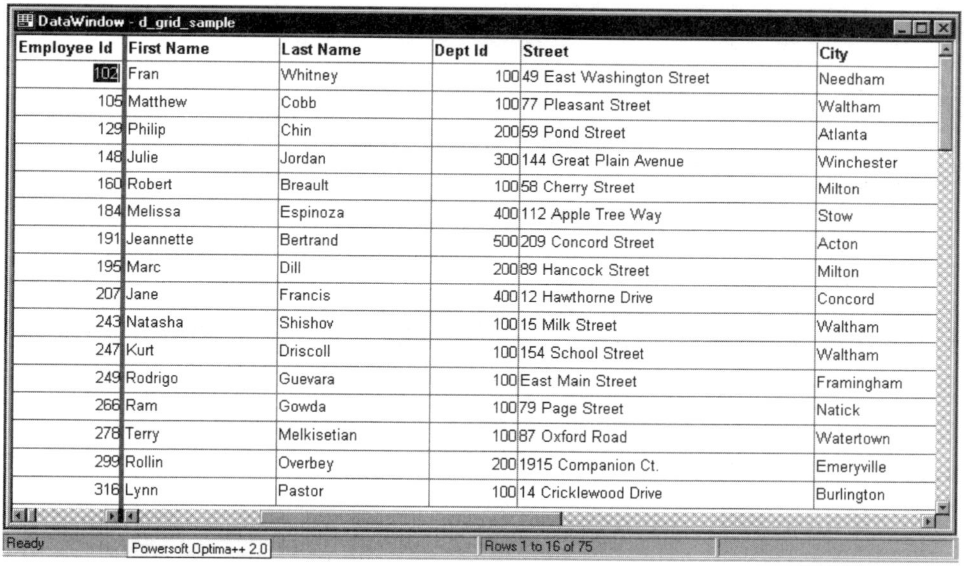

Employee Id	First Name	Last Name	Dept Id	Street	City
102	Fran	Whitney	100	49 East Washington Street	Needham
105	Matthew	Cobb	100	77 Pleasant Street	Waltham
129	Philip	Chin	200	59 Pond Street	Atlanta
148	Julie	Jordan	300	144 Great Plain Avenue	Winchester
160	Robert	Breault	100	58 Cherry Street	Milton
184	Melissa	Espinoza	400	112 Apple Tree Way	Stow
191	Jeannette	Bertrand	500	209 Concord Street	Acton
195	Marc	Dill	200	89 Hancock Street	Milton
207	Jane	Francis	400	12 Hawthorne Drive	Concord
243	Natasha	Shishov	100	15 Milk Street	Waltham
247	Kurt	Driscoll	100	154 School Street	Waltham
249	Rodrigo	Guevara	100	East Main Street	Framingham
266	Ram	Gowda	100	79 Page Street	Natick
278	Terry	Melkisetian	100	87 Oxford Road	Watertown
299	Rollin	Overbey	200	1915 Companion Ct.	Emeryville
316	Lynn	Pastor	100	14 Cricklewood Drive	Burlington

Figure 19-26. *An example of the Grid presentation style (pictured with Horizontal Split Scrolling enabled).*

19.5.4 Freeform Style

The Freeform presentation style, as shown in Figure 19-27, is one of the most flexible of the different presentation styles. Usually only one row of data is displayed at a time with the column individually labeled and arranged like the fields on a paper form. Columns, labels, text, pictures, and other drawing objects can be arranged anywhere on the DataWindow in an unstructured format. The Freeform style is often used for data entry screens or paper based forms. This style can be used to display multiple rows of data on the screen, but this can be confusing to the end user, so usually only one is displayed.

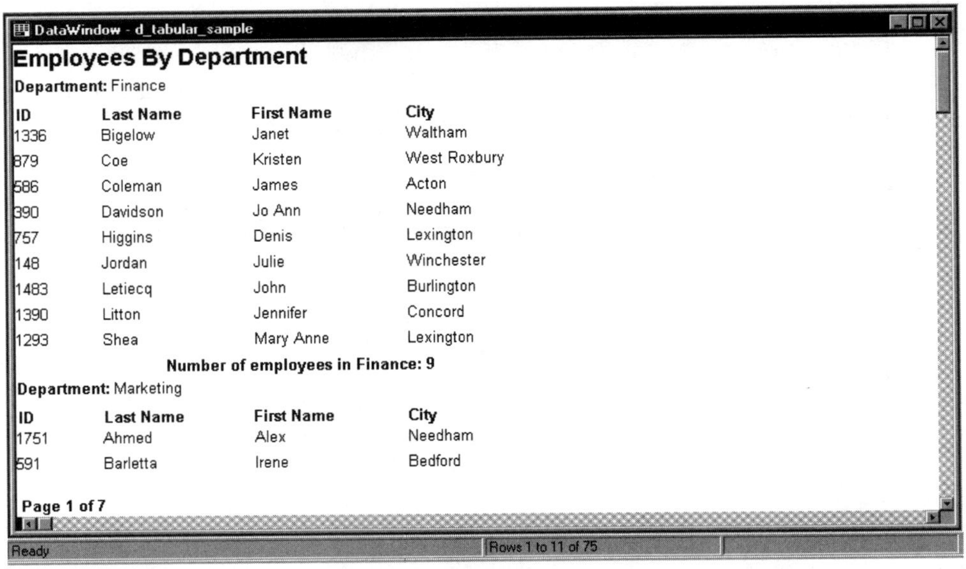

Figure 19-27. An example of the Freeform presentation style.

19.5.5 Crosstab Style

The Crosstab presentation style enables you to analyze data in two dimensional spread-sheet like format. Data is retrieved into the DataWindow, where the Crosstab process the data and presents it in a summarized format. For example, a table in the database holds orders for each customer, with columns for the customer placing the order, the item ordered, and the amount of the order. A Crosstab could be build to yield the total sales amount for each customer for each item, as shown in Figure 19-28.

Once the result set has been defined, the Crosstab Definition dialog window appears as shown in Figure 19-29. Here you must choose which data from the result set you want to represent the columns (x-axis), the rows (y-axis), and the values (date) on the crosstab. You can drag the appropriate column from the Source Data list box to the columns and rows list box. Multiple columns can be placed in each list box allowing you to build complex crosstabs. The values list box will automatically convert the dragged source data into what the DataWindowPainter thinks is the appropriate aggregate function (usually a sum of the data, or if it is non-number, a count of the number of rows). You can double click on this field to alter the definition (such as changing the sum of a dollar field to an average function to get the average purchase).

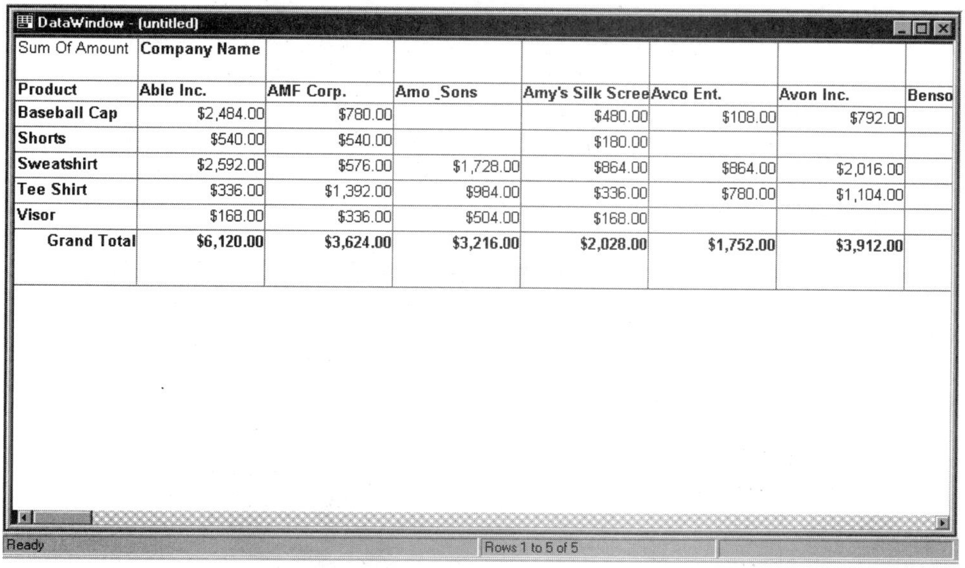

Sum Of Amount	Company Name						
Product	Able Inc.	AMF Corp.	Amo _Sons	Amy's Silk Scree	Avco Ent.	Avon Inc.	Benso
Baseball Cap	$2,484.00	$780.00		$480.00	$108.00	$792.00	
Shorts	$540.00	$540.00		$180.00			
Sweatshirt	$2,592.00	$576.00	$1,728.00	$864.00	$864.00	$2,016.00	
Tee Shirt	$336.00	$1,392.00	$984.00	$336.00	$780.00	$1,104.00	
Visor	$168.00	$336.00	$504.00	$168.00			
Grand Total	$6,120.00	$3,624.00	$3,216.00	$2,028.00	$1,752.00	$3,912.00	

Figure 19-28. An example of the Crosstab presentation style.

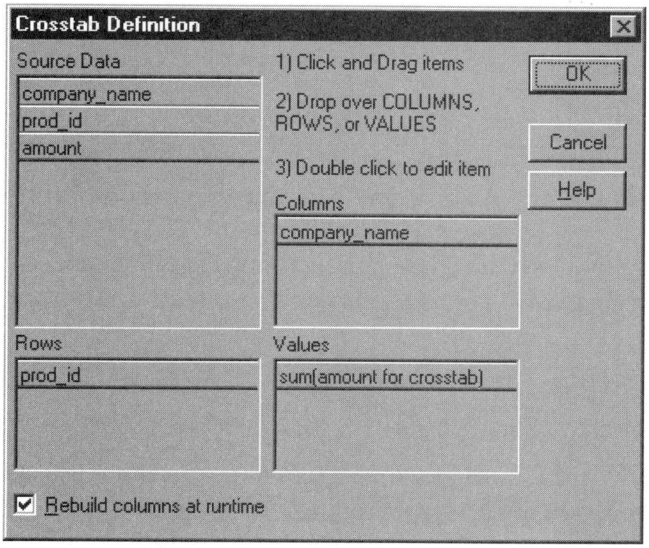

Figure 19-29. The Crosstab Definition dialog window.

The Crosstab is discussed further in the "Advanced Reporting" section in Chapter 22.

19.5.6 Graph Style

The graph presentation style, is one of the best ways to display information visually. This is a powerful and sophisticated style of DataWindow and will be addressed further in the section on Advanced Reporting at the end of this chapter. Any information can be graphed in any one of several different graph types including line, pie, bar, scatter and column graphs.

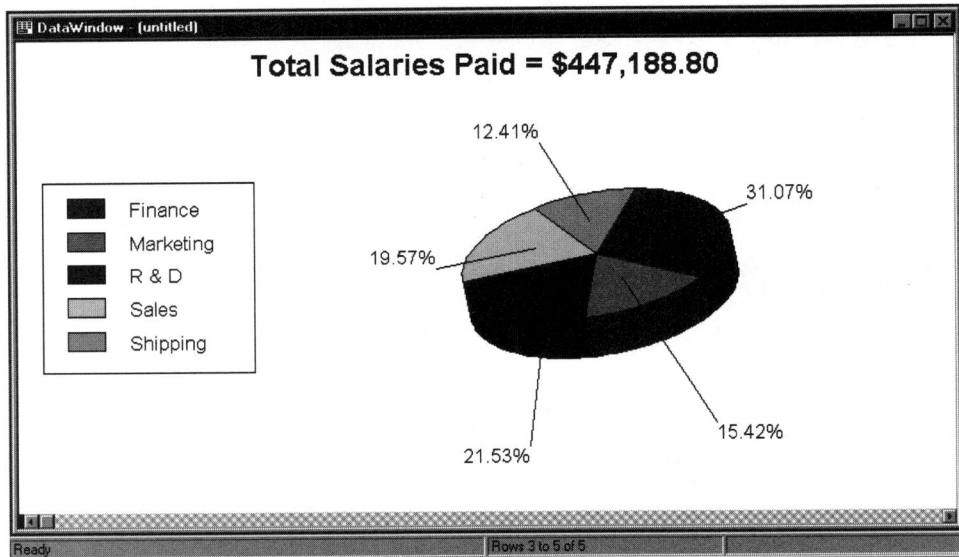

Figure 19-30. An example of a Graph presentation style.

Details on how to build these complex objects is also address in Chapter 22—"Advanced Reporting."

19.5.7 Group Style

The Group presentation style, as shown in Figure 19-31, is a tabular style DataWindow that has be preformatted to provide some client data grouping. It is intended as a short-cut to building grouped tabular DataWindows.

After you define the result set, the Group Report dialog window will open. There are two tabs on this window. The Definition will ask you to select the row, or rows, that you want to represent the main group in the DataWindow.

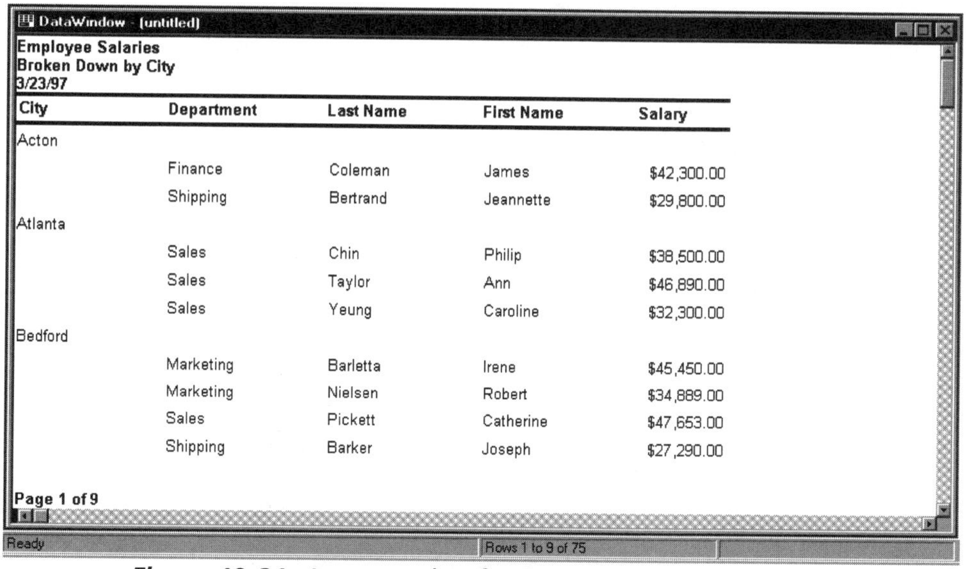

Figure 19-31. An example of a Group presentation style.

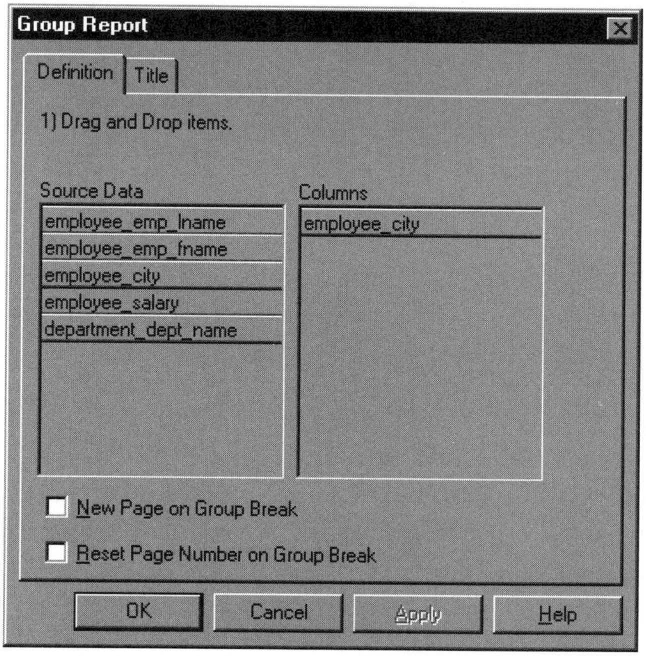

Figure 19-32. The Definition tab of the Group Report dialog window.

Once you have defined the rows to group by, you can move to the Title tab to specify a page header which will be inserted in the header region of the DataWindow as a title.

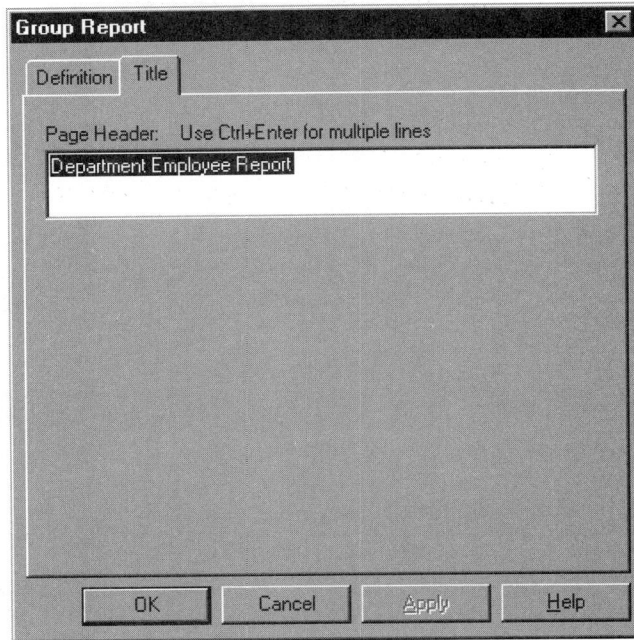

Figure 19-33. The Title tab of the Group Report dialog window.

19.5.8 Label Style

The Label presentation style, as shown in Figure 19-34, is used to present data in the form of mailing labels or other types of labels. Avery brand mailing labels are predefined in a list that appears in the label specification screen. If the label size/type you want isn't available, you can specify a custom configuration.

The Label Specifications dialog window, shown in Figure 19.35, appears after you select the data source details. This is where the predefined labels can be selected from the drop down list, or a custom label can be defined. The order in which you want your labels to appear on the page can also be defined here.

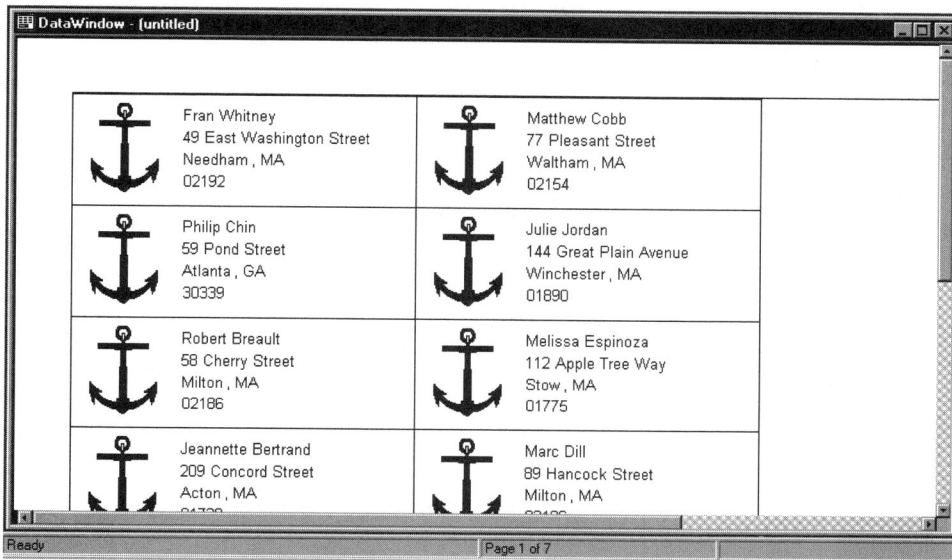

Figure 19-34. An example of the Label presentation style.

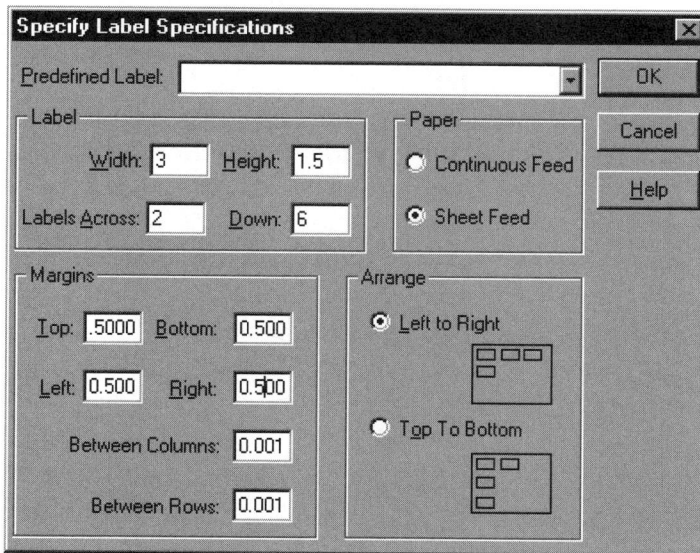

Figure 19-35. The Label Specifications dialog window allows
you to define label characteristics.

19.5.9 N-Up Style

The N-up presentation style displays data in a format that utilizes available space more efficiently. It presents rows of data side-by-side, similar to the layout of a phone book, as shown in Figure 19-36.

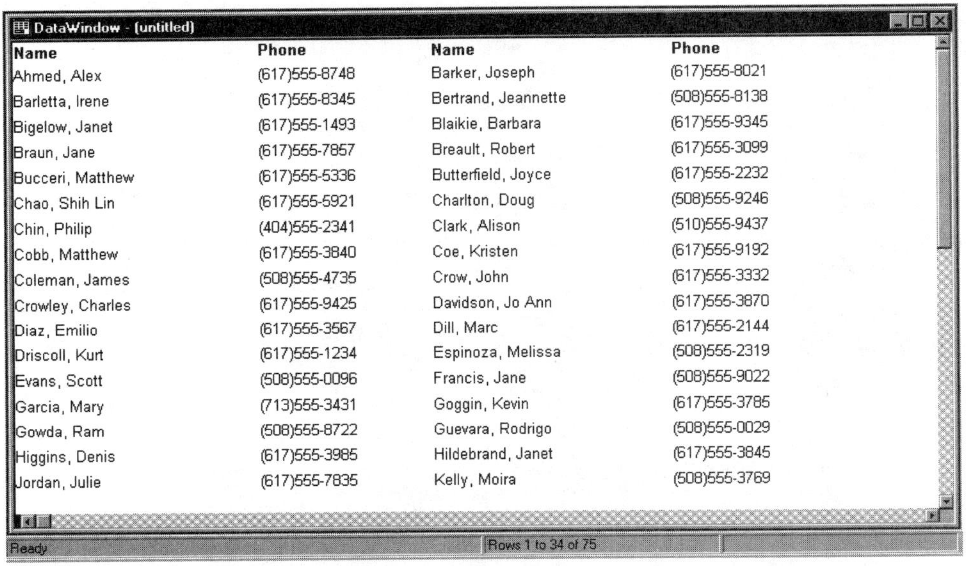

Name	Phone	Name	Phone
Ahmed, Alex	(617)555-8748	Barker, Joseph	(617)555-8021
Barletta, Irene	(617)555-8345	Bertrand, Jeannette	(508)555-8138
Bigelow, Janet	(617)555-1493	Blaikie, Barbara	(617)555-9345
Braun, Jane	(617)555-7857	Breault, Robert	(617)555-3099
Bucceri, Matthew	(617)555-5336	Butterfield, Joyce	(617)555-2232
Chao, Shih Lin	(617)555-5921	Charlton, Doug	(508)555-9246
Chin, Philip	(404)555-2341	Clark, Alison	(510)555-9437
Cobb, Matthew	(617)555-3840	Coe, Kristen	(617)555-9192
Coleman, James	(508)555-4735	Crow, John	(617)555-3332
Crowley, Charles	(617)555-9425	Davidson, Jo Ann	(617)555-3870
Diaz, Emilio	(617)555-3567	Dill, Marc	(617)555-2144
Driscoll, Kurt	(617)555-1234	Espinoza, Melissa	(508)555-2319
Evans, Scott	(508)555-0096	Francis, Jane	(508)555-9022
Garcia, Mary	(713)555-3431	Goggin, Kevin	(617)555-3785
Gowda, Ram	(508)555-8722	Guevara, Rodrigo	(508)555-0029
Higgins, Denis	(617)555-3985	Hildebrand, Janet	(617)555-3845
Jordan, Julie	(617)555-7835	Kelly, Moira	(508)555-3769

Rows 1 to 34 of 75

Figure 19-36. An example of the N-up presentation style.

A major limitation of this presentation style is that sorted data is presented across the page instead of down the page vertically like a phone book. To create a vertical presentation format, you can use a Tabular format and set up "newspaper column" printing which is discussed at the end of this chapter.

19.5.10 OLE 2.0 Style

The OLE 2.0 presentation style is a gateway to a world of new and exciting possibilities. What it allows us to do is to take our data from a SQL select statement and pass it to a valid OLE 2.0 server. That server can then be made to perform functions with the data that we pass to it. For example, we could take our result set and pass it to the media player allowing us to integrate the playing of .WAV (sound files) and .AVI (video) files into our DataWindows. Or we could use MS-Graph as an engine for performing some advanced graphic that perhaps PowerBuilder does not support. One industry group I have been heavily involved in where this will be invaluable is in the energy, forestry, and natural resource industries where integration with GIS (Geographic Information Systems) is critical. The opportunities are endless and will continue to grow as more and more software becomes OLE 2.0 compliant.

We can link any OLE 2.0 server product into the DataWindow as long as it supports the OLE standard Uniform Data Transfer (UDT). You should be able to learn if the application supports this from the vendor documentation, and you can learn what data is expected to be passed. This topic is discussed further in the "Advanced Reporting" section in Chapter 22.

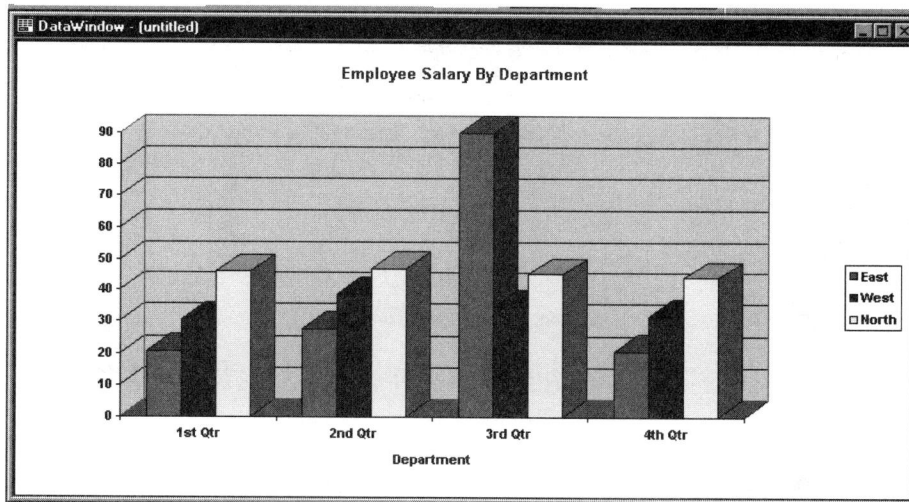

*Figure 19-37. An example of an OLE 2.0 presentation style
using MS-Graph as an OLE server.*

19.5.11 Composite Style

The primary purpose of the Composite presentation style is to allow you to create a DataWindow shell to act as a container for multiple DataWindow objects that you want to group together as a single report. The DataWindows that are included can be data independent. That means that they do not have to have expressions that provide a link between them, and could have completely unrelated data inside. This presentation style allows you group and print more than one DataWindow on a page.

Since the composite DataWindow is only a shell, it has no SQL statement of it's own, and you will not be able to select a data source option. All the DataWindow objects that you embed into the composite DataWindow will have their own data sources. You can however define as many retrieval arguments as you like and those arguments can be linked to the individual retrieval arguments in the embedded objects.

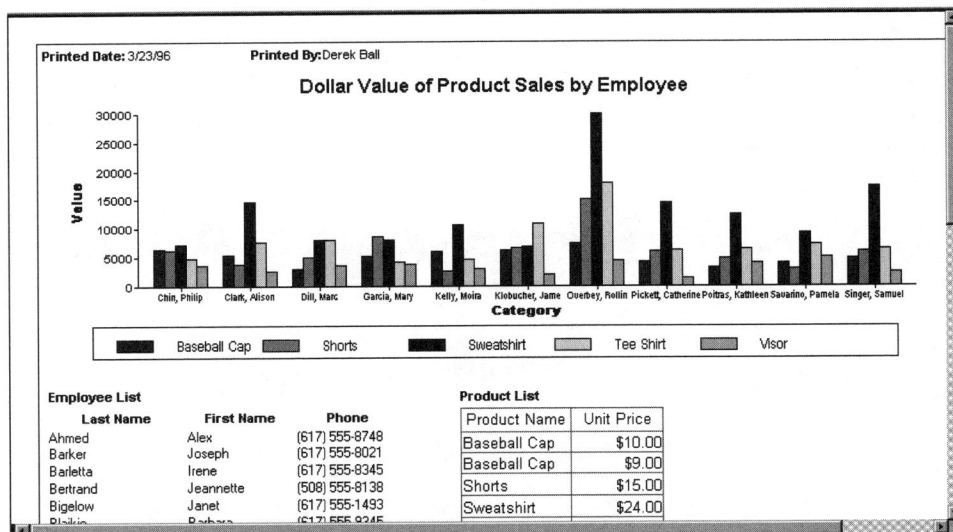

***Figure 19-38.** An example of a Composite presentation style.*

Composite presentation styles as shown in Figure 19-38are read only and are often referred to as Composite reports. They are discussed in more detail in Chapter 22.

19.5.12 Rich Text Style

The Rich Text presentation style, as shown in Figure 19.39, is used to generate DataWindows that involved substantial amounts of text and need to have information from the database embedded in the text. In this style, you can mix text and images of any shape, size, and color you desire. This format is best used for document generation and creation of form letters.

The Rich Text presentation style is discussed in more detail in Chapter 22—"Advanced Reporting."

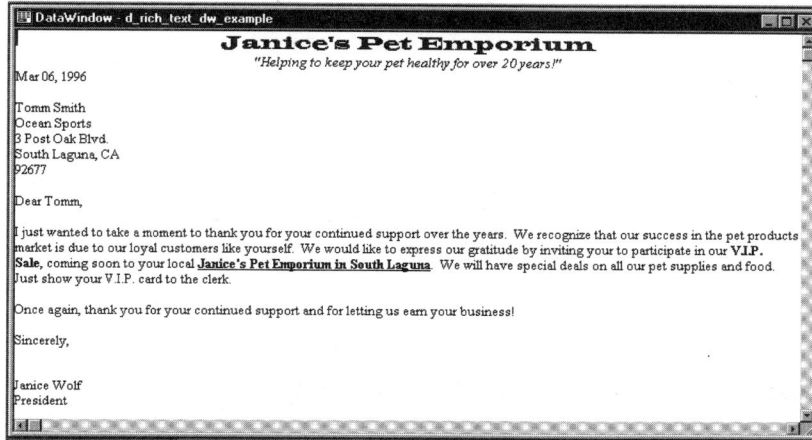

Figure 19-39. *An example of a Rich Text presentation style.*

19.6 Saving a DataWindow

To save a DataWindow object, select Save from the File menu. If the DataWindow-Painter already knows the name of the object (that is, if it's been saved before), it saves this object in the same library, overwriting the old object. If this object hasn't been saved before, the DataWindowPainter opens the Save DataWindow dialog window as shown in Figure 19-40.

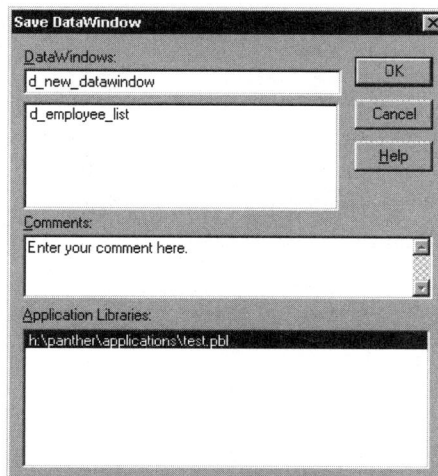

Figure 19-40. *Saving a DataWindow.*

This window is similar to the Select DataWindow dialog window you saw when you first entered the DataWindow painter. You must enter the name of the object your saving in the single line edit box at the top of the screen. The comments box can be used to enter any comments you would like to save with the object. Although comments are optional, it is strongly recommended that you use them. They make it easier to pick out the DataWindow object you are looking for when your library has grown to 50 or 60 DataWindows.

The bottom list box allows you to select which library in your library search path in which you want to save this DataWindow.

19.7   Modifying a DataWindow Data Source

After the DataWindow has been created, you may decide you want to make a change to the data source. To do this, select the SQL icon on the toolbar or choose **Data Source...** from the **Design** menu (this works for External data source DataWindows too). This returns you to the appropriate window or painter to make the modifications you desire. For example, if you created a DataWindow with QuickSelect or SQLSelect, you will be returned to the SQLSelect painter.

19.8   Customizing Your DataWindow

Having completed the steps necessary to define the data source for your DataWindow and the default presentation style, you now find yourself in the DataWindow painter workspace, also known as the DataWindow *designer*. The DataWindowPainter has generated a default DataWindow object for you to use as a starting point. The default layout of these objects is often not quite what you envisioned when you started creating the DataWindow, and so it must be enhanced. In this workspace, you can customize the DataWindow to look and behave exactly as you specify.

You may want to change its appearance by rearranging columns and adding computed fields, summaries, headers, footers, graphics, and other visual enhancements. You can alter column colors, fine tune reports, add graphs, and make other visual enhancements to the DataWindow.

Functional enhancements can also be added. For example, data can be grouped so as to better convey the information to the users, and redundant repeating rows can be suppressed.

The behavior of the DataWindow can be customized as well. Perhaps you want to adjust the columns so the user can't update them, or can update specific columns. You can adjust the DataWindow to retrieve rows from the database only as it needs them, or to pull them all back at once and buffer them in memory.

The DataWindow can be tested now to ensure that it looks and behaves as you desire before you include it in your application. This test mode can be used to view and modify actual database data and to test the real-time retrieval performance of the DataWindow.

19.8.1 Bands

Reports are all around us. We see them at work, such as reports on productivity, shipping reports or inventory descriptions. We see them at home, in our credit card bills or the phone book. Since we all see and deal with information in this format, it is easy to recognize some common components that make up all reports, as shown in Figure 19-41.

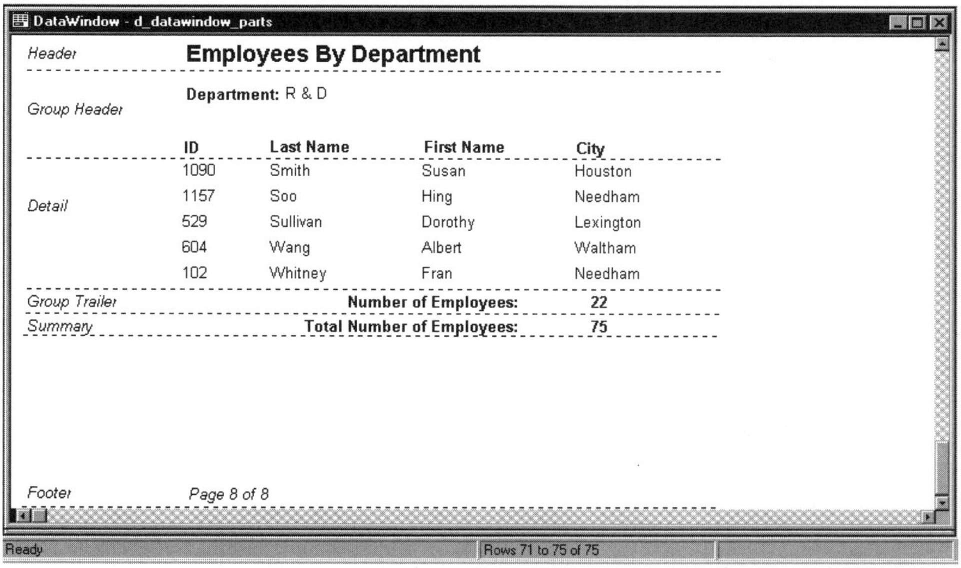

Figure 19-41. Common components of a report.

A DataWindow is divided into sections that correspond directly to the components of a report. These sections appear as bands within the DataWindow workspace.

Below each band is a gray bar with the band's name on it. These bars are for your reference only and don't appear on the DataWindow when you display or print it.

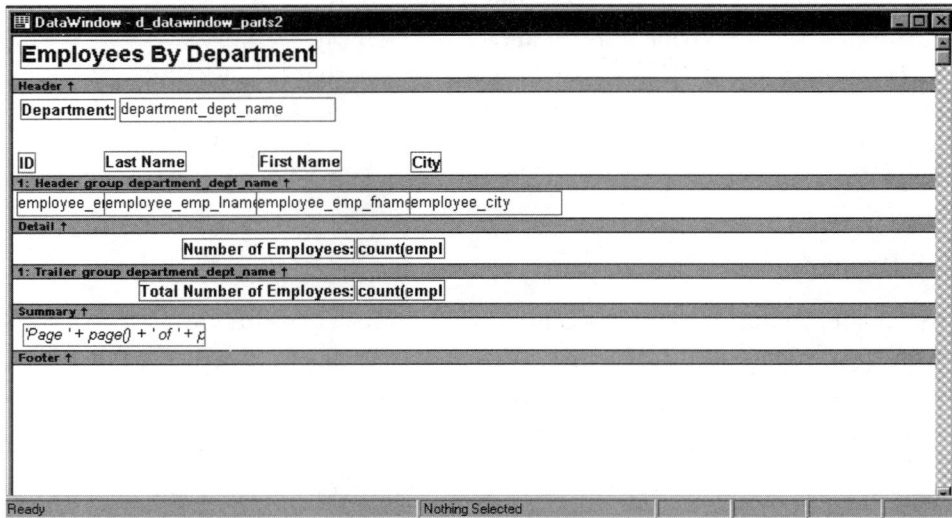

Figure 19-42. The bands in the DataWindow painter correspond to the sections of a report.

19.8.1.1 Header Band

The information you place in the header area appears at the top of your DataWindow and at the top of each page as you page through the data (this also means it appears at the top of each page as you print it out).

What appears in this space when PowerBuilder first builds the DataWindow depends on the presentation style selected. If you chose Tabular, Grid or N-Up presentation style, you will see the column headings in this space.

Quite a few items can be added to this band to enhance the appearance of the DataWindow. You might choose to add a computed field to show the data that a report was run. Text objects can be added as titles or other information.

Developer's Note: Text, bitmap images, and drawing objects such as lines, rectangles, round rectangles, and ovals can be placed in any band of the DataWindow. All of these items can be selected by clicking the respective icon on the PainterBar.

19.8.1.2 Group Header Band

The DataWindowPainter only places this band in your default DataWindow if you have selected Group as your presentation style. This band appears if you create groups in your DataWindow (as you will do later in this chapter). This band displays the information that you want to appear at the start of each group, such as the group identifier (such as the department name, if grouping by department). Summary information for the group can be included here by creating computed fields and placing them in this band. This information could include a total sum of salaries for a grouping of employees in a certain department, or the number of employees in that department.

Developer's Note: You have one group header band for every group that you define, but that doesn't necessarily mean that you have to place objects in all of them.

19.8.1.3 Detail Band

The data retrieved in your result set appears in the detail band, along with any applicable labels associated with that data (such as in the Freeform presentation style). The DataWindow repeats the detail band for as many rows as it can fit in to the visible space on the DataWindow or the report page (taking into consideration the space left over between the header and the footer).

For Tabular, Grid, N-up, and Label presentation styles, the detail band holds fields representing a detail row for each column of each record in the result set (identifiable by the column name). In a Freeform style, labels for each column in the result set appear with the column detail field immediately to its right.

Each row doesn't necessarily have to be on one line. You can create a report that looks like this:

Greenwell, Pat	123 Main Street	Home: (317)555-1212
	Anytown, State	Work: (317)555-2345
	91125	
Jones, Tom	5678 Side Street	Home: (317)555-1213
	Anothertown, State	Work: (317)555-9999
	92345	

You do this by creating a detail band like the one shown in Figure 19-43.

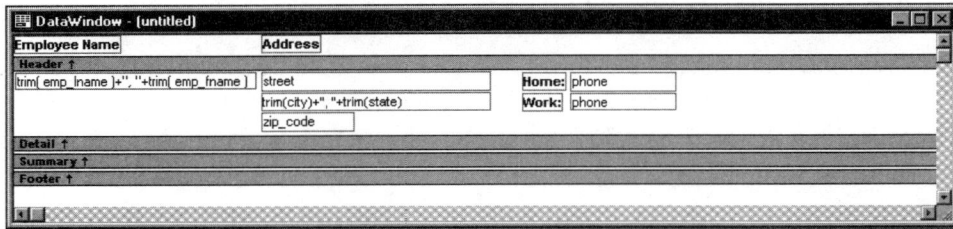

Figure 19-43. Detail band with multiple lines.

Computed fields used in the detail band should only refer to the data used in that particular row. For example, a DataWindow that displays the quantity and price of an item might use a computed field to compute the total cost for that item on that row. It wouldn't be appropriate to use a computed field in this band to display summary information for the group, as this field will be repeated with each row of data in the group (in other words, with each iteration of the detail band).

19.8.1.4 Group Trailer Band

Like the group header band, this band only appears if you use the group presentation style or have added groups to your DataWindow. The information in this section appears after the last item in each group in the DataWindow. Computed fields are often used here to provide summary or total information for each group.

One group trailer band is created for each group in your DataWindow.

19.8.1.5 Summary Band

The information in the summary band appears only on the last screen or page, at the end of the data. It is often used to display summary information for the entire DataWindow. Examples of what can be included here are a count of all the rows of data or total of all the outstanding invoices. If you are required to insert an end-of-report statement or flag, this is the band in which to place it.

19.8.1.6 Footer Band

The footer band is very similar to the header band except that its data appears at the bottom of each screen or page. A common use for this area is to display a computed field showing the current page of the report and how many pages there are in total.

19.8.1.7 Resizing Bands

You can slide the bands up and down the workspace to give you more or less room in which to work. You can select the gray band label by clicking and holding the left mouse button, and then the bar can be moved up or down as desired. Releasing the left button drops the bar in its new location. The amount of physical space between bars will be represented in the actual DataWindow or report, so it is important to size everything appropriately.

19.8.2 Selecting Objects

All of the items in all of the DataWindow bands are objects that you can select. Just as in Window Painter, an object must be selected before you can work with it. You can tell that an object is selected if it has a small black box in each corner. These small black boxes are called handles.

A single object can be selected by clicking it with the mouse. If another object is clicked, the previous one is deselected and the new object becomes the selected item. Multiple objects can be selected simultaneously with the mouse by holding down the CTRL key while clicking the new object. All the selected objects together make up a group. Individual objects can be removed from the group by holding the CTRL key and clicking those objects again. The handles of those objects will then disappear.

There are a few additional ways of selecting groups of objects. It is possible to "lasso" a group of objects by pressing and holding the left mouse button somewhere within the band in an area of empty space. As you drag the mouse (still holding down the left mouse button) a box appears, and grows as you move the mouse. All objects inside the lasso are selected when you release the mouse button.

Another method for selecting a group is to select an option from the Select menu item under the Edit menu on the menu bar, as shown in Figure 19-44.

The Select menu enables you to form a group by selecting all of the objects or a subgroup of objects. By selecting a single object, you can then select all of the objects to its right or left, and the ones above or below it (or them). Two of these actions can be combined to select a range of objects. For example, to select everything above and to the right of the object that is currently selected, choose Select Right and then Select Above. The shortcut keys for these are very intuitive and easy to use. Simply select a single object, and then, holding the CTRL key, select an arrow key in the direction that you want to select other objects. **<CTRL + A>** selects all the objects in the current

DataWindow. Two options that don't have shortcut keys are the options to select all the columns or all the text fields. This can be very useful for general formatting such as setting all the column headers to bold text and 3D Raised styles, but setting the columns themselves to regular text with a white background and 3D lowered.

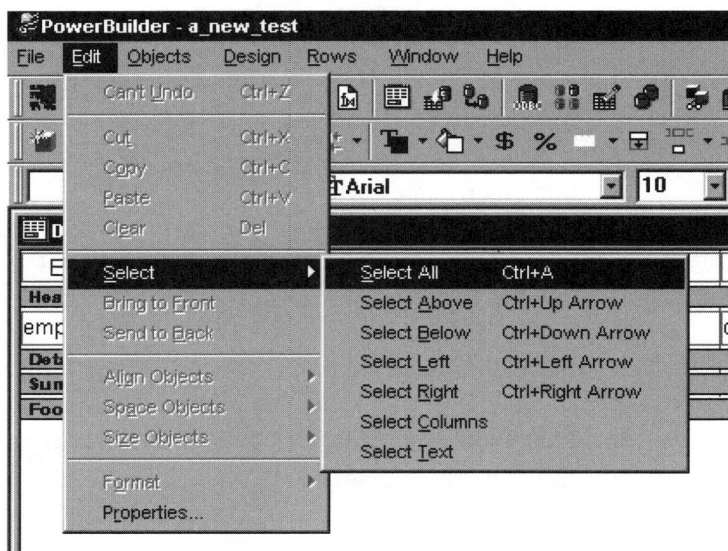

Figure 19-44. The Select menu provides another method for selecting objects.

19.8.3 Manipulating Objects

Items can be moved around in the DataWindow workspace by selecting them and then dragging them around with the mouse. They can be moved individually or as a group.

An object can be resized by selecting it and then moving the mouse pointer to an edge or corner. When the pointer is over one of these places, the normal pointer arrow is replaced with a resize arrow (the one with two heads). Grab the border by holding down the left mouse button. You can now drag the border and resize the object as you desire.

Making very small adjustments with the mouse can be a near impossible task. To move an object or a group by a very small or precise amount, the keyboard arrow keys can be used. Then move the selected object (or objects) one grid space or one unit of measure (if the grid is turned off) in the direction indicated (see Using Alignment Grids and Rulers in this chapter).

The same technique can be used to resize an object or group of objects by holding down the SHIFT key while pressing an arrow key. This has the same effect as dragging the lower left corner of the selected object(s). This lower left corner will now move in response to your arrow keys to make the object larger or smaller. This is also very useful for resizing an entire group of objects simultaneously.

To help make groups of objects appear more cohesive and professional you can use built in DataWindowPainter features to align them along a common axis, space them an equal distance apart and adjust them to all be the same size. The aligning of objects is useful in a wide variety of situations for example, you can line up all the column headings in a tabular report, or line up all the radio buttons in a group. It is also useful to make columns or rows of data appear to be equally spaced. In addition, groups of columns that hold the same data type (date fields are an example) should all be the same size.

The options for performing these operations are located under the Edit menu as shown in Figure 19-45.

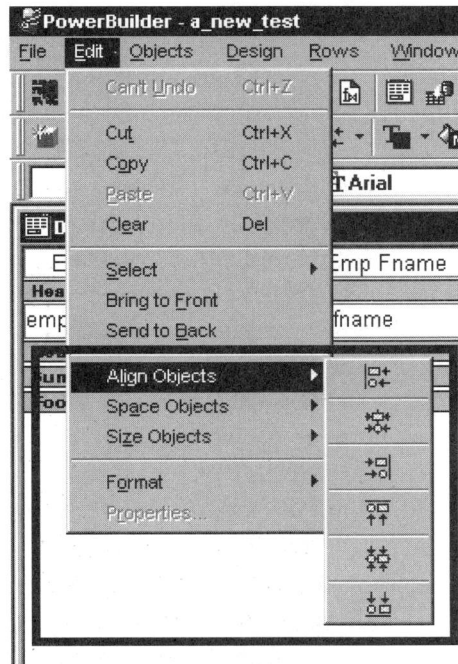

Figure 19-45. The DataWindowPainter has built in features for Aligning, Spacing, and Sizing objects.

When aligning or sizing, all objects in the group are aligned or sized to the first object that was selected in the group. When spacing, all objects are spaced based upon the distance between the first and second objects selected. This presents a small issue when you are using the "lasso" technique to select objects, because the DataWindow-Painter will select the objects in what ever order is most efficient, and this may not be the left to right or top to bottom order. Therefore, if you are planning to do aligning, spacing, or sizing, we strongly recommend that you select your first (and if applicable, second) object manually.

19.8.4 Setting Options

From the Design menu bar item you will be able to select a menu choice called **Options....**This choice will open up the DataWindow Options dialog window where you can set options that define how the DataWindow painter behaves. These options are divided into three categories General, Zoom, and Generation.

19.8.4.1 Using Alignment Grids and Rulers

One of the first sets of options that you will see on the General tab are choices for controlling the alignment grids and rulers. Alignment grids and rulers are tools that will help you to align, space and size objects within the DataWindow painter.

The options that we are looking at right now are all within the group box labeled Alignment Grid in Figure 19-46. The Snap to Grid check box causes objects to automatically align themselves with the nearest gridlines when moved and dropped. This makes it easier to adjust objects precisely to ensure alignment and spacing.

The X and Y single line edit boxes are used to specify the width and height of each cell in the grid. These sizes are measure in pixels.

The Show Grid check box draws the grid lines in the DataWindow workspace. This makes it easier to visually line up objects and ensure straight lines in your DataWindow. These grid lines don't appear when you use your DataWindow in your application or when you print it out. You can turn on the visual grid even if your Snap to Grid option is set to FALSE.

The Show Ruler checkbox displays rulers at the top edge and left side of the workspace to assist you in visually measuring the size of the DataWindow. The ruler displays the units of measurement specified in the DataWindow style (see DataWindow Properties and Style in this chapter).

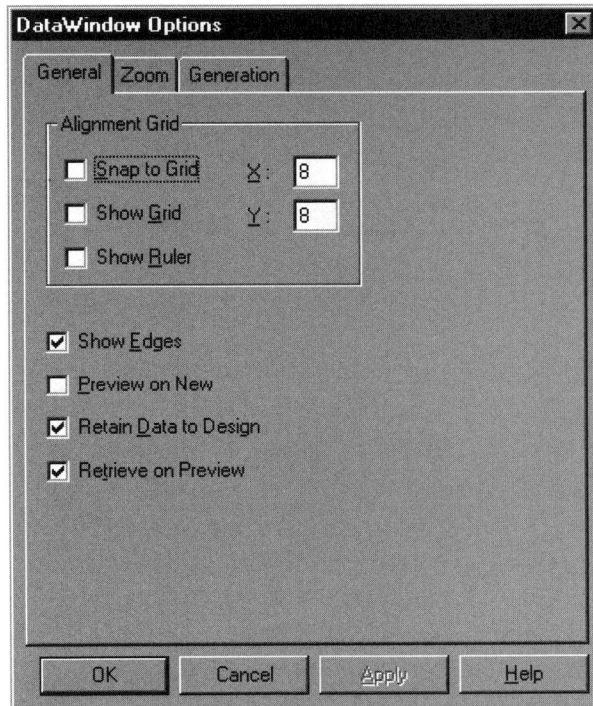

Figure 19-46. The General tab of the DataWindow options dialog window.

Developer's Tip: If you turn on the Snap to Grid option part way through the building of your DataWindow, the objects currently in the workspace don't automatically snap to the grid that you have now imposed upon them. They must be selected, either individually or all together, and then moved a small distance to get them to snap into alignment on the grid.

Displaying the grid will slow down the repainting of your DataWindow workspace during design. If you have a slower computer, you may want to use this option only when necessary. You can still use Snap to Grid, but just don't display it on the screen.

19.8.4.2 Using Show Edges

Another very useful option you will find on the General tab is Show Edges. This option toggles on and off the box that appears around each object showing where its boundaries are. This is a useful visual aid for laying out a DataWindow. By showing the exact space a field will occupy, you can watch for overlapping fields, and fields that aren't large enough to display the entire value they hold.

19.8.4.3 Other General Options

There are three other options on the General tab Preview on New, Retain Data to Design ,and Retrieve on Preview.

Preview on New is the same as the Preview When Built option on the New DataWindow dialog discussed earlier. It indicates that then you first finish building your select statement and are moving to the DataWindow design workspace, you will be given a preview of the data that is being retrieved from the database to ensure that you are returning the correct information.

Retain Data to Design is a useful option that causes the DataWindowPainter to buffer the first result set retrieved when previewing the DataWindow and reuse that result set in future previews. This saves network traffic and time, particularly if you are retrieving a large result set. The result set will automatically be reretrieved in the event that you make a significant change in the DataWindow design that would make a buffered result set inaccurate. You can also manually refresh the result set by pressing the Retrieve button on the toolbar while in Preview mode.

Retrieve on Preview will cause the DataWindowPainter to automatically retrieve a result set from the database when you enter preview mode. If set to false, then you must manually push the retrieve button to obtain the result set. Retain Data to Design takes precedence over this option.

19.8.4.4 Using Zoom

Sometimes workspace isn't large enough to display the entire DataWindow that you are working on, or you may need to see a particular part of the DataWindow up close. To do this, you can enlarge or reduce the view of the workspace using the features on the Zoom tab of the DataWindow options as shown in Figure 19-47.

The Zoom tab has four preset magnification choices: 200% (2X larger), 100% (normal view), 65% (slightly smaller), and 30% (much smaller). You can choose a custom zoom amount by selecting Custom and then entering the percentage you desire. Anything greater than 100 magnifies your view, and anything less shrinks it.

Now comes the bad news: This may sound like a great option, but developers almost never use it. Why? Because at anything other than 100% magnification, the

DataWindow becomes read only and you cannot manipulate any of the objects in the DataWindow.

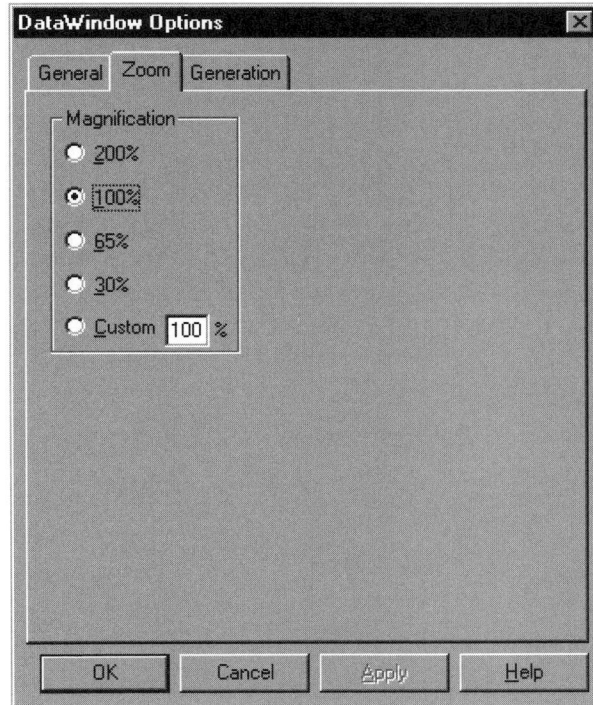

Figure 19-47. The Zoom tab of the DataWindow Options dialog window.

19.8.4.5 Generation Options

The Generation tab serves the exact same purpose as the Options command button on the New DataWindow dialog discussed in the section entitled, "DataWindow Options" earlier in this chapter.

19.8.5 The Toolbars

There are two default toolbars that are specific to the DataWindow design workspace which provide specific types of functionality as the DataWindow is built. These are the Style Bar and the Painter Bar. These toolbars can be customized and new toolbars added. The discussion of toolbars in this section discusses only the default toolbar layouts.

19.8.6 The Style Bar

The Style Bar is located immediately above the workspace. This bar, shown in Figure 19-48, enables you to format the text of any selected object or objects, such as a column or text label. You can choose a font type and size, turn the bold, italic and underline options on or off, and make the text left-justified, centered or right-justified. If you are working with a text object, the text appears in an edit box to the left of the bar and you can edit it there.

Figure 19-48. *The Style Bar is used to manipulate the text of the selected object(s).*

The text in an object can be manipulated by adding special control characters. A normal text header might look like the following:

EMPLOYEE NAME

If you want it to be formatted to display on two lines like:

EMPLOYEE
NAME

enter the following as the text string in the edit box:

```
EMPLOYEE~n~rNAME
```

The "~" character is called a tilde. The ~n and ~r combination produces a new line and a carriage return.

19.8.7 The Painter Bar

The Painter Bar contains buttons to allow you to perform basic operations on the current DataWindow such as saving and loading. It also contains a drop down toolbar icon for placing objects on the DataWindow such as drawing objects and computed columns. Several buttons also exist to help with formatting (changing colors, border styles, alignment, etc.), previewing, tab orders and return to the SQL editor.

Figure 19-49. *The DataWindow Painter toolbar.*

19.8.8 Popup Menus

When you move the mouse pointer over any object in the workspace (or even the empty workspace area) and click the right mouse button, a popup menu will appear with different options that are relevant to the selected object. The standard options are shown in Figure 19-50 and include opening the Properties sheet for the object, cutting, copying or pasting the object and bringing the object to the front of the page or sending it to the back.

Figure 19-50. The Popup menu for a DataWindow item.

The options that you can access via the Properties tab will be discussed as we progress through this chapter.

19.8.9 Keyboard Shortcuts

As you get comfortable with the DataWindowPainter, you will start to use keyboard shortcut keys to perform some of the common and repetitive tasks such as formatting on your selected objects. The keyboard interface is usually faster if you know the correct command. The commands you use often will stay in your mind, but the following table will help you learn the shortcut keys you can use.

Table 19-1. Keyboard Shortcuts.

Action	Keystrokes	Description
Text Functions		
Bold Text	CTRL + B	Toggles bold on and off.
Italicize Text	CTRL + I	Toggles italics on and off.

(continued)

Table 19-1. *(continued)*

Action	Keystrokes	Description
Underline Text	CTRL + U	Toggles underline on and off.
Selecting Objects		
Select All	CTRL + A	Selects all objects in the current DataWindow.
Select Above	CTRL + Up Arrow	Selects all objects directly above the currently selected object or group.
Select Below	CTRL + Down Arrow	Selects all objects directly below the currently selected object or group.
Select Right	CTRL + Right Arrow	Selects all objects directly to the right of the currently selected object or group.
Select Left	CTRL + Left Arrow	Selects all objects directly to the left of the currently selected object or group.
Object Functions		
Open	CTRL + O	Opens the Open DataWindow dialog to select a DataWindow to open.
New	CTRL + N	Creates a New DataWindow object (closing the current DataWindow that is open).
Close	CTRL + W	Closes the currently open DataWindow.
Print	CTRL + P	Prints the current DataWindow.
Save	CTRL + S	Saves the current DataWindow.
Exit	CTRL + Q	Exits the DataWindow Painter.
Preview	CTRL + SHIFT + P	Enter Preview Mode.

19.8.10 Tab Orders

Tab order in a DataWindow is the same as tab order in a form, which was discussed in an earlier chapter. The tab order in a DataWindow indicates which field receives the focus next as the user tabs through the fields. A tab order of zero indicates that the user can't enter a value in that field. This is useful for preventing users from updating values in columns that you don't want them to change.

You enter tab order mode in one of two ways, by selecting Tab Order from the Design menu, or by pressing the Tab Order toolbar icon on the Painter Bar. These options are toggle switches and must be selected again to exit tab order mode (in tab order mode, the only thing that you can modify in the DataWindow is the tab order).

The red tab order labels appear when you enter tab order mode. They appear immediately above the fields in the result set. Text objects, drawing objects, bitmaps, and computed fields don't have a tab order.

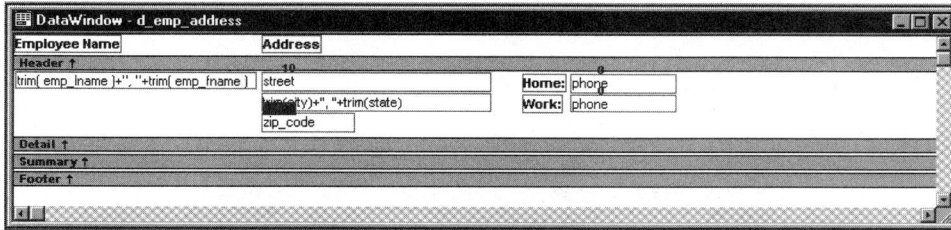

Figure 19-51. DataWindow in tab order mode.

Valid tab values are from 0 to 9999. The exact value that you enter for an object's tab order doesn't matter because the DataWindowPainter automatically renumbers all the tab orders in increments of 10. If you exit tab order mode and then reenter it, you will see that all the tab orders have been renumbered.

Developer's Note: If your DataWindow contains a join between two or more tables, the default tab order on all fields is 0. This is because the DataWindow objects cannot, by default, update multiple DataWindows (Multiple DataWindows can be updated, but that is an advanced topic that is beyond the scope of this book).

The tab order in a DataWindow can be changed dynamically at runtime using the function dw_control.SetTabOrder(x).

19.8.11 DataWindow Properties and Style

Similar to the forms that we built earlier, every DataWindow object has its own style and properties. You can open the DataWindow Object properties page by double-clicking in an empty space on the DataWindow or by clicking with the left mouse button and selecting **Properties...** off the pop up menu.

There are three tabs on the properties page for a DataWindow General, Pointer and Print Specifications.

19.8.11.1 General Tab

On the general tab you can specify the units of measure that is used in the DataWindow.

Your options are:

- PowerBuilder units—this is a hold over from Powersoft's 4GL product, PowerBuilder, and is measured by 1/32 of the system font size.

- Pixels.

- Thousandths of an inch.

- Thousandths of a centimeter.

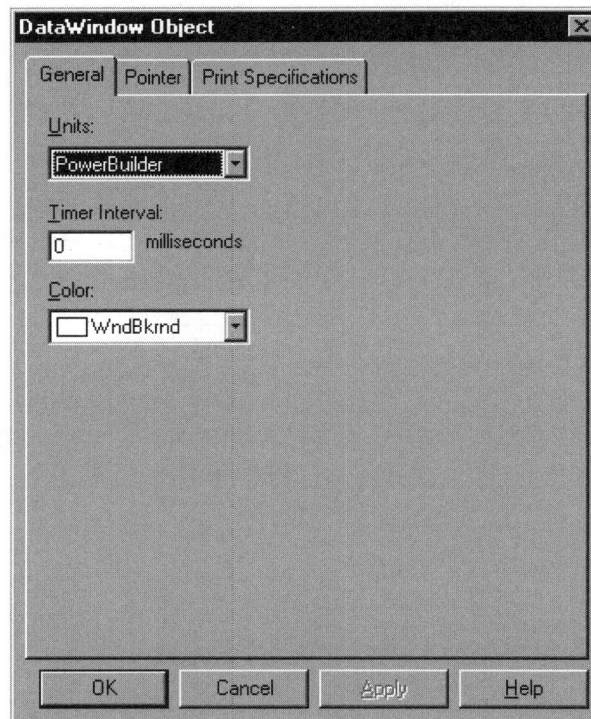

Figure 19-52. *The DataWindow properties page with the General tab visible.*

You can also specify the interval between firings of the DataWindow's internal timer event. This is only relevant if you are using a current time field in your DataWindow. The zero in the entry field is the DataWindowPainter default, which indicates that the DataWindow updates the time field every minute (60,000 milliseconds). If you want to update it more or less often, that can be specified here. The background color for the DataWindow can be specified here as well.

19.8.11.2 Pointer Tab

On the Pointer tab you can select the pointer that will appear when the mouse is over this DataWindow.

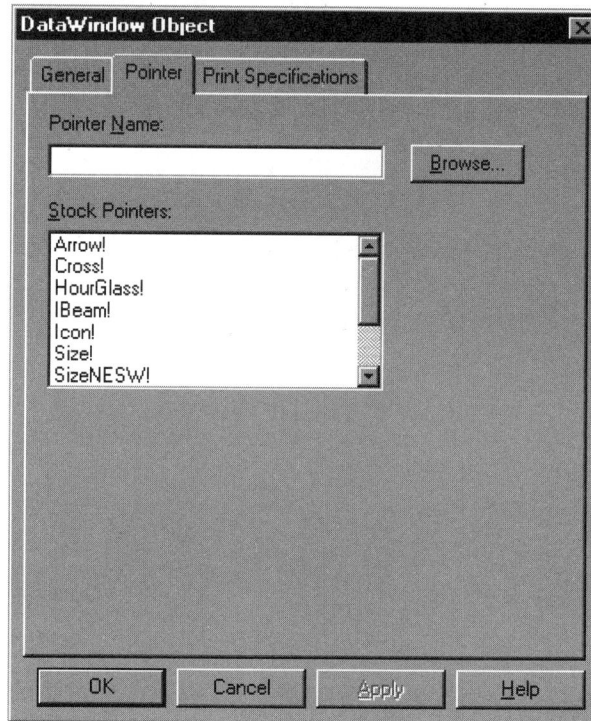

Figure 19-53. The Pointer tab.

The mouse pointer is a very useful tool for conveying information to the user. Just as you can change it to an hourglass shape to tell the user that the system is busy, you can change it as it passed over your DataWindow or portion of your DataWindow.

In the Pointer tab you can select from the list of stock pointers built into the DataWindowPainter, like the arrow and the hourglass, or you can choose any valid pointer file (a valid pointer file has a .CUR extension and can be created with the Image Editor application that comes with PowerBuilder 6.0). An image of the selected pointer will appear to the right of the list of stock pointers.

It is possible to specify one pointer for the DataWindow and then specify other pointers for each column in the DataWindow as will be discussed later.

19.8.12 Display Formats and Edit Styles

The way that the end user views and works with the data in the DataWindow does not necessarily have to reflect how it is stored in the database. The classic example of this is a phone number. When you display a phone number to the user, you probably want it to appear as

(403)555-1212

but you only want to have

4035551212

in the database.

We have two mechanisms available in the DataWindowPainter to translate the data from what is stored in the database to the interface with which the user interacts. These mechanisms are *display formats* and *edit styles*.

19.8.12.1 Display Formats

Display format are definitions stored along with a column that specify how the data in the column is to be displayed to the user. These display formats can be different for each column in the DataWindow.

Display formats are *unidirectional* which means that they will only format the data when it is displayed to the user, but when they enter data into a field, they do so in a raw format. For *bidirectional* data formatting, we will use the edit styles discussed below. Unidirectional behavior makes display formats ideally suited for working with two types of data: currencies and percentages.

Let's consider a currency. The standard accounting format for a negative number would place the negative number in parenthesis with all the currency formatting (dollar sign, commas, decimal points) contained within such as:

($1,256.56)

This is great for display purposes, but when it comes to entering data, the user will not enter negative numbers by typing them within parenthesis, the user will enter them by using the minus sign such as:

-1256.56 [ENTER]

This is where the unidirectional behavior of the display format is very valuable. As soon as the user hits enter, they indicate to the DataWindow that they are finished entering the data and the DataWindow will apply the display format. The user can always enter their numerical information in the raw data mode that they are accustomed to.

19.8.12.1.1 Defining a Display Format

The DataWindowPainter has the most commonly used display formats already predefined such as standard currency formatting which inserts dollar signs and commas where required. If the predefined set of formats are not sufficient you can create your own, although very seldom have I every needed to do this.

Display formats can be created in the Database painter and then applied to a column in a table through the extended attributes. Then when this column is used in a DataWindow, that display format is picked up and used automatically. This is the default display format.

Alternatively, in the DataWindow painter you can override the default display format and change it to another format already predefined for defined in the Database painter (represented by the icon showing two tin cans on the main toolbar), or you can make up your own from scratch.

In the Database Painter

To define an edit style in the Database painter select the **Display Format Maintenance...** from the **Design** menu bar option. This will open the Display Formats window as shown in Figure 19-54.

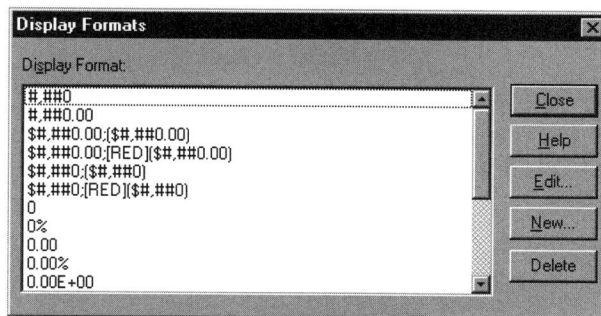

Figure 19-54. *The Display Formats window is the entry point into defining display formats in the Database painter. The same window is used for both editing and creating new formats.*

Selecting an existing display format and pressing the **Edit...** or **New...** command button will open the Display Format Definition dialog window as shown in Figure 19-55. This window is used for both editing existing display formats and creating new ones.

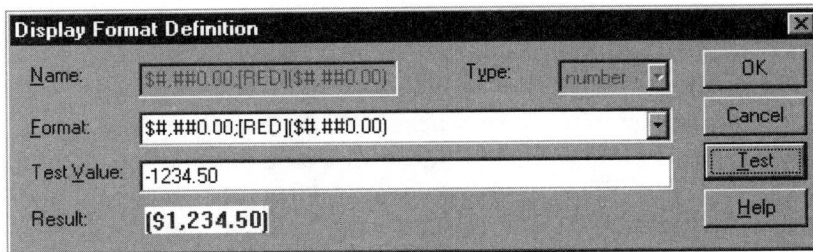

Figure 19-55. *The Display Format Definition window is used for both creating new display formats and editing existing formats.*

When you are editing a display format, you will not be able to change the name or data type of the display format. If this is a new display format you can assign a name up to forty characters long and select a data type of either string, numeric, date, time or datetime.

You will need to create a new definition, or edit the existing definition for the display format. You can enter standard characters that you want to include in the format and special characters such as:

@—to represent any character

#—to represent numeric characters

mm/dd/yy hh:mm:ss—to deal with date and time formatting components

For example, the definition for a string field containing a phone number would be:

(@@@)@@@-@@@@

which would result in a standard telephone format.

As a second example, we could define a currency format that would display the currency formatted to show a dollar sign, commas between the thousands, two decimal places and display the negative values the same way but in parenthesis and in a red color. The definition would look like:

$#,##0.00[RED]($#,##0.00)

Once the definition is complete, we can test it to be sure it is working correctly. The test field allows you to enter some raw data, press the **Test...** command button and see how the display format would format the data you entered.

When you have the display format defined correctly, press the **OK** command button to save it. This definition is stored in the database extended attributes tables and can be attached to any column in the database that you choose, or selected at a later time from the DataWindow painter (as will be shown below).

To assign this display format to a specific column in a table in your database (as opposed to assigning it in the DataWindow painter), you would open up the table that the column is on in the Database painter and open the table definition by double-clicking on the table.

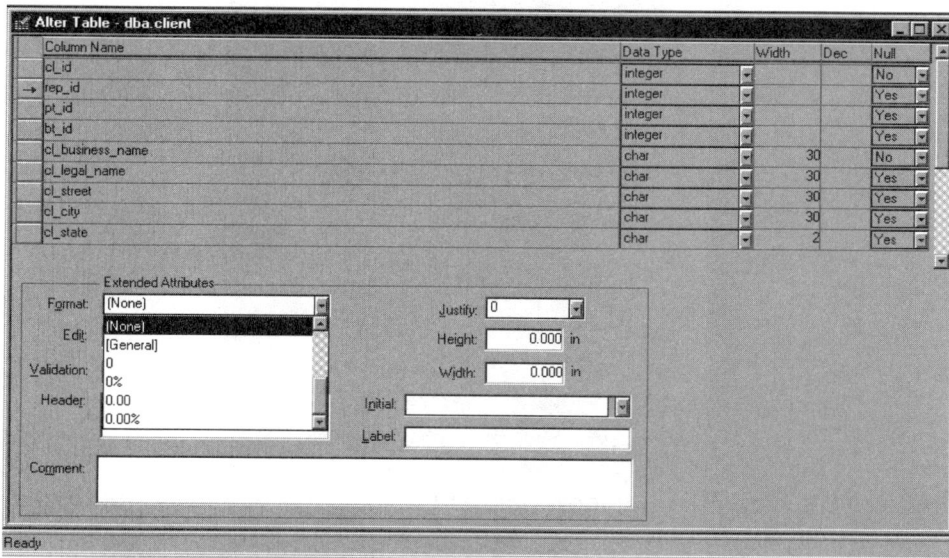

Figure 19-56. The display format for a particular column is defined as an extended attribute in the table definition window.

Select the column that you want to set a display format for. The extended attributes section at the bottom of the window only applies to the currently selected column. In the Display field you can drop down the listbox and select from any of the formats listed (only formats that apply to the column data type will be shown) which includes the predefined formats and the ones that you have custom created.

This format will become the default display format for any DataWindows created using this column. Note that this will apply to any DataWindows that will be created in the future. Existing DataWindows using this column will not be affected.

In the DataWindow Painter

When you create a DataWindow object, the display formats for the columns involved will be defaulted to whatever format was defined in the extended attributes. If no format is defined there then the display format for the column will be [General]. You can override the default in the DataWindow painter through the **Format** tab of the Properties page.

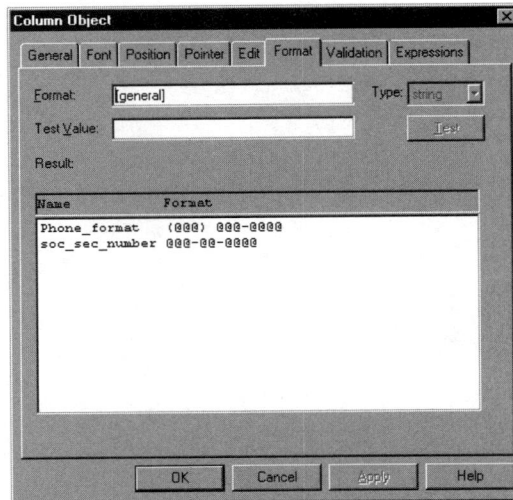

Figure 19-57. *In the DataWindow painter we can override the default display format for an object on the Format tab of the Properties page.*

To change the format for an object, select the object and then open the Properties page. On the Format tab you will see the same fields that you saw in the Display Format Definition window in the Database painter. In fact, this window works exactly the same except for the list at the bottom. This list displays all the predefined formats from the database that apply to this column type. You can select any of these format types, or you can define your own for this specific purpose. When you define your own on this tab, you will not be able to reuse this format in another column or DataWindow. To do that you would have to have defined it in the Database painter as discussed earlier.

Pressing the **OK** command button will apply the changes that you have made to the currently selected column.

In the DataWindow designer, you can change a whole range of columns to a standard currency or percentage display format by selecting all the columns that you want to alter and then pressing either the Currency Format or Percent Format icons in the toolbar as shown in Figure 19-58.

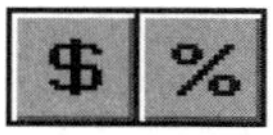

Figure 19-58. *You can change the display format of a group of columns together by selecting all the relevant column and pressing the Currency Format or Percent Format icons in the toolbar.*

19.8.12.12.2 Dynamically Altering a Display Format

The display format for a column on a DataWindow is stored as a string. This makes it easy for us to read and alter dynamically at runtime. There are two techniques that you can use to do this using DataWindow Control component functions SetFormat() and GetFormat().

GetFormat() returns the current display format of a DataWindow column. The syntax for GetFormat() is:

```
dw_control.GetFormat(column_name)
```

where

dw_control is the name of the DataWindow control, DataSource or child Data-Window that contains the column you want the display format of.

column_name is the name of the column (as a string) or the number (as an integer) that you want to obtain the display format of.

GetFormat() returns a string containing the display format of the column. If there is no currently defined display format, the return value will be NULL. An empty string will be returned if an error occurs.

The syntax for SetFormat() is:

```
dw_control.SetFormat(column_name, format_string)
```

where

dw_control is the name of the DataWindow control, DataSource or child Data-Window that contains the column you want the display format of.

column_name is the name of the column (as a string) or the column number (as an integer) that you want to obtain the display format of.

format_string is a string containing the new format that you want to apply.

I have not encountered the need to dynamically alter the display format very often. Situations where you might include systems where the users have the ability to define their own display formats (for example, if they want to see currencies with decimal places or without) or if you don't know what kind of data a field will be displaying until runtime (for example, your system may hold the e-mail address of an individual which may be formatted differently depending on whether it is an Internet, CompuServe, AOL id, or some other format).

Another place where I have seen column formats used dynamically is when working with credit card fields. Different credit cards expect to have the number segments separated in different areas (i.e., American Express has a different format than Visa). This technique can be used to set the correct format for the type of credit card.

19.8.12.2 Edit Styles

The second mechanism that we can use to alter the format and user interface for the data we present to the end user is the edit style. Edit styles differ from display formats in three key areas. First, edit styles are *bidirectional* which means that they affect not only the display of the data to the user, but also are active in formatting the data while the user is entering it. This means that if we were using an edit style to mask a phone number field, the DataWindow would automatically add the parenthesis around the area code and the dash in the middle as we were typing the characters in, although these formatting characters are still not stored in the database.

The second key difference between an edit style and display format is the variety of edit styles that you have available to use. These styles include the standard edit box, the edit mask, a drop down listbox, a drop down DataWindow, check boxes or radio buttons. These styles are designed to improve the user interface and make your application more intuitive.

The example that I use most often to describe the functionality of these styles is the storing of gender in a database. Very likely your database will store only M or F instead of "male" and "female." In order to improve the user interface we could define an interface with two radio buttons, one for Male and one for Female. When the user selects the Male radio button, a "M" is put into the gender column, and when the user selects the Female radio button, an "F" is placed there. The user interface is improved in a number of ways such as there is no need to validate the input, the amount of information being stored in the database is minimized, and the radio buttons make the system easier for the user to run.

Like the display format, a default edit style for a column in a DataWindow is established based upon the edit style assigned to the column in the extended attributes section of the Database painter. Also like the display format, there are a number of predefined edit styles that you can use, or you can define your own in the Database painter, or you could create an edit style for a specific instance of a column in the DataWindow painter.

19.8.12.2.1 Defining an Edit Style

The techniques for defining and edit style are similar to those that we used to define the display formats. You can define edit styles in the Database painter. By doing so, the edit style can be used in multiple places. This is the place to define your edit style if you want to reuse it across multiple columns or if you want to define a default edit style for a column in a table that will be used any time that column is used in a DataWindow.

To create or alter an edit style in the Database painter, you select the **Edit Style Maintenance...** menu option from the **Design** menu. This will open a window listing all the currently defined edit styles—a combination of the predefined DataWindow Painter edit styles and any others that you have added.

We can also define edit styles in the DataWindow painter when they will only be used once or we want to override the default edit style assigned in the Database painter. This is done by selecting the column that you want to define the edit style for and opening the Properties page. The **Edit** tab is where the current edit style is defined.

The technique for defining the edit style depends on which edit style type you select. As the technique is the same in both the Database painter and the DataWindow painter, we will address them both at the same time by examining each of the edit style types. The one difference to remember is that once the edit style is defined in the Database painter, you must still apply it to a specific column or columns by defining the extended attributes for that table.

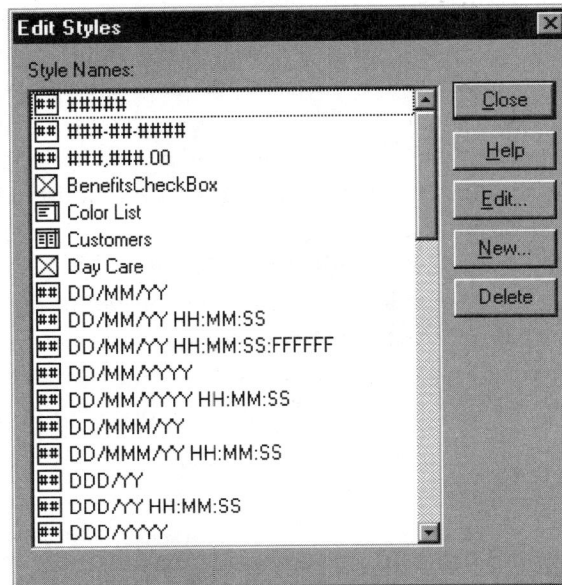

*Figure 19-59. In the Database painter you can edit an existing edit style by selecting it from the list and pressing the **Edit...** command button. Pressing the **New...** command button will allow you to define a new edit style.*

19.8.12.2.2 Edit

If you don't specify an edit style for a column it will default to a style simply called Edit. It is a standard single line edit box like the ones that you use in the Form designer. It still has a number of properties that you can modify to your needs.

The properties of the Edit style are:

Name (this is the same for all edit styles and won't be repeated in subsequent descriptions). This drop down list box contains the names of all the Edit type edit styles stored in the database (these are the ones defined in the Database painter). If the column has a predefined edit style from its extended attributes, that style will be named here. If you want to use a different previously created style you can select it from the list. If you want to define your own custom version of the Edit style, this will be blank.

Style (this is the same for all edit styles and won't be repeated in subsequent descriptions). This is the drop down list box containing all the valid edit styles.

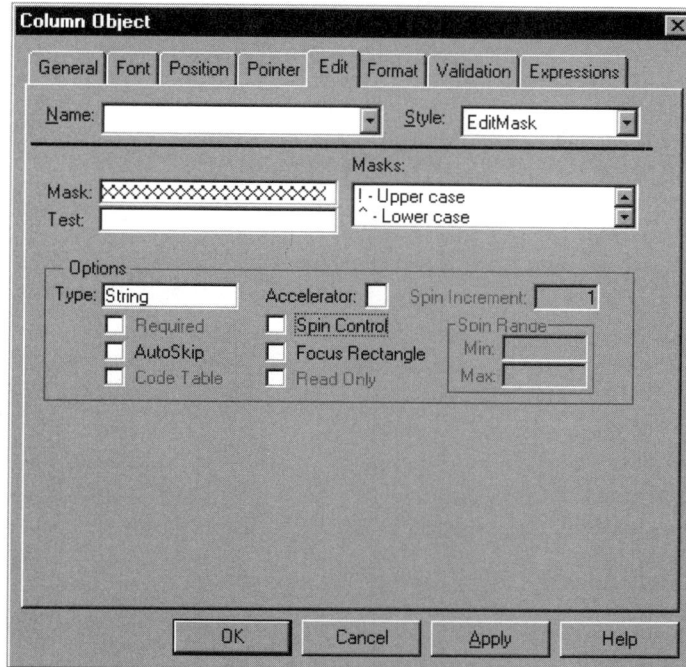

Figure 19-60. The default style for a column is called "Edit."

Limit sets the limit of the total number of characters the user is allowed to enter into the edit field. If the limit is 0, then there is no limit to the number of characters that can be entered.

Case defines what case the entered text will be in. The options are Any (mixed), Upper or Lower. Text that is entered in the wrong case will be converted.

Accelerator allows you to specify a letter that is used in conjunction with the ALT key to allow the user to set focus to this field immediately.

Format this field allows you to define a format that will apply to the value returned by the GetText() function. Normally GetText() will return to you the raw data the user entered into the edit control. If you have a format defined here, this raw data will be formatted as specified.

Password causes the field to display an asterisk for each character for each character that is entered.

Auto Selection causes all the text in the field to be selected when the user tabs into the field (when the user types data into the field it will replace the characters that are currently there).

Required indicates that this is a required field and users are not permitted to tab out of this field until they have entered a valid value. Note that in order for this to take effect the user must have tabbed into the field in the first place.

Empty String is NULL indicates that if the user enters an empty string in the field (which occurs when you type data into a field, and then decide to use backspace or delete to remove the data) the field is set to NULL.

Auto Horiz(ontal) Scroll as the user types text into the box and the box fills to its physical capacity, the text will automatically scroll to the left (horizontally) allowing the user to enter more characters. If this attribute is unchecked (FALSE) then the user cannot enter more characters into the field than will fit physically even if this is less than the amount specified in the Limit attribute.

Auto Vert(ical) Scroll works the same as horizontal scroll except that it scrolls the text vertically.

Horiz(ontal) Scroll Bar and Vert(ical) Scroll Bar will cause the appropriate scroll bars to be displayed as needed (when data extends beyond the boundaries).

Display Only prevents the user from entering any data into the field.

Show Focus Rectangle will cause PowerBuilder to display a focus rectangle around the field when it has focus.

Use Code Table indicates that the data that is entered by the end user should be translated by a code table to display something different in the field. In the example in Figure 19-61, the Use Code Table option is checked and a code table has appeared below the options dialog box. In this table we have two values defines with decode values. If the user types "cal" in the field, this will be translated to "Calgary" when they tab away from the field, but only "cal" will be stored in the database. Values in the database that are not part of the code table, or values that the user enters that do not match the code table will be displayed as they are without any translation.

Validate Using Code Table indicates if the data entered by the user will be validated against the code table. This would restrict the user to only be able to enter values that exist in the code table. Values in the database that do not match the values in the code table would still be displayed as they are without any translation. Only user input is validated.

Display Value contains the value that will be displayed in the field when the field value is equal to what is stored in the corresponding Data Value column. (only applicable when using a Code Table).

Data Value contains the code value that is the raw data. This code value will be translated to the corresponding Display Value when the field is displayed to the user (only applicable when using a Code Table).

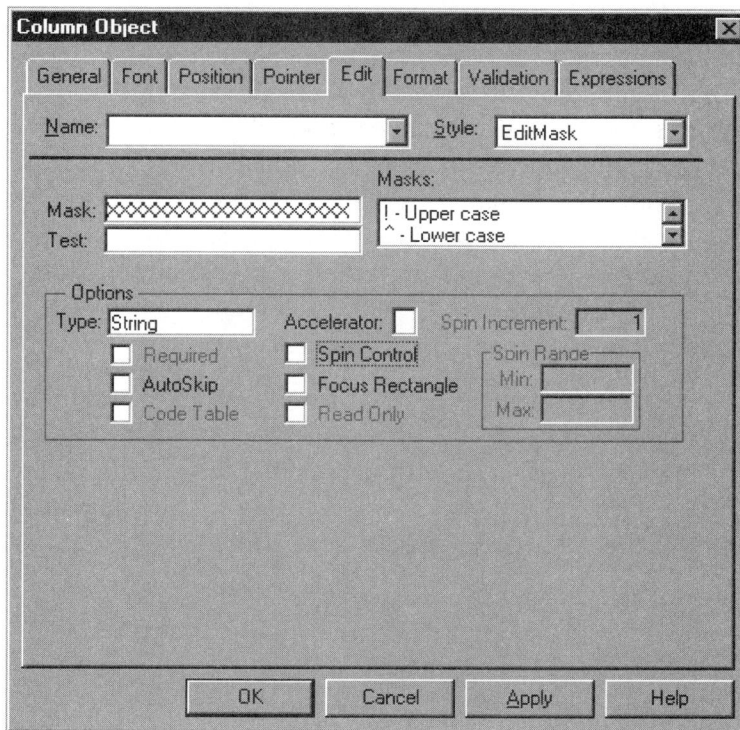

Figure 19-61. The regular Edit Mask enforces a specific format on the data that is displayed and entered.

19.8.12.2.3 Edit Mask

An Edit Mask edit style is used to enforce a specific format on the data that is displayed and entered in a field. It is very similar to the Edit Mask control that you have used in the Window painter. It will automatically insert various formatting characters as required into a field. For example, in the case of a phone number field, it will automatically insert an open bracket, accept three numbers, insert a close bracket, accept three more numbers, insert a dash and then accept four more numbers.

There are two basic subcategories of edit masks regular edit masks and those that use spin controls.

Regular Edit Masks

Regular edit masks accept user input in the standard fashion, through the keyboard. One of the most important attributes is the type which defines if this mask applies to a string, numeric, date, time or datetime related field. Because of its importance, I would have preferred it if Powersoft chose to place this field above the Mask and Masks fields as these fields are dependent upon the type, but this is not the case.

The Edit Mask edit style is often used to format strings such as phone numbers or Social Security Numbers. Currencies are often left for display formats because they allow the user to enter data in raw format. Edit masks are also very popular for fields involving dates and times as they require the user to enter valid values. (See Figure 19-61.)

The properties that you can set for the regular edit mask are:

Type as mentioned above, specifies the data type of the field that this mask is applied to. This is only selectable by you if you are defining an Edit Mask in the Database painter. In the DataWindow painter, the type will be defined by the data type of the column that you are applying the mask to. The valid data types for this field are String, Numeric, Date, Time or DateTime.

Mask contains the character mask that you will use to format the data in the field. The types of characters that apply depend upon the data type selected in Type. The available mask characters are displayed and can be selected from the Masks field.

Masks a listbox of all the available mask characters that apply to the selected Type. The characters can be selected and placed in the Mask field at the point of the cursor by clicking on them. Each character listed also has a description as to the type of character it represents (i.e., a "!" is listed as an upper case character). There are also a number of predefined combinations of mask characters such as "###-##-####" for a Social Security Number or "dd/mm/yyyy" for a standard date field.

Test allows you to enter characters as if you were entering data into the field in the DataWindow and test to ensure that the mask is working correctly.

Accelerator allows you to specify a letter that is used in conjunction with the ALT key to allow the user to set focus to this field immediately.

Show Focus Rectangle will cause PowerBuilder to display a focus rectangle around the field when it has focus.

AutoSkip when all the characters required by the mask are filled focus will automatically shift to the next field in the tab order.

Spin Control turns the standard Edit Mask into an Edit Mask with spin boxes that allow the user to click on up or down arrows within the field to change the value (see the following section for further details).

Edit Mask with Spin Control

The Edit Mask with a spin control attached to it behaves somewhat differently than the standard Edit Mask and it also has additional properties that need to be considered. The Edit Mask will look and behave very similar to the standard Edit Mask until you select the up or down arrow images which are embedded within the field. (See Figure 19-62.)

***Figure 19-62.** The Edit Mask with a spin control has spin boxes embedded within the field that allow the user to click on the up or down arrows to change the value in the field.*

The spin control can be applied to any data type, but will behave differently for each one. With a date, time or datetime data type, the spin control will affect the segment where the cursor is currently positioned. For example, if you place the cursor in the day field and click the up arrow, the day number will increase by one, then if you click in the year field and press the down arrow, the year will decrease by one.

With a numeric data type the field will simply increase or decrease the value as specified by the other properties that you must set.

With a string data type you must define a **Code Table** (which is optional for the other data types). The code table will contain a set of predefined values and as you click on the up or down arrows you will scroll through this table. Code tables can also be used for the other data types when spin controls are enabled.

The other properties that you will need to consider when using spin controls are:

Code Table is described above, allows you to specify a predefined set of values that will be scrolled through as the user clicks on the up or down arrows.

Read Only enabled when you are using a code table. This means that the field can only be accessed by scrolling through the fields in the code table. If this is turned off, the user can still enter data directly as if the field had no spin control.

Required is the same as the Edit style.

Spin Increment specifies how much you want the field to increment or decrement each time the user clicks on the up or down arrow. The default value is 1. This property does not apply to string data types.

Spin Range.Min specifies the minimum value that you will not decrement the field below. This property does not apply to string data types.

Spin Range.Max specified the maximum value that you will not increment the field above. This property does not apply to string data types.

19.8.12.2.4 Radio Button

This edit style is appropriate when you are using a small number of possible values for a field. Each option in the field must be mutually exclusive, for example, employee status of "active," "terminated" or "on-leave" are all mutually exclusive and therefor valid for a Radio Button edit mask. This type of a mask allows users to select their data by selecting one of the available options with the mouse.

Radio button edit styles are always driven by a code table which contains a display value and a data value for each item. The properties for radio buttons are quite straightforward:

Columns Across allows you to specify how many columns you want the items to be displayed in. The example shown in Figure 19-63 is displayed in only one column across (the default) but had we specified 3 columns across, all the items would have appeared horizontally.

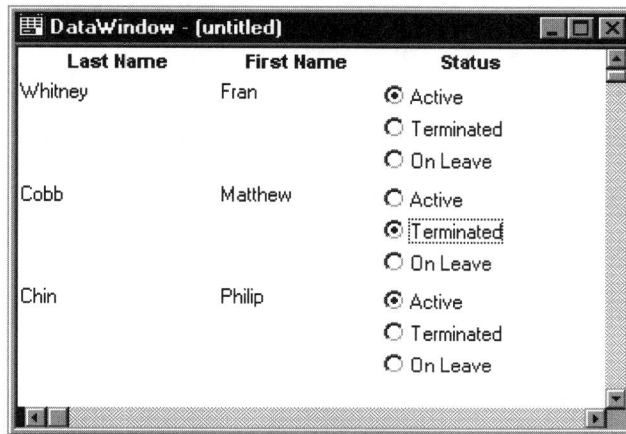

Figure 19-63. *The Radio Button edit mask is useful to select from a small number of mutually exclusive options.*

Left Text causes the text to appear to the left of the radio button when checked, to the right when unchecked.

Scale Circles will cause the radio button circles to be scales to the size of the font when checked. When unchecked the circles will appear in their default size.

3D Look will cause the radio button to be displayed in 3D.

You can provide an accelerator key for each display value by placing an ampersand (&) character before the letter in the display that you want to be the accelerator key. When the user presses the ALT key with that letter, that option would be selected.

Developer's Tip: You may need to adjust the size of the field in the DataWindow designer to accommodate the radio button edit mask. All the options may appear stacked up on top of each other until you increase the size of the field. The items will spread themselves evenly throughout the available space.

The Radio Button edit style should only be considered if you have six or fewer options that are unlikely to change. If you want to have more than six options, or if you don't have sufficient screen real estate to display all the radio button options, then you should consider using a drop down list box.

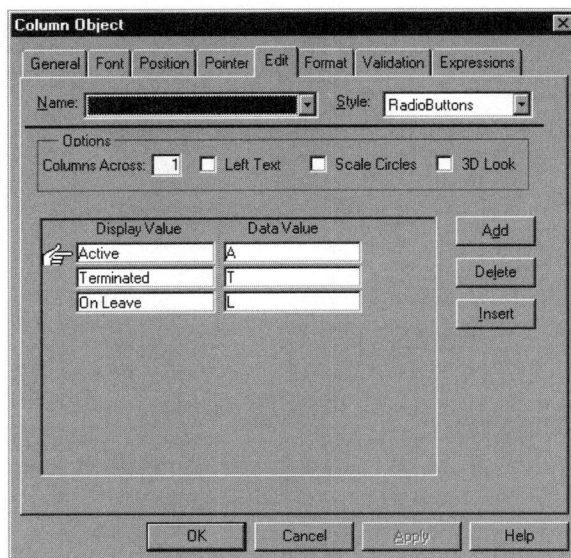

***Figure 19-64.** Radio button edit masks are always driven by a code table.*

A second consideration when dealing with radio button edit styles is that the values are hard coded into the columns and if you want to alter them you must recompile the object and possibly build and distribute a new .PBD or .EXE file if the application you are building is already in production. If you want to be able to change the list dynamically at runtime your best option would be to use a drop down DataWindow and load your data from a table.

19.8.12.2.5 Check Box

We can create a check box as our edit mask for a field. This style fits when the acceptable value is restricted to two values (or three if you include the "unknown" state option). The most common use for the check box edit mask is for a column that contains either a "yes" or "no" value.

The employee table in the sample database has three fields that are defined as having check box edit masks health insurance, life insurance, and day care. Each of these fields is either a yes (the do have this benefit) or no (the don't have this benefit).

If we enable the third state option, we can record if an employee has a benefit, doesn't have a benefit, or we don't know whether they do or don't.

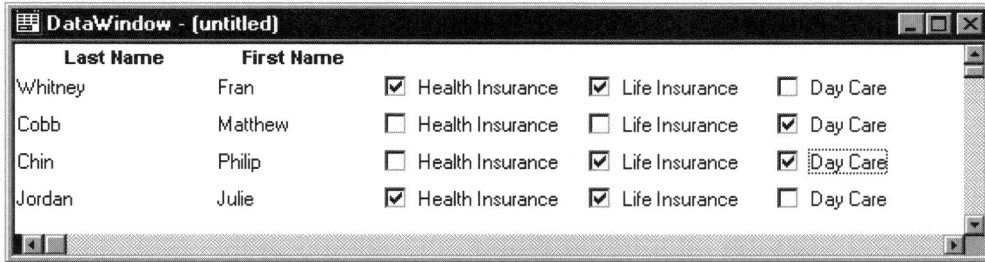

Figure 19-65. The check box edit style is used for fields that have two possible values.

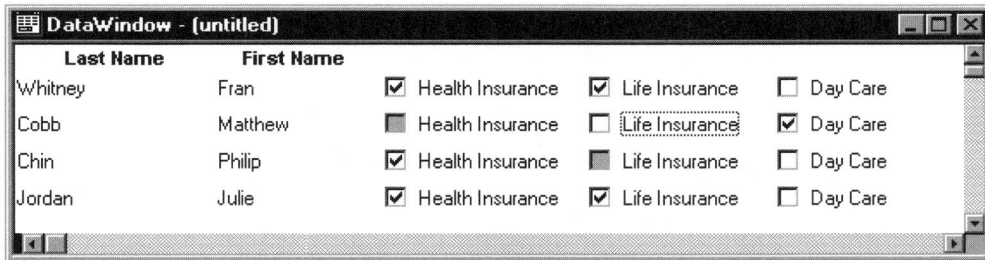

Figure 19-66. The check box options can be set to allow a third state when applicable. The third state shows by shading the inside of the box gray.

The properties for the check box edit mask are:

Text is the text that you want to appear beside the checkbox.

DataValue.On is the value that you want stored in the field when the check box is checked.

DataValue.Off is the value that you want stored in the field when the check box is unchecked.

DataValue.Other (only available when 3State property is true) is the value that you want stored in the field when the check box is in the third "unknown" state.

Left Text controls if the text in the text property is displayed to the left or the right of the box.

Scale will drawn the box to scale with the font when checked.

3 States when checked allows the checkbox to be in three possible states checked, unchecked or unknown.

3D Look draws the box in 3D.

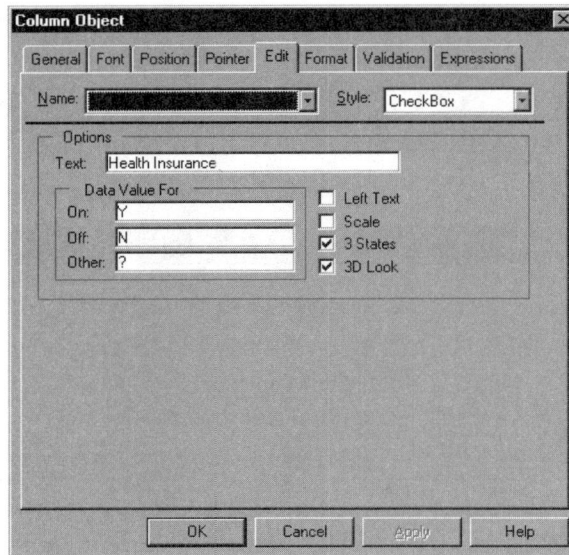

Figure 19-67. The properties of a check box edit mask.

19.8.12.2.6 Drop Down List Box

The drop down list box edit mask allows you to define a selection list for a field and have the user select a single option from the list. The items in the list will need to be relatively static as the values are hard coded into the edit mask and, like the radio button, can only be changed by recompiling the object.

An example of this type of edit style would be a drop down list box with a list of states. The full name of the state is used for the display value, but only the two character abbreviation is stored in the field.

The drop down list box edit style relies on a code table, very much like the Radio Button edit mask code table. The properties for this edit style are:

Limit specifies the maximum number of characters that can be entered. A zero indicates no limit. This is only applicable if the field is set to Allow Editing.

Case controls the case of the text in the drop down list box. The choices are Any (mixed), Upper or Lower.

Accelerator specifies a key that will be used in combination with the ALT key to bring the user directly to this field.

Sorted specifies if you want the data in the list sorted or not.

Required same as in other styles.

Allow Edit specifies if the user can type into the field, or if they must select from the list.

Always Show List specifies if you want the list to always be dropped down when the field has focus.

Always Show Arrow specifies if you want the field to always display the drop down list box arrow.

Empty String is Null same as in other styles.

Auto Horiz(ontal) Scroll same as with the edit style.

Vert(ical) Scroll Bar specifies if you want to display a vertical scroll bar within the data list (you should if you have more data than will fit in the drop down window).

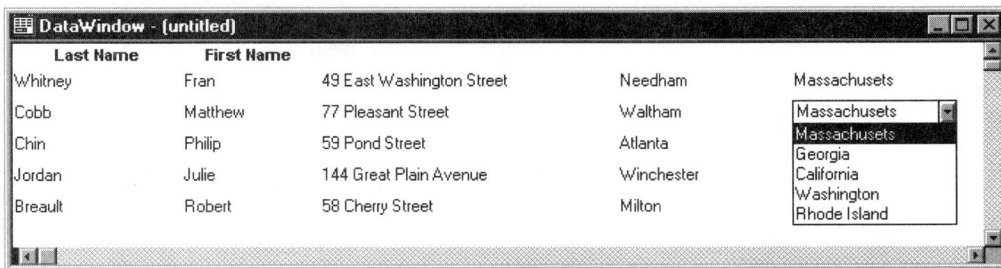

Figure 19-68. The drop down list box edit style allows the user to select a single value from a list of values in the drop down list.

19.8.12.2.7 Drop Down DataWindow

The drop down DataWindow edit mask is very similar to the drop down list box except that the data is for the display and data values is dynamically loaded at runtime from a table in the database.

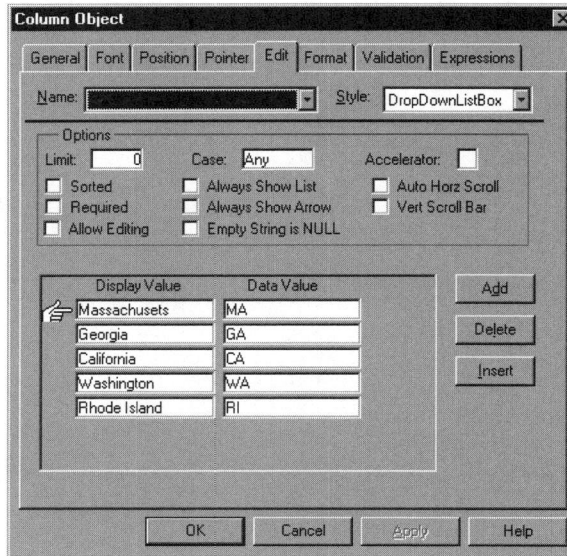

Figure 19-69. *The drop down list box edit mask also relies on a code table to provide display and data values.*

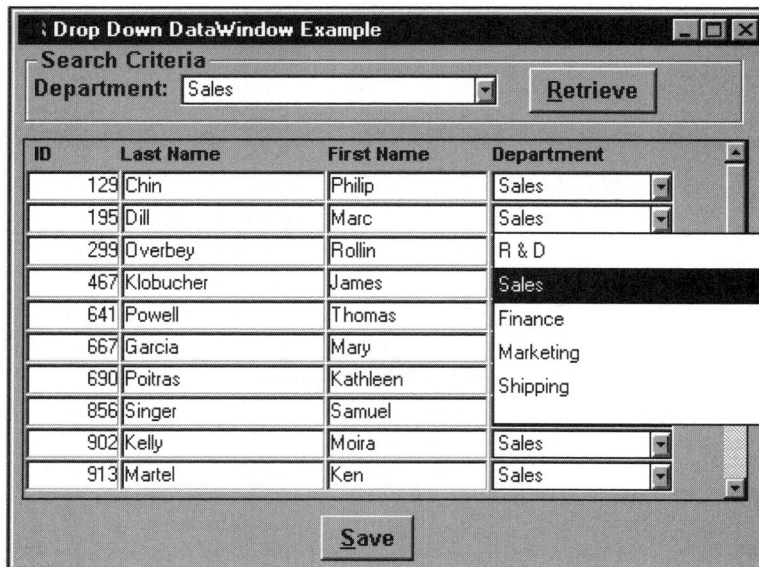

Figure 19-70. *The Drop Down DataWindow allows us to have a column in a DataWindow act like a drop down list box populated with values from our database.*

The drop down DataWindow is like a DataWindow nested inside another DataWindow. It can contain multiple columns and rows and is retrieved when the DataWindow that it is inside (the parent DataWindow) begins a Retrieve() or InsertRow() function. We refer to a DataWindow nested inside another as a *child DataWindow*. We will refer back to this concept as we progress through this example.

Drop Down DataWindow Example

The first step in building a drop down DataWindow is to build the DataWindow object that will eventually become the child DataWindow (the one nested inside the parent). For our example, we will use the department table from the PowerBuilder Demo Database as our drop down list. We want to display the list of department names, but store the department number in the field in the parent DataWindow.

Step 1   To start, build a tabular DataWindow selecting the department table as the SQLSelect data source. Select the dept_name and dept_id columns as in Figure 19-71.

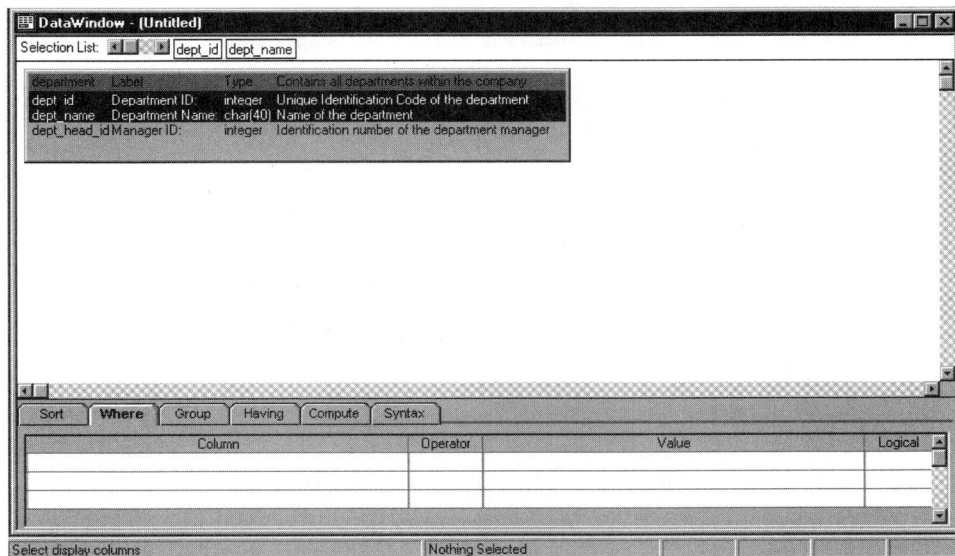

Figure 19-71. Step 1: Build a tabular DataWindow object with a SQL Select data source. Select the dept_name and dept_id columns from the department table.

Step 2   In the designer, remove the text fields and delete the dept_id field (it still exists as part of the result set, it just isn't visible). Now rearrange the bands so that everything is neat and clean like in Figure 19-72.

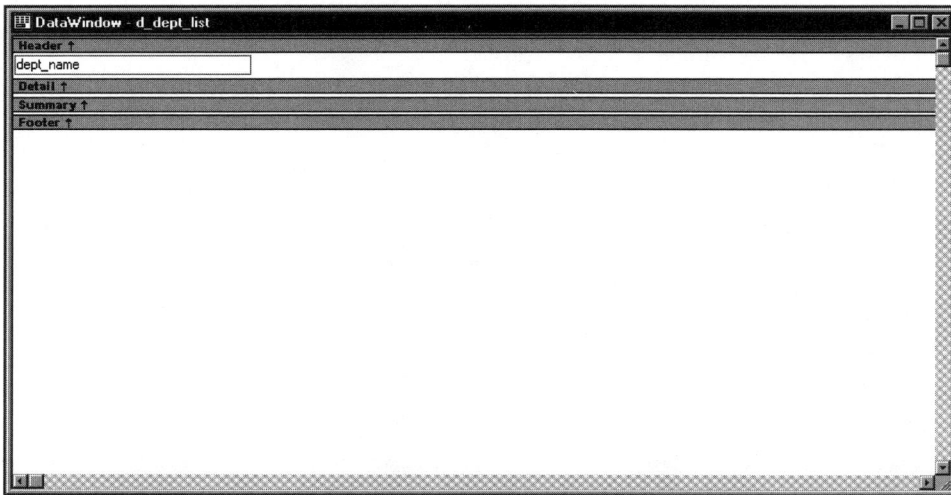

Figure 19-72. Step 2: Remove the test fields and the dept_id. Then size the band appropriately.

Step 3   Now save the DataWindow as d_dept_list (don't forget to give it a comment). You now have a DataWindow that you can use as the child in a drop down DataWindow.

Step 4   There are a variety of approaches for the next step depending on where you want to the DDDW to appear. If this object is intended to stand alone (as opposed to being part of a larger DataWindow), you could build a new DataWindow object and insert the child inside it. This technique is discussed in Option A, below. A second approach would be to insert a DDDW into another existing multiple column DataWindow where we want one of the columns to be a DDDW. This is demonstrated in Option B.

OPTION A: We need to place the drop down list inside another DataWindow object. Alternatively, you could be recursive and place it inside itself. The method that I prefer for this is to create a new DataWindow object.

Developer's Tip: A second common way to implement Option A is to use an External source DataWindow. To do this, replace step 5 below with:

Step 5 Create a new freeform external DataWindow. Define a single column called "dept_id" with a data type of "string" and a size of 3.

This will eliminate the excess overhead that you incur creating a DataWindow that originates from a SQL select statement, but it will require you to manually set the transaction object in order for your InsertRow() to succeed, even though external DataWindows do not normally require an associated transaction object.

Step 5 Create a new freeform DataWindow with a SQLSelect data source. Select the department table from the list. Select only the dept_id column. Switch to the designer by pressing the SQL icon on the toolbar. If you enter preview mode, exit and continue to the designer.

Step 6 Change or remove the text label that appears before the column as desired. Make the dept_id column wide enough to accommodate the longest department name plus enough room for the drop down arrow which will appear inside the field.

Step 7 Open the Properties page for the dept_id column (this should be the only column showing). (See Figure 19-73.)

Step 8 Switch to the **Edit** tab. Select **Drop Down DataWindow** as the Edit Style.

Step 9 Selecting the DataWindow field in the **Options** group box will open a drop down listbox with a list of all the available DataWindow objects. Select the DataWindow d_dept_list that you created in Step 3 above for your drop down list. Choose the dept_id column as the Data Column and dept_name as the Display Column. Add a vertical scroll bar to your DDDW and select Always Show Arrow. (See Figure 19-74.)

Step 10 Select **OK** to apply your changes.

Step 11 Preview your DataWindow. You will see a separate instance of your DDDW for each row in the Department table. Notice that each one behaves as its own independent DDDW. Now you have a Drop Down DataWindow list of departments that you can use on any of the windows in your application. To use this object in your application you associate the appropriate transaction object component followed by an InsertRow() function to make this object work in your form. This will create a single row where the user can select from the list of departments.

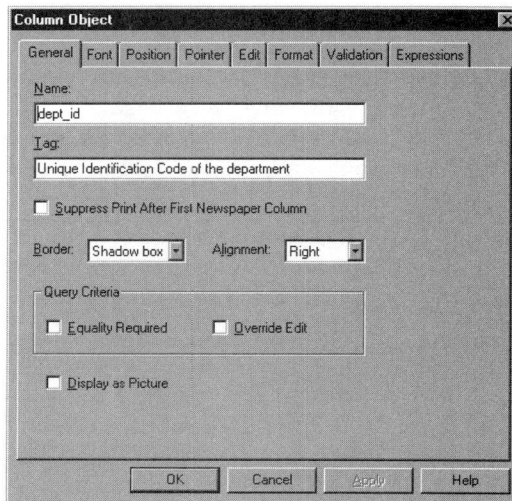

Figure 19-73. Step 7: Open the Properties page for the dept_id column.

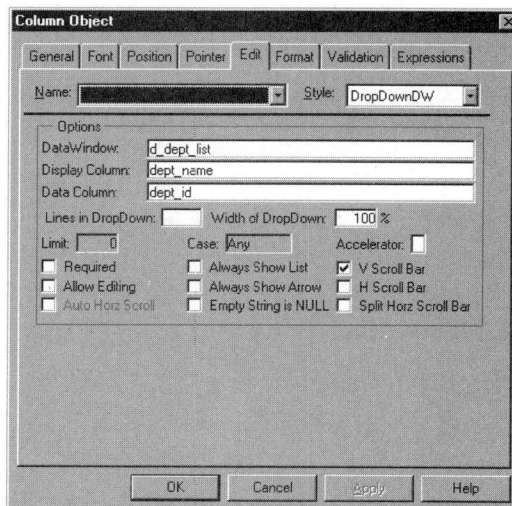

Figure 19-74. Step 9: You must select the Drop Down DataWindow that will appear inside this field and the columns which you want to represent the data and to display.

OPTION B: We want to insert the DDDW into a column of an existing DataWindow object.

Step 5 Open (or build) the DataWindow object that you want to attach your DDDW to. Build a simple tabular DataWindow with a SQLSelect data source as shown in Figure 19-75. It will show a list of all employees and the department id that they work in (selecting only from the employee table). If you want, you can add a retrieval argument that only shows the employees from a specific department. We are going to add a drop down list of departments to the department column in the employee list.

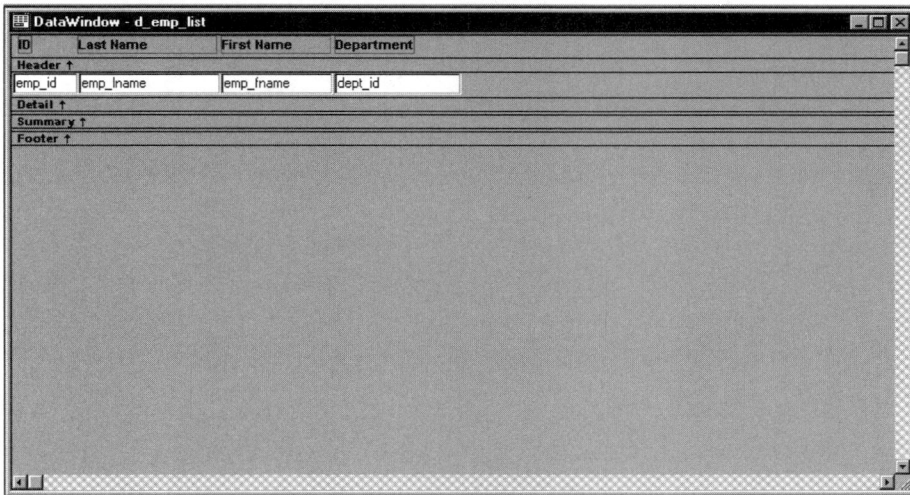

***Figure 19-75.** Create the DataWindow object d_emp_list. We will insert a drop down list of departments in the department column.*

Step 6 Open the Properties page for the dept_id column. Select the Edit tab and make the changes described in Step 9 in Option A.

Step 7 Save the DataWindow object. You can preview it to see how it behaves.

The above steps can be used to create Drop Down DataWindows and add them to your applications.

19.8.13 Validation Rules

Every column in a DataWindow has a validation rule attached to it. This rule is a logical statement that is used to ensure that the data entered by the user is valid. Like Display Formats and Edit Styles, the Validation Rule can be defined in the Database painter and extended to the DataWindow by default any time the DataWindow uses the specified table column. Or you can build a new Validation rule right in the DataWindow painter.

To access the Validation rule for a column open the properties page for the column and select the Validation tab as shown in Figure 19-76.

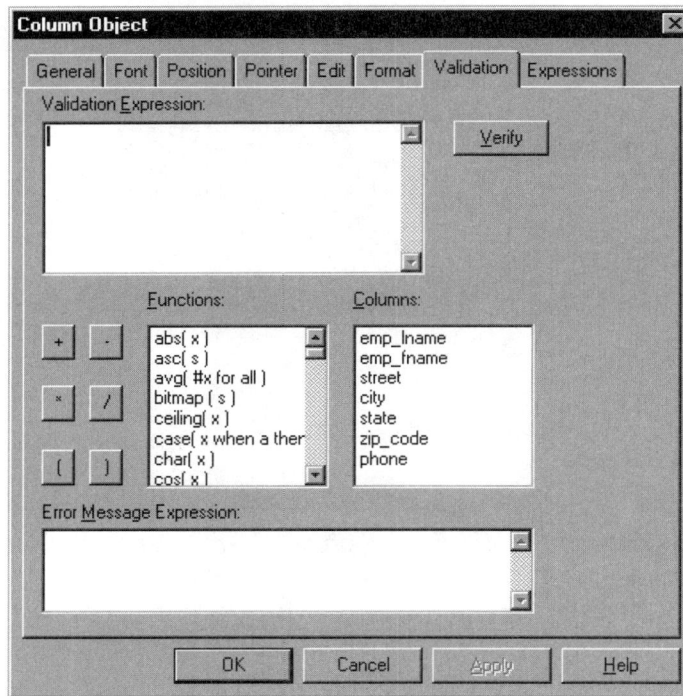

Figure 19-76. The Validation tab allows you to build an expression to validate the data entered by the user.

The validation rule that you define can contain column names, literals, arithmetic operators, and function names. The expression must evaluate to a logical TRUE or FALSE. If the data entered does not pass the validation rule, then the DataWindow will display the error message expression that you specify in the Error Message Expression text box at the bottom of the tab.

To build the validation rule you can use the function GetText() to get the value entered by the user. This value is always a string, even if the field is a numeric or date field. You can then use other functions to convert the entry to the proper data type such as Long() to convert the string to a long or Date() to convert it to a date.

The following example would validate the user entry into a field called age to ensure that the value being entered is greater than 18.

```
Long(GetText()) > 18
```

If this evaluates to TRUE, the user entry is accepted and the ItemChanged event is fired on the DataWindow control. If the entry does not pass the rule then the value is rejected and the user is given an error message based on what you have entered in the Error Message Expression box. If you leave this box blank, the user will get a generic error message stating that the value they entered does not pass the validation rule. The ItemError event will be triggered.

19.8.14 Deleting And Adding Columns

When working on a DataWindow you might find that you want to add or remove a column from the DataWindow. If you are adding a column, and the column does not currently exist in the SQL statement, you will need to select the SQL icon on the toolbar to return to the SQL painter and add the column to the result set. When you return to the DataWindow design painter you will see the column appear and you can begin to work with it.

If the column that you want to add is already part of the result set, but not visible, then you must select the Column button on the toolbar. Then you must click in the DataWindow workspace where you want the column to appear. This will open the Select Column dialog window shown in Figure 19-77.

From this window you can select any column in the result set and paste it back into your DataWindow workspace. This is usually used to paste columns that aren't currently present in the workspace, but all the columns in the result set are listed. Thus, it is possible to paste a column into your workspace that is already there, resulting in more than one instance of the same column in your DataWindow.

To remove a column from the DataWindow workspace isn't nearly as complicated. Just select the column (or columns if you want to remove several) and press the Delete key (or click the Delete button on the tool bar). The DataWindowPainter will not ask you to confirm the deletion, it will just do it. If you make a mistake and wipe something out accidentally, don't worry. You can bring it back by using the technique described above. Deleting a column in this way does not remove it from the result set, only from the visible area. To remove it from the result set, you must go to the SQL data source using the SQL button on the toolbar and remove the column.

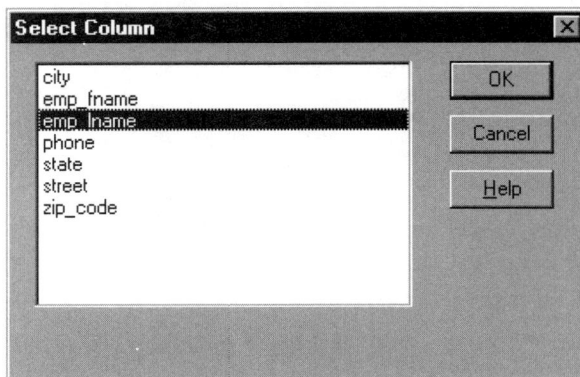

Figure 19-77. The Select Column dialog.

Sometimes you will want to keep non visible columns in the result set such as this example. If you have DataWindow A, which provides a list of employees, and DataWindow B, which provides a list of all the projects that employee is working on.you probably want to retrieve employee ID in the result set of DataWindow B to make sure that you have the key field available for doing updates to the database, but you probably don't want to display it.

19.8.15 Computed Fields

Earlier in this chapter we discussed including computed fields in the result set for the DataWindow. A server based computed column is computed when the data is retrieved. The value remains static until another retrieval occurs. This means that the DBMS actually does all the work, and as far as the DataWindow is concerned, that computed column in the result set is just another static value.

You can build computed columns and fields in the DataWindow workspace that result in calculations being performed on the client. The values in the fields are dynamic, meaning that values in the DataWindow change, any computed values which are based upon the changing values will change also.

To compare these two methods, consider the inventory table for a warehouse. This inventory table holds each item's inventory code, its description, the quantity and the cost per unit.

Inventory Code	Description	Quantity	Cost / Unit
TN-203	Needlenose Pliers	100	$4.25
RL-156	Ruler (metric)	15	$3.60
PB-008	Paintbrush (small)	25	$1.00

You are going to generate a DataWindow that lets you view the total value of the inventory that you hold of each item. It might appear as follows:

Inventory Item	Quantity	Cost / Unit	Value of Inventory
Needlenose Pliers	100	$4.25	$425.00
Ruler (metric)	15	$3.60	$54.00
Paintbrush (small)	25	$1.00	$25.00

The Value of Inventory column could be computed in our SQL select statement, or by a computed field in the DataWindow painter. Either way the result is the same. The difference arises when you modify the data in the columns. If you change the cost per unit of the needlenose pliers from $4.25 to $7.50, you can see the difference:

With a SQL select computed column:

Inventory Item	Quantity	Cost / Unit	Value of Inventory
Needlenose Pliers	100	$7.50	$425.00

With a DataWindow computed field:

Inventory Item	Quantity	Cost / Unit	Value of Inventory
Needlenose Pliers	100	$7.50	$750.00

Note that the value of inventory changed in the DataWindow computed field, but not in the SQL select computed column. The DataWindow is intelligent enough to recognize that the computed field "Value of Inventory" is dependent upon the "Cost/Unit" column. When you changed the value in the "Cost/Unit" column to $7.50, the DataWindow automatically recalculated the value for that row's "Value of Inventory" field.

Developer's Note: If you know that your DataWindow is only going to display information, and you don't want the user to enter data that would require the recalculation of a computed field, you are usually better off to put your computations into the SQL select statement. Most DBMSs are very efficient at generating the computed fields in the result set and also run on larger, more powerful hardware. Take advantage of this when it is applicable.

The above example demonstrates using a computed field in the detail band of a DataWindow. Computed fields are also useful in generating summary statistics or building concatenated fields.

You can use computed fields to calculate summary statistics for a result set or a group in a result set (for example, to count the number of employees in each department, or the sum of all the salaries being paid out by the company).

A computed field is very useful for concatenating two or more fields together. When composing a mailing label, you want to concatenate the first name of the addressee with the last name. You want a single space between the two, not a large gap. To accomplish this, you can create a computed field with a string that trims the leading and trailing blanks from the first name column, adds a string with one blank space in it, and then adds the trimmed last name column. The result is a properly formatted full name. The column would be defined as follows:

```
Trim(first_name) + " " +Trim(last_name)
```

The addition sign (+) is the symbol used for concatenation in the DataWindow-Painter.

To define a computed field to use in the DataWindow workspace, select the Compute button from the toolbar (as shown in Figure 19-78) or select Computed Field from the Objects menu.

Figure 19-78. The Computed Field icon on the toolbar.

Where you place the computed field depends on what you want the field to do. If you want a field that varies with each row of data, you should place it in the detail band. If you want the field to show summary statistics for a group, it should go in the group header or group trailer bands. Summaries based on the entire report and items you want to report and items that you want to appear on each page (such as a page number and page count) should appear in the header or footer band.

Once you have chosen the appropriate place for your computed field, the Computed Object properties window appears, as shown in Figure 19-79.

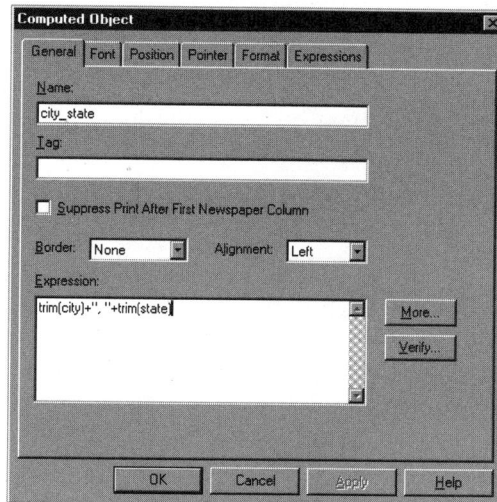

Figure 19-79. The Computed Object properties window.

You define all the properties for the computed object here including giving it a name, setting its font and display format. To get the full Modify Expression dialog window, press the **More...** command button. This will open the window shown in Figure 19-80.

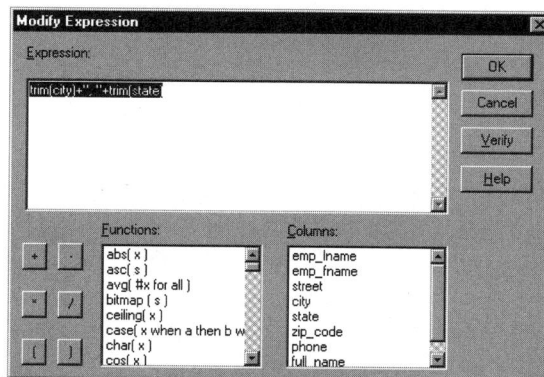

Figure 19-80. The Modify Expression dialog window is used for entering the computed field expression.

In this window you can enter an computed field expression, similar to the process that we followed earlier in the chapter when we defined a computed SQL column in the SQL Painter. That expression was a SQL expression, here you must enter a DataWindowPainter expression. The functions that were available when building the SQL computed field were database functions, now the functions that are available to you are DataWindowPainter specific functions.

The large multiline edit box in the middle of the window is where you enter the expression of rhte column. The expression can consist of DataWindowPainter functions (listed in the Functions list box), column references (listed in the Columns list box), literals and arithmetic operators (remember that the addition sign is used to concatenate strings).

Once you have entered your expression, you can click the **Verify** command button to test the expression and make sure it is valid.

There are a number of computed fields that you will use often. The DataWindowPainter has some built in computed fields to save you from redefining fields every time you want to use them. These are all available under the Objects menu.

Once common computed field is a page count that is placed in the header or footer band. It provides the current page number and the total number of pages in the report:

```
Page 1 of 22
```

which is a computed field defined as:

```
'Page ' + page() + ' of ' + pageCount()
```

It can be selected by using the Page computed field button on the toolbar (shown in Figure 19-81) or by selecting "Page n of n" from the Objects menu.

Figure 19-81. The Page computed field toolbar button.

Reports often have the current date in one of the bands, usually the header or footer. To get the current date in one of the bands such as the header or footer. To get the current date, you can use a predefined computed field that returns the current date to the field with the Today() DataWindowPainter function. It can be selected by using the Today computed field button in the toolbar (Figure 19-82) or by selecting "Today()" from the Objects menu.

Figure 19-82. The Today() computed field toolbar button.

You can place a computed field in the summary and group trailer band to provide the sum of a detail band column. The sum shortcut provides the computed field of the column that you have currently selected, and sums by group if your data is grouped or by the whole report if your data is ungrouped.

The process for doing this is to select the column for which you desire a sum, and then click the Sum computed field icon (Figure 19-83) or select "Sum" from the Objects menu. The new computed field appears in the appropriate group trailer or summary band.

Figure 19-83. The Sum computed field toolbar button.

There are also shortcuts for finding the average value of a field, or a count of the number of records. The process for using either of these is the same as for the Sum field. The toolbar buttons for these options are shown in Figure 19-84 or you can select the appropriate menu option from the Objects menu.

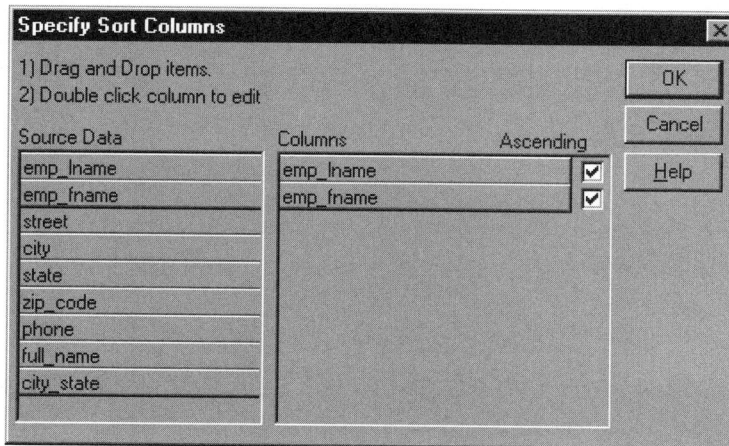

Figure 19-84. The Average and Count computed field toolbar buttons.

19.8.16 Filtering Data

There are times when you want to display only a small subset of the result set returned by the SQL statement for a DataWindow. For example, the user might want to see only the people in a department who have salaries under $30,000. Then the user might want to look at the same department and see only salaries over $50,000. This would result in two separate queries to the DBMS, which may not be the most efficient way to perform this operation.

Instead, you can do one call to the DBMS, bring back the whole result set, and buffer it in memory. Then, have the client apply a filter so that the DataWindow displays only the subset of records that you specify. This filter can be adjusted dynamically at runtime to show any subset your require. A filter can also use DataWindowPainter functions, such as an IF/THEN function to limit the data displayed.

To specify a filter for a DataWindow, select **Filter...** from the Rows menu. This opens the Specify Filter dialog window as shown in Figure 19-85.

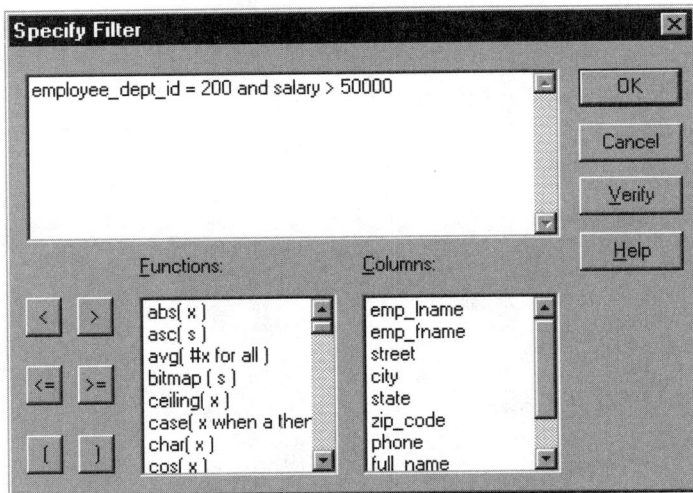

Figure 19-85. *The Specify Filter dialog window.*

The example in Figure 19-85 shows a filter expression which will only show the rows in the result set where the employee's department ID is equal to 200 and their salary is over $50,000.00. The format of this window should be familiar to you by now. It is similar to some of the other expression specification windows such as the validation definition window. In the multiline edit box, you enter an expression which evaluates to a Boolean TRUE or FALSE that determine whether the row will be displayed (TRUE) or not (FALSE).

You can use any valid DataWindowPainter functions in the expression. These functions can be pasted into the expression definition area by double-clicking them in the Function list box. The columns in the result set can be pasted into the expression from the Columns list box in the same way.

You can use any combination of the logical operators OR and AND to join expressions. The validity of your expression can be tested by clicking the Verify command button.

The results of defining the new filter can be seen by testing the DataWindow (see "Previewing and Testing a DataWindow" later in this chapter).

There are two functions that you can use in your code to dynamically change the filter during runtime: SetFilter()—to set the filter expression and Filter() to cause the DataWindow to redisplay its contents with the new filter applied.

19.8.17 Sorting Data

Just as the filtering of a DataWindow is similar to the WHERE clause in a SQL select statement, the sorting functions of a DataWindow are similar to the ORDER BY clause in a SQL select statement. In the SQL painter, you set the order in which the DBMS returns the result set to the DataWindow (this is built into the SQL select statement as an ORDER BY expression).

After retrieving data into the DataWindow, you may sometimes want to view the data in a different order. You could adjust the SQL select statement and then re-retrieve, but that would be a waste of resources when you already have the data sitting in memory.

You can take advantage of the DataWindow's sort function to shuffle the data on the client and display it in the correct order. This helps to relieve the DBMS of the unnecessary burden of reprocessing the result set, and also enables you to sort based on a variable expression that would not be allowed in a SQL select statement.

To set the initial client sort order in the DataWindow, select **Sort...** from the Rows menu. This opens the Specify Sort Columns dialog window as shown in Figure 19-86.

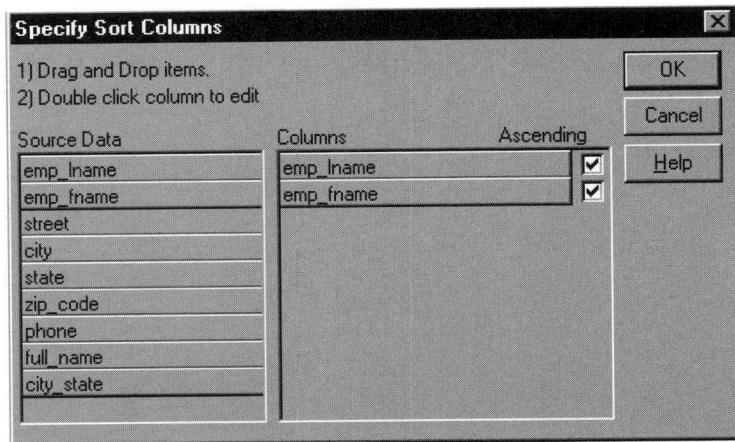

Figure 19-86. You can set the sort order for your DataWindow data in the Specify Sort Order dialog window.

In this window you specify the columns by which you want to sort the result set, and whether you want to sort in an ascending or descending manner. The example in Figure 19.86 sorts first by the employee's last name in an ascending manner. If there is more than one record with the same employee last name, then it sorts within the subset with the employee's first name in an ascending manner.

The Specify Sort Columns window allows you to specify as many levels of sorting as you desire simply by dragging the column that you want to sort by from the left hand list box to the right. You can reorder the sort criteria also by using drag and drop. To remove a sort criteria, drag it back from the right list box to the left.

You can specify if you want to sort in an ascending or descending manner by checking the Ascending check box next to each sort criteria as appropriate. The default sort order is ascending.

It is also possible to sort by using an expression. For example, if you have a list of products that your company sells ad you want to sort them by the ones which are most profitable, you might set your sort expression to be Selling Price—Item Cost. To turn a column into an expression, double-click on the column to open the Modify Expression dialog window.

19.8.18 Suppressing Repeating Values

When rows in your result set have a column or columns that are the same for every row of data, it becomes very tedious to look at. You can set the DataWindow to only display the first occurrence of a value in a column and suppress that value until either the page breaks or the group changes.

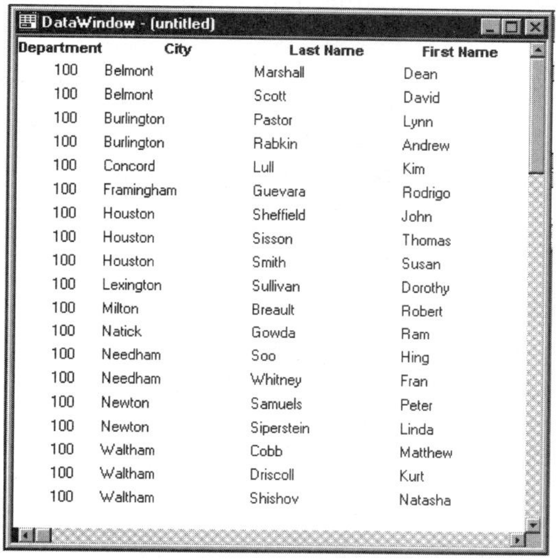
DataWindow - (untitled)

Department	City	Last Name	First Name
100	Belmont	Marshall	Dean
100	Belmont	Scott	David
100	Burlington	Pastor	Lynn
100	Burlington	Rabkin	Andrew
100	Concord	Lull	Kim
100	Framingham	Guevara	Rodrigo
100	Houston	Sheffield	John
100	Houston	Sisson	Thomas
100	Houston	Smith	Susan
100	Lexington	Sullivan	Dorothy
100	Milton	Breault	Robert
100	Natick	Gowda	Ram
100	Needham	Soo	Hing
100	Needham	Whitney	Fran
100	Newton	Samuels	Peter
100	Newton	Siperstein	Linda
100	Waltham	Cobb	Matthew
100	Waltham	Driscoll	Kurt
100	Waltham	Shishov	Natasha

Figure 19-87. *A tabular DataWindow without row suppression.*

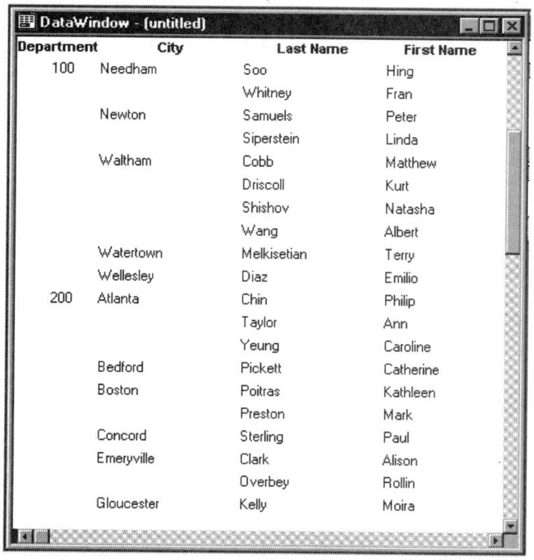
DataWindow - (untitled)

Department	City	Last Name	First Name
100	Needham	Soo	Hing
		Whitney	Fran
	Newton	Samuels	Peter
		Siperstein	Linda
	Waltham	Cobb	Matthew
		Driscoll	Kurt
		Shishov	Natasha
		Wang	Albert
	Watertown	Melkisetian	Terry
	Wellesley	Diaz	Emilio
200	Atlanta	Chin	Philip
		Taylor	Ann
		Yeung	Caroline
	Bedford	Pickett	Catherine
	Boston	Poitras	Kathleen
		Preston	Mark
	Concord	Sterling	Paul
	Emeryville	Clark	Alison
		Overbey	Rollin
	Gloucester	Kelly	Moira

Figure 19-88. *The same tabular DataWindow with row suppression.*

As you can see, Figure 19-88 is much easier to read and obtain details from. To set up the row suppression, select **Suppress Repeating Values...** from the Rows menu. This opens the Specify Repeating Value Suppression List dialog window as shown in Figure 19-89.

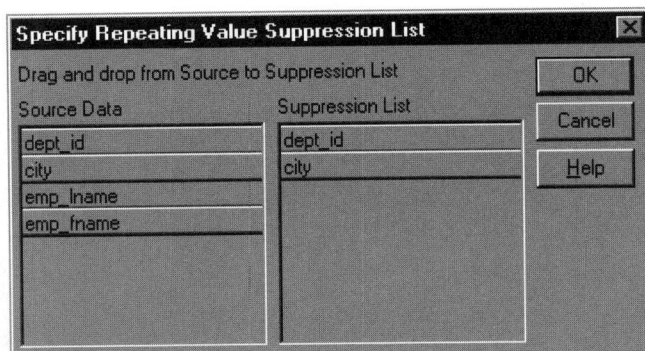

Figure 19-89. The Specify Repeating Value Suppression List dialog window.

This box has two list boxes. The list box on the left displays the columns in the result set while the box on the right lists the hierarchy of columns that will be suppressed if they repeat. The right list box is blank when you first enter because the DataWindow Painter does not assume any default row suppression. The order of the items in the list is very important. When a higher level of suppression changes (in the example, the highest level is department ID), the lower levels must all repeat. You can move columns into the suppression list, or change the order of the suppression list, using drag and drop.

The suppressed values are displayed at the start of each new page and whenever the value in a higher ranked suppressed value changes. This provides a visual link to users so that they don't have to search for the value in a column if it was suppressed on a previous page or group.

19.8.19 Creating And Using Groups

Earlier in the chapter we discussed a DataWindow presentation style called "group" that provided you with one predefined group in your result set. The intention behind grouping is to organize the rows of data in the result set into logical groups. This is beneficial for both displaying the data and doing analysis on each of the groups individually. For example, if you group by department, you can run a report that shows you the average salary in each department.

Groups are based upon columns that are displayed in the DataWindow. You can create as many groups as you require, but they must be structures and sorted hierarchically.

For each group you create, you can specify a custom group header and group trailer (as explained earlier in this chapter). The example in Figure 19-90 retrieves a list of employees grouped by the department they are in. You can retrieve statistics on each department and get a count of the number of employees in each. The name of the department appears in the group header, and the summary calculation appears in the group trailer. If you want a count of how many employees are in the whole company, you can put a similar computation into the summary band of the DataWindow.

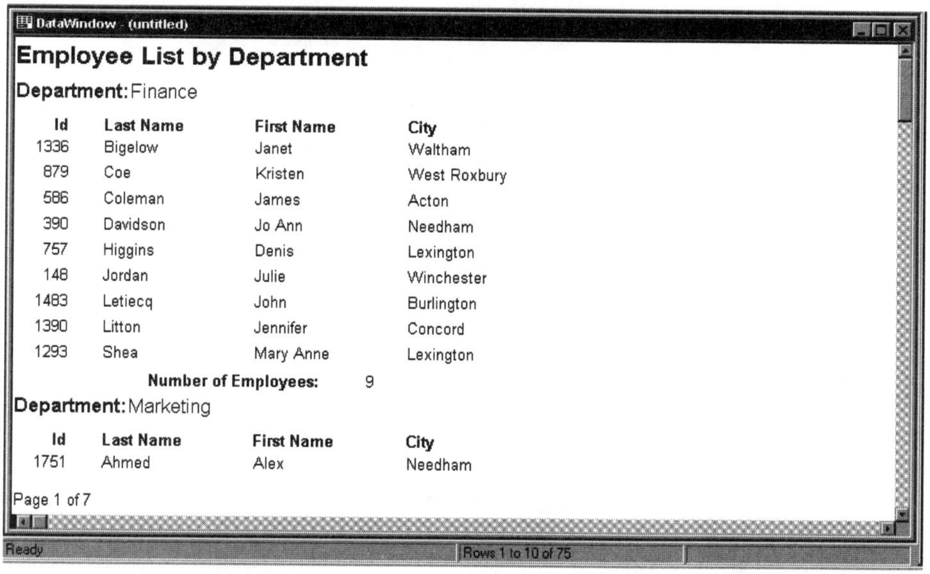

Figure 19-90. A grouped tabular DataWindow.

To define a group to use in your DataWindow, select **Create Group...** from the Rows menu. This opens the Band Object dialog window as shown in Figure 19-91. The act of creating a group is essentially creating a new band. In this properties window you can define how you want the group to be created using the Definition tab which will be the default tab selected.

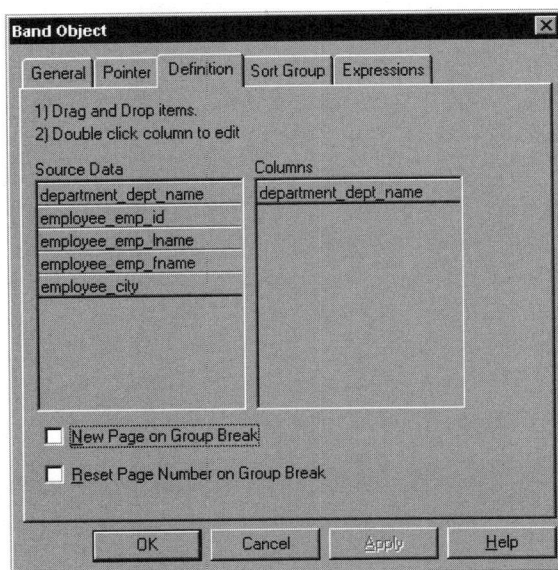

***Figure 19-91.** The Band Object dialog window with the Definition tab visible by default.*

You identify which column, or columns, you want to use to define this specific group (multiple groups will have their own Band and properties). To do this you drag from the available list of columns on the left list box to the right

You can also create an expression to define the group by double clicking on the column in the right list box and opening the Modify Expression dialog that we have used several times in this chapter already. An example of using an expression might be to group a set of accounts receivable records by the current date minus the invoice date to group them by how many days old they are.

If the New Page on Group Break property is set to TRUE, the DataWindow will start a new page each time the group changes. You can identify this option for each group level individually (you could create a page break when the department ID changes, but not when the city changes, etc.). The Reset Page Number on Group Break property allows you to have the page number set back to zero when the group changes. This can also be specified for each group individually.

Every group you use has its own Band, and hence it own Band Object properties window. If you wanted to group our employee list by City and then by Department within that city, you *do not* drag the City column and then the Department column within the same Band Object dialog window. Instead you create the City group band first and then go through the process of create a whole new group again.

Every group as it is created is assigned its own group number. This number represents the position of that group in the hierarchy. The highest group number is 1, then next is 2 and so on.

When using computed fields in a DataWindow's group trailer band to provide a computation based upon the group, you must alter the syntax slightly by providing a link to which group you want to compute for such as:

```
avg (employee_salary for group 1)
```

This computed column will calculate the average salary for all the records within group 1. If we had group 1 defined as department, at the end of each department list we would see the average salary within that specific department. This is different from:

```
avg( employee_salary for all)
```

which calculates the average salary for all employees regardless of department.

One final note: The DataWindow does not sort data by groups automatically. You must specify this yourself in either the SQL painter sort order or the DataWindow sort criteria. If you don't specify a sort order, the DataWindow creates a new group every time the value in the column changes, which can be quite a mess!

Also keep in mind that with new group headers, you might want to move the column headings into the group header area so that they repeat each time the group changes.

19.8.20 Specifying Update Characteristics

One of the most powerful features of the DataWindow is that after modifying some rows, deleting others and insert a few new rows of data, all you have to do to apply these changes to your database is call the Update() function (which will be discussed in more detail later). This function handles generating all the SQL statements necessary to make the database changes you have requested and communicating them to the database.

Even though there is a default DataWindow setting to handle the generation of these statements, there will be times when you want to change how the DataWindow builds the SQL commands. These defaults may need to be changed to address your issues of security, integrity, and concurrency. For example, if your defaults are set so that when a key column is modified it is first deleted and then inserted back into the database, this works fine for most situations. However, if you have built a trigger into your DBMS that cascades that deletion (so that any dependent records are also deleted), you might lose previous data.

A real-world example of this: You have two tables, one for companies and another for orders from those companies. The ACME company has placed 10 orders with your firm. For whatever reason, you update a key field in the ACME records in the companies table. This causes your SQL statements for first delete the ACME record and then insert it back into the database with your modifications. If you have the cascading deletion trigger in place, your DBMS deletes all the orders for the ACME company in the orders table when you issue the deletion (to ensure referential integrity). Obviously, this would not be a good thing.

Thus, when building your DataWindows, it is important to be sure your update characteristics are set up appropriately. If they're not, users that are accessing a record concurrently might wipe out each other's modifications, data might be lost in a cascading deletion, referential integrity might be violated, or other problems could arise.

To modify the update characteristics of the DataWindow we open the **Specify Update Properties** dialog window shown in Figure 19-92. This is done by selecting the **Update Properties...** menu option from the Rows menu.

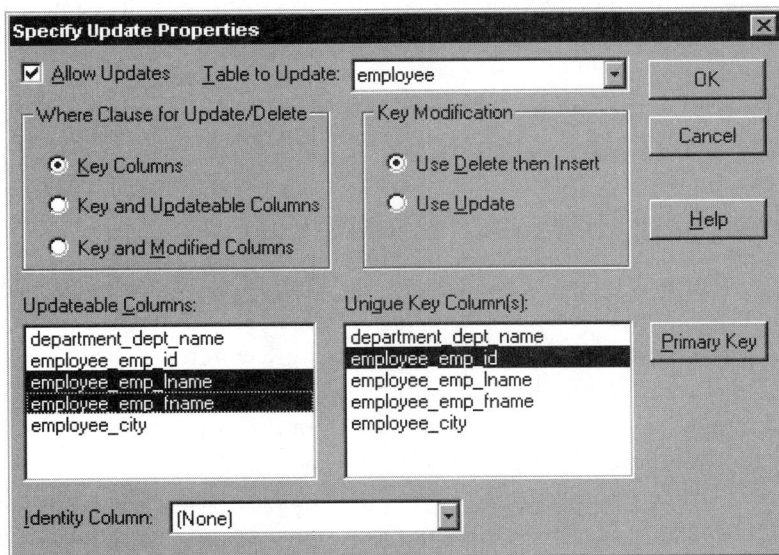

Figure 19-92. The Specify Update Properties dialog window.

In this window we can specify if the DataWindow is updateable at all by selecting the Allow Updates checkbox. By default DataWindows can only update a single table (multiple table updates are possible, but this is an advanced technique that won't be addressed in this chapter.). The Table to Update drop down listbox shows the table that is set as the updateable table.

All the columns in the DataWindow are listed in the Updateable Columns listbox. All the columns that you will include in your SQL statement (if appropriate) should be selected. Any columns that are not selected will never be updated in the database even if the user changes them in the DataWindow.

In the Unique Key Column(s) listbox you select the columns in the DataWindow that will uniquely identify one row from another. The vast majority of the time this will be the primary key (which can be automatically selected by pressing the **Primary Key** command button).

The Key Modification groupbox allows you to specify what kind of SQL statement that you want the DataWindow to generate when the user modifies the key columns. The default option is to have the DataWindow generate a DELETE statement to remove the initial row and then to perform an INSERT of a new row with the new key. This could have implications if dependent records exist for the row being modified. Depending on how your database is set to handle this, the dependent records could be deleted, updated or orphaned.

The second option for Key Modification is to Use Update. This means that the DataWindow will generate an UPDATE SQL statement when the user modifies a key value. Which option is appropriate will depend on how you have your referential integrity set up in your database. Your DBA should be able to inform you which option is correct to use.

The final (and most complex) attribute that you can control is how you want the DataWindow to generate the WHERE clause for the SQL statements it builds. This choice will have some serious impacts on your concurrency and data integrity issues. There are three options Key Columns, Key and Updateable Columns or Key and Modified Columns. We will look at the positive and negative aspects of each. Note that these example are assuming a minimum of interference from the server database. Some server databases will take control of this aspect of the transaction and make your decision easy.

19.8.20.1 Key Columns

With this option, the DataWindow will use only the columns that you have specified as key columns to uniquely identify a row.

Let's look at an example. We have two users who are going to access our database, User 1 and User 2.

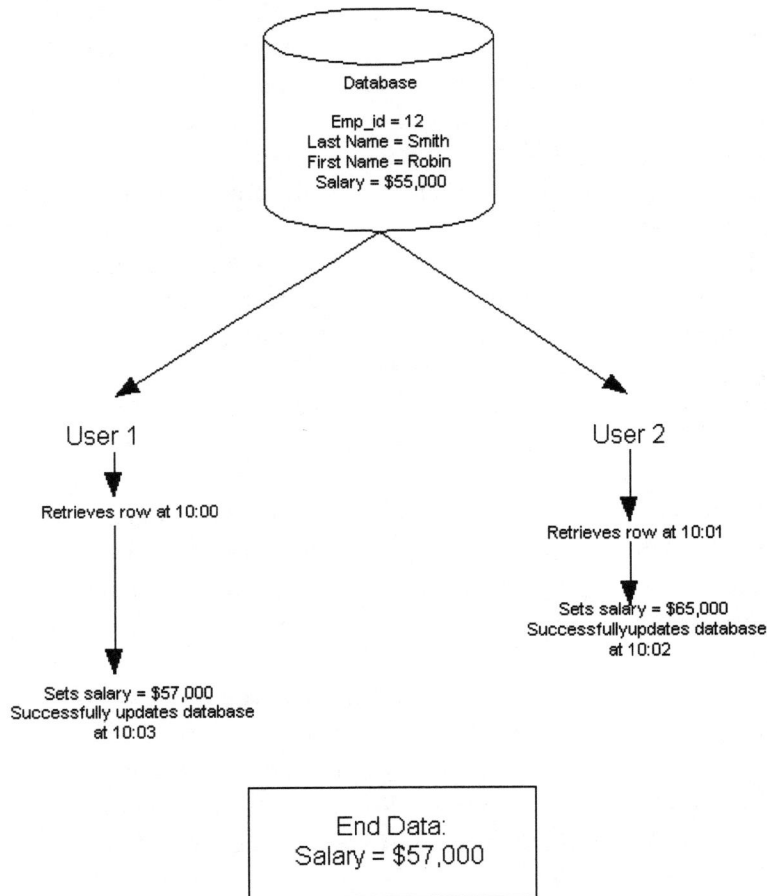

Figure 19-93. *Key Updates scenario.*

User 1 retrieves the row of data (without locking) from the database at 10:00. User 2 retrieves the same row of data at 10:01. User 2 makes a change to the employee's salary, giving them a nice big raise. The SQL statement looks like:

```
UPDATE employee SET salary = 65000.00 WHERE emp_id = 12
```

User 2 saves the data to the database successfully. User 1, unaware of what user 2 has done, changes the employee's salary to a small raise and then updates the database at 10:03. This SQL statement looks like:

```
UPDATE employee SET salary = 57000.00 WHERE emp_id = 12
```

This statement is also successful as it does not check to see if the data has changed since it was retrieved. The net result is that User 1 has overwritten the work done by user 2 and neither of them knows it!

This option works satisfactorily when you have low concurrency and strict locking in your database, but for high concurrent access systems, this option could result in lost data!

19.8.20.2 Key and Updateable Columns

With this option the DataWindow will build a WHERE clause that includes the key value for the row and all the columns that could be updated (based upon their original values as originally retrieve or last updated to the database).

Using our same example from above we can see that the update of User 1 is rejected because the salary has changed.

The SQL that is generated by User 2 is:

```
UPDATE employee SET salary = 65000.00 WHERE emp_id = 12 AND last_name =
'Smith' AND first_name = 'Robin' AND salary = 55000.00
```

The SQL that is generated for User 1 is:

```
UPDATE employee SET salary = 57000.00 WHERE emp_id = 12 AND last_name =
'Smith' AND first_name = 'Robin' AND salary = 55000.00
```

This SQL fails because the salary is no longer equal to $55,000.00.

This option will generally ensure the most consistent data in your database. For that reason alone, it is usually my preferred approach. There may be possible update situations that are logically acceptable that could be rejected with this approach. Consider the example in Figure 19-95.

In this example, User 2 updates the employee's salary and User 1 wants to update the employee's name. User 2 succeeds, but User 1 is rejected even though the data being changed is not interdependent.

The benefit here is maximized data consistency, but you may have user transactions that are rejected even though they are logically valid.

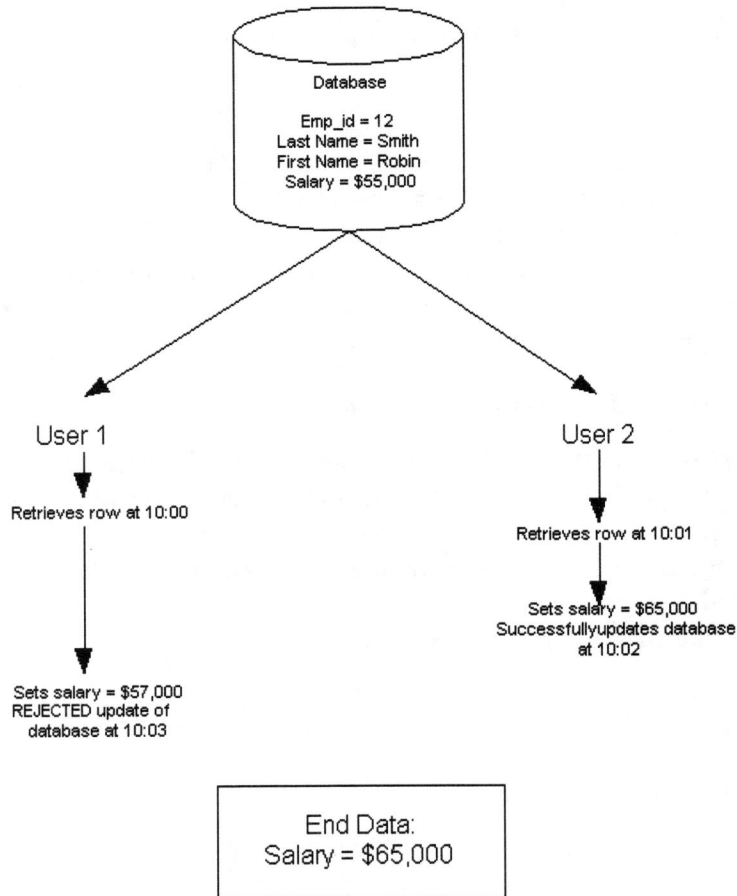

Figure 19-94. *Key and Updateable Columns option would cause the update of User 1 to fail.*

19.8.20.3 Key and Modified Columns

The final option, Key and Modified Columns, will have the DataWindow generate a SQL statement that includes the key value and any columns that the user has modified in the WHERE clause. In our example scenario if User 1 tries to update the salary column after User 2 has changed it, the statement would fail. Salary was modified by both, so it was included in the WHERE clause for both.

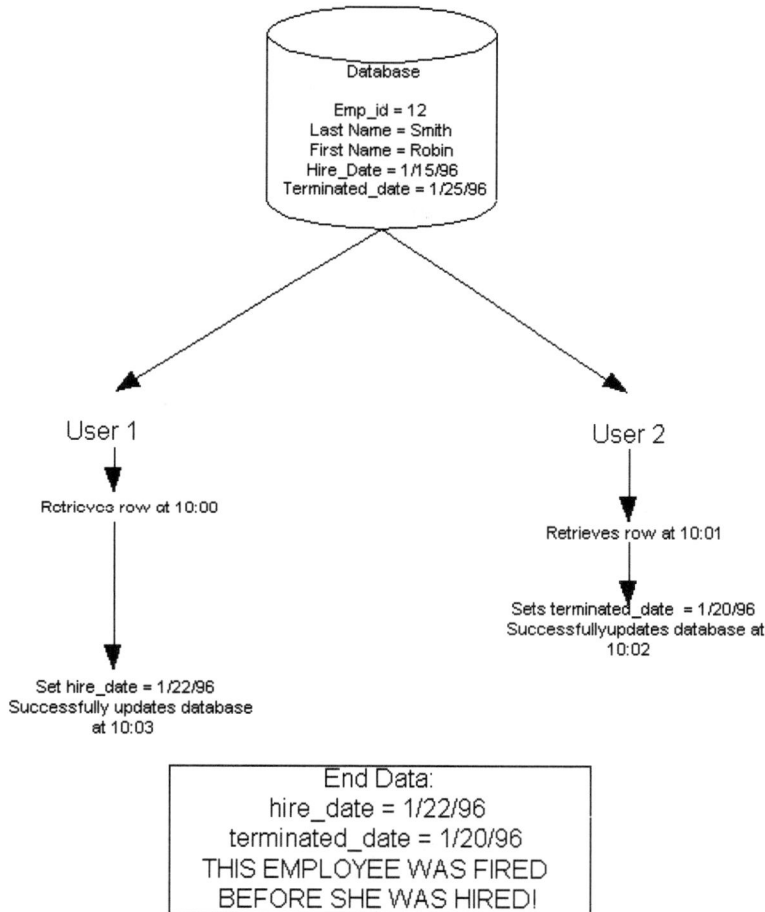

Figure 19-95. Even though the two users are updating different unrelated data, User 1 will have their update rejected.

If we look at the second example, where User 2 is changing the salary and User 1 is changing the last name, then our DataWindow would now behave as illustrated in Figure 19-96.

User 2 sends an update statement to the database like:

```
UPDATE employee SET salary = 65000.00 WHERE emp_id = 12 AND
  salary = 55000.00
```

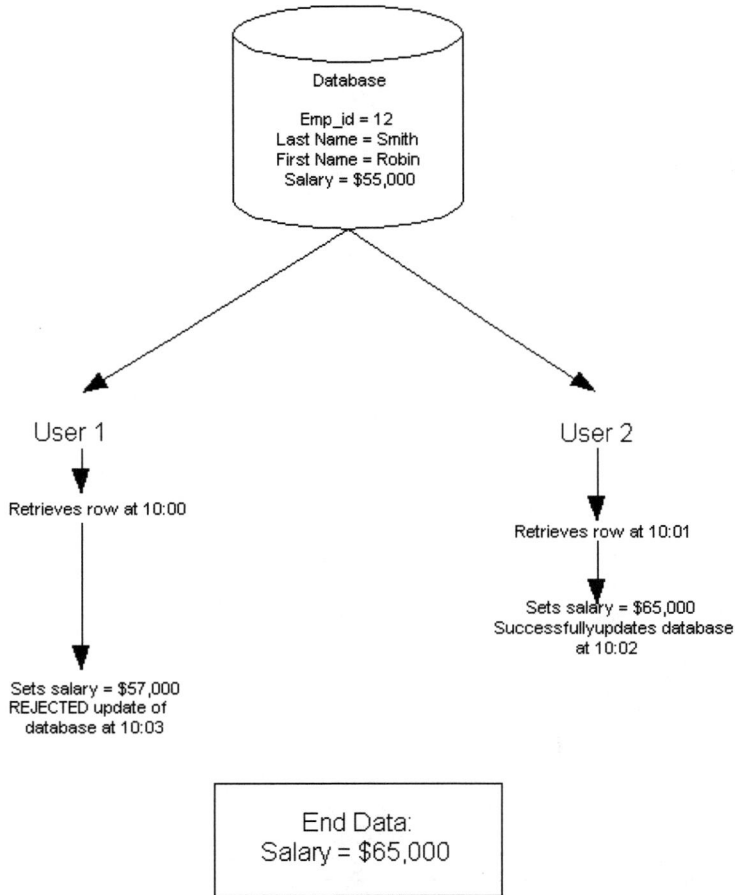

Figure 19-96. Using Key and Modified Columns as the WHERE clause, both user updates are successful.

This update is successful. Then User 1 sends a SQL statement with:

```
UPDATE employee SET last_name = 'Smithers' WHERE emp_id = 12 AND
last_name = 'Smith'
```

Both updates would succeed and neither user has interrupted the other. This may seem at first glance to be an ideal solution, but it has one severe limitations. When you have columns with cross column dependencies you can end up with inconsistent data. Let's look at the example in Figure 19-97.

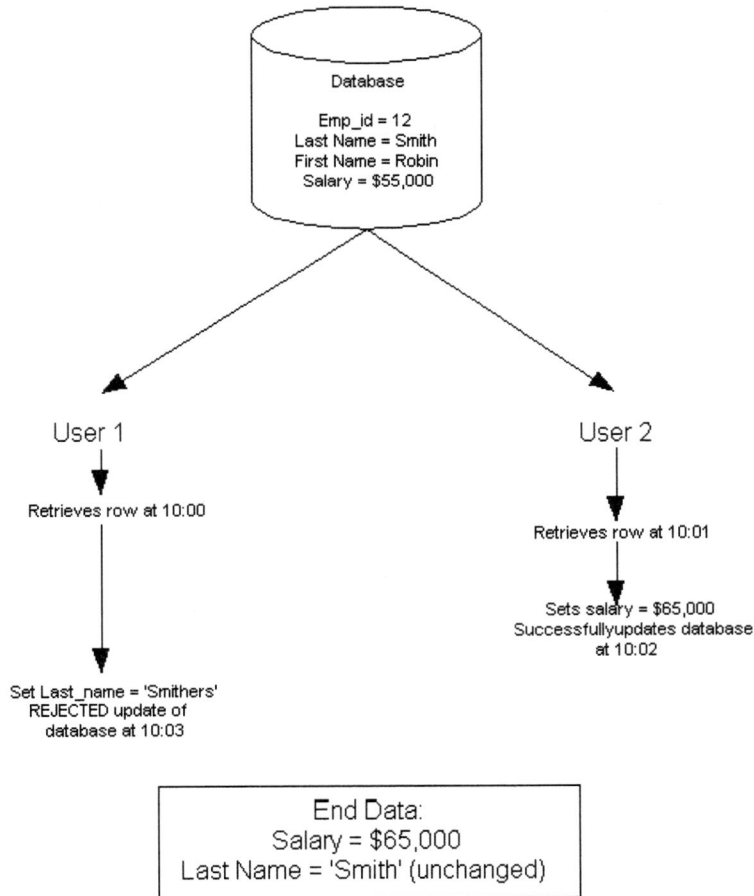

Figure 19-97. Both updates succeed and we end up with illogical data in our database.

In this example, both users make updates that appear from their point of view, but when combined the resulting data is illogical. If your database supports triggers and rules this type of inconsistency can be avoided, but from a client perspective this is definitely unacceptable.

19.8.20.4 ReselectRow() Function

If a user attempts to update the database but has their transaction rejected because the data in the database has changed between their retrieve and their update you can use the ReselectRow() function to retrieve the updated data for just that row in the database leaving the rest of the DataWindow buffers intact.

In order to use this function, you must use a database that supports timestamps and the timestamp column must be included in your result set.

The syntax for the ReselectRow() function is:

```
dw_control.ReselectRow(row_number)
```

where

row_number is the row that you want to reselect the current data for. This can be obtained in the DBError event of a DataWindow control. In this event the row argument will tell you which row caused the error.

If the row in the database was deleted by another user or the function was unable to obtain the updated row information this function will return a -1.

19.8.20.5 Autoincrement Columns

Some databases (including Sybase SQLAnywhere) allow you to create columns in your tables that are defined as "autoincrement." In these columns the database will automatically generate a unique value for all new rows that are inserted. Autoincrement columns are also known as identity columns and sequences.

The DataWindow Painter will expect you to specify a key for a DataWindow object if you intend on allowing the object to perform updates. If the key is an autoincrement column this can pose some problems. With autoincrement columns, you cannot include these columns in your INSERT SQL statement, but they must be part of the result set you request from the database. In the DataWindow Painter we can identify autoincrement columns by specifying the column for the updateable table in the Identity Column field in the Specify Update Properties dialog window (refer to Figure 19-93). A table can only have one autoincrement column so only one field is used.

Specifying the autoincrement column will also cause the DataWindow Painter to refresh the buffer and display the autoincrement value for the newly inserted row after a successful update.

Developer's Tip: Although you must include the autoincrement column in your result set for the DataWindow, it does not necessarily have to be shown to the user. If it is shown to the user ,be sure to identify it as a read only column and protect it from user input.

19.8.21 Previewing and Testing a DataWindow

When you are working with the DataWindow painter, it is useful to test the DataWindow to see how it will appear and make certain that it is behaving as you expect. You can examine the layout and retrieve data into the object. If you set up your DataWindow to be updateable, you can use it to enter and manipulate the data in the database.

To put your DataWindow into preview mode you can: click the Preview toolbar button (Figure 19-98) press <CTRL + SHIFT +P> or select **Preview** from the Design menu.

Figure 19-98. The DataWindow preview toolbar button.

In preview mode, a new window will open replacing the DataWindow workspace. The new window will show the DataWindow as it would appear if it was executed. By default, the DataWindow Painter executes a retrieve function and retrieves data into the DataWindow (except for external data source DataWindows). This action can be overridden by setting the Retrieve on Preview DataWindow option to FALSE (unchecked) in the DataWindow properties page discussed earlier in this chapter.

In preview mode you will see a different toolbar which allows you to works with and navigate through the data. The **Retrieve** button executes the Retrieve() function on the DataWindow and brings back a result set from the database based upon the SQL select statement or other data source that you defined for the DataWindow. If the DataWindow has been designed to be updateable, you can then proceed to make changes, insert new rows, and delete rows from the DataWindow. There are buttons on the toolbar for inserting a row into and deleting a row from the result set. Any changes that you make while in preview mode can be saved to the database using the "Update" toolbar button.

The four navigation buttons all appear as black arrowheads. These buttons are used to help you move through the data in the result set efficiently. The "First" button scrolls to the first page of data in the result set, while the "Last" button will scroll to the last page. The "Prior" and "Next" buttons scroll to the previous page of data or the next page of data respectively.

Pressing on the **Preview** button again (currently it will appear to be depressed) will toggle you out of preview mode.

While in preview mode, the data in the result set can be saved to disk in a number of different formats. To do this, select **Save Rows As...** from the File menu. This will open the Save As dialog window shown in Figure 19-99.

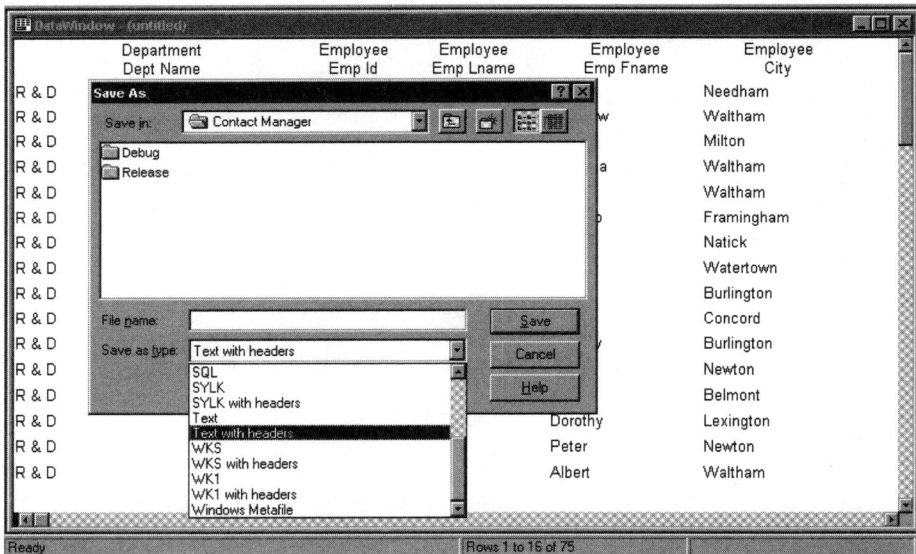

Figure 19-99. Use the Save Rows As dialog window to save the result set to a flat file.

In this dialog window you can save the rows of the result set to a DOS file in one of 19 possible formats:

- **CSV.** Comma separated values. Can be created with or without headers.

- **dBase.** A dBase file, either format 2 or 3.

- **DIF.** Data interchange format.

- **Excel.** Standard Microsoft Excel™ file. Can be created with or without headers.

- **HTML Table.** Saves the basic report format and data as an HTML formatted file.

- **Powersoft Report.** Saves the complete report format and data as a standalone file.

- **SQL.** Saves the SQL syntax for the report.

- **SYLK.** Standard Microsoft Multiplan format. Can be created with or without headers.

- **Text.** Tab separated columns with a return at the end of the row. Can be created with or without headers.

- **Lotus Worksheet.** Standard Lotus 1-2-3™ worksheet file. Can save in formats WK1 or WKS. Can be created with or without headers.

- **Windows Metafile.** Standard Microsoft Windows™ metafile.

This same functionality can be obtained to save values stored in a DataWindow at runtime using the SaveAs() function.

While in preview mode you can also use the menu to sort, filter, and import data. **Selecting Sort...** from the Rows menu opens the Specify Sort dialog window that we saw earlier in the chapter allowing you to resort the result set on the client.

Filters were discussed earlier in this chapter as well. You can apply a filter to your result set by selecting **Filter...** from the Rows menu. This will open the standard Specify Filter dialog window allowing you to define a filter to use with this result set.

You can use the **Import...** menu option from the Rows menu to import data from a standard text or dBase file (.TXT or .DBF). Selecting this option will open the Select Import File dialog window as shown in Figure 19.100.

The data in the file must be in the same order as the data in the result set in order for the import to succeed.

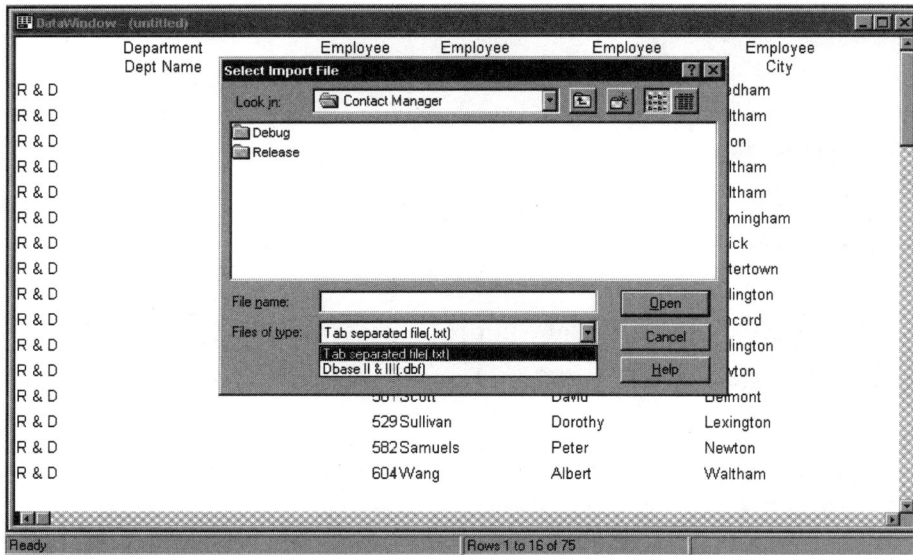

***Figure 19-100.** The Select Import File dialog window allows you to import data from text or dBase files.*

19.9   Using the DataWindow In Your Application

To this point in the chapter, the DataWindow object is basically complete. It has been defined and customized to reflect the needs for which is was designed. It can retrieve or update data, or perhaps generate a report.

The next step it to learn how to use the DataWindow object in our application. Learning how to place this object on a Window and make it do the things you want is the subject of the rest of this chapter.

19.9.1 DataWindow Controls vs. DataWindow Objects

At this point you have used the DataWindow Painter to create an object that interfaces with both the database (in retrieving and updating data) and with the user (in displaying and enabling the modification of data). What you need to do it place the DataWindow in the Window that you are building using the Window Painter.

To do this you must place a DataWindow control component on the Window where you want the DataWindow to appear. The DataWindow control component can be with the other Window components on the PainterBar and appears as shown in Figure 19-101.

Figure 19-101. *The DataWindow control component icon from PainterBar is the same as the DataWindow Painter icon.*

When initially dropped on to a form, the DataWindow control will appear like an empty box as shown in Figure 19.102. Like other controls, it can now be moved and resized to take up the appropriate position in your form.

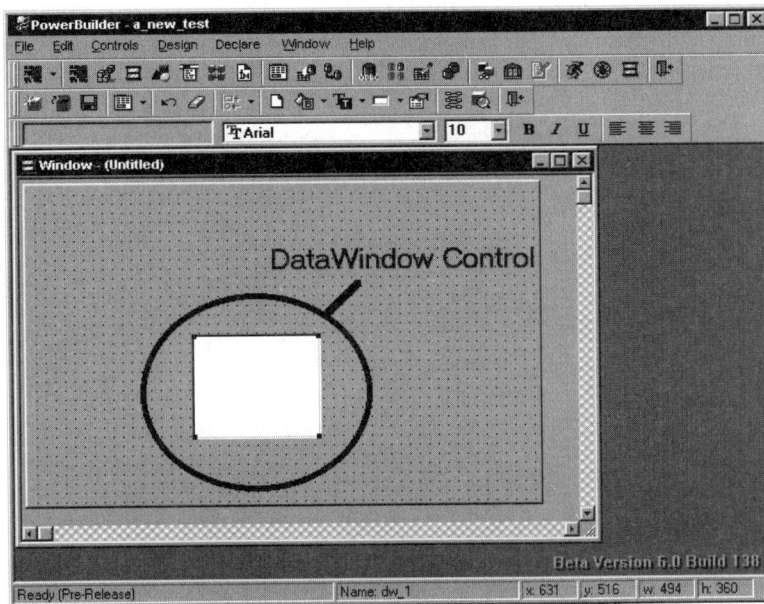

Figure 19-102. *A Window with a DataWindow control component placed on it.*

The next step is to form a relationship between the DataWindow control and the DataWindow object that was built with the DataWindow Painter. To associate (link) a DataWindow object with the DataWindow control you must open the DataWindow Control properties page by clicking with the right mouse button and selecting Properties from the popup menu. (See Figure 19-103.)

On the General tab of this window you will specify the name of the DataWindow object that you want to link to.

At this point we won't go over all the properties of the DataWindow control, but will assume that you have enough PowerBuilder experience to understand the standard properties. Some of the DataWindow specific properties we will explain.

The "H Scroll Bar" and "V Scroll Bar" check boxes allow you to specify if you want horizontal and vertical scroll bars to appear within the DataWindow control if the result set extends beyond the physical space available in the DataWindow control. These scroll bars will be invisible to the user if the data is contained entirely within the available area.

The "H Split Scrolling" enables the user to split the visible area of the DataWindow control into panes and enable separate scrolling in each pane (on the horizontal axis only).

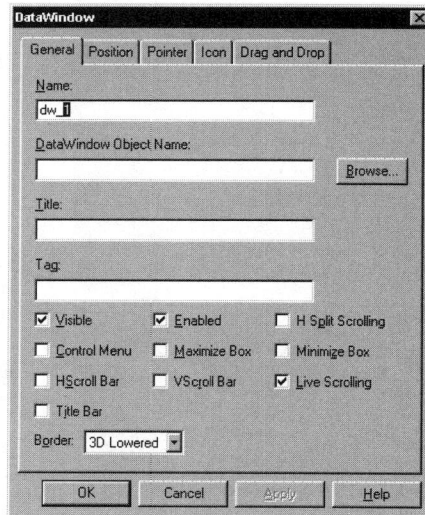

Figure 19-103. The DataWindow Control Properties window with the General tab open.

The "Live Scrolling" option will cause the DataWindow to scroll through the result set as the user performs actions that require rows of data that are out of view to come into view. For example, using the down arrow keys to move thorough rows of data until you are moving through rows in the result set that are out of the visible area. If live scrolling is turned on, then as the user moves down, the result set will scroll up.

Developer's Note: In this section we describe how to statically associate a
DataWindow control with a DataWindow object. There may be situations
where you want to dynamically change which DataWindow object is associated with a DataWindow control. This can be accomplished by changing
the DataObject property of the DataWindow control in your script at runtime like this:

```
dw_1.DataObject = "d_new_datawindow_object"
```

19.9.2 Associating the Transaction Object

At this point you have completed the conceptual link from the user to the DataWindow.
However, there is still one critical step missing. We haven't specified which database our
DataWindow control will be using to connect and manipulate the data. To do this, we
must link this DataWindow control to a transaction object that we have previously
defined. (Remember that SQLCA has been predeclared for you in all PowerBuilder
applications).

To specify which transaction object we will be using we must use the SetTrans-
Object() function as follows:

```
dw_control.SetTransObject(transaction_object_name)
```

An example of associating the DataWindow dw_customer with the transaction
object SQLCA would be:

```
dw_customer.SetTransObject(SQLCA)
```

This script can be put in any number of places like the DataWindow constructor event, the Window open event or another logical location, but it must be called
prior to calling a Retrieve(), InsertRow() or Update() function. The SetTransObject()
function must also be called whenever you dynamically change the DataWindow object
a DataWindow control is associated with.

Now the link is complete and your DataWindow is able to connect to the database at runtime.

19.9.3 What Is the Edit Control?

Before we get too far into the realm of DataWindow functions, let's examine how data
gets from the user's mind to the database. When you tested the DataWindow, you were

able to change the column you were working on (remember this is called changing "focus") using the TAB key and the arrow keys. The field that had focus would become highlighted and the cursor would flash within it. You could enter a new value into this field, thus moving the data from your mind into the system.

You weren't really putting that information into the DataWindow. You were placing it into the Edit control. The edit control takes the data that was entered by the user and holds it until the field loses focus (when you tab or click elsewhere within the DataWindow). When this happens the edit control tries to validate the data to ensure that you have entered data that makes sense. If the data is correct, it will be placed into the appropriate *DataWindow buffer* which will be discussed next.

19.9.3.1 Buffers

Behind the scenes of every DataWindow object are a number of buffers that store and manage the data for which the DataWindow is responsible. Four buffers form the foundation of everything that the DataWindow does. These buffers are the primary, filter, delete, and original.

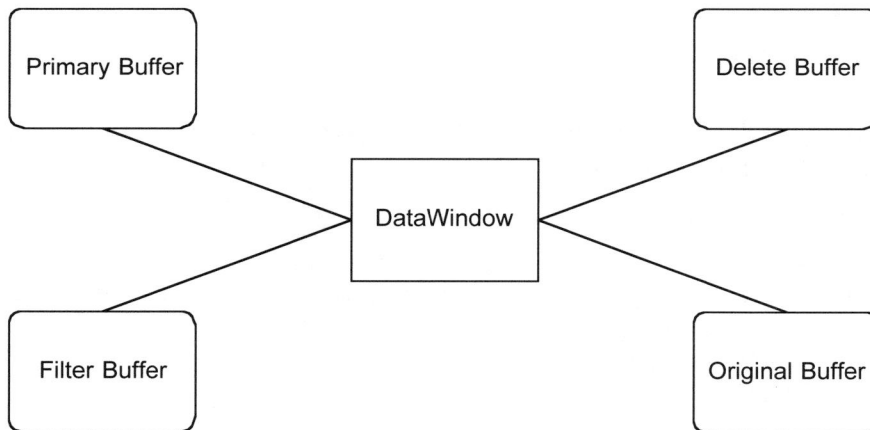

Figure 19-104. The DataWindow buffers store and manage all the data in the DataWindow.

19.9.3.1.1 Primary

The primary buffer is the one that you will interact with most often. This buffer contains all the currently active data. Active data is defined as data which has not been deleted or filtered out. When the user sees data in a DataWindow control in an application, they are looking at the data that is in the primary buffer.

Data is placed into the primary buffer primarily through the Retrieve() and InsertRow() functions although other functions can also move data into this buffer such as RowsCopy(), RowsMove(), and ImportFile().

19.9.3.1.2 Filter

The filter buffer contains data that has been filtered out of the primary buffer though the filter expression of the DataWindow. The filter expression on a DataWindow behaves like a client based WHERE clause that only allows the rows that meet certain criteria to stay in the primary buffer.

19.9.3.1.3 Delete

This buffer contains rows that have been deleted from the primary buffer using the DeleteRow() function, but have not yet been deleted from the database. You can think of the delete buffer as a temporary holding area where rows awaiting deletion are gathered until an Update() function is called. Data could also be placed into this buffer through the RowsMove() function.

19.9.3.1.4 Original

The original buffer contains a snapshot of all the data values before they were changed. This information is critical to allow the DataWindow to build the SQL statement where clauses to perform updates against the database. The original buffer is updated when data is first retrieved and also upon a successful DataWindow update.

19.9.3.2 Manipulating Data Stored in Buffers

Whenever you are manipulating data in a DataWindow you are effectively working with the buffers. When the user types new data into the edit control and presses the tab key, they are trying to insert data into the primary buffer.

There are also other functions that are available to help you manipulate the data in the buffers such as the RowsMove(), RowsCopy(), and RowsDiscard() functions which shift data around in the buffers.

19.9.3.2.1 RowsMove()

The RowsMove() function will take a complete set of rows from a specific buffer on one DataWindow and will move them into another buffer on the same DataWindow or onto any buffer from another DataWindow with a matching result set.

The most common uses in production applications for RowsMove() is to perform a mass deletion or to provide "undelete" functionality.

The syntax for RowsMove() is:

```
dw_control.RowsMove(start_row, end_row, move_from_buffer, dw_target,&
insert_before_row, insert_into_buffer)
```

where

start_row. The first row to move from the source DataWindow control.

end_row. The last row to move from the source DataWindow control.

move_from_buffer. The buffer in the source DataWindow where the rows will be moved from.

dw_target. The DataWindow control that contains the buffer that will be copied into.

insert_before_row. The row number in the target DataWindow that you want to insert before. A number greater than the number of rows in the target will result in the rows being appended to the end of the selected buffer.

insert_into_buffer. The buffer in the target DataWindow into which you want to insert the rows from the source DataWindow.

19.9.3.2.2 RowsCopy()

The RowsCopy() function is almost identical to the RowsMove() function except that rows are not removed from the source DataWindow buffer. This function is particularly useful for copying existing rows of data into the same buffer with a new row status so that they can be modified by the user. This has been used in many production applications and is often referred to as a "New Using" function. It allows the user to use existing data as a template for new data.

This function can also be used to copy a range of rows to a second temporary DataWindow where they can be printed and then discarded.

The syntax is identical to the RowsMove() function except that we use the RowsCopy() function instead. Please refer to the previous section for descriptions of the function arguments.

19.9.3.2.3 RowsDiscard()

The RowsDiscard() function allows you to take a row or range of rows from a DataWindow buffer and wipe them out. The effect of this will depend on which buffer you are removing the data from.

If you remove rows from the primary or filter buffer any updates that have not been saved will be lost. These rows are not removed from the database and could be brought back by issuing another retrieve function. The user will see rows disappear from the primary buffer because they are part of the visible data, but rows that are discarded from the filter buffer will not affect the users current view of the data.

If you remove rows from the delete buffer then these rows will not actually be deleted in the database.

The syntax for the RowsDiscard() function is:

```
dwcontrol.RowsDiscard ( start_row, end_row, delete_from_buffer )
```

The arguments are the same as those from the RowsMove() section above. In an effort to keep the redundant information in this book to a minimum, please refer to that section for descriptions of arguments you are unsure of.

19.9.3.3 Four Levels of Validation

When the user tabs off a field and the edit control there are four validation steps which are executed prior to the data being inserted into the primary buffer:

1. *Is the data of the correct data type?* The DataWindow will check to ensure that the data in the Edit control is of the correct data type (for example, a numeric value, not a string value is entered in a numeric column). If the data isn't of the correct data type, the ItemError event will be triggered (see ItemError event below). If the data type is correct, then the DataWindow will move on to the second level of validation.

2. *Does the data pass the validation rules?* The data in the edit control is compared against the validation rules for the column (these were discussed earlier in this chapter). If the data doesn't pass the validation rules (for

example, if the user enters an age of 3 for an employee, but the validation rule says all employees must be over the age of 18) the ItemError event will be triggered. If the validation rules are successfully passed, the DataWindow will proceed with the third level of validation.

3. *Has anything really changed?* Now the Edit control will check to see if anything has really changed in the field. If the field previously contained "Johnson" and you erased it and entered "Johnson," the DataWindow is intelligent enough to figure out that you really haven't changed anything. Thus it won't pass this value through to the DataWindow buffer and the validation process will stop here.

4. *Does the data pass the ItemChanged event?* The final level of validation for the data in the edit control is to pass any custom validation which has bee coded in the DataWindow's ItemChanged event (this validation is in the form of code that you will enter in the Form designer). If the data is rejected in the ItemChanged event, the ItemError event will be triggered. If the value is accepted, the DataWindow will move the data from the Edit control to the DataWindow buffer and allow the focus to change.

19.9.3.4 Functions Related to the Edit Control

There are functions that you will need to use in your scripts to work with the Edit control. You may need to find out what the value is in the control, or you may want to place a new value in it.

19.9.3.4.1 GetText()

In events such as ItemChanged and ItemError, you want to perform processing based upon the value in the edit control. To find out what that value is, use the GetText() function. The syntax for this function is:

```
dw_control.GetText()
```

The function will return a string regardless of the data type that the column may be. If the user enters 21 into a numeric column representing age, it will be returned as a string "21."

19.9.3.4.2 SetText()

You may choose to place a value into the Edit control for the user. By placing a value into the Edit control, the value you place there acts just like a value entered by the user, including the fact that it must pass through the validation process. (The alternative is to use a function to place the value directly into the DataWindow buffer and bypass the validation.). The syntax for the SetText() function is:

```
dw_control.SetText(string_value)
```

Like GetText(), the value passed as an argument must be a string. The function will return a 1 if it succeeds and a -1 if it fails.

AcceptText()

If the user clicks the mouse outside the DataWindow, the last value the user entered is still sitting in the Edit control waiting to be validated. To ensure that the value is validated and stored in the DataWindow buffer, you can force the DataWindow to validate and deal with the value in the Edit control by using the AcceptText() function as follows:

```
dw_control.AcceptText()
```

There are no arguments for this function. It will return a value of 1 if the data was successfully validated and a -1 if an error occurred.

> **Developer's Note:** The AcceptText() function may trigger the ItemChanged and/or ItemError events. Therefore, AcceptText() should not be placed in the scripts for these events or an endless loop could result.

19.10 Making the DataWindow Perform

Now that all the pieces are in place and all your objects are successfully talking to each other, you need to know how to write the code to make the DataWindow perform the retrieving, updating, and manipulating of data. The DataWindow has many built in functions that make this process quite simple.

19.10.1 Retrieving Data

To populate your DataWindow objects with data, use the Retrieve() function. This function takes one of two formats, depending on how you built the associated DataWindow object. If the DataWindow does not require any arguments, you perform the retrieval as follows:

```
dw_control.Retrieve()
```

For example:

```
dw_customer_report.Retrieve()
```

This causes the DataWindow to execute its data source (Select statement, stored procedure, and so on).

If you have built your DataWindow object to require one or more retrieval arguments (for example, if you are retrieving employees from a specific department), you must specify those arguments in the Retrieve() function as follows:

```
dw_control.Retrieve(Arg 1 {, Arg 2, Arg 3, …})
```

For example, to search for customers in a certain city with account balances exceeding a certain amount, you could use something similar to the following:

```
dw_control.Retrieve("Boston",2000)
```

The Retrieve() function returns an integer equal to the number of rows retrieved from the database. If no data was returned, the value will be 0 and if an error occurs, it will return a value of -1.

If a Retrieve() function fails, it may trigger a DBError event (discussed later in this chapter).

There are three other events that may be triggered by the Retrieve() function:

- **RetrieveStart.** Occurs when a retrieval begins. Could be used to show a visual cue to the user that the data is being retrieved.

- **RetrieveEnd.** Occurs when the retrieval is complete. Could be used to remove the visual cue place in the Retrieve start event.

- **RetrieveRow.** Is triggered after each row in the result set is retrieved. Could be used to provide the user with a row by row count of the retrieval, although, because this code will execute with every row, for large retrievals, this could result in a significant drag on application performance.

19.10.2 Updating Data

To update the data in the database with the changes that have been made in the DataWindow, use the Update() function. After this function is executed, the DataWindow will send all the insertions, updates and deletions to the database. The syntax is very straightforward:

```
dw_control.Update()
```

This book will only address this format of the Update() function. Other formats for this function are used with advanced techniques that require the passing of arguments for the Update() function to update multiple tables or multiple databases, but we will concentrate on the preceding basic form of the Update() function.

As example of this form is:

```
dw_customer_list.Update()
```

This cause the DataWindow to build and execute all the SQL statements, thus passing all the changes in the DataWindow to the database.

The return value of an Update() function is 1 if the update is successful and -1 if an error occurs.

The Update() function can also cause the following events to be triggered:

- **DBError.** Occurs when an update fails.
- **UpdateStart.** Occurs when an update begins.
- **UpdateEnd.** Occurs when an update is completed.

19.10.3 Inserting Data

To insert a blank row into your DataWindow, use the InsertRow() function. This function inserts a row before the row that is specified in the argument. The syntax is:

```
dw_control.InsertRow(rcwnumber)
```

To insert a row before the sixth row in the customer list DataWindow:

```
dw_customer_list.InsertRow(6)
```

The return value of the InsertRow() function is a long data type with the row number of the row that was inserted, or a -1 if the insert failed.

It is common to scroll to the row that was just inserted to be sure that it is visible. And example of the code to this is:

```
long ll_NewRow
ll_NewRow = dw_customer_list.InsertRow(6)
dw_customer_list.ScrollToRow(ll_NewRow)
```

19.10.4 Deleting Data

To delete a row from your DataWindow, use the DeleteRow() function. This function deletes the row you specify in the argument. The syntax is:

```
dw_control.DeleteRow(rownumber)
```

To delete the sixth row of the customer report DataWindow:

```
dw_customer_list.DeleteRow(6)
```

The return value of the DeleteRow() function is 1 if it succeeds and -1 if it fails.

Remember that these deletions and insertions are only happening in the DataWindow buffers, not in the database. The Update() function must be executed to pass these changes on to the database.

19.10.5 Row Methods

There are other functions that you will want to know about when working with DataWindows in your applications. These include functions for determining the current row, bringing rows into view and highlighting a row.

19.10.5.1 GetRow()

Just as every form has only one control that is currently in focus, every DataWindow has only one current row. To obtain the row number of that current row use the GetRow() function as follows:

```
dw_control.GetRow()
```

There are no arguments for GetRow(). The return value of this function is a long data type containing the current row number. You can store this number in a variable or embed this function within another function. This function returns a 0 if no row is current and a -1 if it fails.

An example of this function is:

```
long ll_CurRow
ll_CurRow = dw_customer_list.GetRow()
```

which could then use the variable in another function, like:

```
dw_customer_list.InsertRow(ll_CurRow)
```

This full example would insert a new blank row immediately before the current row in the result set.

Developer's Note: Remember that the current row does not necessarily have to be visible. You could select a row and then use the scroll bars to scroll the row out of the visible area, but it would still be the current row.

19.10.5.2 ScrollToRow()

When you make changes to the DataWindow result set, such as inserting a row, the change may end up outside of the visible area, and the user might not be able to see that a change has taken place. It is important to use the ScrollToRow() function to scroll the DataWindow result set to ensure that the row that was changed is visible. Calling this function will also set the row that is being scrolled to as the current row (the current column is not changed). The syntax for this function is:

```
dw_control.ScrollToRow(rownumber)
```

Where the argument that is passed is the row number that you want to bring into view and make current.

The following example shows a full insert before the current row:

```
long ll_CurRow
ll_CurRow = dw_customer_list.GetRow()
ll_CurRow = dw_customer_list.InsertRow(ll_CurRow)
dw_customer_list.ScrollToRow(ll_CurRow)
```

19.10.5.3 SelectRow()

To highlight or unhighlight a row, you use the SelectRow() function. The syntax for SelectRow() is:

```
dw_control.SelectRow(rownumber, action)
```

Where the first argument is the row number that you want to affect and action is a boolean (TRUE or FALSE) to indicate if you want the row to be highlighted or not. For example, to select the current row in the customer list DataWindow:

```
long ll_CurRow
ll_CurRow = dw_customer_list.GetRow()
dw_customer_list.SelectRow(ll_CurRow,TRUE)
```

Using the value 0 for the row number will cause the action to affect all the rows in the result set. You can use this to select or deselect all the rows in the DataWindow simultaneously. In the final argument, TRUE selects the row and FALSE deselects it.

This function will return a long value of 1 if it succeeds and -1 if it fails.

19.10.5.4 GetColumn()

To find out which column in the DataWindow is current, we call the GetColumn() function as follows:

```
dw_control.GetColumn()
```

There are no arguments for this function. This function returns a long with the current column number, a 0 if no column is current (or if the current column has a tab order of 0) and -1 if it fails.

19.10.6 Getting Data In and Out of the DataWindow

In almost every application that uses DataWindows, you will need to extract data from and insert data into the DataWindow buffers. The best tools for doing this are the GetItemx() functions and the SetItem() function.

19.10.6.1 GetItemx()

The GetItemx() functions return data from a specific row and column that you specify. There is a function for each of the data types of string, number, decimal, datetime, time, and date. Each of these functions returns the value for the row and column specified, in the same data type, and each returns a different value to represent an error (GetItemString() returns an empty string ("") to indicate an error, but GetItemDate() returns the date 1900-01-01 to indicate an error). The basic syntax for these six functions are:

```
dw_control.GetItemString(row, column, buffer, original_value)
dw_control.GetItemNumber(row, column, buffer, original_value)
dw_control.GetItemDecimal(row, column, buffer, original_value)
dw_control.GetItemDate(row, column, buffer, original_value)
dw_control.GetItemDateTime(row, column, buffer, original_value)
dw_control.GetItemTime(row, column, buffer, original_value)
```

where

row is the row number that you want to extract the information for.

column is the column name or number where the information is stored.

buffer is the DataWindow buffer that you want to get the information from. Valid values are Primary, Delete, and Filter.

original_value is a boolean value (TRUE or FALSE) indicating if you want to return the value originally retrieved from the database or not.

You could use these functions to get the employee id from a specific row of data like in the following example:

```
Wlong ll_CurRow
Wlong ll_EmpID

ll_CurRow = dw_employee_list.GetRow()
ll_EmpID = dw_employee_list.GetItemNumber(ll_CurRow, "emp_id", Primary, FALSE)
```

19.10.6.2 SetItem()

You can assign a value to a specific cell in a DataWindow by using the SetItem() function. This function bypasses the validation rules and inserts the value directly into the DataWindow buffer. The syntax for this function is:

```
dw_control.SetItem(row, column, value)
```

where

row is the row number that you want to insert information into.

column is the column name or number for the information being inserted.

value is the literal or variable containing the value that you want to set into the DataWindow primary buffer.

If we wanted to set the employee id value for the current row to 6 we could use the following example:

```
Wlong ll_CurRow

ll_CurRow = dw_employee_list.GetRow()
dw_employee_list.SetItem(ll_CurRow, "emp_id", 6)
```

19.10.7 Other Useful Methods

Here are a few more functions which are used a great deal in production applications with which you may want to familiarize yourself.

19.10.7.1 Reset()

To reset a DataWindow and clear all the rows out of it, use the Reset() function. This function is different from deleting rows from the DataWindow because it has no effect on the database. If you call a Reset() function, it returns the DataWindow to the state it was in prior to issuing a retrieve. The syntax for this function is:

```
dw_control.Reset()
```

The function will return a 1 if it succeeds and a -1 if it fails. The DataWindow does a reset automatically before it retrieves data, so you don't need to do a reset before a retrieval.

19.10.7.2 SetSort() and Sort()

To resort the data without having to make another request to the database, use the SetSort() and Sort() functions. The SetSort() function defines how you want the DataWindow to be sorted, and the Sort() function actually initiates the sort. The syntax for these functions is:

```
dw_control.SetSort( sort_expression)
dw_control.Sort()
```

where

> **sort_expression** is a string that contains the column name to sort by and the order to sort in.

The column name in the sort expression must be followed immediately by an A or a D to indicate sorting in ascending or descending order. Multiple column sorts can be performed by separating the column names by a comma. You may also use the column number if you precede the number with the pound sign ("#").

Some examples of valid sort expressions are:

Sort By	Expression
Client name is an ascending manner.	"client_name A"
Employee last name in an ascending manner followed by salary in a descending manner.	"emp_last_name A, salary D"
First column in a descending manner followed by the second column in a descending manner.	"#1 D, #2 D"

An example of using these functions to re-sort a DataWindow by the customer city and then by the customer name would be:

```
dw_customer_list.SetSort("city A, customer_name A")
dw_customer_list.Sort()
```

19.10.7.3 SetFilter and Filter()

To refilter the data in the DataWindow without having to make another request to the database, use the SetFilter() and Filter() functions. The SetFilter() function defines the filtering criteria, and the Filter() function initiates the filtering. The syntax for these functions is:

```
dw_control.SetFilter( filter_expression)
dw_control.Filter()
```

where

> **filter_expression** is a string that contains the complete logical filter expression.

The best way to explain the format for the filter expression is to give an example. To filter out employees whose salary is less than $50,000.00, use the following filter expression:

```
dw_emp.SetFilter("salary >= 50000")
dw_emp.Filter()
```

You can have filter expressions that use multiple criteria by using the logical operators OR and AND:

```
dw_emp.SetFilter("salary >= 50000 AND city = 'Boston'")
dw_emp.Filter()
```

19.10.8 Using DataWindow Events

Like on other components that we have used, within the DataWindow control are the events where you will place the code that performs actions such as error handling, custom validation, selecting rows, and more. There are many different events. We have selected some of the most commonly used events to discuss here. For a complete list, refer to your PowerBuilder 6.0 documentation or on-line help.

19.10.8.1 ItemChanged

The ItemChanged event is triggered when the user changes a value in the DataWindow and then presses the TAB key or clicks in another part of the DataWindow. This event could also be triggered by the AcceptText() and Update() functions. This is the fourth and final level in the DataWindow validation process.

Here is where you will place custom validation that will vary at runtime. You also have arguments that are passed into the event to gather information about what is being changed. These arguments include:

- **row.** The number of the row containing the DataWindow item whose value has changed.

- **name.** The name of the column containing the DataWindow item whose value has changed.

- **data.** A string containing the new data the user specified for the item (this will always be a string, even if the data type is of another variety. A data column, for example, might contain the string "1997-04-01."

If you use the RETURN statement to end the event you can pass an action code as part of the return to instruct PowerBuilder what to do next. Action codes are numeric values and are used as follows:

```
RETURN action_code
```

such as

```
RETURN 0
```

The valid values for action code in this event are:

- 0—(Default) Accept the data value.

- 1—Reject the data value and don't allow focus to change.

- 2—Reject the data value but allow the focus to change.

For example, suppose we only allow updates of the salary field of the employee list DataWindow if the employee's status is "Permanent." This validation happens in the ItemChanged event and appears as follows:

```
String ls_Status

IF (Name = "salary") THEN

ls_Status = dw_emp.GetItemString(Row, "status")

IF (ls_Status <> "Permanent") THEN
    MessageBox("Change Discarded",&
      "You can only change salaries for Permanent employees.")
    RETURN 2
END IF
END IF
```

19.10.8.2 ItemError

When an item in the edit control fails one of the levels of validation that requires processing by the system, the ItemError event is triggered.

The DataWindow will provide a standard error message of any of these errors, but by using the ItemError event you can handle the error and provide a custom-made, user-friendly error message. You can then use the action code to stop the DataWindow from displaying the default system message.

The following example checks to see if the column that was in error was the employee age column and then displays a custom error message to the user.

```
IF Name = "emp_age" THEN
MessageBox("Invalid Age",
           "Employees must be between the ages of 18 to 65.")
    RETURN 1
END IF
```

We use an action code of 1 in the above example to reject the data value, but tell the DataWindow not to display the standard error message because we have already displayed our own. The valid values for action code in this event are:

- 0—(Default) Reject the data value and show the system error message.
- 1—Reject the data value but don't show the system error message.
- 2—Accept the data value (in case you change your mind about the validity of the data).
- 3—Reject the data value but allow the focus to change.

19.10.8.3 Clicked

The Clicked event occurs when the user clicks a mouse button in the DataWindow. You can use the arguments in this event to obtain the information you require for your script. The elements of this structure are as follows:

- **xpos.** The x co-ordinate of the location of the mouse click.
- **ypos.** The y co-ordinate of the location of the mouse click.
- **row.** Contains the row number of the row that was clicked on. If the pointer is not above a valid row, the value of the row argument will be 0 (i.e., in the text area, in space in between a row, in the header, footer, summary or trailer).
- **dwo.** Contains a reference to the object in the DataWindow object that was clicked on, such as a specific column or text object.

The following example selects or deselects the row that the user clicks on:

```
dw_emp.SelectRow(Row, NOT dw_emp.IsSelected(Row))
```

In the example, we call the SelectRow() function for the dw_emp DataWindow. For the first argument, the row number that we want to affect, we use the Row argument. For the second argument we embed another function of the DataWindow called IsSelected() which will tell us if the row specified is currently selected or not. We use the NOT operator to provide us with the opposite of the boolean returned by the IsSelected() function. Thus, if the row is already selected, it will be deselected, and if it is currently unselected, then we will select it.

19.10.8.4 Double Clicked

The DoubleClicked event is triggered when the user rapidly clicks twice in the DataWindow with the left mouse button. This event is often used as a "drill down" or to launch into an area to provide more information about a specific row of data. It can also be used to open search boxes in the DataWindow field that the user clicked. For example, if the user is entering an order in an order entry DataWindow and then forgets the part number being ordered, she can double-click the part number field to open up a Part Number Lookup window.

The DoubleClicked event arguments are identical to the Clicked event arguments.

19.10.8.5 RowFocusChanged

The RowFocusChanged event is one of the most useful events in the DataWindow control. The code for selecting rows and changing row focus can be located in this event. When you please the row selection code in the clicked event, row can only be selected with the mouse. According to GUI design principles, an application should have a complete keyboard interface. If you use the Clicked event, this leaves out the keyboard interface and forces the user to use the mouse. The RowFocusChanged event enables you to include that keyboard interface by allowing the user to use the arrow keys to change the current row in the DataWindow.

The RowFocusChanged event contains one argument that it is important to remember and that is *currentrow* which contains a number identifying the new current row in the DataWindow. We can use this information to always keep the current row highlighted using code like the following:

```
dw_emp.SelectRow(CurrentRow,NOT dw_emp.IsSelected(CurrentRow))
```

19.10.8.6 DBError

The DBError event occurs whenever a DataWindow function results in a database error. This is the event that should hold all your error handling for functions like Retrieve() and Update().

When the DBError event is triggered, you can find out more information about the through the event arguments. These arguments contain the database error code and the specific error message. You can then pass this information on to the user and take the appropriate action.

The DBError event arguments include the following:

- **SQLDBCode.** Contains the database specific error code. This code will be unique to your database and you will need to refer to the DBMS documentation for information on the meaning of the code. When the error that caused the DBError to fire was not directly caused by the database you may find the following values in this element:

  -1 Missing values in the transaction object.

  -2 Unable to connect to the database.

  -3 The key data in the row in the database is different from the data in the DataWindow. This usually means that another user modified the row after you had retrieved it into your buffer.

  -4 An attempt to write a blob to the database failed.

- **SQLErrText.** Contains the database specific error message.

- **SQLSyntax.** Contains the full text of the SQL statement that was sent to the database when the error occurred.

- **Buffer.** Specifies which buffer was the source of the SQL statement that caused the error.

- **Row.** Specifies the row number in the buffer that initiated the database activity that caused the error.

The valid action code values for this event are:

- 0—Display the default error message.

- 1—Do not display the default error message. Usually you will then display your own error message.

19.10.8.7 RetrieveStart

The RetrieveStart event occurs immediately prior to the DataWindow executing the SQL select statement, but after you execute the Retrieve() function. This event is often used to provide a visual cue to the user that a retrieval is underway, such as a custom icon or pointer, a popup window, or a progress meter that graphically displays the progress of the retrieve.

This event is a good place to find out how much data is going to be retrieved. You can use embedded SQL to count the number of rows to be returned, and then decide if you want to retrieve the rows or not based on the results. Users have been known to make data requests that would result in 50,000 rows being retrieved. This is probably an unreasonable amount, so you may decided to stop the retrieval, or warn the user before proceeding.

At this point you can still halt the retrieval using action code in the RETURN statement. The valid values for action code are:

- 0—(default) Continue with the retrieval as normal.
- 1—Don't perform the retrieval.
- 2—Perform the retrieval, but do not perform a reset before retrieving. This means that all the rows retrieved will be appended to the rows already stored in the DataWindow buffers.

19.10.8.8 RetrieveEnd

The RetrieveEnd event is very similar to the RetrieveStart event except that it occurs after the retrieval is completed. It may be used to remove any visual cue that you set in the RetrieveStart event.

The RetrieveEnd event argument rowcount will tell you the total number of rows that have been retrieved into the DataWindow.

19.10.8.9 RetrieveRow

The RetrieveRow event occurs after each row of data is retrieved by the DataWindow. This event can be used to provide a row-by-row count or to update a progress meter.

The retrieval can also be halted here if the number of rows gets too large using the RETURN action code syntax with the following values:

- 0—(default) Continue with the retrieval.
- 1—Stop the retrieval.

The event argument row contains the number of the row that was just retrieved.

> **Developer's Note:** Placing any code in the RetrieveRow event can signifi-
> cantly slow down the process of retrieving data as the code is executed
> after each row is retrieved. It is not generally recommended to use this
> event if your DataWindow is expected to retrieve significant amounts of
> data.

19.10.8.10 UpdateStart

The UpdateStart event occurs when the Update() function has been called on the DataWindow, but prior to any SQL statements being passed to the database. This can also be a good place to give the user a visual cue that an update is occurring.

The other key use of the UpdateStart event is to allow any external factors to decide if you want to proceed with the update or not. You can control if the update continues using the action code parameter of the RETURN statement. The valid values for action code are:

- 0—(default) Continue with the update.
- 1—Do not perform the update.

19.10.8.11 UpdateEnd

The UpdateEnd event occurs when the DataWindow finishes its update of the database. This event can be used to remove the visual cue placed by the UpdateStart event.

You can obtain some useful summary data about what kinds of actions occurred during the update by accessing the event arguments:

- **RowsInserted.** Contains the number of rows inserted in the update process.
- **RowsUpdated.** Contains the number of rows updated in the update process.
- **RowsDeleted.** Contains the number of rows deleted in the update process.

19.10.9 DataWindow Linking Example

It is common to have two DataWindow controls (and thus two DataWindows) in a form within an application. One DataWindow contains a high-level list of information, such as a list of employees. The second DataWindow contains details about the item selected in the first DataWindow. Alternatively, you can use this as a drill down technique where the first DataWindow contains the high level list (such as a list of departments within the company) and the second DataWindow contains the drill down information (such as a list of employees within the selected department).

To accomplish this functionality, these two DataWindows must be linked through the code in their events. When the user selects a row in the master DataWindow you want to populate the detail DataWindow. The code in the Clicked event of the master DataWindow might appear as follows:

```
dw_detail.Retrieve(dw_master.GetItemNumber(row,"dept_id"))
```

If we break down the above statement we see that we are executing a GetItem() function in the dw_master DataWindow control to obtain the department id that was clicked on. We know which row this is by getting the row argument from the Clicked event.

The department id that we obtain is then passed directly into the Retrieve() function for the dw_detail DataWindow which has been set to retrieve only those employees who are in the department that we specify.

19.10.10 Using the CloseQuery Event on a Form

The Close event is an event on a Window, not the DataWindow, but it has an important role to play in the DataWindow. If users change any values in the DataWindow, you want to be sure to ask them if they want to save the new data before they exit. You do this in the Close event.

This event executes after the form receives the instruction to close, either through the Close() function or through a system message like the user clicking on the close icon in the title bar of the Window. The script in the Close event can use the DeletedCount() and ModifiedCount() functions to find out if there is any unsaved data in the DataWindow and take appropriate action.

19.10.10.1 DeletedCount()

The DeletedCount() function determines the number of rows that have been deleted from the DataWindow (by counting the number of rows in the delete bufffer). The syntax for this function is:

```
dw_control.DeletedCount()
```

This function returns a long with the number of rows deleted but not updated to the database. It will return a 0 if no rows have been deleted since the last update or retrieval and a -1 if an error occurs.

19.10.10.2 ModifiedCount()

The ModifiedCount() function determines the number of rows that have been modified in the DataWindow (including inserted rows) in the DataWindow but not updated to the database. The syntax for this function is:

```
dw_control.ModifiedCount()
```

Like DeletedCount() this function returns a long containing the number of rows modified since the last update or retrieval, a 0 if no rows have been modified or inserted and a -1 if an error occurs.

19.10.11 DataWindow Reporting

The DataWindows that we have been discussing so far are all visual in orientation. You build them exactly how you want them to look. If you want to generate a report, you build the DataWindow in the format you want the report to be in. You can group the data into single or multiple groups, do calculations on the data, including custom formatting, sort and filter to organize the data and even add pictures and graphs. These reports can then be printed by the application using one simple function, Print().

19.10.12 Printing DataWindows

One of the real strengths of DataWindow is its ability to be both a strong visual interface, but also to be able to print its contents in a WYSIWYG (what you see is what you get) format. You can print DataWindow using the Print() function. The syntax for this function is as follows:

```
dw_control.Print( canceldialog )
```

where *canceldialog* is a boolean argument (TRUE or FALSE) specifying if you want to display a popup window allowing the user to cancel the print job while it is in progress.

This function will send the contents of the DataWindow to your default printer as a print job.

19.11 Summary

DataWindows are a key component of any client/server PowerBuilder application. The first step in building a DataWindow is determining what the source of the data should be. There are five possible data sources: QuickSelect, SQLSelect, Query, External, and Stored Procedure.

The next step is to determine how the data should be presented to the user. There are ten standard presentation styles: Tabular, Grid, Freeform, Group, N-Up, Crosstab, Graph, Label, Composite, Rich Text, and OLE 2.0.

Once these decisions have been made the result set for the DataWindow must be defined. This forms the foundation for the DataWindow. To customize the DataWindow (other than the result set) we close the SQL painter and enter the DataWindow design workspace.

In the design workspace you will customize the DataWindow by modifying the objects in the DataWindow bands. The DataWindow may contain a header, group header, detail, group trailer, summary, and footer bands.

All objects in the DataWindow can have their own properties defined including formats, edit styles and validation rules. Sorting and filtering can be used to modify how the user views the result set in the DataWindow by reordering it or only displaying rows of data that match certain criteria.

The DataWindow's powerful update capability is controlled by setting the update characteristics in the design workspace to control which table is updated and how the update will be performed.

Once the DataWindow is built, it then needs to be integrated into your application using a DataWindow control component which is placed on a form. All code that you write to work with and manipulate the DataWindow object will be contained or will address the DataWindow control.

Data that is entered by the user into the DataWindow is managed by the Edit Control which executes for levels of validation before accepting the data and storing it in the DataWindow buffer.

In this chapter we also reviewed many DataWindow functions and events that you will use often when dealing with DataWindows in your PowerBuilder applications.

By the time you complete this chapter, you should be able to create DataWindow objects and reports using DataWindows, attach them to your forms and use them in your applications to retrieve and update information in the database.

The DataWindow is a flexible and powerful tool. We have only addressed the most fundamental aspects of this complex control in this chapter. Future chapters in this book will take you into more advanced features of the DataWindow.

Advanced DataWindow Techniques

*O**ne of the number one reasons thousands of organizations have selected PowerBuilder as their standard development tool is the DataWindow. This object, recently patented by Powersoft, makes data access from your client/server applications a breeze. There is so much functionality in the DataWindow that in addition to learning the basics of the DataWindow in the FastTrack to PowerBuilder course, Powersoft offers a pair of two day advanced courses which covers nothing but advanced techniques for using DataWindows more effectively.*

We will assume that you are already familiar with the fundamentals of using a DataWindow, and we will focus on specific techniques to help you make better use of this powerful object. In this chapter, we will examine passing data to a user object, child DataWindows, sliding columns, edit masks and formats, dynamic DataWindow modification and creation, and advanced result set handling.

20.1 Copying Data Directly to a Non-visual User Object

With the growing usage of non-visual objects to provide services and business rule functions to our applications, we now have an easy way to transfer data from a Data-Window buffer directly into a non-visual (custom class) user object.

To do this you must declare instance variables in the custom class object in the same order and of the same data type as the column data being copied in. For example, if we want to copy a row of data from a table called bonus into a non-visual user object called nvo_bonus we would need instance variable declarations like those shown in Figure 20-1.

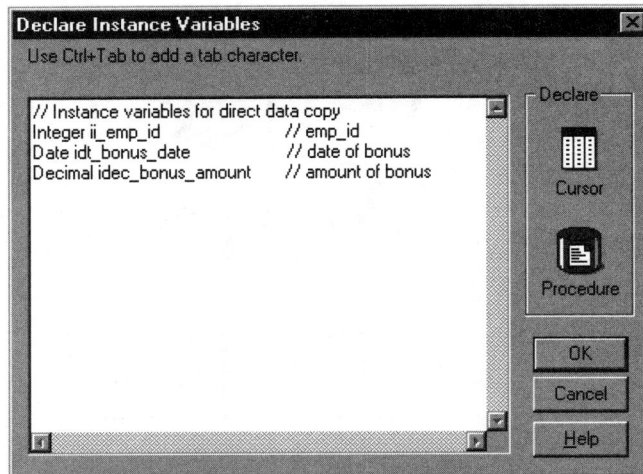

Figure 20-1. *Instance variables in nvo_bonus to allow us to move data directly into the non-visual object.*

To initiate the move of the current row of data from our bonus list DataWindow into our business object we would use the script:

```
invo_bonus = dw_bonus_list.Object.Data[dw_bonus.GetRow()]
```

These variables are now populated and ready for use in our custom class business object invo_bonus.

20.2 Child DataWindows

Sometimes you may want a Drop Down DataWindow to show a different list of options depending on some other outside value. To accomplish this we have to examine the concept of the child DataWindow a little closer. A child DataWindow is any DataWindow which is nested inside another DataWindow, and therefore dependent upon, another (the parent) DataWindow. Child DataWindows include Drop Down DataWindows, DataWindows inside a nested report and DataWindows placed onto a composite DataWindow.

Child DataWindows have most of the same functionality that their parents do. You can access all the methods and attributes inside the child, but to do so you must first obtain its handle. The child doesn't have a name at the window level like "dw_emp" or "dw_dept_list" which we can use to reference it. Instead we use a variable to trap the system handle, which uniquely identifies the object and allows us to reference it. We use a PowerScript function called GetChild() to obtain the handle.

20.2.1 Using the GetChild() Function

The GetChild() function allows us to obtain the handle for a child DataWindow which is nested inside its parent. The syntax for this function is:

```
dw_control.GetChild (column_name, child_handle)
```

where

dw_control is the name of the DataWindow control on the window which contains the parent DataWindow object.

column_name is the name of the column or object that contains the child DataWindow

child_handle is a reference variable of type DataWindowChild which is passed by reference. It will contain the handle of the child DataWindow upon successful execution of the function.

The function returns a value of 1 if the execution was successful or a -1 if it failed.

By default, the child DataWindow works in very close conjunction with its parent. It automatically picks up an uses the parent's transaction object and will retrieve its result set from the database when the parent is retrieved or has a blank row inserted into it. You can easily choose to override these defaults yourself.

20.2.1.1 Assigning a Different Transaction Object to a Child DataWindow

Let's say that you want the data in the DataWindow to use the transaction object SQLCA, but the data for the drop down DataWindow is to come from the database specified in the transaction object gtr_DB2TRANS. To make this work, you would have to obtain the handle of the child and then call the SetTransObject() function for the child before retrieving or inserting into the parent. Here is an example:

```
// Declare local variables
DataWindowChild ldwc_current
integer li_return
```

```
// Set Transaction object for parent
dw_parent.SetTransObject(SQLCA)

//Obtain handle of child DataWindow in the department column
li_return = dw_parent.GetChild("department",ldwc_current)

IF li_return = 1 THEN
        // Set the child transaction object
        ldwc_current.SetTransObject(gtr_DB2TRANS)
        ldwc_current.Retrieve()
        dw_parent.Retrieve()
ELSE
        MessageBox("DataWindow Error",&
        "Unable to obtain child DataWindow |
                handle.")
END IF
```

After setting a different transaction object for the child, you would retrieve the result set for the child and then retrieve the result set for the parent.

20.2.1.2 Populating the Child DataWindow

There are also multiple methods that you could use to retrieve the result set for the child DataWindow. You could let the parent manage all the needs of the child, you could retrieve the result set manually (with or without retrieval arguments), you could share the result set from another DataWindow object or you could create your own result set with the InsertRow() function.

20.2.1.2.1 Letting the Parent Manage the Child

The default process is that the result set for the child is retrieved from the database when the parent window receives a Retrieve() or InsertRow() function. If you have a number of drop down DataWindows in your parent DataWindow, you could incur significant overhead in trying to retrieve the first row of the parent result set because it will also be retrieving all the result sets for the child DataWindows.

For drop down DataWindows where the data is not used very often, the result set is small and the performance implications of the drop down DataWindow default process has minimal impact on the application, use the default process. It takes the least amount of code to manage and is generally very robust.

If you are using the same result set over and over throughout your application, it doesn't make sense to keep retrieving the same result set from the database. Or if you are retrieving a large result set and it has a significant performance impact on the speed of your application, you may want to consider buffering the data on your client workstation. The techniques and implications of this are discussed later in this section when we discuss "Buffering and Sharing a Result Set."

The default processing method will also not work if you have defined any retrieval arguments for your child DataWindow. You can use retrieval arguments in a child to customize the data that they will show at runtime, but if you let the parent manage the child, the result of a retrieve function on the parent would be to pop up a window that asks the user to specify a retrieval argument *for each row in the parent DataWindow result set*. Obviously not a desirable behavior. To manage this, we must manually retrieve the child result set ourselves. The technique and implications of this are discussed in the next section.

20.2.1.2.2 Manually Retrieving the Result Set

The parent DataWindow will only automatically retrieve the result set of the child if the child does not currently contain a valid result set. You can override the default functionality of the parent, but retrieving the result set into the child manually prior to issuing a Retrieve() or InsertRow() function on the parent. This also allows you to utilize retrieval arguments in the result set for the child DataWindow.

The technique for manually initiating a retrieval is very similar to the technique for manually setting the transaction object. The following example would retrieve a result set for the child that needs to know the security level of the user as a parameter as the child will only show options that are available for that security level.

```
// Declare local variables
DataWindowChild ldwc_current
integer li_return, li_security

// Set Transaction object for parent
dw_parent.SetTransObject(SQLCA)

//Obtain handle of child DataWindow in the "function" column
li_return = dw_parent.GetChild("function",ldwc_current)

IF li_return = 1 THEN
        // Retrieve the child result set, passing the users security
        // level (obtained from security non-visual object
        // on this window).
        li_security = THIS.invo_security.GetAccessLevel()
        ldwc_current.Retrieve(li_security)
        dw_parent.Retrieve()
ELSE
```

```
            MessageBox("DataWindow Error",&
            "Unable to obtain child DataWindow
                    handle.")
    END IF
```

This is the only option available if you are wanting to use retrieval arguments in your child DataWindows. If you want to simply retrieve the parent window populating the child DataWindow, this can be accomplished by creating a dummy result set for the child. Instead of performing the retrieve in the above example, use InsertRow(0) to insert a single blank row into the child. This is a valid result set, so the parent won't try to retrieve the child when it populates itself.

20.2.1.2.3 Buffering and Sharing a Result Set

A technique becoming more and more common in enterprise applications today is to buffer result sets for DataWindows and share them whenever a child window requires that same result set. For example, if you have a list of states and provinces that you use as a drop down DataWindow in a number of places throughout your application, this is a good candidate to buffer on your client. The result set for this commonly used data set could be retrieved and stored on a non-visual user object with a DataStore (in release 4.0 and earlier versions of PowerBuilder this functionality was achieved using a hidden window in your application with hidden DataWindows used specifically for storing shared data sets). Then when you use a DataWindow object that has a drop down list of states/provinces inside of it, you can share the result set with your non-visual data store. This will reduce the load on the server and make your application perform faster. For more detail on result set sharing, refer to the section on "Sharing Result Sets."

The important thing to remember when using a shared data store as the source of data for your drop down lists (and other child DataWindows as appropriate) that the data that you are accessing is only as recent as the last retrieval of the data store. This means that this technique is not good for data that changes frequently. Our example of a list of states and provinces above is a good use for this technique because this data is not likely to change with the context of your user session. Data such as inventory for a parts delivery system would probably not be appropriate information to buffer as other users activities will change the information in the database and the data that you have in your buffer may no longer be accurate.

The technique for sharing a result set would be to first of all create a non-visual user object or hidden window in your application which is populated at some convenient time. Usually they are populated as the application starts up. The users would usually prefer to take an initial ten to twenty second performance hit upon startup than to have regular half to one second delays as they are trying to process transactions. Let's assume that we have created a non-visual user object called u_nvo_data_storage. On this object is a DataStore called ds_states. We want to populate the result set for our DataWindow's states column drop down DataWindow by sharing it with the one in u_nvo_data_storage. Here is the code that would let us do this (the non-visual object has been instantiated on this window with the name iuo_data_store, although it could easily have been instantiated on the frame, or if necessary, the application object):

```
// Declare local variables
DataWindowChild ldwc_current
integer li_return

// Set Transaction object for parent
dw_parent.SetTransObject(SQLCA)

//Obtain handle of child DataWindow in the "states" column
li_return = dw_parent.GetChild("states",ldwc_current)

IF li_return = 1 THEN
    // Share the result set from the data store for states
    iuo_data_store.ds_states.ShareData(ldwc_current)
    dw_parent.Retrieve()
ELSE
    MessageBox("DataWindow Error",
    &"Unable to obtain child DataWindow handle.")
END IF
```

You can make use of filters and sort criteria to alter the display of the data in the result set, but you must remember that altering these criteria alters the primary buffer of the child, the original data store and also any other DataWindows currently sharing that result set! They all point to the same memory location at the same time, so any changes you make are universal.

20.2.1.2.4 Manually Creating a Child Result Set

The result set for a child DataWindow does not necessarily have to come from a relational database. You can create any result set you desire by using the InsertRow() function and then manually setting the values into the new row.

I have often needed to combine the manual retrieval of a result set and the manual insert of new rows to add options to the list that might now otherwise be there. For example, on one project, we wanted to provide a list of products in a drop down

DataWindow. This organization had new products that would be produced fairly regularly, so the database may not have always had the newest product in it. Within the list of products, they wanted to add an option called "<NEW PRODUCT>" at the top of the list, and if it was selected, to launch a dialog window that would create the new product in the database.

To accomplish this, we would manually retrieve the list of products and then perform an InsertRow() function adding the "<NEW PRODUCT>" at the top of the list. We would have to check in the item changed event of the DataWindow to see if the user selected this custom option, and if they did, take the appropriate action. The script for doing this was a simple variation of the ones that we have already discussed:

```
// Declare local variables
DataWindowChild ldwc_current
integer li_return

// Set Transaction object for parent
dw_parent.SetTransObject(SQLCA)

//Obtain handle of child DataWindow in the "product" column
li_return = dw_parent.GetChild("product",ldwc_current)

IF li_return = 1 THEN
        // Retrieve the child result set
        ldwc_current.Retrieve()

        // Insert a blank row at the top of the child DataWindow
        ldwc_current.InsertRow(1)

        // Populate the row to have a display value of "<NEW PRODUCT>"
        // and a code value of "*NP"
ldwc_current.object.data[1,1] = "<NEW PRODUCT>"
ldwc_current.object.data[1,2] = "*NP"

        dw_parent.Retrieve()
ELSE
        MessageBox("DataWindow Error",
        &"Unable to obtain child DataWindow handle.")
END IF
```

This example uses the PowerBuilder direct data manipulation syntax that was introduced in the 5.0 release of PowerBuilder. You can still use the PowerBuilder 4.0 SetItem() function if you desire. I still find that I am using SetItem quite a bit although this is most likely due to familiarity. If you wish to use the PowerBuilder 4.0 syntax it is:

```
ldwc_current.SetItem(1, "product_name", "<NEW PRODUCT>")
ldwc_current.SetItem(1, "product_code", "*NP")
```

20.2.1.2.5 Using Other Functions to Populate Your Child

In addition to the techniques we have discussed so far, you could also populate your child DataWindow through the use of ImportFile(), ImportString() or Import-Clipboard() functions of a DataWindow. These functions will expect to receive tab delimited data from a file, string or the windows clipboard. Alternatively, ImportFile() can also use dBase (.DBF) file as its data source.

20.2.1.3 Building a Linked Child DataWindow

It is possible to have a child DataWindow, as shown in Figure 20-2, within a window that will show a different list of options depending on what value is in a different column in the parent DataWindow. To build this link between the master column in the parent and the child, you should build a function which will adjust the result set displayed in the child.

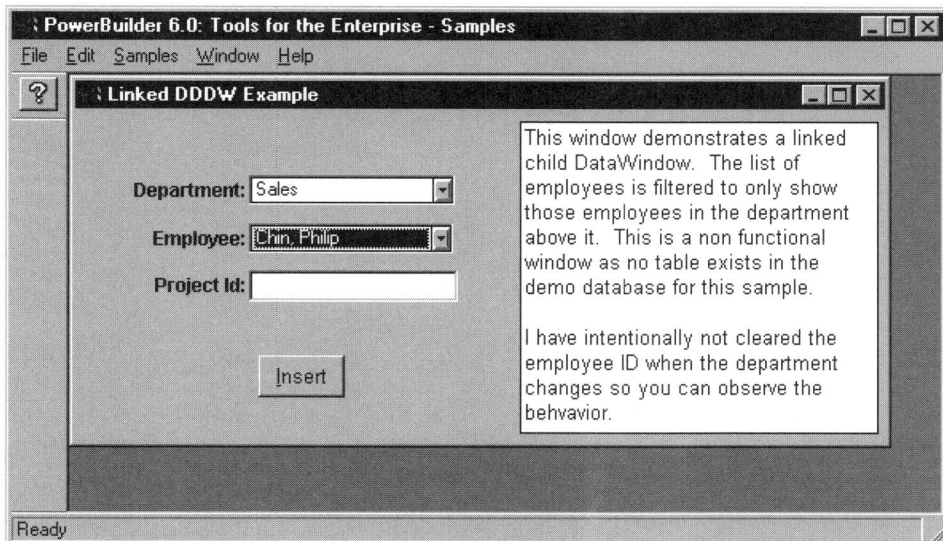

Figure 20-2.*The Employee DDDW in the sample Linked Child DataWindow is linked to the Department field. As the different departments are selected, only those employees in the departments are available for selection.*

The technique for altering the result set will vary depending on many different external factors such as the type of DataWindow presentation style being used. Most commonly, the result set is filtered differently in the ItemChanged event. Alternatively, you could do a ShareData with another data source, or re-retrieve the result set based upon new criteria.

20.3 Sliding Columns

Individual columns can be set to slide around within the DataWindow to eliminate excess space between column and/or rows. Look at Figures 20-3a and 20-3b. They show a set of mailing labels without any sliding columns, and then the same labels with the name fields and state field set to slide left and the address fields all set to slide up.

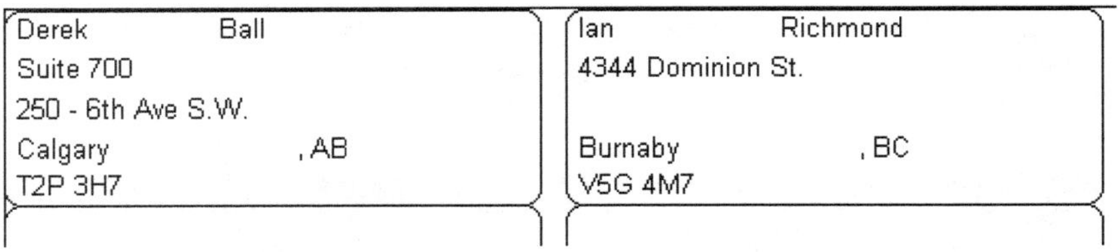

*Figure 20-3a. A pair of mailing labels with no sliding.
These appear blocked and unprofessional.*

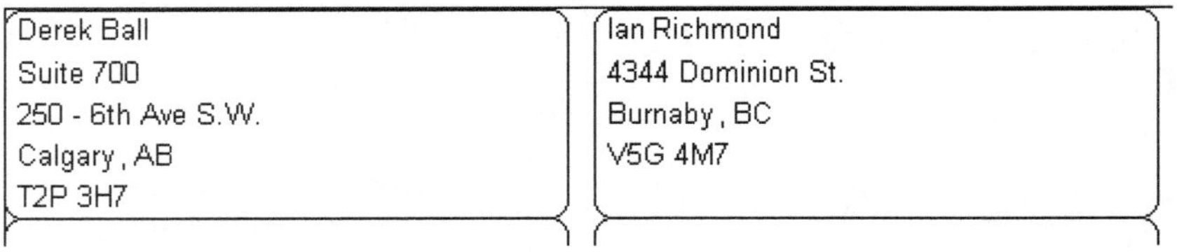

*Figure 20-3b. The same mailing labels with the name fields (including the comma)
and the state field (also including the comma) set to slide left and the entire
address set to slide up where applicable. This looks far more professional.*

The sliding options, as shown in Figure 20-4, allow us to build much more flexible DataWindows. They are particularly useful for forms and reports. They also eliminate the need for many of the standard computed fields that we have used in the past, such as combining an individuals full name into a concatenated field.

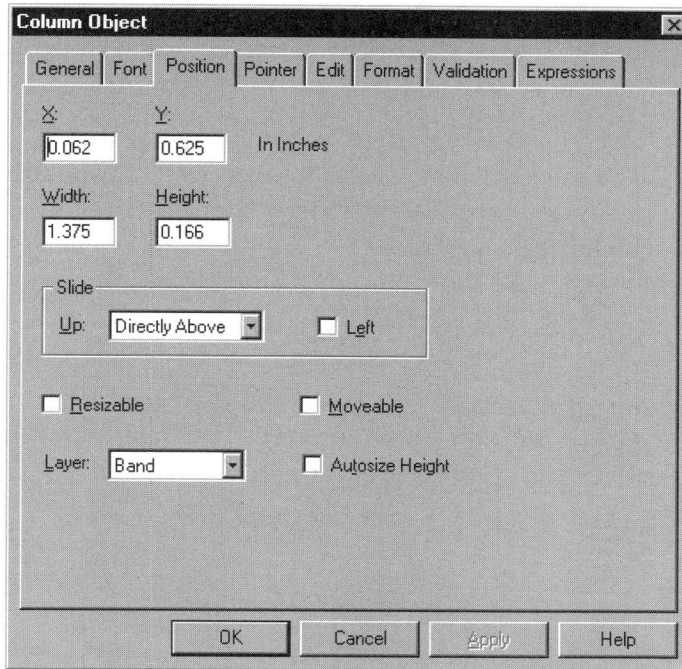

Figure 20-4. *Sliding options can be set on the Position tab of the Properties page for any object on the DataWindow*

The different sliding options can be set on the Position tab of the Properties page for any object on the DataWindow. There are two properties in the Slide group box:

Up. This property defines how you want this object to slide up. Your options are:

None: The object will not slide up.

All Above: This object will slide up as long as there are no objects containing data anywhere in the row above it. This includes objects which may be in the row, but not directly over the sliding object.

Directly Above: This object will slide up as long as there are no objects containing data directly above it in the DataWindow. Objects that are in the same physical row above the sliding object but are not positioned directly above it will not affect its slide.

Left. This property can be set to either checked (TRUE) or not-checked (FALSE). When set to true, this object will slide to the left and take up any excess space between it and any object to the left.

If you use the properties page, you can only change these properties for one object at a time. If you want to set the sliding properties for a whole group of objects, you can select the group and then use the toolbar icons to set the properties. There is an icon for slide left shown in Figure 20-5 and a drop down toolbar for the slide up property as shown in Figure 20-6.

Figure 20-5. A group of objects on a DataWindow can be selected and then all set to slide left by pressing the Slide Left toolbar icon shown here.

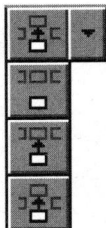

Figure 20-6. The same principal applies to setting a group of objects to slide up. You can select the appropriate slide up setting from the drop down toolbar shown here.

20.4 Dynamically Altering a Display Format

Display formats and edit styles are addressed in Chapter 19. There are some advanced functions which were not appropriate for including in that chapter, including dynamically altering a display format.

The display format for a column on a DataWindow is stored as a string. This makes it easy for us to read and alter dynamically at runtime. There are two techniques that you can use to do this; using PowerScript functions SetFormat() and GetFormat(), or through direct DataWindow object attribute manipulation.

The GetFormat() and SetFormat() PowerScript functions cross all versions of PowerBuilder and are still supported in PowerBuilder 5.0. GetFormat() returns the current display format of a DataWindow column. The syntax for GetFormat() is:

```
dw_control.GetFormat(column_name)
```

where

dw_control is the name of the DataWindow control, DataSource or child DataWindow that contains the column you want the display format of.

column_name is the name of the column (as a string) that you want to obtain the display format of.

GetFormat() returns a string containing the display format of the column. If there is no currently defined display format, the return value will be NULL. An empty string will be returned if an error occurs.

The syntax for SetFormat() is:

```
dw_control.SetFormat(column_name, format_string)
```

where

dw_control is the name of the DataWindow control, DataSource or child DataWindow that contains the column you want the display format of.

column_name is the name of the column (as a string) that you want to obtain the display format of.

format_string is a string containing the new format that you want to apply.

To do the same thing through direct manipulation you would use the syntax:

```
string_variable = dw_control.object.proj_id.format
```

String variable is a variable that you have declared to store the returned format string. Of course, you could use this property without having a storage variable by embedding it directly where it is required.

To set the format you would use the reverse syntax:

```
dw_control.object.proj_id.format = string_variable
```

Developer Note: The direct manipulation specified above replaces the functionality formerly provided with the Modify() and Describe() functions in earlier versions of PowerBuilder. You can still use the Modify() and Describe() functions to alter the column display format by using the syntax:

```
string_variable = dw_control.Describe("ColumnName.format")
dw_control.Modify("ColumnName.format = 'string'")
```

I have not encountered the need to dynamically alter the display format very often. Situations where you might include systems where the users have the ability to define their own display formats (for example, if they want to see currencies with decimal places or without) or if you don't know what kind of data a field will be displaying until runtime (for example, your system may hold the e-mail address of an individual which may be formatted differently depending on whether it is an Internet, Compuserve, AOL id or some other format).

Another excellent example of dynamically changing a display format. He uses it when working with credit card fields. Different credit cards expect to have the number segments separated in different areas (i.e., American Express has a different format than Visa). You can use this technique to set the correct format for the type of credit card.

The sample application on the companion CD contains an example of dynamically changing the display format of a field.(See Figure 20.7.) It uses an external DataWindow with a string field. You can experiment with altering its display format. You can choose between using direct manipulation or functions to change the format. Look at the code behind the command buttons to see how the above functions are applied.

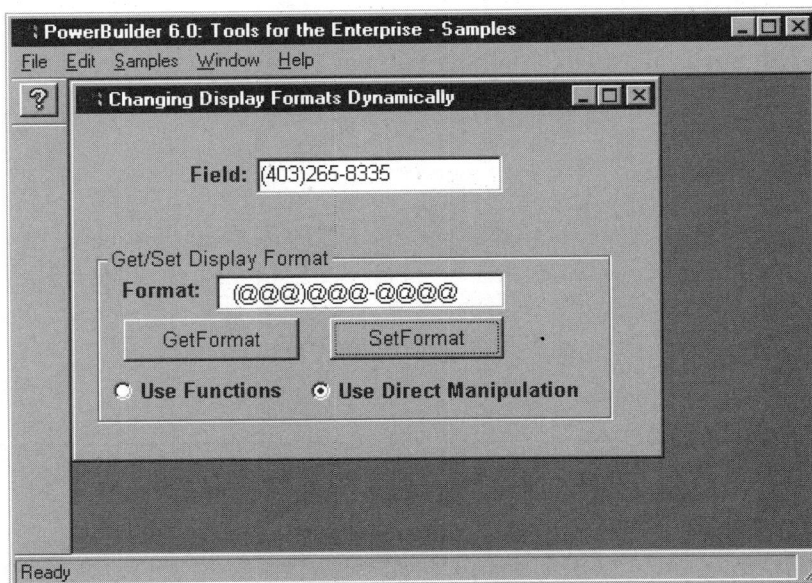

Figure 20-7. *The companion CD contains an example which allows you to dynamically read and alter the display format of a generic field in an external DataWindow.*

20.5 *Creating DataWindows Dynamically*

DataWindow objects can be generated dynamically at runtime. This feature of PowerBuilder is extremely useful when you don't know what information the end user is going to want to deal with until the application is running.

I have used dynamic DataWindows often for two specific types of situations. The first situation is for low level maintenance of tables. If you want to build the ability to select and maintain tables at a low level into your application you don't want to build and store a separate DataWindow for each table. This would be an efficiency and maintenance nightmare. Instead we read the list of tables from the system table and let the user select the one they want to maintain. Then we dynamically create a DataWindow to allow the user to browse and tweak the data in the table. Obviously this has some limitations, you don't want to allow the user to perform a retrieval on a table with 3 million rows of data!

The second situation where dynamic DataWindows are often used is with user ad-hoc queries. Based upon user input, we can dynamically generate the DataWindow at runtime. I don't recommend going too overboard here and recreating InfoMaker. Use this for simple ad hoc queries. If the users need really powerful ad-hoc querying, you should obtain one of the third-party tools on the market specifically designed to do this.

The complete process for dynamically creating a DataWindow object is to:

1. Create a SQL statement.

2. Describe the form and style of the DataWindow object.

3. Generate the DataWindow object syntax using the SyntaxFromSQL() function.

4. Create the DataWindow object within an existing DataWindow control using the Create() function.

20.5.1 Building the Data Object Syntax

To build the syntax for the DataWindow object that is to be created, we must have created two strings. One string will contain the SQL statement that will be the data source for the object. The second string will contain the definition for the presentation style for the object.

We will use an example that will walk us through the process of creating the DataWindow dynamically. To begin, we need to set up our necessary variables:

```
// Declare local variables
string ls_SQL,          // holds the SQL statement
  ls_presentation,      // holds the presentation string
  ls_dwsyntax,          // holds the complete DataWindow syntax
  ls_errormsg           // holds any error returned by generation func.
```

20.5.1.1 The SQL Statement

The first component, the SQL statement could be derived from a variety of formats. You could allow the user to select the table, then the columns to include and then specify the where clause if you desire. To keep our example simple, we will use a SQL statement stored directly in the string variable ls_sql.

```
ls_sql =    "SELECT      company_name," +&
                         "fname," +&
                         "lname," +&
                         "city" + &
                         "FROM customer" +&
                         "WHERE ·city = 'Boston'"
```

Developer's Tip: If you want to dynamically build a DataWindow and then allow the users to use the same SQL statement many times but with different where clauses (very good for what if analysis of ad-hoc queries), build the SQL statement without a where clause and then use the Modify function later to add the where clause.

20.5.1.2 The Presentation Style

The second component that we require is the presentation string. This string is used to define all the details that you would normally have defined in the DataWindow designer. The syntax that we use is the same syntax that you see if you export a DataWindow object from the library painter and examine the text file.

Within the string we must specify a series of key words followed by attributes and values for those attributes in parenthesis such as:

```
"Style(Type = value)"
```

For a given keyword, multiple attributes can be set at one time by adding them all within the parenthesis such as:

```
"Style(Type = value    attribute2 = value2   attribute 3 = value3 …)"
```

The keywords that are valid to use in your syntax are:

- Style.
- Column.
- Text.
- DataWindow.
- Group.
- Title.

There is a huge number of combinations of attributes and keywords that you can use to build your DataWindow. These can get very complex, so PowerBuilder has a tool attached to it to help you build your syntax. It is a separate standalone application that can be found in the PowerBuilder main directory. The name of the application is dwSyntax and should be found as dwsyn050.exe. This useful tool will allow you to browse all the attributes, keywords and values and then cut and paste this into your scripts.

For our example, we are going to define the style of this DataWindow as grid. I would not recommend trying to build extremely complex DataWindows dynamically as this is very labor intensive work and suggests that maybe you should be using a reporting tool. Ad hoc queries are usually relatively simple. The code to set our variable ls_presentation is:

```
ls_presentation = "style(type = grid)"
```

If you do not specify a style type, PowerBuilder will default your dynamic DataWindow to be tabular. For other attributes, PowerBuilder will read the defaults from the system catalog. These are the same defaults that you have set up when you create a DataWindow object in the DataWindow painter. You can alter these defaults through the **Options...** command button on the window where you specify your data source and presentation style.

20.5.2 Rolling It All Together

Now that we have defined our SQL statement and our presentation string we need to combine them together to form a complete DataWindow syntax definition. To do this we use the function SyntaxFromSQL(). The syntax for this function is:

```
string_variable = SyntaxFromSQL( transaction_object, SQL_string,&
    presentation_string, error_string)
```

where

> **string_variable** contains the complete DataWindow syntax string.
>
> **transaction_object** is the transaction object with the details for the database that this object will be querying.
>
> **SQL_string** contains the SQL statement that is the data source for the DataWindow
>
> **presentation_string** contains the presentation style details for the DataWindow.
>
> **error_string** is a reference variable that will contain any errors that occurred in the syntax generation process. If this variable is empty then no errors occurred.

For our example, the code that we will enter is:

```
ls_dwsyntax = SyntaxFromSQL( SQLCA, ls_SQL, ls_presentation, ls_errmsg)
```

20.5.3 Creating the Object

The final step that we must complete to create this dynamic DataWindow is to call the Create() function. This function will take the generated syntax string and use it to define a DataWindow object within an existing DataWindow control.

The syntax for the Create() function is:

```
dw_control.Create( syntax_string, error_string)
```

where

> **dw_control** is the name of the existing DataWindow control within which you want to create the dynamic DataWindow object.
>
> **syntax_string** is the string that has been created using the SyntaxFromSQL() function.
>
> **error_string** is a reference variable that will contain any errors that occurred during DataWindow creation. This variable will be empty if no error occurred.

For our example, the script that we will use is:

```
dw_adhoc.Create( ls_dwsyntax, ls_errmsg)
```

Then we want to complete our retrieval process by coding a SetTransObject() and Retrieve() function.

```
dw_adhoc.SetTransObject(SQLCA)
dw_adhoc.Retrieve()
```

We can now perform all regular DataWindow activities upon our dynamically created DataWindow object.

20.5.4 Using a .PBL For Runtime Ad-Hoc Query Storage

You can use a .PBL as a mechanism for storing ad-hoc queries generated by users. Using the LibraryCreate(), LibraryImport() and LibraryExport() functions you can create your own user defined report library!

LibraryCreate() will allow you to create a .PBL dynamically to store your ad hoc reports in. LibraryImport() will allow you to take the object that is currently associated with a DataWindow control (this could be a dynamic DataWindow that you have created) and save it as a DataWindow object in a .PBL. LibraryExport() allows you to export the syntax from a DataWindow object in a .PBL into a string and use the Create() function to dynamically instantiate the object.

20.6   *Modifying DataWindows Dynamically*

A critical skill to master when working with PowerBuilder is the ability to dynamically modify a DataWindow object at runtime. In the past this was handled through a pair of functions called Modify() and Describe(). You can still use these functions in PowerBuilder 6.0, but now you can also read and modify all the attributes of the DataWindow through direct referencing. Direct referencing is generally preferable to using the Modify() function because the syntax throughout your scripts would be more uniform. I have heard (although not proven yet) that the Modify() function is marginally faster than using direct referencing, although the difference is very small.

Although direct referencing could replace much of the functionality of the Describe() and Modify() functions, it cannot eliminate them completely. Using the Modify() function is still the only way to create and destroy objects within a DataWindow object or to alter an expression within a DataWindow attribute.

Now that the direct referencing technique has been on the market for over a year, I still find most advanced Developers using Modify and Describe as their primary techniques for dynamic DataWindow modification, possibly due to familiarity with these functions.

Let's take a closer look at these two functions.

20.6.1 Describe

The purpose of Describe() is to return information to you about the various attributes of a DataWindow. For example,

```
dw_sample.Describe("DataWindow.Zoom")
```

would return a string containing an number indicating the current zoom factor of the DataWindow such as "100."

This function can also be used to return lists of information. I can request a number of complex attributes which will all be concatenated together in the result set. The function call

```
dw_sample.Describe("DataWindow.Bands DataWindow.Objects")
```

would return a string that contains a list of all the bands in the DataWindow separated by a tab character a "~t". When the bands are all listed the string will include a new line character a "~N" to separate the different elements. Then the string will list all the DataWindow objects each separated by a tab character. The string value would be:

```
'header~tdetail~tsummary~tfooter~Nemp_id_t~temp_fname_t~temp_lname_t~tsalary_t~
temp_id~temp_fname~temp_lname~tsalary'
```

I have inserted "~t" for tabs and "~N" for new lines. If you were to take this string and assign it to a multiple line edit you would see actual tabs and carriage returns.

In PowerBuilder 5.0 and 6.0 we can achieve the same result by using direct referencing:

```
mle_1.text = dw_employee_list.object.DataWindow.bands+"~n"+&
dw_employee_list.object.DataWindow.objects
```

The Describe() function will return the value for the attribute in a string format. If an error occurs the value will return a "!". When you are requesting multiple attributes and an error occurs in a later attribute, the string will contain all the values that were evaluated up to where the error occurred. If an attribute that is requested contains no value the result string would contain a "?".

One other use for the Describe() function which is not possible with direct referencing is the ability to apply an expression to a specific row and column and evaluate the result. This is accomplished through the format:

```
dw_control.Describe("Evaluate('expression','row')")
```

where

> **Evaluate** is a reserved word that activates the evaluate function of the Describe() method.
>
> **expression** is the expression that you want to apply to the column.
>
> **row** is the row number that you want to apply the expression to.

An example of the evaluate reserved word would be:

```
dw_control.Describe("Evaluate('If(age < 16 , 1, 0)', 15')")
```

This function would evaluate the age column in row fifteen. If the age is less than 16 then the function will evaluate to '1' otherwise it will evaluate to "0."

20.6.2 Modify

The Modify() function allows us to dynamically modify the properties of a DataWindow object at runtime. This function has been one of the best weapons in a PowerBuilder Developers bag of tricks. You can use the Modify() function to create objects within a DataWindow, destroy an object with a DataWindow object, or modify any of the attributes on a DataWindow or any of its objects.

20.6.2.1 Creating DataWindow Objects

To create an object within a DataWindow dynamically you embed the CREATE reserved word at the beginning of the modify string. Next you must add to the string the necessary information to define the minimum requirements for the object. These minimum requirements will vary for each different type of object. This is another situation where the dwSyntax program can be a tremendous asset as it will help you construct your CREATE statement through a point and click interface.

If we wanted to use the Modify() function to add a bitmap in the footer band of our DataWindow we would specify our Modify() function as follows:

```
dw_control.Modify("CREATE bitmap(band=header x='1' y='1' height='125'"+&
     "width='125' filename='c:\trash1.bmp' name=picture)")
```

This would create a "trash1.bmp" bitmap in the header band at the coordinates 1,1 with a width and height of 125 units and a name of "picture."

Refer to the dwSyntax program or the PowerBuilder documentation to see examples for creating other objects dynamically within a DataWindow.

20.6.2.2 Destroying DataWindow Objects

To remove an object dynamically from a DataWindow object we embed the DESTROY reserved word at the beginning of the modify string. This only removes the object from this specific instance of the DataWindow object.

To destroy an object you follow the DESTROY reserved word with the name of the object that you want to destroy. For example,

```
dw_control.Modify("DESTROY picture")
```

would destroy the object that we created in the previous section. This will work for all object types except for columns. When working with columns you can name the column directly or precede the name of the column with the reserved word "column" such as:

```
dw_control.Modify("DESTROY column emp_salary")
```

is the same as:

```
dw_control.Modify("DESTROY emp_salary")
```

Destroying cannot be undone, so be sure when you destroy an object that you really don't want it anymore. If you think you may need that object it the future, perhaps you only want to modify its visible attribute so it cannot be seen any more.

20.6.2.3 Changing DataWindow Attributes

The third reason for using the Modify() function is to change the attributes of a DataWindow object or an object within a DataWindow object. This is essentially the reverse of the Describe() function, and for the most part, this capability of the Modify() function has been replaced by direct manipulation of DataWindow attributes.

This variation of the Modify() function is still used if you want to assign an expression to a DataWindow attribute. For example, you want to apply an expression to the Salary.color attribute to be red if the salary is over $50,000 and green otherwise. To do this we would call the following Modify() function:

```
dw_control.Modify("salary.color=' "+ string(RGB(255,0,0)) +&
    " ~t IF(salary > 50000, 255,"+ string(RGB(0,255,0)) +&
    ")'")
```

The value that we specify for the attribute is a default value plus a tab (~t) followed by the expression that we want to use, all within quotation marks.

One of the drawbacks of the Modify() function comes when you need to debug a problem with your statement. The only parameter that the Modify() function takes is a string, so whatever you enter in the string is valid as far as the compiler is concerned. You won't know about any errors until runtime. The function returns a string value to you which will be empty if there were no errors encountered in the execution. If something failed to execute inside your Modify() function then the return string will contain an identifier to help you locate the error such as:

```
Line 1 Column 18:incorrect syntax
```

Then you have to go back to your code, and start counting the characters until you find column 18 and find the character that PowerBuilder didn't like. This can be a frustrating task.

If you are going to perform a large number of modifications to objects in a DataWindow, you could execute multiple Modify() function calls or multiple direct DataWindow manipulation statements. After either of these, the DataWindow will redraw itself. If you are performing a large number of changes this can have a negative performance impact.

There are two possible solutions to this; combine all the statements into a single Modify() function or create a DWObject variable to use in the direct manipulation. If you have a number of Modify() calls to the same DataWindow control, they can all be placed within the same string as long as you separate them with a "~t" character (an embedded tab) such as:

```
dw_control.Modify("emp_lname.visible = '1' ~t "+&
"emp_lname.color = '255' "
```

which would change the emp_lname to be visible and change the text color to red.

Because only one Modify() function is called, the DataWindow is only redrawn once.

Alternatively, you could declare a variable of data type DWObject. DWObject can contain any of the component objects of a DataWindow object. You assign the object that you want to modify and alter those elements as desired. For example:

```
DWObject ldwo_modify

ldwo_modify = dw_control.Object.emp_lname
ldwo_modify.Color = 255
ldwo_modify.Visible = 1
DESTROY dwo_modify
```

This would perform the same functionality as the Modify example above. When you are addressing a number of the properties of a specific DataWindow object, this code is more efficient that long hand direct manipulation. Once critical thing to remember however is that you must explicitly destroy the DWObject variable. If it passes out of scope the object within it will become "orphaned" and will remain in memory taking up space but serving no function.

20.7 Dealing with Large Result Sets

In client/server applications we strive to reduce the size of result sets that we request from the database. Large result sets tie up the server, the network and memory on our client. Reducing the size of the result set will improve the performance of the application and will improve the overall enterprise environment as less system resources are used. We have a number of different techniques that we use to either reduce the size of the result set, or try to deal with it in a more efficient way.

20.7.1 Retrieve As Needed

Retrieve As Needed is a property of DataWindow object that we can use to have the DataWindow only retrieve the result set in small blocks as the data is required by the user. When this property is set to true on the DataWindow and the Retrieve() function is called, a cursor is set up on the server and only enough rows to fill the available physical space (plus one) are fetched from the cursor. When the user cursors down or scrolls to the next page of data the next page is fetched and so on until the entire result set is retrieved.

This technique does not actually reduce the result set, but rather gives the user the perception that the performance of the application has increased because the first page of data appear very quickly. With a standard retrieval the first page of data will not appear until the entire result set is in memory. This option *may* reduce the result set retrieved because the user may only need to see a limited portion of data before finding what they require. At this point the retrieval can be canceled (the technique for doing so is described in the "Proving a Cancel Retrieval Option" section.

To activate this property you select from the menu in the DataWindow painter **Rows → Retrieve → Rows As Needed**. This can also be turned on in your script prior to issuing the Retrieve() function by coding:

```
dw_control.Object.DataWindow.Retrieve.AsNeeded = 'yes'
```

> **Developer's Tip:** Retrieve As Needed is automatically set to "no" if you have any sorting or filtering of the result set on the client (does not apply to sorting or where clauses executed on the server) or if you are using any aggregate functions (such as sum, average or count). These conditions override the Retrieve As Needed property because by definition, PowerBuilder requires the entire result set in order to complete those conditions.

Some of the functions that you use may be impacted by the Retrieve As Needed property. When used, the Retrieve() function will not return the total number of rows in the result set, but only the number of rows fetched in the first set (which is the number of rows it takes to fill the physical space allocated for the DataWindow control plus one). The RowCount() function will return to you the total number of rows that have been fetched into the client buffer so far. The only way to know how many rows are in the cursor on the server in total would be to perform a Count(*) embedded SQL statement prior to issuing the Retrieve() function (see the section entitled "Perform a Count(*) Calculation," for details on performing a Count(*) statement).

The events in the DataWindow are unaffected by this property. The RetrieveStart will be triggered at the beginning of the retrieval, the RetrieveRow will occur after each row is retrieved into the buffer and the RetrieveEnd will be triggered when the full result set is retrieved or the retrieval is canceled.

Developer's Tip: When using Retrieve As Needed, you must be careful as opening and keeping open a cursor on the server may tie up system resources and stop other users from accessing the table that the current user is retrieving from. This lock will stay in place as long as the retrieval is incomplete. This is a bigger issue on databases that lock at the page level (like Sybase) than those that lock at the row level (like Oracle).

To help prevent users being locked out while the user holding the lock goes for lunch, you may want to code a script in the idle event which will check for incomplete retrievals and cancels them after a period of inactivity.

An approach that I recommend for providing the user with the perception of improved performance would be to begin your retrieval with the Retrieve As Needed property set to yes. After you have retrieved the first page of data, turn the property off with:

```
dw_control.Object.DataWindow.Retrieve.AsNeeded = 'no'
```

This will cause PowerBuilder to retrieve the rest of the result set in the background. The user perceives faster performance because the first page of data appears much faster than if they had to wait for a large result set to be retrieved (although the system will be a little sluggish until the entire result set is brought down) and the user can begin reading and looking at the data while the system continues to work.

If you code your retrieval in an event that has been posted to execute after the Open event (meaning that the window has been painted) then you can turn the Retrieve As Needed to no immediately after the Retrieve(). If you coded the retrieval in the Open event of the window you will not want to turn off the Retrieve as Needed property until the window has painted (meaning that you must post an event with the above code in it).

20.7.2 Limiting the User's Query

Limiting the user to using a more specific query is a generic concept that you can implement in many ways. The concept behind it is that users are often prone to ask for more data than they require, particularly if they are coming from the mainframe world where large result sets are common. You can require the user to be very specific in deciding what limiting criteria will be applied to reduce the result set to a smaller and more manageable size than they might otherwise select.

The advantages to this are obvious; improved performance, less network traffic and fewer system resource used. However there are tradeoffs as you are probably limiting the flexibility of the user by forcing them to take specific actions. Also, even with limiting criteria, this does not necessarily guarantee a smaller result set. To help alleviate this issue, this technique can be tied in with the Count(*) SQL calculation.

20.7.3 Perform a Count(*) Calculation

Executing an embedded SQL Count(*) calculation before trying to retrieve a result set will allow you to determine how many rows will be returned by the database. Then you have the option of deciding to cancel the retrieval and require the user to specify a more limited result set if the total number of rows to be retrieved exceeds some maximum threshold that you have established.

This type of a process can cost you in terms of server load as you are essentially having to execute the same SQL statement twice to get your result set. The first SQL call counts the number of rows and the second returns all the rows that were counted in the first call. This can effectively double the amount of server time necessary to complete the transaction.

20.7.4 The RetrieveRow Event

The RetrieveRow event is triggered after every single row that is retrieve from the database and placed into the DataWindow buffer. In this event you can keep count of all the rows that are coming back and stop the retrieval at any given point. You could also give the user the option of choosing to continue with the retrieval or stop with the data that they have so far.

This script will count the number of rows retrieved in the DataWindow and ask the user if they want to quit after every 250 rows (we are assuming the creation of an instance variable of type double called idb_rows).

RetrieveStart Event:

```
// Reset Row Counter
idb_rows = 0
```

RetrieveRow Event:

```
// Increment the row counter (which was set to zero in
// the RetrieveStart event)
```

```
idb_rows ++
IF ((idb_rows/250) - INT(idb_rows/250)) = 0 THEN

        // Exact multiple of 250 rows
        CHOOSE CASE MessageBox("Continue?","We have retrieved a total of "+&
                     string(idb_rows)+" rows.  Do you want to continue?",&
                     Question!, YesNo!,2)

               CASE 1 // Keep Retrieving
                      // Do Nothing
               CASE 2 // Cancel the retrieval
                      RETURN 1
        END CHOOSE
END IF
```

The biggest problem with the RetrieveRow event is that coding any script in this event (even a comment) will cause your retrieval to slow down noticeably because it is having to do work in between each row retrieved. I would not recommend this technique as a general practice, although it has its obvious uses in certain situations.

20.7.5 Storing Data to Disk

When you cannot avoid having to retrieve really large result sets you can avoid trying to store all that data in RAM by setting the StoreToDisk property. This will cause PowerBuilder to create a temporary file on your hard disk. This is a valid option that you can choose when you have no other option, but you have to remember that accessing data stored on disk is substantially slower than accessing data stored in memory.

You can turn this property of the DataWindow object on by selecting **Rows** → **Retrieve** → **Rows To Disk** from the menu in the DataWindow painter.

You can also toggle this property in your scripts with direct manipulation with:

```
dw_control.Object.DataWindow.Table.Data.Storage = 'memory' OR 'disk'
```

One final word about this option: it only works in 32 bit environments. If you are planning to roll out your application in a 16 bit environment, you can't use it.

20.7.6 Provide a Cancel Retrieval Option

You can provide the user with a mechanism to cancel a retrieval in progress by using the function DBCancel() like this:

```
dw_control.DBCancel()
```

This function must be placed somewhere that a user can trigger it such as a command button. If you are using Retrieve As Needed, after each page of data is retrieved, the user can choose to go on as normal, or click on the "Cancel Retrieval" command button with the DBCancel() function scripted in the clicked event. For regular retrievals, you must provide a way for the system to allow another action to be processed. This can be accomplished by placing a line of code in the RetrieveRow event (even a comment will do). This will force the DataWindow to yield to other processing messages as they come in.

Developer's Tip: Whenever you have a long running script and want to provide a way for other windows tasks to process simultaneously you can add a *Yield()* function to your code. This allows the system to check the message queue and execute them if they exist. This will function better in a 32 bit environment. In the 16 bit environment, Windows will try to "time-slice" which can make your application jerk along in a rather unprofessional fashion.

You can also cancel a DataWindow retrieval by coding a

```
RETURN 1
```

in the RetrieveStart (to cancel before beginning a retrieve), SQLPreview or RetrieveRow events. This is the PowerBuilder 4.0 equivalent of a SetActionCode(1) function.

20.8 Sharing Result Sets

In PowerBuilder we have the ability to have multiple DataWindows share the same result set. This is extremely useful when you want to show two different views of the same data in different DataWindows.

An example of how this is often used in production enterprise applications is the list/detail paradigm. In this paradigm you have a window with two DataWindow controls on it. The first DataWindow control contains the entire result set, but only shows the necessary columns to differentiate one row from the next. The format of the first DataWindow is either tabular or grid. This DataWindow is called the list DataWindow.

The second DataWindow control is called the detail DataWindow. It displays all the information about the currently selected row in the list DataWindow, usually in a freeform format. Both DataWindows share the same result set, but display the information in different ways. This interface allows the user to move quickly through the data and perform updates on the rows that they want to change. (See Figure 20-8.)

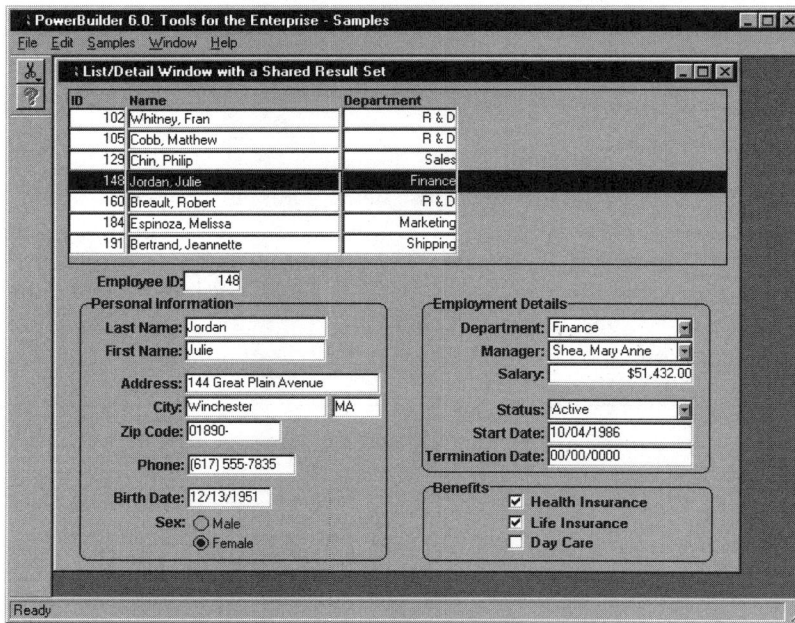

Figure 20-8. Sharing a result set has many uses such as the sample List/Detail window on the companion CD.

The sharing of result sets alleviates two problems with this type of retrieval. You only need to hit the database once to get all the information you need and you don't need to try and synchronize the data between the two windows. The two windows actually directly access the exact same set of buffers. When you make an update in one window, you are effectively updating them both. Sending a function call like Update() to a DataWindow control will cause the primary buffer to update regardless of which of the DataWindows you call the function on.

The result set actually belongs to one of the DataWindow controls. This control is called the Primary control. When you decide to link it to another DataWindow control, this control is the secondary control. You can share to as many secondary controls as you like.

The critical factor when using ShareData() is that all DataWindows sharing the same buffers must have identical result sets. If you try to do a ShareData() function but no data shows up, check to ensure that the result sets are identical. The where clause and sort order statements in your SQL will not affect the share. For example, results sets from these SQL statements can all share data together:

```
1.  SELECT emp_fname, emp_lname FROM employee

2.  SELECT emp_fname, emp_lname FROM employee WHERE emp_id > 250

3.  SELECT emp_fname, emp_lname FROM consultants ORDER BY consultant_id
```

Some developers like to use the query object as the data source when they know they will be sharing result sets to ensure that the result sets are identical. (See Figure 20-9.)

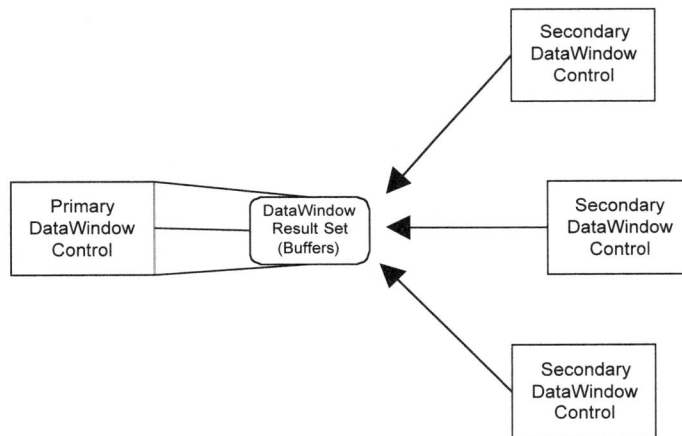

Figure 20-9. When sharing buffers between DataWindows, one DataWindow control is the primary control (it owns the buffers) all others are secondary controls.

The syntax for the ShareData() function is:

```
dw_primary.ShareData(dw_secondary)
```

where

dw_primary is the DataWindow control (with object) that will be the primary DataWindow. This is the DataWindow that has custody over the result set.

> **dw_secondary** is the DataWindow control (with object) that will share the result set of the primary DataWindow.

To stop the link between a primary and secondary DataWindow you use the function:

```
dw_control.ShareDataOff()
```

where

> **dw_control** is either the primary or secondary DataWindow control. If it is a secondary DataWindow control, then the link between those two DataWindows will be severed and the secondary control will appear blank. If it is a primary control then the links to all secondary DataWindows will be severed and they will appear blank.

You can potentially gain performance improvements with ShareData by reducing the number of hits on the database server. Another common use is to have a single DataStore or DataWindow which contains the data for frequently used drop down DataWindows and to share the data with the drop down DataWindows whenever they are used. This technique is discussed in the "Buffering and Sharing Result Sets" (for Child DataWindows) section earlier in this chapter.

There is one thing to be aware of when using ShareData. Since the actual buffers are shared, if you filter one of the DataWindows involved, you are actually going to filter them all. This means that you cannot retrieve your entire code table into one DataStore and then simply filter it for each drop down DataWindow you have.

Developer's Tip: You are not limited to sharing data only on the same DataWindow. You can, in fact, share data anywhere within an application. You can pass a DataWindow as a reference variable to another object and have the second object share data with the first. Of course, if the primary DataWindow is closed, the link will be severed to secondary DataWindows will be severed.

20.9 Using Bitmaps

Working in a GUI environment implies a strong use of visual cues and images. One way of adding to the visual side of your application is to take advantage of bitmap functionality in PowerBuilder. There are a number of different ways that you can use bitmaps in your applications. You can place them in picture controls, picture buttons, or in DataWindows as a visual enhancement, but you can also use them within the working area of a DataWindow to convey meaningful information.

20.9.1 Display As Picture

Text columns in the database can be used to store the name of a bitmap file stored locally or on a network file server. To activate this options, you must turn on the Display As Picture property which is on the General tab of the properties page for the column that contains the bitmap name. When this property is set to true, the column will be a display only column. (See Figure 20-10 and 20-11.)

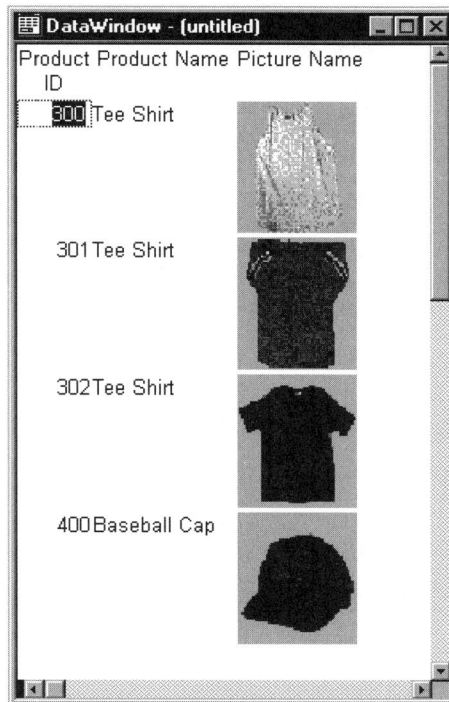

Figure 20-10. Using Display As Picture to display a meaningful bitmap in a column in the detail band.

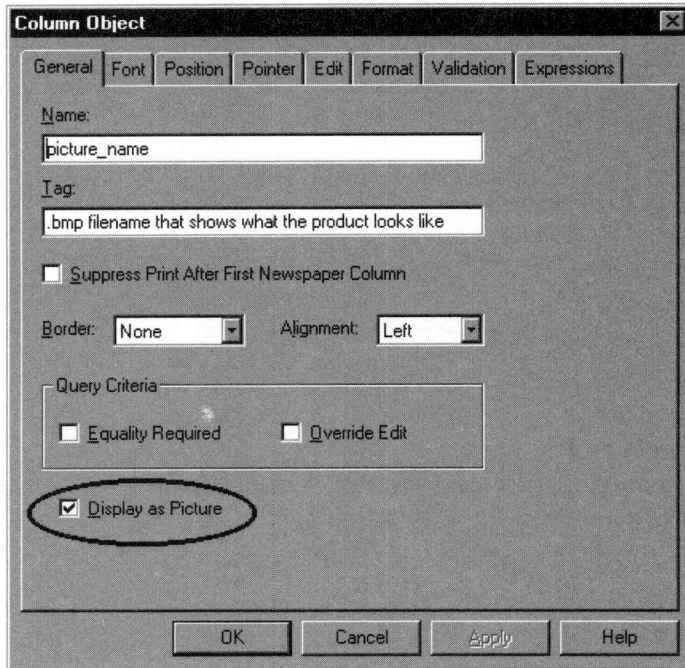

Figure 20-11. *The Display As Picture property will read a text column in the database and convert the text into a name for a bitmap file stored locally or on a networked server. The bitmap is displayed in the column space.*

20.9.2 Pictures in Computed Fields

Display As Picture can also be used in combination with a computed field to relate information to your user. You can define an expression and then use the Bitmap() function to convert a string to a bitmap image. In the sample application on the Shared Result Set example, we examine the employees salary and if it is over $45,000 we put a happy face bitmap, if it is below that we put a blue sad face. (See Figure 20-12.)

The syntax in the computed column is:

```
bitmap(if( salary >45000, 'happy.bmp', 'frown.bmp'))
```

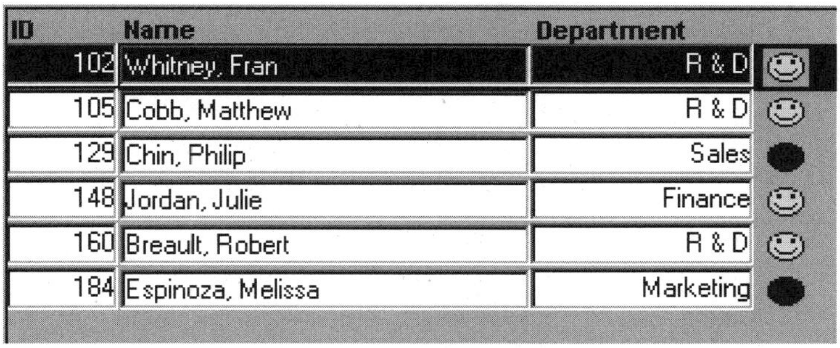

Figure 20-12. Computed fields can be used to display bitmaps based upon computed expressions.

20.10 Using the SQLPreview Event

The DataWindow has a special event called the SQLPreview event which fires immediately before the DataWindow sends a SQL statement to the database. In this event you can examine the SQL statement and decide to allow it to pass, stop it from going to the database, or replace it with a different SQL statement.

This event has a number of arguments that contain key information about the SQL statement that is being passed to the database:

request this argument will tell you which PowerScript function caused the current SQL statement to be generated. It will return an enumerated data type with one of the following values:

PreviewFunctionReselectRow! SQL statement was initiated by the

ReselectRow() function.

PreviewFunctionRetrieve! SQL statement is from the Retrieve() function.

PreviewFunctionUpdate! SQL statement is from the Update() function.

sqltype this argument will indicate what kind of SQL statement the current statement is. The value in this argument is an enumerated data type that equates to:

PreviewDelete! SQL statement is a DELETE statement.

PreviewInsert! SQL statement is an INSERT statement.

PreviewSelect! SQL statement is a SELECT statement.

PreviewUpdate! SQL statement is an UPDATE statement.

sqlsyntax this argument contains the complete SQL statement.

buffer this argument contains an enumerated data type that will tell you the identity of the DataWindow buffer that is either sending or receiving the data for this SQL statement. The possible values are:

Primary!

Filter!

Delete!

row this argument tells you the row number that is being updated, selected, inserted or deleted.

In your script for the SQLPreview event you can elect to continue, abort (if updating) or skip the current request and begin the next one (if one exists). This is accomplished through the return codes:

RETURN 0—continue

RETURN 1—Abort Update

RETURN 2—Skip current request

You can also alter the current SQL statement by using the SetSQLPreview() function as follows:

```
dw_control.SetSQLPreview(new_sql_string)
```

All of the above concepts are demonstrated in the sample application. This example has been added to the User Events window. You will see a checkbox at the bottom of the window which says SQL Preview. When this is checked, the SQL Preview event will open the SQL Preview response window (that is part of the sample application) where you can alter the SQL, Abort it, Skip it or Continue. (See Figure 20-13.)

In the open event of the window we have set the DBParm attribute of SQLCA to:

```
SQLCA.DBParm = "disablebind = 1"
```

disable the use of bind variables. If we leave the bind variables enabled, our update previews would have all the values filled with question marks ("?"). Disabling the use of bind variables while previewing allows us to see the actual SQL statement.

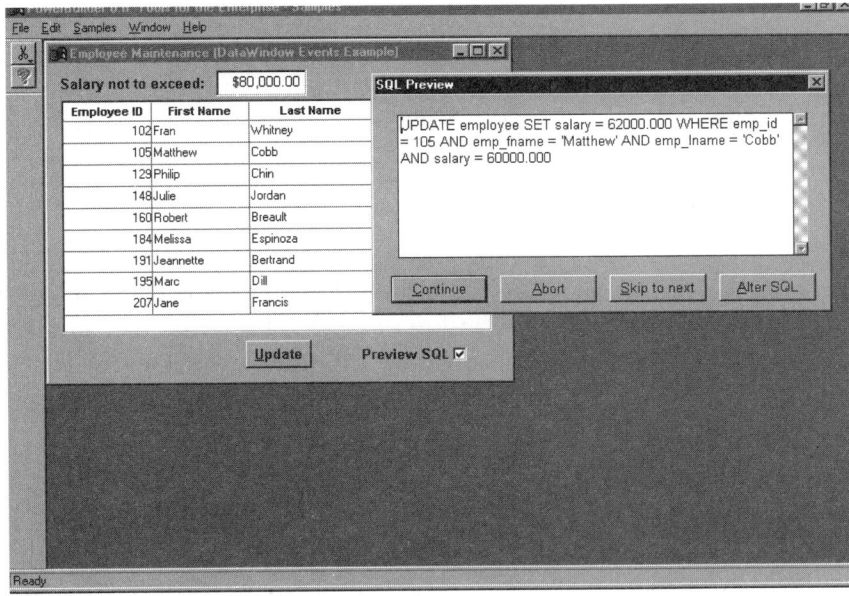

Figure 20-13. *The SQL Preview example in the companion CD application lets you preview and alter each SQL statement the DataWindow sends to the database.*

The DataWindow control has the following script in the SQLPreview event:

```
s_sqlpreview lstr_sqlpreview

IF cbx_preview.checked THEN

        lstr_sqlpreview.s_sql = sqlsyntax
        IF sqltype = PreviewUpdate! THEN
                lstr_sqlpreview.b_update = TRUE
        ELSE
                lstr_sqlpreview.b_update = FALSE
        END IF

        OpenWithParm(w_sqlpreview,lstr_sqlpreview)

        lstr_sqlpreview = Message.PowerObjectParm
```

```
        CHOOSE CASE lstr_sqlpreview.i_return

            CASE 0   // Continue
                RETURN 0
            CASE 1// Abort the process
                RETURN 1
            CASE 2// Skip the current request, but continue with
                // the next
                RETURN 2
            CASE 3// Alter the SQL then continue
                THIS.SetSQLPreview(lstr_sqlpreview.s_sql)
                RETURN 0
        END CHOOSE
    END IF
```

The window w_sqlpreview has a multiline edit where the user can edit the SQL statement and the four buttons shown in Figure 20-13. Each one will specify a different return value. If the return value is 3, then we will use the SetSQLPreview() function as shown above to alter the SQL statement that the DataWindow is sending. Give it a try in the sample application.

20.11 Advanced Updating

When you first start programming with PowerBuilder, you learn how to update one table at a time using the DataWindow in a very simple fashion. As an advanced developer you will encounter situations where you want to control this update at a much lower level, update multiple tables from a single DataWindow and use existing data rows as templates for new data rows.

To accomplish any of these things, it is important to understand the concept of status flags and how they are used in PowerBuilder.

20.11.1 Status Flags

As your user works with the data in the DataWindow buffers PowerBuilder assigns flags to the different rows and columns where the user has made changes. There is a single flag on each row. There are four possible row statuses and they are represented by enumerated data types:

New! indicates that the row has just been inserted, but that the user has not yet added any data to this row. When an Update() function is issued, rows with a status of New! will be ignored.

NewModified! indicates that this is a new row and the user has added data for at least one column in the row. When an Update() function is issued this row will result in an INSERT statement being passed to the database.

NotModified! indicates that this row was retrieved from the database and the user has not modified any of the rows. This row will be skipped in an Update() situation.

DataModified! indicates that this row was retrieved from the database and the user had made modifications to at least one column within the row. When an Update() function is called, this row will result in an UPDATE statement being passed to the database.

The flag on the row identifies to PowerBuilder what rows need to be updated and what kind of statement should be used. PowerBuilder still needs to know which columns in the DataWindow should be included. To this end we also have update flags attached to each column. There is a separate flag for each column of data. These flags have two possible values:

NotModified! indicates to PowerBuilder that this column has nothing new to report and should not be included in any SQL statement being generated.

DataModified! tells PowerBuilder that the user has changed the value in this column and PowerBuilder should build this column into any SQL statement being generated.

Upon a successful Update() function call, all the flags in the buffer are reset and the process begins anew. In a simple update situation, this default behavior is quite acceptable, but in our more complex updating this can cause problems. We will examine some complex updates in the following units.

20.11.1.1 Examining and Changing Status Flags

You can programmatically examine and alter the status flags on a row or column in your DataWindow. You can use this data for a variety of functions. One place that I like to take advantage of this functionality is to define an expression in the DataWindow that will show the user any data in the DataWindow that has not been saved. You can do this by changing the background color of the row. By clicking with the right mouse button on the "Detail" separator line in the DataWindow painter (the gray bar that you drag up and down to change the size of the detail band) we open up the Properties page dialog for the band. On the Expressions tab we set up an expression like the one in Figure 20-14.

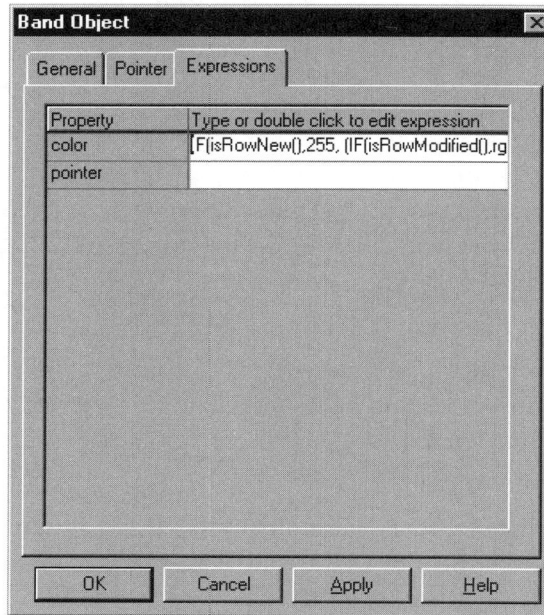

Figure 20-14. *We can use the status flags to define an expression for our DataWindow that will change the color of a row based upon its status.*

The expression that we would enter is:

```
IF(isRowNew(),255, (IF(isRowModified(),rgb(0,0,255),rgb(255,255,255))))
```

We can also access the status of a row in our scripts using the GetItemStatus() function. The syntax for this function is:

```
dw_control.GetItemStatus ( row, column, buffer )
```

where

row is the row number for which you want the status.

column is the column for which you want the status. A column value of 0 would return the status for the row. You can use either column number or column name.

buffer is an enumerated data type specifying which buffer you are getting the item status from. The valid options are Primary!, Filter! or Delete!

The return value for this function is an enumerated data type called dwItemStatus which would evaluate to one of the enumerated data types specified in the valid status types in the "Status Flags" section.

20.11.1.2 Coordinating Multiple DataWindow Updates

Although the bulk of your DataWindow updates will involve only one DataWindow, you will be faced with a number of situations where you will have two or more DataWindows that must be updated together within the same logical unit of work.

The natural tendency would be to update the first DataWindow and check the return code, update the second DataWindow and check the return code and if they were both successful, commit the transaction to the database. Let's look at an example that will book a ticket for a customer on an airline by recording the ticket in the dw_ticket_issued DataWindow and reserve a seat for them in the dw_seat_res DataWindow.

```
// Update the new ticket and seat selection
IF dw_ticket_issued.Update() = 1 THEN
    // Ticket Update successful, now update the seat selection
    IF dw_seat_res.Update() = 1 THEN
        // Both updates successful, commit changes to database
        COMMIT USING SQLCA;
    ELSE
        // Seat selection failed, rollback transaction
        ROLLBACK USING SQLCA;
    END IF
ELSE
    // Ticket update failed, rollback transaction
    ROLLBACK USING SQLCA;
END IF
```

This works fine as long as you don't encounter any errors. If the update of the ticket table fails then the transaction rolls back and everything is fine. The user can correct the error and try again. If the seat selection update fails, then we have a different situation.

The ticket DataWindow updates successfully and PowerBuilder clears all the update flags, thinking that everything is fine. The seat selection DataWindow then tries to update and fails. This failure causes a rollback of both the seat selection and the ticket updates. The update flags in the seat selection DataWindow are maintained because that is the DataWindow that failed, but the ticket DataWindow has cleared its flags.

Now if the user corrects their error and tries to execute the update again, the DataWindow is out of sync with the database and no changes will be sent to the ticket table. This second attempt will fail.

The obvious solution is that we need to stop PowerBuilder from automatically clearing the update flags and we will manually clear them when we are sure that the transaction has committed successfully.

To accomplish this, we have the ability to pass arguments with the Update() function to alter PowerBuilder's default behavior. The full syntax for the Update() function is:

```
dw_control.Update( accept_text, reset_flags)
```

where

> **accept_text** this argument controls if PowerBuilder will perform an accept text, validating any data in the edit control and passing it into the primary buffer before executing the update. If the data in the control does not pass validation, the update will abort. The default for this argument is TRUE.

> **reset_flags** this argument controls whether PowerBuilder will automatically reset the update flags upon a successful update. The default for this argument is true.

To take manual control of the flags we need to use the following syntax for our Update() function:

```
dw_control.Update(TRUE, FALSE)
```

If we look at our previous example, can directly substitute this version of the Update() function for the ones that we were using. Now that we have relieved PowerBuilder of the burden of worrying about the update flags, that task now falls upon our shoulders. If the updates are successful we must issue the **ResetUpdate()** function against all the DataWindows involved. The function must be called for each DataWindow individually using the syntax:

```
dw_control.ResetUpdate()
```

with no arguments.

Our example from earlier would now look like:

```
// Update the new ticket and seat selection
IF dw_ticket_issued.Update(TRUE, FALSE) = 1 THEN
        // Ticket Update successful, now update the seat selection
        IF dw_seat_res.Update(TRUE, FALSE) = 1 THEN
                // Both updates successful, commit changes to database
                COMMIT USING SQLCA;
                IF SQLCA.SQLCode = 0 THEN
                                // Successful commit
                                dw_ticket_issued.ResetUpdate()
                                dw_seat_res.ResetUpdate()
                ELSE
                                // Commit failed, call error handler
                                ROLLBACK USING SQLCA;
                                {insert your error handling code here}
                                // do not reset flags
                END IF
        ELSE
                // Seat selection failed, rollback transaction
                ROLLBACK USING SQLCA;
        END IF
ELSE
        // Ticket update failed, rollback transaction
        ROLLBACK USING SQLCA;
END IF
```

Now if the update encounters errors at any point, the updates will stop, the database will be rolled back to its previous state, and because the update flags are still in place, the user can retry the update after correcting the error.

20.11.1.3 Using Status Flags to Update Multiple Tables from One DataWindow

If I was to try and estimate the ratio of different types of DataWindow updates in an "average" application, I would say that around 80% of your DataWindows will be simple single DataWindow updates. Another 19% would be coordinated DataWindow updates involving two or more DataWindows. The remaining 1% (or less) would be single DataWindows that, when updated, need to update data in two or more tables on the Database. It is quite rare that I run into this situation, but knowing how to handle it has been has been invaluable on at least a few projects.

Let's examine the hypothetical situation where an employee table is joined to an address table on a one to one basis. We want to see the emp_id, emp_fname, and emp_lname columns from the employee table. In our DataWindow, these will be joined to the address table which has an address_id and address_description.

Our DataWindow will consist of a joined set of columns, as shown in Figure 12-15. The select statement would be:

```
SELECT employee.emp_id, employee.emp_lname, employee.emp_fname,
    address.address_id, address.address_description
FROM employee, address
WHERE employee.address_id = address.address_id
```

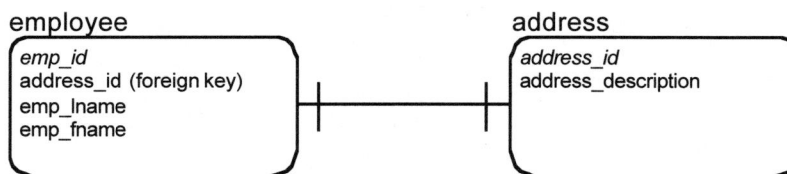

Figure 20-15. *The data model for our example.*

We will set up the DataWindow to update the employee table (remember, the DataWindow can only be set to update a single table in the DataWindow painter). We will update the DataWindow, stopping PowerBuilder from resetting the update flags. We can then point the DataWindow towards the address table using Modify() functions, or through direct manipulation. Then you adjust the flags that indicate which columns are updateable, set the key columns and reissue the update. This time, if the update is successful, we will commit and clear the update flags.

The script to do all this would appear like:

```
// Step 1:  Update the employee table
IF dw_data.Update(TRUE,FALSE) = 1 THEN
        // Update of the employee table was successful
        // Now we need to alter the characteristics of the columns
        // Step 2: Stop the employee columns from updating.
        dw_data.Object.employee_emp_id.Update = 'No'
        dw_data.Object.employee_emp_lname.Update = 'No'
        dw_data.Object.employee_emp_fname.Update = 'No'
        dw_data.Object.employee_emp_id.Key = 'No'

        // Step 3: Change the updateable table to address
        dw_data.Object.DataWindow.Table.UpdateTable = 'address'

        // Step 4:  Enable updating of address data
        dw_data.Object.address_address_id.Update = 'Yes'
        dw_data.Object.address_address_description.Update = 'Yes'
```

```
        dw_data.Object.address_address_id.Key = 'Yes'

        // Step 5:  Update the address table
        IF dw_data.Update(TRUE,FALSE) = 1 THEN
             // Update was successful
             COMMIT USING SQLCA;
             IF SQLCA.SQLCode = 0 THEN
                     // Successful commit
                     dw_data.ResetUpdate()
             ELSE
                     // Commit failed, call error handler
                     ROLLBACK USING SQLCA;
                     {insert your error handling code here}
                     // do not reset flags
             END IF
        ELSE
        // Update failed, call error handler
             ROLLBACK USING SQLCA;
             {insert your error handling code here}
             // do not reset flags
        END IF
    ELSE
        // Update failed, call error handler
        ROLLBACK USING SQLCA;
        {insert your error handling code here}
        // do not reset flags
    END IF

    // Step 6:  Set all the DataWindow characteristics back to the way
    // they were when we started.
    // Enable the updating of employee data
    dw_data.Object.employee_emp_id.Update = 'Yes'
    dw_data.Object.employee_emp_lname.Update = 'Yes'
    dw_data.Object.employee_emp_fname.Update = 'Yes'
    dw_data.Object.employee_emp_id.Key = 'Yes'

    // Change the updateable table to employee
    dw_data.Object.DataWindow.Table.UpdateTable = 'employee'

    // Disable updating of address data
    dw_data.Object.address_address_id.Update = 'No'
    dw_data.Object.address_address_description.Update = 'No'
    dw_data.Object.address_address_id.Key = 'No'
```

20.11.1.4 Using Status Flags to Create Templates

Another useful way of using the status flags in your applications is to use existing data
as a template for user input. I have been involved in many applications where the users
have indicated that most of the data that they enter is very similar to some data that they

have entered previously. They want to identify the row to use as a template and then just change the parts that are different.

To do this, retrieve the row that is being used as a template. Use the SetItemStatus() function to change the status from NotModified! To New!. The syntax for this would appear as follows:

```
dw_control.SetItemStatus(row, column, buffer, new_status)
```

where

row is the row number that you want to alter. For our example, this would be the retrieved row.

column is the number of the column whose status you want to alter. In our example we want to change the row status so we would use a column value of 0.

buffer is a enumerated data type with the identity of the buffer that you wish to change status in. Valid values are Primary!, Filter! and Delete!.

new_status this is an enumerated data type indicating the new status that you wish to change the item to.

For our example, the syntax would be:

```
dw_control.SetItemStatus(1,0,Primary!,New!)
```

You would then need to alter the key values programmatically, or blank them out and have the user enter them as appropriate. As soon as the user makes any changes to the row (or you do with the SetItem() function) the row status will change to NewModified! and will result in an INSERT statement being generated instead of an UPDATE statement.

20.12 DataStores

In pre release 5.0 versions of PowerBuilder it was very common for developers to use DataWindows in their applications that spent their entire life hidden. We were using these DataWindows as places to store and manipulate data, and we never required any of the front end functionality. This caused us to incur excess overhead in our applications because these hidden DataWindows had all the functionality necessary to interact with the user even though we never used it.

To remove this burden of overhead Powersoft has provided an object called a DataStore which is simply a DataWindow control with no visual component. This object was introduced in the last version of PowerBuilder, 5.0. You can associate a DataWindow object with a DataStore and avoid the overhead incurred by all the visual user interface functionality of a DataWindow control.

All the data manipulation functionality of the DataWindow control is present in the DataStore. You can still call functions such as Retrieve(), InsertRow(), DeleteRow(), RowsCopy(), and so on. The functions that you don't have access to anymore are the visually related functions such as SetRowFocusIndicator().

DataStores are non-visual objects. That means that they must be created in the same fashion as other non-visual objects, instantiating them in your scripts with the CREATE function. For example

```
// Declare DataStore variable
DataStore lds_datastore

// Instantiate DataStore
lds_datastore = CREATE DataStore

// Assign a DataWindow object to the DataStore
lds_datastore.DataObject = 'd_employee'

// Retrieve Data
lds_datastore.SetTransObject(SQLCA)
lds_datastore.Retrieve()
```

DataStores can also be created as standard class user objects (see Chapter 22—User Objects for more details on standard class user objects). Doing this allows you to encapsulate custom business rules or services into a DataStore object and reuse these objects throughout multiple applications.

Developer's Tip: Remember that any DataWindow objects that you are going to use with your DataStore are all dynamically referenced objects and must be included in either a .PBD (or .DLL) or brought into the .EXE file with a .PBR (PowerBuilder Resource File).

20.13 Summary

Use the information in this chapter to take your DataWindows to the next level. With these techniques you can improve your user interface, speed up your application execution, and manage your code more effectively.

There are still many more excellent DataWindow techniques that are in use, but this chapter has covered some of the most important. You should keep your eyes on the trade magazines where many new and emerging techniques are often featured.

CHAPTER 21

Advanced Reporting

*D*espite a wealth of third-party tools for report generation on the market, most *PowerBuilder projects choose to generate the bulk of their output directly from PowerBuilder. Why is this? Largely it is because of the flexibility and power of using the DataWindow to create reports. With the latest enhancements from PowerBuilder 5.0 and 6.0, almost any report that you can dream up can be constructed.*

At this point, I am going to assume that you have already built standard reports with PowerBuilder. This implies that you are familiar with the DataWindow painter at a fundamental level and can perform all the basic operations. We will not be reviewing these here. If you need more information on basic DataWindow construction, please refer back to Chapter 19. Instead, we are going to focus on more advanced reporting techniques; nested reports, composite reports, graphs and crosstabs.

21.1 Nested Reports

One of the tools that you have available to you for the building of sophisticated reports in PowerBuilder is the nested report. Nested reports are DataWindows that have other DataWindows embedded inside them. You can daisy chain as many of these DataWindows together as you desire and can effectively create a chain of DataWindows of different types and data sources within your parent DataWindow. Nested reports are sometimes referred to as "Basic Plus" reports in PowerBuilder documentation. (See Figure 21-1.)

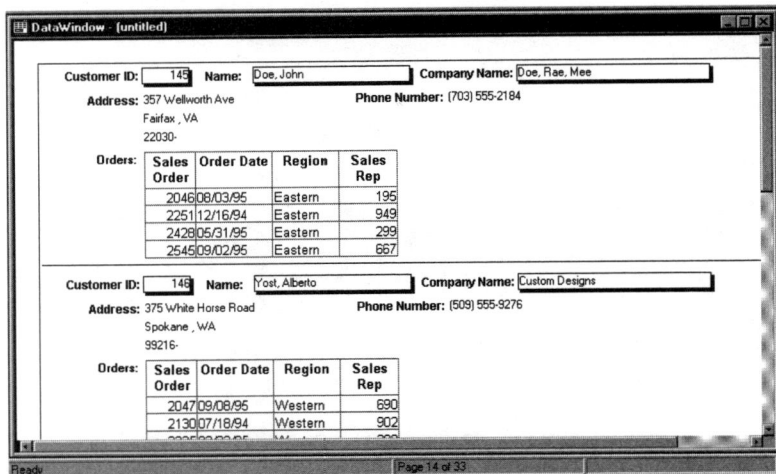

Figure 21-1. *A nested report is a DataWindow which has other DataWindows embedded within it.*

When you nest DataWindows, the object becomes exclusively a reporting object, you cannot use the data input and update DataWindow functionality in a nested report DataWindow object.

Your nested reports can be as many levels deep as you desire, or as your system resources can handle. You can accomplish this by building a nested report with an embedded DataWindow object, then you take that entire report and embed it into a new nested report, and so on. Each new report or DataWindow object can have its own presentation style and data source. You have the ability to link or daisy chain these reports through the definition of retrieval arguments that are linked to columns in the parent DataWindow. This will be demonstrated in the "Creating a Nested Report" section.

Developer's Tip: Nested reports can take a while to retrieve. Each level in the nesting can cause the retrieve time to increase almost exponentially. Try to keep the number of levels at a minimum, and for large reports, you will need to provide visual cues to the end user about what the system is doing.

If you have one nested report the DataWindow will first retrieve the master report. If this report brings back 100 rows then the DataWindow will need to execute 100 more retrieves (one for each instance of the nested DataWindow). This is a total of 101 retrieves. If the nested DataWindow itself contains a nested DataWindow, the retrieval effort could increase exponentially.

When you embed a DataWindow object into another (creating a nested report), you are adding an object to the parent DataWindow. This is accomplished by pressing the Nested Report icon in the DataWindow painter. The object that is created on the DataWindow cannot be treated exactly the same as other objects on the DataWindow such as columns, text fields and bitmaps. This is because within the embedded DataWindow there could be a number of rows of data, all containing multiple columns, and so on. This will restrict you from using the embedded DataWindow in a computed expression, filter, grouping, sorting or other activities which assume a much less complex object.

21.1.1 Creating a Nested Report

Nested reports are particularly useful for creating reports that rely upon a master/detail relationship in the data being reported on. Our example will use data from the PowerBuilder sample database that has just such a relationship.

We are going to build a report that will show all the sales orders for a particular customer, as illustrated in Figure 21-1. The database contains a table called Customer with the primary key cust_id. This links to the foreign key cust_id in the table Sales_Order. We will create a list of all the orders for a customer and embed that DataWindow into a freeform list of all the customers in the database.

Step 1   Create a DataWindow object to show all the orders for a specific customer. Open the DataWindow painter and select **New...** from the Select window. Then select SQL Select as the data source and Grid as the presentation style for your new DataWindow. Press **OK**.

Step 2   Build a SQL Select data source. Choose the sales_order table from the list. When the table appears, select the id, order_date, region and sales_rep columns.

Step 3   Define a retrieval argument. From the **Design** menu bar item, select **Retrieval Arguments...**. This will open the Specify Retrieval Arguments dialog window. Define a single numeric argument called ai_cust_id as in Figure 21-2. This will be used to link the embedded DataWindow to the parent DataWindow. When you are finished, press the **OK** button.

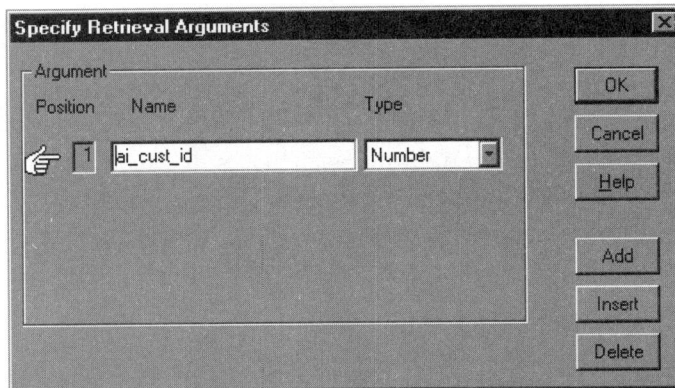

Figure 21-2. *Define a numeric retrieval argument called ai_cust_id. This will be used to link the embedded DataWindow to the parent.*

Step 4   Build the where clause. In the Where tab on the SQL Toolbox (at the bottom of your SQL Select painter) define a where clause to set the cust_id column equal to the argument defined in Step 3. The result should appear as in Figure 21-3. Remember that all arguments are host variables and must be preceded by a colon (":").

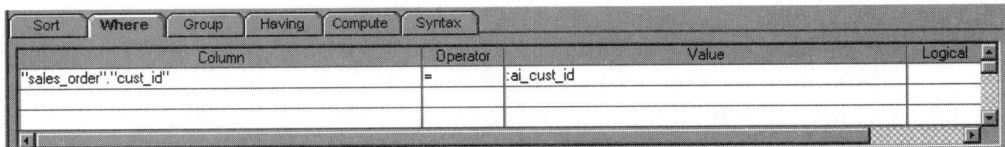

Figure 21-3. *Define a where clause in the SQL Toolbox where cust_id equals the argument defined in step 3.*

The complete SQL statement for this object is:

```
SELECT     id,
           order_date,
           region,
           sales_rep
FROM       sales_order
WHERE      cust_id = :ai_cust_id
```

Step 5   Go to the designer. Press the SQL icon in the painterbar to close the SQL. Select painter and move to the DataWindow designer (sometimes referred to as the "user interface painter").

Step 6 Customize to your specifications. Adjust the DataWindow object so that it conforms to your user interface specifications for reports. You can alter fonts, colors, column widths and other visual aspects. I have changed the edit style for region so that the drop down DataWindow arrow does not appear.

Step 7 Save the DataWindow. Save the DataWindow with the name d_orders_for_a_customer. You have now created the DataWindow object that we will embed into the parent DataWindow. Close the DataWindow painter.

Step 8 Create the DataWindow to show all the customers and their orders. Open the DataWindow painter. Select a new DataWindow and define it as having a SQL Select data source and a Freeform presentation style. Press **OK**.

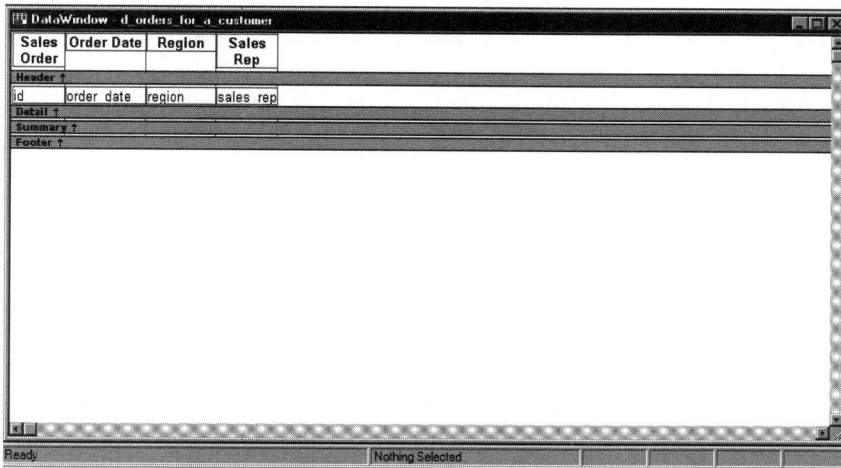

***Figure 21-4.** Adjust the DataWindow object so that it conforms to your user interface specifications for reports.*

Step 9 Define the SQL statement. Select the customer table from the Select Tables dialog window. When the table appears, select all the columns. The complete select statement for this table should be as follows:

```
SELECT   id,
         fname,
```

```
          lname,
          address,
          city,
          state,
          zip,
          phone,
          company_name
FROM      customer
```

Step 10   Go to the designer. Press the SQL icon in the painterbar to close the SQL Select painter and move to the DataWindow designer.

Step 11   Customize the interface. Customize the interface to make room for the embedded DataWindow. You can alter the column layouts and design as I have in Figure 21-5.

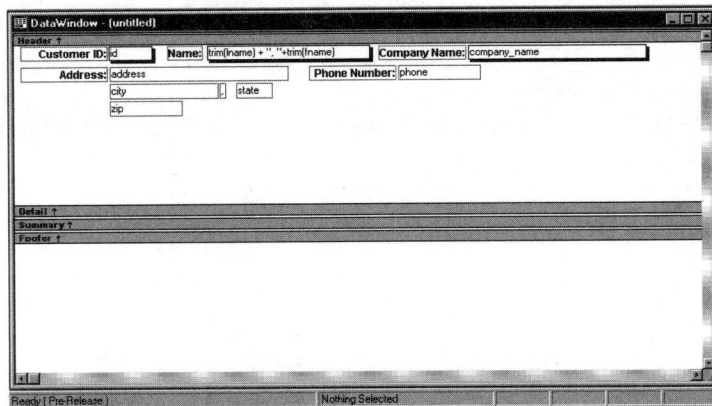

Figure 21-5. *Customize the interface allowing room for the embedded DataWindow and changing the fields to meet the report definition and standards.*

We have removed the first and last name columns and replaced them with a computed field called full_name. The computed field contains:

```
trim(lname) + ", "+trim(fname)
```

We have also added a text field between the city and state fields which contains a single comma. Both this text field and the state field have been set to slide left and eliminate the gaps between city and state.

Step 12 Add the nested report. To embed the nested DataWindow in this one, we first select the Nested Reports icon from the objects drop down toolbar. The icon is pictured in Figure 21-6

Figure 21-6. *The Nested Reports button in the toolbar is used to place a nested DataWindow on the current DataWindow.*

Next you will select where in the current DataWindow you wish to nest another DataWindow. When you do this, a small box will appear and the Report Object dialog window will open as shown in Figure 21-7.

The Report Object dialog window allows you to access and modify all the properties of the report object which you are nesting in the current DataWindow. The tab that comes up selected is the Select Reports. You will choose which DataWindow object you want to embed as a report in the current DataWindow. Select d_orders_for_a_customer from the list.

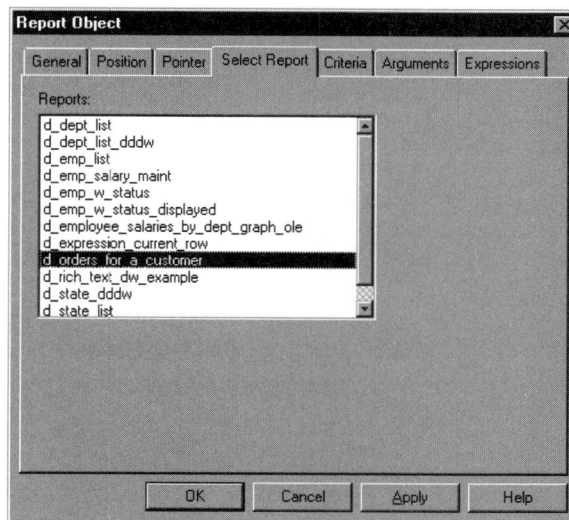

Figure 21-7. *The Report Object dialog allows you to access and modify all the properties of the report object which you are nesting in the current DataWindow.*

When you have done this, press the **OK** command button. Your designer should now show an object that has been resized to the width necessary to contain the report. The height of this object will be automatically adjusted at runtime to a height suitable to contain the number of rows being retrieved. Unfortunately, you don't see the DataWindow object that is nested inside the report object, although this isn't necessary for the object to function correctly.

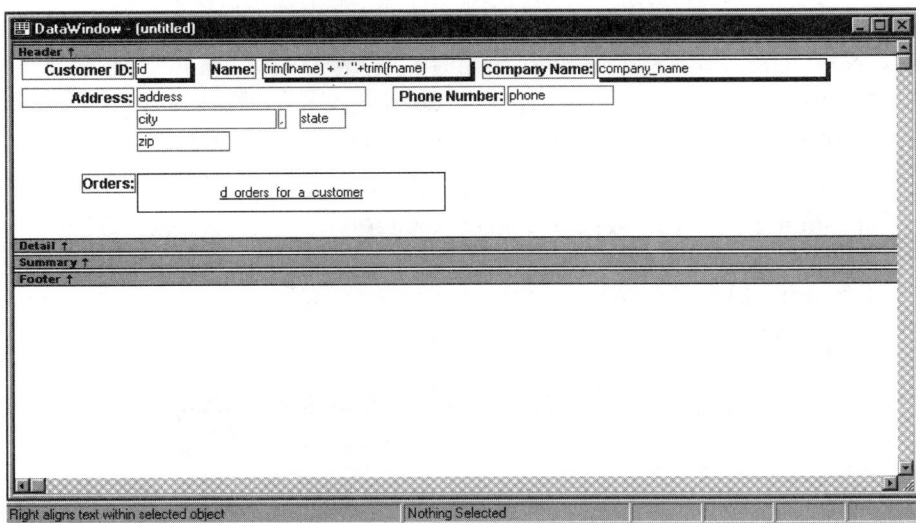

Figure 21-8. *The designer will show a report object on the current DataWindow that is wide enough to contain the nested DataWindow within.*

Add a text field with the label "Orders:" as a header for the report object.

Step 13   Link the embedded DataWindow to the current DataWindow. We must provide a mechanism to relate the embedded DataWindow to the current row of the current DataWindow. This will allow us to only show the orders for a specific customer as their details are displayed in the report. We do this by linking the retrieval arguments on the report object to something inside the current DataWindow. In our case we will link ai_cust_id, the retrieval argument in the nested DataWindow, to the id column in the detail band.

Click on the report object with the right mouse button. A popup menu will appear containing options such as Modify Report, Cut, Copy, and so on.

Select the **Properties...** option. This will reopen the Properties page for the report dialog. From here, select the **Arguments** tab as shown in Figure 21-9.

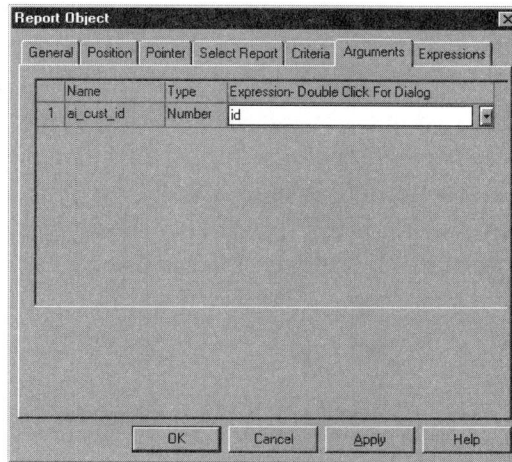

Figure 21-9. *The Arguments tab on the report object Properties page allows you to link the retrieval arguments of the nested DataWindow to an object or expression on the current DataWindow.*

This tab displays all the retrieval arguments defined for the nested DataWindow. You can link each retrieval argument to any referenceable object or valid expression on the current DataWindow. We are going to keep it simple and link the nested DataWindow retrieval argument ai_cust_id to the current value of the id column. Click on the drop down arrow and select id from the drop down list. For a more complex expression, double-clicking in the entry field would open up the expression dialog window.

When you are finished, press the **OK** command button.

Step 14 Save the DataWindow. Save the current DataWindow object as d_customers_orders_report. You can now preview the report by selecting the Preview icon in the painterbar. Your DataWindow should appear similar to the one shown in Figure 21-1 at the beginning of this unit. Watch the row count at the bottom of the screen and you can understand why it takes longer to retrieve the data set for a nested DataWindow object.

21.1.2 Using the Report Objects Properties Page

All the properties of a report object are conveniently located on the Report Objects Properties page which you can open by clicking on the report object in the designer with the right mouse button and selecting **Properties...** off the popup menu. Alternatively, you could open the dialog window by selecting the report object and clicking on the Properties icon in the painterbar.

There are seven tabs in the tab control inside the properties page. They cover general, position, and pointer properties as well as allow you to select the DataWindow object associated with this report object, set retrieval criteria, set values and expressions for the DataWindow arguments and to define expressions to dynamically change the overall attributes for the report object.

21.1.2.1 General Properties

The General tab on the properties page allows you to access the general attributes that affect the overall embedded object. (See Figure 21-10.)

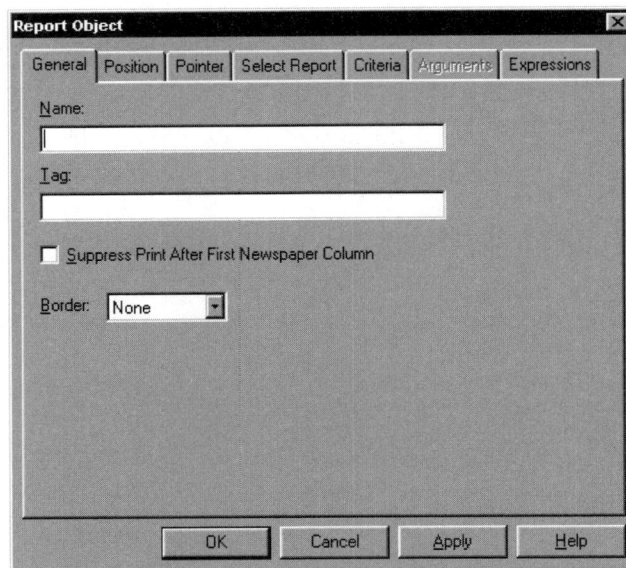

Figure 21-10. The General tab on the properties dialog allows you to change the name, tag, and border of the embedded report object. You can also enable the Suppress After First Newspaper Column attribute, which will stop this object from printing multiple times if the DataWindow is set to display in multiple columns.

These properties are:

Name defines the name by which the embedded DataWindow will be referenced from within the parent DataWindow.

Tag defines the tag value for the embedded DataWindow object. This is a string value which can be accessed at runtime. By default, it will not cause or affect any specific functionality. It can contain any information you would like it to such as a text string for Microhelp. Some third party class libraries access this field to determine how to set protection, colors or other properties at runtime.

Border defines what type of border will appear around the entire embedded DataWindow. In addition to the standard borders of 3D Raised, 3D Lowered, Shadow Box, and Box, you can also use an Underline border or a Resize border (the border does not provide resizing functionality, but only the visual double line around the object). Of course, you still have the option of no border at all.

Suppress Print After First Newspaper Column can be set to either TRUE or FALSE (checked or not checked). When displaying or printing your DataWindow using newspaper column formats, you can stop this object from repeating in columns subsequent to the first by checking this property. This is usually used in objects contained in bands other than the detail band.

21.1.2.2 Position Properties

The Position tab on the report object properties page contains properties that control the physical position of the embedded object in the parent DataWindow. Also contained on this page are the properties that control the sliding and resizing of this object.

In most applications, the Y position and the height of this object are not significant, as the object is repeated with multiple Y positions when it is instantiated, and the height is usually automatically sized at runtime based upon how much data is contained within the embedded DataWindow. The X coordinate and the width are more significant, as they will affect the physical position and size of the object. These attributes are not usually set on the tab, but rather are set in the parent DataWindow designer, where you can use drag and drop to position and resize the object. (See Figure 21-11.)

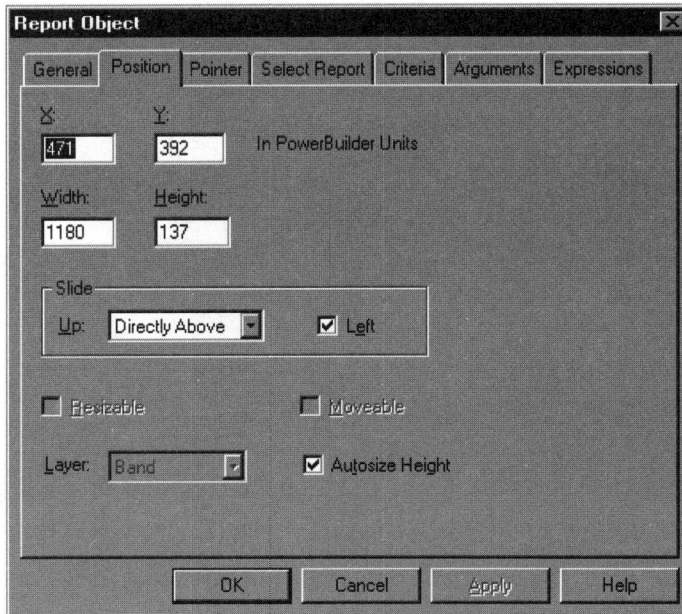

Figure 21-11. *The Position tab allows you to review and alter the physical position properties as well as the sliding and autosizing properties of the embedded DataWindow object.*

The Position tab properties are:

X. Defines the distance of the embedded DataWindow from the left edge of the parent DataWindow in whatever units the parent DataWindow is defined in (by default this is PowerBuilder units).

Y. Defines the distance of the first instance of the embedded DataWindow from the top edge of the parent DataWindow in whatever units the parent DataWindow is defined in. This attribute will dynamically change with each instance of the embedded DataWindow (assuming the embedded DataWindow is contained in the detail band) object, but will automatically maintain is position relative to the other objects that are also repeated with each instance of the detail band.

Width. Defines the width of the embedded DataWindow object in whatever units the parent DataWindow is defined in. The default width that will be assigned is the width of the embedded DataWindow object plus a small amount of space as a border (whether the border is visible or not).

Height. Defines the height of the embedded DataWindow object in whatever units the parent DataWindow is defined in. By default, the height will be set to automatically change based upon how much data is retrieved in each instance of the embedded DataWindow (see the Autosize Height property below).

Slide Up. Defines the upward slide properties of the embedded DataWindow object. The slide properties are similar to the slide properties for a column as discussed in Chapter 9—Advanced DataWindow Concepts. You can cause the embedded report to slide upwards, if there is empty space above it, or slide left if there is empty space to the left (see the Slide Left property). The choices that you have for sliding up are:

> *None:* the object will not slide up, even if empty space exists above it. *Directly Above:* the object will slide up if there is empty space directly above the space which it occupies.

> *All Above:* the object will slide up only if the space above the embedded report is empty for the entire width of the parent DataWindow.

Slide Left. Sets the DataWindow object to slide to the left if empty space or null fields exist to its left. It will slide until it finds an object that is not null. By default, this attribute is set to checked (TRUE). Setting it to unchecked (FALSE) will stop any left sliding from occurring. Slide up and slide left operate independent of one another.

Resizeable. This property is disabled for the embedded report as they cannot be resized by the user at runtime. You may notice the checkbox will become checked if you set the border to be Resize in the General tab, however, your embedded report will still not exhibit this functionality.

Moveable. This property is also disabled for the embedded report. The user cannot move the embedded report at run time.

Layer. This property is also disabled for the embedded report as all embedded reports must appear in the band layer.

Autosize Height. This property is by default set to TRUE. This will cause each instance of the embedded DataWindow to automatically adjust its height at runtime based upon the quantity of data which is contains. This will usually be left in its default state. If you uncheck this attribute (setting it to FALSE) each instance of the embedded report will be the fixed height defined in the height attribute, regardless of how much or how little data they have to show.

21.1.2.3 Pointer Properties

The Pointer tab for the embedded DataWindow object allows you to alter the pointer characteristics when the pointer is positioned above the embedded object (See Figure 21-12.)

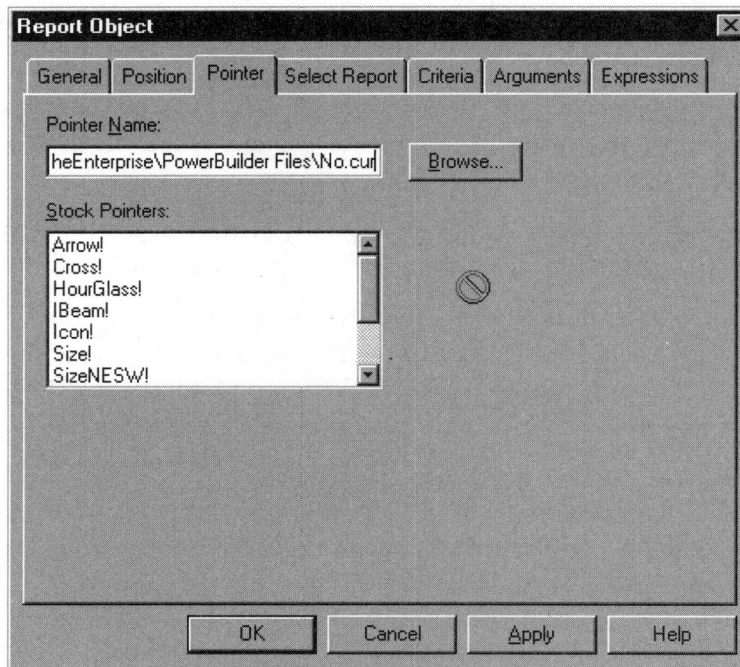

Figure 21-12. *The Pointer tab allows you control which pointer you want to appear when the mouse is positioned over the embedded object.*

The single Pointer tab property is:

> **Pointer Name.** Contains the name of the file which is a valid cursor file (.CUR) that you want to use for the pointer when the mouse is positioned above this object. The **Browse** button will allow you to search through your directories to find the cursor file, or you can use the **Stock Pointers** list box to select from the built in set of pointers. The standard windows pointers are built into the stock

pointer set (i.e., Arrow, HourGlass, Ibeam). If no pointer is defined, the object will use whatever pointer is defined for the parent DataWindow.

21.1.2.4 Select Report Properties

The Select Report tab we have already seen during the creation of our nested report in Step 12 of the above example. This tab contains the Report property (which is the DataObject attribute when accessing this in your scripts). You select the currently associated report from the list of available DataWindows in all the libraries in the application object library search path. (See Figure 21-13.)

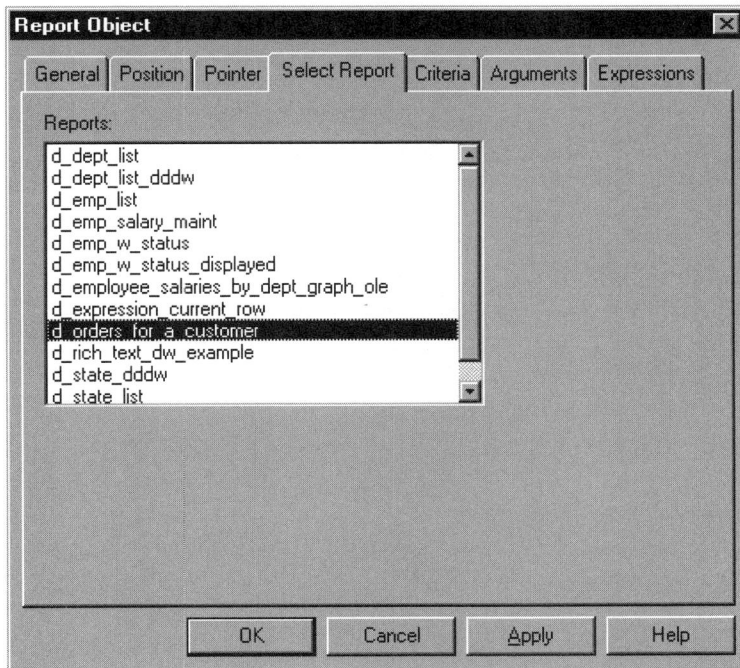

Figure 21-13. The Select Report tab allows you to select or change which DataWindow will be contained within this embedded object.

21.1.2.5 Criteria Properties

The Criteria tab allows you to define limiting criteria for the retrieval of data into this embedded DataWindow object. The method for doing so is very similar to the criteria window of a QuickSelect DataWindow.

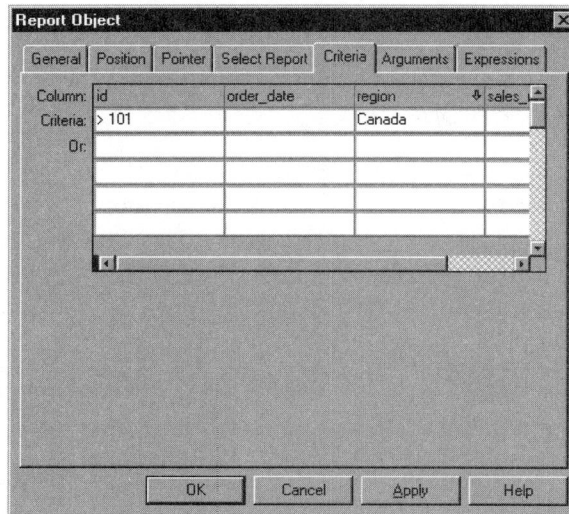

***Figure 21-14.** The Criteria tab contains a table where you can enter limiting criteria for the retrieval of data into the embedded DataWindow object.*

Criteria entered across a physical line will be linked together using a logical AND, whereas, criteria placed on two different physical lines will be linked together with a logical OR. The example in Figure 21-13 would result in the query being limited by a where clause of:

```
id > 101 AND region = 'Canada'
```

The actual where clause would contain the region code. The table automatically takes advantage of the predefined edit style to make our data entry easier. As you can see in Figure 21-14, the edit style defined for region allows us to pick the region from a Drop Down DataWindow.

In Figure 21-15, we see an example of a where clause that would be equal to:

```
region = 'Canada' OR region = 'Western'
```

Developer's Tip: Criteria placed on the same physical line can be ORed together simply by typing "OR" in front of the value. The same technique can be used to AND together criteria placed on two different physical lines.

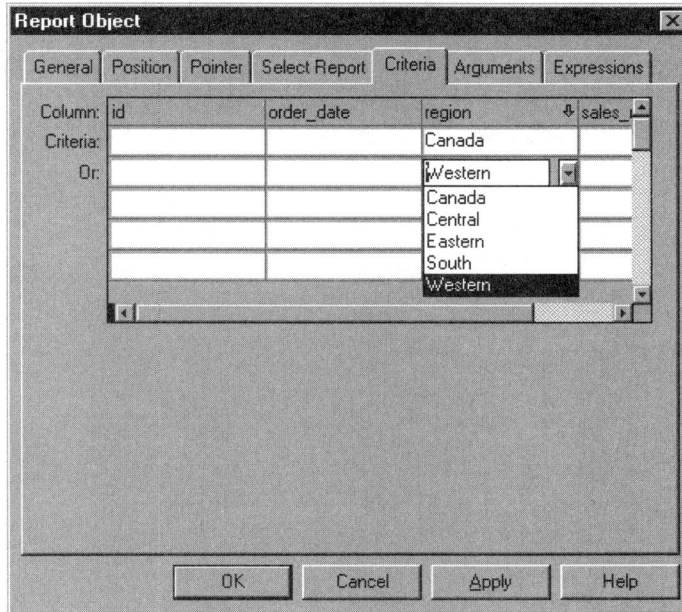

Figure 21-15. *Predefined edit styles are available to help you to enter criteria, like the Drop Down Listbox.*

21.1.2.6 Arguments Properties

The Arguments tab has been demonstrated in Step 13 of the example above. It is used to link any retrieval arguments defined for the embedded DataWindow object to columns and referenceable objects in the parent DataWindow. You can create any valid expression to pass information into the retrieval arguments for the embedded DataWindow. See Step 13 in the section "Creating a Nested Report" for more details.

21.1.2.7 Expressions Properties

The Expressions tab allows you to enter static and dynamic expressions for some of the general properties for the embedded DataWindow object. Although static expressions could be used, this tab is most often used to create dynamic expressions that are evaluated at runtime. An example might be to set the visible attribute to be as follows:

```
IF (state = 'CA',1,0)
```

This would have the effect of making the embedded DataWindow visible only if the customer was from California. (See Figure 21-16.)

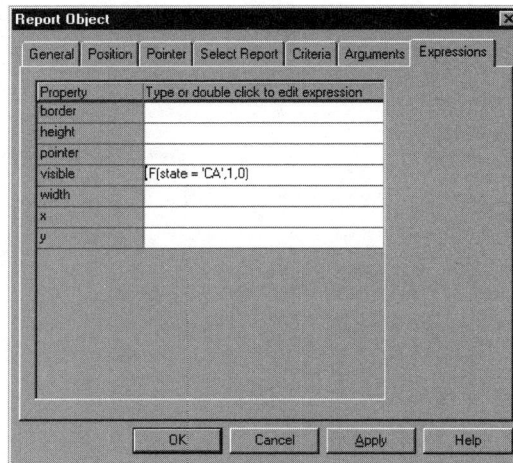

Figure 21-16. The Expressions tab is used to enter dynamic (or static) expressions that will change the properties of the embedded object dynamically at runtime.

PowerBuilder 4.0 to 5.0: This same functionality was available in PowerBuilder 4.0 through the popup menu that appeared when you clicked the right mouse button on a nested report.

21.1.3 Referencing a Nested Report In Your Script

From the applications that I have been involved with, the need to access a nested report from your script arises very seldom. This is largely because nested reports are read only and don't allow any database updates. However, should you need access to a nested report the technique is very similar to accessing a DataWindow object inside of a Drop Down DataWindow with one notable exception; you can read the properties of a nested report, but you can only change a few of them such as the border or the list of arguments. The nested DataWindows are also *child* DataWindows, however, you cannot use the GetChild() function to get the handle of the nested report.

If you are unsure if the parent DataWindow actually possesses any nested reports, you can check the *nested* property. This is done through direct referencing as follows:

```
ls_nested = dw_control.Object.DataWindow.nested
```

This syntax allows you to determine the nested attribute the DataWindow object associated with the DataWindow control you name. The variable, ls_nested, will contain either "yes" or "no" after this line of code is executed.

Direct Referencing Note: Determining if the DataWindow associated with a specific DataWindow control contained a nested report was accomplished with the Describe() function in PowerBuilder 4.0. This syntax will still function in PowerBuilder 6.0. If you are maintaining a PowerBuilder 4.0 application, the PowerBuilder 4.0 equivalent expression would be:

```
ls_nested = dw_control.Describe("DataWindow.Nested")
```

Remember that we cannot alter a property within the nested DataWindow object. Trying to code

```
dw_nested.Object.order_list.Object.DataWindow.color = 255
```

will pass the compiler, but will cause your application to terminate. You could read the color value and store it in a variable like:

```
li_color = dw_nested.Object.order_list.Object.DataWindow.color
```

As a reminder: refer to the dwSyntax program to see what attributes of the nested report you can dynamically modify and the correct syntax for doing so.

21.2 Composite Reports

The primary purpose of the Composite presentation style is to allow you to create a DataWindow shell to act as a container for multiple DataWindow objects that you want to group together as a single report. The DataWindows that are included can be data independent. That means that they do not have to have expressions that provide a link between them, and could have completely unrelated data inside. This presentation style and the nested report functionality overcome what was a major liability of PowerBuilder prior to version 4.0; the inability to print more than one DataWindow on a page.

Since the composite DataWindow is only a shell, it has no SQL statement of it's own, and you will not be able to select a data source option. All the DataWindow objects that you embed into the composite DataWindow will have their own data sources. You can however define as many retrieval arguments as you like and those arguments can be linked to the individual retrieval arguments in the embedded objects. The technique to do this is the same as the attribute linking technique described in the section called "Creating a Nested Report," Step 13.

You can also add other objects to a composite DataWindow including static text, bitmaps, drawing objects and computed fields. The computed fields can incorporate values passed as retrieval arguments. This allows you to do things like customize report titles based upon parameters passed at runtime.

Each of the embedded reports in a composite DataWindow are child DataWindows. You can use the GetChild() function to get a handle for the embedded report. Once you have this you can manipulate the child from your scripts.

21.2.1 Creating a Composite DataWindow

We will walk through the steps of creating the composite DataWindow that is included in the sample application on the companion CD.

Step 1   Create all the DataWindows which will be embedded within the composite DataWindow.

We will be including a list of employees, a list of products and a graph summarizing employee sales by product.

If you are feeling adventurous, create the following three objects:

Employee List—A SQL Select / Tabular DataWindow showing the employee last and first name (concatenated, separated by a comma and space) and phone number.
Product List—A SQL Select / Grid DataWindow showing a list of product names and unit prices.
Graph of Product Sales by Employee—A SQL Select / Graph DataWindow showing a for each employee, the total sales for each product type in a bar graph.

If you prefer to focus on only the composite DataWindow at this time, these three objects can be obtained from the sample .PBL on the companion CD. The object names are d_emp_list_comp1, d_product_list_comp2, and d_emp_sales_by_prod_comp3.

Step 2   Create a new composite DataWindow. Open the DataWindow painter and choose to create a New DataWindow. Choose the Composite presentation style. The data source and **Options...** button will become disabled once you select the composite presentation style. Press the **OK** button.

Step 3   Select DataWindows to include. A list of all the DataWindow objects in the current library search path will appear. You should select the objects that you want to include in your composite report. These will be the objects you created in Step one, or the objects provided on the companion CD. (See Figure 21-17.)

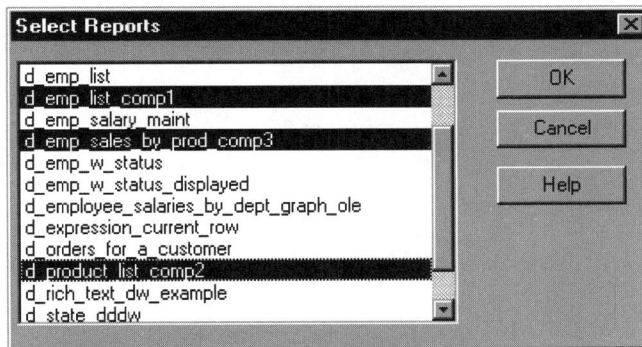

Figure 21-17. In the Select Reports dialog window, you will choose all the DataWindow objects that you want to embed in the composite DataWindow.

Step 4   Rearrange objects and alter the report. Press **OK**. Pressing the **OK** command button will take you to the designer. PowerBuilder will layout the selected objects in a default format. You will want to rearrange this in the fashion that you envisioned the report.

         We want to move the objects to present their information in a more clear. Let's place the graph at the top and resize it so that it takes up the width of the composite DataWindow. Place the employee list and the product list below it as in Figure 21-18

Step 5   Add headers and labels. Now let's add a header to the report which shows the date the report was run and who ran it (which we will pass as a retrieval argument). While we are at it, let's add static text labels for the list of employees and products.

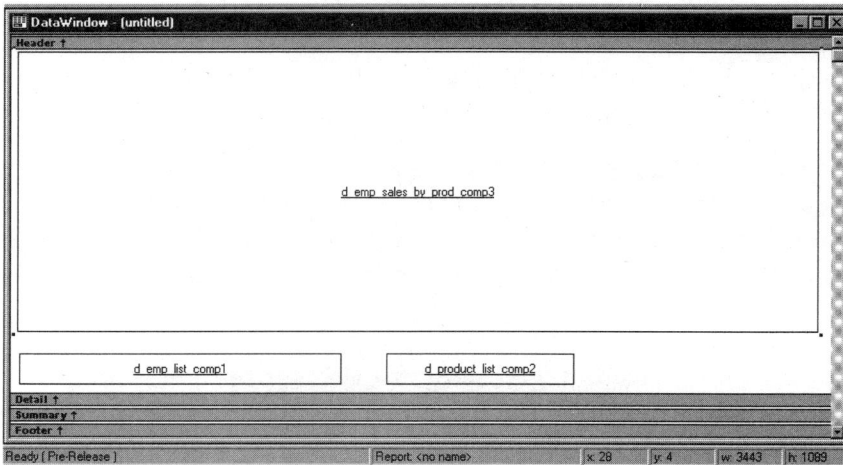

Figure 21-18. *We will rearrange the objects from their default positions to present our report in a clearer way.*

To add the retrieval arguments, click with the right mouse button on an empty area of the DataWindow object. Select the **Properties...** menu option. This will open up a properties page for the DataWindow object. Select the Retrieval Arguments tab as shown in Figure 21-19. Define a retrieval argument called "as_requested_by."

Increase the size of the header band to allow room to insert a "Printed Date" and "Printed By'" field. Adding the date field is quite easy. Select the Today's Date icon from the toolbar and place it in the header. Insert a static text field before it that contains the text "Printed Date:".

Adding the Printed By field is a little trickier. You have to fool PowerBuilder. By default, the computed field icon is disabled, so you cannot place a regular computed field in your report. However, we can place another Today's Date field and then edit the expression to be whatever we want! Add a second Today's Date field now. Add a second static text field with the text "Printed By:".

Now click on the second computed field that you added with the right mouse button and open the properties page. (See Figure 21-20.)

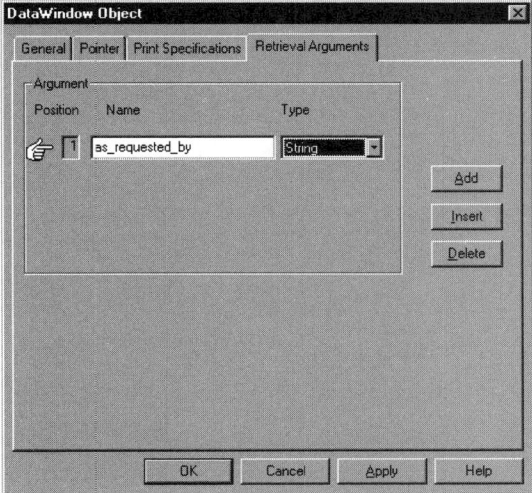

Figure 21-19. *Retrieval Arguments are defined on the properties page for the DataWindow object.*

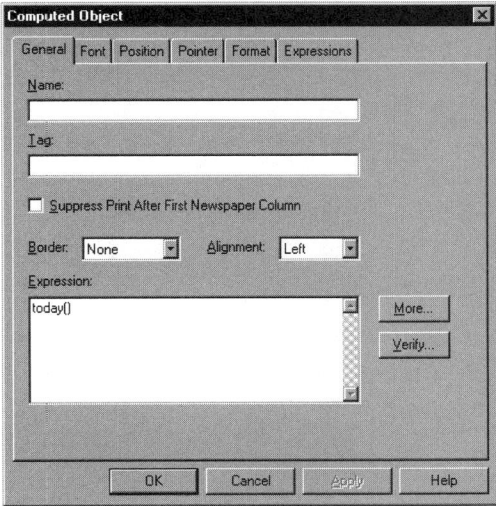

Figure 21-20. *We can fool the composite DataWindow into allowing us to create computed fields by adding a predefined computed field and then modifying it to meet our needs.*

Press the **More...** button to enter the expression editor dialog window. Clear the existing expression, Today(), and replace it with the retrieval argument listed in the columns box (you can do this in one step by highlighting the Today() expression and then clicking on the as_requested_by retrieval argument). (See Figure 21-21.)

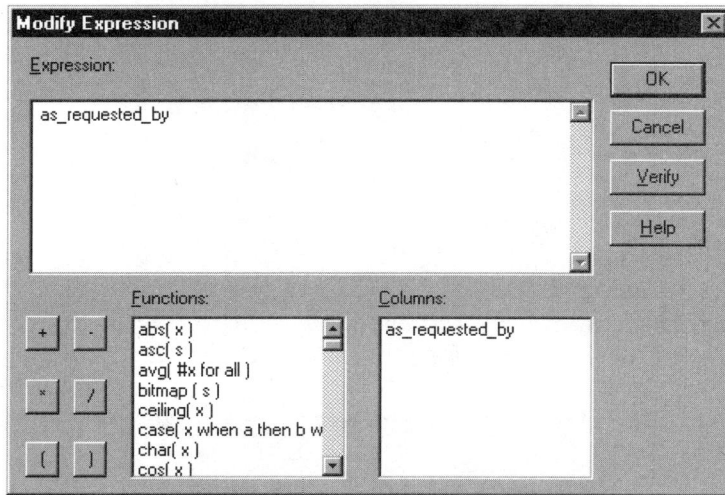

Figure 21-21. Replace the Today() expression with the retrieval argument as_requested_by.

Press the **OK** button on the Modify Expression dialog window to close it. Press **OK** on the Computed Object properties page to close it and apply the new expression to the computed field.

Add static text labels above the employee list and the product list. Your DataWindow should appear similar to the one in Figure 21-22.

Step 6   Preview the result. When you preview the DataWindow, it will ask you to fill in the retrieval argument. Enter your name. I will take a moment to retrieve all the data, remember, there are actually three DataWindows being retrieved. You should see a result something close to Figure 21-23.

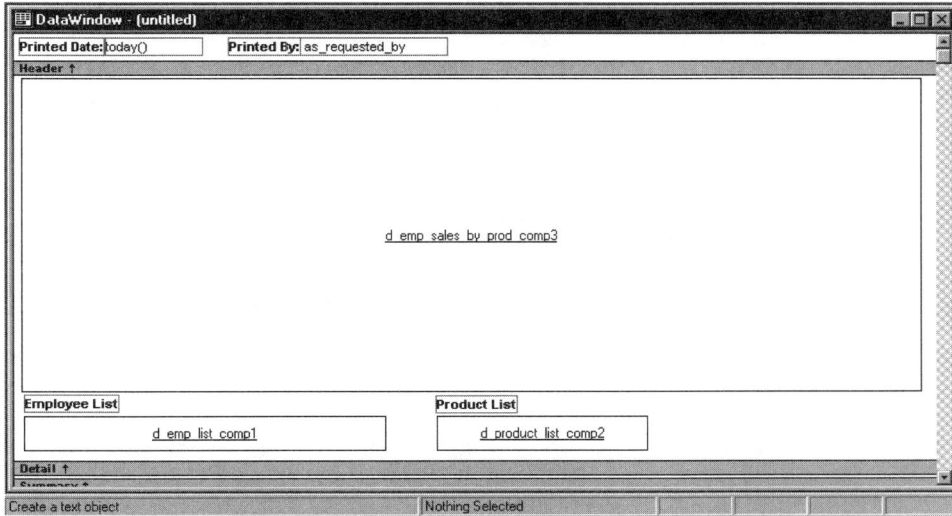

Figure 21-22. We can add static text, computed fields, bitmaps, and drawing objects to our composite DataWindows.

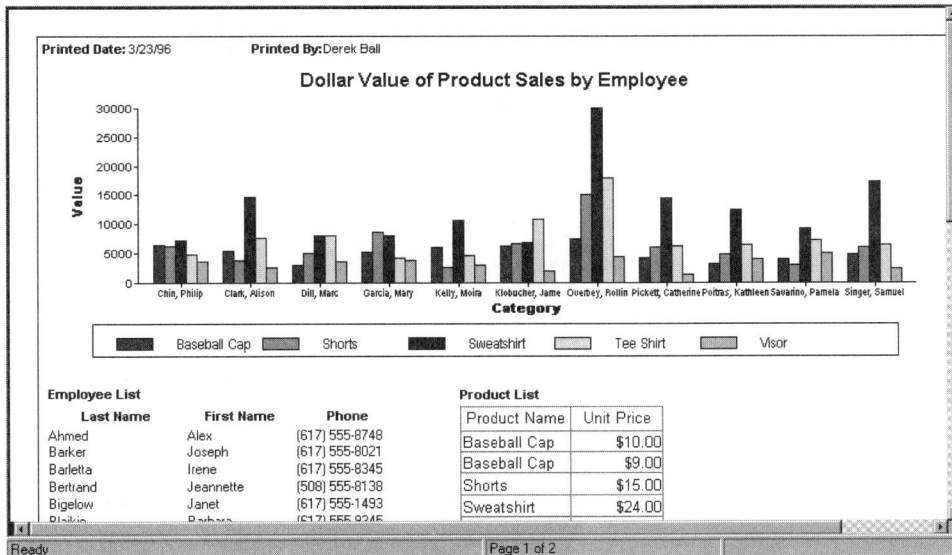

Figure 21-23. Our finished composite DataWindow.

21.2.2 Properties for Composite Reports

The properties for a composite report are very similar to those for a regular DataWindow. On the individual embedded reports, there are two new properties which you will find on the general properties tab. These properties are Start On New Page and Trail the Footer. (See Figure 21-24.)

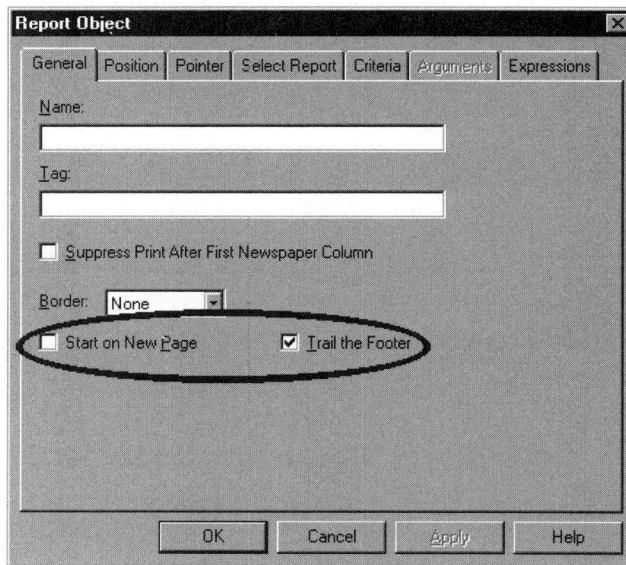

Figure 21-24. The embedded reports on a composite DataWindow have two new attributes on the General tab, Start on New Page and Trail the Footer.

The details of these new properties are:

Start On New Page. When this option is checked (TRUE) each new instance of this embedded DataWindow object will print at the top of a new page. By default this is set to false.

Trail the Footer. When this option is checked (TRUE) the footer for an embedded DataWindow will print immediately following the end of the embedded report. When this option is unchecked (FALSE) the footer will print at the bottom of each page of the report. You can see how this might cause problems if you had multiple embedded DataWindows each with their own footer! The default setting for this attribute is TRUE.

21.3   Graphs

Coming from an analytical and business background, I have long been an advocate of the power of graphs in application development. You have probably heard the axiom "A picture is worth a thousand words." That definitely applies to graphs which excel at conveying information in a quick, succinct an intuitive manner. From the picture is becomes easier to analyze data and determine trends and anomalies.

Everyone is familiar with the graph. We see them around us every day. From early childhood we understand how to read these information loaded pictures. Your users can glean information from a graph regardless of their level of technical expertise. These are major reasons for the tremendous amount of graphing in EIS (Executive Information Systems) and DSS (Decision Support Systems) applications.

In many EIS and DSS systems developed in PowerBuilder to date, graphs are tremendously under utilized. We expect our users to make their decisions based upon lists of data and summary values. This is truly a shame when you consider how easy the PowerBuilder graphing capabilities are to use. By simply specifying the data set that we wish to graph and what type of graph we wish to create, PowerBuilder will do the rest. It will extract the data from our relational database (the most common source) and present it to the user as a bar, line, column, pie or other type of graph.

PowerBuilder 6.0 continues the enhancement of the graphing capabilities of PowerBuilder first introduced in version 3.0. I am particularly pleased that the interface in versions 5.0 and 6.0 has been made more accessible by integrating a properties page that brings all the properties of the graph object together into one dialog window. The tab control is utilized to provide all this functionality in one window.

Developer's Tip: There are numerous ActiveX controls available on the market now for doing very powerful graphing. Visual Components, a company acquired by Powersoft, produces one which you can get an evaluation copy of for free from the Powersoft website at www.powersoft.com. An example of how to build OLE DataWindows is given in Chapter 19 using MS-Graph™ as an example.

21.3.1 How Do I Add A Graph To My Application?

Graphs can be added to your applications in one of three ways:

* In the window painter there is a graph control. The control can be placed on your window like any other window control. These controls are not

specifically tied to a relational database, so you must pass the data to the control via a script. PowerBuilder has a long list of graph functions such as AddData(), AddSeries() and so on. This can become quite an arduous task unless your graph is quite simple. This is the least common use of PowerBuilder graphing capabilities because of this. This type of graph may be used to graph things such as system resources or other runtime information that is unrelated to the data being worked with.

• One of the DataWindow presentation styles is graph which allows you to make the entire DataWindow object a graph. Individual row details are not displayed to the end user.

• Graphs can be used to supplement and provide a pictorial summary view of data in a non-graph DataWindow. In this situation you can have both the low level detail information and the graph available to the user simultaneously. This type of graphing is quite flexible. It allows you to have the graph floating in the foreground layer of the DataWindow so that the user can move it around and keep it handy as they scroll through the data (of course, when it is in the foreground, then they can't print it). Alternatively, you could place in the background layer and you could have the graph display behind the printed detail rows. As another alternative, the graph could be placed right in the band layer and placed side by side with the detail rows.

21.3.2 Components of PowerBuilder Graphs

When you build graphs, there are a number of common elements. This is part of what makes a graph such a universally easy and effective tool to use. These elements have specific names in PowerBuilder:

Category. Defines the major grouping of your data. This is also known as the X axis or the "independent variable" in your graph. Our sample graph in Figure 21-25 shows a simple bar graph displaying employee salaries by department. Department is the category.

Value. Defines the dependent variable in your graph. This is also often referred to as the Y axis. In our sample graph this would be represented by the sum of the employee salaries for a given department.

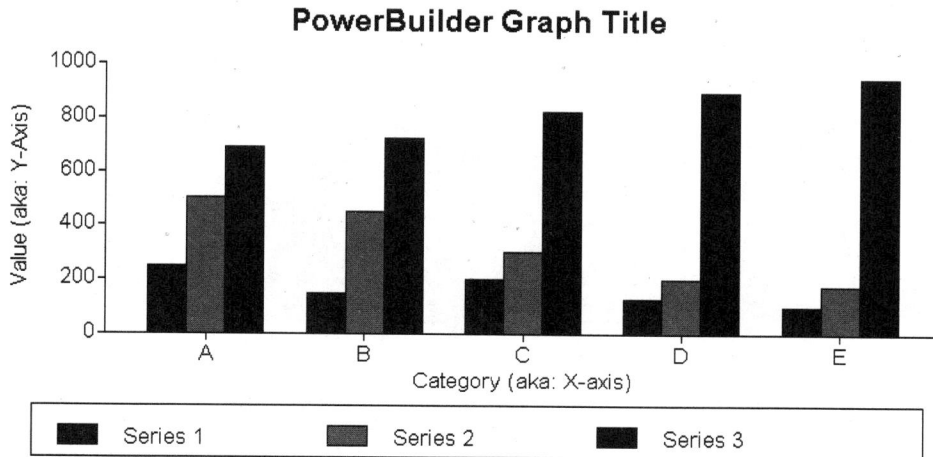

PowerBuilder Graph Title

Figure 21-25. All graphs have a number of common elements which help to make them a very universally effective tool.

Series. Adds a third axis (the Z axis) to provide an extra level of detail in your graph. The series is not a required element of your graph, you can graph by only the X and Y axis if you choose. Graphs with a series are sometimes referred to as 3D because they graph data using three dimensions. You must remember that this is different from a 3D presentation style which is strictly a visual change as opposed to a change in the data. In our example, we have added a series to break down salaries within a department by gender.

Titles and Legends. Titles, labels, and legends can be added to a graph as desired. They are useful for labeling the components of the graph. Legends are often only used if a series is included, or if you are using a pie graph. (See Figure 21-26.)

21.3.3 Two Dimensions or Three?

The expressions 2D and 3D get a little confused in the area of PowerBuilder graphs, because the same expressions are used to mean two different things. We can define both the number of data components or the graph type in terms of the number of dimensions.

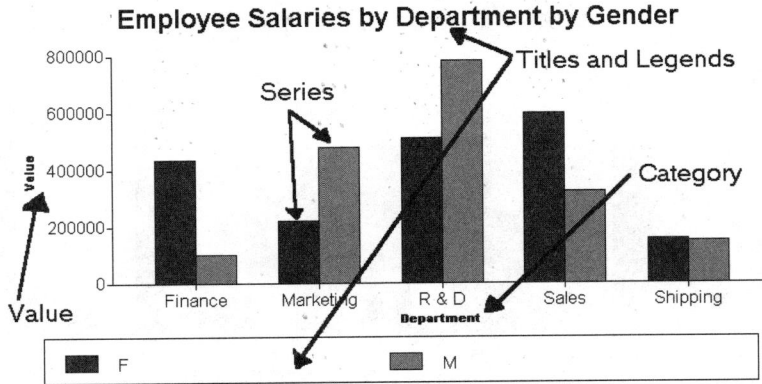

Figure 21-26. A sample graph showing total employee salaries within a department grouped by gender.

In the case of the number of data components, a 2D graph will contain only a category (X-axis) and values (Y-axis). A graph showing the total employee salaries for each department (regardless of gender) would be a 2D graph. A 3D graph will contain a category, values and a series (Z-axis). The series further subdivides the information into smaller groupings such as our graph in Figure 21-26, Employee Salaries by Department by Gender.

When referring to the graph type as being either 2D or 3D, this is purely a visual difference and has no functional or analytical implications. For most of the graphs types you can choose to show your graph rendered in a two dimensional or a three dimensional format as shown in Figure 21-27.

Developer's Tip: Some 3D graphs can be difficult to read. For providing some of the slick visual effects of 3D without going overboard, try using the "solid" graph types for bar and column graphs. These are discussed in the following sections.

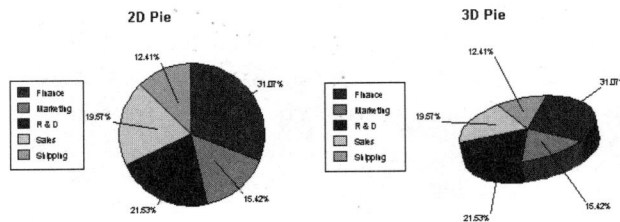

Figure 21-27. Many of the available graph types can be visually rendered in two or three dimensions.

21.3.4 Graph Properties

When you create a graph you will need to assign, at a minimum, values for its category and value properties. There are a vast array of properties that you can manipulate to customize the graph to your specific requirements. These properties are all located on the Graph Objects properties page. The page is divided into tab folders which group the properties into logical sets.

21.3.4.1 The Data Tab

The Data tab contains the most critical properties of any graph; the category, value and series. This tab does not exist on a window graph control as it is not linked to the database. (See Figure 21-28.)

The properties contained on this tab are:

Category. Defines what will appear on the major independent axis (as described in the section "Components of PowerBuilder Graphs"). This field contains a drop down listbox. The list will contain all the possible categories that PowerBuilder thinks you may want to assign as the category. You can select from the list, or you can type in your own logical expression. Any valid expression will work. For example, you may decide to graph your accounts receivable into segments of "Under 30 days," "30 to 60 days," and "Over 60 days."

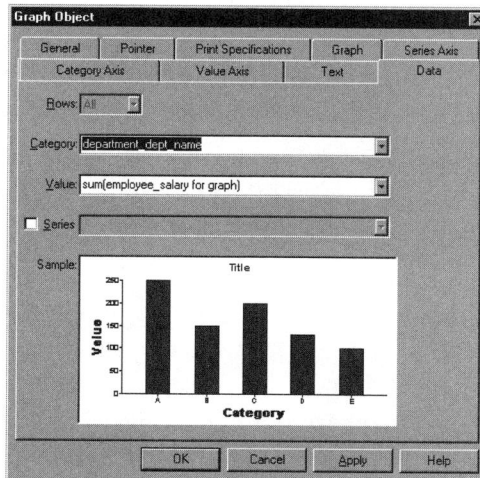

Figure 21-28. The Graph Object properties page requires you to enter a category and value before you can modify any of the other graph properties.

Value. Defines the expression used to evaluate the dependent, or Y axis, of the graph. Usually, some sort of mathematical or aggregate functions are involved. The drop down list box will provide you with a set of possible values that PowerBuilder thinks you may want to define as your value.

Series. Defines the expression used to sub group the value property. For example, our graph showing the total salaries within a department is sub grouped into genders within the department. In order to be able to add a series expression (which by default is disabled), we must check (set to TRUE) the checkbox beside the series field.

Rows. Defines which rows in the DataWindow will make up the data used in the graph. This option is only enabled if you are adding a graph to an existing DataWindow. If you are using the graph on a window control, or making the whole DataWindow a graph, it does not apply. The options in the listbox are:

All: (Default) to include all the rows in the graph.

Page: To have the graph display detail for the current page only. This means that the graph will have to dynamically change as you page through your data. If you decided to embed the graph in the footer of a report and only show the data for that current page, then this would be an option you would consider.

Group n: To have the graph display the data from a specific grouping as defined by the group parameters of the DataWindow. Since a DataWindow could have multiple groups that you might choose to graph by, the n represents the group number.

The sample region at the bottom of the tab is use to remind the developer of the type of graph that is currently selected.

21.3.4.2 The Text Tab

The Text tab is used to control all the text fields that print on the screen. You have the ability to customize every label, font and color used in the text that appears. You can set a value for the graph title, category label and value label here, but you should usually change these three on the Graph, Category Axis, and Value Axis tabs respectively. On these tabs you define the literal that will appear in the label, in the text tab, you can define a custom expression that includes the literal defined in the previous tabs. (See Figure 21-29.)

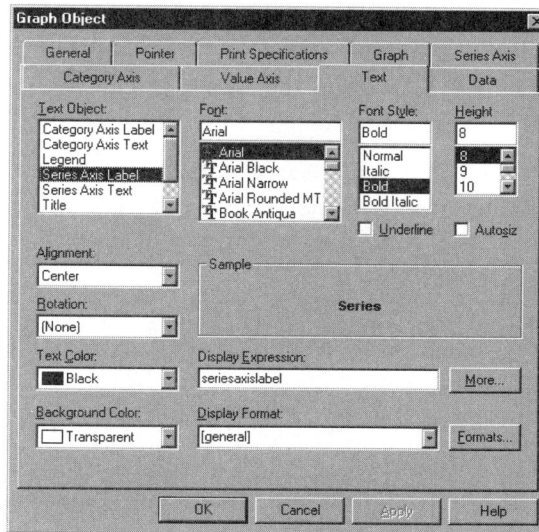

Figure 21-29. *The Text tab allows you to control all the formatting and display aspects for all text fields in the graph.*

The properties on this tab include:

Text Object. The currently select item in this list box is the text object from the graph that you are currently defining. All the other property fields on this page relate to the selected text object. The text objects that you can select are: Category Axis Label, Category Axis Text, Legend, Series Axis Label, Series Axis Text, Title, Value Axis Label, and Value Axis Text.

Font. Defines the currently selected font for the text object. All the available windows fonts will appear inside the drop down listbox.

Font Style. Defines the style of the font for the current text object. You can make the font Bold, Italic, Bold Italic or Normal.

Font Height. Defines the size of the font for the current text object. The standard sizes are listed in and can be selected from the drop down list box, but you can edit the size to be whatever size you prefer. This field is only enabled if Autosize is unchecked (FALSE)

Underline. When checked (TRUE) this will cause the currently selected text object to appear underlined, regardless of font style.

Autosize. When checked (TRUE) will automatically size the current text object font to the size that PowerBuilder deems to be most appropriate. When unchecked (FALSE) you must manually select the font size you desire from the font height field.

Alignment. Allows you to left, center, or right justify the current text object. This option is not available for any of the axes text objects or for the legend.

Rotation. Allows you to display the text of the current text object to some degree of rotation. The options available to you are: None, 45 Degrees Left, 90 Degrees Left, 45 Degrees Right, and 90 Degrees Right. This option is disabled for title and label text objects.

Text Color. Allows you to select a color for the currently selected text object.

Background Color. Allows you to select a color for the background of the currently selected text object. The default color is *transparent*.

Display Expression. Allows you to define a custom expression for what will display in the currently selected text object. This can be any logical expression. Pressing the **More...** command button will open up the Modify Expression dialog window and allow you to access all the DataWindow functions and fields that you can use in your expression. You can include any combination of the following fields (many of them are already defaults for specific text objects):

Title: Contains the string or expression defined in the Graph tab as the title for the graph.

SeriesAxisLabel: Contains the string or expression defined in the Series Axis tab as the label for the series.

CategoryAxisLabel: Contains the string or expression defined in the Category Axis tab as the label for the category.

ValueAxisLabel: Contains the string or expression defined in the Value Axis tab as the label for the value.

Category: Contains the actual category value for the current category. Only available in the Category Axis Text and Legend object.

Series: Contains the actual series value for the current series. Only availabe in the Series Axis Text and Legend object.

SumForGraph: Contains the numeric total of whatever is being evaluated as the dependent axis. For example, if the value axis is defined as "sum" (employee_salary for group) then SumForGraph would be all the employee salaries added together.

SumForCategory: Contains the numeric total for the value axis for the current category. Only available in the Category Axis Text object.

SumForSeries: Contains the numeric total for the value axis for the current category. Only available in the Series Axis Text and Legend text objects.

SeriesCount: Contains the total number of series represented in the graph.

CategoryCount: Contains the total number of categories represented in the graph.

SeriesNumber: Contains the number of the current series. Only available in the Series Axis Text and Legend text objects.

CategoryNumber: Contains the number of the current category. Only available in the Category Axis Text object.

CategoryPercentForGraph: Contains a percentage of the value for the current category versus the total value for the graph (SumForCategory/SumForGraph). Only available in the Category Axis Text object.

SeriesPercentForGraph: Contains the percentage of the value for the current series versus the total value for the graph (SumForSeries/SumForGraph). Only available in the Series Axis Text and Legend text objects.

GraphType: Contains a number representing the type of graph that this is. This can be used in conditional expressions if you want the graph to display different expressions depending on the graph type. The number will match to a graph type as follows:

    1—Area
    2—Bar
    3—Bar3D
    4—Bar3DObj
    5—BarStacked
    6—BarStacked3DObj
    7—Col

        8—Col3D
        9—Col3DObj
        10—ColStacked
        11—ColStacked3DObj
        12—Line
        13—Pie
        14—Scatter
        15—Area3D
        16—Line3D
        17—Pie3D

Some examples of expressions that you might use would include:

```
for title: "Total Salaries Paid = " + String(SumForGraph)

for category: category + String(CategoryPercentForGraph, "0.00%")
```

Display Format. Contains the formatting string for the value returned by the display expression. This defaults to [General] which will display the data exactly as it exists. If you are using a field that calculates a percentage, you could use a display format such as "0.00%" to format the percentage to two decimal places and add a percent sign at the end. Pressing the **Formats...** command button will open up a dialog window where you can select from existing display formats or create and test a new one.

21.3.4.3 The General Tab

The General tab contains properties that relate to the overall DataWindow object graph. These are high level properties and are essentially the same as other general DataWindow properties. (See Figure 21-30.)

        The properties on the General tab are:

Units. Defines the type of units used to measure and layout objects on the DataWindow. The possible values are: 1/1000th of an inch, 1/1000th of a centimeter, pixels, or PowerBuilder units. PowerBuilder units (PBU) are the default and equate to 1/32nd of your system font size. PBUs exist to allow you to create applications that will look the same regardless of your terminal settings.

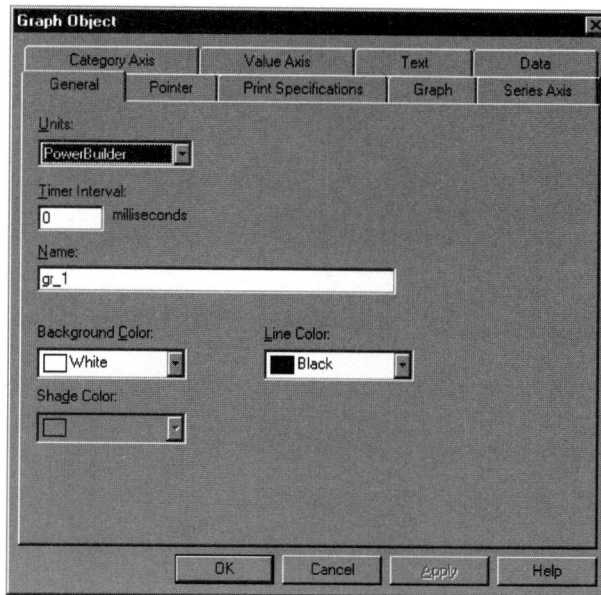

Figure 21-30. The General tab contains properties that relate to the overall DataWindow graph object.

Timer Interval. Defines the amount of time in milliseconds that you want to wait between timer events within the DataWindow object.

Name. The name for the DataWindow object (defaults to gr_1 for the graph object).

Background Color. Background color for the graph (defaults to white).

Line Color. Line color for the graph (defaults to black).

Shade Color. Defines the color used for the 3D base in any 3D graph having a base (pie does not have a base, it floats). This option will be disabled unless you have defined the graph as 3D.

21.3.4.4 The Graph Tab

The Graph tab is where you will define the properties that affect the general type and appearance of your graph. You can choose your graph type, change its 3D properties (if applicable) and modify any other general appearance characteristics (Figure 21.31.)

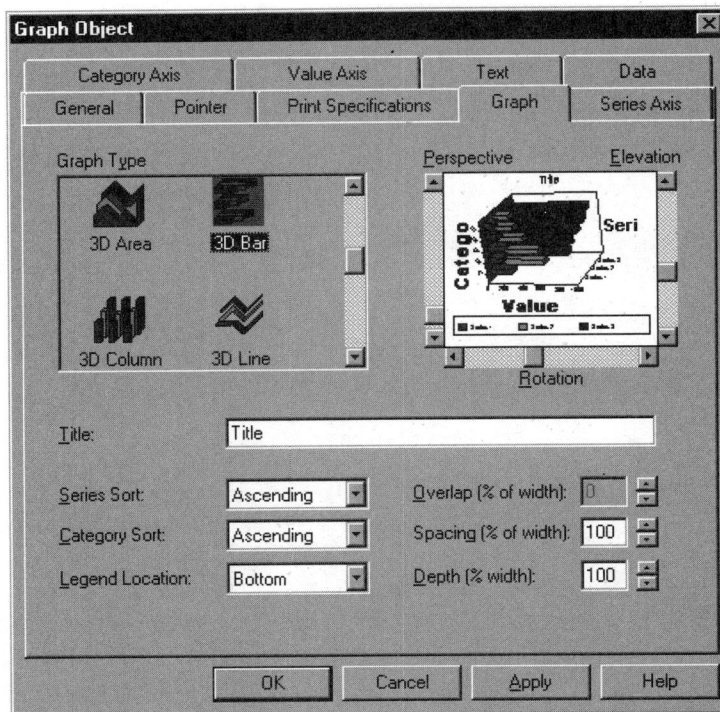

Figure 21-31. The Graph tab is where you will define the properties that allow you to select the type of graph and how it will appear.

The properties that you can work with on the Graph tab include:

Graph Type. Defines the style of graph that you want to create. There are seventeen different types of graphs from line graphs to pie graphs. If you are unfamiliar with the different types of graphs that are available, they are all reviewed in section entitled, "Types of Graphs."

Perspective, Elevation, and **Rotation.** All define the 3D characteristics of a 3D graph. These options are disabled if you are not using a 3D graph. You can use the slider bars to adjust these three attributes (relating to the roll, pitch and yaw) of the 3D object. The results can be viewed in the sample image.

Title. This is the title for the graph. Anything you enter in this field will appear in the title area of the graph, exactly as you type it. Expressions are entered in the text tab.

Series Sort. Defines the sort order for the series axis. Valid choices are: Not Sorted, Ascending or Descending.

Category Sort. Defines the sort order for the category axis. Valid choices are: Not Sorted, Ascending or Descending.

Legend Location. Controls where in relation to the graph the legend will appear. Valid choices are: None, Top, Bottom, Left or Right.

Overlap. Controls how much the different series overlap each other as a percentage of their width. For example, Figure 21-32 shows a bar graph with 35% overlap. This property is only valid for 2D bar and 2D column graphs.

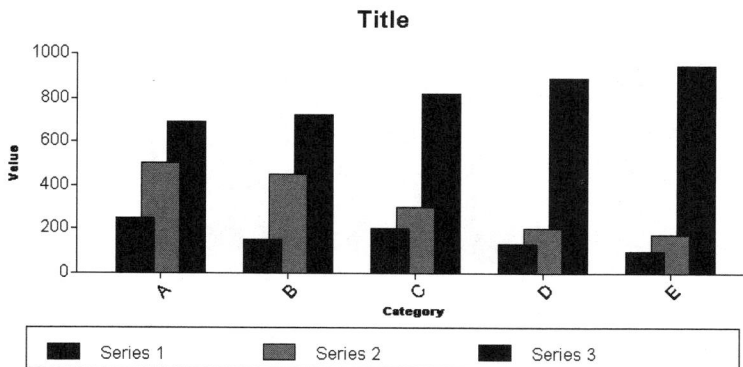

Figure 21-32. This graph has an overlap property of 35% causing the different series to overlap each other by 35% of their width.

Spacing. Controls how much space appears between the data markers for different categories. It is measured as a percentage of width of one data marker. For example, a bar graph with a spacing value of 150 would have a space equal to one and a half times the width of a bar between the categories. This property is not applicable to two dimensional scatter, pie, line or area graphs.

Depth. Controls how deep a 3D graph is in relation to its width. By default the graph will be equally deep as it is wide (depth = 100%).

The Category Axis Tab

Most of the attributes on the Category Axis tab will be disabled for most graph types. Only the scatter graph has any substantial degree of access to the properties contained on this tab due to its unstructured nature. (See Figure 21-33.)

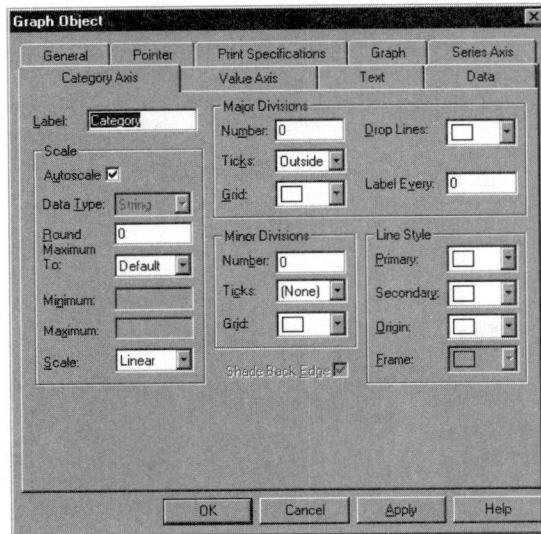

Figure 21-33. *The Category Axis tab properties are largely not accessible for most graph types.*

The properties on the Category Axis tab are:

Label. This property is accessible for most graph types, with the exception of pie. It is the text label that you want to appear on the category axis. Like the Title property on the Graph tab, this is only a character string and will not evaluate expressions. If you want to use an expression for the category axis, you must define it on the Text tab.

Scale.Autoscale. When checked (TRUE), PowerBuilder will automatically determine the appropriate scale for the graph. For most graph types, this is always set to true and is inaccessible.

Scale.DataType. This property is only applicable for non-database graphs, such as those placed directly onto a window. Otherwise, the data type is determined by the expression that is used to define the category.

Scale.RoundTo. Specifies what value you want to round the category axis values to (i.e., 10).

Scale.RoundUnits. Specifies the units that the axis will be rounded in. The default is called "units" which essentially means undefined. You can only define specific units if you are dealing with some measure of dates or times. There are seven possible unit types you can select when dealing with data of this type: Years (a value of 1), Months (2), Days (3), Hours (4), Minutes (5), Seconds(6), and Microseconds (7).

Scale.Minimum. The minimum value for the category axis.

Scale.Maximum. The maximum value for the category axis.

Scale.Scale. Specifies the type of scale used for the category axis. The possible options are: Linear (a value of 1), Log 10 (a value of 2) or Log e (a value of 3).

MajorDivisions.Number. Specifies the number of major divisions on the axis.

MajorDivisions.Ticks. Specifies the type of major tick mark. There are four possible values: None (a value of 1), Inside (2), Outside (3), Straddle (4).

MajorDivisions.Grid. Specifies the type of line used to draw the grid for the major tick marks within the graph. These lines are intended to make it easier to determine where data plots on your graph appear. This setting only affects the grid line for this axis (thus only vertical lines would appear). To have a true grid appear, you would need to define a value for this property and for the equivalent property in the value axis. The valid options all represent different variations of dots and dashes: None (0), Solid (1) , Dash (2), Dot (3), DashDot (4), and DashDotDot (5).

MajorDivisions.DropLines. Specified the type of line that will be used to draw the intersection point of a data point on the graph. Like the grid property, this line will only be drawn for the current axis. If you want to show intersection lines for both axis on the graph, you would need to define the same property for the value axis also. The acceptable values are the same as for the grid property.

MajorDivisions.LabelEvery. Specifies how often you want PowerBuilder to draw labels on the tick marks. The default (0) or a value of 1 will tell PowerBuilder to add a label to every tick mark. A value higher than 1 would cause PowerBuilder to only add labels to specific tick marks. A value of 2 would draw a label on every second tick mark, a value of 3 on every third, and so on.

MinorDivisions.Number. Specifies the number of minor divisions you want to appear on the axis. The default is none (0).

MinorDivisions.Ticks. Specifies the type of tick mark you would like to use for minor divisions. The options are the same as the are for major division tick marks.

MinorDivisions.Grid. Specifies the type of line that you want to use to draw grid lines for the minor tick marks. This property behaves exactly the same as the major divisions grid property, but for the minor divisions.

LineStyle.Primary. Specifies what style of line you want to draw for the axis itself. You can choose from the same styles that are available for drop and grid lines. If you specify None (which is equivalent to transparent) no lines will appear for the axis.

LineStyle.Secondary. Specifies the style of line you want to draw for lines other than the primary axis, that run parallel to the primary axis. The value options are the same as for all the other lines styles.

LineStyle.Origin. Specifies the style of line that you want to draw for the origin line. The origin line is the one that represents zero for this axis (if applicable). The value options are the same as for all the other lines styles.

LineStyle.Frame. Specifies the style of line that will be drawn for the frame of this axis of your graph, if your graph has a frame. The value options are the same as for all the other lines styles.

ShadeBackEdge. Allows you to choose whether you want to shade the back edge of your 3D graph or not. This property is either checked (TRUE) or unchecked (FALSE).

21.3.4.6 The Value Axis Tab

The properties on the Value Axis tab are identical to those properties that are on the Category Axis tab. Which properties are enabled and which are disabled will depend upon which graph type you have selected. Please refer to the property definitions in 21.3.4.5 The Category Axis Tab for the specifics of the value axis tab properties.

21.3.4.7 The Series Axis Tab

The properties for the Series Axis tab are also identical to the properties of the Value and Category Axis tabs. However, these properties will only be enabled if you have defined your graph as having a series in the Data tab. As the definitions for the properties are the same as in the previous two tabs, please refer to the section called "The Category Axis Tab" for property definitions.

21.3.4.8 The Print Specifications Tab

The Print Specifications tab is only available if you have created a graph presentation style DataWindow. It does not apply to graphs created on a window or to graphs added to an existing DataWindow. (See Figure 21-34.)

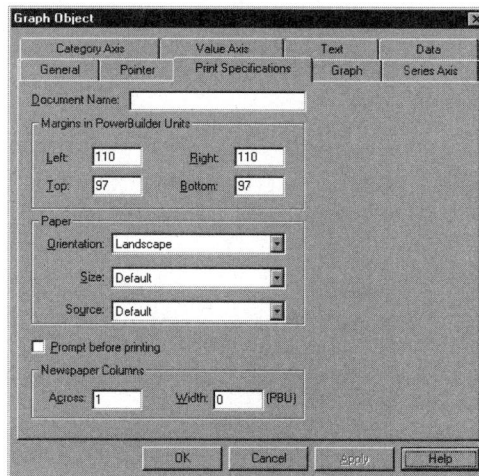

Figure 21-34. The Print Specifications tab allows you to set the properties that define how the graph will print at runtime.

On this tab you can specify all the details that relate to how the graph will print at runtime. The properties that you can control include:

Document Name. Specifies the name that you want to provide for the document to the print server. This name does not appear anywhere else and has no other useful function. If you leave this blank, the default will be no name at all.

Margins. Specifies the margins for the **Left**, **Right**, **Top,** and **Bottom** of the page. These are specified in the same units as the DataWindow is set to use. By default this is set to PowerBuilder Units (PBUs), but remember that you can set the DataWindow to work in 1/1000th of an inch or of a centimeter if that is more convenient for you. The margins will default to (?) of an inch on each side regardless of the units you have selected. If you have left the DataWindow with all of its default settings, you will notice that (?) inch in PBUs is different for width than it is for height. This is because PBUs are based upon the system font size, which is taller than it is wide.

Paper.Orientation. Allows you to override the default orientation of the printer and print this graph in a specific way. Your options here are default (whatever the printer is set for normally), landscape (horizontal) or portrait (vertical).

Paper.Size. Allows you to specify the size of paper that the graph will be printed on. By default, it will use the standard settings of the printer. You can alter this to any of the built in paper sizes like letter, legal, executive, A4, envelopes, etc.

Paper.Source. Allows you to specify where the paper that the graph will be printed on will come from. By default, it will use the printers default paper source, but you can specify whatever valid sources are available for your printer.

Prompt Before Printing. Allows you to present the user with a popup print dialog box as shown in Figure 21-35. This dialog allows the user to select print options such as which printer to use, number of copies and print range. It also allows the user to cancel the printing of the current graph if they choose.

Newspaper Columns. Are intended to allow you to print your data in multiple columns. This does not really apply to graph DataWindows and should be disabled (it may be in the production version, but is currently enabled in mine).

21.3.4.9 The Pointer Tab

The Pointer tab works like any other pointer selection option in PowerBuilder. When the mouse passes over the graph, you can have the pointer change to a different icon. You can select from one of the standard stock icons, or you can select any valid cursor file (cursor files are those with .CUR extensions—these can be created using the Watcom Image Editor that comes with PowerBuilder).

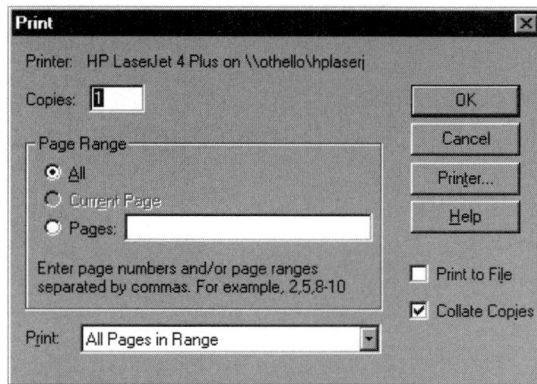

Figure 21-35. *The Prompt Before Printing property allows you to display a dialog window to the user to allow them to select print options or to cancel before printing.*

21.3.4.10 The Expressions Tab

The Expressions tab is only available to graph objects that are embedded into an existing DataWindow. It allows you to dynamically modify some of the attributes of the graph object at runtime. (See Figure 21-36.)

The behavior of this expression dialog is identical to those that we examined in the last chapter. You can enter an expression that will be evaluated at runtime for each of the listed attributes. If you want to use the expression dialog window, you can double click in the field that you want to create an expression for.

The Drag and Drop Tab

The Drag and Drop tab is only available to graph objects that are placed directly on a window, as opposed to those that are created as a DataWindow or embedded into a DataWindow. This tab is used to define the two drag and drop attributes of all dragable windows controls: DragAuto and DragIcon. For a full description of how to use drag and drop, refer to Chapter 8 the section entitled, "Implementing Drag and Drop."

The DragAuto attribute is checked (TRUE) if you want the graph to automatically enter drag mode when the user clicks on it with the mouse. If this attribute is set to false, you must manually initiate drag mode using the Drag() function if you want to drag and drop the graph.

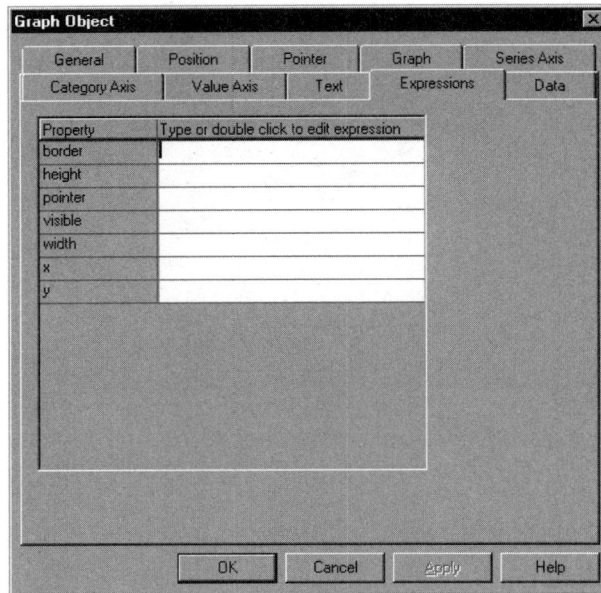

Figure 21-36. *The Expressions tab allows you to dynamically modify the attributes of a graph object that is embedded into an existing DataWindow object.*

The DragIcon attribute sets the icon that will appear in place of the cursor to indicate that the object is in drag mode. If you leave this undefined, the default icon is an outline of the current object (not particularly user friendly when dragging a large graph). You can assign one of the stock icons, or you can use any valid icon (.ICO) file.

An example of implementing drag and drop with a window graph would be to allow the user to drag a graph onto a bitmap of a printer to initiate printing.

21.3.5 Types of Graphs

PowerBuilder has an ample supply of useful graph types. Most major graph types that you will need in a business environment are supported. In the event that you need some graph functions that are not supported in PowerBuilder, there are a number of third party vendors that make OLE 2.0 compatible graphing applications that you can integrate into your PowerBuilder application.

21.3.5.1 Column

When you first create any graph object, the default graph type will always be column. A column graph allows you to show your data as a range covered by the column on your graph area. Column graphs show increasing values on the value axis by increasing the height of the column.

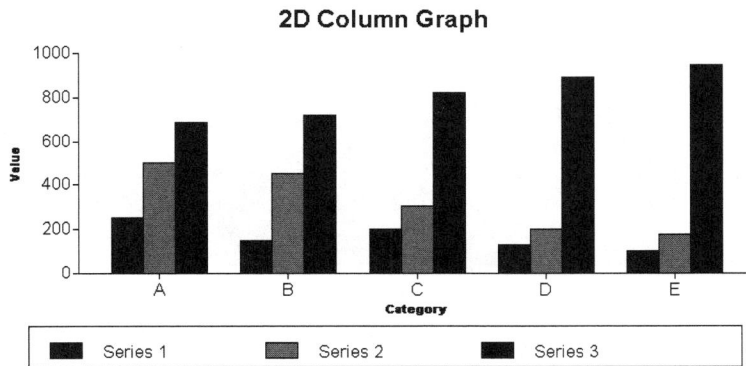

Figure 21-37. *The column graph is the default graph type for any new graph object. It will show data as a range covered by the column on your graph area.*

Column graphs can be either two dimensional or three dimensional. (See Figure 21-38.)

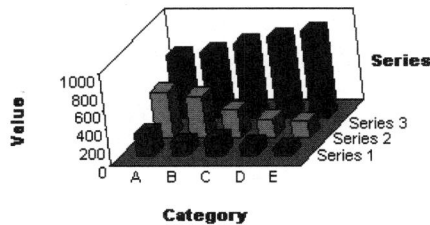

Figure 21-38. *Column graphs also come in a three dimensional variety.*

If you find three dimensional a little too 3D, then there is a graph type called "solid" (available for both column and bar graphs) which takes the 2D graph types and gives their columns some depth. Only the columns themselves are 3D, the rest of the graph is drawn exactly the same. (See Figure 21-39.)

Solid Column Graph

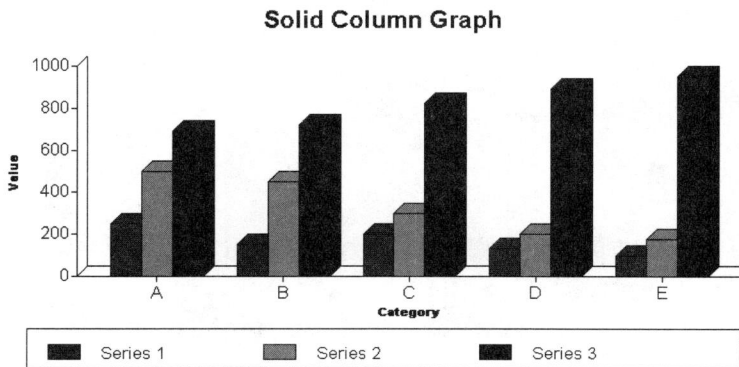

Figure 21-39. *A graph type of Solid Column gives the columns depth but the rest of the graph is drawn the same. This results in a partial 3D graph.*

For business graphing purposes, the 2D or the Solid Column graphs will provide the clearest message. 3D graphs tend to be more difficult to read, although they may look slick in your annual report!

21.3.5.2 Bar

Bar graphs are identical to Column graphs, but the value and category axes are swapped. The category is on the left (vertical) axis which the values are stretched across the bottom. (See Figure 21-40.)

Bar graphs are excellent for communicating information where there is a large range of values, but only a limited number of categories. The Bar graph comes in all the same flavors as the Column graph; 2D, 3D, or Solid Bar.

Bar Graph

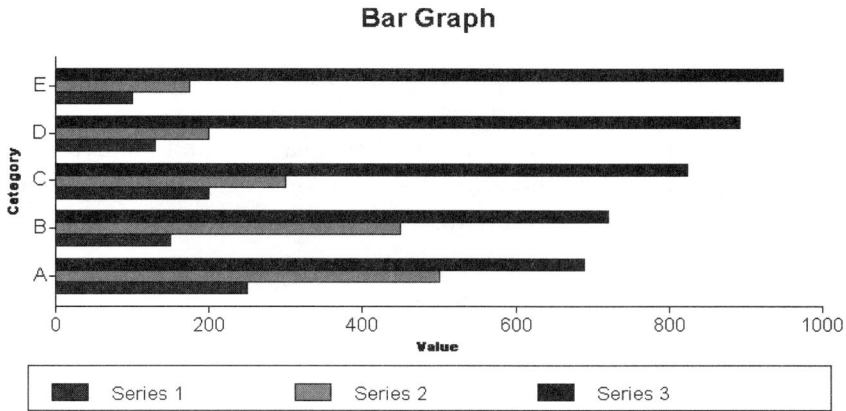

Figure 21-40. The Bar graph is identical to the column graph, however, the category axis is the vertical axis and the value is the horizontal. This will make your bars (columns) stretch from left to right on your graph.

21.3.5.3 Stacked Graphs

When you add a series to a graph, normally this implies adding new bars or columns extending from the appropriate axis, but grouped into a specific category. However, data from a series could also be stacked on top of data from other series within the same category. This allows you to build a cumulative total for all the series within the category.

The stacked variety of graph is available for column and bar graphs only. You can select between 2D or 3D variations. (See Figure 21-41.)

Stacked Column Graph

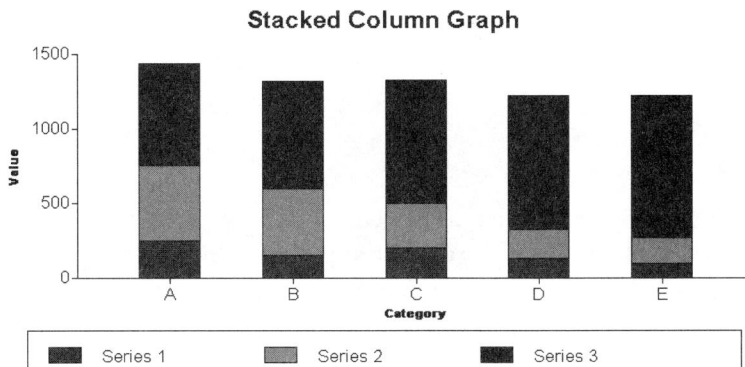

Figure 21-41. The Stacked Column graph allows you to stack series on top of each other within a category building up a cumulative total.

21.3.5.4 Line

Line graphs have discrete data points that are graphed against two axes, the value and the category. The related data points are connected together by a continuous line. If you add a series to a line graph, a separate line will be created for all the data points within that series. Each data point will be given a symbol that will match the symbol for the series as shown in the legend. (See Figure 21-42.)

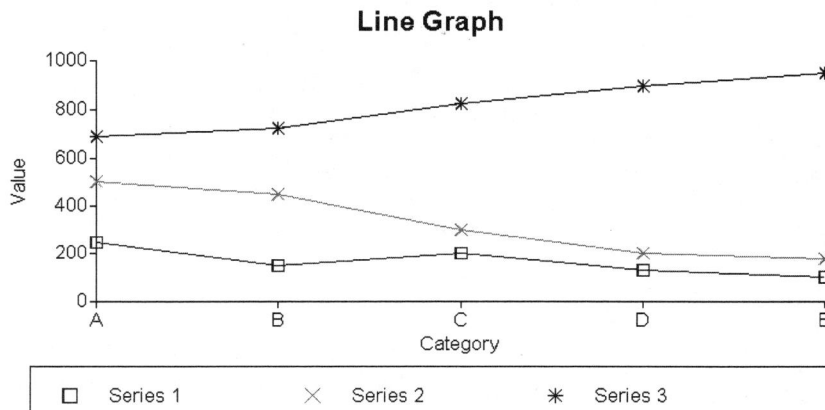

***Figure 21-42.** The Line graph connects discrete data points with a continuous line. Multiple series are shown as separate lines.*

The line graph is most commonly used to show trend analysis. The category axis is often related to time or changes in time. A typical example of a line graph might be total sales of different products over 12 months. Each series would represent a different product.

21.3.5.5 Area

Area graphs are very similar to line graphs. They graph discrete points on two axes (category and value) and draw a line between the points. The difference between the two is that the area graph fills in the area under the line with a solid color.

An example of the use of this type of graph in a business application would be in the financial industry. Area graphs are often used to indicate financial performance or market share as the filled in area is easy to equate with a cumulative or increasing amount. Adding a series to an area graph would result in multiple lines, similar to the example in Figure 21-43.

The area graph has both two dimensional and three dimensional variations. The two dimensional version is shown in Figure 21-43 and the three dimensional in Figure 21-44.

Area Graph

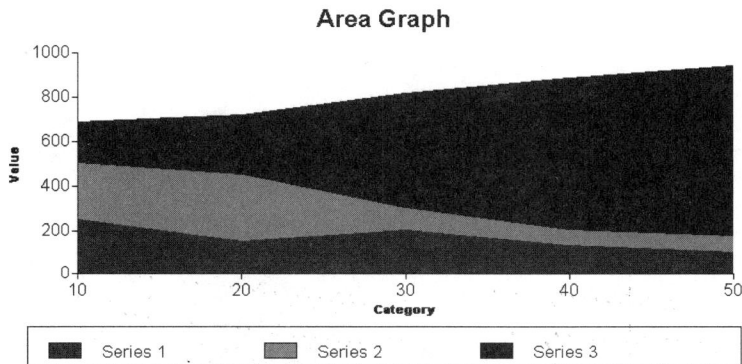

Figure 21-43. *The area graph is similar to a line graph except that the area under the line is filled in with a solid color.*

3D Area Graph

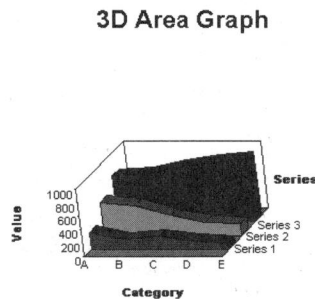

Figure 21-44. *The area graph can be created in both 2D and 3D formats.*

21.3.5.6 Pie

The Pie graph is a favorite of many business analysts. It is frequently used in decision support, executive information and market analysis systems. The data in a Pie graph is contained within a category. Each category shows up as a distinct piece of the pie. The size of the piece of pie represents the value for that category in relation to the cumulative total for all the categories (the entire pie). (See Figure 21-45.)

The Pie graph is also one of my personal favorites because of its flexibility. It comes in 2D and 3D varieties and you have the ability to add a series if you choose. (See Figure 21-46.)

Employee Salaries

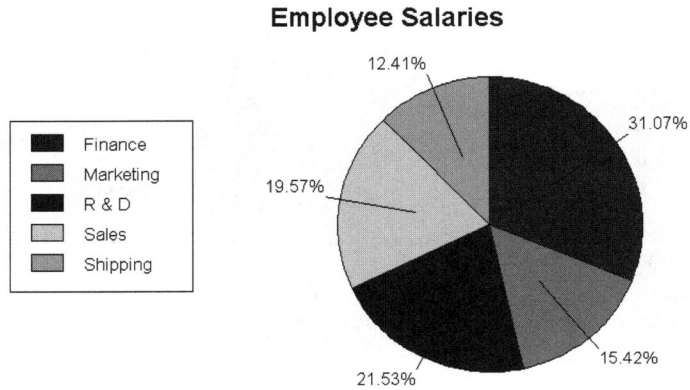

Figure 21-45. *The Pie graph displays the data within a category as a single slice of a pie (which represents the cumulative total of all the data in the graph).*

3D With a Series

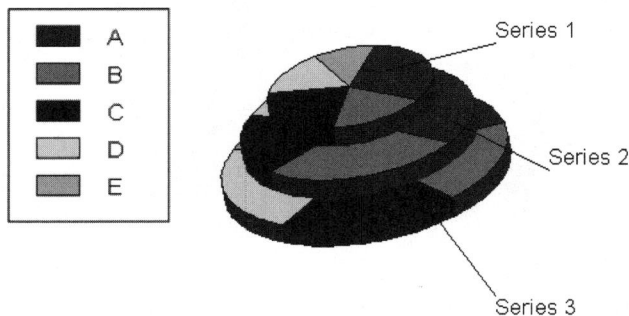

Figure 21-46. *The pie graph comes in 2D and 3D varieties and you can stack the pies up by adding a series.*

Scatter

The Scatter graph allows you to map out discrete points of data against two axes. This type of graph is most often used to provide a mechanism for visually ranking data. (See Figure 21-47.)

Scatter Graph of Construction Firms

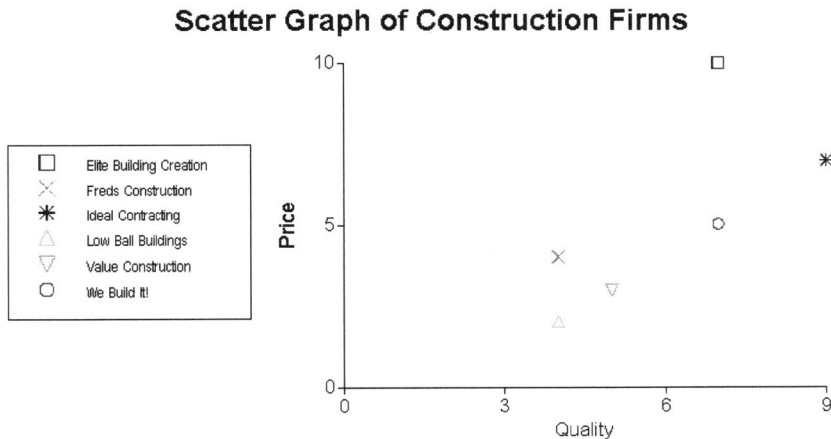

Figure 21-47. The Scatter graph allows you to map out discrete points of data against two axes.

Let's consider an example. We need to select a construction company to build our new office building. There are six construction companies in town and we have them in our database. Each construction firm is ranked for price and quality of work. We want to show a graph of this. The graph in Figure 21-47 allows us to examine which construction firm will give us the most value for our dollar.

Scatter graphs are also often used in research and testing environments where multiple test results from various test runs need to be referenced on the same graph.

21.3.6 Building a Graph Presentation Style DataWindow

The techniques for building a graph are very similar regardless of whether you are adding a graph to an existing DataWindow, or creating a new graph presentation style DataWindow. We will base our example upon the latter, to keep things simple.

Step 1   Open the DataWindow painter. Open the DataWindow painter and select SQL Select as the data source and Graph as the presentation style. Press the **OK** button.

Step 2   Define your data source. In the SQL Select painter we must define the data set that will make up our graph. We will use two tables; department and employee. From the department table we will select the dept_name column. From the employee table we will select the emp_id, status, and salary columns. Press the SQL icon button on the painter bar (remember it appears as a push on/push off button)to close the SQL Select painter and move to the DataWindow designer.

Step 3   Define the category and value. The Graph Object properties page will appear. It contains a number of tabs with all the modifiable properties of the graph object. The Data tab is preselected for you and you are required to define a category and value before trying to select any of the other tabs.

For the category, we will be using the department_dept_name column. When you are dealing with multiple tables, PowerBuilder prefixes the name of the column with the name of the table and an underscore.

You can easily select the column from the list of recommended categories by clicking on the drop down listbox arrow in the category field. The list will contain all the items that PowerBuilder thinks you may want to use as a category, but you can enter any valid expression you desire (refer to the "Graph Properties" section for a complete walk through of all the properties page tabs).

For the value, select sum(employee_salary for graph) from the drop down listbox. We will not be using a series at this point.

Step 4   Change the text labels. We could use the Text tab to change the labels for our graph. On this tab here we can change all the text on our graph including changing the font, color and expression. This tab is also addressed in detail in the "Graph Properties" section.

Alternatively, the title could be changed on the Graph tab, the category label on the Category Axis tab and the value label on the Value Axis tab.

Change the title to "Employee Salaries by Department." Change the category label to "Department" and change the value label to "Amount."

Press the **OK** button.

Step 5   Preview the graph. Your graph should appear similar to the one in Figure 21-48.

Employee Salaries by Department

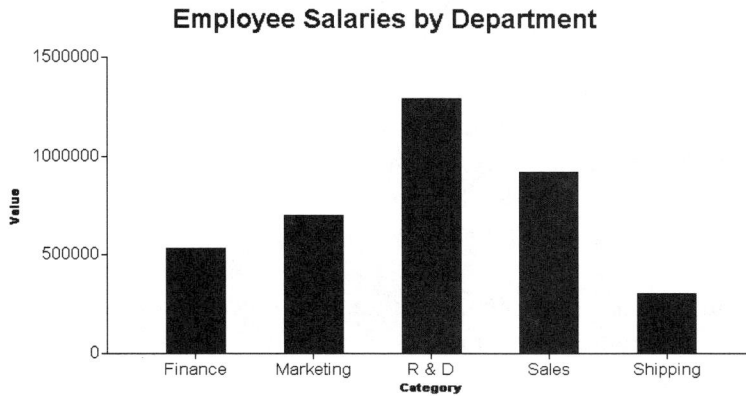

Figure 21-48. Your graph should look similar to this. When you have finished, return to the designer .

Step 6   (Optional)—Change the formatting of the value column to provide currency formats to labels. Open the Properties page by clicking with the right mouse button and selecting **Properties...** from the popup menu.

Select the Text tab and change the display format to an appropriate currency setting as shown in Figure 21-49.

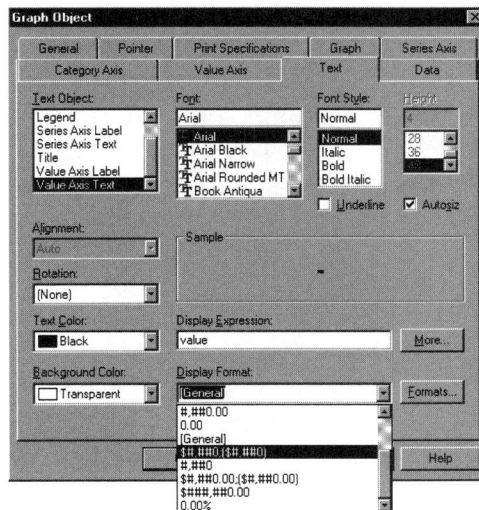

Figure 21-49. Display format can be changed in the Text tab.

Press the **OK** command button to apply the changes. Preview the results to see the new format.

Step 7   (Optional)—Change the title expression. Alter the title expression to include a dynamic evaluation of the total amount of all salaries paid in the company. Open the properties page and select the Text tab. Select the Title text object and change the expression to be:

```
title + " - Total Payroll: "+ String( sumforgraph ,'$0,000')
```

If you had used this field to change the graph title earlier instead of the Graph tab, then your expression will look like:

```
"Employee Salaries by Department" + " - Total Payroll: "+ String( sum-
forgraph ,'$0,000')
```

Apply the changes by pressing the **OK** command button. Preview your graph. It should appear similar to the graph in Figure 21-50.

Employee Salaries by Department - Total Payroll: $3,749,147

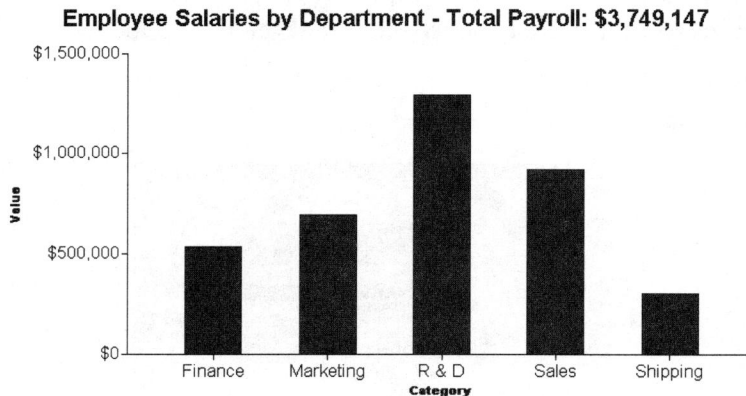

*Figure 21-50. After completing Steps 6 and 7, your graph should
appear similar to this.*

Step 8   (Optional)—Change the graph type. Open the Properties page and select the Graph tab. Select the 3D Pie graph option. Apply the changes and preview the graph. You should now see a 3D pie with all the same properties as you defined in the column graph.

21.3.7 Using Overlays

It is possible in PowerBuilder to overlay a second graph over top of your first graph. The two graphs must be related. This allows you to identify trends or provide supporting information for the graph. You define an overlay in the Graph tab of the Properties page. This is demonstrated below. The new data will appear as a line graph and will be added to the legend like a new series.

Employee Salaries by Department - Total Payroll: $4,196,336

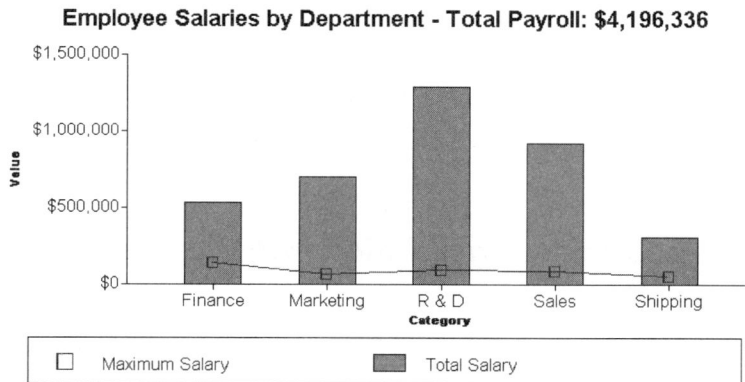

Figure 21-51. Overlays allow us to show supporting information on top of an existing graph object. This is the result of the example steps in the section called, "Using Overlays."

The example below uses the graph you built in the section "Building a Graph Presentation Style DataWindow," as the primary graph. We will overlay the average salary in each department on our salary graph.

Step 1   Define the value axis for the overlay. We only define the value axis for our overlay and not the category as the overlay must use the same category in order for the data to make any sense. Open the Properties page and select the Data tab. In the value list box we are going to append the new expression for our overlay. We separate the two expressions with a comma. The complete new expression will be:

```
sum(employee_salary for graph),max(employee_salary for graph)
```

The first expression is our existing graph, the total employee salaries for a department. The second component will show the highest salary within a department.

Step 2   Define the series for the overlay. In order to make the overlay work, we must have a series defined. This is because PowerBuilder treats the overlay like a new series. The expression that we will use in our series is:

```
"Total Salary" , "@overlay~tMaximum Salary"
```

The first component gives a static label that will appear in the legend to show that our columns represent the total salary within a department. The second component instructs PowerBuilder to generate an overlay based upon the second component of the value axis and label it as "Maximum Salary" in the legend.

Step 3   Preview your graph. Your graph should appear similar to the one in Figure 21-51.

21.3.8 Runtime Graph Manipulation with PowerScript Functions

After you have created a graph object, you can manipulate and alter it at runtime through the use of various PowerScript functions. All aspects of the graph object can be altered. The full set of functions that can be used are listed in the PowerBuilder Function Reference manual that is part of your PowerBuilder documentation or in the online help.

21.3.8.1 Changing A Series Color

One function that I want to mention is the SetSeriesStyle function. I am often asked by students in PowerBuilder training how they can change the color for a graph. The default color for a single series graph is red, and some people don't want to have the bars showing up in red because of the negative financial connotations attached to red.

We can't change this color when we are painting the graph, but it can be altered at runtime through the use of the SetSereiesStyle() function. This function allows us alter any of the style attributes for a particular series. The color attribute that we want to alter is referenced using an enumerated data type called ForeGround!

The syntax to change the color is:

```
control.SetSeriesStyle ({graph_control,} seriesname, colortype, color)
```

where

control is the name of the object that contains the graph control. This could be a graph control on a window, a graph type DataWindow or another DataWindow that has a graph object embedded in it.

graph control is the name of the graph control within the object that you want to alter stored in a string. This is only applicable to DataWindow objects as with graph controls in a window the graph control name is the same as the control name.

seriesname is the name of the series stored in a string for which you want to set the color.

colortype is an enumerated data type containing which color attribute you wish to modify. The valid attributes are: ForeGround!, BackGround!, LineColor! or Shade! (applicable to 3D or Solid graphs only).

color Is a long containing the color that you wish to change the color type to. Remember that you can use the RGB() function to help you get the right color.

If we wanted to change the salary series of a graph to green instead of red, we would write a script such as:

```
dw_salarygraph.SetSeriesStyle("gr_1","salary", ForeGround!, RGB(0,255,0))
```

21.3.9 Creating a Drill Down Graph with PowerScript

Another series of functions that I find useful when working with graphs are those that allow me to turn the graph into a useful tool in the user interface. For example, the user can click on a section of a pie graph to get the detail of the data that is within that pie.

To accomplish this kind of functionality, we need to write a script for the clicked event on our DataWindow control. In this event, we need to find out which part of the graph the user clicked on. To do this we use the function ObjectAtPointer() which will return to us the object type that was clicked on and, through reference variables, will also provide us with the series number and data point that were clicked on.

The syntax for ObjectAtPointer() is:

```
control.ObjectAtPointer( { graphcontrol, } seriesnumber, datapoint )
```

where

control is the name of the object that contains the graph control. This could be a graph control on a window, a graph type DataWindow or another DataWindow that has a graph object embedded in it.

graphcontrol is the name of the graph control within the object that you want to alter stored in a string. This is only applicable to DataWindow objects as with graph controls in a window the graph control name is the same as the control name.

seriesnumber is an integer reference variable which, when the function completes, will contain the number of the series that the user clicked on.

datapoint is an integer reference variable which, when the function completes, will contain the number of the data point that the user clicked on.

The return value for this function is an enumerated data type called grObjectType (for "graph object type") and has the possible values of:

TypeCategory! The user clicked on a label for a category.

TypeCategoryAxis! The user clicked on the category axis or in between the category labels.

TypeCategoryLabel! The user clicked on the label of the category axis.

TypeData! The user clicked on an individual data point or other data marker such as a bar.

TypeGraph! This is the catch all that is returned when the user clicked anywhere in the graph that is not represented by one of the other values for grObjectType.

TypeLegend! The user clicked inside the legend box, but not on a series label.

TypeSeries! The user clicked on the line that connects the data points of a series in a line graph, or the user clicked on the series label in the legend.

TypeSeriesAxis! The user clicked on the series axis (only applied to 3D graphs)

TypeSeriesLabel! The user clicked on the label of the series axis (also only applies to 3D graphs).

TypeTitle! The user clicked on the graph title.

TypeValueAxis! The user clicked on the value axis or the value labels.

TypeValueLabel! The user clicked on the label for the value axis itself. (See Figure 21-52.)

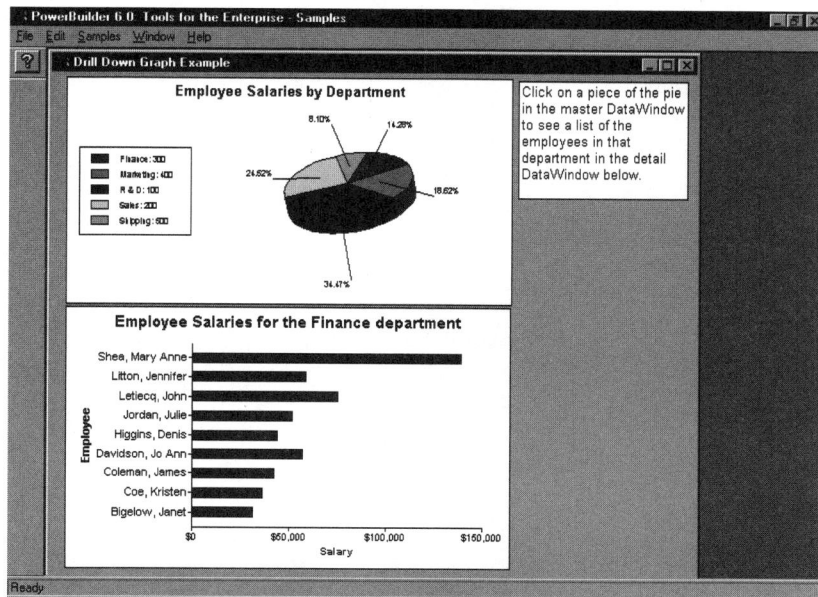

Figure 21-52. The sample application on the companion CD contains an example of a drill down graph.

You can examine the functionality of the ObjectAtPointer() function by looking at the drill down example on the companion CD. In this example, we have created two graph objects. The master object is a pie graph that shows all the departments and the total salaries paid in the departments. The detail object shows all the employees and their salaries within a specific department as a bar graph. The example I deliberately kept as simple as possible so that you can see the functionality of the ObjectAtPointer() function. The only scripts on the window are in the open event and the clicked event on dw_master.

The open event sets up the transaction objects and retrieves the master:

```
dw_master.SetTransObject(SQLCA)
dw_master.Retrieve()
dw_detail.SetTransObject(SQLCA)
```

The clicked event calls the ObjectAtPointer() function and checks to see if the user clicked in either a data area (pie slice) or category (legend). If they did, then it gets the category name. It retrieves the detail DataWindow based upon the department id component of the category name and it changes the title of the detail DataWindow based upon the department name component of the category name.

```
// Declare local variables

grObjectType len_object
integer li_series, li_datapoint, li_dept_id
string ls_catname

// Where did the user click?

len_object = dw_master.ObjectAtPointer("gr_1", li_series, li_datapoint)

// Did the user click on a datapoint or category?
IF len_object = TypeData! or len_object = TypeCategory! THEN

    // User clicked in valid area
    // Get the Category name
    ls_catname = this.CategoryName("gr_1",li_datapoint)

    // Strip the department id from the category name
    li_dept_id = Integer(Mid(ls_catname, Len(ls_catname) - 3))

    // Retrieve the detail DataWindow
    dw_detail.Retrieve(li_dept_id)

    // Modify the title of the detail DataWindow to include
    // the department name
    dw_detail.Modify("gr_1.title= 'Employee Salaries for the "+&
        Mid(ls_catname,1,Len(ls_catname) - 5)+" department'")
END IF
```

21.4 Crosstabs

Crosstabs are very useful tools when you need to perform analysis of your data. They allow you to scan through a large quantity of information and present a two dimensional summary of the results. The columns across the top of the cross tab represent the first dimension and the rows down the side of the crosstab represent the second. The intersection point in the grid between any individual row and column will contain the summary information about the data for that row/column combination. For example, in the crosstab in Figure 21-53, the first dimension is the product, the second dimension is the customer. At the intersection point between any row and column we see the total value of purchases made by that customer of that product.

Customer Purchases	Product					
Customer Name	Baseball Cap	Shorts	Sweatshirt	Tee Shirt	Visor	Grand Total
Agliori, Michael	$2,052.00	$1,080.00	$2,304.00	$108.00	$1,176.00	$6,720.00
Colburn, Kelly	$1,140.00	$1,620.00	$1,728.00	$1,668.00	$588.00	$6,744.00
Devlin, Michaels	$684.00	$360.00	$2,016.00	$1,992.00	$756.00	$5,808.00
Gagliardo, Jessie	$240.00	$900.00	$2,880.00	$1,332.00	$420.00	$5,772.00
Goforth, Matthew	$804.00	$180.00		$1,284.00	$252.00	$2,520.00
Mason, Meghan	$324.00	$1,080.00	$2,304.00	$2,220.00	$756.00	$6,684.00
McCarthy, Laura			$1,728.00	$984.00	$504.00	$3,216.00
Niedringhaus, Erin	$564.00	$180.00		$2,724.00	$504.00	$3,972.00
Phillips, Paul	$912.00	$180.00		$504.00		$1,596.00
Reiser, Beth	$780.00	$540.00	$576.00	$1,392.00	$336.00	$3,624.00
Ricci, Dylan	$1,356.00	$540.00		$276.00	$924.00	$3,096.00
Grand Total	**$8,856.00**	**$6,660.00**	**$13,536.00**	**$14,484.00**	**$6,216.00**	**$49,752.00**

Figure 21-53. *Crosstabs allow you to present the results of scanning through a large amount of information and summarizing it by two primary categories. The example above summarizes the total amount spent on each product type by each customer.*

Crosstabs have the look and feel of a spreadsheet. They use the basic grid format for displaying their information which means that the user has the ability to dynamically rearrange and resize columns at runtime. If you have a particularly large crosstab, you can enable split scrolling too.

Crosstabs can be found in many types of systems, particularly in decision support and analytical systems.

A system that I was involved with for a large university used crosstabs to analyze the number of applicants to each faculty within the university and break them down by their status: within state, out of state and foreign. This was important as they were required to report the ratios of in-state, out-of-state and foreign students who were attending to the government board that providing their funding.

21.4.1 Creating A Crosstab

Let's walk through the steps of creating a crosstab DataWindow. We are going to create two crosstabs, the first one is a fairly simple crosstab, the second becomes a bit more complex. The first crosstab we will build will be the one shown in Figure 21-53.

21.4.1.1 Sample One—A Simple Crosstab

Step 1   Build the SQL statement. Open the DataWindow painter and select SQL Select/Crosstab. Select the Customer, Sales Order, Sales Order Items and Product tables. Remember to double check the table joins to be sure that they are correct! From these tables select the customer.fname, customer.lname, sales_order_items.quantity, product.name, and product.unit_price columns. Close the SQL painter and move to the designer.

Step 2   Define the crosstab. Closing the SQL painter will cause the Crosstab Definition dialog window to open as in Figure 21-54. In this window you will define what data will represent the columns, rows and the intersection point between the rows and columns in the crosstab. Multiple data fields can be included in the definition and we will examine this in the second example. This example will use only one data field in each dimension.

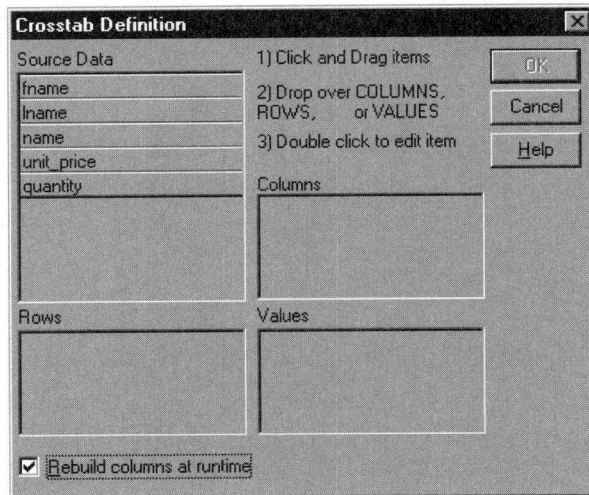

Figure 21-54. *The Crosstab Definition dialog window is where you define what data will represent the columns, rows, and intersections in the crosstab.*

We want to use the product name as our first dimension (our columns). Drag the "name" field from the Source Data listbox into the Columns listbox.

For the second dimension, the rows we want to use the combination of first and last name. This will be a custom defined expression. To provide for this, we will drag the "lname" field from the "Source Data" listbox and drop it in the "Rows" listbox. Now we must double click on the field with the left mouse button to open the Modify Expression dialog window (Figure 21-55.)

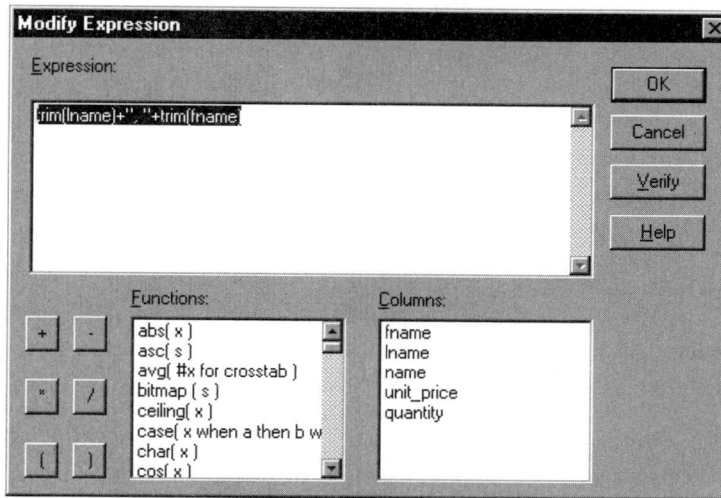

Figure 21-55. *We will double-click on the field to open the Modify Expression dialog window and change the field to a custom expression.*

Change the expression to combine the first and last name like:

```
trim(lname) + ", " + trim(fname)
```

Now we have to define our intersection point. This is represented by the data displayed in the "Values" listbox. Drag the "unit_price" field from the "Source Data" to the "Values" listbox. PowerBuilder will take a guess at building an expression that you might want to use. In this case it will produce:

```
sum( unit_price for crosstab)
```

which is not really what we are after. What we really want to show is the sum of the (unit_price X quantity) for all the items that match the current product and customer. We need to double click on the field and modify the expression to be:

```
sum( ( unit_price * quantity) for crosstab)
```

Now we have fully defined our crosstab. At any time in the designer, if you click with the right mouse button in an empty area of the DataWindow, you will see a popup menu with an option that says **Crossstab...** which will bring you back to the Crosstab Definition dialog. Press the **OK** command button to close the dialog.

Step 3   Modify the crosstab. Now you will see a DataWindow in the designer that appears very much like a grid DataWindow. In fact, it behaves very much like a grid. You cannot add overall titles, but you can add a title in the upper left cell of the grid. You can change the field types, alignments, colors and so on just like you would in a grid DataWindow.

You should change the column label to "Products," the row label to "Customer Name" and the crosstab label to "Customer/Products." Apply a currency format to the intersection cell so that the amounts are formatted as currencies.

Step 4   Modify computed fields. By default, PowerBuilder will have created a grand total column for you that runs in both dimensions. In the summary band, you can create any computed field you desire. If you would rather show an average, you can use the AVG (#x for all) function. All the standard aggregate functions apply.

Where things become a bit different are when you want to add computed fields for the summary of a row. Notice the computed field in the detail band contains the CrosstabSum() function. This function will provide you with the sum of all the fields in the row that are part of the crosstab. The complete set of crosstab specific functions that you can use in computed fields on a row are:

CrosstabSum()—Sums all the fields in the row that are part of the crosstab.
CrosstabAvg()—Averages all the fields in the row that are part of the crosstab.
CrosstabCount()—Counts the number of values returned by the expression for rows included in the crosstab.
CrosstabMax()—Returns the maximum value for the fields in the row that are part of the crosstab.
CrosstabMin()—Returns the minimum value for the fields in the row that are part of the crosstab.

All of these functions have a simple and a complex syntax. In the simple syntax, they have a single parameter which is an integer. This integer indicates which expression that the function must act upon. Since our simple example has only one expression, this value will always be 1. Figure 21-56 demonstrates the use of the CrosstabSum() function in our example.

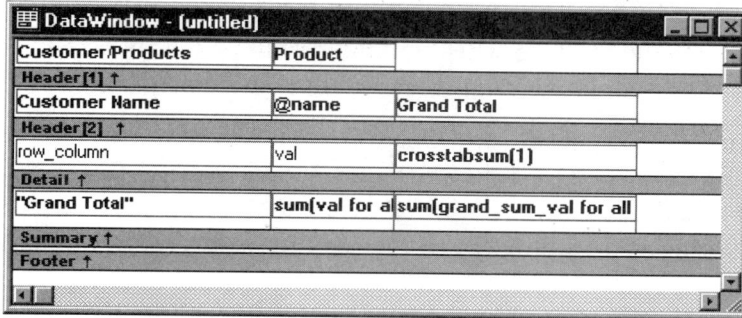

***Figure 21-56.** The CrosstabSum() function is used in a computed field within the detail band in our example. This field is automatically generated by PowerBuilder for us.*

Step 5   Preview your data. Your finished crosstab should appear similar to the one in Figure 21-57.

Customer/Products	Product					
Customer Name	Baseball Cap	Shorts	Sweatshirt	Tee Shirt	Visor	Grand Total
Agliori, Michael	$2,052.00	$1,080.00	$2,304.00	$108.00	$1,176.00	**$6,720.00**
Andrews, Ling Ling			$3,456.00	$108.00		**$3,564.00**
Arlington, Randy	$696.00	$1,260.00	$288.00	$672.00	$504.00	**$3,420.00**
Beldov, Rosanna	$336.00	$360.00		$840.00	$924.00	**$2,460.00**
Belmont, Serop	$444.00		$288.00	$840.00	$84.00	**$1,656.00**
Bensoul, Sebouh	$564.00		$576.00	$108.00	$84.00	**$1,332.00**
Berejiklian, Herbert	$240.00	$1,800.00	$864.00	$1,176.00	$336.00	**$4,416.00**
Berenberg, Vartan	$456.00	$720.00	$576.00	$672.00		**$2,424.00**
Bilhome, Moe		$1,260.00		$2,148.00	$420.00	**$3,828.00**
Boyle, Laura	$912.00	$360.00	$1,440.00	$2,208.00	$336.00	**$5,256.00**
Cara, Nicklas	$480.00			$600.00	$168.00	**$1,248.00**
Cass, Jack	$804.00		$288.00	$612.00		**$1,704.00**
Chau, Helen		$540.00	$576.00	$3,372.00	$924.00	**$5,412.00**
Chen, Sheng	$2,484.00	$540.00	$2,592.00	$336.00	$168.00	**$6,120.00**
Chermak, Maio	$228.00	$1,080.00	$864.00	$216.00	$252.00	**$2,640.00**
Chin, Jen-Chang	$672.00	$720.00			$504.00	**$1,896.00**
Chopp, Shane		$540.00	$2,880.00	$1,716.00	$252.00	**$5,388.00**
Clarke, Belinda		$1,440.00	$288.00		$924.00	**$2,652.00**
Colburn, Kelly	$1,140.00	$1,620.00	$1,728.00	$1,668.00	$588.00	**$6,744.00**

Ready   Rows 1 to 19 of 109

***Figure 21-57.** Our end result.*

21.4.1.2 Sample Two—Crosstab With Complex Dimensions and Grouping

Now we are going to push our crosstab a little bit further by building one which has complex dimensions with multiple data elements. In our example we will build a crosstab that is going to tell us the purchases that each customer made for each product broken down by year and quarter (whew!). The result is shown in Figure 21-58. The whole crosstab didn't fit, so when you build yours, you can scroll back and forth, or you can see the result in the sample application on the companion CD.

Step 1   Build the SQL statement. Open the DataWindow painter and select SQL Select/Crosstab. Open the Customer, Products, Sales Order, and Sales Order Items tables. Check the joins to ensure they are correct. There will probably be an incorrect join between the products and customers table. Delete this join.

Customer Purchases

Customer Name	Product	1994 Q3	1994 Q4	1994 Total	1995 Q1	1995 Q2	1995 Q3	1995 Q4	1995 Total
Agliori, Michael	Baseball Cap	$1,020.00		$1,020.00		$108.00	$240.00	$684.00	$1,032.00
	Shorts	$180.00		$180.00	$360.00		$540.00		$900.00
	Sweatshirt			$0.00		$2,304.00			$2,304.00
	Tee Shirt			$0.00	$108.00				$108.00
	Visor		$924.00	$924.00				$252.00	$252.00
Agliori, Michael Total		**$1,200.00**	**$924.00**	**$2,124.00**	**$468.00**	**$2,412.00**	**$780.00**	**$936.00**	**$4,596.00**
Andrews, Ling Ling	Sweatshirt		$1,152.00	$1,152.00			$576.00	$288.00	$864.00
	Tee Shirt			$0.00		$108.00			$108.00
Andrews, Ling Ling Total		**$0.00**	**$1,152.00**	**$1,152.00**	**$0.00**	**$108.00**	**$576.00**	**$288.00**	**$972.00** $
Arlington, Randy	Baseball Cap		$360.00	$360.00	$228.00		$108.00		$336.00
	Shorts			$0.00		$720.00	$540.00		$1,260.00
	Sweatshirt		$288.00	$288.00					$0.00
	Tee Shirt			$0.00				$672.00	$672.00
	Visor	$336.00	$168.00	$504.00					$0.00
Arlington, Randy Total		**$336.00**	**$816.00**	**$1,152.00**	**$228.00**	**$720.00**	**$648.00**	**$672.00**	**$2,268.00**
Beldov, Rosanna	Baseball Cap	$216.00	$120.00	$336.00					$0.00
	Shorts		$360.00	$360.00					$0.00
	Tee Shirt	$336.00	$168.00	$504.00		$168.00		$168.00	$336.00

Figure 21-58. Sample two builds a crosstab that will show us the total purchases that each customer made for each product broken down by year and quarter.

Select the customer.fname, customer.lname, product.name, product.unit _price, sales_order_items.quantity, and sales_order.order_date columns. Your complete SQL statement should appear as follows:

```
SELECT "customer"."fname",
       "customer"."lname",
       "product"."name",
```

```
        "product"."unit_price",
        "sales_order_items"."quantity",
        "sales_order"."order_date"
  FROM "customer",
        "product",
        "sales_order",
        "sales_order_items"
 WHERE ( "sales_order"."cust_id" = "customer"."id" ) and
        ( "sales_order_items"."id" = "sales_order"."id" ) and
        ( "sales_order_items"."prod_id" = "product"."id" )
```

Close the SQL Select painter and move to the designer.

Step 2   Define the crosstab. The Crosstab Definition dialog window will open as you move from the SQL painter to the designer. We need to define the dimensions (rows and columns) and intersection (values) for this crosstab.

Drag the "lname" field into the "Rows" listbox. Double-click on it to open the Modify Expression dialog. Change the expression to:

```
trim(lname) + ", " + trim(fname)
```

Close the Modify Expression dialog window. Drag the "name" field into the "Rows" listbox. Make sure that you drop it below the customer name field that we defined as we want the product name to be subordinate to the customer name. If we dropped the product name field above the customer name, then product name would become the primary group. We don't need to modify product name, we will use the field as it is.

Now drag the "order_date" field to the "Columns" listbox. Modify the expression so that we only use the year component of the date. To do this we use the Year() function in the expression as follows:

```
year(order_date)
```

Close the window. Now drag the "order_date" field to the "Columns" listbox a second time. Drop it after the year field. Modify the expression to provide us with the quarter that the order was placed in. We can do this by using the new PowerBuilder 5.0 case expression function as follows:

```
case(month(order_date)
when 1 to 3 then 'Q1'
when 4 to 6 then 'Q2'
when 7 to 9 then 'Q3'
when 10 to 12 then 'Q4'
else '??')
```

Now that we have both our dimensions defines, we have to define our intersection. Drag the "quantity" field to the "Values" listbox. Modify the expression to give us the unit price multiplied by the quantity for each cell in the crosstab. The expression will be like this:

```
sum((quantity * unit_price) for crosstab)
```

The expression is quite simple. PowerBuilder takes care of the more difficult grouping and interpretation of the expression.

Press the **OK** command button to close the Crosstab Definition dialog.

Step 3   Modify columns and text fields. PowerBuilder automatically generates all the necessary groups and fields for you (hurray!). All that you have to do is tweak them until you get the formatting that you desire. (See Figure 21-59.)

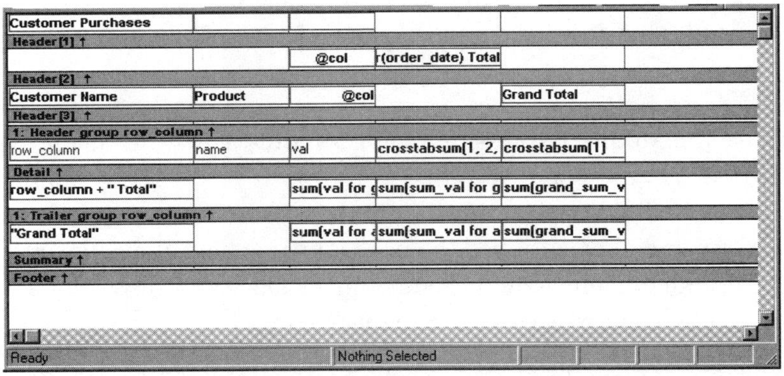

Figure 21-59. Tweak the fields in the designer until you have the crosstab formatted as you desire.

You can change the text field at the top of the crosstab to "Customer Purchases"and remove the other fields from the header [1] area.

In the header [2] area, you should select the third column with the "@col" value and change its alignment to centered. This is the column that will display the year, and it looks better if the year is centered over the four quarters.

In the header [3] area, you should change the label above the customer name column to read "Customer Name" and the label above the product column to read "Product."

In complex crosstabs, the volume of information can make it them difficult to read. Here is an excellent application for the use of color in your user interface. In the detail band, I have changed the customer name and product columns to have dark green text. You can't see it in the black and white picture above, but you can in the sample application. I also have changed the fourth column, the year subtotal, to a dark blue text.

In the group 1 trailer band, I changed all the text to a dark blue except the last column ("Grand Total") which I left black. The summary band I left unchanged.

You should alter the column widths to more appropriate settings, otherwise some of your columns will be difficult to read.

Step 4   Modify general settings. Clicking with the right mouse button in the unused area of the DataWindow will open up a popup menu. Select the **Properties...** option. This will open the Properties page for the DataWindow. On the General tab you will see a set of options that will allow you to change the grid settings. (See Figure 21-60.)

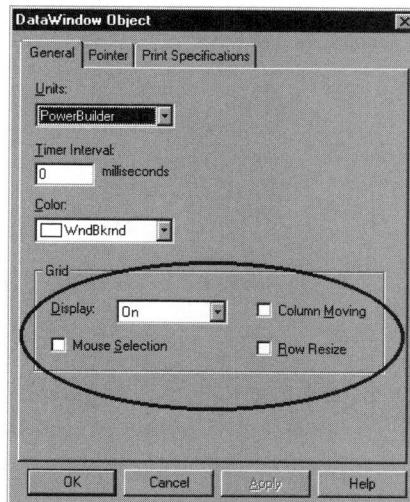

Figure 21-60. *On the Properties page you can change the grid settings for the crosstab.*

The Display drop down list box allows you to toggle the displaying of the grid lines for the cross tab. You can have them on, off, display only (not visible when printing), or print only (not visible when displayed on the screen. You can also enable or disable the end users ability to rearrange columns, select columns and resize rows at runtime.

Step 5   Preview your crosstab. Your end result should be similar to the original picture in Figure 21-56. If you run the version in the companion CD, you can see the crosstab functioning in an application. Notice the built in functionality for horizontal split scrolling.

This example is a more sophisticated crosstab, but they can get even trickier. Notice in the above example, our subtotal columns use a more complex variation of the CrosstabSum() function. All the crosstab functions have an alternate syntax which is:

```
crosstabsum( value_exp, column_exp, groupvalue)
```

where

value_exp. Is the expression in the Values listbox of the Crosstab Definition window that you want to perform the function upon. In our example, this value is 1. This must always be a numeric value.

column_exp. Is the expression in the Columns listbox of the Crosstab Definion window that you want to perform the calculation upon. In our example, we want the sum for each of our product lines, so our value is 2 (product is the second expression in our Columns listbox). This also must always be an integer.

groupvalue. Is a string which is used to control the grouping for the calculation. Group value is usually a value from another column in the crosstab. In our example, we are wanting to group by the year. To define this, we would build a string for groupvalue that begins with the "@" symbol (which is a required element) and then add the name of the column (defined in our crosstab at "year(order_date)"). The resulting groupvalue string is "@year(order_date)").

21.4.2 Dynamic vs. Static Crosstabs

There is an attribute of crosstabs which is often overlooked by most developers. Consider this problem which I encountered at one client I was working with. They had to track ships that were coming and going from their dock. They wanted to build a crosstab that would show how many ships were scheduled on Monday through to Sunday broken down by the company that the ships belonged to. The crosstab would appear something like:

Ship Schedule	Monday	Tuesday	Wednesday	Thursday	Friday	Saturday	Sunday
Company A	0	2	5	1	0	3	2
Company B	1	0	3	1	0	2	1
Company C	3	1	2	1	0	1	0

They wanted to produce this schedule every week with all seven days listed. The only problem is that on days like the Friday shown above, the column would not appear at all. This is because by default crosstabs are dynamically rebuilt with every result set retrieved. If there is no data for Friday, the Friday column would be removed.

You can override the dynamic setting and build static crosstabs that will always come out the exact same way every time they are run. This is accomplished by deselecting the **Rebuild Columns at Runtime** checkbox in the Crosstab Definition dialog window as shown in Figure 21-61.

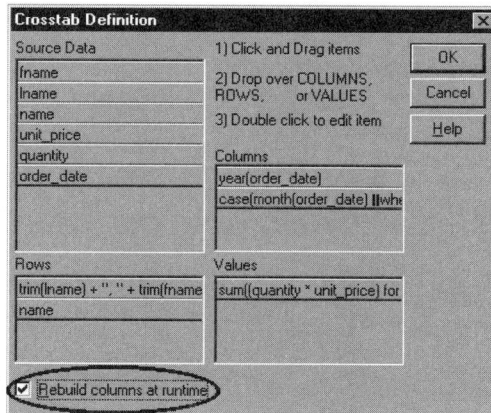

Figure 21-61. Static crosstabs can be generated by deselecting the Rebuild Columns at Runtime checkbox in the Crosstab Definition dialog window.

Now when you press the **OK** command button to close the Crosstab Definition window, PowerBuilder will retrieve the data from the database and will set up a series of static columns that will be the same for every retrieval of this crosstab. In order to ensure that all the columns that you want included will exist, there must be data in the database for each column (in our example, we must have at least one ship arriving each day). This is only necessary at the time that you create the crosstab. At runtime, it won't matter if there are no ships coming in on Friday, the Friday column will show up anyhow. You may need to create some fake data to meet your short term crosstab creation needs. (See Figure 21-62.)

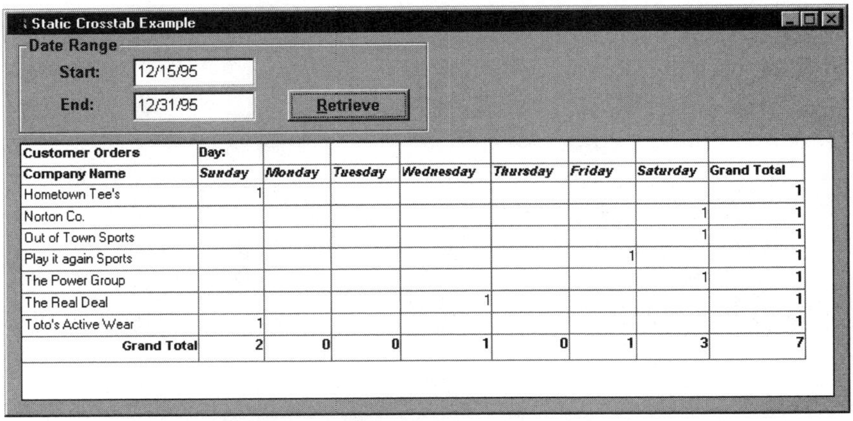

Figure 21-62. *Our Static Crosstab demonstration window on the companion CD allows you to pick a range of dates and then see which days orders were placed for each company.*

21.5   OLE 2.0 DataWindow Presentation Style

The OLE 2.0 presentation style is a gateway to a world of new and exciting possibilities. What it allows us to do is to take our data from a SQL select statement and pass it to a valid OLE 2.0 server. That server can then be made to perform functions with the data that we pass to it. For example, we could take our result set and pass it to the media player allowing us to integrate the playing of .WAV (sound files) and .AVI (video) files into our DataWindows. Or we could use MS-Graph as an engine for performing some advanced graphic that perhaps PowerBuilder does not support. One industry group I have been heavily involved in where this will be invaluable is in the energy, forestry and natural resource industries where integration with GIS (Geographic Information Systems) is critical. The opportunities are endless and will continue to grow as more and more software becomes OLE 2.0 compliant.

We can link any OLE 2.0 server product into the DataWindow as long as it supports the OLE standard Uniform Data Transfer (UDT). You should be able to learn if the application supports this from the vendor documentation, and you can learn what data is expected to be passed.

For our example, let's use Microsoft Graph as our OLE 2.0 server. This is an application that is installed with the Microsoft Office suite of tools, if you don't have it, you won't be able run this sample from the companion CD. (See Figure 21-63.)

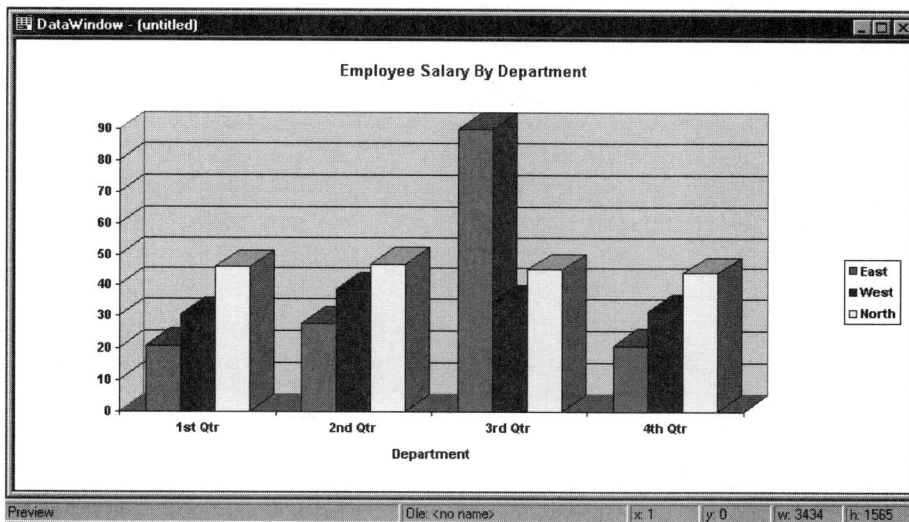

Figure 21-63. *The OLE 2.0 presentation style can use any OLE 2.0 server that supports UDT (Uniform Data Transfer) to display data from the database. In our example, we will use Microsoft Graph as an OLE 2.0 server within a DataWindow object.*

Creating a Microsoft Graph OLE 2.0 DataWindow

Step 1   Start the DataWindow painter and select **New....** Select **SQLSelect** as your data source (or other as appropriate) and OLE 2.0 as your presentation style. Notice that the **Options...** button is disabled as the display of the data will be handled by the **OLE 2.0** server and not by PowerBuilder. Select the **OK** button.

Step 2   Select the appropriate tables and columns for your data source. In our example we selected the employee and department tables. (See Figure 21-64.)

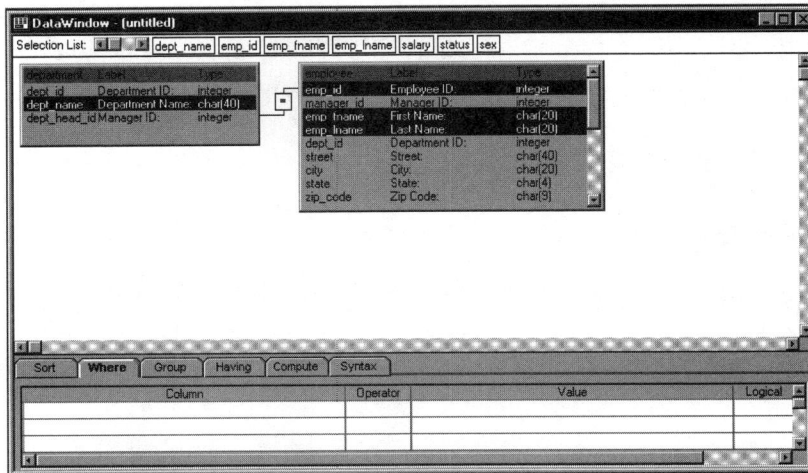

Figure 21-64. *Select the data columns you wish to pass to the OLE 2.0 server.*

Step 3   Note that to move from the SQL Painter to the Design window inside the DataWindow, you select the **SQL** button, which is a push on/ push off button that will bring you in and out of the SQL painter. Do this now to move from the SQL Painter to the Designer.

Step 4   When moving into the designer, PowerBuilder will need to know what OLE 2.0 server you will be using. It opens the window in Figure 21-65 to ask you to select one (alternatively you could open an .OCX control as the container for the data). In our example, we are selecting Microsoft Graph 5.0. Selecting the **Browse...** command button will take you to the Object Browser where you can examine the inside of your selected OLE 2.0 server. You will see options such as where the server is physically located, which .DLL it uses, and so on. (See Figure 21-65.)

Step 5   You will return now to the DataWindow designer. The OLE 2.0 server will be visible and selected in the middle of the DataWindow painter. Notice that the toolbar at the top of the painter is actually the tool bar for Microsoft Graph. While the OLE 2.0 server object is selected, you have access to all the functions and features of MS-Graph. If you click outside the OLE 2.0 object, on the blank area of the DataWindow, you will revert back to the PowerBuilder DataWindow toolbar. To go back to MS-Graph, click on the OLE 2.0 server object at any time you are in the designer. Click outside the OLE server now. (See Figure 21-66.)

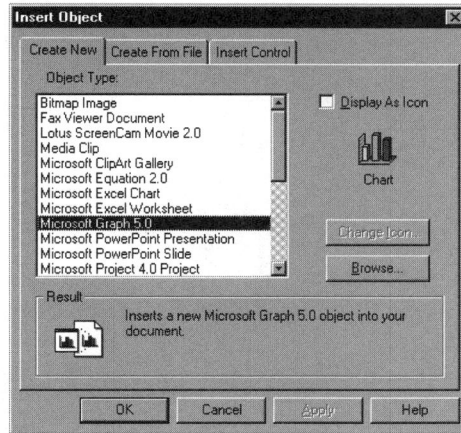

***Figure 21-65.** Select the OLE 2.0 server. We are using Microsoft Graph.*

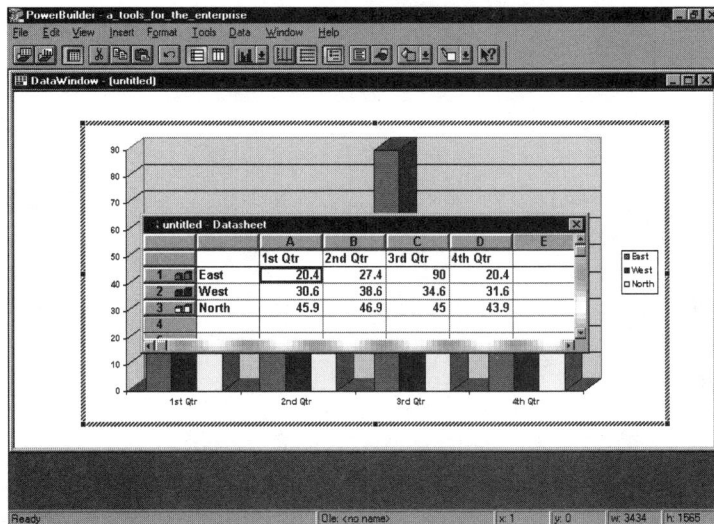

***Figure 21-66.** When you enter the designer, you will notice that the OLE server object is selected. When selected, the menu for MS-Graph appears in the toolbar. You have access to all the features of MS-Graph.*

Step 6 When you clicked outside the OLE server object in Step 5, you returned to the normal DataWindow painter designer. Then, a dialog window appeared asking you to define the object as in Figure 21-67. Specifically, the object needs to know what data it is receiving.

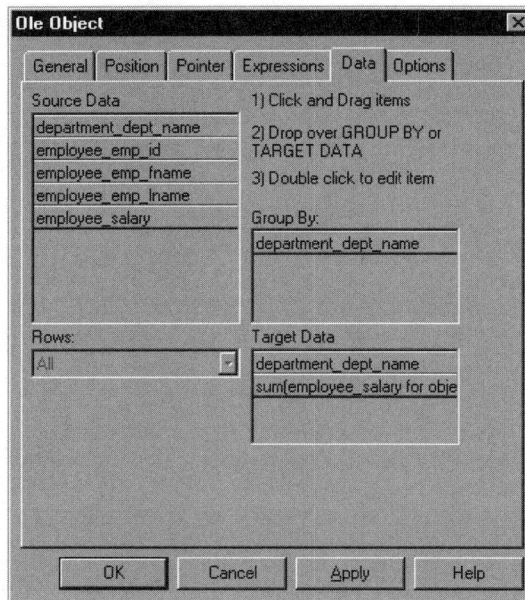

***Figure 21-67.** The OLE server now needs to know what data we are passing it.*

In this window we have to specify which data we are sending to the OLE 2.0 server and how we are grouping it. We do this using drag and drop. First, let's drag the column department_department_name into the Group By box. This specifies that we are going to group by the department name. Next, drag the same column into the Target Data box, indicating that we are going to pass the department name to the OLE server. Then drag the column employee_salary to the Target Data box. Notice that the field in the target data box changes to sum(employee_salary by object). PowerBuilder makes the guess that you want to graph this data by the sums of salaries within a department. If this is true you can leave it, if you want to change the expression, you can double-click on the column in the Target Data box and it will take you to the expression editor dialog window. For our purposes, this is the correct value, so we do not need to alter it.

There are other tabs on the window for modifying the attributes of the OLE server object including expressions, OLE options, which pointer to use and where to display the object. We will look at these later, for now, just select **OK**.

Step 7   Now we are in the DataWindow painter. Let's preview our data. Select the Preview button from the DataWindow painterbar. Your DataWindow should appear similar to the one you see in Figure 21-68.

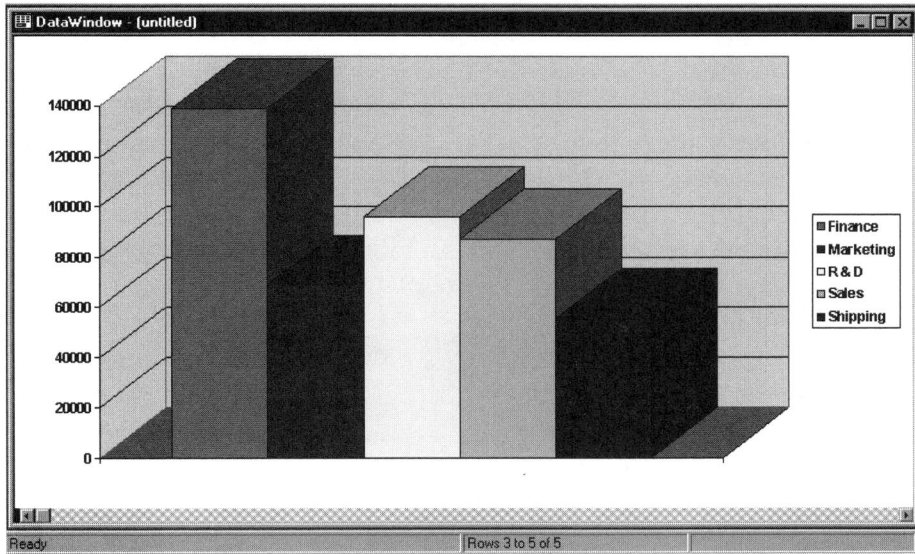

Figure 21-68. Your data should appear something like this.

By double-clicking on the object the end user will be able to bring up the MS-Graph server and begin changing the properties of the graph. If you want to provide this kind of functionality to the user, then you can just leave the settings as they are. Some of the benefits of leaving this functionality in place is that the user now has a high degree of control over the data they are being presented with. They have the ability in our example to change the graph type, colors, and formatting, or view the data sheet, or almost any other functionality that MS-Graph provides. The drawback is that you also cannot limit that functionality. If there are some features of MS-Graph that you don't want the to have access to, like importing an external chart, that functionality comes along with the package and you cannot selectively restrict the user. It also increases the complexity of the user interface, and depending on your user group (remember Chapter 4 when we talked about analyzing your users) you may want to keep the interface as straightforward as possible.

If you want to override the double clicked functionality which activates the OLE server, this can be accomplished on the tabbed window where we specified the data. If you started up the MS-Graph server, switch back to the DataWindow by clicking on the white space outside the OLE object. Now press the preview button again (it is another push on/push off button) to return to the designer. Within the designer, if you click on the OLE object with the right mouse button you will get a popup menu. Select the **Properties...** menu item. This will open up the OLE properties dialog window again. Select the **Options** tab. On this tab, change the Activation setting to Manual. Now the user cannot start up the MS-Graph server. Although launching the server application is disabled for the user, you can still start it up through your script. (See Figure 21-69.)

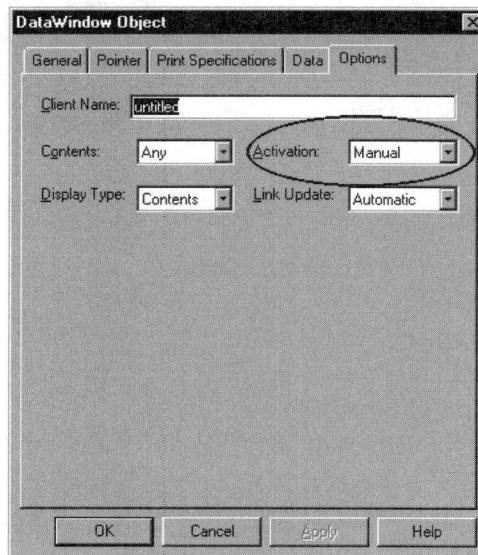

Figure 21-69. You can deny the user access to the functionality of your OLE server by overriding the activation setting and changing it from DoubleClicked to Manual.

Step 8   Let's enhance our graph by adding some labels. Double click on the OLE server object. This will start up the MS-Graph server inside our DataWindow painter (alternatively, to start up MS-Graph outside of our DataWindow painter, click on the server object with the right mouse button and select

Open... off the popup menu). Click with the right mouse button inside the graph. This will bring up a popup menu. Select the **Insert Titles...** option. You will then be given the option of attaching a title to the entire chart, or to the axes. The options are check boxes, so you can select whichever ones you desire. Choose Chart and Value Axis. (See Figure 21-70.)

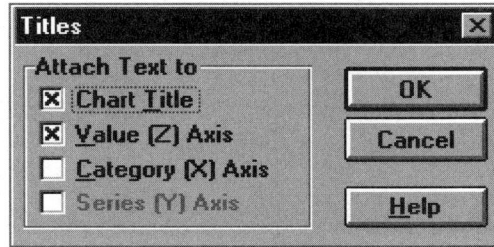

Figure 21-70. *The Insert Titles dialog from MS-Graph allows us to customize our OLE object.*

Now you can select the titles in the graph and enter new text for them. Like in PowerBuilder, you can select an object and then with the right mouse button, you can change it's properties. Change the properties of the Value Axis label by clicking with the right mouse button and adjusting the font alignment to display the text vertically. Now let's move the legend to the bottom of the window. Do this by selecting the legend, clicking with the right moue button and selecting **Format Legend...** from the popup menu. On the Format Legend dialog window, you can go to the Placement tab and change the position to the bottom of the window. Now return to the DataWindow painter by clicking outside the OLE object and let's preview our work. Your DataWindow should look similar to the one in Figure 21-71.

To see the completed version of the above example, examine the sample application on the companion CD.

21.5.1.1 Rich Text Edit Presentation Style

If you have ever had to produce a report or DataWindow object that involved substantial amounts of text and the need to embed information into the text, you will be very pleased to learn about the Rich Text Edit presentation style. It will allow you to mix text and images of any shape, size and color you desire. This particular format is extremely valuable for document generation and creation of form letters. (See Figure 21-71.)

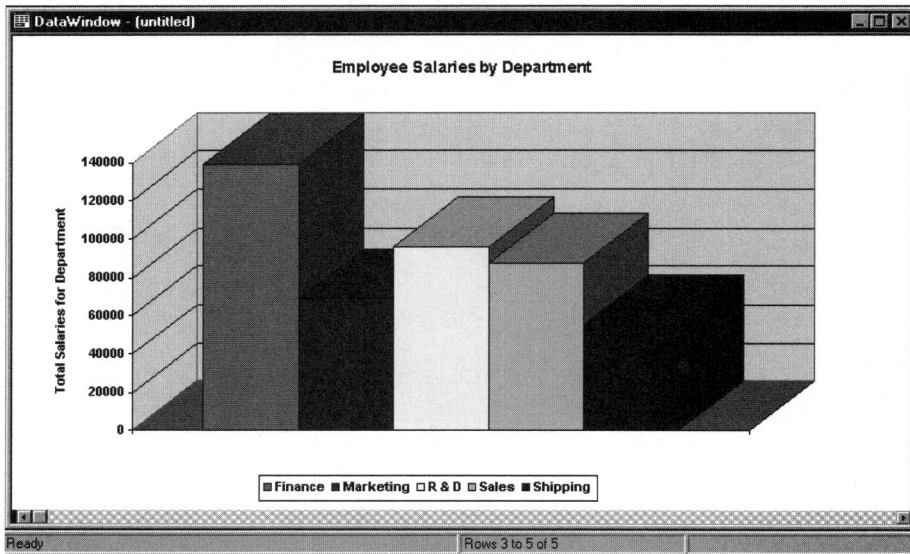

Figure 21-71. *Our enhanced OLE object takes advantage of the functionality of the OLE server.*

Enterprise applications are often called upon to generate form letters. In the past, we have accomplished this through a variety of means including the generation of a mail merge file and then using DDE to command Microsoft Word or WordPerfect to perform a mail merge with some predefined template. Now we have the ability to generate these documents directly in PowerBuilder.

We can provide the end user with the ability to edit and modify these letters at runtime. All this functionality is encapsulated within the RTF presentation style, all you have to do it turn it on! The end user can also be provided with a popup menu that will allow them to take their modified letter and cut and paste it into their word processor of choice to manipulate. We have the ability to add headers and footers to our text, mix fonts and perform automatic word wrapping and column sliding.

Let's create a sample RTF DataWindow object using data from our Customer table in the PowerBuilder sample database. We want to send out a letter to all customers in a particular state informing them that there is a special sale coming up which is custom tailored to customers from their state!

Step 1   Launch the DataWindow painter and select SQL Select as the data source and RichText as the presentation style (notice that the **Options...** button is disabled). (See Figure 21-72.)

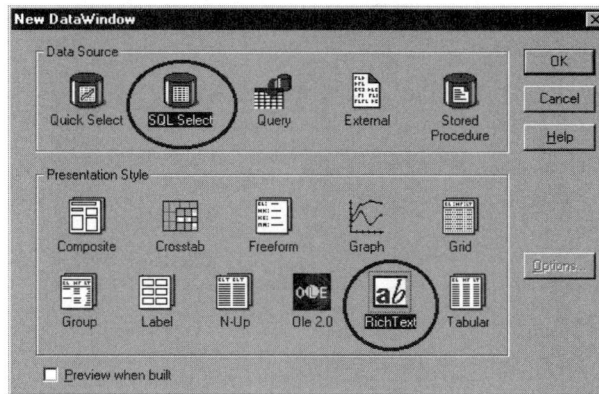

***Figure 21-72.** Launch the DataWindow painter and select SQL Select as the data source and Rich Text as the presentation style.*

Step 2   You will enter the standard SQL Select painter. Let's select the Customer table. From this table, select all the columns except Customer_ID and Phone_number. (See Figure 21-73.)

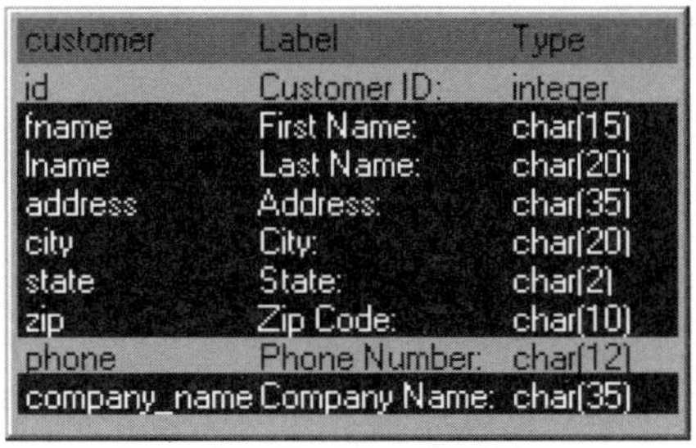

***Figure 21-73.** Open the Customer table and select all the rows except ID and Phone_Number.*

Step 3   Define a retrieval argument for the State. From the **Design** menu bar item, select **Retrieval Arguments....**. This will open up the Retrieval Arguments Dialog window as shown in Figure 21-74. Here, define one string argument called as_state.

Step 4   Declare a where clause in the SQL Toolbox at the bottom of the SQL Painter. Set the column "customers"."state" to be equal to your retrieval argument defined in Step 3. (See Figure 21-74.)

```
"customers"."state" = :as_state
```

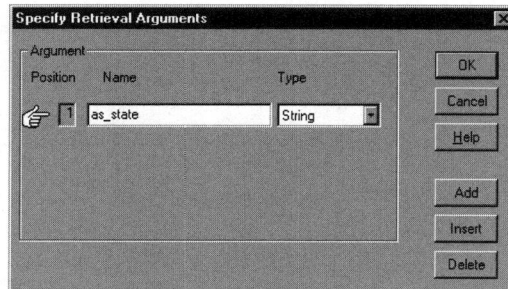

***Figure 21-74.** Define one string argument called as_state.*

Note: Remember that the colon (":") in front of the argument name denotes it as a host variable. (Figure 21-75.)

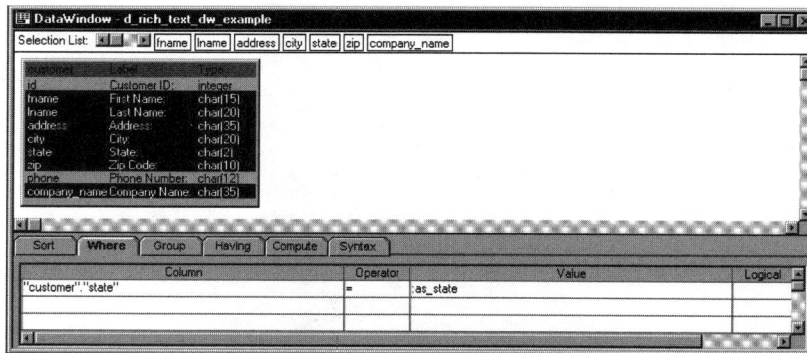

***Figure 21-75.** Declare a where clause in the SQL Toolbox*

Step 5   Return to the Designer by clicking on the SQL button in the toolbar and turning the SQL painter off.

Step 6   Before the designer appears, you will be asked to fill in the details of the properties for this RTF object. The Rich Text Definition dialog will appear. We want to deselect Header/Footer as we won't be requiring these for our letter. We want to enable Word Wrap so that our text will wrap to fit the page as appropriate. Under the Rich Text Bars group we have the option of providing the user with a toolbar, tab bar and ruler at runtime with which they can edit the RTF DataWindow. We want to provide the user with the RTF Tool Bar.

The Popup menu option enables the menu that allows the users to cut, copy and paste text from the RTF DataWindow. It also allows them to access the properties page and alter the properties settings for the object, turning toolbars on and off, enabling viewing options, and so on.

You can also make the DataWindow Display Only. This means that the user cannot alter the text inside your document. In the are of presentation, you can choose to show embedded characters for returns, tabs, and spaces. This is very similar to a feature that most major word processors have. The colors for the background of the DataWindow and the embedded fields can be selected here.

Another major option that can be selected is the option of using a RTF file that you have built prior to the creation of the DataWindow. To do this you indicate Use File and then specify the file you with to include. (Figure 21-76.)

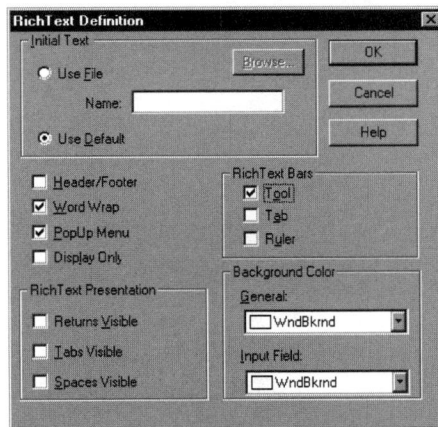

Figure 21-76. The Rich Text Definition dialog allows you to select options for your RTF DataWindow object.

Step 7   Within the designer you will see all the fields that you selected in the SQL Painter. These fields are enclosed in braces to indicate that they are RTF fields. Before each field is the traditional DataWindow label. We don't want these labels in our letter, so we are going to remove them. Delete these labels from view now. (See Figure 21-77.)

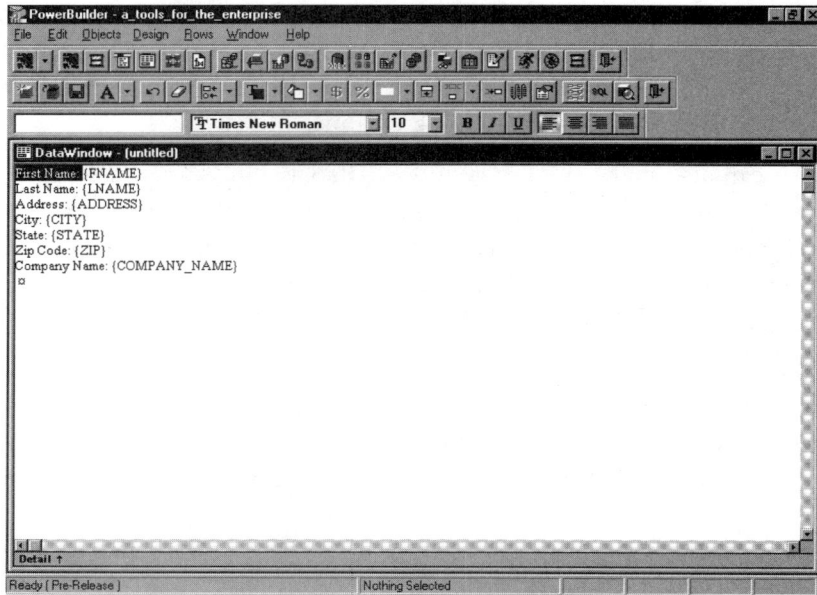

Figure 21-77. All the fields selected in the SQL painter will appear enclosed in braces to show that they are RTF fields. Remove the labels from these fields as they are not necessary for our letter.

Step 8   Now that the labels are gone, rearrange the fields so that Last Name comes after First Name (separate them with a space) and that State comes after City (separate these with a comma and a space). Move Company Name to the line below the customers name.

Now we want to insert a date field at the top. Move the cursor to the top and insert two blank lines. To insert a computed field, select **Computed Field...** from the **Objects** menu bar item. Then click where you want the computed field to appear, at the top of the page. (See Figure 21-78.) Now define the computed field. Give the computed field the name of Date_String and define it as:

```
String(Today(),"MMM DD, YYYY")
```

Step 9   Now we enter the body of the text. On the first line we want to enter "Dear" and then follow that with the first name of the customer again. To do this, we have to make the same column appear twice. Select the **Column** menu item from the **Objects** menu bar item. Then select where you want the column to appear (click after the text "Dear"). You will be given a window with all the columns in it as shown in Figure 21-79. Select the "fname" column. This field will now appear after your text. Follow it up with a comma.

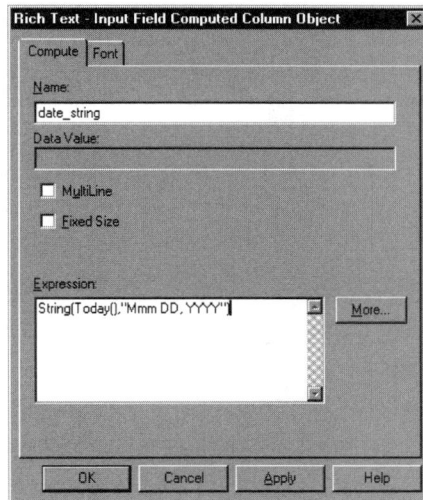

Figure 21-78. The Rich Text Input Computed Column Object dialog window allows you to define your own computed column. We will use it to show the current date formatted as Mmm DD, YYYY.

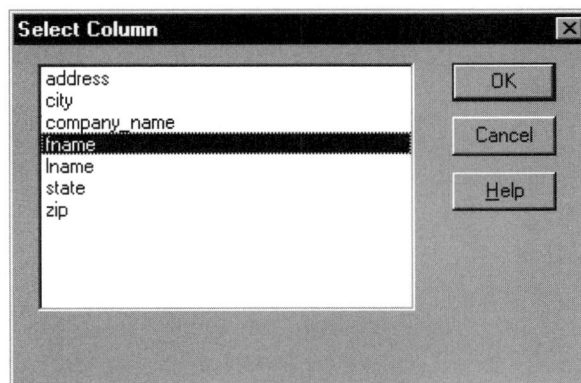

Figure 21-79. The Select Column dialog window is used for insert fields into our RTF DataWindow.

Use this same technique to insert the name of the city into the body of your text You can make the body of your text anything you want. Our sample uses:

Dear {FNAME},

I just wanted to take a moment to thank you for your continued support over the years. We recognize that our success in the pet products market is due to our loyal customers like yourself. We would like to express our gratitude by inviting your to participate in our **V.I.P. Sale**, coming soon to your local <u>Janice's Pet Emporium in {CITY}</u>. We will have special deals on all our pet supplies and food. Just show your V.I.P. card to the clerk.

Once again, thank you for your continued support and for letting us earn your business!

Sincerely,

Janice Wolf
President

For some finishing touches, we bold the name of the sale and underline the name of the store and the customer's city. Then we add at the very top of the page some letterhead like text. We could also, if we desired, insert a bitmap with the president's signature at the bottom in the signature area, and maybe add a bitmap logo to the top of the letter.

Step 10   Now save your RTF DataWindow before previewing. This is just being cautious, but I believe in saving these objects regularly. After saving, preview your object by selecting the Preview button on the toolbar. Enter a valid state (I will use "CA"). You should see all your letters appearing in your DataWindow. Along with viewing these letters, you can print them too! Note that if you scroll up and down in the DataWindow using the vertical scroll bar, it will only scroll within the existing page and will not take you to the next page. To page forward and backward you must use the toolbar buttons or the PAGE UP and PAGE DOWN keys on your keyboard. Keep this in mind when you build your applications as you may want to provide "forward" and "backward" buttons to your users. (See Figure 21-80.)

Figure 21-80. Our finished RTF DataWindow object can be incorporated into an application.

21.6 Summary

Good quality reporting is an essential element of any successful business system. The ability to provide feedback to the users of the system is a key factor in why PowerBuilder has been so successful in the client/server business application development arena.

There are many advanced features in PowerBuilder that you can use to provide reports and feedback for your user. We have examined nested reports, composite reports, crosstabs, graphs, OLE 2.0, and Rich Text DataWindows.

Take full advantage of these features to improve the quality of reporting that you integrate into your system. The features that are discussed in this chapter are some of the most powerful that PowerBuilder has to offer, yet they make up probably less than 10% of the reports currently in use in production systems.

CHAPTER 22

User Objects

A critical requirement to develop object oriented applications within any environment is the ability to define and reuse your own object classes. In PowerBuilder, one of the vehicles for providing this functionality is the user object.

Although you are not required to utilize user objects when creating applications in PowerBuilder, they are essential if you want to build applications that are distributed, tiered, and/or low maintenance. When you take advantage of user objects your development teams will be able to avoid repetitive coding, improve the maintainability of your application(s), standardize the interface and processing, and more!

User objects can be broken down into two general types: visual and class (non-visual).

22.1 Visual User Objects

Visual objects are objects that the user can see and will interact with in your application. In general, these objects are intended to be used as controls on window objects. You can use the visual user object to customize the appearance and behavior of standard PowerBuilder visual controls or you can integrate controls written in other languages like C, Delphi, or Visual Basic into your PowerBuilder applications.

Visual user objects usually consist of one or multiple controls that are used for a specific function or business purpose. These objects can be used in the Window painter, but only external properties can be modified there. External properties are things like the position, size, color that are not encapsulated within the object. To modify the encapsulated properties of a visual user object you must use the User Object painter. In PowerBuilder we have four different types of visual user objects; custom, external, standard, and VBX.

22.1.1 Visual: Standard

Standard visual user objects allow you to customize the standard PowerBuilder visual objects such as command buttons, DataWindow controls, radio buttons and so on. These are particularly useful if you want to reuse this new object in multiple places. Consider the standard close command button. This button is used in many different windows throughout multiple applications. You could create a standard visual user object of this button encapsulating the button label and clicked method.

Let's walk through the process of creating the standard visual object cb_close.

Step 1   Open the User Object painter. Select the user object icon. The standard selection dialog window will open. Notice that it looks very much like the Window painter selection window. You can create a new user object or you can inherit from an existing user object. This allows you to inherit from and extend your own class definitions. Select the **New...** command button. This will open the New User Object window in Figure 22-1.

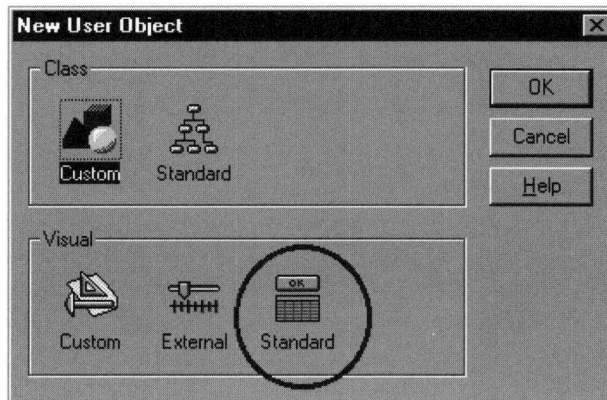

Figure 22-1. The New User Object dialog window allows you to select the kind of user object you want to create.

Select the standard visual user object and press the **OK** command button.

Step 2   Choose object type. The Select Standard Visual Type window will open. This window contains a list box with all the standard PowerBuilder visual objects that you can inherit from. Select the *commandbutton* from the list and press the **OK** command button. (See Figure 22-2.)

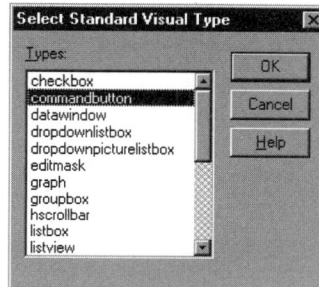

Figure 22-2. *The Select Standard Visual Type dialog window allows you to select the type of standard object that you are going to create from a list of all the standard PowerBuilder types.*

Step 3   Modify object. In the user object painter you will see a standard command button that has been created. You can now modify this object by altering its properties and adding methods and instance variables (which become new properties for this object when it is instantiated). (See Figure 22-3.)

Figure 22-3. *In the user object painter you can alter the properties of the command button and add methods and instance variables.*

In the style bar, change the text on the button to "&Close" and make it bold (using the bold toolbar icon). Now resize the button to the size that you want it to be by default.

Next we want to add a method to the clicked event of this object. Click on the command button with the right mouse button and launch the script painter from the popup menu. By default, you will enter the clicked event. Like in any other instance of the script painter, you can move between events using the drop down list box at the top of the painter.

We want the clicked event to close the window that this object has been placed on. We want to code this script to be generic so it can be used on any Window. We will use the PARENT pronoun to accomplish this.

```
Close(PARENT)
```

Save the object and give it the name u_std_cb_close.

Step 4   Create a new window. Open the window painter and create a new window (or use an existing window that has a Close button). To place the object on the window, select the user object control from the control palette. This will cause the Select User Object dialog window to open. (Figure 22-4.)

Figure 22-4. When placing a standard user object on a window you will be presented with the Select User Object dialog window from which you will choose the object you want to work with.

Choose your u_std_cb_close object. Place this object on your window. Give the object a meaningful name like cb_close. Save your window.

Step 5 Run your window. Run your window and observe the behavior of the user object that you placed. When clicked, it will close the window it is sitting on.

This user object could be used on any window in any application and it would function exactly the same. In order to use the user object we simply had to place it on the window and its encapsulated functionality did the rest.

This was a simple example, but you can think of many different uses, particularly for objects like the DataWindow control. If you are building a "fat" two tiered application, you could build a DataWindow object that has all the logic for row selection, error handling, searching, sorting, and so on built right in. Then all the DataWindows in your application could take advantage of all this functionality that you only had to build once!

If you are building a "thin" three tiered or n-tiered application, or if you are taking advantage of a service based architecture, you could build your own standard visual DataWindow control that has built in links to all the required service objects and business objects.

22.1.2 Visual: Custom

The custom visual user object can be though of as a way of grouping other objects together into one common container. This container is a fully encapsulated and reusable object. These objects are usually relatively generic in orientation. One project that I was involved with used a group of commandbuttons with the same functions as a custom popup toolbar throughout all their applications. When you clicked with the right mouse button, this user object was dynamically created (see the section called, "Creating User Objects").

A common type of custom user object is a DataWindow VCR Controller. This type of a control combines a number of standard buttons that are combined into a custom visual object. This object can be used in conjunction with any DataWindow control as a user interface device for moving through the Data. (Figure 22-5.)

Figure 22-5. A DataWindow toolbar, or DataWindow VCR Controller allows you to use everyday controls to navigate through the data in a DataWindow.

We will walk though the construction of this custom visual user object.

Step 1   Open the User Object painter. As you did in the previous section, open the user object painter, and create a new user object. This time select the Custom Visual User Object Icon. This will open the user object painter window.

Step 2   Create the custom object. The workspace in the user object painter when creating a custom user object is very much like working in the window painter. You have the palette of standard PowerBuilder controls that you can build into your custom object. You can even embed other user object into this custom user object.

Place four picture button controls in your workspace. Double-click on each picture button and change its properties as follows (set Original Size to true for all):

1. name: pb_first enabled picture: BFIRST.BMP (or you can use FIRST.BMP from your PowerBuilder directory)

2. name: pb_prev enabled picture: BPREV.BMP (or PREV.BMP from the PB directory)

3. name: pb_next enabled picture: BNEXT.BMP (or NEXT.BMP)

4. name: pb_last enabled picture: BLAST.BMP (or LAST.BMP)

Arrange these buttons in the top left corner of the workspace in the format of the toolbar pictured in Figure 22-5.

Step 3   Define an instance variable. We need to create a reference variable of type DataWindow that we can use at runtime to reference the DataWindow control that we want these buttons to work with. To do this we define an instance variable for the user object. This is done in the same fashion as in the window painter.

Define the variable as protected so that it cannot be accessed from outside this control. This keeps our object properly encapsulated. (Figure 22-6.)

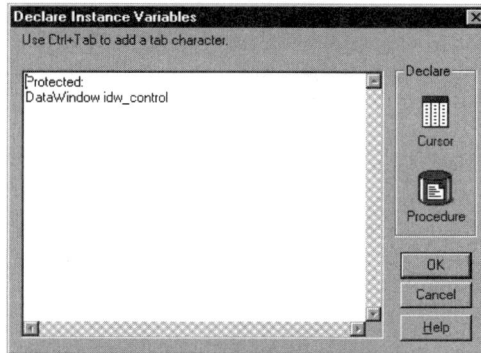

Figure 22-6. *Define a protected instance variable that will contain the runtime reference to the DataWindow control we want to tie this toolbar to.*

Step 4   Define a public function to set the runtime instance variable. We defined the instance variable as protected to encapsulate our user object. We need to provide a runtime interface to allow the parent object to interact with our toolbar. We will define an object level function called SetDW() which will accept a single argument of type DataWindow. This argument will be passed by reference and inserted into our protected instance variable. This will provide our methods in the picture buttons with a handle of a DataWindow control with which they can work. (Figure 22-7.)

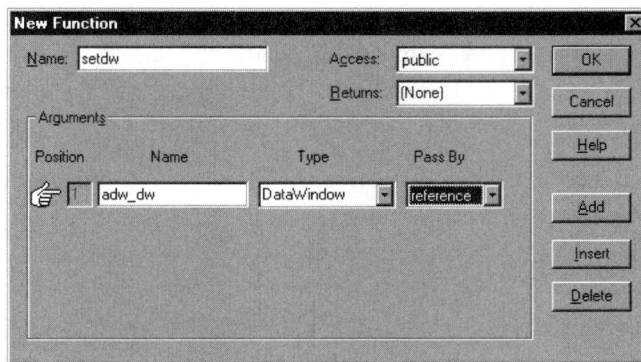

Figure 22-7. *The function declaration for SetDW().*

The function declaration is shown in Figure 22-7. The script for this function is:

```
idw_control= adw_dw
```

Step 4 Add scripts to the buttons. We need to add a script to each button in the toolbar. The scripts will be as follows:

cb_first will scroll to the first row in the DataWindow control. The script is:

```
idw_control.ScrollToRow(1)
```

cb_prev will scroll one row up in the DataWindow control. The script is:

```
idw_control.ScrollPriorRow()
```

cb_next will scroll to the next row in the DataWindow control. The script is:

```
idw_control.ScrollNextRow()
```

cb_last will scroll to the last row in the DataWindow control. The script is:

```
idw_control.ScrollToRow(idw_control.RowCount())
```

Step 5 Fine tune the control. Change the background color of the control to a gray. Make sure that the border property is set to None. Resize the edge of the control so that it wraps neatly around the picture buttons.

Step 6 Save the control. Save the user object with the name u_cst_dw_toolbar.

Step 7 Place the control on a window. Select a window that has a DataWindow control on it. From the sample application you could select the w_emp_maint_dw_events window. Open the window and place the control on the window.

Step 8 Link the DataWindow control to the toolbar. We can link the DataWindow control to the toolbar by calling the SetDW() function that we defined in the user object. In the constructor event for our user object control enter the following script:

```
THIS.SetDW(dw_employees)    // Use the name of the DW control on this
                            // window.
```

Step 7   Run the window and observe. Now that the object is created, it can be used on any window, anywhere with only one line of code to link it to the appropriate DataWindow control.

22.1.3 Visual: External

The external visual user object is used to bring objects and controls created in languages outside of PowerBuilder into a PowerBuilder application. The most common of these are probably controls written in C, C++ or Delphi, but you could encounter controls from any number of languages. Almost any language that builds a true windows .DLL (Dynamic Link Library) can be tied into PowerBuilder.

In order to use an external .DLL it is critical to have the appropriate documentation from the producer of the .DLL so you know the correct class name and style settings.

To define an external visual user object you select that option from the New User Object window. PowerBuilder will ask you to identify the .DLL file that will be the source for this object. Select it and press the **Open** command button.

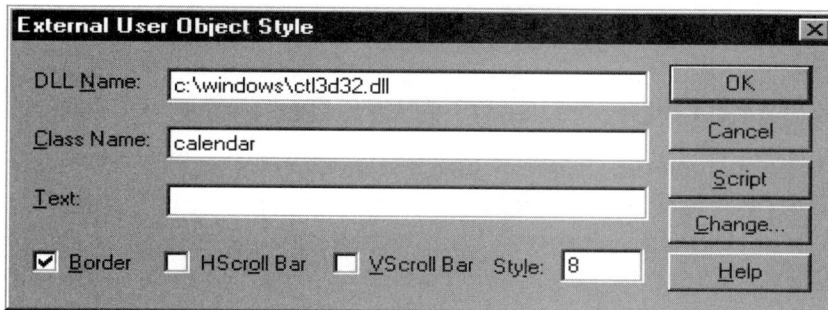

Figure 22-8. The External User Object Style dialog window.

This will open the External User Object Style dialog window pictured in Figure 22-8. The .DLL name will be filled in. This .DLL must be available at runtime which means it must be distributed along with your .EXE and other files to your end user. The Class Name comes from the documentation of the vendor. A single .DLL could contain multiple classes that you could use. The other critical property that you must set is the

Style value. This value will control the attributes of the class. These values will also be specified in the documentation. If everything is set up correctly, when you press the **OK** command button, you should be able to see the control in the user object workspace. You will need to define custom user events that are linked to the appropriate windows messsages (refer to Chapter 8, the section entitled, "Setting Up Object Events") as specified in the vendor documentation.

22.1.4 Visual: VBX

The VBX user object is only available if you are using the 16 bit version of PowerBuilder. These have generally been replaced by the 32 bit OCX controls. Chances are you won't be working with VBXs, but just in case, here is how they work in a nutshell.

VBX controls are those written in Visual Basic. There are many third party VBX controls on the market for using in your applications. These objects work very similar to external user objects in PowerBuilder, except that they are a little easier to set up. You merely specify the VBX file to use, select from the list of control in that VBX file and that is all. You will automatically have a set of VBX events defined. You can continue to extend these methods as you see fit.

22.2   *Class (Non-visual) User Objects*

Class, or non-visual objects are encapsulated containers for attributes and methods that the application will use but are never created visually or seen by the user. These objects are essential for distributed PowerBuilder, integrating OLE automation and the use of business objects and service based architectures.

22.2.1 Class: Standard

The standard class user object are objects that allow you to extend the properties and methods of standard PowerBuilder non-visual classes. The classes that you can build on are seen in Table 22-1.

Table 22-1

Standard Class	Description
Connection	Object containing connection information for distributed PowerBuilder objects.
DataStore	A non-visual version of the DataWindow class. Used for manipulating data but not displaying it to the user.
Dynamic Description Area (SQLDA)	Object which stores the input and output information for type 4 dynamic SQL statements.
Dynamic Staging Area (SQLSA)	Object which stores type 4 dynamically generated SQL statements. This object acts as the only connection between the dynamic SQL and the transaction object.
Error	Object which stores information on errors and the location where the errors occur.
MailSession	Object which contains the context information for Mail Application Program Interface (MAPI) processing.
Message	The standard message object which is passed to and used during the processing of events.
OLEObject	Object which acts as a proxy for a remote OLE object.
OLEStorage	Object which acts as a proxy for an open OLE storage area.
OLEStream	Object which acts as a proxy for an open OLE stream.
Pipeline	The standard pipeline user object which contains the context information for execution of a pipeline object (see Chapter 15 for more information on Data Pipelines).
Transaction (SQLCA)	The standard transaction object which serves as a communications area between the database and the PowerBuilder application component (such as a DataWindow).

The objects that you create from these ancestors can have expanded functionality that the ancestors don't have. For example, we could define our own transaction object that has all its methods encapsulated inside it. We could add a method that will automatically read in the property settings from an .INI file, another that will manage the connection process and so on (the current transaction object is very poorly encapsulated requiring you to do a great deal of work outside of the object).

Let's create our own transaction object as an example of how we create a standard class user object.

Step 1   Open User Object Painter. Open the user object painter and choose a new object. Select the Standard Class object from the Class group box. PowerBuilder will open up the Select Standard Class Type dialog window and let you select what kind of class to use as the ancestor for your object. (See Figure 22-9.)

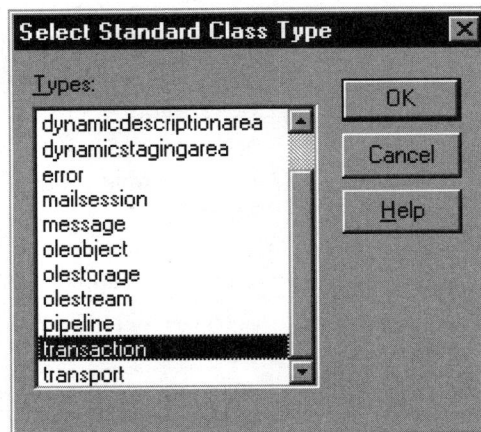

Figure 22-9. Select the object to use as the ancestor for your standard class user object from the Select Standard Class Type dialog window.

Step 2   Define any custom attributes and methods. The painter will open up with what looks like a window workspace, but you can't place any controls on it because it is non-visual! You can, however, define new attributes for the class (as instance variables) and new methods (as object functions).

We will define a custom method called GetINIParms() which will load the database parameters for the transaction object from an INI file. Select the **Declare** → **User Object Functions...** option from the menu. This will open the Select Function Window. Press the **New...** command button to create a new function.

In the function declaration window, declare your function as in Figure 22-10.

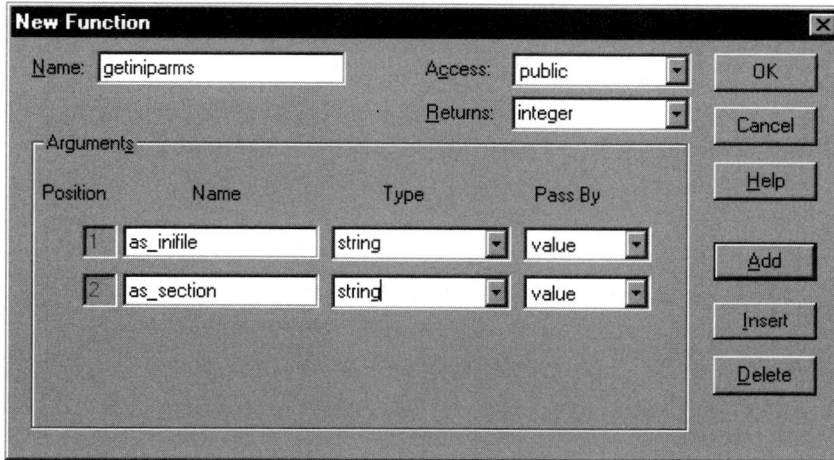

Figure 22-10. Declaration for the GetINIParms() function.

Define two string arguments, one to contain the path and name of the .INI file and the second to store the name of the section in the .INI file where the database profile can be found. The script for the function should be something like:

```
IF FileExists(as_inifile) THEN
    // Retrieve Parameters
    THIS.DBMS = ProfileString(as_inifile,as_section,'dbms','')
    THIS.Database = ProfileString(as_inifile,as_section,'database','')
    THIS.ServerName = &
    ProfileString(as_inifile,as_section,'servername','')
    THIS.Logid = ProfileString(as_inifile,as_section,'logid','')
    THIS.Logpass = ProfileString(as_inifile,as_section,'logpass','')
    THIS.Userid = ProfileString(as_inifile,as_section,'userid','')
    THIS.DBPass = ProfileString(as_inifile,as_section,'dbpass','')
    THIS.DBParm = ProfileString(as_inifile,as_section,'dbparm','')
    RETURN 1
ELSE
    // File Not Found
    MessageBox("Connection Error","Unable to read connection information."+&
        ".INI file '"+as_inifile+"' not found.",StopSign!)
    RETURN - 1
END IF
```

This example reads even the user id and password from the .INI file. Most likely these would come from other places.

If you were to substitute this transaction object for the standard SQLCA transaction object (the technique for doing this is discussed in the "Creating User Objects" section below) you would get SQLCA to populate itself from your .INI file simply by calling the following function:

```
SQLCA.GetINIParms("myapp.ini", "[database]")
```

I am sure you can think of many other methods that it would be useful to have inside your standard transaction object such as a Connect() function that connects and checks for errors.

Step 5   Save the new object. Save the object as u_nvo_transaction.

22.2.2 Class: Custom

The custom class user object is a place where you can build any kind of non-visual object you desire. This is the place where you will build your service objects, or your distributed objects for PowerBuilder.

When you first open a new custom class user object, it will have only one pre-defined property called *proxyname* that is used for distributed computing (as discussed in Chapter 9—Building Distributed Applications). The only functions it supports are ClassName(), GetParent(), PostEvent(), TriggerEvent(), and TypeOf().

It is up to you to create the properties and methods that are necessary for what you intend this object to do. This is done in the same was as we have accomplished this in previous units, through instance variables and object functions.

Let's create a non-visual service object for handling errors.

Step 1   Open the user object painter. Open the painter and select Custom Class as the type of object that you want to create. This will open up the user object painter with a workspace that looks the same as it did in step one for the Standard Class object. Like that object, there is no visual component here, so you will not be able to place controls in the workspace.

Step 2   Define any custom attributes and methods. This is the meat of creating a non-visual user object as it serves no purpose without the specific attributes and methods that you define. For our example, we are going to define a two standard methods; one for checking for errors after embedded SQL calls, and a second for generic database error handling.

The generic error handling method will be created as HandleError(). The function definition for this is shown in Figure 22-11.

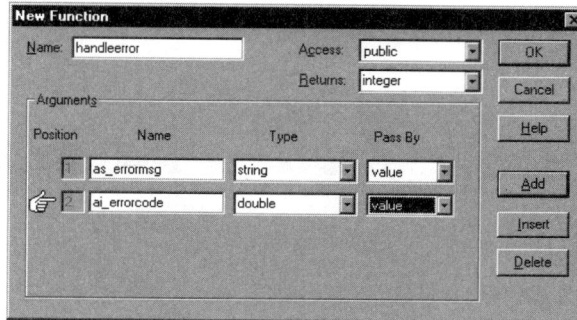

Figure 22-11. Function declaration for the HandleError() method.

The processing in this function could get quite complex. You could put in custom handling based upon error code and even use different non-visuals for different databases to allow for easier DBMS independent development. For our example, we will simply display the error message:

```
// Custom error handling based upon error code
// could be inserted here.  Different non-visuals
// could be implemented for different databases
// simplifying database independent development.

RETURN MessageBox("Database Error", "Error: "+as_errormsg + &
    "~n~rError Code: "+String(ai_errorcode), StopSign!)
```

The second method that we will add is the CheckSQLError() method. This method could also be incorporated into the transaction object in the previous section, but for the purposes of demonstration it is included here. The function definition for CheckSQLError() is shown in Figure 22-12.

This script will check the transaction object that was passed to determine if the SQL executed correctly. If not it will immediately rollback the transaction and call the error handling function (that is conveniently located within itself). The script for this is as follows:

```
IF atr_trans.SQLCode <> 0 THEN
     // Rollback immediately so that other users aren't
     // locked out of the table.
     ROLLBACK using atr_trans;

     // Call the Handle Error event to process error
     THIS.HandleError(atr_trans.SQLErrText,atr_trans.SQLDBCode)
     RETURN TRUE
ELSE
     RETURN FALSE
END IF
```

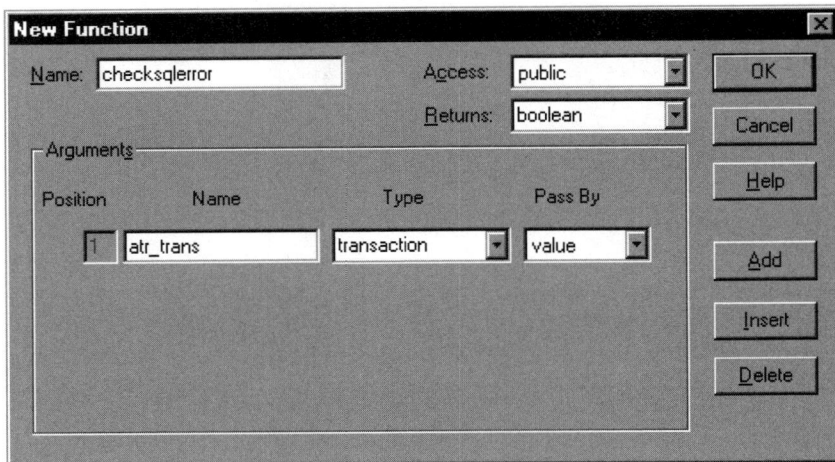

Figure 22-12. *Function declaration for CheckSQLError() method.*

Step 3   Save the object. Save this object as u_nvo_errorhandler.

The next step to using this object is to create it in the location where it is required. Refer to the following section for details on how to do this.

22.3 *Creating User Objects*

Creating user objects is only half of the skill that is necessary to realize their benefits. The second step is to integrate them into your application. The techniques for doing so are very different for visual and non-visual user objects.

22.3.1 Instantiating a Visual User Object

Visual user objects play a critical role in interfacing with the user. You can think of them like a custom control that you place on a window. There are two methods for instantiating a visual user object; you can do it directly in the window painter, or you can write a script to dynamically create them as required at runtime.

22.3.1.1 In a Painter

To add a user object to your window in the window painter, you simply select the user object icon from the window painterbar (Be careful not to select the icon from the PowerBar as this would launch the User Object painter. Note that the icons are the same.) When you do so, you will be asked to select the object that you wish to paint on the window from the Select User Object dialog window.

> **Developer's Note:** Although non-visual user objects will appear in the list when you choose your user object to place on a window, attempting to place one will result in a warning message that you cannot place non-visual class objects on the window.

Once you have chosen the user object that you want to place, you simply click on the window where you want it to appear. From that point it behaves exactly like any other windows control.

22.3.1.2 In a Script

If you are already familiar with instantiating non-visual objects, you will be familiar with the reserved word CREATE. This is the same reserved word we use to define our own transaction objects, which at this point I will assume that you are already familiar with. We could use the CREATE syntax to instantiate a visual class of object like this:

```
u_std_cb_close cb_close
cb_close = CREATE cb_close
```

This script would indeed create an instance of the class in memory. We could assign values to its attributes and so on. There is one critical reason why we don't do this; the object never appears on the window. Using the create statement on a visual class will not cause it to appear within the visible interface. To do this we need to use a special function called OpenUserObject().

The OpenUserObject() is specifically designed to allow us to instantiate and visually provide the user with a user object at runtime. The syntax for this function is:

```
window.OpenUserObject(user_object {, x , y })
```

where

window is the window that you want the user object to be instantiated within

user_object is the user object that you want to instantiate

x is the x coordinate of where in the window you want the user object to open (the default if you don't specify is 0)

y is the y coordinate of where in the window you want the user object to open (the default if you don't specify this is also 0)

This function will return a 1 if the open succeeds, a -1 if it fails.

Developer's Note: Prior to version 6.0 of PowerBuilder, when you opened a user object dynamically at runtime, the object was NOT be placed into the window control array. Now with version 6.0 it is. If you manually tracked this in applications that you migrated from version 5.0, you may want to modify this code.

Developer's Tip: If you issue an OpenUserObject() function for the same user object, PowerBuilder will open the object the first time, but only activate it the second time (not create a second instance). This behavior is the same as when you open a window. If you want to mulitply instantiate a user object, use the same technique you would with a window. Declare a reference variable instead of opening up the object itself.

The OpenUserObjectWithParm() function works exactly the same way, but you are able to pass a parameter to the user object through the message object, just like you would with OpenSheetWithParm() or OpenWithParm().

If you want to close a user object that you have dynamically opened, you can do so with the CloseUserObject() function. The syntax for this function is:

```
window.CloseUserObject(user_object)
```

where

> **window** is the window that contains the user object

> **user_object** is the user object that you wish to close

This function also returns a 1 if successful and a -1 if not successful. When called, the object is removed from the window and removed from memory. You do not need to script a DESTROY statements in order to release the resources back to the system.

22.3.2 Instantiating a Non-Visual User Object

When you want to instantiate a non-visual user object you must declare the object in your scripts so that the object manager will create the object in the appropriate memory pool. Some non-visuals are already declared for you. These are the system non-visual objects such as the error, message and SQLCA transaction object.

22.3.2.1 Default System Non-Visual Objects

You can change the standard system objects that PowerBuilder defines for SQLCA (communications area—transaction object), SQLDA (dynamic description area), SQLSA (staging area), the message object and the error object. If you would rather have SQLCA be created from the transaction object that we described above in the section called "Class: Standard" we can switch it in the Application painter.

The definitions for these standard system objects is established in the application object. If you open the properties page for the application object you will see a tab marked Variable Types as shown in Figure 22-13.

To use your object instead of the standard transaction object, simply replace the name of the object in the SQLCA field to your non-visual object name, u_nvo_trans.

22.3.2.2 In Script Creation

Most non-visual objects will be instantiated as required in your scripts. The usual process is to declare a reference variable that contains the handle for the object. This handle is how you will reference the object in your scripts.

The syntax for instantiating a non-visual object is:

```
u_nvo_errorhandler luo_errorhandler
luo_errorhandler = CREATE u_nvo_errorhandler
```

If you wanted to call a function in the error handler you would do so by using the reference variable like this: (See Figure 22-13.)

```
luo_errorhandler.HandleError(dw_1.DBErrorMessage(), dw_1.DBErrorCode())
```

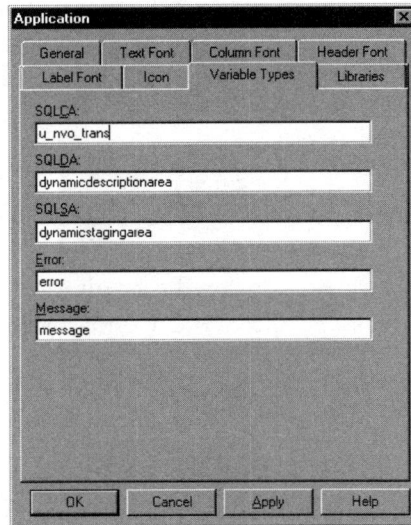

Figure 22-13. *You can substitute your enhanced standard non-visual user objects for the standard system objects that PowerBuilder creates in the application object.*

The scope of the reference variable that you declare will determine where you can reference this object. The error handler object example could be declared locally if you only needed the error handle within that object, or you could go to the other extreme and declare it globally so that the error handle could be used by any object in the application at any time.

Developer's Tip: In the latest two versions of PowerBuilder we have a new variation on the CREATE syntax that allows us to be extremely generic when writing our scripts. We can now call CREATE and append the keyword "using" to dynamically specify an object that we want to create.

For example, let's say that we have two ways of searching through a set of data on library books, by Author Name or by Title. We could have two specific search non-visual object each inherited from the generic search non-visual object. We could dynamically determine which object we needed and instantiate only the appropriate object like this:

```
luo_nvo_search u_nvo_generic_search
string ls_specific_search

IF rb_searchbyname.checked THEN
    // Search by name
    ls_specific_search = "u_nvo_name_search"
ELSE
    // Search by title
    ls_specific_search = "u_nvo_title_search"
END IF


luo_nvo_search = CREATE USING ls_specify_search
```

Now calling the methods on the non-visual object luo_nvo_search will cause the appropriate Name or Title specific method to be implemented automatically.

When you CREATE an object, you must remember to DESTROY the object when you are finished with it and before the reference variable passes out of scope. If you fail to destroy the object and the handle passes out of scope, then you have no way of removing this object from the memory pool. The object has now been "orphaned." It is occupying memory, but there is not way to reference it to use it or remove it. When your application exhibits this kind of behavior, we say that it has a "memory leak." The longer you run the application, the more orphaned objects are created and the fewer and fewer resources are available to the application.

The syntax to destroy our error handler object is:

```
DESTROY luo_errorhandler
```

Developer's Note: If you issue multiple CREATE statements for the same object such as:

```
u_nvo_errorhandler luo_errorhandler
luo_errorhandler = CREATE u_nvo_errorhandler
luo_errorhandler = CREATE u_nvo_errorhandler
```

This will result in the creation of two instances of this object. The first one would be orphaned because the reference variable will point to the last object that was created. Be careful that you don't create any orphaned objects.

22.3.2.3 Without Reference Variables

It is possible to instantiate a non-visual user object (it must be a user object, non a system class) without explicitly declaring a reference variable first. PowerBuilder will automatically declare a global reference variable with the same name as the object class. For example:

```
u_nvo_errorhandler = CREATE u_nvo_errorhandler
```

would create an instance of u_nvo_errorhandler and provide us with a global reference variable of the same name to reference the object.

22.3.2.4 Autoinstantiate

Since PowerBuilder 5.0, we have had a feature called *autoinstantiate* that is available for custom class user objects. The autoinstantiate property, when set to true, will cause PowerBuilder to automatically create an instance of the object in the appropriate memory pool when you declare a reference variable for it in your script. This eliminates the need for a CREATE statement.

This property can only be set in the user object painter. You access the property from the popup menu that appears when you right mouse click on the custom class object as shown in Figure 22-14.

There is one behavior that you need to be aware of when using the autoinstantiate property. Usually if you set one reference variable to be equal to a second, the first reference variable merely picks up the pointer of the second object. When autoinstantiate is on, the entire object is copied and a new instance created when one reference variable is set to be equal to the second.

```
luo_errorhandler1 = luo_errorhandler2
```

would result in two separate instances of luo_errorhandler2. Note that if you already had an instance of your non-visual error handler in luo_errorhandler1 it would now be 'orphaned' and unreachable by you. This orphan will continue to consume system resources and can degrade the performance of your system.

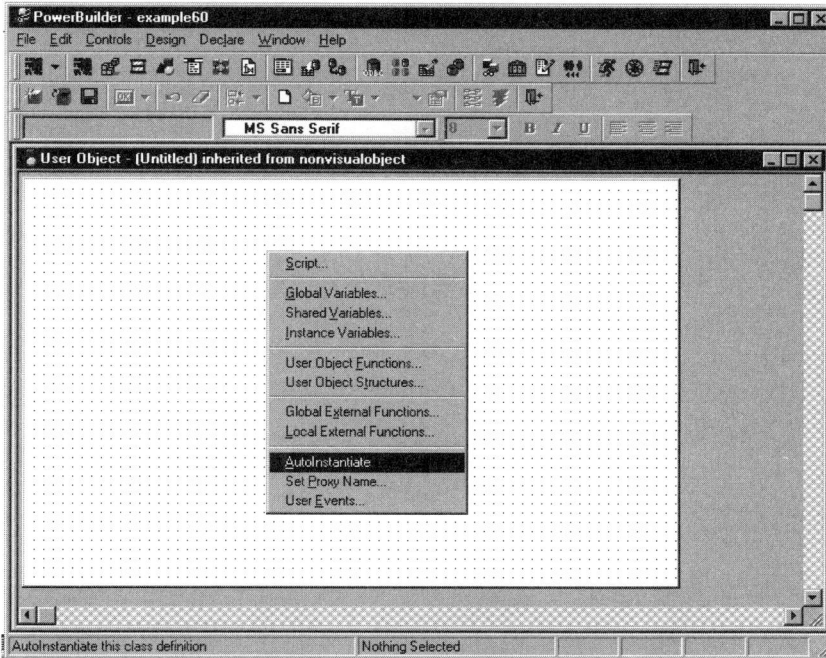

Figure 22-14. *The autoinstantiate option in a custom class user object will cause PowerBuilder to automatically instantiate the object in memory when you declare a reference variable of that object type.*

22.4 Summary

In any quality enterprise application built with PowerBuilder, user objects will play a critical role. They help with standardization, encapsulation, reduced maintenance, and increased developer productivity. When used correctly, they can improve the performance of your application also.

Take a close look at the PowerBuilder Foundation Class library (PFC) that comes with PowerBuilder enterprise to see an example of the extensive use of user objects.

Using SQLCentral

*W*hether you are a new user of Sybase SQLAnywhere or a veteran of the Watcom *database engine, there is a new tool that ships with the 32 bit versions of PowerBuilder 6.0 (actually it comes with the 32 bit versions of Sybase SQLAnywhere) which will make your life as a DBA much easier. This tool is called SQLCentral. In this appendix we will explore this new tool and demonstrate how to perform most standard database administration tasks within its point and click interface. The interface is very full featured and we will endeavor to cover most of the functionality, however just because we do not mention a specific feature here doesn't necessarily mean that SQLCentral doesn't support it. We encourage you to explore the interface and discover all the different capabilities of this flexible tool.*

SQLCentral only runs in the 32 bit environment. If you are administering your SQLAnywhere database from a 16 bit environment you will not be able to access any of this functionality. I would strongly encourage you to administer your SQLAnywhere database from a 32 bit platform. Aside from the benefits of robustness and speed, you will be able to utilize the SQLCentral tool.

What Is SQLCentral?

SQLCentral is a tool for graphical database administration. Through a Windows 95 "explorer" type interface a DBA can examine multiple SQLAnywhere databases. In each database the DBA can examine and manipulate database objects such as tables, views, triggers, indexes, and stored procedures. The graphical environment helps to insulate the DBA from many of the idiosyncrasies of SQL and also makes it easier for less experienced DBAs to manage the database.

Many other DBA activities can also be automated within SQLCentral. Procedures such as database backup and recovery can be made easier. Database compression, extraction, loading and translating can be performed through a point and click GUI interface. Many of these advanced features utilize a 'wizard' to step you through to process of performing the task.

SQLCentral will work with Watcom 4.0 databases, but not with releases earlier than that. The upgrade wizard in SQLCentral will upgrade Watcom 3.2 and 4.0 to SQLAnywhere 5.5.

Using the SQLAnywhere Utilities

When you first start SQLCentral you will not be connected to any databases. The only functionality available to you will be to connect to a database or to begin working with the SQLAnywhere Utilities. All these utilities are stored in a folder in the explorer interface. Selecting the folder will cause the list of utilities to be displayed on the right side of the explorer as in Figure A.1.

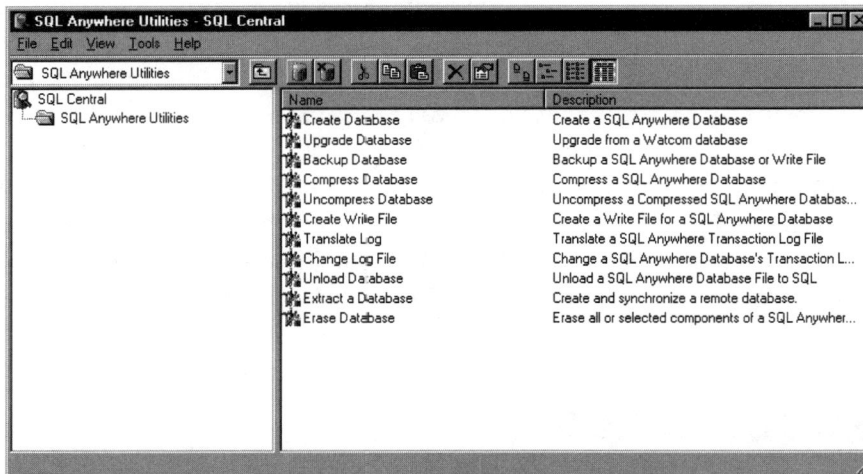

Figure A-1. Selecting the folder for SQLAnywhere Utilities will cause a list of the available utilities to be shown on the right side of the explorer interface.

These utilities will make the task of administering SQLAnywhere databases very straightforward. Previous tasks that required mysterious command line statements can now be executed by pointing and clicking to select your options.

Any of the utilities can be executed by double clicking on the utility with the mouse. A wizard will run that will walk you through the process. An alternative method for running a utility is to use drag and drop to drag the icon for a database that you have opened in SQLCentral (as discussed later in this appendix) and dropping it on the appropriate utility folder.

Backing Up

Backup up a database is one of the most common and definitely most critical operations for a DBA. Database backup from the command line prompt has been discussed earlier in this book. We will not revisit the theories of backup here, but will show you how it is done with SQLCentral.

Run the Backup Database utility. The first page of the wizard, shown in Figure A-2, asks you to specify if you are backing up a running or a non-running database. The tool can create backups of both, but the process that it will use is different.

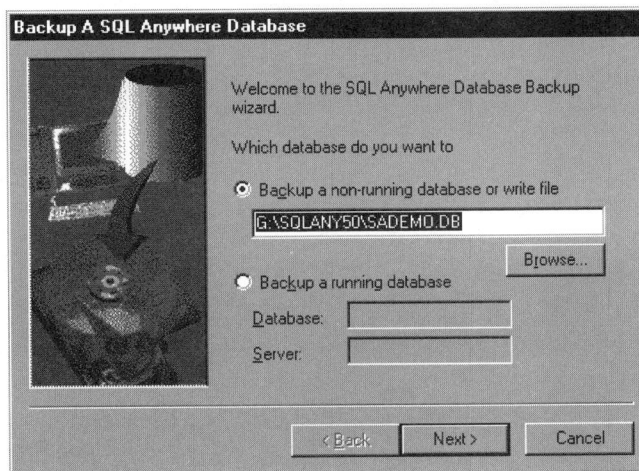

Figure A-2. The first page of the backup wizard will ask you to specify if the database that you wish to back up is running or not.

After selecting the running/not-running option you will have to tell SQLCentral where the database is. If it is not running you do so by providing the name of the database file (.DB) and its full path. If you don't know the full path or correct name, you can push the **Browse…** command button to search for it. If the database is running you will have to specify the database name and the server on which it is running. Pressing **Next** after you have done so will take you to the next page.

The next page will ask you to specify a valid DBA account name and password. If you are using the standalone or single user SQLAnywhere engine, this will be a user id of "dba" and a password of "sql." (See Figure A-3.)

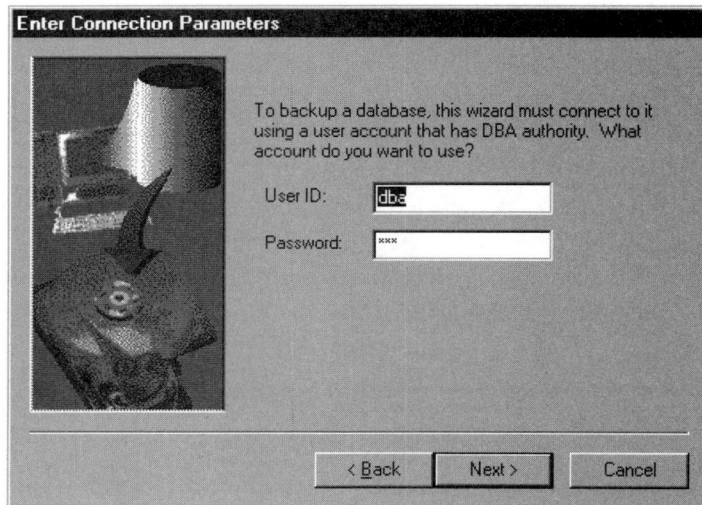

Figure A-3. The second page of the backup wizard will ask you to specify a user id and password that has DBA level access to the database.

The third page is where you will specify where the backup file will be stored. This can be anywhere in your visible directory structure. You can specify a directory that does not exist and SQLCentral will ask you if you wish to create a new directory.

Next you must specify what parts of the database you wish to back up. You can choose any combination of the database main file (which contains all the database objects and data including stored procedures, indexes and triggers), the transaction log and, if applicable, the database write file. (See Figure A-4.)

If your database is using a transaction log, the fourth page will specify how you want to deal with the log after the backup. By default, the system will continue to use the existing log. Alternatively, you could erase the old log and start a new one, or rename the old one and start a new log file with the original name. (Figure A-5.)

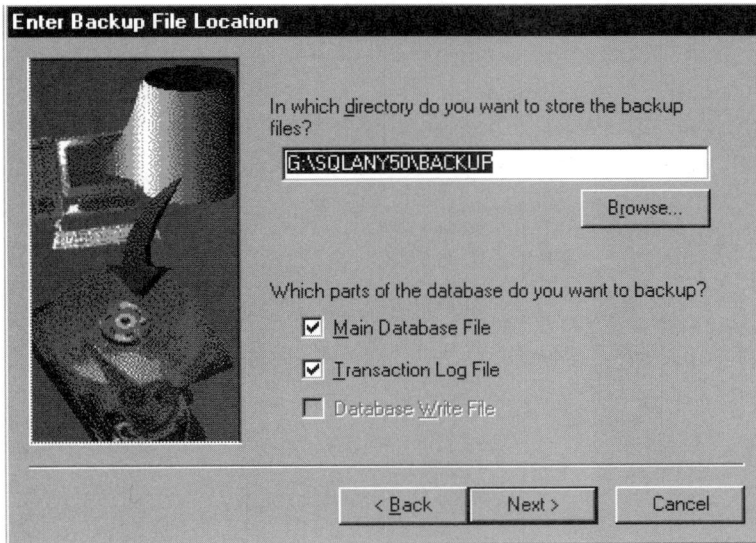

Figure A-4. *The third page allows us to specify where the backup file will be stored and what components of the database we wish to back up.*

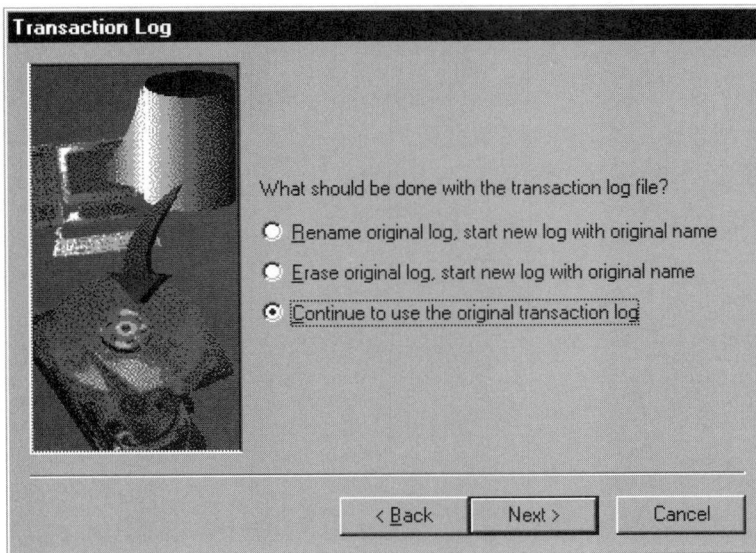

Figure A-5. *The next page allows you to specify how you want to deal with the transaction log. By default, the system will continue to use the original transaction log.*

The final page will display the database to be backed up and where the backup files will be stored. This is your final confirmation. Once you press **Finish** SQLCentral will create the backup. A progress screen will appear showing how much of the database has been backed up. The backup log window will display any messages relating to the backup and tell you of the success or failure of the operation as shown in Figure A-6.

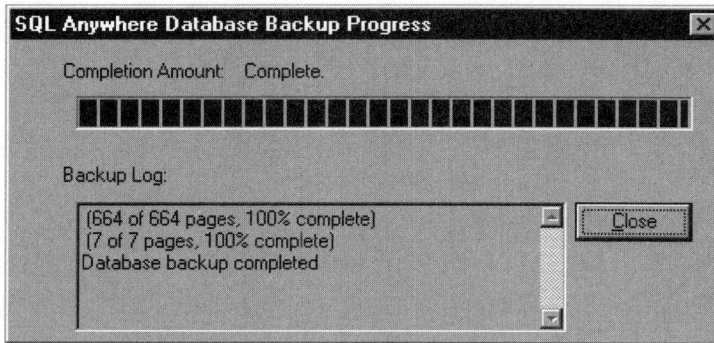

Figure A-6. During the backup process, SQLCentral will display a progress window allowing you to watch the progress of the database backup and observe any messages relating to the backup in the backup log area.

If there were no messages you will see backup copies of all the requested database components (.DB, .LOG and/or .WRI files) in the subdirectory you specified.

Database Compression

Sometimes, when storage space for a SQLAnywhere database becomes an issue (like in installations on portable computers) we can compress our database to a smaller size. Access times for a compressed database are slower, and the database cannot be updated directly anymore. Updates are performed through write files. If these limitations are acceptable for your situation, you can compress a database in SQLCentral by launching the Compress Database wizard.

Compressing

The Compress Database wizard will not affect the database file that you tell it to compress. It will instead create a new compressed file. On the first page of the wizard you will specify the database that you wish to compress. You need to include the file name and the path name. You can use the **Browse...** command button to select a file and path if desired. (See Figure A-7.)

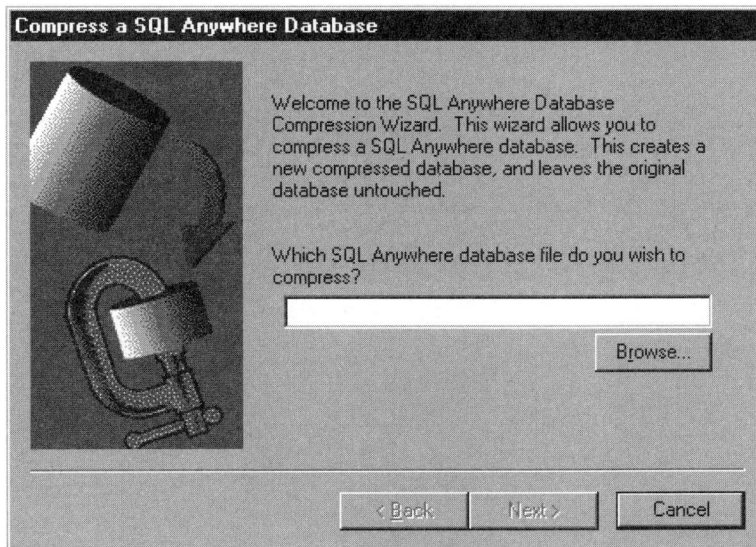

Figure A-7. *The Compress Database wizard is used to create a new compressed database file that is smaller than the original file. On the first page you will specify the database filename and path name.*

Developer's Note: Compressed databases can be reexpanded using the Uncompress Database utility discussed below.

Compressed databases will be stored with a filename extension of .CDB instead of the standard .DB for database files. The second page of the wizard will ask you to specify the name of the compressed database and where it should be stored. If you do not specify the .CDB extension, the wizard will add it for you.

Developer's Note: The .CDB file extension used by compressed SQLAnywhere databases is also used by another Sybase product S-Designor Data Architect to represent a conceptual data model. If you have S-Designor installed and you look at your compressed database in Explorer, it will show up as an S-Designor file even though it is not.

The final page of the wizard will ask you to confirm the detail you entered on the previous pages. When you press the **Finish** command button a progress window will appear showing you the progress of the compression and any informational messages in the log area. Upon completion of the compression process, SQLCentral will display a window showing the details of how the file was compressed as shown in Figure A-8.

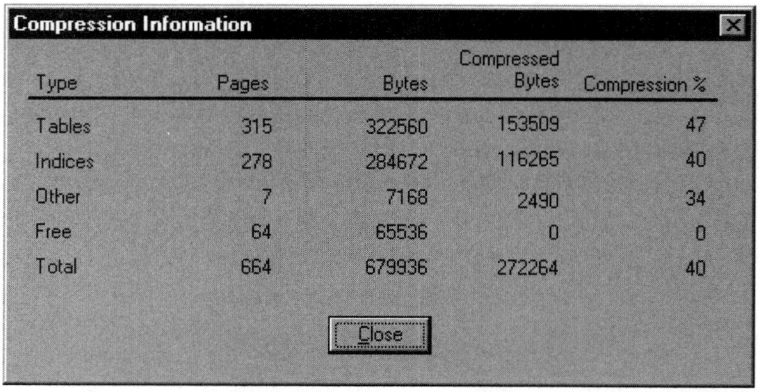

Type	Pages	Bytes	Compressed Bytes	Compression %
Tables	315	322560	153509	47
Indices	278	284672	116265	40
Other	7	7168	2490	34
Free	64	65536	0	0
Total	664	679936	272264	40

Figure A-8. The Compression Information window is displayed after compressing a database. It will tell you how much compression was achieved.

Uncompressing

The Uncompress Database utility works the same as the compression utility in reverse. It takes a compressed database file and expands it into a standard uncompressed database file. A new file is created leaving the original compressed file alone.

The wizard will ask you to specify the file and path name for your compressed database file (with a .CDB extension), the name of the database file to create (with a .DB extension), and then will ask you for confirmation.

The progress window will display and will show you any messages that relate to the decompression. When the utility has finished executing you can use the new .DB file just like you would any other SQLAnywhere database.

Creating a Database

Creating a new (empty) SQLAnywere database is as simple as running the Create Database utility and specifying the file and path name for the new database file on the first page of the wizard as shown in Figure A-9.

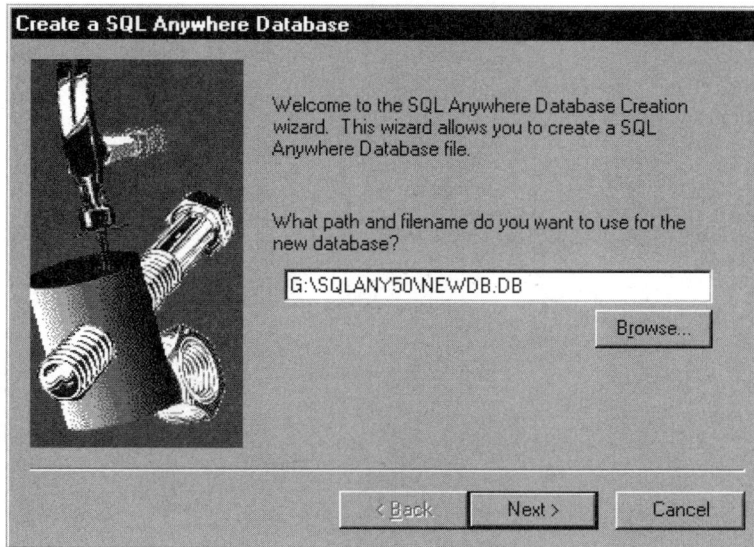

Figure A-9. *The Create Database utility makes creating a new SQLAnywhere database very simple.*

On the second page is where you will specify if you want the database to use a transaction log or not, and if so, where the log is going to be located (file and path name). Transaction logs have .LOG extensions. The default for a new database is that it will use a transaction log and the log will have the same name as the database (except for the .LOG extension) and will be stored in the same location.

For extra protection against a device failure, the third page of the wizard will ask if you want to maintain a mirror transaction log. This is an identical file to the original transaction log, but it has a different extension (.MLG) and should be stored on a different physical device. In the event that the physical device storing the original log is unrecoverable you can use the mirrored transaction log to recover your data. By default, no mirrored log is created. To create on, click on the checkbox and specify a name (and device by path) for the log file.

The fourth page of the wizard allows you to specify options for the database. The first option is encryption. An encrypted database makes the database file unreadable in a standard text editor (not that it is that readable to begin with!). Remember that encrypting a database reduces the ability of the compression utility to compress the data. By default, databases are created unencrypted. (See Figure A-10.)

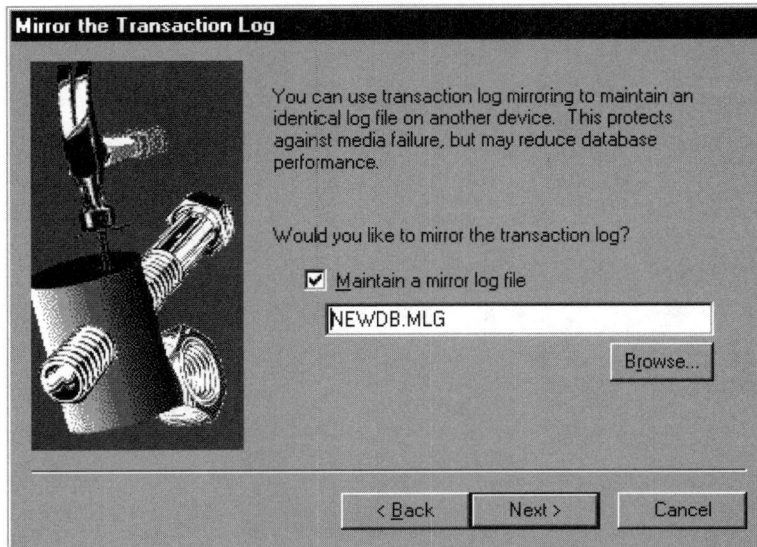

Figure A-10. *You can choose to create a mirrored transaction log as an extra degree of security in the event of physical device failure.*

The second option is to ignore the trailing blanks when doing string comparisons. This means that a string consisting of:

```
"Smith      "
```

would be equal to a string without the blanks after it like

```
"Smith"
```

By default, this option is off, meaning that strings must match exactly, blanks and all.

The third option is if you want to set case sensitivity for identifiers and values in the database. By default this is set to false. If true, then if you specify a column of "EMP_ID" in your SQL statement, but the column is saved as "emp_id" then the two will not match up. This option is provided to maintain ISO/ANSI SQL standard compatibility.

Finally, on this page, SQLCentral asks you to specify the user id for the 'DBO' id. This id will be the owner of a set of system view that mimic the system tables of Sybase SQLServer. You would only ever change the default DBO value if you are using the id DBO to represent something else in your database. (See Figure A-11.)

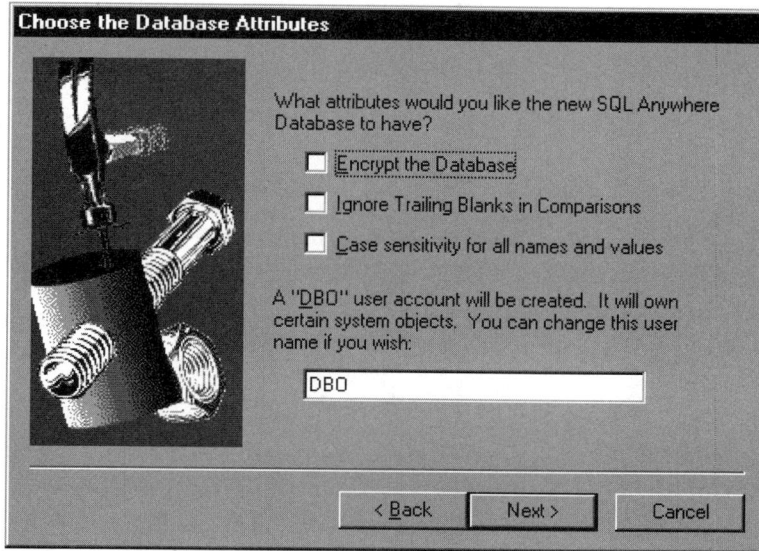

Figure A-11. *On this page of the wizard you will specify database options for encryption, case sensitivity, trailing blanks, and the system DBO id.*

The fifth page allows you to customize the page size of the database. You can choose from 512, 1024 (default), 2048, and 4096. As a general rule of thumb, small databases should use a small page size and larger databases a larger page size for efficiency.

The sixth page allows you to specify how you want SQLAnywhere to build collation sequences for performing string comparisons. This is particularly significant for people operating in a multilingual environment. There are different collating sequences for US standard, Canadian French, Norwegian, and others. Refer to the SQLAnywhere manual for the full description of all the possible collating sequences. By default the collating sequence is an ANSI standard ASCII multilingual sequence.

The final page asks if you want to connect to the database as soon as SQLCentral is finished creating it. When you press the **Finish** command button, SQLCentral will generate the database. Instead of a progress window, you will see a message window which will show you the part of the database that is currently being created. (See Figure A-12.)

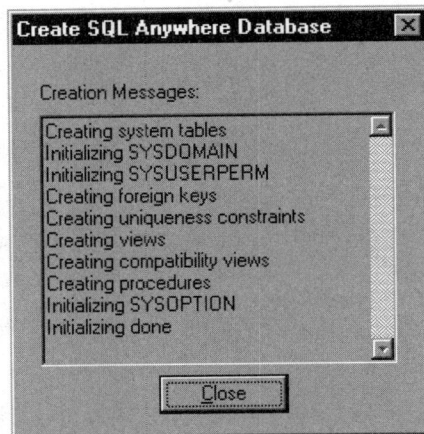

Figure A-12. When creating a database, instead of a progress window you will see a message window which will tell you which part of the database is currently being created.

Creating a Write File

A write file is a special file for a database. When a database that uses a write file is updated, the changes are not made to the database. Instead, they are made in the write file. This is useful for developers who are developing against a production database (so they don't want their changes to affect the database), for read only databases, and for compressed databases (which cannot be updated directly).

To create a write file using the SQLCentral tools select and run the Create Write File tool. This will execute the appropriate wizard. The first page of the wizard will ask you which database you wish to generate a write file for. Specify the database file and full path name.

On the next page you will specify the path that will be used for the write file and the file name that you want. Write files have the extension .WRT.

The third page asks you if you wish to maintain a transaction log for the write file. This transaction log will contain a record of all changes made to the write file. If you do want a transaction log, you must specify the file name which will have a .WLG extension.

Like with a regular transaction log, if you desire, you can create a mirror transaction log for the write file (which is usually stored on a different physical device to protect against device failure) on the fourth page of the wizard. You would specify the full file name and path name for the mirror log which would have a .MWL extension.

Finally the fifth page will provide you with a summary of what you have requested and allow you to cancel to request or to go ahead and generate the write and log files requested. If successful, a message box will display telling you where each file was created.

Erasing

The Erase Database tool allows you to delete a database (the database to be deleted must not be running at the time), compressed database or write file. When you run the wizard it will ask you to specify which object you want to delete. You can specify the file and path name for the object to be removed or you can press the **Browse...** command button. (See Figure A-13.)

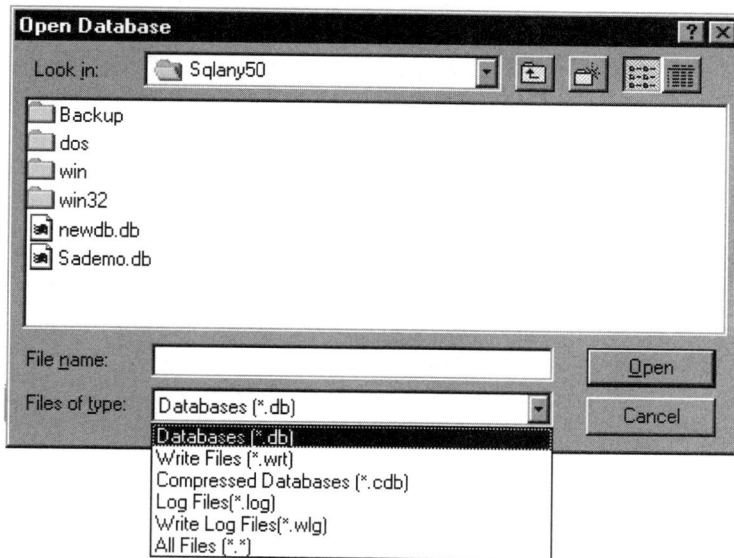

Figure A-13. *In the Erase Database tool you can erase databases, compressed database files, log files, write files, and write log files.*

On the second page of the wizard you can choose to delete any related files to the file you selected on the first page, such as transaction logs and mirrored transaction logs for a database file.

The final page of the wizard asks you to confirm that you really want to delete the specified objects, because deleting these is like deleting a file. Once it is gone, you probably won't be able to recover it.

Extracting (Remote Databases)

The Extract Database tool is intended to be used to extract and synchronize the data in a remote database with the data in the consolidated database. The consolidated database is usually your primary database which contains all the data from a number of different remote databases (which only contain a subset of the consolidated database).

Usually remote and consolidated databases are kept synchronized using the SQLRemote. Extracting is a different way of achieving the same result. You unload the data from the consolidated database and load it into a remote database. This technique is different from the SQLRemote utility because it uses the direct manipulation of files instead of the SQLRemote messaging utility.

The extract utility actually completes a number of steps for you. If you are extracting from a running database it creates the remote database, extracts the data and structure from the consolidated database and loads those files into the new remote database. If your database is not running, it will not create and load the remote database. For this reason, you should usually perform your extraction from a running database.

When you start the Extract Database wizard, the first page will ask you to specify either a consolidated database file (which isn't running) or the name of the database and the server it is running on in the case of a running database. The second page will ask you to specify the user id and password to access the database.

On the third page you will specify the remote user that you are creating an extraction for and if you want the wizard to automatically start the subscriptions for you (which is recommended). For more in depth information on subscriptions and publications, refer to the *SQLAnywhere Developer's Guide* by Ian Richmond, Derek Ball ,and Steve Clayton from Powersoft Press. (See Figure A-14.)

On the fourth page you will choose which elements of the database schema that you want to extract. You can choose any combination of foreign keys, stored procedures, triggers, and views.

The fifth page allows you to specify the name that was used for the DBO user (if you specified an alternative DBO name when you created the database). On this page you can also specify the isolation level. The isolation level can be anywhere from 0 to 3. The higher the number, the more restrictive the locking and the greater the chance that creating the extraction would impede the functioning of the running database by locking other users out.

You will specify the path and file name for the SQL command file that is necessary to reload the data on the sixth page. The seventh page allows you to choose to unload the structure and data, or just the structure or just the data. Then on the eighth page you will specify the path and name for the file that will contain the unloaded data. You can also choose to order the data or take it as it comes.

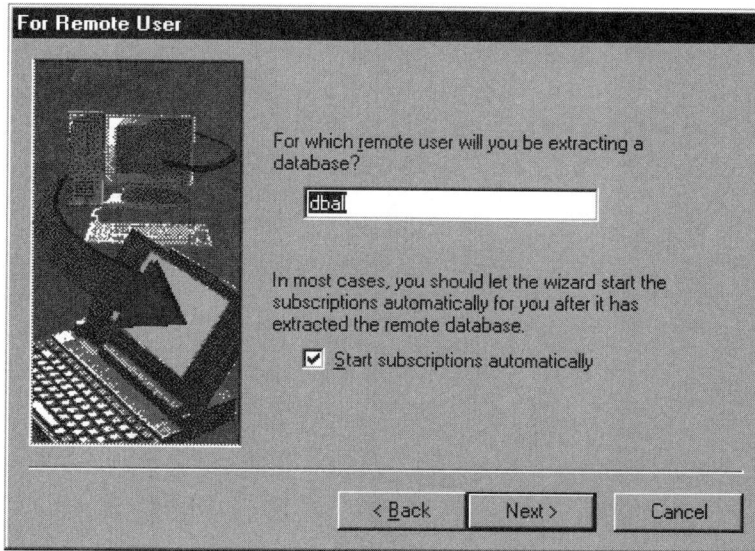

Figure A-14. *You must specify to the remote user that you are creating an extraction and if you want the wizard to start the subscriptions for you automatically.*

The final page of the extraction wizard asks you if you would like to confirm the extraction. When you have finished, you will press the **Finish** button and the extraction will begin. You will be given the option after the data is extracted to load the remote database.

Transaction Log Files

The SQLCentral utilities provide a wizard to assist you with translating a log file into a text file of SQL commands that you can extract and use. Another wizard is provided to help you with changing the log file to a different file.

Translating

The first two pages of the Translate Log File wizard ask you to specify the name of the log file to translate and the path and file name of the SQL command file that will be created.

The third page of the wizard allows you to select some options for the generated SQL. You can choose to:

- include transactions that have not been committed yet.

- generate only ANSI standard SQL (if you wanted to execute the commands against a database other than the SQLAnywhere database).

- translate from the last recorded checkpoint.

- generate SQL statements for all users, or for specific users that you specify. (See Figure A-15.)

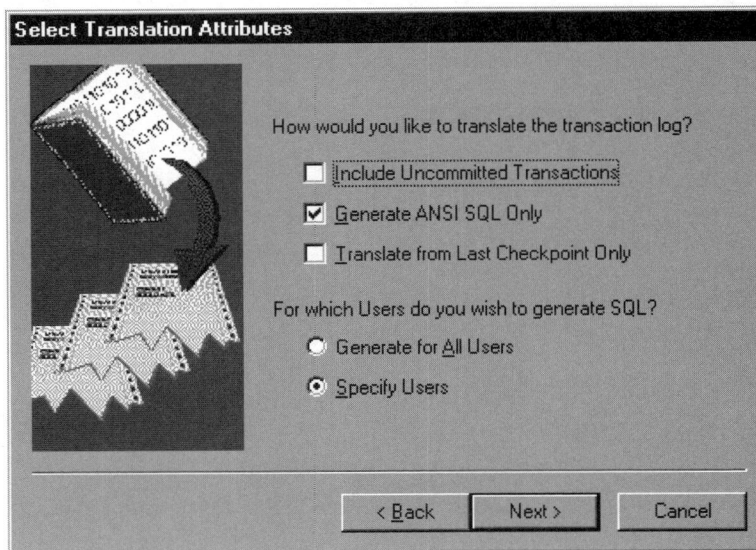

Figure A-15. *The Translate Log File wizard allows you to specify a variety of options when generating the SQL commands.*

If you choose to generate the SQL commands for only specific users, the next page of the wizard will ask you to specify a set of users to either include or exclude.

The next page gives you the option to include, exclude or include as comments any transactions which have been generated by triggers. This becomes significant when you try to execute the generated SQL commands against a database. If the target database has the same triggers defined as the current database, the same trigger transaction should occur automatically. In this case you would exclude the trigger generated transactions. If you were to want to apply the SQL statements against a database that didn't have the triggers defined you would probably want to include the trigger generated statements to keep the data consistent.

When you press the **Finish** command button a status dialog window will appear (with a funky animated icon) showing you the progress of the translation. You can see in this window if the translation was successful or not.

Changing

With the Change Transaction Log wizard you can alter how a database or a write file uses a transaction log. You have three options that you can execute with the wizard:

- **Rename the transaction log file.** This will actually create a new log file with the new name when the first transaction is committed. You will have the option of deleting the old transaction log or keeping it.

- **Stop using a transaction log file.**

- **Create a transaction log file** (if the database does not currently use a log file).

- **Create a mirror log file** (if the database does not currently use a mirror log file).

- **Rename the mirror log file.** Like with the transaction log file, this will actually create a new mirror log file with the new name when the first transaction is committed. You will have the option of deleting the old mirror log or keeping it.

- **Stop using a mirror log file.**

The pages of the wizard will ask you to specify the name of the database or write file that you want to alter the log attributes for. Then you will go through two pages. The wizard will then examine the database or write file to determine what the current log file settings are. Based upon this, the appropriate options from the above list will be made available to you. You will get separate wizard pages for the transaction log options and the mirror log options, as shown in Figures A-16 and A-17.

Depending on which options to choose you will be given the opportunity to specify new path and file name settings for the transaction and mirror logs, and what to do with any transaction and mirror log files that are no longer required.

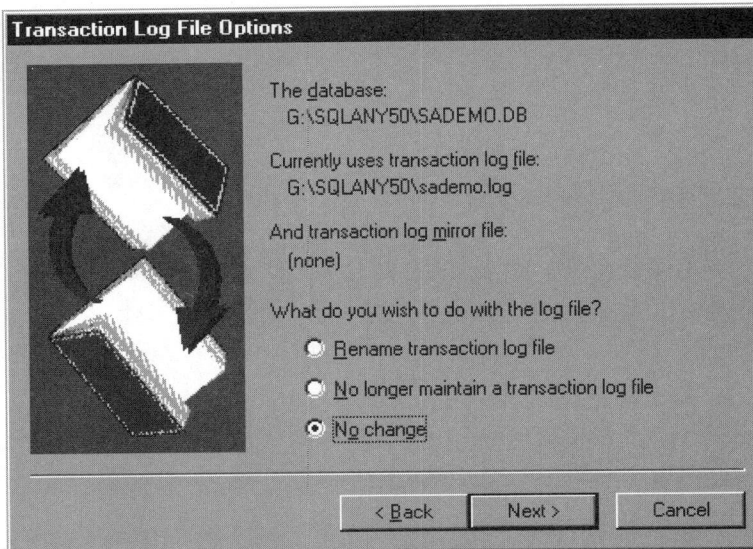

Figure A-16. *The wizard will present you with the appropriate options for changing the transaction log attributes based upon the current settings.*

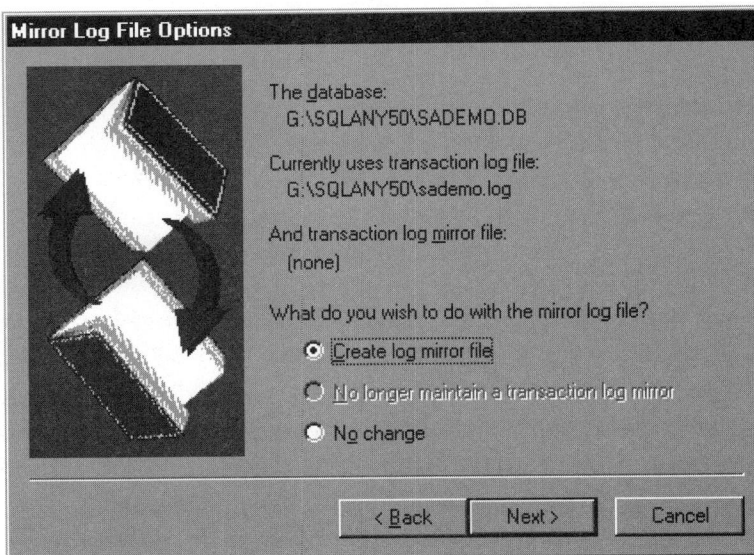

Figure A-17. *The options for changing a mirror log file will appear on a separate page of the wizard.*

Unloading

The Unload Database wizard allows you to unload the structure and/or data of a database file (running or not) into a SQL command file. The first three pages ask you the standard questions of which database file to unload, what user id and password to use (must have DBA permissions) and what file and path to store the SQL command file in.

The fourth page of the wizard will give you the option to unload:

- The structure and data.

- The structure only.

- The data only (See Figure A-18.).

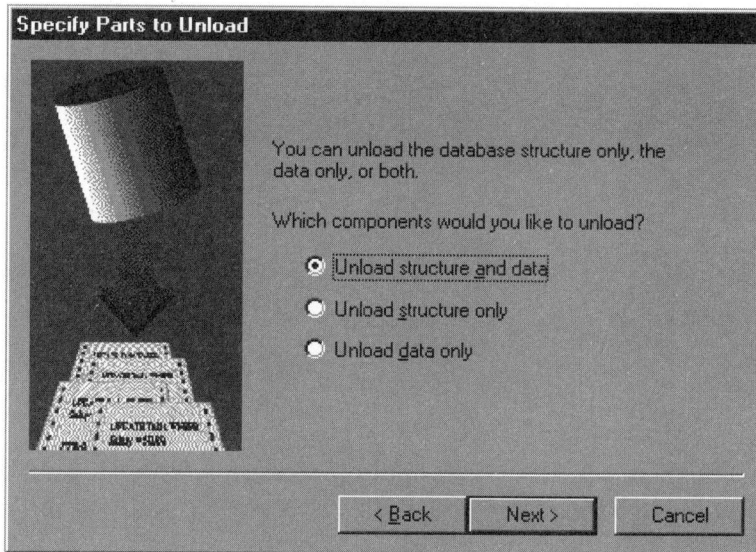

Figure A-18. The Unload Database wizard allows you to unload the structure and data of a database into a SQL command file.

On the next page of the wizard you will specify if you want to perform an "internal" unload or an "external" unload. An internal unload (the default) assumes that the directory that you are specifying (when you specify the path and filename for the unload) is relative to the physical location of the server. If your server is on a physically remote machine, performing an internal unload is usually faster because the data does not have to cross the network.

The second option, an external unload, assumes that the path and file name that you specified for the unloaded SQL file is relative to the client. That means that the data will be passed to the client before being placed in the SQL file (which is assumed to be on the client). This will usually cause your unload to perform slower unless the client and server are running on the same physical machine. (See Figure A-19.)

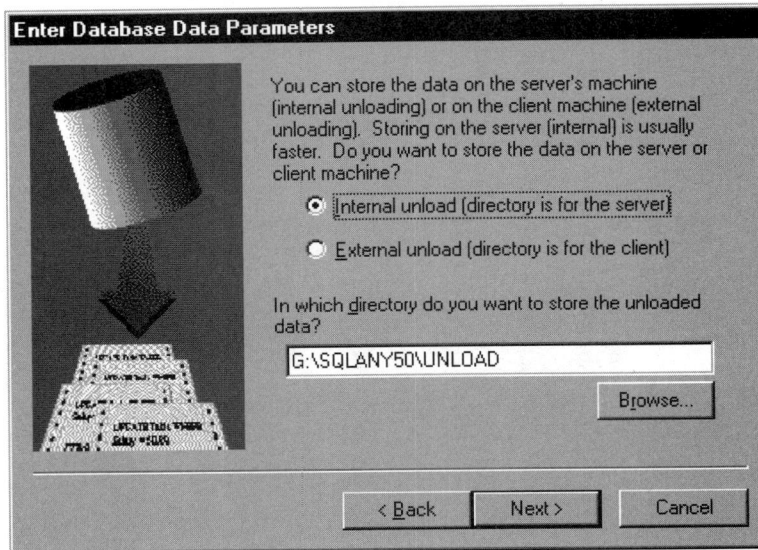

Figure A-19. The "internal" versus "external" unload option specifies if the SQL file will be generated in a directory that is relative to the server or the client.

Before finishing you can set an option to order the data (default) or leave it as it is. You also need to specify the id for the DBO user. This defaults to DBO and only needs to be changed if you specified a different id for the DBO when you created the database (see the section above on database creation).

When you press the **Finish** command button on the final page of the wizard, you will see a dialog window with the details of how the unload is progressing (and a funky animated icon to keep you entertained). When the unload is complete the window will inform you of the success or failure of the operation.

Upgrading

The Upgrade Database wizard allows you to upgrade a Watcom SQL 3.2 or 4.0 database to Sybase SQLAnywhere 5.0. (Remember Sybase bought Powersoft who bought

Watcom thus making the Watcom database now the Sybase database). On the three pages of the wizard you will indicate the filename for the database to be upgraded (non-running), the DBA user id and password and then if you want to use a different id for the DBO (other than 'DBO' which is the default).

When you press finish, the utility will complete the upgrading of the database and inform you of the status when it is complete.

Database Management

Along with the specific utility functions discussed in the first part of this appendix, SQLCentral also assists you with the more routine tasks associated with database management. You can use its point and click interface to perform many common processes such as table maintenance, setting up triggers, creating indexes and developing stored procedures. The security of a database can also be managed from SQLCentral where you can add and maintain users, manage their permissions and define and manage user groups.

The User Interface

SQLCentral is designed to have the common look and feel which is becoming standard in the 32 bit windows environment. This interface style is often referred to as the "Explorer" interface, after the Windows 95 explorer. (See Figuare A-20.)

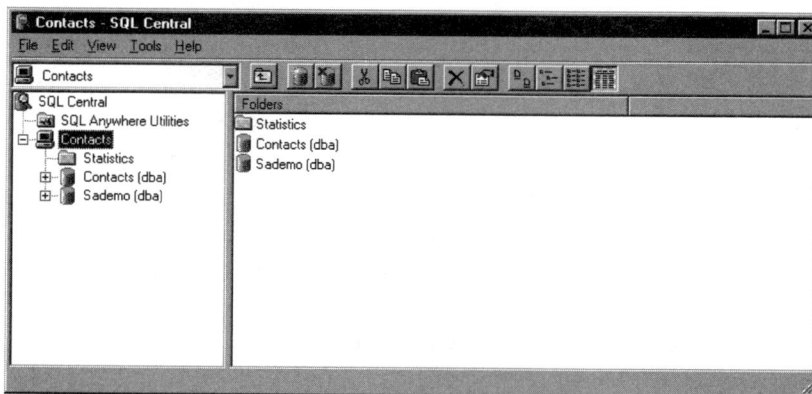

Figure A-20. *SQLCentral adopts what is rapidly becoming the standard interface for 32 bit windows applications, the "Explorer" interface.*

This interface is divided into two primary workspaces. The workspace on the left is the *object tree* and the workspace on the right shows all the elements that compose the object selected in the object tree on the left. In Figure A-21 we can see that the database SADemo is selected in the object tree and all the folders that compose SADemo are displayed in the large workspace on the right (those of you coming from a Windows development background may recognize this workspace as a List View).

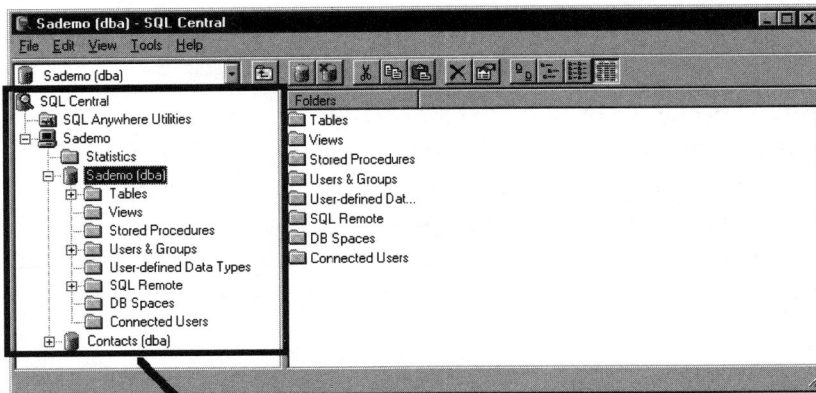

Object Tree

Figure A-21. The Object Tree in the left workspace of SQLCentral shows a hierarchical listing of objects, utilities, and components that can be accessed through SQLCentral.

SQLCentral always shows only one root level icon, the icon for SQLCentral itself. Expanding this icon will show you the SQLAnywhere utilities folder which was discussed in an earlier section above. To see more icons you will connect to other databases (as discussed in the following section). The level below the SQLCentral icon will show icons that represent servers that you can access and which may have SQLAnywhere databases running on them. If you are only running your SQLAnywhere servers locally, the name that will appear beside the server icon will be the same as the name of the first database that you connect to. Otherwise these icons will display the names of the respective servers that they represent.

When you expand a server you will see icons for:

- **Statistics.** Which will let you select different database performance statistics and execute them in the performance monitor. This feature is discussed in detail in the section on "Using the Performance Monitor."

- **Connected Databases.** These are SQLAnywhere databases that SQLCentral is aware of and are available for you to work with.

Once you select a connected database you will see icons that appear like folders. Each of these icons holds specific database objects or information. There are separate folders for tables, views, stored procedures, users and groups, user defined data types, SQLRemote, DBSpaces, and Connected Users. All of these folders contain database objects, and some contain other subfolders. Each of these is discussed below.

You can continuously drill down to lower levels of detail until you hit a level where no further subdetail is feasible.

The other elements of the user interface serve merely to support the two main workspaces. The menu allows you to connect and disconnect from databases (as outlined in the following section) and change your view of the data (from report view to small icons and so on as is consistent with the 'explorer' interface style) and the toolbar allows you to access the same functions that are available on the menu, but with a GUI interface.

Connecting to Databases

When you want to connect to a database, you must discern if the database is running or not, and if it is, is it running on a server that you can see.

If the database is running and you can see the server that it is running on in your SQLCentral object tree, you must expand that level of the tree by double clicking on it, or choosing **Open** from the pop up menu that appears when you click with your right mouse button. You should then see all the running databases on that server, although they will appear with a small red X on their database icon to indicate that you are not currently connected to the database. To connect to the database select the database with the right mouse button and choose **Open** off the pop up menu (or you can double-click on the database name/icon to achieve the same result). A dialog window will appear asking you to enter your User ID and Password that you are going to connect with. Once successfully connected, the red X will disappear from the database icon.

If the database isn't running, or is running on a server that is not visible in SQLCentral, then you must select **Connect** from the **Tools** menu item, or click on the Connect icon in the toolbar. A connection dialog will appear. Depending on what you are trying to connect to you will need to fill in the appropriate information:

- To connect to a single user stand alone database already running on your PC, you simply need to enter your User ID and Password.

- To start and connect to a database that is not currently running you must enter a valid User ID, Password, Server Name (if applicable, by default the server—which is the database engine—will pick up the name of the database that is opened), Database Name (the unique name of the database which is usually the same as the database filename without the .DB extension), and then the Database Startup information. This last parameter will contain the path and file name of the database file that you want to connect to. If you are running the database locally, select the Local radio button. This will start up the database engine with the standard local settings. If you are running the database engine on a networked server, then you will select Network radio button to cause the engine to execute on the remote networked machine. The third radio button, Custom, allows you to manually customize the database start up options (such as changing the default size of the cache). (See Figure A-22.)

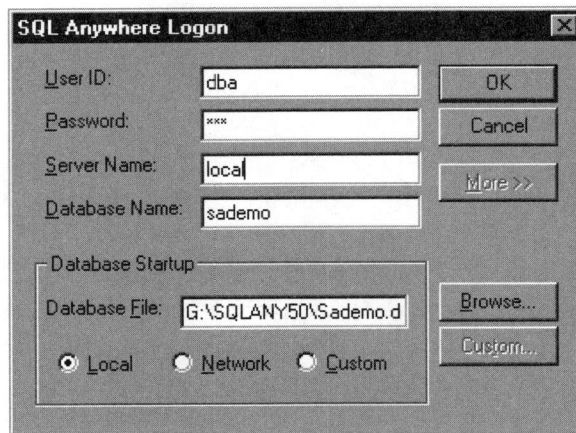

Figure A-22. *The connection dialog is where you will enter the connection details of the database to which you are trying to connect.*

Using Connection Profiles

If you need to connect to the same database often (which is you are a DBA or a developer you probably do) then you should create a *database profile*. The database profile remembers all the settings for connecting to a specific database and when you want to connect to that same database in the future, you merely have to select the name of the database from the list of profiles.

To access the database profiles, choose the **Connection Profiles...** menu item from the **Tools** menu. This will cause the window in Figure A-23 to open.

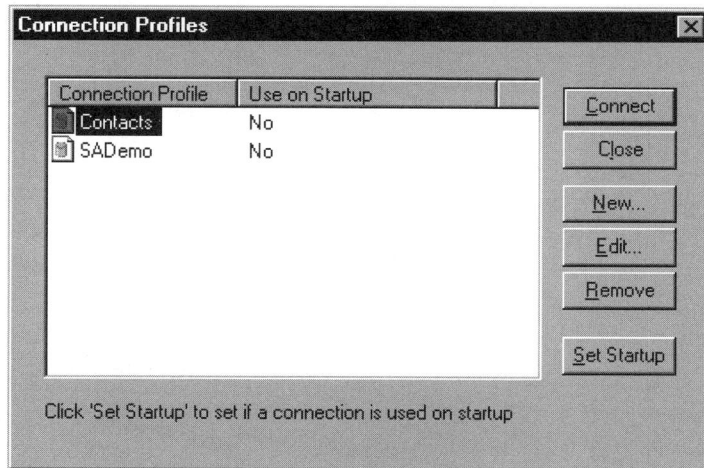

Figure A-23. The connection profile remembers all the settings for a specific database connection and makes it easier to connect to that database in the future.

You can select a database from the profile list and press the **Connect** command button and SQLCentral will connect to that database using the parameters that you had specified previously.

To set up a new profile, select the **New...** command button. This will cause a sequence of two windows to appear. The first window, shown in Figure A-24 requires you to enter a name for the database profile and specify its type.

Next you will see the connection dialog window discussed in the previous section. You must specify all the database connection parameters that you want this profile to use. When you are finished you will press the **OK** command button and the profile is now ready to be used.

If you always use SQLCentral to manage the same database, or set of databases, you can have SQLCentral automatically connect to those databases when it starts up. To enable this, select the profile that you want to have automatically connected and press the **Set Startup** command button. You will notice the indicator in the window for "Use on Startup" switch from a "no" to a "yes." You can toggle this back and forth by pressing the **Set Startup** button again.

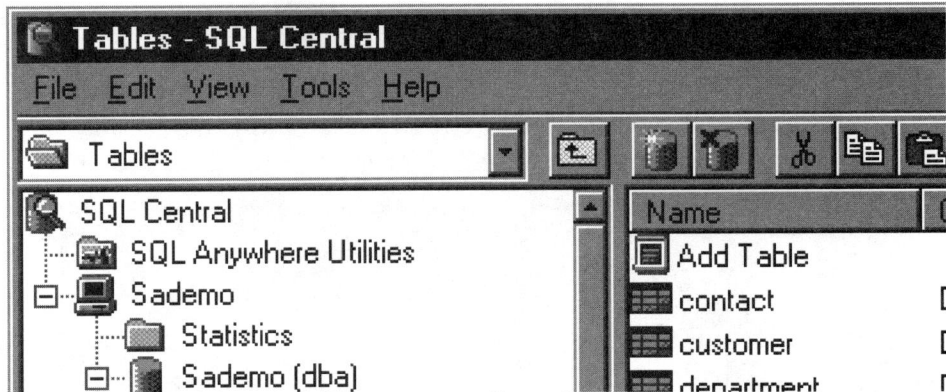

Figure A-24. *To define a new profile you must first give the profile a unique name and specify the type of profile (SQLAnywhere).*

Tables

SQLCentral contains a very complete set of tools for creating and maintaining tables in your database. You can manage the physical make up of the tables, the referential integrity, permissions, and more. In order to manipulate a table, you must be connected to the database in which you want to alter the table. (See Figure A-25.)

Adding/Deleting Tables

To add a new table to a database you must connect to that database and then select the Tables folder from the tree view, as shown in Figure A-26.

Selecting the Add Table option will launch the table creation wizard. The first page of this wizard will ask you to specify the name of the table and which user should own the table (which defaults to who you logged on to the database as) which can be changed to any group that you are a member of.

Also on the first page you must choose if this table is to be a base table or a global temporary table. You are probably most familiar with base tables. A base table stores data on a permanent basis. When you insert data into a base table, terminate your connection and then reconnect, the data is still there. The second type of table is a global temporary table, which you may not be familiar with. This table is permanently defined in the database, but the data only exists within the context of your current connection. When you add data, then disconnect and reconnect, the data from your first access is no longer in the table. (See Figure A-27.)

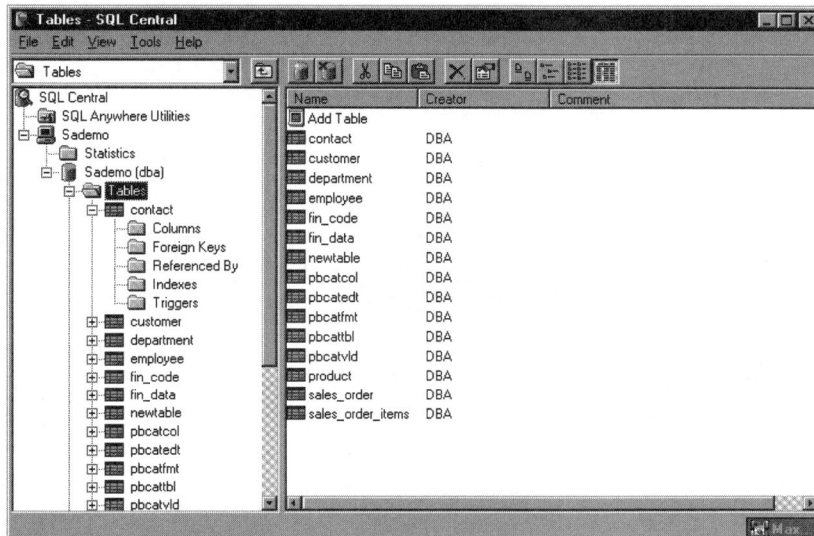

Figure A-25. *You can manipulate all aspects of the tables in your database using the graphical SQLCentral interface.*

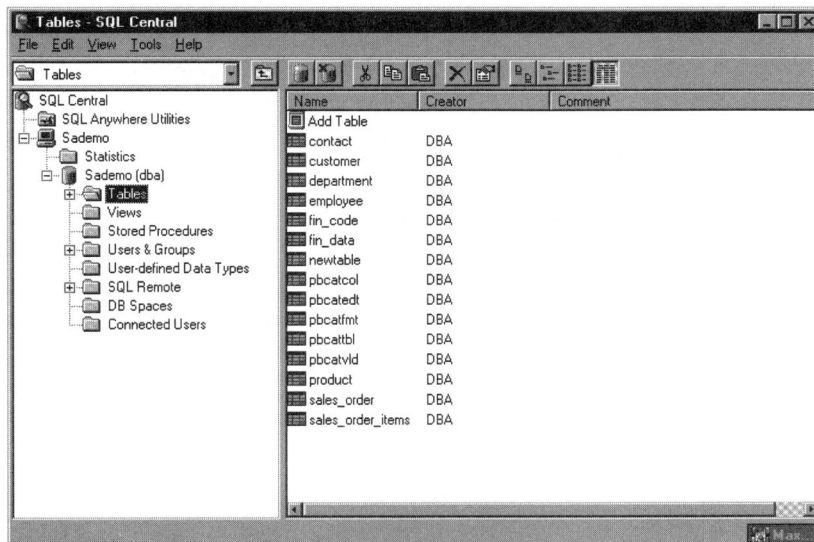

Figure A-26. *When you select the Tables folder in the tree view you will see a list of tables in the list view and a utility for creating new tables.*

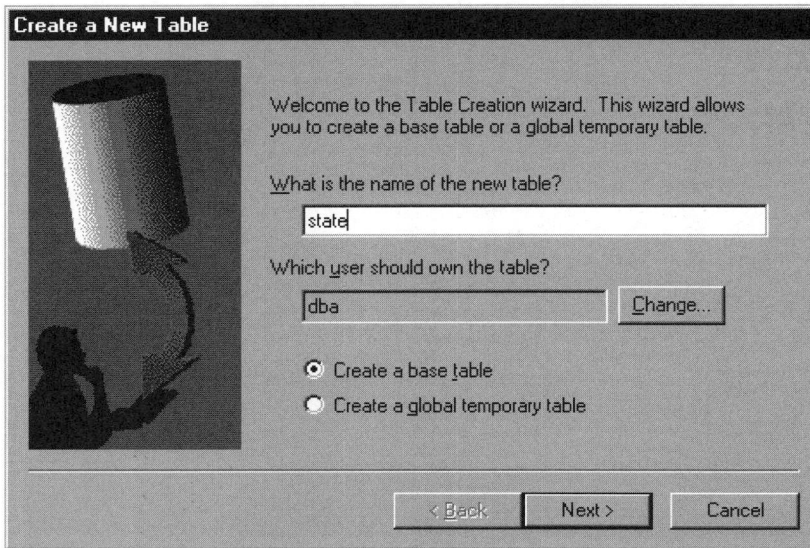

Figure A-27. The table creation wizard will ask you to specify the table name, owner, and type of table to create.

The second page of the wizard will ask you to specify which DB Space you want to store the table in (DB Spaces are discussed in the section below). Specifying multiple DB Spaces will allow you to have your database span multiple physical files. An important option to understand is the **Properties...** button on this page. Pressing this button will open the Properties page as shown in Figure A-28. You can specify a different database file and also add pages to this database. Adding pages preallocates space within the DB Space to be used exclusively by this table. This will improve performance if you are bulk loading data into your table. Each page that you add increases the amount of preallocated space by the page size that you defined for this database when you created it (the default was 1024 bytes).

On page three you will add a comment for the table and press the Finish button to generate the empty table in the database. Now you must define columns for the table.

To delete a table, select it in the list of tables and press the delete key. Alternatively, you could click on the table with the right mouse button and select Delete from the pop up menu.

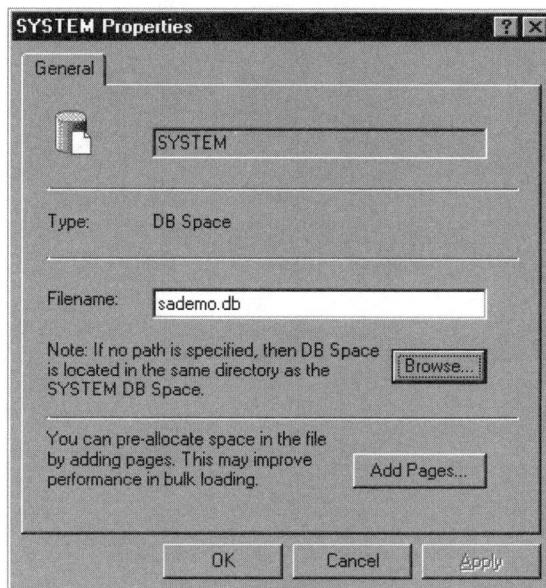

Figure A-28. *On the second page you will specify which DB space that you want this table to be stored in.*

Columns

Once you have created a table you must add columns to it in order to store data. If you expand the table folder you will see a list of all the tables. If you double click on the table in the tree view you will see a list of folders that relate specifically to that table. The first folder is for all the columns in the table. Selecting the Columns folder will cause a list of all the columns in the current table plus, at the top of the list, a utility for adding columns to be displayed in the list view.

The add column utility will open up the Properties Sheet for a column where you can give the new column a name and a comment as shown in Figure A-29.

On the Data Type tab you can select the column data type and view a summary of the advanced column properties for the default value, constraint rule, null settings, and uniqueness as shown in Figure A-30.

The Advanced Column Properties dialog window allows you to select a user defined default. This can be any value that is consistent with the data type. Alternatively, you could select the pre-defined default. Depending on your column type, different options will be available. Table A-1 details the list of pre-defined options.

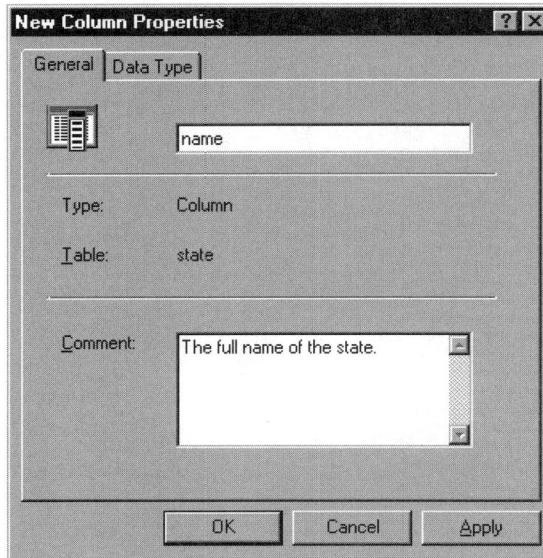

Figure A-29. *The Properties Sheet for a column allows us to define the column name, comment, data type, column type, default value, null acceptance, and constraint rules.*

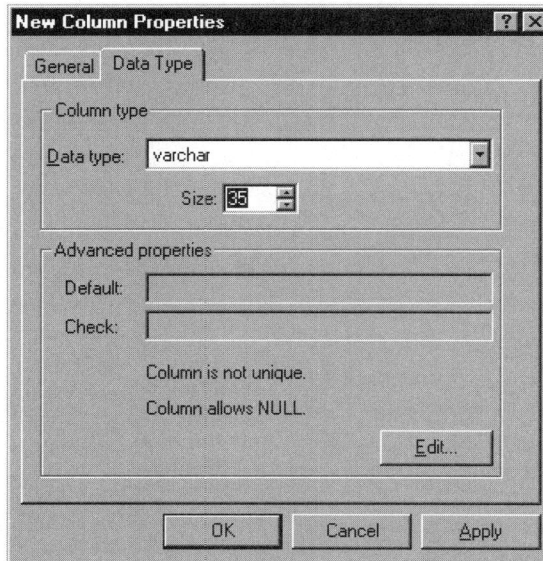

Figure A-30.*You can select the data type for the column and alter the advanced properties.*

Table A-1

Default	Data Type	Description
AutoIncrement	smallint, integer, numeric, float, double, tinyint, money, smallmoney, bit,	Inserts a numerical value one greater than the current maximum value in the table.
Current Date	date, char, varchar, long varchar, binary, long binary, text, image	Inserts the current system date into the column.
Current User	char, varchar, long varchar, binary, long binary, text, image	Inserts the user ID of the current user into the column.
Current Database	char, varchar, long varchar, binary, long binary, text, image	Inserts the name of the current database into the column.
Current Publisher	char, varchar, long varchar, binary, long binary, text, image	Inserts the user ID of the publisher of the database for SQLRemote replication.
Current Time	char, varchar, long varchar, binary, long binary, time, text, image	Inserts the current system time into the column.
Current Timestamp	char, varchar, long varchar, binary, long binary, timestamp, datetime, smalldatetime, text, image	Inserts the combination of the current date and the current time into the column.

For the column constraints you can choose if the column allows NULL values or not. If you decide not to allow NULL values, then you can choose to define this column as only allowing unique values. (See Figure A-31.)

You can also assign the column a *check condition*. This is a rule that all values in the column must adhere to, such as requiring age to be between 0 and 125. The syntax for the check condition is:

```
CHECK (condition)
```

where "condition" is an expression that can be used to validate the data in the column. You can validate the data in many ways such as checking for a range of values with:

```
CHECK ( age BETWEEN 0 AND 125)
```

or

```
CHECK (active_date BETWEEN '1996/01/01' AND CURRENT DATE)
```

where CURRENT DATE is a SQLAnywhere constant.

Alternatively, we could require a value to conform to a specific set of possible values with:

```
CHECK (gender IN ('M','F','?'))
```

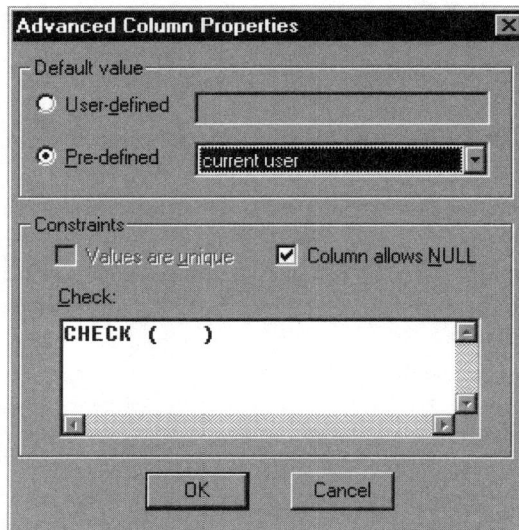

Figure A-31. The Advanced Properties dialog window.

Primary Key

You won't see a folder for the primary key in the subfolders below the table. This is because the primary key is considered a property of the table. Once you have added the columns to the table, to add the primary key you select the table in the tree view with the right mouse button and choose **Properties...** off the pop up menu. This will cause the table Properties Sheet to display as shown in Figure A-32.

If you select the **Columns** tab you will see a list of all the columns currently defined for this table (as shown in Figure A-33). You can view the detailed information about the column by pressing the **Details...** command button.

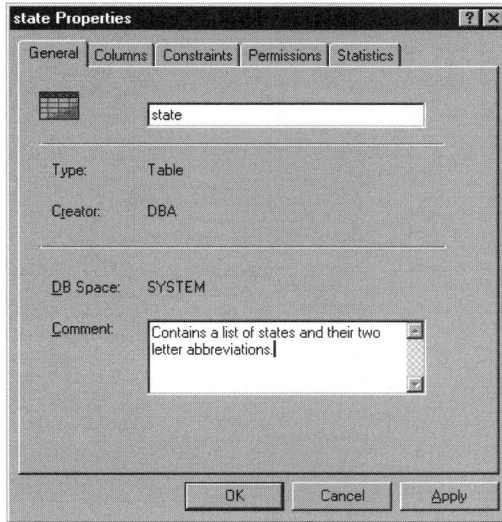

Figure A-32. *You can alter the properties of a table on the Property Sheet including the name, comment, primary key, constraints, security, and statistics.*

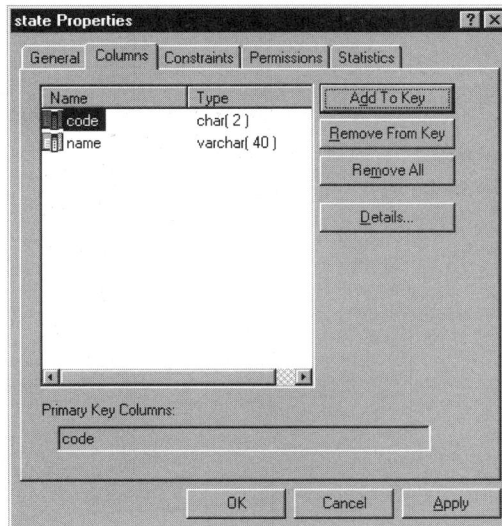

Figure A-33. *You can modify the primary key for a column on the Columns tab of the Properties Sheet. The current primary key for our State table is the Code column.*

You can also build the primary key for the table here. When you select a column, you can press the **Add To Key** button to have the current column appended to the key. The whole key is displayed at the bottom in a read only single line edit field. To remove a specific element from the key, select the column you wish to remove and press the **Remove From Key** button. To clear the primary key and start over you can press the **Remove All** key.

Foreign Keys

Foreign keys are managed in the Foreign Keys folder located under a specific table in your tree view. When you open the folder you will see a list of all the foreign keys currently defined for a table, if any exist. You will also see the **Add Foreign Key** utility. When you double click on this utility it will launch the Foreign Key Creation wizard.

On the first page you must specify the table that contains the primary key, or uniquely constrained column(s), that you want to link your new foreign key to. In our example, we are defining a foreign key for the Customer table. We will link the State column in the Customer table to the Code column in the State table (Customer.State must exist in Table.State).

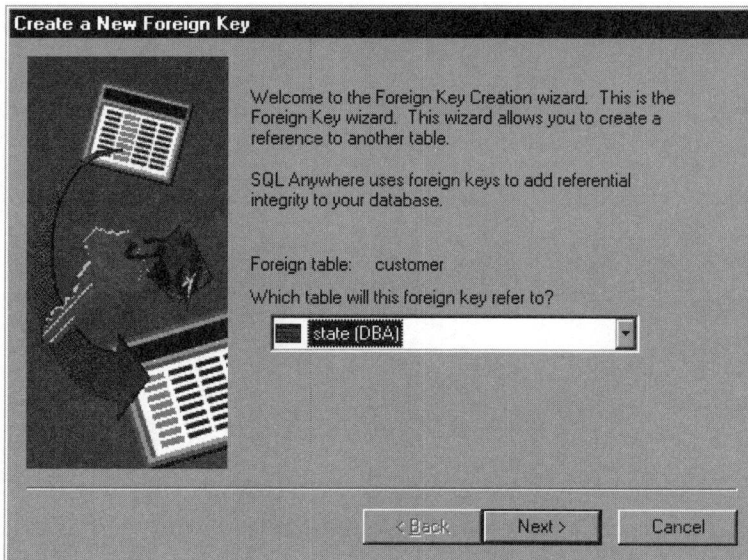

Figure A-34. The table creation wizard allows us to build a foreign key for the current table. The first page asks us to specify the table which contains the primary key that we want to link our current table to.

On the second page of the wizard you must specify if you want to connect to a Primary Key column or to a Unique constraint. If you select "primary key," the primary key of the table you are linking to will appear, otherwise you will see the unique constraints and must select the appropriate one. Most often, foreign keys are linked to primary keys.

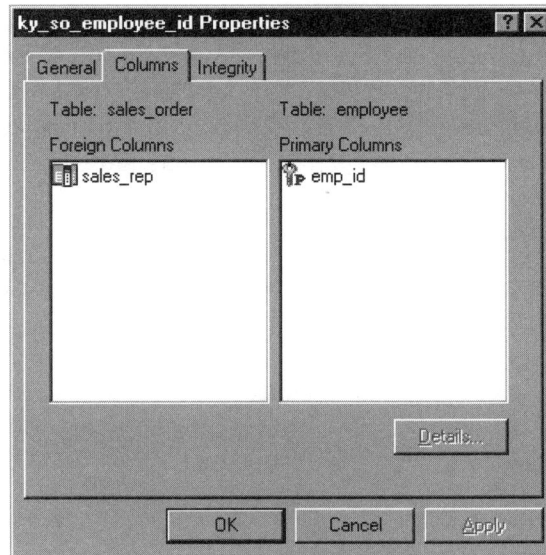

Figure A-35. *You must choose if you want to link to a primary key or to a unique constraint. Once you have selected, you must choose which column in the current table is going to be linked.*

In the list box, you must specify which column in the current table you are going to link to the primary key of your master table. All columns that have matching data types will appear in the drop down list box as shown in Figure A-35. Alternatively, you could create a new column that will provide the link by selecting "<Create Column>."

On the third page you will specify a name for the primary key and give it a comment if you desire. If the column that you have specified for the foreign key is set to allow NULL values, you will be given an option to specify if the foreign key is allowed to contain NULLs. This practice is usually discouraged as it violates referential integrity. On the same page you will also specify if you want SQLAnywhere to check the foreign key integrity at the time of the updating of the table, or if you want it to wait until a COMMIT is issued. The default is to check immediately.

Next you must specify how you want the foreign key to handle updates and deletes. Depending on how the columns involved are defined you will have four possible options:

1. **Restrict.** Restricting an update means that you cannot change the primary key value if it has dependent foreign key values in the table for which the foreign key was defined. For example, we couldn't change the state code for California from CA to CL if the customers table has records for customers belonging in state CA. The database would reject the update transaction. The same concept applies for restricting a delete. You cannot delete the state of California from the State table if customers exist in the customer table for that state.

2. **Cascade.** Cascading an update means that if you change the primary key value, the foreign key values are all updated also. For example, if we changed the state code for California from CA to CL, all the customers in the Customer table from California would have their state fields updated to CL. In the case of a cascaded delete, if we deleted the state of California from the State table, all the customers in the state of California would also be deleted.

3. **Set NULL.** In this case, if you update or delete a primary key, the linked foreign keys would be set to null. This option is only available if the foreign key columns are defined as allowing NULL values in the first place.

4. **Set Default.** If you update or delete a primary key, the linked foreign keys would be set to the default value for the field. This option, like the Set NULL option, is only available if the column has be defined to have a default value.

You will set one method for handling updated and another for handling deletes. For example, we could have our foreign key for the customer table set to cascade changes in the state code, but to restrict the deletion of a state that has existing customers.

The final page in the wizard asks you to verify the data that you entered and then press the **Finish** button to create the foreign key. Note that in our example, the creation of the foreign key would fail because we have customers in our customer table, but we have no states currently in our state table. Therefore by definition our creation would fail.

To maintain an existing foreign key definition, double click on the foreign key in the list view. This will open the Properties Sheet for the foreign key. There are three tabs on this sheet which allow you to maintain the name of the key, the comment, columns involved and integrity rules.

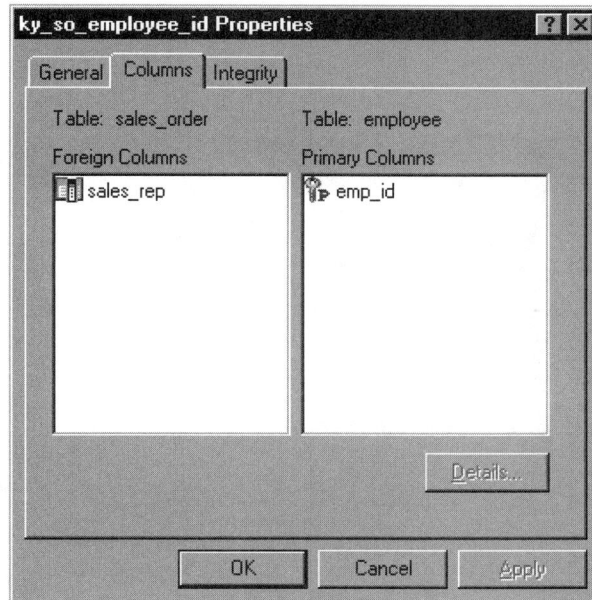

Figure A-36. We can maintain an existing foreign key by opening its Properties Sheet and altering the name, comment, columns, and integrity rules for the key.

Referenced By

The Referenced By folder under a table will show you all the tables that have foreign keys that reference the primary key of this table. If you double click on a table in the list view, it will open the Properties Sheet of that table.

Indexes

The Indexes folder will show you all the indexes that are defined for the current table. To maintain an existing index you will double click on the index in the list view opening up the Properties Sheet. On this sheet you can only alter the comment for an index. If you want to change the definition of the index you must drop it and recreate it.

Drop an index, select it, and press the delete key. Alternatively, you could select it with the right mouse button and choose **Delete** from the pop up menu.

To create a new index, double click on the Add Index utility. This will cause the Create New Index wizard to execute. On the first page of the index you will specify a name for the index that you are creating.

The second page of the index is where the real work is done. Here you must select the columns that you want to index by and decided whether to index them in an ascending or descending manner by pushing the appropriate command button.

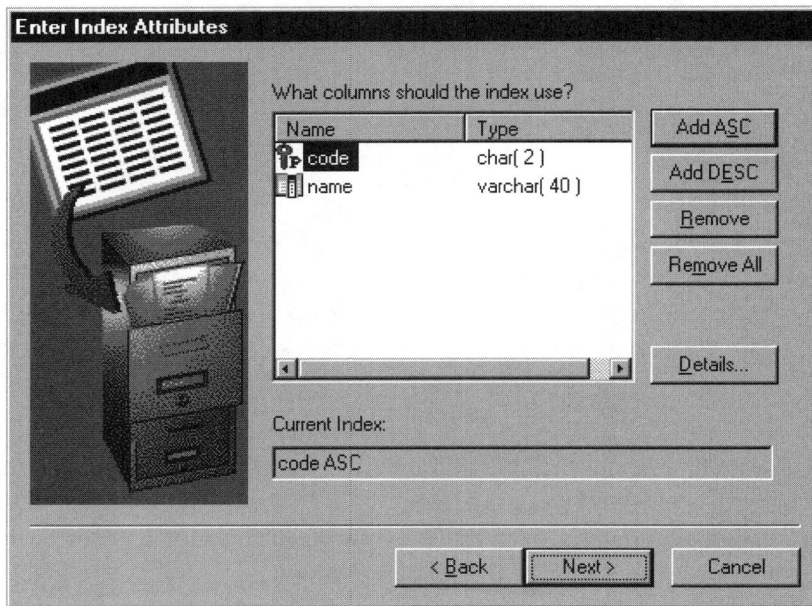

*Figure A-37. The wizard will ask you to specify which columns make up the index by selecting them and pressing the **Add ASC** or **Add DESC** buttons.*

On the third page you will select the DB Space that you want the index to be stored on (it is perfectly acceptable to have the index on a different DB Space than the table resides on). You will also specify here if the index is unique (no two rows can have the same key value) or duplicate (allowing duplicate key values).

On the final page you can add a comment for the index and then press the **Finish** command button when you are ready to create the index.

Triggers

As we learned earlier in this book, a trigger is a predefined block of code that executes when some action in the database initiates it, such as deleting a row. Triggers are defined for a table. To view the triggers that exist for a specific table, open the Triggers folder under the table in the tree view. The right panel will show a list of the triggers.

You can maintain a trigger by double clicking on it to open the code editor. When the code editor opens it will display the trigger in the code that it was last saved in. Remember that SQLAnywhere supports two dialects of SQL, Watcom SQL and Transact SQL. You can choose to open the trigger and display the code with either dialect by clicking on the trigger with the right mouse button and then selecting **Open as Watcom SQL** or **Open as Transact SQL** as appropriate.

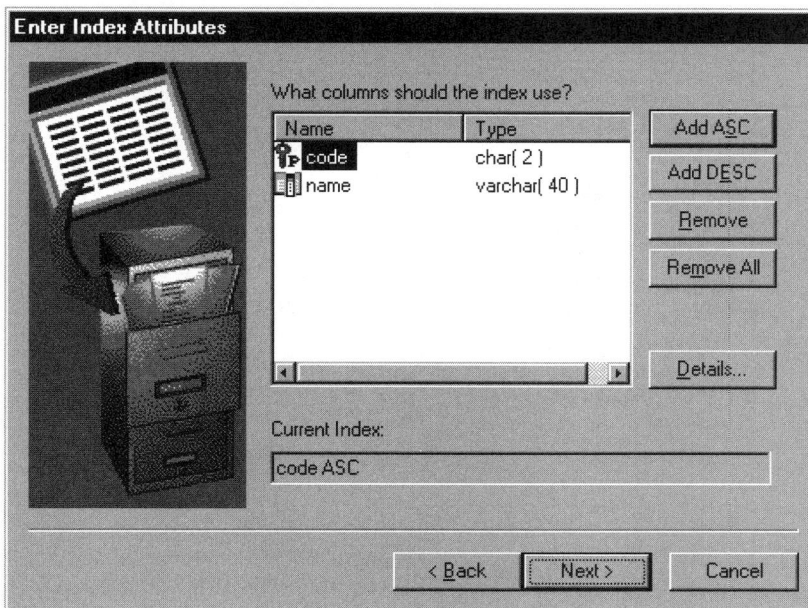

Figure A-38. The code editor window allows us to maintain our triggers in either Watcom SQL or Transact SQL.

Once the code editor is open you can examine and modify the trigger script. To regenerate the trigger and incorporate any changes you must select File -> Execute Script from the menu. The Trigger Manager Code Editor windows are modeless allowing you to open multiple triggers at the same time and cut and paste code between them.

To create a new trigger we will use the Add Trigger utility that appears in the Trigger folder. The first page will ask you to provide a name for the trigger.

On page two you will identify what causes this trigger to fire. You can pick any combination of Insert, Update, Delete or Update of a specific column. When selecting Update of a specific column, you will also have to specify which columns, when updated, cause this trigger to fire.

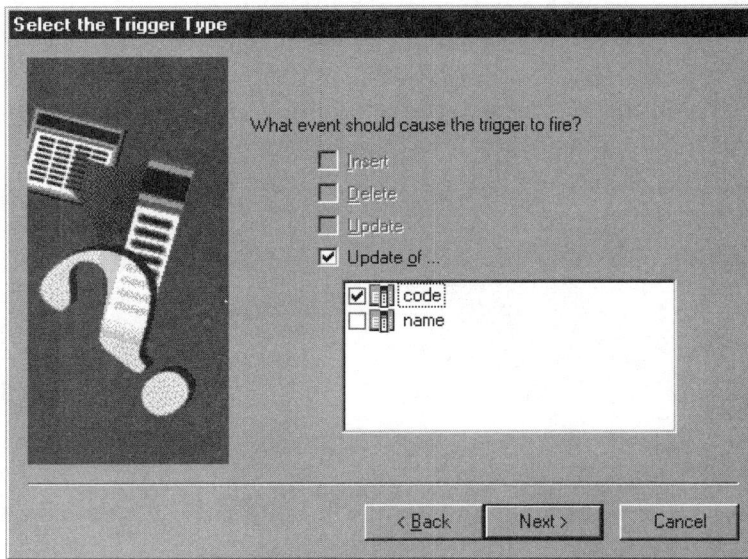

Figure A-39. *You must specify when you want the trigger to fire, either on Insert, Update, Delete, or Update of a specific column.*

On the third page of the wizard you will be asked to specify if this trigger is a row level or a statement level trigger. The difference is that row level triggers can occur multiple times within a single SQL statement and can be set to execute before or after the execution of that statement on a row. A statement level trigger can only occur after the SQL statement has executed. This option can be set on the following page of the wizard where you will be given three radio buttons to select if you want the trigger to execute before or after the statement, or on a SQLRemote conflict.

Also on this page you can specify a firing order for the trigger. This is used to determine the order in which triggers will execute if multiple triggers are defined for this operation on this table.

The final page of the wizard allows you to define a comment for the wizard. When you press the **Finish** button the Trigger Editor window will open as in Figure A-40. This syntax for the trigger is laid out for you in a handy color coded format. All you have to do is fill in the process that you want to execute.

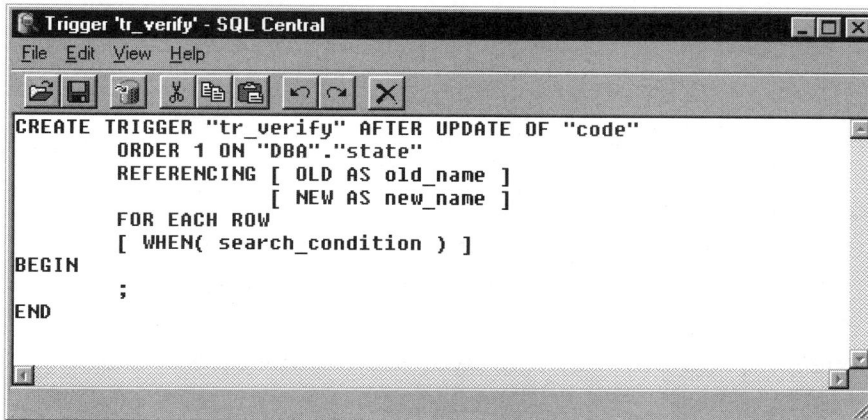

```
Trigger 'tr_verify' - SQL Central
File  Edit  View  Help

CREATE TRIGGER "tr_verify" AFTER UPDATE OF "code"
          ORDER 1 ON "DBA"."state"
          REFERENCING [ OLD AS old_name ]
                      [ NEW AS new_name ]
          FOR EACH ROW
          [ WHEN( search_condition ) ]
BEGIN
          ;
END
```

Figure A-40. The final step in creating a trigger is to define the syntax. The wizard provides a template to get you started.

Views

You can use SQLCentral to manage the views in your database. As you learned earlier in this book, views are virtual tables that you can query like regular tables, and in certain situations, update.

When you select the Views folder, you will see all the views defined in this database. When you double click on a specific view the View Editor window will open allowing you to see and edit the definition of the view.

To create a new view in SQLCentral you double click on the Add View option inside the folder. There isn't really a wizard for this function. The View Editor window will open with a blank view template, but you must build the view yourself. Perhaps a future enhancement would be a drag and drop view builder like we see in the Powersoft PowerBuilder tool.

To delete a view, simply select the definition and press the delete button. Alternatively, you could select the view with the right mouse button and choose **Delete** off the popup menu. This same menu allows you to view the current data visible with the view by selecting the View Data option. This will open an ISQL session and automatically execute a select query on the view.

In the properties page for the view (also accessed with the right mouse button) you can alter the comment and permissions for the view.

Stored Procedures

Opening the Stored Procedures file allows you to see all the procedures that have been defined for the database along with who created them and if they are in Watcom SQL or Transact SQL.

Double clicking on a specific stored procedure will open up the procedure definition in the Procedure Editor window as shown in Figure A-41. You will notice that the definition is already formatted as an "alter" statement to facilitate editing of the procedure.

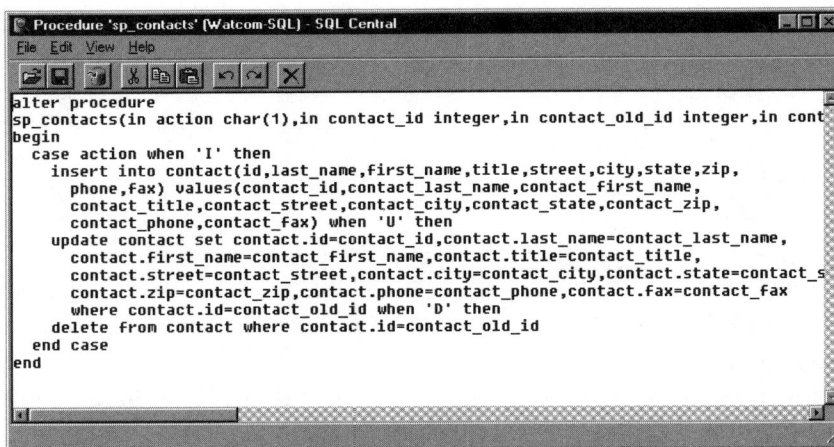

Figure A-41. Stored procedures can be edited within SQLCentral by double clicking on the procedure name and altering the procedure in the Procedure Editor.

Adding a procedure is very similar to the process for adding a view. When you select the Add Procedure utility, it will open up the Procedure Editor with a blank template for your new procedure. You can then choose to generate the procedure from the menu in the editor.

If you select a procedure with the right mouse button, the popup menu will allow you to open the procedure in its default format, or to convert the procedure to Watcom SQL or Transact SQL (assuming that the script is convertible).

Another option on the popup menu is **Test Procedure** which will generate a test script that you execute in ISQL to ensure that the procedure is working correctly. The following script was generated for testing the "sp_product_info" procedure in the SADemo database:

```
%
% % SQL Central generated procedure test script
%
% % Ensure any previously executing procedures are completed
RESUME ALL;
%
% % Ensure our test variables do not already exist
SET OPTION On_error = 'continue';
DROP VARIABLE "prod_id";
SET OPTION On_error = 'prompt';
%
% % Create input/output variables
CREATE VARIABLE "prod_id" integer;
%
% % Edit the following lines to set the input values
SET "prod_id" = '1';
%
% % Execute the procedure
CALL "DBA"."sp_product_info"( "prod_id" );
% % Use the RESUME command to view multiple result sets
```

In order for this script to work we would have to alter the line which sets the product id to 1 to a valid product id from our database.

Like in other areas, we can manage the permissions and comments for a specific procedure by opening the Properties Page with the right mouse button.

Managing Users and Groups

One of the most useful functions of the SQLCentral program is to manage the security, permissions and users for a database. When you open the Users and Groups folder for a database you will see a listing of Users, Groups, and Publishers for the database. Each will have a different icon to assist you in differentiating them.

Maintaining Users

You can select any user shown and double click on their id to open up the User Properties Page as shown in Figure A-43.

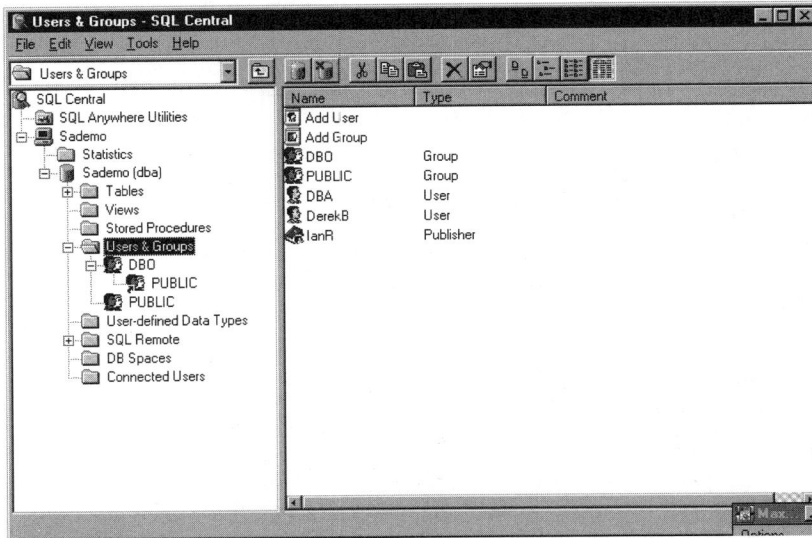

Figure A-42. *One of the most useful functions of the SQLCentral program is in the management of database security and permissions.*

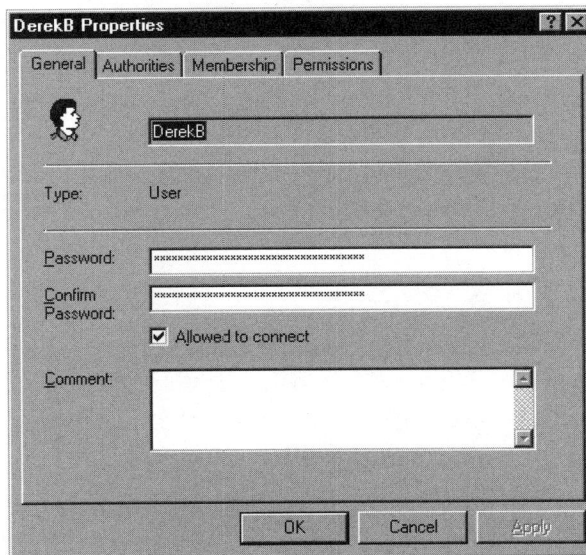

Figure A-43. *The User Properties Page allows us to manage all aspects of a users permissions and level of access.*

On the first page we can alter the user's id, define a new password (notice that we cannot see the users existing password), give them connect privileges and add a comment about the user account.

The Authorities tab allows us to define the user as any combination of:

- **DBA** full database access.

- **Resource** able to create objects in the database.

- **Remote DBA** generally not used by a real user, but as an access account for the SQLRemote Message Agent.

The Membership tab allows the assignment of this user to database groups. The groups that the user currently is a member of are displayed. You can add the user to another group by selecting the **Join Group...** button and then selecting the group from the popup list. Conversely, you can terminate a users membership in a group by selecting the group from the list and pressing the **Leave Group** command button.

The **Permissions** tab is where you can specify, at a very low level, the exact permissions that this user has within the database.

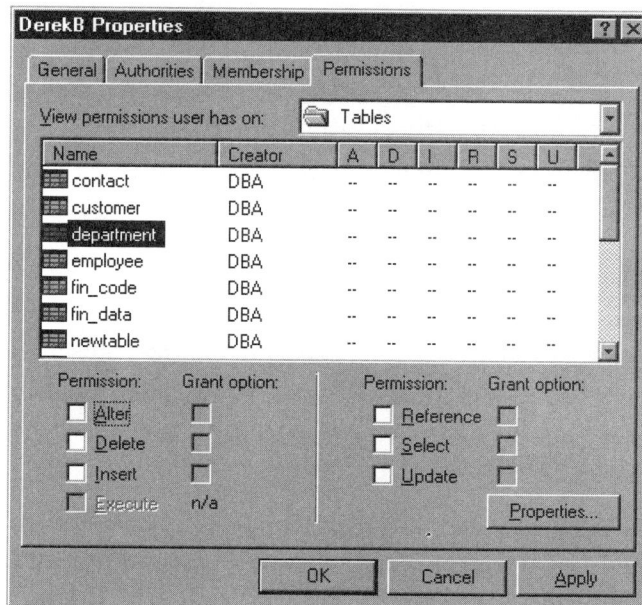

Figure A.-44. On the Permissions tab we can define the specific permissions that the user has on each object in the database.

You can manage permissions on Tables, Views, and Procedures. Individually granting the following permissions:

- **On Tables:** Select, Insert, Update, Delete, Alter, and Reference.

- **On Views:** Select, Insert, Update and Delete.

- **On Stored Procedures:** Execute.

For each of the permissions that can be assigned on a table or view, you can also allow the user a "grant option." This means that you are allowing this user to grant this same permission to other users.

The **Add User** utility in SQL Central is a wizard that takes you through each of the properties pages and has you fill in the information for the user id, password and access level. It does not assign permissions or groups. You must do this after creating the user account.

Groups

When you want to assign an identifiable group of users the same set of access rights you can do this with a group. When a users belong to a group they get all the rights and permissions of that group. The membership of a group can be seen in the right list view of SQLCentral when the group is selected in the tree view. To view the general permissions for the group, open the Properties Sheet for the group by clicking with the right mouse button. Administering these permissions is identical to the way you administered permissions for an individual user.

Adding a User To a Group

You can add a user to a group through the Membership tab of the User Properties Sheet as discussed earlier. You can also use drag and drop to select a user and drop them over the group that you wish to add them to.

Maintaining User Defined Data Types

A user defined data type is a standard data type which has a default value and check condition defined for it. You can create your own, or examine any existing user defined data types by opening the User Defined Data Types folder. If you run the Add User Defined Data Type utility, you will see the Data Type Property Sheet where you must define a name for your new data type and then select what the base data type is, the default value, if it allows nulls and any check condition that you want to apply.

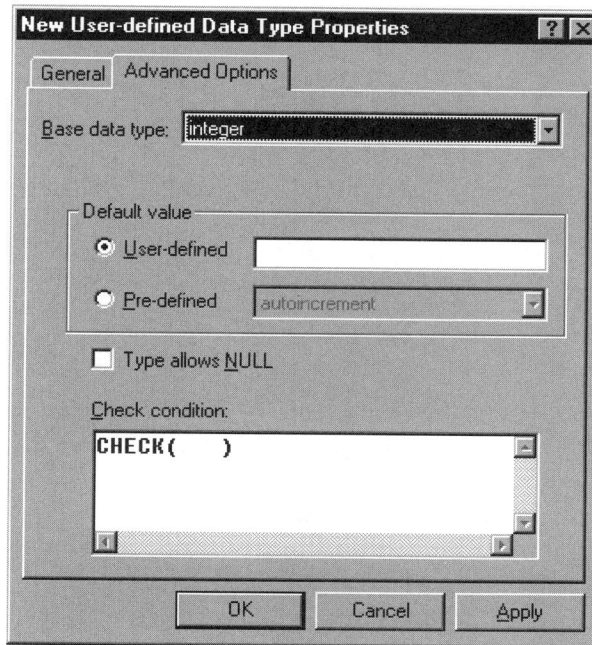

Figure A-45. *The User Defined Data Types can be viewed and maintained through SQLCentral.*

Connected Users

The Connected Users folder allows you to view any users who are currently connected to the selected database. You can view the user id, connection id and network node from within the SQLCentral window.

If you click on a user with the right mouse button you will be given the options to **Disconnect** that user (if you have that authority) or view the users **Properties**. The Properties Sheet has two tab pages. The first tab page will tell you all the details about the user as shown in Figure A-46.

On the Statistics page of the Properties Sheet you can examine the statistics of this specific user such as the number of different types of reads and writes or the number of commit requests.

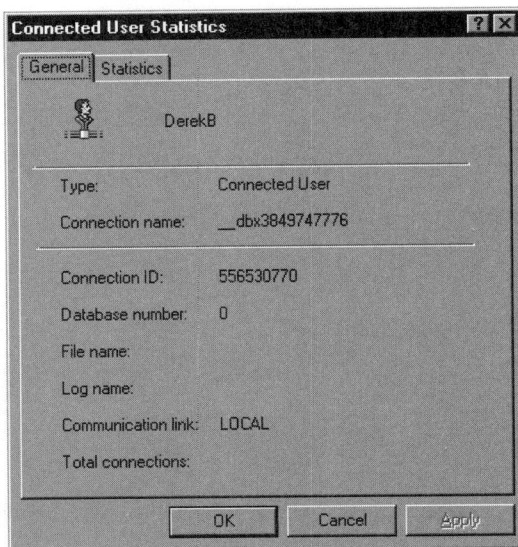

Figure A-46. *You can view all the properties of a connected user on the General tab page.*

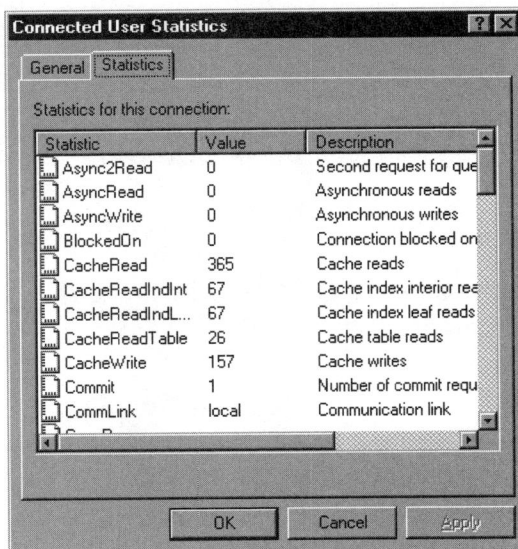

Figure A-47. *The Statistics tab allows you to examine all the statistics for the selected user.*

Database Spaces

A SQLAnywhere database is initially created in only one physical file. This file is called a DB Space. The initial DB Space is given the name *system*. You can manage and add new DB Spaces to your database. Having multiple files for your physical database can provide advantages such as being able to separate the data file and the transaction log file into two different storage areas (remember that the table data and the indexes on that table must be stored in the same DB Space).

You can examine an existing DB Space by double clicking on it or by selecting it with the right mouse button and choosing **Properties**. On the properties page you can see the name of the space and the physical file that it uses.

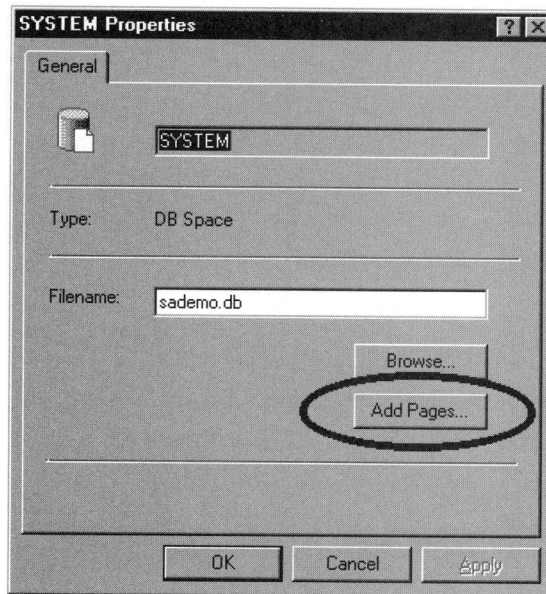

Figure A-48. *You can add more pages to a DB Space by clicking on the **Add Pages...** command button.*

Normally, SQLAnywhere will add pages to your DB Space (database file) when they are required. To improve performance you can choose to add pages manually by pressing the **Add Pages...** command button on the properties sheet. This will pre-allocate space for this DB Space to use. If you over allocate space, you cannot unallocate pages, so be sure not to use this option arbitrarily.

You can remove a DB Space by clicking with the right mouse button and selecting **Delete** off the pop up menu. In order to delete a DB Space you must have already deleted any tables stored in this DB Space.

Using the Performance Monitor

The SQLCentral Performance Monitor is a utility that you will find in the Statistics folder for the current database. This tool will display a graphical representation of any set of statistics that you request. The graph will be updated in real time as requests are made to the database (thus one of the reasons for a 32 bit operating environment).

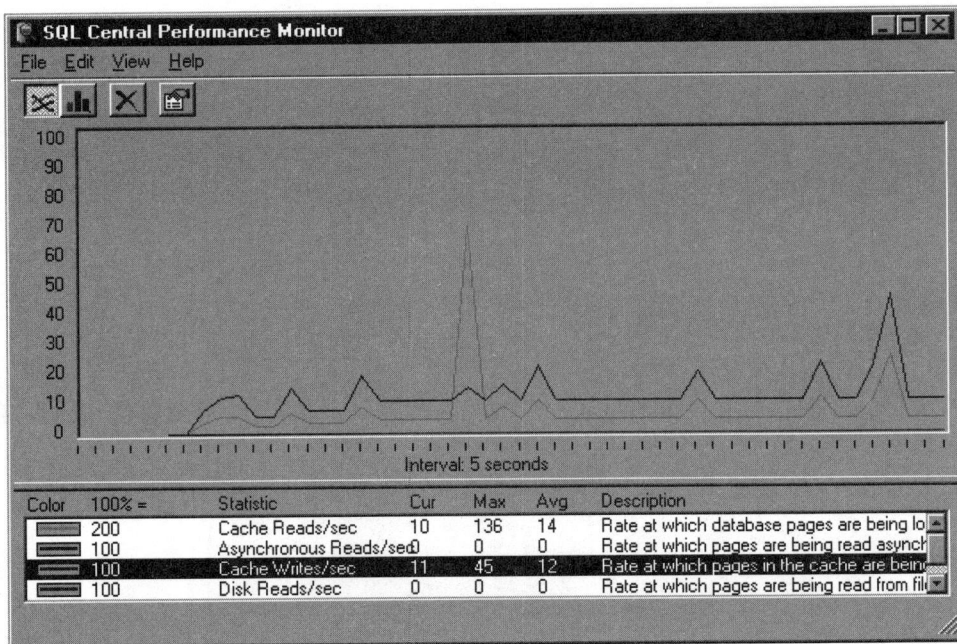

Figure A-49. The SQLCentral performance monitor allows us to monitor a specific SQLAnywhere database.

Developer's Note: Remember that the performance monitor will skew your results as the queries that it uses to determine the performance of the database server will cause database activity. You can get around this if you use the Windows NT performance monitor (assuming your database is running on Windows NT). The Windows NT performance monitor will not skew your results because it operates in a non-intrusive fashion. It also provides you with options to monitor network statistics which aren't available in the SQLCentral performance monitor.

Selecting Statistics to Monitor

In order to open the performance monitor, you must first select which statistics you want to monitor. When you open the Statistics folder you will see all the available statistics listed in the right panel. The icon beside each statistic will show you if it is currently set to graph in the monitor or not (a red graph line indicates that it will show in the monitor).

Double-clicking on a particular statistic will open the Properties Sheet. On this sheet you will see a checkbox at the bottom allowing you to flag this statistic for monitoring. The monitor can display many statistics at the same time, but be careful, because more than a handful will make the monitor hard to read.

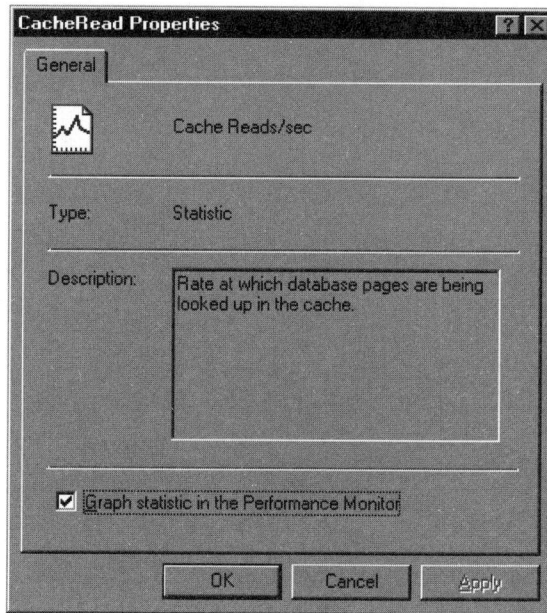

Figure A-50. On the Properties Sheet you can get a description of a statistic and flag it to be displayed in the performance monitor.

Alternatively, you can select a statistic with the right mouse button. From the pop up menu you can choose to add or remove the selected statistic from the set being shown in the performance monitor. As soon as you select one of these options, the performance monitor will be opened (if it isn't open already).

Running the Performance Monitor

When you open the monitor, it will by default display information in a line graph format as shown in Figure A-49. The graph will be updated in realtime at an interval of x seconds. The initial setting for the interval is 1 second. If you want to slow this interval down, you can do so by opening the Preferences window as shown in Figure A-51. The Preferences window can be opened by selecting the **File → Preferences** menu option.

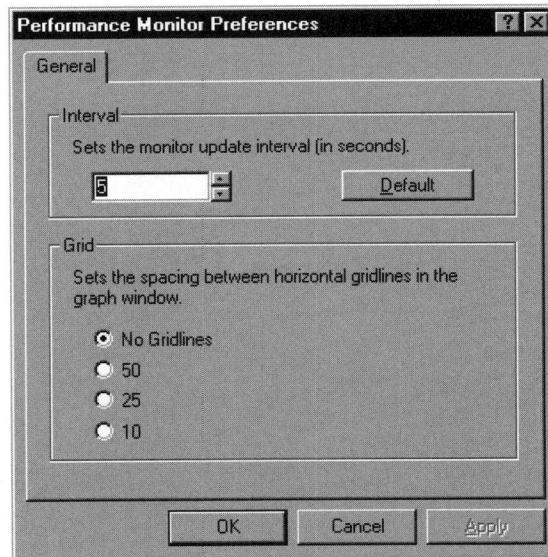

Figure A-51. On the Preferences window you can set the interval for the performance monitor graph and also select options for displaying gridlines in the graph area.

In the Preferences window you can also choose to display gridlines within the graph area. The default is to not show any gridlines at all. You can change this to show gridlines every 50, 25, or 10 units.

Under the **View** menu item you have options to alter the display of the performance monitor. You can choose to individual show or hide the legend, status bar and toolbar. You can also choose to display the results as a fluctuating bar graph instead of a line graph. A bar graph only shows you the current interval for your statistics. This can be easier to read if you have many statistics showing, but doesn't allow you to see a history or trend line for any particular statistic.

To clear the monitor and start your graph over, select the **File** → **Clear** menu item.

Managing SQLRemote through SQLCentral

If you are unfamiliar with SQLAnywhere's replication capabilities, can refer to *The SQLAnywhere Developers Guide* by Ian Richmond, Derek Ball, and Steve Clayton from Sybase/Powersoft Press.

You can use SQLCentral to set up SQLRemote replication between a consolidated database and one or many remote databases. This includes server to server, server to desktop and server to laptop situations. To begin, you must connect with SQLCentral to your consolidated database with an account that has full DBA privileges, preferably before you have extracted your remote database(s) from it.

Publishers

The next step is to identify a user, or group, as the publisher of the database. This is the user id that will be used to exchange messages with the remote databases.

When you open the SQLRemote folder for the consolidated database, you will see three subfolders; Publications, Remote Users and Message Types. These will be discussed shortly. You will also see a utility for defining a *publisher* for this database.

When you run this utility, the window in Figure A-52 will appear. From this list you must select a user id or group to act as the publisher for this database. Select the appropriate id and press the **OK** command button.

Alternatively, on the consolidated database property sheet there is a tab for **SQLRemote**. On this tab you will see the name of the publisher for the database. You can press the **Change...** command button to select a different user id or group.

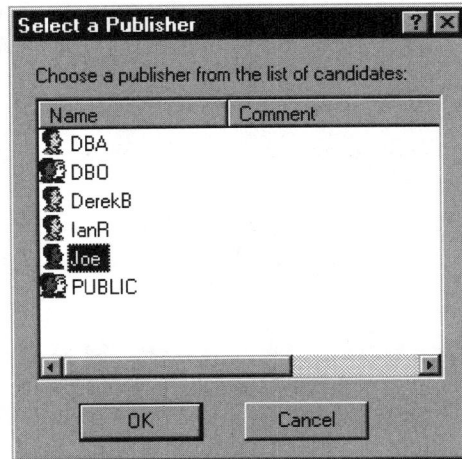

Figure A-52. The first step in setting up replicated databases with SQLRemote is to set the publisher.

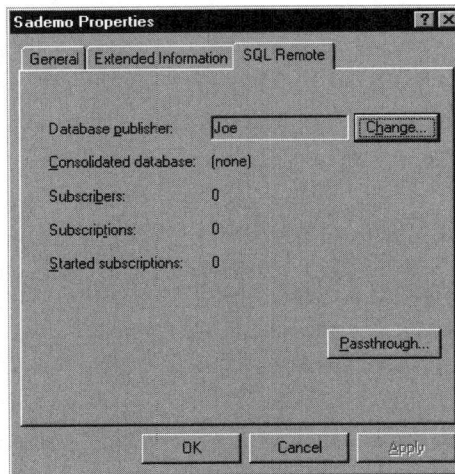

Figure A-53. The database properties sheet has a tab control for SQLRemote which will display the summary information for SQLRemote settings for this consolidated database.

If you want to revoke publication rights from a publisher, you can select their id from the SQLRemote folder with the right mouse button and choose **Revoke Publisher** from the pop up menu.

Message Types

Next you will be defining the message types that this consolidated database will use. You can open the Message Type folder and select the message type(s) that you are using. Next you must define the publishers address for that message type.

By default, message types for four standard replication protocols are included. These are:

- **MAPI** (Mail Application Program Interface—used by many popular e-mail packages such as Microsoft Mail™ and Lotus Notes™) such as "dball" or "irichmond."

- **VIM** (Vendor Independent Messaging used by cc:Mail™) such as "dball" or "irichmond."

- **File** (to used shared files to provide replication instead of a e-mail based message system) such as "s:\shared\message\sademo.msg."

- **SMTP** (Simple Mail Transfer Protocol—such as used by many Internet based mail systems) such as "dball@cadvision.com."

You can add your own message types using the **Add Message Type** utility.

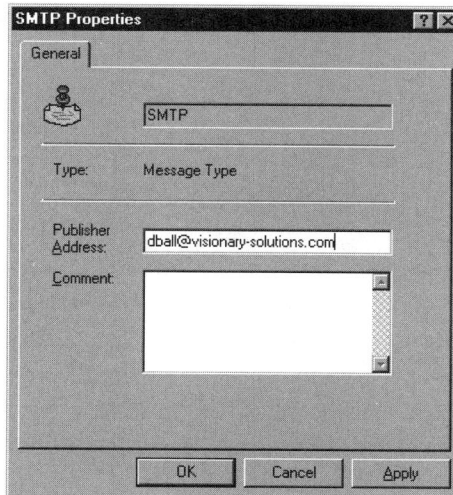

Figure A-54. In addition to the SMTP message type shown here, SQLRemote also supports VIM, MAPI, and File based messaging.

Remote Users

Each remote database also requires a "publisher." These publishers are identified to the consolidated database as a *remote user*. You define remote users in SQLCentral by opening the Remote Users folder in the SQLRemote folder.

Initially there will be no remote users for a new consolidated database. You will run the **Add Remote User** utility to generate new remote users. The wizard will ask you to specify the name and password (plus confirm the password) for the new remote user.

On the second page of the wizard you must specify the message type that this particular remote user will use (as discussed above) and what their specific address (or file name) is.

On the third page you will specify how often you want the publisher to send messages to this specific remote user. Your options are:

- **At a scheduled time.** To send a message at a specific time each day.

- **At a specific interval.** To send a message after a certain number of hours and/or minutes.

- **Upon closing.** To send a message when closing the database.

The next page of the wizard asks you to assign permissions for this user. These are the same as the permissions that we discussed under the Users and Groups section in this appendix. This user can have DBA access, Resource access or Remote DBA access (refer to the section "Maintaining Users" for details).

Finally you can add a comment and click on **Finish** to create the new user.

Publications and Articles

In order to have replication occur, you must first define your *publications*. A publication is a databaes object that describes the data that is to be replicated. Each publication consists of *articles* (sounds like we are actually making a magazine!). An article describes specific tables and/or table components to be replicated.

Publications are stored in the Publications folder (within the SQLRemote folder). Initially, your consolidated database will have no publications. You must run the **Add Publication** wizard to create new publications.

The first page of this wizard asks you to give the publication a unique name and specify which user will own the publication (all database objects require an owner, this will default to the DBA).

The second page of the wizard will ask you to specify the articles that will compose the publication.

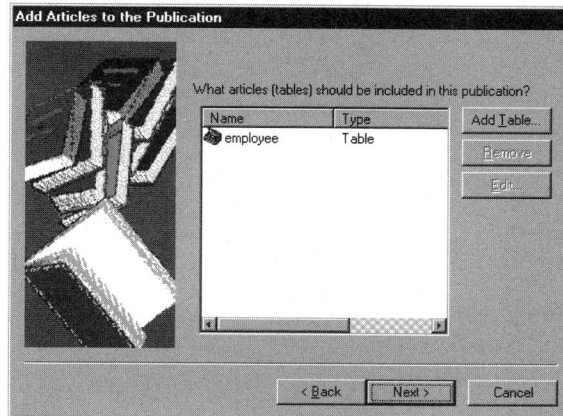

Figure A-55. *The second page of the Add Publication wizard asks you to define the articles that will compose the publications. Click on the* **Add Table...** *button to select tables and table components.*

You will need to select the **Add Tables...** command button to define the tables and table components that you wish to include in this publication. By doing so, you will see the New Article dialog window shown in Figure A-56.

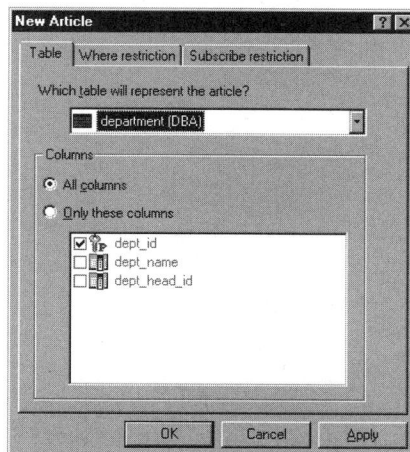

Figure A-56. *The New Article dialog window allows you to select the table, or table components, which rows, and any subscription restrictions that you wish to define.*

In this dialog window you will choose the table that you want to replicate. You can then choose to replicate all column, or only a subset of the columns. You can also restrict which rows are replicated by defining a where clause. An example of this would be a situation where the remote database only contains data for a particular department, so you would only want to replicate data from that department. You can also define any subscription restrictions that you wish to impose.

Finally you will add a comment and click on the **Finish** button to create the publication.

Subscriptions

Now that we have remote users and publications we must link these two entities together through a *subscription*. This is required to allow the remote user to replicate data between the remote database and the consolidated database.

Subscriptions for a publication are properties of that publication. To add a subscription to the publication you either click on the publication with the right mouse button and select **Subscribe for...** from the pop up menu, or you open the publication's Property Sheet and select the Subscriptions tab. You will see a command button labeled **Subscribe for....** Both of these options will bring up a list of valid remote users. You can then select the remote users that you wish to subscribe to this publication.

Developer's Note: You can also generate subscriptions by dragging remote users and dropping them on top of subscriptions.

Extracting and Deploying

The extracting of the remote database is accomplished using the Extract Database utility described in the earlier section "Extracting (Remote Databases)." This will generate the extracted database. This is as far as you can go with SQLCentral. SQLCentral will not deploy the database for you. To complete this final step you must manually install the extracted database on the remote server and test the communications structure.

What is Sybase SQLAnywhere?

*T*he Sybase SQLAnywhere database engine is Sybase's offering in the small footprint, portable workgroup database category. It is intended to be a complimentary component of the System XI database, but it also does very well standing on its own. A single user version of this engine is shipped with the PowerBuilder 6.0 software.

This appendix is intended to tell you a little bit about SQLAnywhere as a database. Depending on the scale of your application, you may decide to use SQLAnywhere as your deployed production database for your PowerBuilder application.

History

Although you may not be familiar with the name "Sybase SQLAnywhere," this is not a 1.0 release database engine. This engine has been around for some time and was formerly known as the Watcom database engine. In late 1994 (approximately), Watcom was acquired by Powersoft Corporation. Then in February 1995, Powersoft was in turn acquired by Sybase. Thus Sybase became the owner of the Watcom database engine. This engine was rechristened the Sybase SQLAnywhere database and released to the public in early 1996. Variations of this product have been included with PowerBuilder since version 3.0. The Sybase SQLAnywhere name has been used since PowerBuilder 5.0 shipped.

Features

The SQLAnywhere database is intended to provide the IT community with a powerful, but compact workgroup database server. It is built to be scaleable and allow you to grow from a handful of users to several dozen.

The small footprint of SQLAnywhere make it very well adapted to use in mobile computing environments. This coupled with its replication capabilities make it an ideal fit for distributed workgroup computing situations.

SQLAnywhere has many of the advanced features of its big brother, System XI. It has full support for triggers, stored procedures and bound rules. You can establish full referential integrity with primary and foreign keys and enforce this with restricted or cascading updates and deletes.

You can implement your SQLAnywhere database on a variety of platforms including Windows 95, Windows NT, Windows 3.x, OS/2, DOS and Netware (as an NLM). The database file created on any one platform can be placed onto another platform without having to go through the pain of loading and unloading of the database. Multiple environments can all be integrated into one cohesive distributed network of replicated databases.

The replication in SQLAnywhere allows for easy to implement bi-directional replication. Ideal for projects where users have to have laptops that are disconnected from the network, such as a mobile salesforce. With the SQLRemote tool you can access standard message based APIs that will synchronize all your remote users. And for large enterprise installations, the SQLAnywhere database will integrate seamlessly with Sybase System XI through the Sybase Replication Server distributed database architecture.

The qualities and features of this little powerhouse can be described in three categories; high performance, scaleable/versatile server, and a ANSI standard SQL query language. (See Table B-1.)

Table B-1. *Qualities and Features of SQLAnywhere.*

High Performance	Scaleable/Versatile Server	Query Language
Cost based query optimizer results in fewer disk accesses and less processing	Full transaction management	ANSI-89 compliant SQL query language featuring ANSI-92 extensions
High speed query optimization	Bi-directional scrollable, updatable cursors	Also supports Sybase Transact SQL

(continued)

Table B-1. *(continued)*

High Performance	Scaleable/Versatile Server	Query Language
Symmetric multi-threading	Automatic data recovery	Easy to use GUI administration tools
	Full ODBC 2.5 level 2 support (for Windows 95 and NT) and ODBC 2.1 support for Windows 3.x	Full support of stored procedures, triggers and rules
	Replication architecture	Complete referential integrity
	Integrates with Sybase System XI	Support for BLOBs (Binary Large Objects)
	Full database security	Updatable multi-table views
	Supports NetBIOS, IPX and TCP/IP	
	Supports peer to peer networks	
	Row level locking	

What's New Since Watcom Version 4.0?

There have been many substantial improvements in the SQLAnywhere engine since its last release as the Watcom 4.0 database. The following list is not exhaustive, but does cover the most significant changes.

Replication (SQL Remote and Sybase Replication Server)

To us, the ability to integrate easy seamless replication into distributed databases is one of the biggest improvements in the SQLAnywhere database. Replication is the ability to share data between physically separate databases and keep that data properly synchronized. Changes made in any one database are replicated through the replication architecture to other databases within the architecture. This replication can be accomplished in SQLAnywhere through two different means; SQL Remote and through the Sybase Replication Server.

SQL Remote is a tool that ships with SQLAnywhere. With it you can build a replication architecture around a number of "occasionally connected" physically separate databases. This is intended to be used in environments that are running SQLAnywhere databases exclusively. The usage of the SQL Remote tool is discussed in detail in Chapter 9—Using SQL Remote.

The second mechanism for replication is the Sybase Replication Server. This is accessed through the Open Server Gateway (discussed below). SQLAnywhere can act as a replicate (slave) site within the Sybase Replication Server architecture (Sybase Replication Server is a separate Sybase product that can integrate many different databases in its architecture). You can get SQLAnywhere to behave as a primary (master) data site within the replication architecture by purchasing the SQLAnywhere Replication Agent product. The Sybase Replication Server is out of scope for this book. Look for other books in the Sybase Press line for detailed information on the Sybase Replication Server.

GUI DBA Tool (SQL Central)

We now have a GUI tool for database administration called SQL Central. SQL Central only runs in Windows 95 and NT, so if you are running Windows 3.x you won't see this utility. You will recognize the familiar "explorer" like interface. Utilities in this graphical tool include:

- **Database Creation** creates a new SQLAnywhere database
- **Backup Database** creates a backup of a SQLAnywhere database or write file. The database can be either running stopped at the time.
- **Uncompress Database** uncompressed a database file creating a new uncompressed database but leaving the original compressed database intact.
- **Translate Log** allows you to translate a transaction log or write file into a file of SQL commands.

- **Upgrade Database** upgrades a Watcom 3.2 or 4.0 database.
- **Compress Database** creates a compressed database leaving the original database file intact.
- **Create Write File** creates a write file from a database.
- **Change Log File** allows you to change the log file that you want a database to use.

- **Unload a Database** allows you to unload the structure and data of a database into a SQL command file (for the structure) and comma separated file (for the data).
- **Erase a Database** allows you to erase a non-running database, compressed database or write file.

- **Extract a Database** allows you to create a remote database by extracting it from your consolidated (primary) database.

Compatibility with Sybase Transact SQL (TSQL)

In order to make it easier to write applications that are portable between SQLAnywhere and System XI, SQLAnywhere's Watcom SQL language has been extended to include a number of standard TSQL functions. The specific intent behind this is to all your stored procedures, triggers, rules and data to be transportable between the two engines. Application developers who are faced with prototyping a new application on SQLAnywhere and then rolling out in production on Sybase System XI will appreciate the amount of code reworking that this saves.

ODBC Enhancements

If you are operating the either the Windows 95 or the Windows NT environment, SQLAnywhere now has level 2 ODBC 2.5 support. If you are operating in the Windows 3.x environment you have ODBC 2.1 support.

Open Server Gateway

The Open Server Gateway serves a similar purpose as the TSQL language extensions. They both are intended to allow client applications access either Sybase or SQLAnywhere. The Open Server Gateway is middleware that allows the client applications that you develop to access your database through the standard Sybase Open Client interface. This interface can in turn communicate to either System XI or SQLAnywhere seamlessly. This is very valuable if you have some users of an application who will be accessing your central System XI database, and others who will be mobile, but use the same application against their portable SQLAnywhere database.

Performance Enhancements and Monitoring

Sybase has incorporated a number of improvements that will increase the performance of SQLAnywhere. In order to help you measure and monitor this performance, they have also added a set of system functions that will provide you with statistics on the performance of your database. If you are running your SQLAnywhere engine on NT you can also access the Windows NT Performance Monitor.

SQL language Extensions

There are many new enhancements to the Watcom SQL language used by SQLAnywhere including pattern matching and the ability to define your own custom user functions. New functionality is also provided in the development of stored procedures, batches, user defined data types, and more.

Mirrored Transaction Logs

As an additional layer of security against disk failure or file corruption, you can have SQLAnywhere maintain two completely separate transaction log files. This way if one gets corrupted, or of the disk that one of them resides on fails, you can recreate the transactions from the other log.

MAPI Compatibility

You can now hook your stored procedures into your e-mail system using the new MAPI functions provided in SQLAnywhere. This can be very useful for keeping key personnel informed of important events such as sending an e-mail to the DBA as the system is running out of disk space, or sending a note to an account manager when a clients balance due exceeds their credit limit.

External .DLL Calls

You can also build your stored procedures to call external Dynamic Link Libraries (.DLLs) when desired.

Installing and Configuring SQLAnywhere

If your Sybase SQLAnywhere came as part of your PowerBuilder or Power++ package, it will install as part of the installation process for that package. If you have purchased the full version of SQLAnywhere, you probably received a CD-ROM which contains all the software for all platforms for both the client and the server.

There are three components that may be involved in installing a SQLAnywhere database:

- Server Engine (with or without SQLRemote).

- Client Software.

- Standalone Engine (with or without SQLRemote).

SQLAnywhere is designed to be installed on any Intel based PC with a 386 or higher processor. If you are running the 16 bit windows engine, it can be run on a 286 PC, but I wouldn't recommend it!

Installing the SQLAnywhere Server

The Server engine can be installed on Windows 3.x, 95 and NT platforms as well as OS/2, DOS and Netware (as an NLM—Netware Loadable Module).

The server engine is a lightweight in terms of required system resources. Although it will run on a 386 processor (or 286 for the 16 bit engine software), I would strongly recommend a minimum of a 486 processor.

The amount of hard drive space required for the engine (not including database space) is:

Platform	Space Required
Windows NT	14 Mb
Windows 95	14 Mb
Windows 3.x	12 Mb
DOS	14Mb
Novel	6 Mb (Netware server)
	14 Mb (Local machine)
OS/2	12 Mb

Upgrading Watcom 3.2 or 4.0 Databases

The new 5.0 version of Sybase SQLAnywhere is fully capable of accessing earlier versions of the database. As previously mentioned, earlier versions of this engine were known as the Watcom database. You simply point the database startup routine at your version 3.2 or 4.0 database file (filname.db). The limitation to doing this is that you will not be able to access some of the new features of version 5.0 such as SQLRemote and Transact SQL procedures. To get the full benefit of SQLAnywhere 5.0, you will want to convert your 4.0 databases to 5.0.

> **Developer's Tip:** The tools available to upgrade your database will upgrade it "in place." This means that the existing database file will be overwritten by the new database file. For this reason, before upgrading a database, be sure you have backed it up!

The upgrade utility that you receive with version 5.0 can be accessed from either SQLCentral or from the command prompt. To upgrade a version 4.0 database you must know the database name, the administrator's id and password. You call the upgrade utility from the command prompt as follows:

```
dbupgrad -c
"dbf={database_name};uid={adminstrators_id};pwd={administrators_password}"
```

where

database_name is the filename for the database, such as "products.db"

administrators_id is the user id for someone with DBA privileges. For many Watcom databases, this will be "dba."

administrators_password is the password for the administrator user id specified above.

An example of this would be:

```
dbupgrad -c "dbf=c:\wsql40\products.db;uid=dba;pwd=sql"
```

In this example, we used the switch "-c" to allow us to specify all the connection information at our command prompt. Table B-2 describes other available switches.

Table B-2 Available Switches.

Switch	Function
-c "keyword1=value1; keyword2 = value2..."	Allows you to supply a connect string containing all the database connection parameters. This is used in the example above.
-g userid	Allows you to specify a user id to have the upgrade utility replace the standard "dbo" (database owner) user it with. See detailed explanation below.
-k	Causes the command prompt window to close upon completion (assumes you are not running a DOS system).
-q	Activates "quiet mode" where no windows or messages are displayed.

Developer's Tip: To upgrade a database with either the command prompt or SQLCentral, the database must not have active connections, including yours! Databases that currently have connected users will cause the upgrade tool to fail.

In the modern world of GUI interfaces, this seems to be an antiquated approach. The technique that we use to convert our Watcom databases to SQLAnywhere 5.0 is through the SQLCentral administration utility.

You can launch this utility by selecting the SQLCentral icon from your SQLAnywhere program group. When it starts, you will see a typical Windows 95 style registry window. In this window you can open the folder for SQLAnywhere Utilities. Inside this folder you will find all kinds of useful utilities for everything from database creation to backup or extraction and more. The tool that we are interested in right now is the "Upgrade Database" tool. Double-clicking on this tool will launch the upgrade wizard as shown in Figure B-1.

Specify the path and file name for the database, a valid administrators id and password. The next window will ask you for a replacement name for the generic user name "dbo" (for "database owner")in SQLAnywhere. If you have a user defined in your Watcom database with the id dbo, this will conflict with the new SQLAnywhere system tables who have "dbo" as the owner by default. If this is the case, you can specify a new user name for the system tables. If you don't have a user with this id, then you can ignore this screen. Pressing the **Finish** command button will initiate the conversion process.

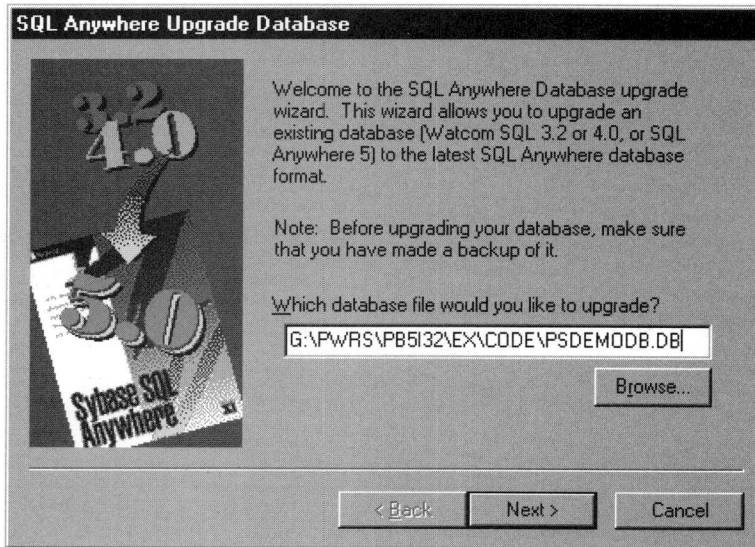

Figure B-1. *The SQLCentral database upgrade wizard makes converting your Watcom 4.0 databases a snap!*

If you wish to use replication on a database that you have upgraded, you must also archive the transaction log and create a new one for your upgraded database.

How to Get Help

Sybase's general address and phone number is:

Sybase Inc.
6475 Christie Ave.
Emeryville, California 94608
USA
Phone: (617) 564-7353
Fax: (303) 294-3739

You can get further help with using the SQLAnywhere database through Sybase technical support, the Internet Web site, CompuServe or through their fax line. The connection information for these services is:

Technical Support	Installation/Registration	North America	(519) 884-0702
		Latin America	(713) 977-0752
		Singapore	65-378-0140
	Annual (Paid) Support		(800) 937-7693
	Pay Per Use Support		(508) 287-1950
	Customer Service Fax		(508) 369-4992
	Online	BBS	(508) 287-1850
		CompuServe	Three forums address SQLAnywhere:
			GO SYBASE
			GO POWERSOFT
			GO WATCOM
		Internet	There are also three World Wide Web sites:
			www.sybase.com
			www.powersoft.com
			www.watcom.com
			And three ftp sites:
			ftp.sybase.com
			ftp.powersoft.com
			ftp.watcom.com
	Fax Line (24 hours)		(508) 287-1600
Sales	Upgrades, product orders, etc...		(800) 8-SYBASE
	To buy annual support		(800) 395-3925

At the moment there are no technical publications dedicated to SQLAnywhere, but you may find references to it in the numerous trade journals that support PowerBuilder, Optima++ and Sybase System XI such as the *PowerBuilder Developers Journal*, *PowerBuilder Advisor*, *Databased Application Development Advisor*, and *DBMS magazine*.

Index